The Palgrave Handbook of Social Fieldwork

Nasir Uddin • Alak Paul
Editors

The Palgrave Handbook of Social Fieldwork

palgrave
macmillan

Editors
Nasir Uddin
Department of Anthropology
University of Chittagong
Chittagong, Bangladesh

Alak Paul
Department of Geography and
Environmental Studies
University of Chittagong
Chittagong, Bangladesh

ISBN 978-3-031-13614-6   ISBN 978-3-031-13615-3 (eBook)
https://doi.org/10.1007/978-3-031-13615-3

© The Editor(s) (if applicable) and The Author(s), under exclusive licence to Springer Nature Switzerland AG 2023

This work is subject to copyright. All rights are solely and exclusively licensed by the Publisher, whether the whole or part of the material is concerned, specifically the rights of translation, reprinting, reuse of illustrations, recitation, broadcasting, reproduction on microfilms or in any other physical way, and transmission or information storage and retrieval, electronic adaptation, computer software, or by similar or dissimilar methodology now known or hereafter developed.

The use of general descriptive names, registered names, trademarks, service marks, etc. in this publication does not imply, even in the absence of a specific statement, that such names are exempt from the relevant protective laws and regulations and therefore free for general use.

The publisher, the authors, and the editors are safe to assume that the advice and information in this book are believed to be true and accurate at the date of publication. Neither the publisher nor the authors or the editors give a warranty, expressed or implied, with respect to the material contained herein or for any errors or omissions that may have been made. The publisher remains neutral with regard to jurisdictional claims in published maps and institutional affiliations.

Cover illustration: © amriphoto / Getty Images

This Palgrave Macmillan imprint is published by the registered company Springer Nature Switzerland AG.
The registered company address is: Gewerbestrasse 11, 6330 Cham, Switzerland

Those social scientists who contributed to developing social fieldwork in its present form

Acknowledgements

Editing a book always holds many people's debt, and this book is no exception. We, first of all, express our deep gratitude to all the contributors to this volume who have been with us throughout the journey that started almost three years ago. The contributors listed in the table of contents are our fellows, colleagues and friends who responded immediately soon after we invited them to join us with the contribution of a book chapter on their research experience. We fairly bestow our deep respect for their professional and personal relations with us. They have been incredibly tolerant and endurant to respond to our numerous editorial queries during this long period of time. The book would not see the light of the day without their sincere support, cooperation and tireless responses on various occasions in the time of its making. We also remember those four contributors who pulled their submissions out at the final stage of preparing the manuscript because of some unavoidable reasons due mainly to the COVID-19 effects. We tried our best to accommodate them but they really couldn't make it. We would be happy if we could house them in this book but they couldn't manage it. Besides, we would like to express our sincere thanks to our colleagues at the University of Chittagong for their all-out support during the time of preparing the final manuscripts. They include Professor S M Monirul Hassan (Department of Sociology), Professor Dr. Abdullah Al Faruque (Department of Law), Professor Dr. Dwaipayan Sikdar (Department of Biochemistry and Molecular Biology), Professor Dr. Mohammed Abul Manchur (Department of Microbiology), Professor Dr. Tarequl Hasan Chowdhury (Department of Economics), Professor Dr. Shyamal Ranjan Chakraborty (Department of Physics), Professor Dr. Khairul Islam (Department of Computer Science and Engineering), Professor Dr. Jamal Uddin (Department of Finance) and Professor Dr. A B M Nazmul Islam Khan (Department of Sociology).

We acknowledge the contributions of Palgrave Macmillan's consulting editor Elizabeth Graber and Sara Hills for their sincere cooperation and constant support through the editing period and publication process.

Nasir Uddin owes his deep debt to his teachers who trained him as an ethnographer. He also acknowledges the contribution of his family members who have been deprived of their demanded space and care during the time of its making. His partner Mrs. Farzana Ahmed and two daughters (Mrittika Rahman and Neelima Rahman) have always extended their hands of cooperation whenever needed while the editorial tasks of the manuscript were going on. Uddin sincerely expresses his gratitude to his family members.

Alak Paul is indebted to all his mentors and teachers both at home and abroad who shaped him to understand geographical fieldwork from different perspectives. He expresses sincere thanks to his elder brother, sisters and family members for their inspiration. Alak expresses his gratitude to his life partner Mrs. Sumana Podder and two boys (Anirudho Paul and Arindom Paul) who supported him throughout this book project.

Chittagong University
February 2023

Nasir Uddin
Alak Paul

Contents

1   Methodological Issues in Social Research: Experience from the
Twenty-First Century   1
Nasir Uddin

Part I   Fieldwork in Challenging Social Settings   21

2   Research in a Moving Field: Doing In-aqua Research in Blue
Space Settings   23
Ronan Foley

3   Researching Garo Death Rites   37
Erik de Maaker

4   Navigating the Tyrannies of Fieldwork: A Nigerian Experience   53
Adebayo Adewusi

5   Trial by Fire: Reflections on Fieldwork in Nagaland,
Northeast India   69
Debojyoti Das

Part II   Field, Relations, and Emotion   83

6   Feeling Unsettled in the Field: Emotions and the Field
Researcher   85
Anuradha Sen Mookerjee

7 Developing Relationships over Many Years: Under Investigated but Important Types of Interview-Based Research 103
Ian G. Baird

8 Sick in the Field: Illness and Interbeing Encounters in Anthropological Fieldwork 121
Olea Morris

Part III Bio-ethics, Fieldwork Practices, and Ground Reality 137

9 At the Organ Bazaar of Bangladesh: In Search of Kidney Sellers 139
Monir Moniruzzaman

10 *"Can we talk about surrogacy?"* Legal Precariousness and Qualitative Research in the Biomedical Context 161
Pragna Paramita Mondal

11 Qualitative 'Fieldwork' in Health Geographic Research: Self-reports from Bangladesh 181
Alak Paul

12 Adolescent Drug Use in Connecticut Private High Schools: Zero Tolerance, Contextual Peer Influence, and Deterrence Effectiveness 197
Minjune Song

13 Dilemmas and Challenges in Qualitative Fieldwork with Climate-Vulnerable Communities 219
Md. Masud-All-Kamal, S. M. Monirul Hassan, and Nasir Uddin

Part IV Gendered Fieldwork and Gender in Social Research 235

14 Risks and Challenges in Fieldwork on Gender-Based Violence: Gendered Identity, Social Taboo and Culture 237
Nahid Rezwana

15 Rethinking Ethnographic Research as 'Gendered and En-casted Labour': Reflections from a Non-metropolitan City of West Bengal, India 253
Ekata Bakshi

16	Capturing the Uncaptured: Photovoice as a Method for Women's Empowerment in Domestic Violence Zuriatunfadzliah Sahdan	271
17	Fieldwork with Opposite Gender: Exploring the Agency of Left-Behind Women of Migrant Households in Rural Bangladesh Main Uddin	295

Part V	Theoretical and Epistemic Challenges in the Field	313
18	Between an Activist and Academic: Contested (Re)positioning of Ethnographers in Refugee Research Nasir Uddin	315
19	Moving Research Methods to the Field: Challenges and Lessons Learnt Across African Contexts Deo-Gracias Houndolo	331
20	Entry, Access, Bans and Returns: Reflections on Positionality in Field Research on Central Asia's Ethnic Minorities Matteo Fumagalli	347
21	Doing Ethnography on Sexuality Among Young Men in Dhaka, Bangladesh: How Has Reflexivity Helped? Sayed Md Saikh Imtiaz	367

Part VI	Nativity, Participant Selection, and Challenges in Archival Research	387
22	A Native Anthropologist's Positionality of Being an Insider/Outsider: A Reflective Account of Doing Ethnographic Research in Nepal Kapil Dahal	389
23	Recruitment of Participants from Vulnerable Groups for Social Research: Challenges and Solutions Melati Nungsari	405

24 Navigating Archival Readings of Rural Technology   417
Sanjukta Ghosh

25 Conclusion: Challenges of Social Research—A Way Forward   441
Alak Paul

Index   459

Notes on Contributors

Adebayo Adewusi has his BA and MA degrees in History from Obafemi Awolowo University, Nigeria. He is currently a PhD candidate at the Department of History, University of Ibadan, Nigeria. He is working on the dynamics involved in commercial tobacco farming in Oke-Ogun, Southwest Nigeria. He was a field research officer in a European Research Council-funded international collaborative research project between the University of Birmingham, UK, and Osun State University, Nigeria. He has contributed many book chapters to edited volumes as well as published articles in many peer-reviewed acclaimed journals.

Ian G. Baird (PhD) is a faculty of Geography at the University of Wisconsin-Madison (UW-Madison), where he teaches courses about nature-society relations, development, Southeast Asian Studies and qualitative research methods, including ethnography. He is also the Director of the Center for Southeast Asian Studies at UW-Madison. He conducts most of his field research in Laos, Thailand and Cambodia, where he has been conducting research for almost 30 years. His most recent book, *Rise of the Brao: Ethnic Minorities in Northeastern Cambodia During Vietnamese Occupation* (2020), was published by the New Perspectives in Southeast Asian Studies series of the University of Wisconsin Press.

Ekata Bakshi is a final-year PhD candidate at the Centre for Women's Studies, Jawaharlal Nehru University, India. Belonging to the third generation of a refugee family, she has been interested in the theme of Partition since the very beginning of her academic career. The questions she is particularly interested in asking are, how does the Partition refugee live today, 72 years after the initial displacement began, and how have their location, both in terms of physical location and structural location (in the caste and gender hierarchies), have come to bear upon the trajectories they have been able to trace for themselves? She has so far published two papers on her research work and presented her work at a number of national and international forums.

Kapil Dahal (PhD) is a lecturer at the Central Department of Anthropology, Tribhuvan University, Nepal, from where he did his PhD in Anthropology in 2017. He obtained MA in Medical Anthropology from the University of Amsterdam, the Netherlands. His recent postdoctoral researches have focused on health governance, confrontations between service providers and health seekers and uterine prolapse in Nepal. He has published articles in various national and international journals and books on different areas, imperative for critical anthropology. He has also participated and presented papers in several anthropological/medical anthropological international/national conferences/workshops.

Debojyoti Das is an anthropologist of South Asia with a focus on the borderlands of eastern India and the Indian Ocean world. His work is deeply interdisciplinary, bridging his training as an ethnographer with extensive use of visual media (photo voice, digital diary) and action-based research. His current work focuses on environmental education, eco-social justice, migration, and sustainable development issues among marginalised littoral communities in the Indian Ocean rim. He is the author of the book *The Politics of Swidden Farming: Environment and Development in Eastern India (2018)*. He is currently exploring less glimpsed but important dynamics of environmental refugees in littoral East Africa and South Asia.

Erik de Maaker (PhD) is an associate professor and Director of Graduate Studies at the Institute of Cultural Anthropology and Development Sociology, Leiden University. He studied at the University of Amsterdam, the Netherlands, where he obtained his first degree in Cultural Anthropology in 1993. He obtained his PhD degree from the University of Leiden in 2006 on a thesis entitled "Negotiating Life: Garo Death Rituals and the Transformation of Society". He has published extensively on the uplands of eastern South Asia, focusing on the challenges people face with respect to cultural change and rapid economic development. At the moment, he is co-leading a multi-national cooperative research project on landscape, environment and climate change in the eastern Himalayas, in partnership with the Himalayan University Consortium and ICIMOD.

Ronan Foley (PhD) is an associate professor in the Department of Geography at Maynooth University, Ireland, and started work there in 2003. His research is primarily in the area of health geography, with significant publications on therapeutic landscapes, healthy blue space and health care services as well as on historical and cultural geographies. Before his arrival in Maynooth, he worked at the University of Brighton from 1988 to 2003. He has also taught at the University of Canterbury in Christchurch, New Zealand, in 2015 and as an occasional lecturer at Queen's University Belfast and Trinity College Dublin.

Matteo Fumagalli (PhD) is a senior lecturer at School of International Relations, University of St. Andrews, UK. His research interests lie at the intersection of the study of identities, ethnic conflict and violence and the politics of natural resources. He has conducted research in the post-Soviet space (especially Central Asia and the Caucasus) and East Asia (especially South Korea, Taiwan, Laos, Myanmar and Bangladesh). He has authored several books, more than 20 peer-reviewed articles and many book chapters. His monograph *New Silk Roads, Growing Inter-Asian Connections: South Korea's Quest for Energy and New Markets in Central Asia* is forthcoming with Palgrave in 2021.

Sanjukta Ghosh (PhD) is an early career researcher in agricultural history with an interest in colonial and post-colonial South Asia, based in SOAS University of London from where she completed her doctorate with a fellowship from the Association of Commonwealth Universities, UK, and has been a Senior Teaching Fellow. Currently, she is on the research group of GRID Heritage, a partnership between SOAS, Sussex University and JNU.

Deo-Gracias Houndolo (PhD) is an Evaluation Specialist and the Regional Coordinator of the West African Capacity Building and Impact Evaluation Programme (WACIE). He is completing a PhD degree in Development Economics at the Erasmus University Rotterdam, the Netherlands. He works with organizations such as the International Initiative for Impact Evaluation (3ie), the World Bank, the African School of Economics and the Partnership for African Social Governance and Research (PASGR). His current researches focus on poverty dynamics and agricultural development.

Sayed Md Saikh Imtiaz (PhD) is a faculty of the Women and Gender Studies Department at the University of Dhaka. Dr. Imtiaz achieved a PhD degree from the University of Amsterdam and completed two post-doctoral assignments: one with a multidisciplinary team from Vanderbilt University, USA, in 2013, and the second in 2018 with a team from Promundo-US, CMMS and Dhaka University. He is the Founder of the Center for Men and Masculinities Studies (CMMS). He has also researched gender issues concerning human rights, climate change, financial inclusion of women, livelihood, poverty, masculinities, fatherhood, youth, sexuality, violence against women and girls, etc.

Md. Masud-All-Kamal (PhD) is an associate professor in the Department of Sociology at University of Chittagong, Bangladesh. He received his PhD from The University of Adelaide, Australia, and completed his MSc in Development Studies from Lund University, Sweden. He is an interdisciplinary researcher, and his research interests include environmental management, climate change adaptation and public policy. His work has appeared in high-quality interdisciplinary journals such as *Climate and Development, Sustainability, Local Environment, Regional Studies & Regional Science, Current Research in Environmental Sustainability,* and *Poverty and Public Policy.*

Pragna Paramita Mondal is a PhD scholar at Women's Studies Research Centre, University of Calcutta, and an assistant professor at Narajole Raj College, India. She completed her MPhil as UGC Junior Research Fellow at the Institute of Development Studies, Kolkata. In 2019, she was awarded the

Calcutta University Travel Grant for attending the *Consuming Gender Symposium* at Wits University, Johannesburg, South Africa. She has published in the *Economic & Political Weekly* (2018) and has contributed to *Population Dynamics in Eastern India and Bangladesh: Demographic, Health and Developmental Issues* (Springer, 2020) that is listed under STICERD LSE India Observatory Publications.

Monir Moniruzzaman (PhD) is a medical anthropologist and an associate professor in the Department of Anthropology at Michigan State University. Monir's research centres on human organ trafficking, focusing on the bioviolence against malnourished bodies of marginalized populations. His work has been published in leading journals and books, including *Journal of the Royal Anthropological Institute*, *Medical Anthropology Quarterly*, *American Journal of Bioethics* and *School for American Research*. His research has transformed into a multi-media installation piece, which was exhibited in *InterAccess*, an art gallery in Toronto. More than one hundred of his interviews have appeared in major media outlets. At present, he is serving as a member of the Task Force on Organ Transplantation at the World Health Organization.

Olea Morris is an environmental anthropologist and PhD candidate in Environmental Sciences and Policy at Central European University, Budapest, Hungary. She has an MA in Anthropology from San Diego State University, and has worked in regenerative agriculture and permaculture projects in Latin American and Europe. Olea is interested in multispecies ethnography, environmental history and regenerative agriculture movements in Latin America.

Melati Nungsari (PhD) is an applied micro-economist who studies labour economics, industrial organization, economic education, public economics and migration. She is Associate Professor of Economics at Asia School of Business in Kuala Lumpur and a Research Affiliate at MIT Sloan School of Management in Boston. She has published research on forced migration in Southeast Asia, two-sided platforms in business, economic pedagogy, retirement markets and social protection. She has also written for the *Chronicle of Higher Education*, and multiple public outlets in Southeast Asia such as *The Edge*, *The Star Group*, and *The Malay Mail Online*. She received her PhD in Economics from the University of North Carolina at Chapel Hill.

Alak Paul (PhD) is a faculty in the Department of Geography and Environmental Studies at the University of Chittagong, Bangladesh. He received his PhD from the University of Durham, UK, in 2009. Being an empirical human geographer, his research and teaching interests span public health, society and environment, disaster management, etc. for the last 20 years. He has over 40 peer-reviewed research publications in reputed journals along with 7 book chapters and 4 authored and/or edited books to his credit. Very recently, Routledge published his co-edited book titled *Geography in Bangladesh: Concepts Methods and Applications* (2019). His latest book title is *HIV/AIDS in Bangladesh: Stigmatized People, Policy* (Springer, 2020).

Nahid Rezwana (PhD) is an associate professor at the Department of Geography and Environment at the University of Dhaka. Nahid Rezwana obtained PhD in Geography from the Durham University, UK, her first MSc degree in Geography and Environment from the Dhaka University and her second MSc degree in Hazard and Disaster Management from the Kingston University London, UK. Her fields of interest are hazards and disaster management, impacts of climate change, gender and health. Her recent book is *Disasters, Gender and Access to Healthcare: Women in Coastal Bangladesh* (2018). A book chapter in the edited collection *The Routledge International Handbook of Gender and Feminist Geographies* was recently published in 2020.

Zuriatunfadzliah Sahdan (PhD) is Lecturer in Human Geography at Universiti Pendidikan Sultan Idris, Malaysia. Dr. Sahdan received her PhD from Durham University. Her research focuses on postcolonialism, space and cultures of domestic violence in Malaysia using participatory methods and storytelling. She co-authored *Trauma, Gender and Space: Insights from Bangladesh, Malaysia and the UK* (2020) which appeared in *Routledge Handbook of Gender and Feminist Geographies*. Some of her recent works include *Demonic Possession: Narratives of Domestic Abuse and Trauma in Malaysia* published in *Transactions of the Institute of British Geographers* and a book chapter on *Recognising and Addressing Secondary Trauma: Stories from the Field*.

Anuradha Sen Mookerjee is a social anthropologist and Visiting Senior Fellow, Institute for Human Development, New Delhi, India. She has undertaken qualitative field research for the last 20 years. Between 2000 and 2010, she worked on issues of feminized poverty, knowledge management, violence against women and trafficking of women and children in South Asia at the Centre for Women's Development Studies, United Nations Development Programme in India, and United Nations Development Fund for Women, South Asia Office, New Delhi. She received her PhD in Anthropology and Sociology of Development from the Graduate Institute of International and Development Studies, Geneva in 2019. Her research interests include ethnography, the Bangladesh-India borderlands, political economy, intersectional feminism, critical mobilities and anthropology of migration. Her latest publication is, *Movement of internal migrants during the COVID-19 pandemic in India: Enacting embodied citizenship (November, 2022)* in the Journal *Citizenship Studies*.

Minjune Song born in Seoul in South Korea, is an independent scholar of the history of technology, public science and the Cold War. He has previously worked on a study of federal laboratories and their privatization in the postwar period. He is also an assistant under Professor Yoon Ji Woong from Kyung Hee University, and works under the GSOC-sponsored research project on the study of (video game) addiction and government regulation. His recent works are on adolescent drug abuse, school discipline and educational policy.

Main Uddin is an associate professor of the Department of Anthropology, Jagannath University, Dhaka, Bangladesh. He is currently a PhD researcher in the Department of Social and Cultural Anthropology, Tallinn University, Estonia. He has experience of conducting qualitative research among men and women of indigenous, minority and mainstream people of different parts of Bangladesh for the last 20 years. His academic interest focuses on migration and Diaspora, trans-border network, globalization, gender issues and South Asian ethnography.

Nasir Uddin (PhD) is a cultural anthropologist and a faculty of Anthropology at the University of Chittagong. Uddin studied and carried out research at the University of Oxford (UK), School of Oriental and African Studies (SOAS) at London University (UK), the London School of Economics (LSE) at London University (UK), Heidelberg University (Germany), VU University Amsterdam (the Netherlands), Ruhr-University Bochum (Germany), Delhi School of Economics at Delhi University (India), the University of Hull (UK), Kyoto University (Japan) and the University of Dhaka (Bangladesh). His latest edited book is *Deterritorialised Identity and Transborder Movement in South Asia* (Springer, 2019 [co-edited with Nasreen Chowdhory]). His latest monograph is *The Rohingya: An Ethnography of 'Subhuman' Life* (2020).

S. M. Monirul Hassan is a professor in the Department of Sociology at the University of Chittagong. His research interests include critical perspectives in sociology, gender perspective in sociology, social cohesion, microcredit and NGOs. His current research focuses on the role of local institutions in climate risk management.

Abbreviations

Chapter 1

CHTs — Chittagong Hill Tracts
GBV — Gender-based violence
MGNREGS — Mahatma Gandhi National Rural Employment Guarantee Scheme

Chapter 2

GIS — Geographic Information system
GPS — Global Positioning System

Chapter 3

IFAD — International Fund for Agricultural Development
NEHU — North-Eastern Hill University
UNDP — The United Nations Development Programme

Chapter 4

ATRs — African Traditional Religions

Chapter 5

FCC — Facilitator of Community Conservation
MGNREGS — Mahatma Gandhi National Rural Employment Guarantee Scheme
MLA — Member of the Legislative Assembly

Chapter 6

BBEECC — Bharat Bangladesh Enclave Exchange Coordination Committee
CRCC — Citizen Rights Committee
LBA — Land Boundary Agreement

Chapter 7

CIA	Central Intelligence Agency
GAPE	Global Association for People and the Environment
HAGL	Hoang Anh Gia Lai
LFNC	Lao Front for National Construction
NGO	Non-government organization
PRK	People's Republic of Kampuchea
PRPK	People's Revolutionary Party of Kampuchea
RLGE	Royal Lao Government in Exile
UFNSK	United Front for National Salvation of Kampuchea

Chapter 9

USD	United States Dollar

Chapter 10

ART	Assisted reproductive technology
CCTV	Closed circuit television
IVF	In vitro fertilization

Chapter 11

AIDS	Acquired immune deficiency syndrome
FGD	Focus group discussion
HIV	Human immunodeficiency virus
IDU	Injecting drug user
NGO	Non-governmental organization
PLWH	People living with HIV.

Chapter 12

APA	American Psychological Association
GFSA	Guns Free School Action

Chapter 13

IPCC	Intergovernmental Panel on Climate Change

Chapter 14

FGM	Female genital mutilation
KII	Key informants interview
SRA	The Social Research Association

VAWG	Violence against women and girls
WHO	World Health Organization

Chapter 15

OBC	Other backward classes
SC	Scheduled classes

Chapter 16

PAR	Participatory action research
WAO	Women's Aid Organization

Chapter 18

INGO	International non-governmental organization

Chapter 19

CAPI	Computer-assisted personalized interviews
DHS	Demographic and health survey
IRB	Institutional Review Board

Chapter 20

EU	European Union
USSR	Union of Soviet Socialist Republics

Chapter 21

CDA	Critical discourse analysis

List of Figures

Fig. 2.1	Representation of GeoNarrative from kayak	26
Fig. 2.2	Representative Image from Ubipix screen grab	30
Fig. 5.1	The compromise letter. (Photo Credit Debojyoti Das)	78
Fig. 9.1	Advertisement for selling kidneys posted on the entrance door of the doctors' seminar room in a leading transplant hospital in Dhaka, October 28, 2004	145
Fig. 9.2	Interviewed sellers on the map of Bangladesh	151
Fig. 16.1	"The Items That Used to Beat Me" Shot by Harini	278
Fig. 16.2	"The Items That Used to Beat Me" Shot by Harini	278
Fig. 16.3	"The Items That Used to Beat Me" Shot by Harini	279
Fig. 16.4	"The Items That Used to Beat Me" Shot by Harini	279
Fig. 16.5	"My Husband Once Stabbed Me in the Neck with Sharp Knives Like This" Shot by Rekha	280
Fig. 16.6	"Life at Home like a Mousetrap" Shot by Ashna	282
Fig. 16.7	"A Restricted Life, Locked Inside the Doors of Violence" Shot by Harini	283
Fig. 16.8	"He Tightly Closed the Door and My Freedom" Shot by Shalini	284
Fig. 16.9	"I Feel My Husband's Shadow Here" Shot by Usha	286
Fig. 16.10	"I Feel My Husband's Shadow Here" Shot by Usha	287
Fig. 16.11	"I Feel the Silhouette of My Husband" Shot by Shalini	287
Fig. 16.12	"An Increasingly Advanced Life" Shot by Rekha	289
Fig. 16.13	"My Confusion and Uncertain Future" Shot by Chumy	291
Fig. 24.1	(**a**) and (**b**) Negalu, dabbi naga, naga, light plough, Deccan harrow	421
Fig. 24.2	(**a**) Dantal, Chokiu, Nangar, Large clod crusher Patiu, Zusari and (**b**) Karpi, Dariu, Hal, Single yoke for the plough, Harrow, Phavdi, Vakhelu, Single yoke for hoes, Tarfen, Dhariu, Karapdi	423
Fig. 24.3	(**a, b**) Manual Power Tillage Implements	424
Fig. 24.4	(**a**) Negalu, Dabbi Naga, Naga, Light Plough, Deccan Harrow and (**b, c**)	425

Fig. 24.5	(a, b)	428
Fig. 24.6	(a, b) Double Mould Board Plough and Furrows Illustration	430
Fig. 24.7	Segregation of Traffic-Cement Concrete Roads for Cart Traffic	436

List of Tables

Table 12.1	Expected frequency of past and licit and illicit drug use	205
Table 12.2	Correlation between licit drug use and peer context factors	206
Table 12.3	Correlation between expected frequency of illicit drug use and peer context factors	207
Table 12.4	Correlation between expected frequency of licit drug use and punishment severity and likelihood	207
Table 12.5	Correlation between expected frequency of illicit drug use and punishment severity and likelihood	208
Table 14.1	Overview of the studies	241
Table 21.1	Fieldwork phases, purposes and rationale for using methods and tools	375
Table 21.2	Dimensions of participant observations in relation to the present study	376

CHAPTER 1

Methodological Issues in Social Research: Experience from the Twenty-First Century

Nasir Uddin

1.1 Primer

The methodology of social research has been transformed along with the metamorphosis of the socio-economic and political rhetoric and the reality across the globe. Because of its various experience and experiments depending on the subjects, contexts and regions, social research methodology itself has become an issue of research in the twenty-first century. The fieldwork challenges vary from discipline to discipline and from region to region because every discipline in social sciences, despite having some identical broader frameworks, has its distinctive tone of interpretation and every region has its own social, political, historical and ecological settings. Social research involves the researcher's engagement, interpersonal attachment, and impersonal affection in dealing with persons; the object of study (See, Uddin, 2011). Since social research and its methodologies tend to change and evolve from time to time, new and newer fieldwork experiences are needed to reformulate the model and module of social research methods and methodologies. Hence, a new form of methodology could be framed that reflects the researcher's personal, political, social, cultural and emotional holdings being developed and formed throughout the researcher's socialization and socio-cultural upbringing across time and space (See, Uddin, 2022). Consequently, social research is not simply a typical 'academic practice' that follows an innocent 'professional genre' and 'research rituals'; rather it heavily entangles with the researcher's lived experiences of

N. Uddin (✉)
Department of Anthropology, University of Chittagong, Chittagong, Bangladesh
e-mail: nasir.anthro@cu.ac.bd

© The Author(s), under exclusive license to Springer Nature Switzerland AG 2023
N. Uddin, A. Paul (eds.), *The Palgrave Handbook of Social Fieldwork*,
https://doi.org/10.1007/978-3-031-13615-3_1

dealing with the object of research, which define and redefine the tools, techniques, notions and application of methodologies in a particular social setting, on the one hand. Amid the researcher's series of engagement and re-engagement in the 'rites of passage' of research, on the other hand, the methodology takes its shape which substantially contributes to the established practices of doing social research with renewed interpretation, transient experiments and upcoming challenges in research methodologies (Clifford, 1986). Since social research takes on pains and pleasures, problems and potentials, challenges and solutions, and hard and soft memories, the personal experience becomes an impersonal subject and an indispensable part of research methods and methodologies. Therefore every research context in the field provides a distinctive and unique experience and understanding which in the end enriches the established genus of social research methodologies. Social research methodologies have thus continuously changed over the decades and continue to change in response to changing socio-economic and political rhetoric and realities on a local and global scale. This introductory chapter sets out all trends and tendencies of methodological issues in social research based on the experience of top researchers' personal experience of doing fieldwork in different social settings across the world. It offers epistemologically and ontologically important personal accounts of academic and professional researchers having long-term intensive, comprehensive and ethnographic fieldwork in various social settings and versatile regional contexts across the globe. The accounts contain regional and local specificity including South Asia, Southeast Asia, Eastern Europe, Latin America, Southern Africa and Middle Eastern countries. Since personal experience holds collective importance and academic significance, the field experience of a galaxy of scholars across disciplines and regions enables them to contribute a distinctive framework to the existing body of scholarship on social research methodologies.

Structurally, the chapter is divided into six sections which house together major methodological issues of contemporary social research across the globe. Section one illustrates conducting fieldwork in challenging social settings particularly in a conflict zone, war-torn areas, geographically isolated sites and thematically sensitive topics. This section presents some exciting personal accounts of doing research in challenging settings in Northeastern India, the Chittagong Hill Tracts in Bangladesh, conflict zones in Africa and the state vs. indigeneity issue in India which unfold the way forward just like a guideline about how to encounter challenges in the field. Section two focuses on field relations to the informants a researcher builds, develops, nurtures and continues even during the post-fieldwork time. This section explains how fieldwork generates relation and emotion amidst various forms of engagement and interaction with the informants, but at the same how to maintain an intelligent balance between emotion and profession which lays down the emotional challenges of fieldwork. Section three discusses bio-ethics in social research since doing fieldwork on bio-social issues involves serious ethical considerations. The human body is not only a biological entity but has strong relations to social, political and economic aspects in the changing and complex global realities. Based on practical experiences of doing fieldwork on bio-social issues, this section touches upon triplicate relations of bio-ethics, its theoretical discussion and ground realities which could provide readers with a new realm of social research. Gender has always been a big question in social research since gender sensitivity involves justification and validity of presentation and representation of the research topic which has been covered in section four of the chapter. With the first-hand experience of doing fieldwork, this section presents some very thought-provoking case studies of gender issues in social research. Section five covers the theoretical and epistemological challenges in social research because established genres of fieldwork frequently face multifaceted challenges in the field which generates new and promising alternatives to the existing scholarship. This section provides some very strong case studies of fieldwork accounts which reveal the theoretical and epistemological challenge of social research in the twenty-first century. Section six discusses the importance of nativity, the technical difficulties of participant selection and the challenges in archival research. Fieldwork always follows some sort of professional code of ethics involving the researcher's personal, socio-cultural and political repositioning. Fieldwork is not an innocent and normative practice of knowledge production as it has its politics and hence it must follow some ethics. Historically, researchers and people researched hold a bi-polar position; colonists vs. colonized, modern vs. traditional, developed vs. underdeveloped, urban vs. rural, and the West vs. the rest which is still dominant in social research in one form or another. This section critically engages in this aspect of social research which is historically and politically loaded. Having discussed all mentioned above, the chapter provides briefly an overall outline of the methodological issues in social research of the twenty-first century.

1.2 Fieldwork in Challenging Social Settings

In many parts of the world, doing fieldwork is becoming challenging day by day due to many reasons including the state's growing intolerant nature to the people of cultural, racial and ethnic differences, mounting polarized political divide, escalating disparity between classes, the state's regimented approached towards Adivasi people, growing religious intolerance in the society and researchers' passion for the object of study. However, challenging social settings offer newer ideas to reintroduce new techniques of data collection and newer research methods which contribute to the scholarship of social research. Therefore, the personal experience of doing fieldwork in challenging social settings becomes a resource for social research in the twenty-first century.

Keeping the premise in mind, in Chap. 2, Ronan Foley offers a wonderful fieldwork experience in his reflexive writing. Foley explains that while much social fieldwork is carried out on terra firma, there is a growing interest in research in the water, based on a recent turn in human geographical research towards blue space (Foley and Kistemann, 2015), especially in relation to a range of leisure practices that promote health and well-being. In parallel, there has been a growing interest in geo-narratives, in which emotional responses and geo-spatial tracking are co-produced in-situ, on or near the water (Bell et al., 2018). In both cases, the fieldwork involves a deeply immersive process, which can be challenging for both the researcher and co-participants. In his chapter, Foley provides an initial survey of such work and the often difficult process of gathering research from, by, in, on and under the water (Foley et al., 2020), as exemplified in fieldwork-driven studies of surfing, kayaking, diving, sailing and swimming. The chapter additionally documents recent field-based research with swimmers in Ireland using swim-along interviews, to suggest the value of such work for enhanced knowledge production, but also considers critically its value over other approaches to water-based fieldwork. Theoretically, such fieldwork approaches draw from an assemblage of health models (Duff and Hill, 2022), where specific social, affective and material properties emerge from the immersive methods used, with a particular interest in how such fieldwork can be health-enabling. Finally, the chapter presents some key critical comments associated with such specifically in-situ research, for different participants and within different settings, incorporating aspects of risk, access, authenticity, technologies and representation (Garcia, 2012).

Doing empirical research in the social settings of indigenous people is always challenging. Based on the long-term engagement of doing research among the Garo indigenous people, Erik De Maaker has explained the challenges of field experience in Northeast India. In Chap. 3, Maaker focuses on fieldwork that he has done between 1999 and 2001 in the Garo Hills of eastern Meghalaya (India). He explores how he, in the course of this PhD research, has related to the people concerned. He describes how relationships emerged and developed, and how people reacted to his involvement in their lives. He concludes by arguing that although his research did not have the intention to expose the village concerned, it did certainly contribute to it being put on the map as a 'traditional' village. As far as Maaker can judge, this seems to have worked out positively for the villagers. It has made people more aware of the importance that is being attributed by an outside world to their cultural practices and ensures that they receive a positive kind of attention from state organizations and the like. Over the last two decades of the previous century, anthropology has moved away from the kind of fields that it used to cherish before. Where previously anthropological research was typically linked to a single field site, now a multi-sited approach became the standard (Marcus 1995). This provided better possibilities for comparison of the data collected, enabling a better and broader understanding of the topic being studied. Nevertheless, certain research topics continue to benefit from (predominantly) single-sited research. The fieldwork that he has conducted on death-related practices required close engagement with a limited number of people. Not only because of the level of 'trust' and 'rapport' required for the fieldwork but also because the research demanded that he took the multiple dimensions of the relationships maintained by the people concerned into account. To achieve this, he had to meet them in various roles: about their land, as traders, as kinsmen or when acting by their religious responsibilities. This could be achieved best by interacting with a (more or less) single set of people over a prolonged period.

Doing ethnographic fieldwork in the African context is quite often challenging. Adebayo Adewusi in Chap. 4 brilliantly explores the tyrannies of doing fieldwork in the African context with the case of Nigeria. He explains that research can be a highly rewarding effort considering the phenomenal discoveries that can be made through the combing of various previously known and unknown sources of information. At the same time, one cannot deny the obvious fact that it can also be very difficult, frustrating and discouraging in terms of the challenges researchers often encounter in sourcing materials. These challenges that he calls the tyrannies of the field can be as diverse as sources of materials for contemporary researchers in Africa. With a particular emphasis on an oral interview, which has become a major research tool across disciplines, and almost indispensable in social sciences and humanities in contemporary society, its significance cannot be over-emphasized. But certain human factors can make such a worthwhile exercise an uphill task for fledging researchers. Extensive oral interviews conducted across the Yoruba-speaking areas in Nigeria, particularly southwest and part of the North-central geopolitical zones, provide an illustration and practical experience on how cultural imperatives, wrong perception about research and researchers, and other socio-economic and political factors can constitute major hurdles for researchers from gaining access to places and, most importantly, informants traditionally invested with the authority to speak on behalf of their communities. These factors can equally serve as a pitfall for an unsuspecting researcher. Despite the highlighted challenges, research is not an impossibility in this area. Considering these issues, this chapter presents diverse research experiences, issues and clarifications on the conduct of interviews and how determined a researcher in the face of tyrannies was able to navigate the convoluted system through understanding and adaptations dictated by the peculiarities of different communities without compromising the ethics of research.

Northeast India has always been a site of challenging social research which is further reflected in the lucid narrative of Debojyoti Das in Chap. 5. Das explains that fieldwork is a 'right to passage' and over time one becomes reflexive during and the afterlives of one experience with his/her interlocutors. Thus, anthropological fieldwork stands out from other social sciences in that intimate fieldwork experience becomes the ethnographer's primary source of knowledge. In this chapter, Das engages with the question of 'violence', 'risk' and the 'ethics of self-harm' in a challenging setting. He reflects on his personal experiences with one of his interlocutors who was in a position of power and temporarily acted as his host. He showcases how emotional detachment is a misnomer and even men can find themselves trapped in a vulnerable and compromising position while undertaking fieldwork. Therefore, the ethics of complicity, collusion and detachment can be a tricky and blurred exercise in the field. He presents a personal narrative of his experience—ethical dilemma with his interlocutor in the first section of the chapter while in the second part he turns on to the hostage encounter. The chapter focuses on the moral and ethical dilemmas of conducting fieldwork in a social context where everyday violence, state pogrom and suspicion feature prominently. In this context, methodological practices such as reflectivity, informed consent, fieldworkers' responsibility, rapport and reciprocity need to be considered to engage with the ethics of fieldwork. In an anthropological investigation, the question of the researcher's self and agency becomes primordial as he or she is expected to be engaged, immersed and at the same time objective and neutral. The chapter is based on fourteen months of ethnographic fieldwork in eastern Nagaland. He conducted fieldwork under ceasefire with the sensitivity and strong desire of being unharmed. However, despite my hopes of being safe, he was caught up in a hostage situation while travelling with my interlocutor to his village. The hostage was triggered by the local factional clash about development money that was spent on public works in the village funded by the Mahatma Gandhi National Rural Employment Guarantee Scheme (MGNREGS), India's largest rural employment programme that he has conversed in detail in this chapter.

1.3 Field, Relations, and Emotion

The field does not essentially mean 'locale' anymore but it involves interpersonal relations and deep emotion generated through reciprocal engagements and re-engagement between the researchers and the participants in the research. Every researcher experiences various forms of relation to and emotion in the field. Anuradha Sen Mookerjee in Chap. 6 explains that every field encounter is unique and has a significant influence on the way data is collected, framed, interpreted and generalized. While the encounter is expected to throw light on social and cultural patterns that we seek to build up through the ethnographic project, its directness, particularity and unexpectedness also influence the broader goals of the project. While part of one's psychological efforts is directed towards oddly limiting the influence of the encounter, in reality, its ambiguousness and often paradoxical nature may influence major aspects of the study, including analysis, interpretation, writing and the theory to which it contributes, adding value to the project (Crapanzano 2010). This chapter based on her fieldwork in the former *ChhitMahals* (enclaves) along the India-Bangladesh border in the Cooch Behar district of West Bengal, India between March 2016 and January 2017, other than two visits in 2015, will address the experience of the encounters and her struggles in finding a balance to accept the 'truth' and feel of the experience while being caught in tailoring it within the broad framework within which her PhD project was located. It looks into her emotional struggles of being committed to certain biases and orientations while at the same time being open to what was supposed to be unfamiliar. She unpacked the binaries of the familiar and unfamiliar that led her to reflect on the category of the 'other', which she experienced as otherness and 'othering'. She experienced shifts in the way she looked at herself, leading to changes in what she considered the 'other'. The shifts in her approach that took place through the ethnographic encounter were intersubjective and can be located amidst my struggles both of commitment to the academic literature to which she was committed to contributing through the project and the implicit moral frame of the encounter. In this chapter, she explores how changes not only shaped the way she related to and experienced the emotions of entrenchment, proximity, identification, distance and rejection, among others, but how the shifting emotions led to the redefining of what is to be included and excluded as data.

It is also undeniable that amid engagement and re-engagement with the field during a long period, a particular kind of relation has been developed which is always instrumental in qualitative research (See Uddin, 2011). Ian Baird in Chap. 7 based on his long-year research in the Southeast Asian region wonderfully illustrates the importance of relations in social research. He explains that qualitative research requires carefully considered and nuanced understandings and approaches, as well as attention to a wide variety of potential pitfalls. Over the last few decades, the literature in Geography regarding ethnography, and qualitative methods more generally, has expanded and deepened considerably, leading to heightened attention to research methods and ethics. One of the topics that feminist geographers have particularly pioneered are ideas about how to approach such issues as 'positionality' and 'reflexivity' in qualitative research. Much has also been written about interviewing approaches, including the importance of navigating relationships with interviewees and other types of research participants, which can be crucial for shaping research outcomes, including how knowledge is co-produced. However, most of the literature, as useful as it has been, focuses on the most typical types of encounters between qualitative researchers and research subjects: short-term encounters that exist for just a few hours, days, months or at the most about a year or two. Longer-term relationships between researchers and research participants have not received nearly as much attention, revealing an important gap in the literature. In this chapter, he focuses on some of his long-term relationships with research participants—some of whom feel more like friends than 'research subjects'—living in Cambodia, Laos, Thailand, the United States, France and Canada. Here, he reflects on these relationships—some of which began over a decade ago—and how these long-term relationships can greatly benefit research. This is especially the case when politically sensitive topics are under investigation. However, developing such long-term relationships also come with potential difficulties, ones that he reflects on here. How can researchers maximize the benefits of developing long-term relationships with research subjects, while minimizing potential problems or other difficulties associated with adopting a long-term approach to qualitative research?

Medical anthropology as a technically specialized area of research always demands the deep engagement of research with the participants which usually generates a passionate field relation. In Chap. 8, Olea Morris attends to the embodied experience of illness in the course of carrying out anthropological fieldwork. Medical anthropologists have long engaged with the social aspects of how illness is constructed, interpreted and treated by their interlocutors. However, there has been little discussion of researchers' personal experiences of illness ('dis-ease') while carrying out fieldwork; indeed, ethnographic accounts tend to downplay hardships experienced in the field and frame researchers as always available, willing participants. Considering the fundamental importance of the body as a tool in anthropological fieldwork, Morris understands illness as a particular state of being through which ethnographic data and everyday experiences are refracted. This chapter questions how being ill affects one's ability to carry out fieldwork research, but also how it influences the construction of anthropological knowledge—by both anthropologists as well as their interlocutors. Specifically, he discusses two periods of illness sustained during the course of his fieldwork in Mexico—a serious allergic reaction to a local plant, and an outbreak caused by an unknown microbial source—using multispecies ethnography as a praxis for understanding these experiences. Encounters with unknown toxins and pathogens pervade fieldwork experiences, highlighting latent interspecies entanglements and the ways they affect human health. This chapter explores how these experiences with illness were interpreted by the communities with which he was working, revealing different perceptions about the social and ecological relationships in which they were embedded. Reflecting on illness in the field reveals the critical limitations of the body as an instrument for certain kinds of participative research, but also the generative possibilities of using sensorial ethnographic approaches.

1.4 Bio-ethics, Fieldwork Practices and Ground Reality

Ethics and politics as well as the politics of ethics in social research have long been a burning issue because ethical guidelines become mal-functional in the field, on the one hand, and ethical questions put the entire research and researcher under a big question of moral challenges. In anthropology, bio-ethics has long been a serious methodical questions. Monir Moniruzzaman in Chap. 9 critically brings in the question of bio-ethics in his ground-breaking research on kidney sellers. In doing his ethnographic fieldwork on the illicit trade in human organs, spanning more than a decade, he faced tremendous difficulties, particularly in gaining access to kidney sellers, an extremely 'hidden population' in Bangladesh. Many kidney sellers did not disclose their actions to anyone, even to their family members, as selling body parts are considered an outlawed and repulsive act. Also, organ sellers reside in every part of the country and are unknown to each other; therefore, he was unable to employ snowball sampling in locating them. While all of my avenues were exhausted, he gained the trust of a major organ broker, who facilitated him to connect with 33 kidney sellers (30 male and 3 female) in Bangladesh. His novel methodological grounding, that is, employing an organ broker to locate organ sellers, however, raises major ethical challenges: should the organ broker be my key informant when he was involved in illegal activities and potentially exploiting others? To what extent should he be involved in my research? Should he comply to reimburse him for his work? In this chapter, he has outlined in detail how he gained access to 33 kidney sellers by employing an organ broker as my key informant. Relevant ethical issues, such as risks and challenges, as well as roles and responsibilities of the researcher in doing ethnographic fieldwork in an underground setting, will also be explored. As his research would not have been possible without the broker's support, he argues that the key informant technique is effective in gaining access to 'hidden populations'.

Ethnographic research has gradually expanded its scope to too many challenging fields which demand serious bio-ethical concerns and one of those is surrogacy. Pragna Paramita Mondal in Chap. 10 deals with the methodological concerns that were experienced as part of intensive multi-sited field research on Indian surrogacy in the cities of Kolkata, Mumbai, Pune, Anand and Howrah between 2014 and 2017. The discussion would offer an insight into the challenges and processes of accumulating diversified qualitative data from the principal stakeholders in three different phases as the surrogacy law in India was constantly undergoing radical shifts and was transitioning from a commercial to a kin-based altruistic model. Family creation through artificial reproductive technology had more or less been a contested issue but the insistence on the scope and appropriateness of the use of the surrogacy services for poor Indian women with socio-economic vulnerabilities changed the entire discourse of assisted reproduction in the country. Consequently, it added to the moral contingency and legal precariousness of surrogacy procedures following the periodic evolution of its legislative mandate in India. This had immense significance in the context of research accessibility and data collection on surrogacy as perceptions of confidentiality and legal immunity were reconfigured because of the transformative guidelines. The chapter is divided into the following sections: section I introduces the concept and methodological outline of the study and discusses the issue of securing institutional ethical clearance for initiating research on human subjects, especially amid the changing legal narratives on surrogacy in India. The emphasis here is on the conceptualization of 'informed consent' as part of the research design and its ramification in the fields of biomedicine, social sciences and feminist legal theory as being layered, subjective and incomplete. Section II describes the experience of field research in the subsequent phases and highlights the aspect of trust-building and anonymity, the use of specific tools for data gathering, the intricacies of pooling respondents in varied region-specific contexts and the alterations in methodology and strategies that impacted the outcome of the research. Section III is an exploration of how the research has sought to overcome the limitations that socio-legal constraints have otherwise generated in the documentation of surrogacy in India. The final section concludes the discussion and proffers recommendations on the future directions of conducting a social-scientific inquiry in the field of biomedicine, law and reproductive health.

The proximity between the researcher and the research participants is always imperative for good quality, but at the same, it poses challenges with the questions of partiality and biasness. Alak Paul in Chap. 11 explains that qualitative inquiry helps understand people's minds when researchers wish to be closed to their research participants. Here, many (researchers) prefer the purposive sampling method, especially when they work on sensitive topics. Generally, sensitive issue deals with society's vulnerable people or stigmatized subjects, accompanied by social prejudices and taboos. In qualitative 'fieldwork', the interviewer needs to keep trust in the interviewees. On the contrary, the respondent has to be emotionally attached to the issue that helps grow convenience. Researchers need to be flexible for 'unexpected information' which might change the research direction. Both parties need to be sensible to research content and respectful of each other's dignity and state of mind. Though it is difficult to generalize the research findings in the qualitative method, this method is still the best option to deal with sensitive issues or subjects. The author was involved with the everyday life of the marginalized and stigmatized people in public health during his doctoral research. The chapter presents a self-reported description developed of his research subjects, support and surrounding environments during his 'fieldwork' in the arena of health geographic study. Here, the researcher discusses how he planned his research settings; managed his diversified participants, both individual and group; developed suitable contacts through 'snowballing' or peers; earned trust using 'body language' and friendly attitude; and showed interest to listen to their 'sad stories' through in-depth interview, group discussion, case study, participant observation, etc. Apart from different experiences in survey planning and data collection experiences, problems faced in the 'fieldwork' and overall limitations of the qualitative research are also described in this chapter.

Doing research in an educational institution is also challenging particularly when it is about adolescents. Minjune Song in Chap. 12 noticed a parallel between equitable student treatment and the unfair reality of school drug and alcohol policies, prompting him to investigate the justification behind zero tolerance. The author's most recent fieldwork involves surveying and interviewing fifty adolescents bound to Connecticut on trends in drug use and their relationship with school policy and peers. In his analysis of the monthly frequency of drug use, he observed an interesting contrast between peer contextual factors and zero tolerance deterrents in impacting adolescent drug use, findings which have come to embody his research. His original plans to conduct in-depth interviews with the selected students were postponed due to the global pandemic. Recently, the author's interests have also expanded to video game addiction and government regulation. After the 1994 Gun-Free School Act, schools expanded the use of a zero-tolerance policy: all Connecticut private high schools have in place drug and alcohol policies that are punitive.

Based on the criminological theory of deterrence, the zero-tolerance policy delivers severe and certain punishments, designed to deter rational actors from engaging in problem behaviours. Existing research suggests that adolescents perceive rewards more strongly around peers and lack impulsive control, raising the possibility that peer pressure may override rational deterrence in an adolescents' decision-making process. An 'immune group' of adolescents predisposed to ignore punitive deterrents may play a sizable role in inducing peer drug use. If peer influence supersedes deterrence in a significant number of cases, adolescents who are affected both by deterrents and peer pressure may be at a higher risk of following the example of the 'immune group'. This study raises the question of whether Connecticut's private high school students' drug use is correlated with perceptions of policy punishment and contextual peer influences. A questionnaire that measured students' drug use on a scale of 1 to 4, perceived severity and likelihood of punishment out of 0 to 10, and interaction with drug-using peers out of 0 to 10, was completed by 50 respondents. While the results of this study are limited to Connecticut private high school students, the observed tendency in students to disregard risks and pursue peer-involved drug use may be generalized in adolescents. Even in places where school discipline is not a wide issue, the impact of contextual factors like peer influence must be re-conceptualized in thinking about school drug policies.

When the vulnerable category of people becomes the object of study, it always poses a certain form of ethical challenges and moral dilemmas regarding whether the researchers could do anything that can directly benefit the people. In Chap. 13, Md. Masud-All-Kamal, S. M. Monirul Hassan and Nasir Uddin have brought a new question of ethical challenges and moral dilemmas in doing fieldwork among the vulnerable community. They have explained that research with groups prone to multiple vulnerabilities places academic researchers in a wide range of ethical dilemmas and risks both methodologically and epistemologically. Drawing on our long-term research engagement with vulnerable coastal communities in Bangladesh, this chapter presents dilemmas and challenges that a researcher faces while undertaking qualitative fieldwork. They find that dilemmas and risks arise from listening to distress stories, knowing participants' problems, balancing demands made by the participants and benefits available to the participants during fieldwork. Ethical issues come up amid dealing with informants in the contexts of personal and collective vulnerabilities, as well as the question of immediate responses from the concerned authorities. A researcher ideally takes from the communities in the form of information but gives nothing material which is deeply needed for the vulnerable communities. Research is not essentially a task of 'give and take', but in the case of vulnerable communities, it puts a researcher in the dilemma of the contribution that could help the community in crisis. They suggest broadening the purview of formalized research ethics to minimize researchers' dilemmas in qualitative research.

1.5 Gendered Fieldwork and Gender Relations in Social Research

Gender relations in fieldwork have also been a much-debated issue in social sciences (See, Uddin, 2011). Since gender relation and the structure of its formation varies from society to society across regions, it upholds various dimensions in social research. Masculinity and femininity in fieldwork produce a different form of research findings since gender relation poses a big challenge in social sciences. Nahid Rezwana in Chap. 14 brilliantly brings in the discourse of identity, social taboo and culture in understanding gender-based violence (GBV) in Bangladesh. This chapter provides an overview of the extent and nature of the risks and challenges of doing fieldwork on GBV, especially on sexual abuse, rape and domestic violence against women. GBV is a pervasive problem in society, however, commonly under-reported and kept concealed within the family or local community. Based on fieldwork experiences in the remote locations of Bangladesh, the chapter presents the difficult situations that researchers face to get access to society and reach GBV victims to collect information. It is a social taboo to talk about domestic violence, which is often considered a family matter, and sexual violence is mostly kept hidden and not commonly shared with strangers. Connection to the gatekeepers, gender identity and interviewing skill of the researcher become the influencing factors in trust-building, access to information and the successful implementation of field-study plans. It becomes a big challenge for the researcher to build trust and conduct fieldwork within a planned period. Researchers in GBV research often apply qualitative research methods to understand the context, which requires longer fieldwork including the necessity of staying in the study area. However, disclosing social taboos and incorporating victims in the study, while discussing the role of perpetrators and society to get the whole picture often increases the insecurity of researchers. They have to be alert about their security as well as of the GBV survivors who may become victims of further harassment, humiliation and abuse. The chapter illustrates the major issues regarding fieldwork on GBV, and how these rising challenges are subdued using different research methods with intelligence and patience. By doing so, the chapter ensures that future researchers have access to relevant evidence of challenges present within the fieldwork and can combat such challenges with more confidence and safety.

Chapter 15 discusses the gendered dimension of social fieldwork. This chapter is an attempt to reflect on my academic journey about the ethical-political concerns that surround the question of methodological challenges in social sciences. While attempting to rethink the question of Partition and Partition-induced migration in West Bengal, Ekata Bakshi explains that in India at the intersections of caste, gender and region, through ethnographic research in a non-metropolitan city, from the initial (before fieldwork) stage, her research had tried to weave in the feminist questions of 'ethics',' self-reflexivity, the relationship between (structural) location and privilege, representation and knowledge production. Yet, when conducting the actual fieldwork, being a woman and third-generation member of a Partition-induced migrant family, she felt challenged by all the established notions of ethics and politics, as she sought to bring in the intersectional-feminist lens to reflect on the process. In her project, she sought to understand the experiences of paid labour of the caste women from the Scheduled Caste and Other Backward caste Partition migrant families to revisit the hitherto documented feminist narratives of the Partition in West Bengal, India. The question that then became ethically and methodologically salient was how an academic enterprise by an upper-caste woman that is enabled by the consumption of devalued, feminized labour of mostly Scheduled Caste and Other Backward caste women can ethically narrate such lives. Following certain strands of feminist thought, she, however, argues that neither a perfunctory acknowledgement of privilege nor complete disengagement from studying the less-privileged 'others' is an adequate way to address such ethical dilemmas. She, therefore, suggests a relational approach that not only tries to understand upper caste and Scheduled Caste femininity as co-constituted but also the researcher–researched relationship, in this context, as an extension of that co-constitution to be a partial way out of this roadblock. She seeks to enter and situate such co-constitution through the gendered and en-casted categories of labour and vulnerability. She does not, in this chapter, seek to provide fully realized resolutions, but focuses more on the mistakes and ignorance(s) that mark her journey and the possibilities of evolving as an anti-caste feminist that they potentially present.

In Chap. 16, Zuriatunfadzliah Sahdan illuminates the issue of women empowerment in domestic violence using the case of Malaysian society. She explains that photographs give voice to many abused women whose voices are unheard and remain unspeakable. Therefore, photographs sometimes turn into a very powerful voice of voiceless and muted groups like abused women. They capture the survivors' visceral experiences of fear of shadows, hearing voices and being haunted by the perpetrators in spaces of the home that have been used to confine them and their children, often for decades. Drawing on qualitative research with survivors in Malaysia, and working from a feminist postcolonial framework, this chapter focuses on how photovoice is used as a participatory method to convey women's spatial experiences of living in an abusive relationship and their feelings after they had escaped. This provides another way for women to speak about domestic violence discourse, which is often difficult in the conservative social climate of Malaysia. Despite facing challenges in the deployment of photovoice in the field, the method proved to be powerful and effective that resulted in solid empirical data regarding domestic violence.

It is always challenging to work with the opposite gender since the articulation of male-hood and female-hood are largely cultural conditions. Therefore, doing social research working with female informants or female research working with male informants has posed a big challenge in terms of validity, authenticity and quality of research due to male-female relations being full of shame, taboo and mutual mistrust. Main Uddin in Chap. 17 brings in the various forms of challenges that a male researcher faces while working with female informants in the case of Bangladesh's rural society. This chapter details his lived experience of year-long intensive fieldwork where, together with a female research assistant, he conducted an ethnographic study from January to December 2017 with the stay-behind female counterparts of the international migrants in a village in Bangladesh. Largely, the rural society of Bangladesh follows patrilocal residence where women are transferred from their natal home to that of their in-laws for which they are in-migrants from other villages. In general, they stay on homesteads and perform merely household activities while men dominate the public sphere and do outside work. In addition, the women are responsible to uphold the image and honour of their household members by following the norms and values of the family and the society where they are kept under invisible surveillance by the villagers including their household men. However, the migration of men brings fundamental changes in the lives of women as they perform both in the household and in the public spheres maintaining contact between homes and abroad. In such a social context, the study intends to investigate the continuity and changes in the discourse and practices of traditional gender roles and the development of the subjectivity and agency among women to explore the transformation in gender relations following the international migration of men. In doing so, the study deals with the gender-sensitive issues of a majority Muslim society where women are kept under a veil in public places and where the cultural and religious norms do not allow women to talk with women individually in separate places. The chapter is a comprehensive account of his engagement with the left-behind women in various challenging social situations. Thus, the chapter contributes to the field of feminism by exploring a range of gendered aspects of social and cultural life in rural Bangladesh.

1.6 Theoretical and Epistemic Challenges in the Field

What the graduate school trains in the class as research methodology and what the social researcher faces in the field have always been an issue of contestation in social science (See, Uddin, 2011). Theoretical understanding and practical experience sometimes differ in the field which generates a kind of epistemological problem. Nasir Uddin has presented such a contestation between academic and activist positions in researching the protracted refugee situations. Uddin explains in Chap. 18 that an unsettled contestation between activist positioning and academic repositioning has long been an issue of powerful debate in social research. It brings certain fundamental methodological questions in social search on board including subjectivity vs. objectivity, emic vs. etic, outsider vs. insider, native vs. foreigner, and 'self' vs. 'others'. Ethnographers frequently struggle to maintain a sensible equilibrium of a dichotomized positioning between attachment vs. detachment, association vs. disassociation, and engagements vs. disengagement with the object of study while doing fieldwork. It becomes more critical when it comes to the question of refugee research since refugees are often depicted with various negative connotations by the host society, but the researchers tend to stand by refugees due to perceived vulnerable conditions of refugeehood. This contested representation is articulated amidst the dynamics of refugee management. For example, human/refugee right activists and different rights bodies often consider refugees living in very inhuman conditions with poor housing, inadequate food and water supply, unhealthy sanitation, and the lack of many everyday essentials whilst the host community depict refugees living in 'rajar halee' (living like a king/queen) receiving more than what they need supplied by national and international aids agencies. Given the context, the chapter, with my decade-long experience of research on/with the Rohingya refugees, presents the contestation of activist and academic (re)positioning in refugee research because an academic cannot 'blame the victims', on the one hand, and cannot ignore the sufferings of the host society, on the other hand. The chapter illuminates the ways how an ethnographer could make an intelligent balance between how to become politically sensitive even without being an activist and deeply committed to the object of study even by maintaining a maximum degree of academic neutrality. Though objectivity and neutrality are relative ideas and subjectively loaded concepts, an ethnographer with his/her training, ethical ground, moral standard and a strong sense of commitment can maximize the degree of academic objectivity to minimize the gap between activism and academia.

Technological intervention in social research has generated another kind of challenge because society was conventionally understood in the form of relations and interactions between and among the social organization and institutions. In Chap. 19, Deo-Gracias Houndolo explains that data quality determines primarily research quality, and it is the first ingredient before analytical techniques and tools can be applied. Research that requires fieldwork and data collection must invest considerable endeavours during the preparation phase, data collection process in the field and data quality check after the field. He learned over twenty years of experience and practice that each fieldwork is unique, and always brings its unique context and challenges that require an adaptation of existing research methods or innovative approaches to address them. In this chapter, he looks over various fieldwork activities he got directly involved in since the year 2000. He shares the challenges faced that cover ample selection, adaptation to cultural and religious norms, the use of computer-based technology in areas with no internet and electricity coverage, and language challenges. He looks at managing the shortage of time allocated for fieldwork, facing budget constraints, health issues in the field, tracking respondents in a panel data surveys, adapting to the high refusal rate of respondents, etc. In addition to the challenges, this chapter also presents the adjustments made to the context and field realities, without compromising data quality. Reflecting on those experiences, he shares key lessons learned over the years. He pulls from African

(Benin, Niger, Democratic Republic of Congo, Chad, Togo, Burkina-Faso, Kenya) contexts where he used or supported questionnaire surveys, field interviews, direct observations and transect analysis for data collection. Those data were used for policy impact evaluation, agricultural development, forestry, humanitarian assistance interventions, gender analyses, etc. The challenges and lessons learned that are presented in this chapter remind researchers and practitioners of how complex fieldworks and data collection processes are, and why it is critical to manage them well to support evidence-informed decision making for development.

The researcher's positionality among the research participants and informants has always been a big challenge in social research because being a human being, objective claim-making is not always taken for granted (See, Uddin, 2011). A researcher has to build his/her positionality in course of time and the 'rites of passage' of fieldwork. In Chap. 20, Matteo Fumagalli, drawing on fieldwork conducted in post-Soviet Central Asia, explores questions of researcher positionality about research on ethnic minorities. This allows him to reflect on his positionality as an international researcher from an institution in the Global North conducting fieldwork in authoritarian, conflict/post-conflict and/or illiberal contexts. The chapter uses experiences and lessons learnt as regards entry and access to 'the field'—as well as bans and subsequent returns—to reflect on issues of privilege and (self-)representation and more generally situated knowledge, to shed light on how his identities impacted on the production of knowledge and how his researcher was shaped by the structures in which it was embedded and being created. The chapter compares challenges and opportunities in entry and access to three field sites different in time, place and openness of the research environment: the case of the Tajik community in Uzbekistan; the position of ethnic Uzbeks in Kyrgyzstan and Tajikistan and their relationship with Uzbekistan; and the ethnic Koreans in Kyrgyzstan and Uzbekistan. The chapter draws on lessons learnt over multiple rounds of fieldwork from 2001 to 2021, amid the COVID-19 pandemic. As it highlights the fluid and relational nature of positionality(-ies), the chapter calls for active reflexivity to more consciously reflect on researcher positionality.

Knowledge production is always challenging in social science because the entire process of empirical data collection involves personal-level engagement and attachment between researchers and the people studied. Good-quality knowledge production is only possible if an ethnographer could make an intelligent balance between relations and professions. In Chap. 21, Sayed Md Saikh Imtiaz explains that knowledge production is a contested process in Anthropology. Anthropologists are critical of the power relation and degree of freedom that an Anthropologist may enjoy in narrating the culture s/he studies. Some Anthropologists like Talal Asad (1973) are particularly critical of the colonial roots while others like Clifford and Marcus (1986) questioned the scientific methods of anthropology in the 'writing cultures'. Such self-criticism of Anthropology has rightly questioned the relationship between the anthropologists, the people represented in the texts and their textual representations.

Therefore, an anthropologist's role in the field as well as her/his interpretations of the texts have ultimately placed the issues of power and representation at the core of the discussion. This questioning has also sparked a significant criticism of ethnography as a method as not 'objective'. This chapter has focused on reflexivity as a tool to ensure objectivity, describing the researcher's experiences in ethnography on sexuality among young men in Dhaka, Bangladesh. It states how the consciousness regarding 'multiple selves' has helped the researcher to identify his values, assumptions and biases, while adopting 'shifting roles' as a 'native ethnographer' has ultimately resulted in increasing trust among the respondents and thereby getting access to the youth culture on sex—an already taboo issue in a Muslim-majority country like Bangladesh. Thus, the chapter provides empirical evidence of how reflexivity may help researchers to conduct an ethnographic study on difficult subjects like sexual practice. The chapter is based on two ethnographic works on sexuality among the young men conducted in Dhaka, Bangladesh 2006–2010 and 2015–2018 as part of two projects; the doctoral and a post-doctoral trajectory.

1.7 Nativity, Participants Selection and Challenges in Archival Research

The idea of the native itself is a problematic one but nativity has always represented an affirmative aspect of social research (See Asad, 1973). But, it creates different kinds of challenges in identifying bthe researcher's positioning in the field and post-fieldwork writing about the product of fieldwork. Kapil Dahal has brought a brilliant analysis of nativity and the dilemmas of ethnographer's positioning using the case of Nepal in Chap. 22. Dahal has explained that native anthropologists have begun to contribute to knowledge production in Nepal for more than three decades, gradually increasing in the last two decades. Nevertheless, being native in a country context can in no way be similar to that of being an insider, and thus being an outsider as well in pursuing ethnography. This chapter highlights that the positionality of the researcher as being an insider/outsider is neither a priori nor an objective status but rather a socially constructed relative identity. This chapter also points out that even research that began with a participatory approach may provide space for the researcher to have such experience of being in the dilemma of inside/outside. This chapter argues that there is no either-or situation, and it depends upon the lens through which the researcher and/or the research participants assess the researcher's positionality largely determines this. In reflecting upon this, this chapter deals with how often gender, caste, ethnicity, educational status and regional origin of a researcher are taken as identity markers along with and sometimes which may differ with his/her research topic at hand. This chapter is based on the reflective experience of conducting anthropological research on health and well-being in Nepal over the last two decades. However, experience, information and reflection are mainly drawn from a multi-sited ethnographic study that was carried out to generate information about the health-seeking practices of Tarai Brahmin women in different periods between 2012 and 2015. To some extent, adopting, and also departing from, conventional community ethnography and its various rites of passage, he followed the people related to health-seeking and their interactions with service providers at a health facility in the locality as well as in the neighbouring towns and cities in India. In ethnographic studies, interaction, participation and observation techniques were employed to generate information which was later analysed reflexively.

A human being studying another human being brings a conflict of interest for sure but a professional treatment could blur the conflict and keep it under a comfortable stage so that a researcher could smoothly complete his/her research (See, Uddin, 2011). In Chap. 23, Melati Nungsari explains that social research begins, fundamentally, with human participants. Hence, the recruitment of participants for research projects in the social sciences is of utmost importance. However, in my personal experience doing fieldwork, this is often the hardest step—significantly more complicated than the conceptualization of the research question and design, or even the analysis of the data collected. This problem is compounded even further when one works with hidden or vulnerable groups. Traditionally, participant recruitment has happened through the use of community leaders (Sigel and Friesema 1965; Natale-Pereira et al. 2008; Chan et al. 2015), with the assumption being that the voice of the community leader represents the will of the community they belong to. However, to what extent can we study the entire population by studying only a few people at the 'top', especially when there usually is no democratic process that governs the selection of leaders? More importantly, if recruitment through community leaders is fraught with problems, what are some better ways of recruiting participants from a vulnerable group for a study? In this chapter, based on her fieldwork with refugees in Malaysia, Nungsari explores a couple of different ways to recruit participants. She also considers, both from experience and the academic literature, the pros and cons of each mode of recruitment.

Social research does not essentially take place in the field since archives could also be a field where social research could be done. In Chap. 24, Sanjukta Ghosh delves into the challenges of historical methods of inquiry based on reading the colonial archives to locate indigenous voices and opinions that questioned authority and vanguards of scientific agricultural knowledge. It entails empirical research open to alternative interpretations, making the field of socio-historical investigation tentative, and a methodologically complex reflexive framing of marginalized archival data. While literary engagement with the archive raises new alarms, it is possible to disentangle the official storyline by looking at the visual language of unintended consequences. One such opening comes in the form of vernacular literature and its myriad uses. Besides, non-officials have often left accounts probing between the documents for stories left untold, and questions left unanswered. A literary reading of the visual in the form of alternate narratives of agency and empowerment can lead to entangled histories of science, colonial history and postcolonial society.

1.8 Conclusion

It is admittable that most of the volumes on social research methodology available in the market tell us about the various issues of social research from different points of view. Most books discuss the theoretical aspects of social research where field aspects receive less attention. Some books provide fieldwork matters but have poor diversity of intellectuality. Some books cover only developed or developing countries. On the contrary, this book accommodates many issues under one cover from epistemological, ontological and methodological perspectives. Researchers around the globe present their fieldwork experiences having different inter-disciplinary backgrounds in social sciences which might be a new dimension in the field of social research publication. This book will be a good sourcebook of various fieldwork experiences including scopes, opportunities and challenges along with their mitigation aspects for fieldworkers in social sciences. It accommodates personal accounts of fieldwork in challenging social contexts of well-trained academic and professional researchers having diversified disciplinary backgrounds including sociology, anthropology, political sciences, geography, international relations, law, area studies and so on. Experiences of intensive fieldwork in different geographical settings on various topics and with newer methodological tools could provide a comprehensive and distinctive framework of social research in contemporary academia and research field. The content of the book thus enables us to refine and fine-tune the social research methodologies for the time to come.

References

Asad, T. (1973). *Anthropology and colonial encounter*. London: Ithaca Press.
Bell, S., Foley, R., Houghton, F., Maddrell, A. and Williams, A. (2018). "From therapeutic landscapes to healthy spaces, places and practices: A scoping review." *Social Science & Medicine*, 196: 123–130.
Chan, Kim-Yin, Marilyn A. Uy, Oleksandr S. Chernyshenko, Moon-Ho Ringo Ho, and Yoke-Loo Sam. (2015). "Personality and entrepreneurial, professional and leadership motivations." *Personality and individual differences* 77: 161–166.
Clifford, James. (1986). "Partial Truth". In Clifford, J., and Marcus, G.E., eds. *Writing Culture: Poetic and Politics of Ethnography*, pages; 01–26. Berkeley, CA: California University Press.
Crapanzano, V., (2010). *At the Heart of the Discipline. Emotions in the field: The psychology and anthropology of fieldwork experience*, edited by J. Davies and D. Spencer, pp. 55–78.
Duff, C. and Hill, N. (2022). "Wellbeing as social care: On assemblages and the 'commons', Wellbeing", *Space and Society*, 3, 100078.

Foley, R. and Kistemann, T. (2015). "Blue Space Geographies: Enabling Health in Place. Introduction to Special Issue on Healthy Blue Space", *Health & Place*, 35, 157–165.

Foley, R., Bell, S., Gittins, H., Grove, H., Kaley, A., McLauchlan, A, Osborne, T., Power, A., Roberts, E. and Thomas, M., 2020. "Disciplined research in undisciplined settings: Critical Explorations of In-Situ & Mobile Methodologies in Geographies of Health and Wellbeing." *Area*, 52, 514–522.

Garcia, C.M., Eisenberg, M.E., Frerich, E.A., Lechner, K.E. and Lust K. 2012. "Conducting Go-Along Interviews to Understand Context and Promote Health." *Qualitative Health Research*, 22(10), 1395–1403.

Marcus, George E. (1995), "Ethnography in/of the World System: The Emergence of Multi-Sited Ethnography." *Annual Reviews of Anthropology*, Vol. 24: 95–117.

Natale-Pereira, Ana, Jonnie Marks, Marielos Vega, Dawne Mouzon, Shawna V. Hudson, and Debbie Salas-Lopez. "Barriers and facilitators for colorectal cancer screening practices in the Latino community: perspectives from community leaders." *Cancer Control* 15, no. 2 (2008): 157–165.

Sigel, Roberta S., and H. Paul Friesema. (1965). "Urban community leaders' knowledge of public opinion." *Western Political Quarterly*, 18, no. 4: 881–895.

Uddin, Nasir. (2011). "Decolonising Ethnography in the Field: An anthropological Account." *International Journal of Social Research Methodology*, 14(6), 455–467.

Uddin, Nasir. (2022). "Research on Rohingya Refugees: Methodological Challenges and Textual Inadequacy." In Nasir Uddin *Voices of the Rohingya: A Case of Genocide, Ethnocide and Subhuman Life*, pages: 27–51. Switzerland: Palgrave Macmillan.

PART I

Fieldwork in Challenging Social Settings

CHAPTER 2

Research in a Moving Field: Doing In-aqua Research in Blue Space Settings

Ronan Foley

2.1 Introduction

While much social fieldwork is carried out on *terra firma*, there is a growing interest in research on and in the water based on a recent turn in human geographical research towards blue space (Foley and Kistemann 2015), especially in relation to a range of leisure practices that promote health and wellbeing. In parallel, there has been a growing interest in geo-narratives, in which emotional responses and geospatial tracking are co-produced in situ, on, in or near the water (Bell et al. 2017). In both cases, the fieldwork involves a deeply immersive process, which can be challenging for both the researcher and co-participant. This chapter will provide an initial survey of such work and the often-difficult process of gathering research from, by, in, on and under the water (Foley et al. 2020). This will be exemplified in fieldwork-driven studies of surfing, kayaking, diving, sailing and swimming (Foley et al. 2019; Peters et al. 2022). The chapter will additionally document recent field-based research with swimmers in Ireland using swim-along interviews, as one specific empirical example, to suggest the value of such work for enhanced knowledge production, while also considering critically its value over other approaches to water-based fieldwork.

Theoretically, such fieldwork approaches draw from an assemblages of health model (Duff and Hill 2022), where specific social, affective and material properties emerge from the immersive methods used, with a particular interest in

---

R. Foley (✉)
Department of Geography, Maynooth University, Maynooth, Ireland
e-mail: ronan.foley@mu.ie

© The Author(s), under exclusive license to Springer Nature Switzerland AG 2023
N. Uddin, A. Paul (eds.), *The Palgrave Handbook of Social Fieldwork*, https://doi.org/10.1007/978-3-031-13615-3_2

how such immersive work can be health-enabling. In terms of socially emplaced fieldwork, key critical comments associated with such specifically in-situ research, consider how such approaches uncover and co-trace the experiences of different participants within different settings. While the focus is always on relational dimensions of health and wellbeing, such methods almost inevitably cover aspects of risk, access, authenticity, technologies and representation; all germane to this chapter (Guasco 2022). Doing research in the very mobile settings of waters, both coastal and inland, can be challenging in terms of practice, ethics and the kinds of contemporary technologies used in such work. Yet, each blue space study, whatever the water, seeks to identify important knowledge from place, recognising that doing research in specific and unique geographical settings can present a range of challenges for social researchers, but provide a depth of understanding of such spaces, settings and practices, precisely from that immersion. As a practice rooted in health-enabling spaces, where embodiment, emotions and experience are all central (Bell et al. 2018), such fieldwork also echoes Anderson and Smith's suggestion 'that social relations are lived through the emotions, but that the emotional qualities of social life have rarely been made apparent within the lexicon of social research' (Anderson and Smith, Anderson and Smith 2001: 9).

2.2 Literature Review

Blue Space, Health and Wellbeing

Blue space is a term whose origins are hard to pin down, but Völker and Kistemann's (2015) study of urban river and lake spaces in Germany was a key early work, as was the identification of the coast as a 'Blue Gym' by Depledge and Bird (2009). More formal definitions and applied studies, at least within health geography, also emerged in a special issue of *Health & Place* (Foley and Kistemann 2015). That text and a later edited collection by Foley et al. (2019) identified assemblages of blue space settings and practices that incorporated work on island spaces, historical settings, canals, coasts and lakes within which a range of practices—sailing, surfing, diving, swimming, kayaking—exemplified how those spaces were used for specific health and wellbeing purposes. There were two strands to this work in terms of extending the field. One was theoretical, in that much of this research was qualitative and invoked links to earlier research on therapeutic landscapes, spoke to a new relational geography of health, but deepened this to consider a range of identifiable embodied, emotional and experiential elements that enabled health and wellbeing in place (Bell et al. 2018; Cummins et al. 2007).

A second strand aimed to match method to theory in combining assemblages of health with parallel assemblages of field methods that were also mobile, active and immersive. Such methods, typically carried out in situ and with a strong go-along ethos, sought to uncover how different users and different places emerged in co-creative ways that also reflected cultural and social affordances (Bell and Bush 2021). It is also important to consider wider research on green space that documents positive links between time spent in nature and benefits to health and the methods used to do this (White et al. 2019). One theoretical socio-ecological model by Lachowycz and Jones (2013) considered the mechanisms of how, in their case, access to green space linked exposure to outcome, how that was moderated in place, what supportive mechanisms existed and how these were, in turn, mediated by immersive engagements to produce health benefits. Other green space research used a range of technological approaches using GIS and GPS to measure and track, for example, physical activity spaces within parks and other public spaces (Mears et al. 2021). Both strands have also informed recent blue space research methods that seeks to uncover similar mediating and moderating factors and processes that enable health and wellbeing in, in this case, a moving blue field.

Geo-narratives

The go-along is an established method globally across human geography and leisure studies (Burns et al. 2020; Foley et al. 2019), with a particular intent to uncover insights on health and wellbeing, literally in place (Garcia et al. 2012). Within work on both green and blue space, one key exemplar of this type of fieldwork were geo-narratives (Bell et al. 2015) as a particular strand of go-along work. Bell's work used a go-along approach walking and talking with participants on coastal cliffs or in the water on kayaks, so literally crossed the land-water threshold. She combined these walking interviews with wearable technologies that digitally mapped the route along with accelerometers that tracked speed of movement but also moments of speeding up and slowing down. Having access to all these dimensions within the field provided rich empirical content that linked specific narratives to specific places and moments, within which place acted as a trigger of reflections on health and wellbeing (Bell et al. 2015). A geo-narrative was a very specific form of sensing place, while capturing mobile traces and emotional responses at the same time and reflected Anderson and Smith's exhortation (Anderson and Smith 2001: 8): '…to embrace … emotive topographies, their "structures of feeling" or … try to capture them in some way'. So, the foundational idea of a geo-narrative as a specifically in-situ practice provides a methodological field route that combines fields, relations and emotions across blurred land and sea settings (Fig. 2.1).

Getting into the Water: Go-alongs in Blue Space

As one key aspect of this chapter is to document fieldwork that does literally get into the water, then recent studies in the area of blue space, health and wellbeing document this more clearly. One key review focused solely on specific interventions in blue space (Britton et al. 2018), where the focus was more evidence and outcome-based. Settings and practices identified in this review included canoeing, fishing, sailing, scuba-diving, surfing and swimming, linked to a wide

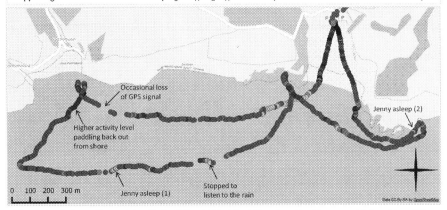

Pete: We went from the car park, hence the very slow walk down with the canoe ((laughs)) and then over to Portholland where our son was on the beach with his cubs, 'cos they had the day there. And then we went out around the corner here to see what was round there. Where it's all plotted together back about here, that's where Jenny fell asleep ((laughs))… It started to rain so we stopped for a while and just listened to the rain on the water. It was very calming. Then you come back and there's a little beach just there, which you can't get to except for on a boat. Then went round to explore all the little coves around this side. We stopped again there and she fell asleep again ((laughs)) It's the only time that she'll relax, she'll be asleep!

N.B. A dot is plotted every 10 seconds (provided the GPS could detect signal). The colour of the dot corresponds to the relative activity level detected by the accelerometer, whilst the location of the dot is determined by the associated GPS reading. Darker coloured dots indicate relatively greater accelerations per 10s time period (i.e. participants were being more active). The greater the distance between the dots, the faster the GPS unit was travelling. This canoe trip lasted approx. five hours.

Fig. 2.1 Representation of GeoNarrative from kayak. (Bell et al. 2015; p. 61)

range of physical and mental health conditions. Immersion across these settings varied; being by, on, in and under the water. Wider blue space research, more qualitative in its approach, further documents this immersive experience with examples drawn from diving (Merchant 2016; Straughan 2012), swimming (Denton and Aranda 2019; Foley 2017; Gould et al. 2021; Moles 2021; Olive and Wheaton 2021), sailing (Brown 2019; Couper 2018), surfing (Anderson, Anderson 2012; Britton et al. 2020; Evers 2009; Lisahunter and Emerald 2016) and canoeing/kayaking (1 Lund et al. 2020). While the specific form of immersion differs in each case, they all require doing in-aqua research in blue space settings. The specific fieldwork methods used in each will be detailed below, but the nature of the different practices each require different approaches, all shaped by the different waters in which they occur. That 'different waters' element is very important to all fieldwork in blue space. It is never solely maritime, as lakes, rivers, canals and other bodies of water are also involved. Equally, there is no specific pristine blue, and different shades and temperatures are invoked, with much of the swimming literature drawn from cold-water swimming, a dimension we note as having specific impacts on field-based methods. The water surfaces can range from still to stormy, while the dimensions of the blue space range from enclosed to open (McDougall et al. 2022). The blue spaces themselves also vary from fully open/public to more enclosed or indeed exclusive, private settings. In the case of the latter aspects of exclusion and the place of bodies of difference have also featured in research and shape field experiences, while other dimensions of ageing, expertise, belonging and identify can also shape the mobile field experience (Costello et al. 2019).

2.3 Methods: Technologies and Ethics

While specific examples will be discussed in the next section, it is worth mentioning that quite often in-situ methods, especially those in hard-to-control blue settings, usually have a rough ride from ethics committees (Foley et al. 2020). This can especially be the case in medical sciences, though slightly easier to negotiate in social sciences and even humanities settings. In all cases, doing fieldwork in the water always has ethical dimensions. Quite apart from risk associated with the uncertainty associated with all waters, coastal and inland, the kinds of in-situ methods increasingly being used do tend to be personal, embodied and often very invasive, especially if working with wearable technologies, tracking devices. Moving beyond the body, blue spaces are sites of significant inhabitation, and research in such spaces can have negative elements: invasion of spaces, privacy, access and place triggers, which are often countered in ethical risk/benefit terms with more positive dimensions of place-care of/for self and others, shared socialisation and deeper awareness of the more-than-human. Some recent papers also consider critically research carried out in certain blue spaces, especially in the Global South, in part based on indigenous ownership, post-colonial privilege and specific masculinist and endangering overtones, though a respect for and co-working with research subjects remains a core positive aspect (Guasco 2022; Olive and Wheaton 2021; Shefer and Bozalek 2022).

2.4 Empirical: Recent In-aqua Research

Blue Space Fieldwork: Key Observations

In looking more closely at the specific field-based research in blue spaces, a number of recent survey papers document these (Britton et al. 2018; Foley et al. 2020) both in terms of the wellbeing practice but also the methods used, mostly in situ and often with visual and technological components to do this. The use of action cameras has, as the name suggests, been a mainstay of mainstream recording of surfing, diving and kayaking, where the recording of the in-the-moment embodied experience is a mainstay of research output, used in subsequent visual analysis and video elicitation (Evers 2015; lisahunter and Emerald 2016). In diving studies, where underwater camera and video is also used, it is difficult to communicate, and the use of post-dive video elicitation is a central aspect of such work, with the researcher and co-diver talking through the dive immediately after its completion (Merchant 2016). Other video recordings, for example, of a swim or sail, can be valuable but can also be a little hands-off and more of a fish-eye lens approach, though more ethnographic and narrative methods can typically capture the feel of a swim or a sail in quite effective ways (Brown 2019; Moles 2021). What does emerge from all these studies is a lively sense of the experiential flow of that blue space practice and the afterglow as an important wellbeing outcome. Many blue space users identified at times an initial reluctance to full immersion, but post-immersion, in whatever sport or leisure pursuit, almost never regretted it. Across all these study settings what emerged, however it was captured, was a recognition that being in blue space provided access to a public health asset, allowed for the expression of identity for oneself and with others and crucially enabled a physical activity which was invariably beneficial, and usually brought mental benefits in its literal wake. The use of some wearable technologies in the water, capturing things like heart rate, cortisol levels or speed and duration, was also effective in capturing this as evidence. Finally, other studies of, for example, swimming with young people with mental health issues such as autism or depression, identified very specific pathways to success in these areas. Britton et al.'s (2020) work, picked up on specific embodied barriers for autistic children, for example, reluctance in putting on restrictive wetsuits, which once in the water, became quickly forgotten. Getting into the water provided a sea-level view that was shared and experienced together with the autistic children and identified evident wellbeing effects linked to enjoyment and relaxation in the water, a response also noted in other blue space research linked to sailing courses with deprived urban youth in Norway (Broch 2020).

Swim-alongs in Ireland

One key developing fieldwork method in blue space is the swim-along interview. Most fully explored by Denton and Aranda (2019) and Denton et al. (2021), the aim of such research is to try and capture a voice from the water, while sharing the same practice and being actively mobile, all at the same time. As these studies, based in the cold-water environment of Brighton, United Kingdom, attest, doing this type of fieldwork is trickier than land-based work for a variety of reasons. These include the temperature of the water, the recording technologies, the specifics of recording effectively in fluid waters, the movement in the water with research participants, the cold and the length of engagement. In all cases, recording effectively in a cold-water swimming environment was fraught with difficulties, but considered worthwhile in uncovering the narratives of transformation, connection and re-orientation, which were enabled by the immersive methodological approach (Denton and Aranda 2019). The rest of the section will document a specific recent study from Ireland that sought to use similar methods but in different waters and using a specific spatial video technology to record the field experience.

The Irish study was based on swim-alongs involving twenty-three swimmers in total (13f, 8 m) at six different locations, three coastal (Killiney, Greystones, Guillemene) and three inland (Lough Derg, Lough Ramor, River Nore), carried out between July and October 2021 during the ongoing COVID-19 pandemic. At each swimming location, an assemblage of evidence was gathered from image and sound and video to swim-alongs recorded using go-pros, smartphone and zoom sound recorder and subsequently uploaded onto Ubipix spatial video software. Ubipix is a free to use spatial video app developed at Maynooth University and downloadable by anyone from the ubipix.com website. Basically, the field research involved taking a video of the swim with a go-pro, though a waterproof smartphone would also work; the hands-free nature of the former was, however, an advantage. When the video clip is uploaded online, the software generates a literal trace but aligns this exactly to the video frames. So, clicking on any point in the geographical trace brings you to the exact location on the video and vice versa. Five distinct bits of information are also generated in the conversion process; video, sound, height and speed but also the direction of the camera gaze. Figure 2.2 below shows a screen grab of a typical Ubipix recording. One key additional potential is that you can tag any point in the video, and it can be stored, but the system will also generate xy co-ordinates for that tag. It is also possible to write short tag descriptions to screen as sort of a memo for thematic analysis. One last thing is that it is also possible to create stills from micro-moments of the swim.

With the conversation in the water, as well as at times, just before and just after the swim, a number of broad questions were to guide the content in the direction of health and wellbeing; though more often than not, the conversations evolved in the water. Typical questions posed included those that sought to uncover swimming history, connection to place, place preference, swimming habits, health and wellbeing responses and other observations in the water. For example, from a river swim, the swimmer noted the wellbeing benefits of being in touch with wildlife in a more organic way; being on the same level as the birds meant not being noticed in the same way but also brought the swimmer down to nature's level. More broadly, all of the swims identified important aspects of attention-restoration, stress-reduction and improved mindfulness in and around the water, something that was augmented specifically by the waterborne conversation. People seemed able to talk and reflect differently in the water than on dry land, though the conversation did often flow across both. In terms of reminiscence and reflection, the swim acted as an in-situ place trigger, stimulating memory, recall and a form of restoration of affect, at least in the moment immediately around the swim. Yet there was also the value of the swim as one in an evolving set of everyday moments/events that build to a longer-term, sustained yet varied wellbeing practice; noted by one lake swimmer: *'it's different every time, every time it's different. It's a different feel, the sky is grey today. It looks different every day. The grass and everything. and the sound of it, you know'* (Ramor, F).

During the swim-alongs, the swimmers were to an extent allowed to set the agenda apart from direct prompts though it was difficult to set a hard and fast rule as each swim and each setting varied hugely. While a structured approach to capturing the swim, with defined pre-, during- and post-swim periods,

Fig. 2.2 Representative Image from Ubipix screen grab

might work better for more robust analysis, the experience of the swim-along felt as if a more open approach was helpful. This applied in part to group swims, where leaving space for the incidental and unplanned at times sometimes felt effective in terms of getting a variety of responses, and it was also the case that health and wellbeing emerged naturally in swimmer's own voices.

Given quite a few of the swimmers were either new or returned swimmers in local blue spaces due to COVID-19 lockdowns, the timing of the swim-alongs uncovered specific momentary effects with river swimmers using the nearest river as a space of respite and a break from home, consistent with wider healthy nature findings on stress-reduction, attention-restoration and a general break in a mobile and populated space, in direct contrast to lockdown domestic environments. These aspects of socialisation were also central to maintaining mental health, something described by another river swimmer, *'Oh it was, it was literally five months of it (lockdown). Now I'm lucky in that it was end of April I started swimming; you know getting back in here (in river). But you are talking then it was really four months without swimming. I felt it, yeah … also for the mind'* (Nore, M).

Hitchings and Latham (2020) note a lack of honesty and elision in many academic papers on difficulties encountered doing fieldwork, and this is a valid suggestion, especially in the complex and mobile settings in which swimming takes place. There is considerable promise in spatial video, though the research process identifies several aspects of bad practice, some of which were researcher-specific. Go-pro usage was an issue with research participants with one popping off a swimmer's head and spending a night at the bottom of the lake, while another swimmer's insistence on dipping their head in and out of the water at all times damaged the screen. Sometimes the on button was switched to image or was accidentally switched off and incorrectly used. So, by a process of trial and error, a dual go-pro approach, one worn by the researcher, one by the swimming participant, provided the best results in the form of back-up and triangulation. But in almost all of the core swims a recording was made of some of the swim, while backup smartphone video and sound recordings were used out of the water to generate what could be called a methodological assemblage. There are also some ethical issues, though the project was approved based on respondent buy-in and signed permission forms. Where possible, the use of the Ubipix material would always try and exclude direct faces, but one of the advantages of the respondent wearing their own go-pro is images taken from their perspective, which maintained privacy; this also applied to any screengrabs from the images. The speed and variety of swimmer's interviewed, especially in group swims (of which there were several), means an interviewer needs to have a decent level of expertise and speed, though many swimmers were hard to keep up with. In general, though slow swims or even wading and chatting was the most productive way to talk, while both river and lake proved to be sonically more reliable than the sea, where sound seemed to diffuse more easily.

2.5 Discussion and Summary

In-aqua approaches to fieldwork are still relatively new, but the renewed fascination with the sea across a range of literature, and its identification as a key multi-disciplinary site for empirical research, means increased attention is needed on how to research on and in the water (Peters et al. 2022). In its material form, and in the field-based methods used to research it, water is complex, mobile and an always unpredictable more-than-human element in such research. This can shape how and when the fieldwork can be done, as well as bringing in other considerations such as risk and access. While this chapter has focused on links between blue space, health and wellbeing, especially its immersive dimensions, there are other geographies—economic, cultural, environmental—that also involved an immersive relationship with water, from fishing and eco-tourism to conservation and marine spatial planning to sustainability and globalisation (George 2013; Winder and Le Heron 2017). Each of these can and do use in-aqua methods, but some of the methods listed here may speak to those geographies as does the wider theoretical focus on assemblage theory (Duff and Hill 2022). Immersive assemblages take many forms in the water and a flexible approach to fieldwork including the kinds of ethnographic methods used by the likes of George (2013), which involved living and working on container ships for a year, shows that immersive methods may take different forms.

In all of the blue space studies, especially those which involved embodied, emotional and experiential imbrications in blue spaces and practices (Conradson 2005), there are always contested elements; one of the values of in-situ research is to provide a close-up view of these contested spaces, whether that be inadvertent or advertent (Foley 2019). This latter term is important, given it means being heedful and paying close attention to the world in which one immerses oneself. Contestation emerges in multiple ways within such fieldwork. There are aspects of access and localism in swimming and surfing research, around who is or isn't allowed into a space, with some interesting knock-on effects on some groups in society. Both Wiltse (2007) and Phoenix et al. (2021) recount how historical exclusion of African Americans from swimming spaces had led to higher drowning rates. The ownership of blue space—think how expensive the words 'sea view' are globally—means that many blue spaces globally are privately owned, so accessing such private spaces is excluding for both the general public but also for researchers. In the water, the need for swimming researchers, for example, to feel they have to 'stroke-the-stroke' is an important dimension that can shape researcher/participant relationships in terms of access to swimming communities more generally. There are transgressive and risky blue space communities who seek danger either in their practice or in the spaces they go; Clifton Evers' (2019) work on surfing in polluted waters in the northeast of England being one example. The practice of research as an act of privilege, especially in post-colonial societies, can also be contested in ways that challenge the rights of the research itself, for example, to trespass on indigenous land or in environmentally sensitive settings and to, in some ways, revisit a colonisation of a shared 'blue commons' (Guasco 2022; Shefer and Bozalek 2022; Wheaton et al. 2021). Yet, it is precisely that sense of a 'blue commons' that also makes such settings so interesting, especially in terms of a wider social fieldwork dimension, where the assemblage of bodies, affects and material social interactions are essential components, within 'blue third places' that have global reach.

In both my own swimming research but also I think evident in wider immersive field-methods is a recognition of the value of such methods in uncovering aspects of both joy and pain. In doing swim-along interviews, what lingered beyond the technological issues was the pleasure in doing research, in their own spaces, with swimming communities. This provided significant learning for the researcher from the exploration and discovery within field-practice, as well as the joy of sharing as a research tool; an emplaced noticing of how health and especially wellbeing emerged in those coastal and inland blue spaces (Foley et al. 2020). From a participant perspective, it felt like taking an everyday leisure practice seriously and engaging with it on that level, helping swimmers re-envisage their own in-situ practice in a positive light, opening up space for different accounts and experiences across a range of neuro and bodily diverse respondents (Bell and Bush 2021). Doing research in the moving field of water meant directly experiencing mobility and motility (Couper 2018) and getting caught up in the swirl and churn of the experience. As swimming often produces an inversion of both person and place, it provides what might be termed a bathymetric understanding of space, providing depth, flow, but also a volumetric insight into water in ways not possible on land. In turn, as with other blue space research, a deeper place engagement often leads to deeper place care and enhanced environmental awareness; by immersing oneself in water on a regular basis for human health and wellbeing, it becomes reflected in better pro-environmental behaviours, such that self-care morphs into place care (Britton and Foley 2021). Finally, one frequent comment from swimmers, whatever the water, was its crucial, yet ironic role in grounding them in ways that were supportive of both physical and mental health. Mobile and liminal assemblages of fieldwork approaches seem appropriate for the investigation of similarly liminal and mobile blue geographies that counter-intuitively find resilient and solid ground in moving waters.

References

Anderson, J. (2012). Relational places: the surfed wave as assemblage and convergence. *Environment and Planning D: Society and Space*, 30, pp. 570–587.

Anderson, K., and Smith, S. 2001. Editorial: Emotional Geographies. *Trans. Inst. Br. Geogr.*, NS 26, 7–10.

Bell, S.L. and Bush, T. 2021. 'Never mind the bullocks': animating the go-along interview through creative nonfiction, *Mobilities*, 16:3, 306–321.

Bell S.L., Phoenix, C., Lovell, R. and Wheeler, B.W. 2015. Using GPS and geonarratives: A methodological approach for understanding and situating everyday green space encounters. *Area*, 47:1, 88–96.

Bell, S. L., Wheeler, B. W., & Phoenix, C. 2017. Using geonarratives to explore the diverse temporalities of therapeutic landscapes: perspectives from "green" and "blue" settings. *Annals of the American Association of Geographers*, 107(1), 93–108.

Bell, S., Foley, R., Houghton, F., Maddrell, A. and Williams, A. 2018. From therapeutic landscapes to healthy spaces, places and practices: A scoping review. *Social Science & Medicine*, 196: 123–130.

Britton, E., Kindermann, G., Domegan, D. and Carlin. C. 2018. Blue care: a systematic review of blue space interventions for health and wellbeing. *Health Promotion International*, https://doi.org/10.1093/heapro/day103.

Britton, E., Kindermann, G. and Carlin, C. 2020. Surfing and the sense: Using body mapping to understand the embodied and therapeutic experiences of young surfers with Autism. *Global Journal of Community Psychology Practice*, 11:2, 1–17.

Britton, E. and Foley, R. 2021. Sensing Water: Uncovering health and wellbeing in the sea and surf. *Journal of Sports and Social Issues*, 45:1, 60–87.

Broch, T.B. 2020. Sensing Seascapes: How Affective Atmospheres Guide City Youths' Encounters with the Ocean's Multivocality. *Journal of Sport and Social Issues*, 45:2, 161–178.

Brown, M. 2019. Sailing, health and wellbeing: A thalassographic perspective. In R. Foley, R. Kearns, T. Kistemann, & B. Wheeler Eds., *Blue space, health and wellbeing: Hydrophilia unbounded*. Abingdon, Routledge, pp. 52–64.

Burns, R., Gallant, K., Litwiller, F., White, C. and Hamilton-Hinch, B. 2020. The go-along interview: a valuable tool for leisure research, *Leisure Sciences*, 42:1, 51–68.

Conradson, D. 2005. Landscape, care and the relational self: therapeutic encounters in rural England. *Health & Place*, 11: 337–78.

Costello, L., McDermott, M-L., Patel, P and Dare, J. 2019. 'A lot better than medicine'—Self-organised ocean swimming groups as facilitators for healthy ageing. *Health & Place*, 60, 102212.

Couper, P. 2018. The embodied spatialities of being in nature: encountering the nature/culture binary in green/blue space. *Cultural Geographies*, 25:2, 285–299.

Cummins, S., Curtis, S., Diez-Roux, A. and Macintyre, S. 2007. Understanding and representing 'place' in health research: A relational approach, *Social Science & Medicine*, 65(9), 9, 1825–1838.

Denton, H. and Aranda, K. 2019. The wellbeing benefits of sea swimming. Is it time to revisit the sea cure? *Qualitative Research in Sport*, 12:5, 647–663.

Denton, H., Dannreuther, C. and Aranda, K. 2021. Researching at sea: Exploring the 'swim-along' interview method. *Health & Place*, 67, 102466.

Depledge, M. and Bird, W. 2009. The Blue Gym: Health and wellbeing from our coasts. *Marine Pollution Bulletin*, 58(7), 947–948.

Duff, C. and Hill, N. 2022. Wellbeing as social care: On assemblages and the 'commons', Wellbeing, *Space and Society*, 3, 100078.

Evers, C. 2009. 'The Point': surfing, geography and a sensual life of men and masculinity on the Gold Coast, Australia, *Social & Cultural Geography*, 10:8, 893–908, https://doi.org/10.1080/14649360903305783.

Evers, C. 2015. Researching action sport with a GoPro TM camera: An embodied and emotional mobile video tale of the sea, masculinity and men-who-surf. In I. Wellard Ed., *Researching embodied sport: Exploring movement cultures*, London, Taylor & Francis, pp. 145–163.

Evers, C. 2019. Polluted Leisure, *Leisure Sciences*, 41:5, 423–440.

Foley, R. and Kistemann, T. 2015. Blue Space Geographies: Enabling Health in Place. Introduction to Special Issue on Healthy Blue Space, *Health & Place*, 35, 157–165.

Foley, R. 2017. Swimming as an accretive practice in healthy blue space. *Emotion, Space and Society* 22, 43–51.

Foley, R., Kearns, R., Kistemann, T., Wheeler, B. (eds), 2019. *Blue Space, Health and Wellbeing: Hydrophilia Unbounded*. (Routledge Geographies of Health Series). London, Routledge, Taylor & Francis.

Foley, R., Bell, S., Gittins, H., Grove, H., Kaley, A., McLauchlan, A, Osborne, T., Power, A., Roberts, E. and Thomas, M., 2020. Disciplined research in undisciplined settings: Critical Explorations of In-Situ & Mobile Methodologies in Geographies of Health and Wellbeing. *Area*, 52, 514–522.

Foley, R. 2019. Cartographies of Health: From Remote to Intimate Sensing. In Atkinson, S. and Hunt, R. (Eds.) *Geohumanities and Health*. (Global Perspectives on Health Geography). Cham, Springer Nature, 261–277.

Garcia, C.M., Eisenberg, M.E., Frerich, E.A., Lechner, K.E. and Lust K. 2012. Conducting Go-Along Interviews to Understand Context and Promote Health. *Qualitative Health Research*, 22(10), 1395–1403.

George, R. 2013. *Deep Sea and Foreign Going*. London, Portobello.

Gould, S., McLachlan, F. and McDonald B. 2021. Swimming With the Bicheno "Coffee Club": The Textured World of Wild Swimming. *Journal of Sport and Social Issues*, 45:1, 39–59.

Guasco, A. 2022. On an ethic of not going there. *Geographical Journal*. https://doi.org/10.1111/geoj.12462.

Hitchings, R. and Latham, A. 2020. Qualitative methods II: On the presentation of 'geographical ethnography'. *Progress in Human Geography*, 44:5, 972–980

Kronsted Lund, L., Petersen Gurholt, K. and Dykes, N. 2020. The vitalizing sea: embodiment and wellbeing on a sea-kayak journey. *Annals of Leisure Research*. https://doi.org/10.1080/11745398.2020.1836663.

Lachowycz, K. and Jones, A.P. 2013. Towards a better understanding of the relationship between greenspace and health: development of a theoretical framework. *Landscape and Urban Planning*, 118, 62–69.

Lisahunter and Emerald, E. 2016. Sensory narratives: Capturing embodiment in narratives of movement, sport, leisure and health. *Sport, Education and Society*, 21:1, 28–46.

McDougall, C., Foley, R., Hanley, N., Quilliam, R. and Oliver, D. 2022. Freshwater Wild Swimming, Health and Well-Being: Understanding the Importance of Place and Risk. *Sustainability*, 14(10), 6364; https://doi.org/10.3390/su14106364

Mears, M., Brindley, P., Barrows, P., Richardson, M. and Maheswaran R. 2021. Mapping urban greenspace use from mobile phone GPS data. *PLoS ONE* 16(7): e0248622.

Merchant, S. 2016. Re constructing the tourist experience? Editing experience and mediating memories of learning to dive. *Leisure Studies*, 35:6, 797–808.

Moles, K. 2021. The Social World of Outdoor Swimming: Cultural Practices, Shared Meanings, and Bodily Encounters. *Journal of Sports and Social Issues*, 45:1, 60–8.

Olive R, Wheaton B. 2021. Understanding Blue Spaces: Sport, Bodies, Wellbeing, and the Sea. *Journal of Sport and Social Issues*, 45(1), 3–19.

Peters, K., Anderson, J., Davies, A. and Steinberg, P. 2022. *The Routledge Handbook of Ocean Space*. London, Routledge.

Phoenix, C., Bell, S.L. and Hollenbeck, J. 2021 Segregation and the Sea: Toward a Critical Understanding of Race and Coastal Blue Space in Greater Miami. *Journal of Sport and Social Issues*, 45:2, 115–137.

Shefer, T. and Bozalek V. 2022. Wild Swimming Methodologies for Decolonial Feminist Justice-to-Come Scholarship. *Feminist Review*, 130(1), 26–43.

Straughan, E., 2012. Touched by water: the body in scuba diving. *Emotion, Space and Society*, 5, 19–26.

Völker, S. & Kistemann, T. 2015. Developing the urban blue: Comparative health responses to blue and green urban open spaces in Germany. *Health & Place*, 35, 196–205.

Wheaton, B., Waiti, J.T.A., Olive, R. and Kearns, R. 2021. Coastal Communities, Leisure and Wellbeing: Advancing a Trans-Disciplinary Agenda for Understanding Ocean-Human Relationships in Aotearoa New Zealand. *Int. J. Environ. Res. Public Health* 18, 450.

White, M., Alcock, I., Grellier, J., Wheeler, B.W., Hartig, T., Warber, S., Bone, A., Depledge, M. and Fleming, L. 2019. Spending at least 120 minutes a week in nature is associated with good health and wellbeing. *Scientific Reports*, 9, 7730.

Wiltse, J. 2007. *Contested Waters. A Social History of Swimming Pools in America*. Chapel Hill, University of North Carolina Press.

Winder, G.M. and Le Heron, R. 2017. Assembling a Blue Economy moment? Geographic engagement with globalizing biological-economic relations in multi-use marine environments. *Dialogues in Human Geography*, 7(1), 3–26.

CHAPTER 3

Researching Garo Death Rites

Erik de Maaker

3.1 Introduction

In this chapter, I am focussing on fieldwork that I have done between 1999 and 2001 in the Garo Hills of western Meghalaya (India).[1] I am exploring how I, in the course of this PhD research, have related to the people concerned. I describe how relationships emerged and developed, and how people reacted to my involvement in their lives. I conclude by arguing that although my research did not have the intention to expose the village concerned, it did certainly contribute to it being put it on the map as a "traditional" village. As far as I can judge, this seems to have worked out positively for the villagers. It has made people more aware of the importance that is being attributed by an outside world to their cultural practices and ensures that they receive a positive kind of attention from state organisations and the like.

Over the last two decades of the previous century, anthropology has moved away from the kind of fields that it used to cherish before. Where previously anthropological research was typically linked to a single field site, now a multi-sited approach became the standard (Marcus 1995). This provided better possibilities for comparison of the data collected, enabling a better and broader

---

[1] This chapter was originally published as 'Researching Garo Death Rites' in the volume 'Fieldwork in South Asia: Memories, Moments and Experiences,' edited by Sarit K. Chaudhuri and Sucheta Sen Chaudhuri. New Delhi: Sage, 2014, pages 167-185.

E. de Maaker (✉)
Institute of Cultural Anthropology and Development Sociology, Leiden University, Leiden, The Netherlands
e-mail: MAAKER@fsw.leidenuniv.nl

© The Author(s), under exclusive license to Springer Nature Switzerland AG 2023
N. Uddin, A. Paul (eds.), *The Palgrave Handbook of Social Fieldwork*, https://doi.org/10.1007/978-3-031-13615-3_3

understanding of the topic being studied. Nevertheless, there are certain research topics that continue to benefit from (predominantly) single-sited research. The fieldwork that I have conducted on death-related practices required close engagement with a limited number of people. Not only because of the level of "trust" and "rapport" required for the fieldwork but also because the research demanded that I took the multiple dimensions of the relationships maintained by the people concerned into account. To achieve this, I had to meet them in various roles: in relation to their land, as traders, as kinsmen, or when acting in accordance with their religious responsibilities. This could be achieved best by interacting with a (more or less) single set of people over a prolonged period of time.

3.2 First Encounters

It is not easy to say where my journey to northeastern India started. I guess that an initial interest was raised by the long talks that I as a teenager had with a secondary school teacher who told me about his extensive travels in India. In his stories, northeast India invariably surfaced as a region that was for its political instability forbidden to foreigners.

My interest in death rites developed several years later, when I was working on an ethnographic film project in Indonesia. We made a film (or as it later turned out—a series of films) (de Maaker et al. 2007) based on the research of Danielle Geirnaert, an anthropologist who had done extensive research among people for whom ancestor-centred belief systems played a major role. These beliefs inspired people to a complex cycle of annual rituals, which was, however, increasingly difficult to maintain, because the younger generations converted to Christianity. But, whereas conversion to Christianity ended people's participation to the annual ancestor-oriented rituals, it had much less of an impact on the death rituals that were conducted. We attended the mortuary ritual of a man who belonged to the local gentry, and what unfolded was a performance stretching over several days, which combined care for the deceased's soul with complex interactions between relatives, neighbours and friends. Following that occasion, it dawned upon me that in societies where social relationships are primarily framed in kin terms, funerals are often attributed to much greater importance than is the case in the West.

In 1995, the restrictions that the Indian state had for decades imposed on foreigners for entry to the northeastern region were partly abandoned, allowing travel on a tourist visa to the states of Assam, Meghalaya and Tripura. Access to the four other northeastern states (Arunachal Pradesh, Nagaland, Manipur and Mizoram continued to be subject to a special permit). In 1997, I had the chance to go to Shillong, the capital of the Indian state of Meghalaya. During this trip, I met many of the people who would come to play an important role in my PhD project. One of them was Tanka Subba, a prolific scholar attached to the Anthropology Department of Northeastern Hill University (NEHU). He would later become my local academic supervisor. I also met with Milton Sangma, a historian who belonged to the community (Garo), with whom I would decide to work. Furthermore, I met anthropologist and linguist Robbins Burling, who was at the time a visiting professor at NEHU. He had just retired as a professor from the University of Michigan. His engagement with the Garo had been lifelong, resulting as early as 1963 in the monograph "Rengsanggri" Robbins Burling (1997 [1963]), which was followed by a large number of articles and several other books.

It soon dawned upon me that most of what had been published on the Garo community religion (the followers of which are referred to as "Songsarek") is to an important extent based on interviews with "knowledgeable people." Interviews tend to force people to generalise about beliefs and practices. Rather than taking such generalisations as a starting point, it seemed worthwhile to attempt to research death rites with a focus on what people actually do (rather than what they say they do). A mortuary ritual demands the involvement of relatives, friends and neighbours of the deceased, allowing them and at the same time forcing them to express their relationship to the deceased and his or her closest relatives. Moreover, a death calls for gifts to be offered, some of which are attributed to great symbolic value. Therefore, I supposed that an analysis of the conduct of Garo death rituals would not only reveal people's perspectives on notions such as life, death and the ancestors but also on practices and ideas relating to kinship and exchange.

During my first visit to northeast India, I did not have the time to actually visit the Garo Hills. A couple of months later, I had another chance to go to India and spent about a month in the Garo Hills. Accompanied by a local folklorist I visited many places, notably in the east and west of the Garo Hills. We did not have a car, so used public transport, or—where that was absent—went around on foot. Moving around like this, carrying backpacks with a sleeping mat and some food, allowed us to stay over where ever we were invited, and meet a large number of people. That way, we also met with the local underground. Rather, they met with us. But at the time I was blissfully unaware of that. My companion did not tell me about it until a couple of months after the trip, and at the time I had only registered a couple of young men who were curious to know my whereabouts. One afternoon we reached a village named Sadolpara. When we came into the vicinity of the village, we heard gunshots. My companion identified these as an announcement of a death that had occurred and told me that by his knowledge it would not be impertinent to attend the event. As with other villages that we had been travelling through, this one had several courtyards, divided by stretches of forest, areca nut gardens and even a paddy field. The courtyards were large sandy patches. Houses were located at the fringes of the courtyards. Near the house from where the gun had been fired was a small group of people, centred around a frail old woman. She was walking slowly towards the house, keeping her body bent to point a stick with feathers towards the house while raising her voice in lament.

The particular village and the larger region in which it was located had a good number of Songsareks (adherents to the Garo community religion).

Along the way, we had come across many remnants of sacrifices, but this was the first time that I saw a Songsarek ritual. My companion asked the bystanders whether we could record the chant of the old lady. Much to my surprise, they had no objections. Perhaps they were used to people being attracted by the exoticism of Songsarek practices. And perhaps they recognised my companion—who is also a famous Garo folk singer—and they wanted to be forthcoming to a local celebrity. Moreover, as I understood much later, they simply did not see any harm in a foreigner making video recordings of the chanting old lady.

The woman whose chanting I recorded did not blink at the sight of the video camera. Once she had finished, we asked her a couple of questions, which she answered briskly and self confidently. Her chanting had concluded a certain phase of the death ritual, and she asked us to come over to her house for a cup of tea. The house was located on top of a low hill, at a slight distance from the part of the village where we had just been. Inside the house, we were joined by children, grandchildren and in-laws. They joked with my companion about me. At one stage, half as a joke, half-serious, the woman told me: "You will be like a son to me."

The old woman's name was Jiji. Jiji's position in life was a delicate one, as her husband had died about a decade ago, leaving her with the responsibility for five children. Attempts to find a new groom for her, as a replacement for her deceased husband, had not worked out. Jiji and her children survived, but in the bargain, she lost much of the wealth that had previously belonged to her household. Moreover, she and most of her children lacked the funds to invest in newly emerging forms of cultivation. By and large, they remained dependent on the swidden agriculture that had made previous generations of Garo villagers wealthy but was for various reasons quickly becoming less rewarding.

Jiji invited us to eat and sleep in her house, but we could not do so. Early that afternoon, before we went to the funeral, we had met a young man who lived in one of the only brick houses in the village. We had left our bags with him and had agreed to eat and sleep in his house. Notwithstanding my boldness when it came to videography, I was careful not to offend people when it came to commitments regarding food and stay. I was afraid that us going back on an earlier made appointment might do damage to my future relationship with the young man.

Now, before I continue these fieldwork-related accounts, I want to fill in the reader on the social topography of the area in which I conducted my PhD research.

3.3 Between Town and Village

Northeast India consists of broad river valleys and the hills and mountains surrounding these. Differences in mode of agriculture and so on create a divide between people in the plains and those in the hills or mountains, although there are also abundant interlinkages. Notably among the people who live away from the plains, great cultural and linguistic diversity exists. Opinions differ on what sets apart a language from a dialect, and on how to define an ethnic group, but according to the official classifications, the region counts several dozen communities, many of which have their own language (Singh 2002). Most of the people who live in the hills and mountains have by the various state governments been classified as "tribal." They belong to numerically relatively small groups that do not only have their own language but are also in a social, economic and religious sense believed to differ from more mainstream Hindu and Muslim communities. For instance, "tribal" groups would have a more egalitarian social structure. Also, it is generally assumed that "tribal" groups attribute greater importance to kinship as a model for the social organisation than "non-tribal" groups. Most states of northeast India have a "tribal" majority, and quite a few "tribal" communities have a certain level of administrative autonomy within the state.

The concept of "tribe" as used in India is rather problematic since there is no single set of criteria that applies to all that have been categorised by the state (Bates 1995; Karlsson and Subba 2006). Hence, I use quotation marks around the term "tribe" to indicate that it refers to an administrative category that does not necessarily link up to the ways in which anthropologists have been applying the term elsewhere in the world. Rather than representing groups that share certain traits, "tribe," as a category, seems to act as an umbrella for all those communities who do not satisfactorily qualify as a Hindu or Muslim caste. Since the Indian state considers "tribes" to be "less advanced," or even "backward," in comparison to the majority communities, they qualify for positive discrimination. People who belong to a "tribal" community tend to have access to a certain quota of dedicated "seats" in schools and universities, but, usually, there are many other benefits associated with having a "tribal" status as well. These kinds of benefits are accessible to every member of a given community, without taking individual needs into account. The Garo have qualified as "tribal" from the time that the category came in use, even though there is great cultural and linguistic variation within the community, and it is not always clear who qualifies as a Garo and who does not.

Early on, in the nineteenth century, when the colonial state expanded towards the northern edge of Bengal and into the plains of the Brahmaputra valley, Garos maintained at times tense relationships with the inhabitants of the plains. The ensuing violence provided an excuse for the colonial state for the conquest of the hill area. Garos, who had their own community religion, proved susceptible to conversion to Christianity. Australian and American missionaries (predominantly) came to play an important role in the emergence of an educated Garo middle class, as well as the formation of a Christian Garo cultural identity. From the second half of the twentieth century onwards, Christianity became the majority religion, leaving the remaining adherents of the community religion as a relatively marginal group in the rural hinterland. The village in which I had met Jiji was located in one such region.

Most of the Garo live in the three easternmost districts (collectively known as the Garo Hills) of the state of Meghalaya. These three districts have a Garo majority, but they are home to people belonging to various other communities as well. Some of these are categorised as "tribals," such as Koch and Hajong. Others are the descendants of migrants from Assam or Bengal, among others.

One of the things that I noted during my first weeks in the Garo Hills was the great disparity that existed between people's lifestyle in the towns as compared to that in villages such as the one in which I had met Jiji.

With about 60,000 inhabitants, Tura is the largest town in the Garo Hills. It harbours about one-tenth of the region's population. Tura is the political, administrative and educational centre of the Garo Hills. It is here that all major government offices are located, as are the principal hospitals, colleges and even a university. In Tura town, people lived with the comforts of a small-town India. Electricity (although with frequent power cuts), telephone (often out of order), running water (during the dry season only for a couple of hours a day), cable TV (about 40 stations from India, Bangladesh and the United States), shops selling a variety of food and consumer items and so on. Most importantly, in contrast to villages where everyone knows everyone else, a town like Tura has such a large number of people that there is scope for anonymity and to have contractual, non-personalised relationships.

In villages such as the one where Jiji lived, modern-day comforts were absent. There was no electricity, no telephone and water had to be collected with a vessel or a bucket from a well. In Jiji's village of about 1600 inhabitants, there were less than 10 TVs (operating on solar-charged batteries). There were two shops, but these only sold basic items such as rice, lentils, salt, dry cells, cigarettes and soap. Once a week there was a market at which villagers sold their produce to wholesalers, and could buy rice, clothing and sometimes vegetables.

Most of the villagers had very little access to money, and would not be able to buy much from the shops or in the market. People did, however, have free access to the forest that belonged to their village and the produce it yielded. Most people cultivated their own land, but if they worked for money salaries would vary from INR 30 to INR 50 a day (US $0.75 to US $1.25). Some families did not have food security throughout the year, which was notably an issue in the months immediately preceding the start of the rains. Tura had the Garo elite, but there are also many poor Garos, as well as a substantial number of non-Garos. Many townspeople commanded by way of their salaries a steady flow of money. Notably, for politicians and wholesale traders, these were very substantial and allowed for them to build large houses, maintain servants, own cars and travel.

In villages such as the one where Jiji lived, educational facilities would be basic or non-existent. During the first year that I came there, there was one primary school in Sadolpara. The teacher would only give classes for one or two hours a day, if at all. Educated in schools, townspeople had access to book-based knowledge, which was out of bounds for the mostly illiterate villagers.

There was a government health dispensary in a village close to Sadolpara, but its doctor would not be present for more than a couple of hours a week, if at all. A larger community health centre was slightly further away. It did have doctors and medicines, but villagers did not like to go there. This had a variety of reasons, one of these being that the medical staff of the community health centre tended to be quite harsh towards the villagers since they in their opinion lacked basic knowledge of hygiene and so on. Regarding medical care, villagers, by and large, managed on their own. Several people were knowledgeable about the use of medicinal plants, and in addition adherents of the community, and religion solved their health problems through sacrifices to the animist deities.

One way to look at the town-village disparity is that the medical posts and schools were exponents of an urban culture that extended into the rural area. From the perspective of the government-salaried medical personnel, and the teachers, the villagers were illiterate, backward and ignorant. Songsareks were referred to as immoderate when it came to drinking rice beer, and lacking the disposition to create savings. From the villagers' perspective, however, educated townspeople had little idea or interest in living in a village, and the difficulties involved. Unless townspeople had spent their childhood in a village, they would invariably lack what was for the villagers' basic knowledge of animals and plants. Townspeople normally lacked the skills required for life in a village environment (bamboo working, house building, hunting, fishing, etc.). And what they lacked most of all was the sheer physical strength and endurance required for doing these kinds of tasks.

Although the contrast between townspeople and villagers was in many respects pretty sharp, this did not mean that there were no connections. Some townspeople enjoyed visiting the villages. And some villagers would travel every now and then to town, trade, talk with their political representatives, and see all that money can buy. Village youth would move to town to work as a domestic helper and get the opportunity to attend a reasonably good school. Likewise, towns had many people who during earlier phases of their life lived in villages, or who would own agricultural land and go there regularly. Most importantly, people living in towns and villages were connected through kinship ties. This allowed them to call upon each other for help and assistance. It also implied that they would meet every now and then at events such as funerals or—in urban Christian settings—weddings.

The disparity between town and village was particularly big where villagers were Songsareks. More and more, for urban youth, the Garo community religion is something of the past. It is an important part of what makes Garos "different" from others, and therefore attention is given to it in textbooks used in schools, through documentaries shown on the regional subsidiary of the state broadcaster Doordarshan on local radio stations, or at exhibitions or festivals that display "traditional" Garo culture. In these representations, Garo culture tends to be represented in a rather essentialist manner that has only a distant relationship with the way in which Songsareks live their lives today.

For the fieldwork that I did among animist Garo villagers, I depended upon university-educated Garos. Two out of the three with whom I worked throughout the two-year period of my stay were former students of the Department of Garo language of the Northeastern Hill University (Tura Campus). They were aware of the particularities of village culture and had a positive disposition towards animism (even though they themselves were Christians). Not only were they willing and able to live in a Garo village for a prolonged period of time they also accepted that animist Garo villagers engaged in practices and used language that is at times not readily understandable to people who belong to the same community, who have been brought up and live their lives in quite a different setting.

3.4 Getting Organised

After the second trip to Meghalaya, I had outlined what I wanted to do my PhD research on, but it would take me a year to secure funding. I applied for a PhD grant with Leiden University, but my application was turned down in the first round of the selection process. "Theoretically not sufficiently innovative" was the reason given. Luckily, an improved version of my proposal passed the first of two rounds for funding from the Dutch National Science Foundation. I reworked the proposal, collected feedback from many scholars and reworked it some more. Once I had submitted the final version, it took many months before I received the reviews, and then again, more weeks before the committee decided which proposals to fund. Throughout this period, I worked as a freelancer on an ethnographic film project, the earnings of which were just enough to pay for my monthly bills. After more weeks of waiting and worrying, word came that I had received the much-desired scholarship, and could embark on my PhD research.

In the meantime, my personal situation had changed. Earlier that year, I had met my to be wife. She was an Indian, at that time residing in Mumbai. A couple of months later we got married, and whenever her activities allowed, she would stay with me in the Garo village. Rather than being alone, which had earlier been my earlier prospect, I would thus be with her. This had important consequences for my position in the field, in a positive sense, as it worked out that she could have a kind of contact with women that was out of reach for me.

Now, in order to do research in India, I needed a research permit. Anticipating that I would eventually manage to secure a grant, I had put in an application for such a permit immediately after having returned from my visit to northeast India. One and a half years followed. The problem was, not surprisingly, a certain apprehensiveness on the side of the Home Ministry about the safety of a foreigner residing for a prolonged period of time in a northeast Indian border zone. These were justified concerns, as I found out once I started reading the local newspapers. Nevertheless, the Home Office eventually relented and granted the visa required.

By the end of August 1999, I returned to Tura, this time with my wife. We took classes in Garo, and after a couple of months, we could shop in the market, ask for directions and so on. However, more complex conversations continued to be cumbersome. Moreover, in Tura, it proved very difficult to practice simple Garo, since almost everyone who had been educated beyond primary school would for convenience's sake talk to us in English. English is the language of tuition in many secondary schools and colleges in the state of Meghalaya. To improve our Garo, we had to get out of town. It was anyway time to leave Tura since my fieldwork would take place in rural West Garo Hills.

To prepare for the move, we made a two-day visit to the village in which Jiji lived. The rainy season was at its height, and the humidity was suffocating. The mud paths were extremely slippery, while the abundant rains chased snakes out of their holes. I nearly stepped on one that crossed the path we walked on. A little while later, there was another encounter with a snake when I was walking on grass (I had not yet learned that one should not do so in the rainy season). As a European, used to nature as pristine and beautiful (since it has been "cleared" from dangerous animals), I was not at all prepared for this. In addition, on the day we left, I developed a high fever: I had contracted malaria.

It took about a month for me to recover from malaria. By then, the rains had stopped, the mud was dry and hard, and the snakes had retreated to their holes. Now, how to move to Sadolpara? Who had the space to put me up, and where was I supposed to keep my laptop, video camera and other equipment? At the time, I was alone. My wife had gone to work in Mumbai, and I had not managed to find a research assistant. To start with, I took a room at the partly abandoned government health dispensary. From there it took about 10 minutes, on a scooter, to reach the village in which Jiji lived. An attendant maintained the dispensary. In the absence of medical staff, relatives of the attendant occupied most of the rooms. Others were used as a storage space for firewood and so on. The attendant granted me a room that was still vacant.

From the dispensary, I began to make trips to the surrounding villages. This way, I thought, I could meet people and begin my research. However, right from the start people discouraged me to drive either after dark or before sunrise. They warned me for tigers, and herds of wild elephants (neither of which I ever saw). This meant that I could not be out after six at night. Likewise, I would never be in any of the villages before six or seven in the morning. Around eight in the morning, and sometimes earlier, people left for their fields, to return by four or five in the afternoon. During the day, villages tended to be depopulated, except for children under four years of age, people who were so old that they could hardly move and those who were ill. In order to collect the kind of data required, there was really no other option than to move to a Garo village.

I did consider other villages than Sadolpara, but nevertheless almost instinctively chose the village in which Jiji lived. More than two years later, her "You are like a son to me" still resonated in my ears. She herself repeated that statement on virtually every occasion that I met her. My wife had joined me again, and we discussed our wish to stay in Sadolpara with some of the villagers. Jiji (or perhaps one of her sons) told me that we could construct a house next to hers. She appeared to be a titleholder to land (as we then found out), which gave her the right to decide so. We discussed this proposition with the village head (*nokma*), who cautioned us that we should not "depend on the village for our rice." When we reassured him that we would buy our rice from the market, he did not object to us staying in the village.

We requested various people if they were willing to construct a house for us, but that proved rather difficult. No one had the time for it, they explained. Thatching grass and wood were scarce, so it would take a lot of effort to obtain these. A long discussion followed, and in the end, a group of men offered to build a house that would last for at least a year, for the price of INR 5000 (about US $125). They did a good job. The house outlasted our entire stay, and after three years, it still stood but was dismantled since people wanted to use the spot on which it stood for something else.

I expected people to get down to building the house straight away, but this was not at all the way it went. The men could only work on our house for one or two days a week, whenever they had some spare time. Dependent on who was available, the size of the party varied from day to day, and from week to week. To begin with, the men went to a part of the forest that had many different kinds of bamboo. There, they harvested particular kinds of bamboo for distinct parts of the house. I tried my best to help, but it was hard work and I was of little use to them. I could not even carry half their load of bamboo. Then the men collected wood for the pillars and beams of our house. A good part of the bamboo that had been collected would be used as a weave for the walls and had to be flattened before the actual building could commence. All these preparations took many days, in the course of which we got to know more and more people. It was a good starting point for an extended stay. After several weeks of construction work, the house was finally ready, and we could move into it.

3.5 Getting Established

Moving into the house transformed the relationship with Jiji and her relatives. From the first day, the youngest daughter of Jiji, who lived with her, provided me with drinking water and firewood. Notably, the drinking water involved no small effort, since it had to be collected from a well at the bottom of the hill at which the house stood. I asked a granddaughter of Jiji, who lived next door if she would be willing to help mornings and evenings in the house. She was 10 or perhaps 12 years old, which is an age that children are anyway expected to contribute to the running of their household. Every day, she would cook lentils and a vegetable, and later on, wash the dishes. We would pay her some money, and provide her with her meals. She readily agreed, and so did her parents.

I used my time in Sadolpara to talk to people, take pictures and so on. Also, I spent many hours a day typing away on my laptop. Obviously, people were curious as to why I was living there. Rather than trying to explain the theoretical framework of my PhD project, I would stick to the much more general (but not inaccurate) statement that I intended to learn about their "customs and culture" (*niam aro dakbewal*). I tried to explain that I was affiliated to a university, but very few villagers could imagine what such an institution might be about.

At the time, Sadolpara did not have much of a place on the tourist map (there were other villages within which the majority of the people were Songsareks closer to Tura), but its inhabitants were well aware of the importance attached by townspeople and foreigners to the Garo community religion. Every year, the villagers participated in the annual Wangala dance competition, a festival organised by the government of Meghalaya state. These dances originated as part of the most important annual celebrations of the Garo community religion, and the dance competition as a whole in many ways presents that religion as the main source of "Garoness." Villagers were not unaware of the importance that was being attributed to their practices and beliefs by the outside world, and I guess that the interest I expressed in their customs and culture was in line with this.

Villagers were very proud, and would never ask to be given anything, even though it was obvious that money provided us with access to a seemingly unending supply of tea, milk, rice, lentils, vegetables and so on. I knew from earlier fieldwork experiences that this could prove to be supremely uncomfortable, so consciously set up an unequal exchange. We agreed with Jiji and her daughter that they would cook our rice. That is, we bought rice (at least 10 kg at a time) or gave them money to buy rice. In return, we received a number of shares of cooked rice twice a day. The amount of rice that came into Jiji's household this way covered our needs as well as those of Jiji and her daughter (compensating them for their cooking effort). In addition, it allowed them to share out or lend out rice to relatives and neighbours. For Jiji and her relatives, it was obvious from the outset that we would leave again, and they made sure never to depend on us in any structural manner.

The granddaughter of Jiji who helped us in the house collected food from us to have it with her own family. So her family had access to our food as well. In addition, there were less regulated food exchanges with other people living in the same area of the village. People would offer us eggs, or a bowl of curry. Invariably, we would reciprocate such gestures. Since there was always a more substantial flow of food (and money) from us to the others than the other way round, we did not burden them in this respect. For us, it contributed to being tied in a web of exchange relationships that extended far beyond food.

Our household helpers would never stay for more than a couple of months. When Jiji's granddaughter decided not to work for us anymore, her elder sister volunteered to replace her. After the elder sister followed the daughter of another neighbour, and then again others. That these commitments were short-lived was not unusual. Every now and then, village youth in search of adventure and education would go to one of the towns in the Garo Hills (such a Tura). There, they would combine work as a domestic helper with attending school. Very few of these youths stayed on for more than just a couple of months, while they actually had intended to be there for several years. The most common reason for leaving was referred to as *kracha'a*, which can probably best be translated as "being ashamed" or "made to feel ashamed." My reading is that after some time, they felt humiliated when they had to accept orders from someone who was not a kin-senior to them. It would normally not be a problem to take orders from relatives who are senior in the kinship hierarchy, such as parents, grandparents, uncles and aunts. However, taking orders from people who are not considered kin would for many of the village youth after a while become difficult to accept. Although Jiji projected a kin relationship between me and her, we were not truly kin, and our household helpers would after some time feel uncomfortable with us telling them what to do.

My relationship with Jiji, which had had such a quick start two years ago, continued to be important. She remained very committed to me, and whoever came with me to the village. She was self-confident, witty, helpful, caring and at the same time able to advance her own interests.

Jiji was a well-respected person in her village, who knew an immense number of people. My affiliation with her and her children and in-laws provided us with a starting point from which to negotiate relationships. During the first couple of months, I often went out with her to meet people. Later on, this happened less, as I had grown confident enough to go out on my own. It was also with Jiji that I attended my first Garo funeral. Funerals were by and large public events, but Jiji was obviously well aware of any sensitivities and knew where and how she could take me without causing offence.

For close relatives of the deceased, the loss of someone dear had a great impact on their lives. But mortuary rituals were not only attended by close relatives and friends but also by many people for whom it was also, or perhaps primarily, a social occasion. It allowed them to express their position within their social network. For me, it was possible to legitimately attend funerals by being included in this latter group. Death was in itself "bad" (*namja*), but that did not mean that funerals did not have enjoyable elements as well. Funerals involved a lot of waiting and hanging around and provided people with an occasion to catch up with friends and relatives. Funerals also implied a relative abundance of food, since close relatives of the deceased had to provide at least one meal to everyone, and if the funeral was hosted by Songsareks, there would be rice beer as well.

Sadolpara had about 1600 inhabitants. Nearby, that is, within a couple of hours' walking distance, were at least six other villages with between 200 and 600 inhabitants. Throughout the nearly two years that the fieldwork lasted, I was notified of about 15 deaths. I attended at least eight mortuary rituals. Most people died inside the house where they had lived, usually after a period of prolonged illness. Very often, given the course an illness was taking, people expected death to occur. They would gather in the house of the ill person, and provide him or her with water or medicines. Immediately after someone had died, the nearest relatives would wash the dead body, and lie it out in state inside the house. Once this had been done, gunshots were fired, and people would send out messengers to convey the news. Soon after, relatives, friends and acquaintances would begin to drop in. Funerals lasted normally two days, the dead body is buried or cremated at the end of the first day.

Rather than just attending funerals, I intended to record them on video. For Jiji, my making video recordings were not at all a problem, which had become clear from our very first encounter. This was also what she communicated to other people, and at funerals, I was generally more or less directly allowed to make video recordings. The video recordings became an essential source for the research. They allow for a detailed observation (both visual and auditive) of the events witnessed, and to ask people to clarify what they or others had said, and why certain things were done or avoided.

3.6   Sustaining Relationships

Throughout the period that I stayed in the village; I did a lot of work in the house that had been built next to Jiji's. There, the research assistants would work on the transcription of the Garo dialogues. It was also there that local people volunteered to discuss the video material shot or just dropped in to chat over a cup of tea. Every now and then, I tried to make appointments with people to come over and work with us, but that proved quite difficult. They usually had other, more important things to do. However, our house was located at a crossroads, and many people passed by when they were on their way somewhere else. Luckily, our house turned into a welcome place to stop, chat, smoke and drink tea. Dropping in was then a spontaneous decision on the side of the person who did so, and they would generally be very committed to the discussions we had.

Certain people proved to be so resourceful that they gradually became key informants. One man made himself available day after day, freeing lots of time for us. After many weeks, I decided that I wanted to compensate him for the time he spent with us. After all, if he did not stay with us, he would spend his days working his fields, or earning money as a day labourer. He had an amazing memory and provided me with the names and kinship designations of an enormous number of people. He could place relationships between people in a historical perspective, providing insights in their economic, social and ritual dimensions.

After a couple of months in the field, I collected many hours of video material. Analysis of the tapes took time, and soon a considerable backlog developed. Consequently, we would mostly be working on events that had been videographed months ago. By then, these events had become "history," and the sorrow that people had felt at the time that a specific mortuary ritual took place had waned. One category for which this did not hold were widows and widowers and the parents of deceased children. People actively discouraged them from watching the video recordings, since it was believed to be unfavourable if they would relive the grief and sorrow that they had felt at the time of the funeral. These sorts of emotions, when relived, were said to make people vulnerable to diseases and affliction by ancestral ghosts.

Even though our relationship with Jiji and her close relatives was the most profound, gradually many other people befriended us as well. Friendship involved sharing time and food, as well as helping each other out whenever that was necessary and possible. If people came to us with requests, which could vary from headaches and infected wounds to the repair of a radio or a ride to town, we tried to accommodate these. I was also regularly asked to loan small sums of money, and much to my surprise, every one but a single person paid back their debts, without me reminding them even once.

Of course, there was also envy. Garo villages are face-to-face communities, in which people have little choice than to get along with one another. This particularly, since land ownership rests with the resident kin group as a whole, and techniques of agriculture and animal husbandry are such that people have to take joint decisions. No one can do without the cooperation of others, but that does not mean that people do not have their likes and dislikes. Some people talked dismissively about the benefits that Jiji and her relatives had secured by having us residing with them. They mentioned the food that Jiji and all had obtained through us, and the monetary inputs that we provided (which were even by village standards very modest). But then, everyone acknowledged that it had been Jiji and her relatives who had come forward and provided us with a very explicit invitation to stay with them, while other people had at that time been much more reserved.

3.7 Conclusion

I don't think that any of the villagers had ever thought that a book might be written on mortuary rituals, or that it might be interesting and worthwhile to videograph these. The analysis of the video recordings, and their use in the research process, resulted in extensive discussions on people's involvement with the mortuary rituals, the activities they engaged in and the conversations they had. Often, we found that these activities and conversations revealed core principles ("*niam raka*"), which were not normally formulated. Among villagers, there was a general consensus that these principles were poorly understood by townspeople (who had lost their connection to the Garo community religion), and even by the village youth (who tended to move towards Christianity, if they were not already Christians).

Most of the people in Sadolpara were illiterate, and those who did read only read Garo. My PhD thesis is in English (de Maaker 2006), and they could unfortunately only appreciate the pictures. I have shown the DVD which came with my thesis to the people filmed, as well as to others. The DVD has video recordings of a mortuary ritual, and I feared that people would not like to watch it. However, between the occurrence of the death filmed, and the finalising of the DVD at least five years had gone by, and the events filmed had become part of their past.

Some of the people among whom I did my fieldwork developed an increased interest in ritual practices, and the kind of explanations that people provide for these. After all, I spent a lot of time talking to old and knowledgeable people (these were also the ones whom the community more or less granted the authority to do so). And perhaps, my listening to these people, and meticulously writing down what all they had to say, resulted in other people paying more attention to their explanations as well.

My research also had other consequences. It resulted in an increased interest of townspeople in the village. Some of these came to visit us, others were perhaps drawn by the stories that were doing the rounds about us. NEHU's Department of Garo shifted its annual outing to the village in which we resided, which meant that about 50 students and staff would attend the most important of the annual year cycle rituals. Sadolpara gained a name with various state organisations, which led to journalists and foreign tourists dropping in to be guided around. In addition, even more than before, the village came to be used as a set for documentaries and docu-dramas shot by local TV stations.

The attention that was drawn from the outside world contributed to the early inclusion of the village in projects run by IFAD (International Fund for Agricultural Development), an ambitious scheme funded by the UNDP. This brought professionals in development to the village, who have guided people in the creation of savings schemes, the management of natural resources, the creation of a joint agenda for village development and so on. The results of some of these programs appear positive, but it remains to be seen what their effect will be over an extended period of time.

Over the years, Jiji has shown great hospitality to many of the strange visitors that came to Sadolpara. Her good-natured, sincere curiosity made her a natural talent when it came to engaging people. She would never give anyone the feeling that they had to support her in one way or the other, but I know from her stories that many of the visitors did. After all, these visitors saw the relative poverty in which she lived, and felt that they should not take her hospitality for granted.

On the whole, villagers reacted positively to these developments. They appreciated the interest shown in their way of living, laughed about the silliness and clumsiness of the outsiders and tried to benefit from the visits. Many years later, Jiji told me how she had once received an old couple, an American and the Japanese. Jiji enacted how the old man and woman had with great difficulty climbed into her house (which has its entrance about 1 meter from the ground level). Clearly, it was not the first time that she narrated this story, as the other people listening knew what was coming and laughed their heads off long before she had made her point. Likewise, Jiji told me about a Mumbai-based filmmaker who had stayed for days in a tree hut in order to shoot a herd of marauding wild elephants—that did not show up. In relation to myself, one of her most popular stories was how I had tried to make rice beer, but burned the grains that I had to roast. The rice beer tasted so bad that it had to be thrown away. I take it that the continuing recounting of these sorts of stories is an expression of what has become a lasting relationship.

I, on my part, do not only cherish the memories of the time that we could spend in Sadolpara but I also hope that relationships with its people will be continued in the years to come. The writing and films that have come out of the fieldwork, and will most probably continue to emerge over the next couple of years, will hopefully contribute to an appreciation for a rich culture among a broad audience.

References

Bates, Crispin (1995), "Lost Innocents and the Loss of Innocence?" Interpreting Adviasi Movements in South Asia.' In: R.H. Barnes (Ed.), *Indigenous Peoples of Asia*. Ann Arbor: Associaton of Asian Studies, Pp. 103–120

Burling, Robbins (1997 [1963]), *Rengsanggri: Family and Kinship in a Garo village*. Tura Book Room: Tura. (Original Publication with The University of Philadelphia Press)

Karlsson, B.G. and T.B. Subba (2006), *Indigeneity in India*. London: Kegan Paul

de Maaker, Erik (2006) *Negotiating Life: Garo Death Rituals and the Transformation of Society*. Ph.D. dissertation: Leiden University

de Maaker, Erik, Dirk Nijland, and Danielle Geirnaert-Martin (2007), *Ashes of Life, the Annual rituals of Laboya, Sumba 1996. An Ethnographic Multimedia DVD* (with). Göttingen: IWF Knowledge and Media.

Marcus, George E. (1995), Ethnography in/of the World System: The Emergence of Multi-Sited Ethnography. *Annual Reviews of Anthropology*, Vol. 24: 95–117.

Singh, K.S. (2002), *People of India: introduction*. New Delhi: Oxford University Press

CHAPTER 4

Navigating the Tyrannies of Fieldwork: A Nigerian Experience

Adebayo Adewusi

4.1 Introduction

Whether academic or otherwise, research is a serious business for those who engage in it. As the aims of researchers differ so also are the procedures employed in carrying out various research. This explains why a number of researchers feel comfortable using oral interviews while some have misgivings about its reliability as a major research tool. For some who employ it in the process of data collection, it is treated as supplementary to other methods.[1] Despite such treatment as second best, there is no doubt that interviews have become an important tool in the data collection process for researchers in social sciences, humanities and medical science, among others. The growing popularity of interviews is evidenced by the prevalence of their use. Atkinson and Silverman underscore the wider use of interviews by many researchers when they declare that the contemporary society is an "Interview Society."[2] Riesman and Benny anticipate a society in which interviews would not only serve as means of collecting data about individuals and institutions only but also as "one of our best laboratories for the study of interactions, of the Simmelian

---

[1] Kleinman, S., Stenross, B. and McMahon, M., 1994. Privileging Fieldwork over Interviews: consequences for identity and practices. *Symbolic Interaction*

[2] Atkinson, P. and Silverman, D., 1997. Kundera's Immortality: The Interview Society and the Invention of the Self. *Qualitative Inquiry*

A. Adewusi (✉)
Department of History, Obafemi Awolowo University, Ife, Nigeria

dyads and of other larger groupings."[3] Among historians, interview is not only considered important and serious evidence for historical reconstruction, the need to give it public respectability being enjoyed by other sources of information has equally been emphasised.[4] Furthermore, outside the social sciences and humanities, interview enjoys some measure of importance as a major research technique in the medical environment in which researchers, especially those of post-positivist inclination, have found some sort of comfort in using it in "understanding people in the social and cultural context within which they live."[5]

The highlighted importance of interview in research methodology notwithstanding, it can be a complex, daunting and frustrating exercise. In such situations, a researcher may feel highly tyrannised. This is usually the case when a researcher lacks a good understanding of the people and cultural constraints in different research areas. Quite unlike previous works on interviews, this chapter uses case studies derived from many years of field research in southwest and north-central Nigeria to explain factors that constitute challenges to researchers who have embraced interviews as an important research tool and are persuaded of their reliability. The focus area is also known as Yorubaland because it is inhabited principally by the Yoruba ethnic nationality. Even though the coverage area is limited to a section of Nigeria, the discussion can also serve as a practical guide to researchers who may wish to conduct interviews in the course of their research in other areas of the country and elsewhere in Africa.

4.2 Conceptual Clarification

"Tyrannies" presents a conceptual problem that needs some clarification here. I use the term advisedly to refer to challenges that researchers face, or are likely to encounter, while engaging in fieldwork, in this case oral interviews. The choice of a pluralised form of the noun, tyranny, is intended to demonstrate the multiplicity of these challenges. Some of these challenges may be socio-cultural, economic, environmental or even personal idiosyncrasies of the interviewees that are capable of frustrating a researcher seeking to access important information through interviews. It is essential to point out that despite the complexity of such challenges, they can be surmounted with resoluteness and willingness on the part of the researcher to understand the terrain of the researc On the surface interviewing may appear an easy task since everyone has been involved in it in one form or another at different times in life. It can, however, be such a difficult exercise in some instances when certain considerations serve as a wall between the interviewers and potential interviewees. In fact, the awareness that

---

[3] Riesman, D. and Benny,M., 1956. The Sociology of the Interview. *The Midwest Sociologist*

[4] Ritchie, D.A., Shulman, H.C., Kirkendall, R.S. and Birdwhistell, T.L., 1991. Interviews as Historical Evidence: A Discussion of New Standards of Documentation and Access. *The History Teacher*

[5] Myers, M. D. (1997). Qualitative research in information Systems. *MIS Quarterly*

the interview has some value for the researcher often increases the possibility of tyrannies as hurdles to be crossed before accessing the needed information. Therefore, my conception of field tyrannies is encapsulated in what a researcher will consider an unwelcoming atmosphere before, during or after the conduct of the interview. My personal experience in the field shows that these tyrannies need to be understood before setting out to some uncharted environments. It must be acknowledged that some of these tyrannies can be inscrutable that a researcher may not be able to circumvent them.

4.3 The Sweet-bitter Pill

On June 25, 2016, I visited Bogije, a lagoon community in southwest Nigeria. The purpose of my visit was to interview the baale (community head) on the migration and peopling of the community. The man consented to my request after I had visited him on two different occasions and he requested that I draw up all the questions I wanted to ask him during the interview. I obliged him. I arrived at his house early enough on the agreed day and I sought his consent to tape-record the interview. To this he raised no objection. His responses to my questions were encouraging; he also allowed me to ask further questions when I felt he had not answered some satisfactorily. About thirty minutes into the interview a young man came in and demanded that I stop the interview. The young man is one of the sons of the *baale* and I had met him twice during my earlier visits. In fact, on a particular day, we spoke at length about the busy schedules of his father, and his inability to grant me the needed audience. On that day, the young man told his father that he ought not to have allowed me to interview him let alone record his voice. I think his fears were genuine: he feared some of his father's adversaries in the community might have sent me to record his (baale) voice so that they could use it against him. I did not understand what he meant by the adversaries of his father, but I made an effort to explain to him that I came from a university and the interview was strictly for research purposes. I even reminded him that I had met him before and I explained that I had carried out similar research in other communities in the area. But the young man remained unconvinced. He demanded that I delete the recording immediately in his presence. He also ordered me to leave the house immediately and threatened to invite some young men in the area to manhandle me out of the house. Should I disobey his order? Incidentally, it was the rainy season and the rain was falling so heavily that morning. When my appeal did not appear to have any effect on him, I knew I was left with no other option than leave. I moved out of the house into the heavy rain to avoid further embarrassment and the possibility of a physical attack on me.

The experience narrated above represents part of the challenges researchers encounter while doing fieldwork in Nigeria. Unarguably, such experience is capable of persuading fledging researchers, and even experienced ones, to recalibrate their methodology to avoid preventable embarrassment or physical injury that may likely occur from hostile individuals in the field. It was a reality that thwarted my initial hope of accessing rich information about the community after the baale had consented to my request for an interview with him. In such a palpably unfriendly situation, it is incumbent on a researcher to re-strategise how best to navigate through without compromising on research ethics. In my case I did not return to the baale's house after the incident because of the obvious danger such an unwary step portended. Meanwhile, before I conclude on my subsequent experience in Bogije, I need to state that it is standard practice in some rural communities that a visitor, especially a researcher in small communities where strangers are easily identifiable,[6] first visit the community head to announce his mission to the place. Failure to do this may deny the researcher the opportunity to carry out the intended research. By making the baale's house my first port of call in the community, I was merely conforming to the tradition as obtained in other places I had visited before Bogije.

I need to stress the fact that Bogije was one of the important lagoon communities I had to include in my research. I felt duty-bound to return there, armed with the conviction I could really meet persons that would be well-disposed to my cause. So, I returned to the community four days later and my experience was quite different from what I had previously. I spoke to a number of people who willingly invited me to their homes and granted me the needed interviews. One thing became clear to me after I concluded my interviews at Bogije: I discovered that there had been a series of crises in the community over land ownership. Since water occupies a substantial part of the community, the available land had been a subject of constant disputes which had led to court cases in the past. I later reasoned that had I spoken to a few people about the nature of intra-communal relationships in Bogije, I would probably have avoided the initial unpalatable experience. And for the interview that was brought to an abrupt end shows the extent to which a third party can influence the course of research/interview even after the interviewees have consented to the researcher's request.

Meanwhile, it is remarkable that as unpleasant as the experience of Bogije was, it became very useful and guided me in my subsequent research work elsewhere. The case of Igbo-Ora is worth stating here. Igbo-Ora is a composite town made up of some six independent communities, namely, Iberekodo-Igbole, Iberekodo-Odan, Pako, Saganun, Idofin and Igbo-Ora. On my first visit, I had some casual discussions with a few people and they made me understand that Igbo-Ora is a complex town considering its social and political structures. These initial enquiries about my research location afforded me the opportunity to understand that the name "Igbo-Ora" can be quite misleading because it signifies a particular community, yet it is also used in the official quarters as a generic name for six different communities and this has been a

---

[6] In 2014, I was accosted on the road by some people in Ogbere-Ijebu who demanded to know my mission in the community. The people said they had observed that I came into the community the previous evening and they were curious to know what I was doing there.

source of resentment for others who have distinct identities from the real Igbo-Ora. Learning about the peculiarities of Igbo-Ora early helped me to avoid asking displeasing questions while conducting interviews in their various communities. Also, when I went to conduct interviews in Ejigbo a few months after the town experienced a religious-driven crisis in a high school which subsequently spilt over to the town, my initial enquiries in form of informal discussions with a few people at a filing station gave me the idea about whom to approach and where I might go to avoid trouble. Being my first time in the town and given the crisis the town had experienced, I took seriously the counsel I received during my casual conversations with people and I successfully navigated through the troubled town when I interviewed right persons.

4.4 Contending with the Realities of Culture

People often speak of cultural inheritance apparently with a view to validating certain practices or claims. Culture may be invoked when some unifying ideals peculiar to a particular group are perceived to be threatened by some externalities. Despite the absence of unanimity in its definition, culture has remained a convenient tool for claims-making and as a sort of shield for projecting the aims and ideals of a political entity.[7] Regardless of the onslaughts it has sustained from colonialism, Islam, Christianity, etc., culture has remained, as Falola has argued, a single word often used to explain and justify most things among Africans.[8] Being at the root of the society, no doubt cultural considerations are capable of influencing the attitude a people exhibit towards members of another group of strangers. However, the lack of understanding of factors that underlie such behavioural patterns may lead a researcher to a hasty conclusion about a people as strange, unaccommodating, hostile or primitive. I illustrate how some of these cultural essentials can serve as constraints to researchers and how they prevented me from accessing relevant information during a field research among the Yewa (Egbado) in Yorubaland (also known as Southwest Nigeria). I need to add here that there is no basis to consider the Yorubaland as a cultural unit, but the land of cultures where an acceptable practice in a community is frowned at in another. For instance, it is considered taboo for the paramount ruler of Abeokuta to see an Egungun masquerade,[9] whereas it is acceptable in Ede in the same Yorubaland that masquerades visit the Oba (king) during the festival.[10] Therefore, it is essential that researchers in Nigeria understand such variations in practices to find accommodation within each locality.

---

[7] Marriot, M 1967, 'Cultural Policy in New States' in Geertz, C. ed., 1967. *Old Societies and New States: The quest for modernity in Asia and Africa.* Free Press.
[8] Falola, T., 2008. *The power of African cultures.* University of Rochester Press.
[9] Nolte, I., 2002. Chieftaincy and State in the Abacha's Nigeria: Kingship, Political Rivalry and Competing Histories in Abeokuta during the 1990s. *Africa*
[10] I covered the Egungun festival in Ede in June 2012, and I was very surprised that by tradition two masquerades must visit the traditional ruler of Ede in his palace on the first day of the festival.

While doing research on *Gelede* masquerade[11] in Iboro my guide took me to an elderly woman whose family is famed as the custodian of the masquerade in the town. The woman welcomed us and listened very carefully to my explanation. She admitted that all the regalia of the masquerades were usually kept in her house, and she even showed me where those regalia and drums were deposited in a special room. But she did not go beyond that. She declined to speak on the history and celebration of *Gelede festival* in the town. The reasons for her refusal was predicated on some laid down rules which she equated with taboo that must not be broken by any member of her family, and in the town in general. According to her, some people must be present before she could speak on the subject, lest she betrayed the family and the deity (*Gelede*). I asked if she could direct me to someone else I could speak to but she told me that no one would dare grant me interview on *Gelede* in the whole of the town. She was confident that anyone I asked would certainly refer me back to her house. She explained further that it is not that the knowledge of masquerade is a monopoly of her family but everyone in the town understands the need to do things the appropriately. By this she meant the laid down procedure must be followed in attending to issues that border on their cultural heritage. It was clear the woman regretted her inability to help me as she later offered her apology that even though what I came to ask her was not a difficult thing to explain and she also has children who might find themselves in my situation, she feared that there would be consequences if she elected to break the taboo. When the woman's action is considered against the backdrop of her socio-cultural orientation, one may find a justification for her unwillingness to break the taboo.

Despite such argument that taboos are for "the most part irrational and hard to defend on the practical or humanitarian ground",[12] it can be sufficiently argued that the phenomenon has not totally lost its significance in many parts of Yorubaland. Taboos have continued to shape opinions, feelings and knowledge of individuals and groups despite their years of exposure to other cultures. Even within the supposed secular Western society, there are some restrictions imposed on social behaviour which are symptoms of enduring taboos. The following observation reinforces such assertion:

> When I decided to put "The Secret Gay Life of Malcom Forbes" on the cover of *OutWeek*, I was conscious of violating a long-standing rule: The homosexuality of public figure is strictly a private matter, to be ignored or even deliberately cover up by the press. Both the mainstream and the gay press had always adhered to

---

[11] Gelede is a popular Yoruba masquerade found among the Yewa sub-group in Nigeria and eastern part of Benin Republic. See Lawal, B 1978. New Light on Gelede. *African Arts* Los Angeles, Cal.

[12] Thody, P.M.W., 1997. *Don't do it! A Dictionary of the Forbidden*. Athlone Press.

that rule. But since last summer a debate had been growing within the gay and lesbian press on the ethics of disclosing the sex of famous gay.[13]

Much as some consider taboo as unwarranted restrictions on human freedom, the phenomenon has continued to serve as an unwritten social rule or mechanism for maintaining social balance in different societies. Even though the level of immersion in taboos varies from one society to another, a researcher, whether conducting ethnography or interview, is likely to find out more about different taboos, their observations and how they can aid or retard fieldwork. In Share and Omu-Aran, two Yoruba towns in north-central Nigeria, I found out that I had to visit the palace of their traditional rulers first before I commenced my research. Even though the traditional rulers have some designated persons to speak to researchers on behalf of the palace, it is a tradition that must be observed. And the palace will have to give approval before the designated persons agree to be interviewed. It is interesting to note that even though the researcher may not be required to show any evidence of approval from the palace, mere mentioning that one has visited the palace is enough to serve as a pass. This shows how what I call the 'culture of trust' operates in some societies and the need for research to understand how it operates.

As I witnessed in Iboro, the idea of having many people around during an interview with strangers is also practiced elsewhere. But I think the nature of the discussion basically determines the number of people that must be present. It appeared to me that when a researcher seeks to know about stuff that concerns the generality of a community such information is better related either by the head who is vested with the full authority to deal with such issues, or by some elders who must do so in the presence of others, probably to guard against misrepresentation, or to promote some parochial interests capable of jeopardising the collective wellbeing of the community. In Ibara, another Yewa town, a notable chief of the town refused to speak to me about the history of the town. The chief maintained that the only person permitted to speak on such subject is the oba and anything outside that would amount to an aberration which he as a chief must guard against. He gave an illustration of a deity and its adherents in which the two mutually reinforce each other. He said that it is the duty of the deity to provide spiritual protection to its adherents, and the adherents must always uphold the sanctity of their deity before outsiders. He said chiefs as representatives of the people installed the king as the overall leader of the town, and it is their duty to accord him respect as the chief custodian of their tradition to have the final say on anything that concerns the town. I observed some situations similar to what I encountered in Ibara at other communities such as Irawo-Owode and Irawo-Ajegunle, two neighbouring communities in Oke-Ogun in the northwest of Yorubaland. In Irawo-Owode, the

---

[13] Rotello, G., 2004. The ethics of "outing": Breaking the Silence Code on Homosexuality. Quoted in Ogunyemi, O., 2008. The Implications of Taboos among African Diasporas for the African Press in the United Kingdom. *JournalofBlackStudies*

king could speak on any issue, and he did speak to me on the history of the town, their peculiar deity known as Orisa Oko, its origin and how the people celebrate their festival, among other issues. The king equally spoke on the introduction of Islam and Christianity to the community, but he referred me to the imam, head of the Muslim community of the town, for a better discussion on the religion.

However, the situation was different at the imam's place. While the king spoke to me without inviting anyone during the interview, the imam decided to bring in some Muslim elders to discuss the history of Islam in the town. In the neighbouring Irawo-Owode, the imam also invited his lieutenants and some other Muslim elders when I interviewed him on the practices of Islam and its introduction into the community. Much more interesting, though surprising, was when I was directed to one of the oldest persons in the town to interview him on the general history of Irawo-Owode because the king, as I learnt, had passed away a few months earlier. On reaching his place, I met the old man seated in an open space in front of his house. After I had explained my mission, he offered me a seat. He then invited many people to listen to the interview. In my estimation, there were about thirty persons in attendance, both old and young, and some people who were not invited also came to listen. If I had the opportunity I would have requested a one-on-one interview, but I felt it was within his right to determine the number of people he wanted around. More so, it appeared such an occasion was a rarity and it was considered an opportunity for many residents of the community to listen to the history of their town from an elderly person.

The situation was completely different when I sought to inquire about some esoteric issues like the secret society in the same Irawo-Owode. Unlike the history of the town and other public religions like Islam, Christianity and Orisa Oko, which is also the principal deity of the town, I think the knowledge of the secret society like the Ogboni[14] is not for public consumption. But members seem willing to relate with researchers especially those from outside their community. Even though the members of such a society are well-known in the community, their supposed secrets are not really known to people and any information from non-members is, at best, conjectural. Perhaps the reason is premised on the idea of whatever is made a secret commands respect. I need to admit that contrary to the popular perception, which I equally held *ab-initio*, that a researcher seeking to know about secret societies such as the Ogboni must first be initiated into the cult and perform some peculiar rituals before gaining access to the members, that perception seems a product of mere speculations occasioned by utter lack of knowledge of the mechanics of their activities.

---

[14] See Denneth, R.E., 1916. The Ogboni and other Secret Societies in Nigeria. *The Journal of the Royal African Society*

4.5 WHEN RELIGION DOES (NOT) MATTER

It is common knowledge that Islam and Christianity are the dominant religions in Nigeria. For over a century, the two dominant religions have always competed with each other for adherents[15] but the competition seems more pronounced in recent years.[16] It has also been observed that the two dominant religions constitute a threat to the African Traditional Religions (ATRs),[17] although the ATRs no doubt are still very active across the Yorubaland. For a number of researchers, religious consideration is a major determining factor in their research interest. Unlike their counterparts in the mainstream sciences who are accustomed to the controlled laboratory experiments, the fact that social researchers deal mainly with humans whose behaviours are not always predictable. The fact that human behavior cannot be ethically controlled like the scientific objects make the conduct of interview with people of other religions a major problem for some researchers. To be confronted with practices incongruous with the researcher's religious belief is what some may wish to avoid. Considering the importance of interviewing as highlighted by scholars, should religious belief stand in the way of the researcher? My thought on this is that the place of belief in the choice of research topic and methodology depends on individual researchers. Since the decision on the research topic solely rests with the researcher, unless such research is being carried out on behalf of someone else, it should be expected that the researcher would have envisaged what the fieldwork entails and be prepared to take on challenges as they may arise. Therefore, if the primary aim of the researcher is to discover new things or access some privileged information through an interview, then the focus needs to be on the interview.

As a non-Muslim, I have had reasons to be invited into the mosque in my quest to interview some Muslim groups. I had to conform to the rules and regulations guiding the conduct of people in the mosque, even though I did not perform ablution nor did I join them in praying. The case of Isiwo-Ijebu is worth reporting here. Isiwo-Ijebu is a small Yoruba community where I had to interview a number of people for my research. The last person I was to interview was the Imam of the town, but I learned he resided outside the community and only came every Friday to lead the weekly prayers. I put a call through to him and he told me to meet him on a Friday in Isoyin-Ijebu. My initial thinking was that he was going to grant the interview after the weekly congregational prayer which he led, but it came to me as a great surprise when I heard my name from the loudspeaker of the central mosque. My name was announced

---

[15] Peel, J.D.Y., 1997. *Engaging with Islam in Nineteenth Century Yorubaland*. North Atlantic Missiology Project.

[16] Adewusi, A., 2012. 'NASFAT and its Giant Strides: A Discourse of a Social and Religious Movement in Nigeria.' in Siyan, O. ed., *Islam and Society in Osun State: Essays in Honour of HRM Oba Olayiwola Olawale Adedeji II, Akinrun of Ikirun*. Megapress.

[17] Danfulani, U.H.D., 2001.Religious Conflict on the Jos Plateau: The Interplay between Christianity and Traditional Religion during the Early Missionary Period. *Swedish Missiological Themes*

demanding that I come into the mosque and I did. Although I was hesitant initially not because I had not entered a mosque as a building before that time, it was the first I would be invited there during a congregational prayer.

What was more surprising upon my entry into the mosque was that instead of proceeding to the interview which we had agreed upon I became the one being interviewed. Questions started coming from different people in the mosque. Some asked me about my religion and why I was interested in the activities of the Muslims in the community. Another person said that as a non-indigene of the community he was not sure I was going to be fair in anything I would write about them. In fact, someone said I was likely to be a spy for people of other religions. But I maintained a façade of calmness and in my response I informed the gathering that as a researcher/historian my religion does not come between me and my research. I also explained that I had been researching Islam long before I came to Isiwo-Ijebu and that I have published a couple of my research on Islam.

It seemed my explanation was not convincing enough to some people in the gathering. Perhaps to confirm the veracity of my claim they demanded that I present a copy of my publication on Islam before the interview I required could be granted. Eventually, I returned to Isiwo-Ijebu with a copy of my publication on Islam which I presented to the Imam the following week. Regrettably, the interview did not take place. Ilusin-Ijebu was another place where my interviewee demanded that I come into the mosque during weekly congregational prayer before we could have the interview. But I did not go through any form of interrogation before we started the interview.

Generally, the practitioners of ATRs are associated with fetish practices which explains why most Christians and Muslims avoid association with them.[18] When the belief is put first there is every likelihood that a researcher of Islamic or Christian persuasion who does not want to get involved in fetish practices will avoid interviews with the practitioners of ATRs. But my field experience and several encounters with practitioners of ATRs in different communities gave me a different perspective on the popular notion about the practitioners of ATRs. I can confidently assert that individuals rather than the religion they practice determine the interview context. I have had varied experiences in interviewing practitioners of ATRs in the southwest and north-central. Few of my respondents insisted on observing certain practices which ordinarily would have dissuaded a researcher of a different religion. For example, in my quest to interview an Ogboni leader in Ilaro my guide told me that I had to take along with me certain items such as kola nut and alcohol drink. But on the agreed date my guide told me that I could buy the drink alone and that the man would accept it. True to his assurance the man accepted the drink alone and agreed that I interview him. The interview was conducted between me and him alone. In a similar interview with a member of the same religion in Irawo-Owode I have not requested a present gift but no one else was allowed to be present

---

[18] McGaffey, W., 1994. African Objects and the Idea of Fetish. RES: *Anthropology and Aesthetics*.

during the interview. It was the same experience with an Ogboni member in Igbo-Ora.

Ethically, and unlike job interviews in which the interviewer determines interview location, for researchers the location or setting of an interview is usually the exclusive preserve of the interviewees, except such a person elects to concede such a privilege to the researcher. I have been asked on a number of occasions by my interviewees to choose the locations and they were comfortable with my choice. But I do not ask any potential interviewee for the privilege of choosing the location. Another major discouragement in interviewing practitioners of ATRs is the location which may be in the shrine or their place of worship. As I have noted earlier, the religion may not necessarily prescribe a particular location for an interview but individuals do most of the time, possibly to subject the research to some temperament test or for other reason best known to them. In Ilashe, a border community between Nigeria and the Benin Republic, I went to interview a priest of Sonpana (the deity of smallpox) and the man insisted the interview must be conducted in the shrine where the deity was. His reason for such insistence was that he could not speak about the deity in its absence. Raising an objection to go into the shrine would mean that he would not grant the agreed interview. Closely related to this were two different occasions at Okeho where I was confronted with certain challenges at interview locations but I diplomatically resolved them. The first was when I wanted to interview a devotee of Sango (Yoruba deity of thunder). Before we commenced the interview the man brought out a gourd which contained some dark powdery substance, poured some on his palm and ingested it. He offered the same to me but I asked him if it was connected to the interview we wanted to have. He said the substance was for the fortification of the body and that he only offered me out of altruism and it was not compulsory that I took it. The interview went on thereafter. The second instance was during a group interview with some practitioners of ATRs and my hosts offered me some decoction which everybody in attendance partook of. I was exempted from taking the decoction upon request but that did not stop the interview from going on.

4.6   The Pitfall for Unsuspecting Researchers: Reliabilities of Information

As the conversation with a purpose and one of the methods used for obtaining information about processes, attitudes and feelings of people interviews can also be misleading when not carefully handled. Naturally, a researcher would appear to have scaled a major hurdle in meeting an important personality like a traditional ruler or chief in a community for an interview, but that is merely a step in many steps to be taken. What about the credibility of the information obtained through interviews, especially with someone in a position of authority? Some researchers attach hardly any importance to interviews because they privilege other methodologies over them, but that does not diminish the invaluable contribution interviews can make to the research process. Getting the best out of interviews can be a herculean task that many fledgling researchers hardly want to undertake. Silverman observed this uncritical use of interviews by "unconscious Naturalists and Emotionalists."[19] In my own line of operation, a historian is required to gather as much information as may be available to him from different sources to avoid the vulnerability of being misled into drawing conclusions on wrong premise. I give an illustration of the possibility of being misled by informants with some field experience, but I need to state that wrong information may not necessarily be a deliberate act by interviewees.

My research on Owu, one of the most scattered sub-groups of the Yoruba people in southwest and north-central Nigeria, underscores the need not only for multiple interviews but also to be critical of information. I visited many Owu towns and villages, and during my visit to Owu Ile, I learned about the migration of the people from the original settlement called Owu Ipole. My interviewee told me that the reason for the migration of their ancestors to their present location was due to the contest for the throne between two brothers in which the younger brother was favoured over the older one. The older brother and his sympathisers felt cheated, seized the crown and left to settle in the place that is known today as Owu Ile. By tradition, the kingmakers could not install the younger brother without the crown. They, therefore, sent emissaries to appeal to the older brother to return home so that the contest could be held again. The older brother and his entourage agreed to return to Owu Ipole. The account states further that upon the return of the older brother the kingmakers gave each contestant a bean seed to plant and the seed that germinated first would determine who would ascend the throne. Unknown to the older brother his own seed had been parboiled and could not germinate. The seed that was given to the younger brother sprouted and He became the king. Because I wanted to determine the pattern of migration of the Owu after the 1825 war, I had to visit as many Owu communities as I could, and in the course of such visit, I discovered something intriguing at Owu Isin, another Owu settlement.

When I visited Owu Isin located in the north-central part of the country I discovered through an oral interview that their story of migration is not only similar to what I was told at Owu Ile but rendered in the same way. The few differences are the locations and names of the two brothers who contested for the throne. On the surface, someone would appear to be dishonest and deliberately seeking to mislead the researcher, but these are the tradition of the people and it is not the responsibility of the researcher to adjudge the people of misrepresentation, after all, the information can only serve as raw materials to be worked upon. As a researcher seeking to make sense of the two different but similar accounts, I looked beyond the similarities between the accounts.

---

[19] Silverman, D., 2013. What Counts as Qualitative Research? Some Cautionary Comments. *Qualitative Sociology Review*

Since interviewers are not free from biases and are not under compulsion to tell the truth to their interviewers always,[20] it is the responsibility of the researcher to determine the use of the information so gathered. I found a solution to the apparent problem in the two interviews by conducting more interviews in other places, and I discovered that both accounts were part of the invented tradition like the Convent of Wesel.[21] As Hobsbawm has noted, invented tradition is a set of practices, normally governed by overtly or tacitly rules and rituals or symbolic nature, which seeks to inculcate certain values and norms of behaviour by repetition,[22] it goes without saying that interview can serve as a major platform to strengthening such traditions. My discovery shows that the claims of migrating from Owu Ipole which was destroyed during the Yoruba internecine wars of the nineteenth century are part of the effort to create a pan-Owu system with Owu Ipole at the centre. As my subsequent interviews and other sources reveal, both Owu Ile in the southwest and Owu Isin in the north-central actually did not migrate from Owu Ipole but from an earlier Owu kingdom that is less talked about in the modern history of Yoruba.

Further on the invented tradition and the vulnerability of researchers through interviewing, the interviews I conducted in two different locations further emphasise the need to treat information with utmost circumspection. I discovered through the interviews the claims and counter-claims over superiority between Telemu and Kuta, both post-Owu war settlements in the southwest. I met the traditional ruler of Telemu first and he agreed to grant an extensive interview in which he narrated how the Owu war led to the dislodgment of his ancestors from their original settlement in Owu Ipole. He stated further how the culture hero of the Owu people named Anlugbua disappeared into the earth in that particular location and that makes the people of Telemu the original descendants of Anlugbua because he still resides with them and has continued to be the protector of the community. Even though their original home was destroyed in the war and was resettled about a century later, the assertion at Telemu is that the original descendants of the earlier inhabitants are not the current occupants of the settlement. However, my interview with the traditional ruler of Kuta introduced a new twist with the counter-claim that Anlugbua actually resides in the domain and that makes Kuta and its people the real Owu than any other group.

---

[20] Benny, J.M., 2002. Validity and Reliability Issues in Elite Interviewing, *Political Science and Politics*

[21] Spohnholz, J., 2017. *The Covent of Wesel: the event that never was and the invention of tradition.* Cambridge University Press.

[22] Hobsbawm, E., 'Introduction: Inventing Tradition' in Hobsbawm, E, and Ranger, T, eds., 1983. *The Invention of Tradition.* Cambridge University Press.

4.7 Victims of Wrong Perceptions and High Expectations

How do the interviewees perceive a potential researcher? There is no doubt people have been interviewed at various times and on different subjects in their homes, on the roads, in hospitals, workplaces, etc., and much as there are experienced and fledgling researchers, the same can be said of respondents. Often times, the attitude exhibited towards a researcher is a function of the past experience of the interviewees. In fact, some people have made up their minds not to grant interviews to any stranger irrespective of the topic or the personality of the researcher. I recall an encounter with the traditional ruler of Idowa-Ijebu who demanded I leave his palace after I had explained to him what my mission was. He told me that he had made up his mind not to grant an interview to anyone. His attitude can be categorised as strange considering the enthusiasm with which most traditional rulers in this part of the country usually want to tell researchers about their community and make claims about their superiority to neighbouring communities. In other words, interviewing is used as an avenue to draw the attention of the outside world to their locality. While I could not fathom the reason behind what appears a bizarre attitude, I could infer from the explanation offered by other people who hold the view that most researchers disguise collecting information on people to be used for purposes they consider inimical to their interest in the respondents.

Apart from this, there are categories of people who hold the view that every researcher must have received funding either from the government or some foreign donor agencies. It is expected that the researcher shares what in the popular parlance is called the "national cake" with them. Even after explaining that not all research is government-funded, some people still believe the interview should be paid for. Questions such as "will the research not fetch you money after the completion?" and "will you remember us after you have started making money from this research?" explain the mind of a number of people about research as a money-spinner they must benefit from as much as the researchers will. In this sense, information is a highly prized commodity that can be sold through interviews.

4.8 Conclusion

Irrespective of indifference of some researchers towards interviewing as a suitable method in social research, there is no doubt that it has become a standard data collection process across disciplines in social sciences, humanities and medical science over the years. The various highlighted hurdles or tyrannies are indications that interviewing is not a cheap, substandard research tool that a novice can employ at will, rather it is a credible process that requires a good mastery before considering its inclusion in research methodology. Moreover, it has been demonstrated here that researchers can successfully conduct interviews without compromising the ethics of research; that the reliability or otherwise of information collection through interviews depends on the skills of the researcher and how these are employed in analysing such information. In essence, an interview is doable but the onus rests on the researcher to determine how to navigate through the convoluted web unscathed.

REFERENCES

Adewusi, A., 2012. 'NASFAT and its Giant Strides: A Discourse of a Social and Religious Movement in Nigeria.' in Oyeweso, S. ed., *Islam and Society in Osun State: Essays in Honour of HRM Oba OlayiwolaOlawaleAdedeji II, Akinrun of Ikirun*. Megapress

Atkinson, P. and Silverman, D., 1997. Kundera's Immortality: The Interview Society and the Invention of the Self. *Qualitative Inquiry* 3(3), pp.304-325

Benny, J.M., 2002. Validity and Reliability Issues in Elite Interviewing, *Political Science and Politics*, 35(4), pp.679-682

Clarke, M., 1975. Survival in the field: implications of personal experience in fieldwork. *Theory and Society*, 2(1), pp.95-123

Danfulani, U.H.D., 2001. Religious Conflict on the Jos Plateau: the interplay between Christianity and Traditional Religion during the early missionary period. *Swedish Missiological Themes*, 89 (1), pp.7-39

Denneth, R.E., 1916. The Ogboni and other Secret Societies in Nigeria. *The Journal of the Royal African Society*, 16(61), pp.16-29

duTiot, B. M.,1980. Ethics, Informed Consent, and Fieldwork. *Journal of Anthropological Research*, 36(3), pp.274-286

Falola, T., 2008. *The power of African cultures*. University of Rochester Press, pp.

Holstein, J. A. and Gubrium, J. F., 2004. The active interview inSilverman, D., ed. *Qualitative Research. Theory, Method and Practice*, Sage. pp. 140-161.

Hobsbawm, E., 'Introduction: InventingTradition' in Hobsbawm, E, and Ranger, T, eds., 1983. *The Invention of Tradition*. Cambridge University Press

Kleinman, S. et al. Privileging Fieldwork over Interviews: consequences for identity and practices. SymbolicInteraction 17(1), pp. 37-50

Lawal, B 1978. New Light on Gelede. *African Arts* LosAngeles, Cal, 11(2), pp.65-70

Myers, M. D. (1997). "Qualitative research in information systems" *ManageInformSystem* 21(1), pp.241–242.

Marriot, M 1967, 'Cultural Policy in New States' in Geertz, C. ed., 1967. *Old Societies and New States: The quest for modernity in Asia and Africa*. Free Press.

McGaffey, W., 1994. African Objects and the Idea of Fetish. RES: *Anthropology and Aesthetics*. 25(1), pp.123-131

Nolte, I., 2002. Chieftaincy and State in the Abacha's Nigeria: kingship, political rivalry and competing histories in Abeokuta during the 1990s. *Africa* 72(3), pp. 368-390

Nolte, I., Ogen, O. and Jones, R., 2017. *Beyond Religious Tolerance: Muslim, Christian and Traditionalistencountersinan African town*. James Curry.

Peel, J.D.Y., 1997. *Engaging with Islam in Nineteenth Century Yorubaland*. North Atlantic Missiology Project.

Philips, R. and John, J., 2012. *FieldworkforHumanGeography*. Sage Publications Ltd.

Riesman, D. and Benny, M., 1956. The Sociology of the Interview. *The Midwest Sociologist* 18 (1), pp.3-15

Ritchie, D.A., Shulman, H.C., Kirkendall, R.S. and Birdwhistell, T.L., 1991. Interviews as Historical Evidence: A Discussion of New Standards of Documentation and Access. *The History Teacher*, 24(2), pp.232-238

Rotello, G., 2004. The ethics of "outing": Breaking the Silence Code on Homosexuality. Quoted in Ogunyemi, O., 2008. The Implications of Taboos among African Diasporas for the African Press in the United Kingdom. *JournalofBlackStudies*, 38(6), pp.862-882

Sanneh, L., 1989. *Translating the Message: the Missionary Impact on Culture*. Maryknoll.

Silverman, D., 2013. What Counts as Qualitative Research? Some Cautionary Comments. *Qualitative Sociology Review*, 9(2), pp. 49-55

Soares, B.F., 2006. *Muslim-Christian Encounters in Africa*. Brill.

Spohnholz, J., 2017. *The Covent of Wesel: the event that never was and the invention of tradition*. Cambridge University Press.

Thody, P.M.W., 1997. *Don't do it! A Dictionary of the Forbidden*. Athlone Press.

CHAPTER 5

Trial by Fire: Reflections on Fieldwork in Nagaland, Northeast India

Debojyoti Das

> *In many areas of the world, anthropological fieldwork is more dangerous today than it was in the past. There are approximately 120 'armed conflicts' ... and given that about one-third of the world's countries are currently involved in warfare and about two-thirds of the countries resort to human rights abuses as normal aspects of their political process to control their population, it is clear that few anthropologists will be able to avoid conflicting situations and instances of socio-political violence in the course of their professional lives.*
> —Sluka (1995: 276)

Sarat Chandra Roy the founding father of Indian Anthropology once admitted to his student Nirmal Kumar Bose that if he was given a second life, he will rewrite his ethnography. Fieldwork is a right to passage and, over time, one becomes reflexive during the aftermath of one's experience with one's interlocutors. In this chapter, I will engage with the ethics of self-harm, not only from the standpoint of conducting fieldwork in dangerous fields where violence features predominantly but also the unknown dangers that can emerge while establishing relationships with interlocutors in the field which cannot be outlined in standard research ethics clearance protocol. In my book titled the *Politics of Swidden Farming*, I have engaged with the question of violence produced by state and non-state actors in a cease-fire environment. In this chapter, I will shed light on my personal experiences with one of my interlocutors who

D. Das (✉)
Department of Education and Sports, University of Edinburgh, Edinburgh, UK

was in a position of power. I will echo how emotional detachment is a misnomer and even men can find themselves in a vulnerable position while undertaking fieldwork in dangerous fields. Therefore, the ethics of complicity, collusion and detachment can be a tricky and blurred exercise in the field (Trundal, 2018). I will present a personal narrative of my experience with my interlocutor in the first part of the chapter and then connect on to the second part where I talk about a violent episode that made a revelation of how political nexus and development programs are embedded in community's will to improve and manifest state's governmentality extended through community-driven development programmed.

Anthropological fieldwork stands out from other social science research in that intimate fieldwork experience becomes the ethnographer's primary source of knowledge. The chapter will also discuss the moral and ethical dilemmas of conducting fieldwork in a social context where everyday violence and suspicion feature prominently. In this context, methodological practices such as reflexivity, informed consent, fieldworkers' responsibility, rapport and reciprocity need to be considered to engage with the ethics of fieldwork. In ethnographic fieldwork, the question of a researcher's subject position becomes primordial, as he or she is expected to be engaged, immersed and, at the same time, objective and neutral.

My reflection is based on fourteen months of ethnographic fieldwork in the Indian state of Nagaland. The Nagas have engaged with the Indian government for recognition of their unique history and culture and have called for self-determination through acts of armed resistance, which have lately resulted in a cease-fire agreement. I conducted fieldwork under conditions of a ceasefire with the impression that things would be normal. However, despite my hopes of being safe, I was caught up in a hostage situation while travelling with my interlocutor to his village. The hostage situation was triggered by the local factional clash about development money that was spent on public works in the village funded by the Mahatma Gandhi National Rural Employment Guarantee Scheme (MGNREGS), India's largest employment programme, which I will discuss in the second part of my chapter.

Fieldwork involves some deep relationships which we develop with our interlocutors, participants and informants. It is different today from what nineteenth-century anthropologists proposed as a detached social activity. In those days, the power dynamics between the anthropologist and the natives they studied were based on the master-subject (we and the other) relationship. Over time, the practice of ethnography has changed, as these colonial privileges came to a close in the era of decolonization. However, official ethnographic exercises carried out by anthropological intuitions like the Anthropological Survey of India have still championed the idea of a detached observer and neutrality in the field. During my fieldwork, it became increasingly difficult to detach myself from everyday village life and the politics of the field. I had to immerse myself amongst my interlocutors. And often, the boundaries between myself and the other collapsed.

But this also opened up many challenges of conducting fieldwork in an unknown field, where violence by state and non-state actors in the borderland regions at the margins of the Indian state was part of everyday life. Besides this, I was perturbed by another challenge in the field: to find the right collaborators for my research. When I initially visited the field, I decided to work closely with project officials who implemented the Nagaland Empowerment of People Through Energy Development (hereafter NEPeD), which focused on the initial intent of my study—an anthropological analysis of how development works through institutional intervention following an actor-network model of development practice. But this attempt was met with challenges. The first trip I took to Kohima made me very enthusiastic that the project staff would extend their help to me, which they did by taking me on a couple of day trips to project villages in the suburbs of Kohima. These interactions were more official-guarded, and I had limited interaction with villagers. The purpose of doing long-term fieldwork while living in a village seemed impossible at that time. The team members were also not prepared to leave me in a project village. I soon realized that in such a targeted intervention, based on the evaluation of programmes implemented in the field through what they called "outcome mapping", extended interaction was not possible. In the NEPeD case, it was the economic and social empowerment of swidden villagers through granting of microcredits, the creation of self-help groups and the popularization of alder-based plantation cropping that was leading farmers away from field rotation under slash and burn agriculture towards permanent crop husbandry. I took some time off to rethink my strategy and decided to write a small piece about the project in a local newspaper, *The Shillong Times*. This immediately created a rift between the research staff and myself. I perhaps misinterpreted my interlocutors, and they decided not to cooperate anymore with me. They claimed that I had misunderstood the project. This was the first setback I received in the field and it also helped me to think about building a more intimate, long-term relationship with my interlocutors so that I could get to know them better and spend time with them in a single field site. The misunderstanding of the project goals and my quick appraisal of the project created some tension, as I was seen as an outsider, with limited knowledge of the project's activities. I did make some visits later to their Kohima office headquarters but slowly realized that they were not interested in sharing more information on the project through personal interviews. Therefore, I reoriented my focus from the study of the project itself to the study of the people who became beneficiaries of the project in a model village where the interventions were carried out.

This prompted me to search for a new set of interlocutors who were not part of the project team but local actors who could provide me with the opportunity to settle in a Naga village and conduct long-term fieldwork. Many of my mentors suggested that I should reside in a nearby village in Kohima and conduct my ethnographic work. I tried very hard to find a study village, and Khonoma emerged as my favourite. After visiting the village, I did get very interesting data on village conservation work and the popularization of the alder-based plantation, which has been the hallmark of NEPeD intervention in another neighbouring district, as the traditional way of farming based on indigenous knowledge of the community. The NEPeD team had made Khonoma one of its early case study villages. Khonoma turned out to be too popular as a touristic village with bird watchers and NEPeD staff, and I found it too close to Kohima to settle down and work. Also, it was, in some ways, researched by other academics who had studied the positive side of alder-based planation. I, therefore, returned to my natal home to rethink my fieldwork. During this time, I contacted several people. My former teacher at North-Eastern Hill University, who was at that time the head of the department, suggested that his past student was now the principal of a college in Nagaland and that he could help me with my fieldwork where the NEPeD intervention was taking place in swidden cultivation villages.

This was an exciting breakthrough for me, and I soon contacted the principal and told him that I would like to visit his home in Mokokchung so that he could introduce me to villages he knew in eastern Nagaland. Our interaction over the phone was very positive. I then made a research plan to visit the field with him. He invited me to come to his home in Mokokchung, from where we proposed to visit the field. I booked a ticket from Shillong to Kohima and then, after a stopover at Kohima, took a transport to Mokokchung. When I arrived at the bus stop, he was already there to greet me. He was wearing a white jacket with ironed jeans and sunglasses. He looked to be in his early 40s and was quite macho in his style. A driver was standing by his side with their white Maruti gipsy. As I disembarked my vehicle, he identified me, and I soon greeted him for welcoming me. He was looking at me, all the time wearing the sunglasses. He was quite friendly and charming, to begin with. After a short drive, we reached his house, which was well-decorated and had all the gadgets for cooking: a rice cooker, an electric cooker for cooking a quick meal, beside the traditional Naga kitchen with firewood. We soon relaxed and started chit-chatting about his life. He explained to me that he lived alone with his young driver, while his family lived in another district.

During the day, he took me to the village headman's home and we had some interaction about how farming in the village had completely transformed with the introduction of plantation crops, such as small tea gardens, passion fruit and pineapple cultivation and stone quarrying in the village. This had also significantly changed the lives of the village's people bringing in cash and generating disposable income with which they can afford to buy few luxury items. In the afternoon, we met a women's self-help group in the village and we also went on to visit the village *morung*[1] house, which was used as an outdoor museum to

---

[1] The *morung* or the bachelor dormitory system used to be an essential part of Naga life. Apart from the family, it was the most important educational system of the Naga people. Announcements of the meetings, the death of the villager, warning of the impending danger were made from the *morung* with the beating of log drums. With the onset of missionary modernity, the *morung* system is no longer practiced among the Naga tribes and is kept in most villages as a living open air museum artifact for visitors to come and see Naga culture and their remarkable past.

showcase visitors' Naga heritage. Once we returned to his home, we relaxed in his kitchen. The driver cooked a meal, in which we all gave a hand. The driver was around 20 years old. When I enquired about his family, he explained that they were from a distant village and visited during holidays. He loved staying alone. During the evening, he took me to another *Gaon Burah's*[2] house and there we discussed the village's past, migration history and the Morung House.

He explained to me that he comes to his natal home on weekends and then travels to his college on weekdays which was quite far. He was very popular with the local political elites and was friends with the chief minister of the state. On a lighter note, he remarked that he had gotten the job of the principal because he was in the good books of his friend in office and the administration. He sounded very confident. As it was getting dark, his driver, who also worked as the housekeeper, started to prepare the evening meal and we switched on the television. By 8 pm, we had finished our dinner and it was time to relax and talk some more before bedtime. As his driver left, I was persuaded by my host to stay awake and watch television, which I was happy to join in. He soon started staring at me and I did not know why, but I felt slightly uncomfortable. I thought it was something normal. As it was nearly 9.30 pm, I politely requested that I should go to bed. He kept on insisting that I stay awake and sit close to him. After a point of time as his staring increased, I felt a little more uncomfortable and finally requested that I should go to bed. After much reluctance, he agreed, and I went to my bedroom and tried to sleep. I was also disturbed why my host was behaving in such an unusual manner. Soon he knocked on my door and jumped into my bed. He pulled the blanket over us and started cuddling with me. At this point, I woke up from my sleep and realized that he was beside me. Soon, he said don't worry, we are going to have a good time now. He started touching my private parts. This created lots of discomfort and I was shocked by his behaviour. I politely requested that he get out of my bed, but he insisted that I drop my shorts and play with him. He was relentless in his effort. This scared me, and I was not sure what to do. He further pressed me to do the act. I resisted and screamed that I had not been expecting this. He replied I like your resistance we should not do this act instantaneously. Maybe you are shy today; we will try another day. He soon remarked "I like your body, and if you are not keen today, you will like it in the coming days", and he left the room, wishing me good night. I was shocked by my host's behaviour and felt like breaking down. I was clueless about what to do then. This intimate encounter, which I was not expecting, made it impossible for me to sleep in his house that whole night and I thought of escaping immediately.

---

[2] The '*Gaon Burah*' as the word suggests in Nagamese and Assamese are the village headmen. They are considered the eyes and ears of the district administration at the village level. In colonial times the British appointed the oldest person in the village as the head, who would oversee matters relating to land and revenue in a particular area. The institution is in practice in many parts of highland South Asia.

I felt like my fieldwork was in ruins after the initial setback with the NEPeD project team. This incident posed a heightened crisis for my fieldwork. The homosexual behaviours of my host made me disconcerted. A person whom I had known for just one day had made such a sly advance at me. The next morning, we had initially planned to travel to Mon where I had planned to visit some Konyak villages, record their stories and find a village where I could settle down. Now, these plans were in danger. The next morning, he came across as though nothing had happened. There was no discussion about the previous night's incident, and the driver returned to the kitchen. I felt it would have been undignified to question his behaviour in front of his driver and was contemplating what I should do to escape him. He was not embarrassed by his action but rather felt that I would welcome his advances and that we would spend time together as lovers. I decided to travel with him till Mon, as had been planned and then to go on my way independently, as his behaviour had come as a blind shock to me. At the same time, I was dependent on him to find my interlocutors in Mon among, the Konyak Nagas. This interdependency increased my precarity and raised my anxiety. Therefore, I decided to travel with him to Mon, as it was an unfamiliar field for me. After a long drive, we reached the town. On our way, we stopped at a roadside tea stall and had some snacks. I soon realized that he was looking at me with his eyes fixed on my face and bottom. Behind his glasses, there was a particular desire. He often commented during our trip in passing that I had a good body and that he loved such people. I kept listening to him and was not sure how to respond and escape this uncomfortable engagement. That night, once we reached Mon, we were tired and decided to retire early. In the middle of the night, he again entered my room and forced himself into the bed. He started to squeeze himself behind my back; at this point I woke up with a shock and my heartbeat went up again. I resisted his act and after some time, he decided to leave unfulfilled. I then decided that only one day was left with him before he got back to work and I left his home. The next morning, I decided to leave his place and return to a friend whom I contacted earlier and who was living with her husband in the town. She was also a college teacher and was looking forward to my visit. Although I visited her house, I was not comfortable and at peace. I was not sure with whom I could share my experience. Would people trust me? How would I respond to my host if he asked to meet me again? I was unsure.

A general sense of mistrust overwhelmed me, and I was unsure what to do at that stage. My host had promised me to meet again, so that I could fulfil his desires by spending time with him in solitude. This sounded like a terrible trade-off to me. After spending some time with my other host in Mon town, who were a lovely couple, I decided to return to my natal home and decide my plan of action. I did not share this bitter experience with my family or friends, as I was quite disturbed and traumatized by the treatment I received from my host. The burden of him being introduced by a university professor, my former teacher, made me feel helpless and lonely. I was also very angry at him. But I could not accuse my teacher of wrongdoing as he genuinely tried to help me find a base in Eastern Nagaland from where I could launch my fieldwork after the initial failed attempt. Neither could I disclose it to my close family members, as they would have just asked me to abandon my project. This personal encounter was a traumatising one, and my host still followed me like a shadow. He kept on sending me text messages with flowery words about when I was coming back to Nagaland and when we could meet privately. I ignored his messages and kept my calm. But things further took a drastic turn when one day, he called me and surprisingly declared that he was in my hometown and was staying for a couple of days at the Nagaland House in Shillong on an official visit. I did not disregard his message but found a way not to meet him again and to avoid another such compromising situation. As a month passed by, I was back in Kohima, still exploring a village in which to launch my fieldwork. During this time, I met Asoba on a bus journey. He was a jolly young man who introduced himself as a facilitator of community conservation (FCC) for the NEPeD project. This rang a bell, as I was reading the NEPeD literature and realized that the NEPeD project had recruited FCC workers from villages on casual contracts who would help project officials liaise with villagers, carry out surveys and work as intermediaries. When I disclosed to him that I wanted to study shifting cultivation he shared his interest and invited me to visit his town and promised to take me to villages that took part in the NEPeD project and were under his regulated field visits. He was much younger than me and was a spirited leader with high ambitions. I somehow felt, after interacting with him, that he could help me locate a NEPeD project village where I could settle to conduct my field research, as he was in regular touch with villagers during his visits and was very active in working with local political and village intermediaries.

We soon exchanged our phone numbers, and after reaching Kohima, I kept in touch with him for my next visit. I had not overcome the traumatic experience I had had with my former host in his residence in Mokokchung and Mon. But after talking to Asoba, I was very confident that he understood what I was looking for. During our bus journey, he also explained to me that they lived in remote borderlands close to Myanmar and almost never received visits from researchers who were keen to study their life and economy. It was not much longer after I had had this conversation that I landed in his natal hometown, after travelling over 200 kilometres from Kohima. Asoba was excited to see me and we immediately discussed a plan to visit a nearby village that had been part of a NEPeD project. We got up early in the morning the next day and drove to the village on his motorbike. On arrival, he took me to the house of my host, with whom I became a friend and that established my enduring bond with the study village. In the next section, I will discuss the events that led to the second perilous encounter in the field.

5.1 The Events

Let me begin by narrating the turbulent encounter. It was on 11th July 2009, after spending 9 months in the field, that I was exposed to a violent event that remains an important mark of my fieldwork. After arriving in my study village, Lanso, I had settled in with the family of John, who was politically influential in the village. My host's nephew and his sons assisted me with my household survey, which focused on livelihoods, household consumption patterns, land use and land relations.

My study was not about violence (at least not in the conventional sense) but focused on the effects of transnational and state-driven development projects. The road connecting Lanso to the district headquarters (Tuensang town) was maintained by local contractors. Although it was risky to travel on such mountain roads during peak monsoon season, with boulders and mudslides cutting off the vital road links, I had visited Shillong, the capital town of Meghalaya, my hometown, and intended to return to my field site on 11th June. In addition, my host from Lanso was in Kohima to visit his political party and do development work for the village and his farm. I had decided to meet up with my host at Dimapur on my return journey and then travel with him back to Tuensang.

On 9th June, I reached Dimapur. On the same day, we travelled through the rugged mountain highways of Kohima and Mokokchung to his leader's plantation near Shamatur sub-divisional headquarters in Tuensang district. Before leaving, my host and his leader's parents prayed for our well-being, holding the Bible in their hands.

As we reached Tuensang town, after much struggle through the monsoon rains, it was already dark. Lanso was still 73 kilometres away. That morning, when I had reached Dimapur, the driver informed me that his boss had left. This turned out to be a miscommunication, but perhaps an intentional one. I later learnt in the field that our journey had been kept secret, known only to the host family and us. The tracked, bumpy road had already made me drowsy, and after travelling for over 270 kilometres and 10 hours, I was falling asleep. As we were running out of fuel, it was necessary to refuel in Tuensang town but, as it was Sunday, the sole petrol pump was closed. Earlier, on our way from Mokokchung, a drunken man had suddenly appeared on the road, waving at us to stop. An accident was averted by our driver, who had driven past him, accelerating sharply. Now, as our vehicle left the petrol station, it was swirling around corners. Half asleep, suddenly I saw our car being stopped by two unidentified armed men. The one on the left was carrying a revolver, and the one man on the right was carrying an assault rifle pointed at the vehicle. The vehicle immediately stopped with a violent jerk that threw us from our seats. Within minutes, one of the armed men had taken control of the vehicle. They had already smashed the headlight, so everything was happening in darkness. Before I could say a word, our driver was bleeding from his forehead, where he had been smashed with a pistol butt. My host, who was trying to intervene at this point, was dragged out of the front seat. In the meantime, a group of armed guards had entered the vehicle from the rear and ransacked my belongings. The armed guards were shouting, "Don't you respect us as soldiers? We are in civilian dress; you don't respect us. You will have to pay for it with your blood." The driver pleaded for mercy but he could not escape. In the meantime, the assailants were holding my host, a man in his mid-50s, by his collar and he had already developed a swollen forehead. I was the only person who had remained untouched at that point.

Amid this violence, I heard one armed guard speak to me from behind, "Run, run, before you are beaten up too. Run for your life!" I called to the driver and we started running in the darkness with a dim torch in my hand that I had fortunately taken out of my bag before the event. After running for around ten minutes on the dark road, I arrived at a college teacher house who lived nearby and whom I had contacted earlier, when the vehicle was being refuelled. We rang the police but to no avail. Soon, I received a frantic call from my host. He tried to convince me that the situation was now settled, and we would soon be on our way to Lanso, so long as we came back to the spot where the incident had happened, or else the situation could get worse. The college teacher appealed to me not to go, as the situation was too dangerous, but I had little choice. I felt it was morally incorrect to leave my host alone with the assailants when he was calling for help. The driver was very reluctant to come, as he was too fearful of being killed, but I managed to convince him. Moving through the darkness towards the scene of the incident, we realized that the armed guards had blocked the road. But soon I saw my host coming down the road with a loincloth across his face, drenched in blood. He identified us as his associates. The next moment we were taken captive and escorted to an unidentified place.

I had no idea where my field notes, my camera and my laptop were. They had been thrown out of the vehicle. Even the vehicle was declared missing. All mobile phones were snatched from us and switched off. We were at once disconnected from the outside world. The dialogue that followed was emotionally charged. The town commander at times exploded, narrating his hard life as a rebel leader hounded by the military. Pointing at me, he denounced me as an Indian: "Your government has repressed our aspiration for self-rule." He also accused my host of misunderstanding them. "The Naga army has been cursed to be *musafir* (wanderers) in the forest and jungle of Saramati mountain." But, by this time, the paramilitary forces had been tipped off and they reached the spot and rescued us all. In the days that followed, there were intense negotiations between the assailants and my host, who was an important political figure in the area. Scores of villagers, party workers and sympathizers came to see him to express their support and sympathy. Party workers argued that the assailants should be punished according to tribal council rules. However, my host's party leader was adamant that a situation of escalation should be avoided and proposed a compromise, which he announced, holding the Bible: he called it a "compromise of forgiveness" as "Jesus did to his enemies."

However, his stance was described by party colleagues and sympathizers from the local town as an act of cowardice, conceding to the power of the guilty. People accused the public leader of bowing down before the pressure of the underground town commander. My host replied, bringing out the Bible from his bag, "I am doing it in the name of the holy God." He seemed convincing enough, but this moral stance also had a political purpose, as people said "He is our next MLA [Member of the Legislative Assembly]; how can he bow down to such people who depend on him and beg him for money when they are in need?" Yet his position was a clever act of disguise. It re-established

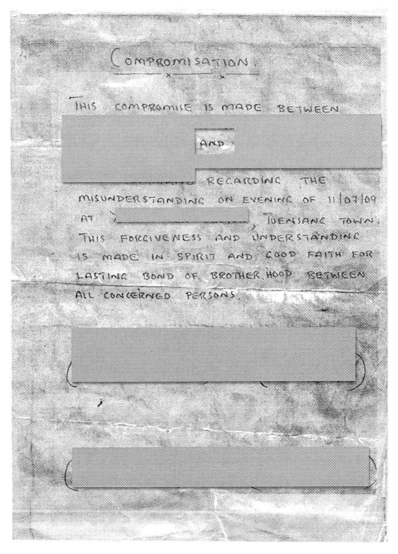

Fig. 5.1 The compromise letter. (Photo Credit Debojyoti Das)

the political patron-client relation that the MLA and his family had established over years.

For my host's party leader, this was a position he had to take to secure his political future. A lot was at stake: his farm, the whole political constituency and an electorate whom he could not possibly take on as opposition or see fractured by antagonized factions. In our later conversations, I came to realize the importance of this compromise. The calm we maintained during the hostage crisis not only minimized the dangers of confrontation but also saved our lives. A letter of compromise was signed between the two parties for reconciliation (see Fig. 5.1).

5.2 Reflections

Reflecting on the event, there were a few inferences that I could draw from it. In the immediate aftermath, I was more preoccupied with ethical questions. One of my host's children asked me why I had initially run away when his father was being beaten up by the town commander. I had no simple answer. In the days following, we again became good friends but the question still haunted me: did I betray my interlocutor to violence that demanded quick action? However, many things were unclear. Why did they take their community members hostage when they constantly stated that "we Nagas are one"? What were the issues of conflict that led to this attack? Was the plot preplanned? What were their motives? Reflecting on what had happened that night, I felt I had no control over the production of ethnography.

As Nilan (2002) has emphasized, in fieldwork, the question of control over the recording and production of data causes much anxiety for the ethnographer in an "exceptional setting," where emotional detachment, objectivity and control over the production of data are difficult to achieve. In the violent encounter that night, the government forces did not apprehend the culprits; rather, they acted as a go-between. Interestingly, nothing appeared in the local newspaper about this event. Every piece of information was concealed from the outside world. It helped in building confidentiality, as I also kept the incident to myself and did not share it with anybody. I thus sought to act as a good ethnographer in the entire research exercise, strictly following my research protocol and ethical guidelines. I only shared it with my research committee after returning from the field, who expressed their empathy and worries about conducting fieldwork in such a precarious area.

To many of my colleagues, friends and relatives, going to Nagaland appeared to be an act of bravery, adventure or foolishness. While this attitude was largely the result of the media-disseminated images of Naga people, or for that matter, of people of northeast India in general, I was more intrigued by what Naga friends and well-wishers told me about eastern Nagaland, the location of my study area. They saw it as a misadventure, given my status as an outsider, a British Indian who had come from London to research the "colonial" unadministered Nagas. These are the "wild spaces" where people still practice *jhum* (slash and burn) cultivation, wear little clothing and are not very civilized. They advised me to conduct ethnography in a nearby village close to Kohima town, from where I could commute easily. Surviving fieldwork can be the most important task in a perilous and intimidating setting. For this reason, field workers working in violent field sites need to possess a sensibility about the field, practical knowledge of local realities, or what Nancy Scheper-Hughes calls "anthropology with one's feet on the ground" and "phenomenologically grounded anthropology" (1992, 4). As Campbell writes, "violence changes the experience of fieldwork and raises new concerns about ethics, research methods and the anthropologist's relationship with the fieldworkers" (2011, 9). The point is to acknowledge the chequered nature of ethical practice in anthropology and the changing relationship between anthropologists and their informants.

Over the last couple of decades, there has been some rigorous introspection about the methodological and philosophical concerns of fieldwork in unstable places, from Nancy Scheper-Hughes (1992) to Antonius Robben and Caroline Nordstrom's examination of "fieldwork under fire" (1995, 1996) What we must consider, however, is how we deal with "violence" in the field alongside ethical issues without undermining our obligation towards society. If anthropology as a discipline is to progress in the twenty-first century, it should address these value-laden issues. The literature currently published on fieldwork practice also demands fresh insights into violent and extraordinary field situations. This brings us to the question of the potential ethics of "putting oneself to danger", which is rarely discussed; anthropological ethics is far more explicit on issues concerning the security and confidentiality of our informants.

My knowledge of violence became clearer after the hostage encounter. Extended fieldwork experience, therefore, becomes critical in producing a valuable qualitative dataset substantive for research. Ethnographers working in dangerous fields are pressed with the challenge of innovating new strategies for their well-being, while at the same time continuing to identify and explain the unique social interrelations that arise amidst crisis and strife. During my 14-month stay in Nagaland, I engaged with the problems and steered my way through them, at times adopting alternative routes and tools of rapport-building with my respondents that were quite unconventional in nature. This not only involved a long-term stay in the village, respecting their customs and culture, but also being empathetic to their cause and worldview. The personal experience of violence also heightened my awareness of how people live with everyday violence in Nagaland, where safety and security hang on delicate political equations with local elites and village potentates who work as brokers in development programmes.

I adopted a method of collaboration in which I shared my field notes with my interlocutors and solicited their opinion on what I wrote or thought about them. Such participation cleared away many preconceptions about the community I lived in, and over time, I came to be recognized by village members as one of them. On one occasion, the village Sunday Bible preacher announced that I was no longer an outsider. Such intimacy grew out of my participation in mundane activities, the sharing of food with residents and staying overnight with them in their paddy fields. This collaborative proactive instilled trust and fostered friendship with the villagers with whom I lived. However, despite such positive assurances, fieldworkers like myself did experience the paranoia and trauma of the event, both psychologically and emotionally, which cannot be redressed. One of the consequences of such an experience was that I could not share the experience with my parents, who would not have countenanced my travel to the region for future fieldwork in the aftermath of the event.

In the 1960s, anthropologists began to respond to the crisis in the discipline created by the post-World War II emergence of new nations from old colonies. Anthropologists increasingly breached research ethics, working as spies or being used as spies by the state in anthropological research (Nash 1976, 225). In the contemporary context, this has included anthropologists working at home (in their own countries) studying ethnonationalism, sub-nationalism and separatist indigenous movements. These roles have been particularly challenging, as they have required anthropologists to engage with politically fiery questions that require acumen and skills which are distinct from those needed just to study "other cultures." I would like to add that the everyday talk of violence was reflective of the politics of violence and helped me understand how violence was indistinguishable from the texture of people's day-to-day life. The result is deep reflections that have helped me to understand and, at least partly, articulate the dangers and complexities involved in fieldwork under violent circumstances.

To conclude, I suggest that the encounter made me realize that there is a problem of "ethnographic refusal" (Simpson 2007) while engaging with questions of research ethics, methodology and political activism within anthropology. My training as an ethnographer made me duty-bound to maintain confidentiality and stopped me from acting as an activist. There were ethical dilemmas that underpinned sharing my experience. It could not be made public beyond the remit of my research community. I was acting more like an ethnographer than an activist who wished to highlight the impact of violence on innocent villagers who are caught in the crossfire. In addition to this, I was wary of the politics of representation, as I consciously chose not to represent the incident as another trailblazing moment in the long history of scholars venturing into unruly spaces as illustrated in colonial and post-independence ethnographic and popular memoirs written by travellers, anthropologists, administrators and journalists.

Referring back to the first homosexual encounter, my experience with my interlocuter posed potential ethical and moral trials that also shaped my engagement with the field. I found objectivity and rationality to be a distant dream, because often the ethnographer is caught up in the dilemma to choose between the field and the interlocutor. The "ethics of self-harm" then becomes paramount. Although I did choose my field, the emotional trauma caused by the violent encounters; first, an intimate encounter with my host, where he solicited sexual favours as a quid-pro-quo without my consent, and, second, where I was taken hostage with my host. Both these events left deep blemishes on my mind and caused me psychological and emotional distress. These kinds of experience were unexpected and challenged the image of fieldwork that is impaired by uncertainty in perilous field sites. Emotional attachment became central to my ethnographic enquiry, and I became more conscious of "voice" and "agency." Through reflection on my fieldwork experiences, I tried to engage with these events as a "right of passage", which brings up deep memories of an engaged and immersed research where the boundary between the "self" and the "other" is blurred by these experiences.

In contemporary times, anthropologists are increasingly working in a violent social context and developing relationships with interlocutors who become friends, interpreters, hosts and not just informants. Therefore, it is very important to build a rapport with interlocutors based on friendship and reciprocity. Often, these friendships can entail compromises that can pose a serious risk to the researcher's safety. The experience of violence in two different contexts was triggered by actions that were related to my interlocutors—one that resulted in a breach of the researcher's trust and the other that unfolded out of a wider political economy of development money. Often, the researcher's social context and lack of access to the study community because of gatekeepers and intermediaries can make it enormously challenging to work with the study community. The ethics of trust, care, conviviality and relational ethics with respondents and interlocutors who become our friends and well wishers is very important in ethnographic research where we spend a lot of time in weaving relationships through long stay with the study community. Therefore, the dangers of breach of trust can leave deep psychological scar on both the researcher and their interlocutors. To conclude, my research alerts us to the pitfalls of doing fieldwork in a politically contested social context. Thus, it is of utmost importance that anthropological ethics communities across the globe recognize the fact that anthropologists are increasingly putting themselves in harm's way and there should be increasing awareness of this fact while training graduate students to embark on fieldwork in perilous and politically challenging landscapes. Also, personal experience should guide us to understand that anthropological fieldwork is no longer a detached, disengaged activity, but is informed by the complex network graduate students build with the host community, who should not be referred to in dichotomous terms such as "we" and the "other."

Acknowledgments The author would like to acknowledge Felix Scholarships for funding his PhD research and to numerous other institutions for supporting his fieldwork such as the Emslie Horniman Anthropological Scholarship Fund, Radcliffe-Brown Sutasoma Award and Central Research Fund.

References

Campbell, J. 2011. The problem of ethics in contemporary anthropological research, *Anthropology Matters*, Vol 10, No 1, pp. 1–17.
Nash, J. 1976. 'Ethnology in Revolutionary Setting' in *Ethics and Anthropology: Dilemmas in Fieldwork*, ed by M. Rynkiewich and J. Spreadley, pp. 144–66. New York: Wiley.
Nilan, P. 2002. "Dangerous Fieldwork" Re-examined: The question of Researcher Subject Position, *Qualitative Research*, Vol 2, no 3, pp. 363–383.
Robben, A. and C. Nordstrom, eds. 1995. *Fieldwork under Fire: Contemporary Studies of Violence and Survival*, Barkley and Los Angel: University of California Press.
Robben, A. C. G. M. 1996. Ethnographic Seduction: Transference and Resistance in Dialogue with Terror and Violence in Argentina, *Ethnos*, Vol 24, no. 1: pp. 71–106.
Schepere-Hughes, N. 1992. *Death Without Weeping: The violence of Everyday Life in Brazil*, Barkley: University of California Press.
Simpson, Audre. 2007. On Ethnographic Refusal: Indigeneity, 'Voice' and Colonial Citizenship, *Junctures*, pp. 67–80.
Trundal, Catherine.2018. Uncomfortable Collaborations: The Ethics of Complicity, Collusion, and Detachment in Ethnographic Fieldwork, *Collaborative Anthropologies*, Vol. 1, no. 1, pp. 89–111.

PART II

Field, Relations, and Emotion

CHAPTER 6

Feeling Unsettled in the Field: Emotions and the Field Researcher

Anuradha Sen Mookerjee

6.1 Introduction

During the course of fieldwork, a researcher has numerous field encounters which lead to the experience of a range of emotions that can offer a nuanced and deeper understanding of people, communities, relationships and interactions that are being investigated. It takes place through countertransference phenomena, that is, "how the observer of human data reacts as a person and as a human being to his own observations", in the words of Weston La Barre in the preface to Devereux (1967, 2014), which, simply put, are the effects that the fieldwork might have on the field researcher, particularly emotional reactions that come about from the encounters in the field. In this chapter, I

Declaration: This fieldwork for my PhD dissertation entitled *Boundaries of Citizenship: Social Practices and Negotiations in the Former Border Enclaves of Bangladesh and India* (2019) was conducted for the project "Changes in Border Policy and Border Identities: A Case Study of the Indo-Bangladesh Border Enclaves", with Principal Investigator Professor Shalini Randeria and Co-principal Investigator Professor Alessandro Monsutti, Partner Principal Investigator Professor Ranabir Samaddar, Calcutta Mahanirban Research Group (MCRG), India, administered by Global Migration Centre, The Graduate Institute of International and Development Studies, Geneva, Switzerland. The project was funded by the Flash Research Programme, Cooperation and Development Centre (CODEV) EPFL, Lausanne, Switzerland.

A. Sen Mookerjee (✉)
Institute for Human Development, New Delhi, India

© The Author(s), under exclusive license to Springer Nature Switzerland AG 2023
N. Uddin, A. Paul (eds.), *The Palgrave Handbook of Social Fieldwork*, https://doi.org/10.1007/978-3-031-13615-3_6

explore how emotions as countertransference phenomena inform the field researcher's understanding of the lifeworld being investigated and have the potential to offer a methodological and epistemological contribution to the investigation. Anthropological scholarship on emotions has advocated the methodological position of *radical empiricism*, a concept derived from the work of the philosopher William James, for whom the subject and the object of research are epistemologically connected (Davies 2010, 3). Radical empiricism consists of a postulate, a statement of fact and a conclusion. The postulate contends that "the only things that shall be debatable among philosophers shall be things definable in terms drawn from experience," the "fact" is that "relations are just as directly experienced as the things they relate", and the conclusion is that "the parts of experience hold together from next to next by relations that are themselves parts of experience" (James [1909] 2010), the latter meaning that one's hypothesis is liable to modification in course of future experience. I analyse my field experiences, particularly emotions, during my PhD project on new citizens of the recently reterritorialized Bangladesh-India border enclaves in the context of the theorisations by William James whose metaphysics of experience has highlighted the importance of direct experience as much as the things (that are formed as meanings and values in a maze of connections) through those relations and in case of field research constitutes the "field" being studied. I trace my field encounters and emotions and demonstrate how they led me to decide upon conducting multi-sited fieldwork and to understand new citizenship in terms of the bodily experiences of the new citizens. I explore the importance of emotional experiences over time in epistemologically informing research. I show how my feelings of disappointment and of being unsettled led me to find meaning in what my field of study represented as an idea and practice and how it could be investigated.

6.2 Preparing for Fieldwork

My PhD project is an ethnography of the experiences of the newly documented Indian citizens of the former Bangladeshi and Indian border enclaves (an enclave being defined as a piece of sovereign territory completely bounded by another sovereign jurisdiction) that were exchanged between Bangladesh and India on 1 August 2015. One hundred and sixty-two "enclaves" popularly known as the "Chhit Mahals" in Bengali, along the Bangladesh-India border located in the Cooch Behar district of West Bengal in India and the districts of Kurigram, Lalmonirhat, Panchagarh and Nilphamari in northern Bangladesh, had existed on both sides of the Bangladesh-India border, constituting the world's largest enclave complex. They were exchanged between Bangladesh and India 41 years after the Land Boundary Agreement between the two states had been signed in 1974.[1] Fifty-one Bangladeshi enclaves (all located in the Cooch Behar district in the state of West Bengal in India) with 7110.02 acres of land became Indian territory, and 111 Indian enclaves with 17,160.63 acres of land became Bangladeshi territory.[2] Through the conduct of a joint survey between 6 and 16 July 2015, residents of the enclaves had the option to register their choice of citizenship of either country. All the 14,864 enumerated inhabitants of the former Bangladeshi enclaves in the Cooch Behar district of West Bengal in India opted for Indian citizenship while 37,532 inhabitants of the Indian enclaves in Bangladesh opted for Bangladeshi citizenship, except for 922 residents of Indian enclaves who moved to India permanently opting for Indian citizenship (Sen Mookerjee 2017). As a result of the exchange, the Bangladeshi enclaves in the Cooch Behar district became Indian territory and the Indian enclaves in northern Bangladesh became Bangladeshi territory.[3]

The residents of these former enclaves as people living in the borderlands of the two postcolonial states had been living in a severely marginal condition being left effectively stateless as the states chose not to be administratively present in these territories nor draft any agreement with guidelines on how these territorially bound populations left to fend for themselves since the partition of India in 1947, and the making of new international borders, and were to carry out their daily lives in the absence of any facilitation by the host states. My initial idea of the enclaves as place and space was informed by the literature on the enclaves including the historical and geographical study of the enclaves by Whyte (2002) who highlighted the challenging everyday life of enclave residents in the absence of the states in their territories. The socio-economic challenges of the residents of the former enclaves had resulted from the absence of any agreement between the Governments of India and Pakistan (since the partition of India in 1947 till 1971) and thereafter with the Government of Bangladesh (since its creation in 1971) regarding the transit of private citizens or their trading of enclave produce outside the enclaves, their social rights in health, education, minimum social welfare and livelihoods, civil rights to a

---

[1] The Agreement Concerning the Demarcation of the Land Boundary between India and Bangladesh and Related Matters of 1974 (referred to as 1974 LBA) attempted to find a solution to the complicated nature of border demarcation, particularly addressing three outstanding issues including an un-demarcated land boundary of around 6.1 kilometres, the exchange of the enclaves and the adverse possessions. The adverse possessions refer to pockets along the India-Bangladesh border that have been traditionally under the possession of people of one country in the territory of another country.
[2] PTI. "Bangladesh, India in Historic Land Swap after Nearly 4 Decades". *Http://Www.hindustantimes.com/*, The Hindustan Times, 31 July 2015, www.hindustantimes.com/india/bangladesh-india-in-historic-land-swap-after-nearly-4-decades/story-gHXVmfal3DFnFdyfObEz1L.html.
[3] https://indiacode.nic.in/ViewFileUploaded?path=AC_CEN_5_40_00001_195557_1517807319455/notificationindividualfile/&file=14864+Bangladesh+Citi.+Notification.pdf.

legal personality and political rights of democratic participation; to visit their mainland, the inhabitants of the former enclaves were required to cross through the territory of the host state (Van Schendel 2002, 124). Left in states of despair without market access to sell their agricultural produce and infrastructure facilities like electricity, schools and health services, residents for 62 years since 1947 were compelled to draw upon facilities of the host state for livelihoods and survival (Whyte 2002, Jones 2009, Shewly 2013, Cons 2014). Consequently, they historically bore the brunt of the border and the bordering practices being socially, economically and politically disadvantaged borderlands people. Their social practices of transborder mobility and community-level activism against their statelessness had articulated their embodied resistance to their historical marginalization by the states (Sen Mookerjee 2017), giving meaning to their culture of standing up for themselves, strongly engaging with the national and international media and claiming recognition as human beings who were part of the global and national communities. While the scholarship on the enclaves theorized their geography of marginalization in connection to territory and the media reports helped shape public understanding of their experiences of abandonment, various forms of harassment, violence and insecurity, what fascinated me about enclave societies was that the residents of the former enclaves survived through transborder movement in everyday life making them demonstrably active social and political actors.[4] Based on readings of the literature and media reports my aim for my research project was to understand how the grant of new legal status as documented Indian citizens infused new cultural meanings to the various facets of their lifeworld amidst external changes being brought about by the reterritorialization exercise.

I entered the field through a community-based activist organization in the former Bangladeshi enclaves in India: Bharat Bangladesh Enclave Exchange Coordination Committee (BBEECC), based in Dinhata town of Cooch Behar, which was present in the former Bangladeshi enclaves as community-based committees. Between 2011 and 2015, there were continuous news articles on the enclaves published in the Bengali vernacular press in India and Bangladesh. *The New York Times* featured a piece entitled "At India-Bangladesh Border, Living in Both, and Neither", in 2011, highlighting the absence of the state in these territories and the ambivalence of belonging for the residents as marginal populations. Both the academic literature and the media reports put out voices of anxiety, harassment and non-citizen status highlighting the trampling of the human dignity of residents of the enclaves. On social media an electronic transborder community of activists and journalists regularly engaged with the enclave issues raised by the activist residents of the enclaves. Following the

---

[4] Reece Jones in his article, *Spaces of refusal: Rethinking sovereign power and resistance at the border*. Annals of the Association of American Geographers, 102(3), pp. 685–699. has proposed that in the "borderlands" people employ "multiple strategies that transgress, reinterpret, and ignore sovereign power but not necessarily rise to the level of overt political resistance", "where situated ways of knowing and being continue to exist".

exchange of the enclaves, the BBEECC as an organization was disbanded in August 2015 and a new organization named Citizens Rights Coordination Committee (CRCC) was formed with the same members, who were now newly documented citizens of the former Bangladeshi enclaves and their supporters both in Cooch Behar and in other parts of India and Bangladesh. Particularly the print media reports informed my imagination of the everyday life in the former Bangladeshi enclaves of Cooch Behar. I was convinced that the district administration and the residents of Dinhata town, along with journalists and other stakeholders who were in some way involved with the reterritorialization process, were all strongly concerned with the long-term marginalization and underdevelopment of the Bangladeshi enclaves in their district and had unquestioned support for their development and welfare. Based on my readings, I had approached the new citizens through the lens of territory and the state.

I visited the former Bangladeshi enclaves in both Dinhata and Mekhliganj subdivisions of the Cooch Behar district for the first time during the conduct of the joint survey in the second week of July 2015. It was a rare historic moment as the enclave residents registered their choice of citizenship and also were visited by state officials in their enclaves. I found many journalists visiting the enclaves during the joint survey and the residents were very comfortable talking to them. BBEECC representatives were warmly welcomed by the enclave residents and the Indian and Bangladeshi officials doing the joint survey, demonstrative of the cordial relations between state agents and the BBEECC. The population of Cooch Behar district, as per the 2011 Indian census data, constituted of 74.06 per cent Hindus and 25.54 per cent Muslims. Within that, the Dinhata subdivision has 36.83 per cent Muslims and 63.17 per cent Hindus, while the Mekhliganj subdivision has 19.26 per cent Muslims and 80.41 per cent Hindus. I observed that while the joint survey experience in the Hindu majority enclaves in the Mekhliganj subdivision seemed to be occurring like a routine state enumeration event, the survey exercise in the Muslim majority Bangladeshi enclaves in Dinhata had a festive character, as most people and children who turned up to register themselves were dressed to attend a festival, generating much excitement in the community. I found the enclaves and their neighbouring Indian villages were however difficult to visibly differentiate, except for electrification in the Indian villages while the enclaves battled with darkness. While the populations of the Indian villages were enumerated and had access to state welfare facilities, which the Bangladeshi enclaves lacked, visibly both the Bangladeshi enclaves and the Indian villages seemed seamlessly to be part of the same rural, non-industrial, underdeveloped borderlands that were under surveillance on both sides, with camps of the Indian Border Security Force spread throughout the stretch of 549.45 kilometres of borderlands in Cooch Behar district. In addition, there was a difference in the nature of excitement among the residents of the Hindu majority enclaves of Mekhliganj and the residents of the Muslim majority enclaves of Dinhata, with so many of the enclave residents in both subdivisions already having

Indian identity documents, which were procured using an Indian address. Discussions with the to-be citizens revealed that they were all very excited that now their lands would have Indian state-led development like electricity, water supply, roads, schools and primary health centres. Several of the Hindu residents of the Bangladeshi enclaves of the Mekhliganj subdivision with whom I spoke to mentioned that India was their "desh" (translated as nation or country) and it was their right to be finally documented as Indian citizens with their own addresses. I found many of them had already accessed many benefits of state welfare as documented Indian nationals and several of them lived a life overlapping India and Bangladesh territorially as many among them had a house or agricultural land in the adjoining areas in the Indian mainland as well. The Muslim residents of the Dinhata's Bangladeshi enclaves on the other hand mentioned that documented citizenship would bring to them legal legitimacy of existence on Indian soil and redeem them of their historical marginality as they did not want to leave the native lands of their forefathers in Cooch Behar despite being Muslims; several of them mentioned that they would now not be looked upon as "foreigners" in the eyes of the Indian Border Security Forces as they were no less Indians than the Hindus. Fewer Muslim residents in the enclaves had houses in Dinhata or in other Indian locations outside their enclaves and every former enclave (now Indian village) in the Dinhata subdivision had large migrant populations to urban centres in India like Delhi.

6.3　Deciding on Multi-Sited Fieldwork

In June 2015, on my way to Cooch Behar for initial field visits during the Joint Survey, I spent a few days in New Delhi where I met Aadil Siddiqui, a 26-year-old migrant worker belonging to the Bangladeshi enclave Chhit Karala in Dinhata subdivision. He had moved to Delhi in 2011 to work at a private company after completing his higher secondary education in Dinhata. Aadil worked to support his parents living in the enclave Chhit Karala, particularly the education of his school-going younger brother. One-third of the population of all Muslim majority enclaves in the Dinhata subdivision, with the exception of Chhit Shiba Prasad Mustafi (the only Hindu majority Chhit Mahal in Dinhata subdivision), work as migrant labour in the National Capital Region of New Delhi (peripheral locations in Delhi, Gurgaon, Faridabad and Noida, which had many construction sites, brick kilns and so on) and other places in India including Dehradun, Bangalore and Kerala. The enclave inhabitants were cultivators holding small and medium-sized land holdings, with about 40 per cent of the population being landless, holding small land plots where they usually had a house but no land to cultivate. Historically, landless peasants from the rural Bangladeshi enclaves in Cooch Behar were circular migrants to Indian cities who worked in the construction sector and in other unskilled work in the absence of alternative livelihoods in their enclaves and places near the enclaves. Cooch Behar has been regarded as one the poorest district in West Bengal and it stood second in the category of having Below Poverty Line (BPL) families, with a large number of economically poor agricultural labourers constituting 34.74 per cent of the total workforce of the district, of whom 30.45 per cent are male workers, who migrate due to the compulsions of unemployment and poverty (Som 2022).[5] It explains why the enclave residents found it difficult to find work in the Cooch Behar district and were compelled to migrate to cities in India. With Aadil, I visited construction worker sites in Haryana, Ghaziabad and Gurgaon and was surprised to discover a large population of migrant workers from the Bangladeshi enclaves in Delhi's National Capital Region (a planning region centred upon the National Capital Territory of Delhi in India; it encompasses Delhi and several districts surrounding it from the states of Haryana, Uttar Pradesh and Rajasthan). In Saidpur, Haryana, as I was speaking to some people belonging to the former enclaves, I was approached by a couple, Rafiq Ali and Naima Bibi who were both workers at the construction site. Naima Bibi was dressed in a Rajasthani skirt and a shirt that showed the adaptability of migrant workers to local conditions. They showed me a framed photograph of themselves and a young child, with Naima Bibi wearing a saree. Speaking in Bengali, they said, "Didi [meaning elder sister], we belong to the Karala Chhit in Dinhata. Please see our picture here with our son who lives in the Chhit [enclave]". They requested me to visit him when I was in Cooch Behar. In a similar incident in early March 2016, when I visited Naved Ali Miah, a 60-year-old landless peasant in the former Chhit Kisamat Batrigach in Dinhata subdivision, he was very persistent that I speak to his son Aftab Ali who was a migrant worker living in Indirapuram in Ghaziabad, Uttar Pradesh, working as a construction worker. He mentioned that visiting him in the village was not complete till I spoke to his sons, including the one who was away from Cooch Behar. He mentioned that along with his other sons, he had worked for long years as a worker in the construction industry in the National Capital Region around New Delhi. Naved Ali Miah's voice was filled with emotion when he said that even though Aftab has been working in Delhi for 15 years now, he "belonged" here, in the former "Chhit" (enclave). "This is his home", he said. Naved Ali Miah while connecting with Aftab Ali on his mobile phone kept trying to reach him for more than an hour as Aftab Ali could speak on the phone only when he had his lunch break. Naved Ali requested me to wait at his house and not leave without talking to his son. I found his emotional connection with his son not merely a father's exuberant reaction to being inclusive about his son but a historically marginal enclave resident's claiming of enclave identity for his family, one which underlined the translocal nature of the Chhit Mahals (i.e. the enclaves) as a place, whose residents included migrants like Rafiq, Naima and Aftab who toiled through labouring lives away from the enclaves and yet were an integral part of it. These field encounters left a deep impact on me and evoked strong feelings of nostalgia. I was led by my field

---

[5] Sarkar (2015), *Migration And Rural Agricultural Labourer Crisis In Nagarerbari Village Of Cooch Behar District, West Bengal, India: A Micro-Level Geographical Analysis,* unpublished paper accessed from Research Gate mentions 66.63 per cent of people from the study area migrate to Delhi.

experiences and emotions to adapt my research methodology, opting for multi-sited ethnography, with a long stay in Cooch Behar and field visits to migrant settlements in Ghaziabad, Gurgaon and Saidpur in the Delhi National Capital Region (NCR).

6.4 Field Encounters: Initial Disappointments

I moved to live in Dinhata town in Cooch Behar in February 2016. The West Bengal State Assembly elections were scheduled for May 2022 and India's Election Commission in March 2016 was vested with powers under a new amendment of Election laws to carry out a limited delimitation exercise in the Cooch Behar district to allow voting rights to the new citizens of the former Bangladeshi and Indian enclaves who opted for Indian citizenship in August 2015.[6] It was a time of political excitement in Cooch Behar as the new citizens were eager to participate in their first election as documented Indian citizens and the political parties participating in the elections were invested in wooing voters among the new citizens. In the Cooch Behar context, it meant that every other influential community member in the former enclaves was directly or indirectly associated with a political party. I chose not to enter the field through any influential person in the enclave community who is known to be associated with a political party as that would have given a political meaning to my field visits to the enclaves before the elections and my presence and interviews might be looked upon as having political intentions of eliciting knowhow for predicting the election outcomes. However, this decision to bypass the influential persons of the former enclaves associated with political parties did not turn out to be very comforting for my research process as the very people I avoided were wielding influence with the district administration.

The period following the enclave exchange between September 2015 and January 2016 had seen a large number of new citizens from the former Bangladeshi enclaves take to the streets in Dinhata under the banner of Citizens Rights Coordination Committee (CRCC) to protest against district authorities in Cooch Behar for moving slow on infrastructure development in the former enclaves and demanding legal papers for their lands. CRCC's activists among the new citizens became identified as critics of the district administration, of the state and of its political leadership, as they had distanced themselves from political parties before the elections in May 2016. I sensed a shift in CRCC's relationship with the district administration just before the West Bengal State Assembly elections in 2016 compared to the time when I had first visited Cooch Behar during the Joint Survey in July 2015. Possibly their vocal activism and questioning of the distribution of welfare and related funds earmarked for the enclaves were not well received by the district authorities. The initial

---

[6]The Kolkata Gazette No. WB (Part IA)/2016/SAR-8, Tuesday, 15 March 2016 https://ceowestbengal.nic.in/UploadFiles/Notification/CEOWB_635937479539893117_Notification6GN.pdf.

openness of the district administration to my queries on the reterritorialization process shifted to gradual delays and I did not manage to secure an appointment with the officer in charge of the subdivisional administration in Dinhata despite repeated attempts. The officials in the district administration had initially shared with me their concern for the historically marginalized enclave residents and yet my attempts to understand from them the challenges they faced in the process of reterritorialization and development of former enclaves and the distribution of welfare for the new citizens met with failure after cooperative initial introductory meetings. I felt exasperated with the district administration on several occasions. I had expected and assumed necessary cooperation from them, partly as a fellow Bengali, for a study which I considered a worthy intellectual exercise aimed at creating an analytical social record of the historic process of reterritorialization of the enclaves. I felt inadequately prepared for the subjective experience of the field. My feelings of disappointment with the district administration led me to rethink my location in the field. Being an Indian, a Bengali and the daughter of a former officer of the West Bengal Civil Services, I had been confident about my field access. Instead, I found myself classified as a researcher from "Switzerland", a country that in people's imagination is the ultimate tourism experience, a paradise of pristine mountains and natural beauty and a place far removed from India. My interlocutors in the administration identified me on the basis of my Swiss institutional affiliation. Through their reactions, I felt that I was a lesser Indian and Bengali, as I was bodily identified through difference. These feelings pained me deeply and forced me to reconsider the way I saw myself in the field, to be accepting of the reality that my presumed cultural "oneness" with several of my interlocutors, particularly in the administration, had failed and what I had considered to be "familiar" had to reconceived as "unfamiliar" and "strange". It led me to readjust my reactions to the district authorities in the later part of my fieldwork and not feel dejected or upset if I did not receive from them a reply to my queries. It also helped me recalibrate my presumptions with other interlocutors and accordingly create alternative opportunities for productive participant observation.

6.5 Field Emotions: Unsettled and Rattled

In Dinhata town I rented an apartment as I had to travel almost daily to the various former enclaves that were now reterritorialized administratively either as an Indian village or as part of an existing village, across the Dinhata and Mekhliganj subdivisions of Cooch Behar. New citizens from former enclaves often came to Dinhata for its markets, for visiting doctors or the subdivisional hospital, the banks and the civil court, among other facilities. Like most field researchers, I was working on a tight time schedule of one year for my fieldwork, more so as the West Bengal State Assembly Elections scheduled in May 2016 made undertaking fieldwork amidst election campaigns rather difficult. I had my list of life histories and interviews to conduct and enable my understanding of the shifting lifeworld of the new citizens I chose to talk and engage with as many of them and build a relationship of trust with them that made them comfortable to share their experiences with me and for me to understand the shifting cultural meanings with which they grappled in their new lifeworld as Indian citizens.

My apartment was located on the first floor of a house that belonged to an Indian Hindu family. The house owner was a man running a small dealership in medicines. A room adjacent to the main entrance was the owner's warehouse, full of medical supplies that filled up the room from the floor to the roof. The room alternated as his office and he sat there through the day till late evening in surveillance mode watching those who entered the house through the front entrance. I had moved to this apartment in the centre of Dinhata town with my mother and Maajid Khan, a long-term employee of my family in Delhi, who used to drive me to the enclaves in the initial months of my fieldwork. During the first two weeks of March 2016, I regularly visited the former enclaves in the Dinhata subdivision, the closest one being about 15 kilometres away from my apartment and the farthest being about 120 kilometres, for four days every week. Rest of the days, I stayed at my apartment in Dinhata. Sometimes new citizens from the former Bangladeshi enclaves and those who had permanently moved to India from Indian enclaves in Bangladesh opting for Indian citizenship and were living in the Dinhata Krishimela Enclave Resettlement Camp would visit me. By spending a lot of time amidst the new citizens, both at the former enclaves and at my apartment, interacting with them and hearing them discuss issues amidst themselves, I was keen to immerse myself into their lives. I was interested in hearing what they had to say about various day-to-day issues, as I sought to comprehend their thoughts and feelings. Sometimes my visitors would come to my place in the mornings and read several newspapers to catch up on the daily news about development activities initiated or announced in the former Bangladeshi enclaves and the upcoming elections. Often, several of them would animatedly discuss the large poster-size map of Cooch Behar and the Indian subcontinent hung on the wall of the living room. Mostly the conversations were about the visible gaps in the state welfare resources reaching the new citizens, the delay on part of the district administration in initiating development in these former enclaves, electricity in particular, and also strategizing on how best to bargain as first-time voters with the political parties in the upcoming West Bengal State Assembly elections. Among my regular visitors, there were three residents of the Dinhata Krishimela Enclave Resettlement Camp who visited me often. They were poor Muslim men, who worked as unskilled labour in informal sector jobs and wore the traditional lungi (a type of sarong or men's skirt wrapped around the lower waist and worn in several South Asian countries) and a half shirt or vest, their visible bare working bodies tanned in the summer sun. For my Hindu house owner and neighbours, my visitors were "Bangladeshis" as most of them were visibly Muslim men and they inquired with me a few times why these people visited me. It did not seem to bother them that my visitors were poor and marginal people from the former Bangladeshi enclaves and the Dinhata Enclave Resettlement Camp who had only recently received documented Indian citizenship, after decades of marginalization. News about their historically difficult lives was not only published in the print media on a regular basis, but the entire Dinhata administration was abuzz with the reterritorialization exercise yet for the Hindu middle-class households of Dinhata, the Muslim men visiting me were bodily identified as "Bangladeshis" and hence the "other".

Within four weeks of my moving into the apartment, after the bathroom fittings had been changed and a telephone landline and an internet connection had been set up, my house owner verbally informed me that I need to leave the apartment with immediate effect as his family was feeling insecure with so many Muslim men visiting me. He mentioned that the women of the family were feeling "uncomfortable" by the continuous visit of Muslim men. It was a major breaking point for me as it totally undermined the stability that I was working to achieve in setting up myself in Dinhata. Crapanzano (2010, 60) has stressed the importance of breakdowns in conversations, which may be understood as misunderstanding, which he observes while being dangerous are a principal path to ethnographic discovery. If we are ready to learn from the breakdowns and misunderstanding, it can enable unlearning and offer rich perspectives. As Victor Turner (1985, 226) elucidated, experience "is a journey, a test (of self, of suppositions about others), a ritual passage, an exposure to peril, and an exposure to fear". I was upset with my house owner's approach to my interlocutors and me and felt extremely disappointed both personally and professionally. I felt it was a violation of the ethics of rental arrangement and also felt disappointed by a fellow Bengali.

In addition, as a married woman, I had been the subject of much curiosity and scrutiny by the family of my house owner. That I had left my school-going teenage son for long months to undertake the research project did not have a favourable impression on my interlocutors and I was repeatedly faced with the question as to why I had embarked on such a long-term study that required me to be away from my family, wondering who would be cooking for them. The stereotyping image of the woman often came in the way of my negotiation of identity as a field researcher. Women interlocutors who sometimes visited with their men folk shared with me their deepest concerns and fears regarding long-distance parenting as many mothers had sons who worked as migrant labour in the Delhi region. They wanted to see the pictures of my family and would always ask about when they might be visiting me. My first house owner's wife had been very surprised that I did not wear the vermillion as a symbol of marriage as a Hindu woman nor any other symbol that indicated my married status. Earlier when I was visiting the Dasiarchara enclave in the Kurigram district of northern Bangladesh, during the conduct of the Joint Survey in July 2015, at the Burimari border check post, standing amidst a group of men who were crowding the immigration counter, I was asked by the immigration official who was stamping my Visa after a close look at my passport picture that why as a Hindu married woman I did not wear the *bindi*, which is the symbolic vermillion dot often worn by married Hindu women on their forehead. I was taken aback for a moment, a bit unprepared for the question as the men at the counter stared at me while some started grinning. I had calmly replied that many married Hindu women no longer wear the vermillion and that there was no social pressure on women in India to wear the *bindi*. Never had I been made aware before of being a "Hindu woman" by people in the communities I had lived in Geneva, Delhi or Kolkata, the three cities where I visited and lived from time to time; nor was I ever questioned on my purpose behind not wearing the vermillion on my forehead as a symbol of marriage. While there is a vast literature on gender and fieldwork, scholars have observed that "the field-worker's marital status is of particular significance to anthropological informants because most 'primitive' cultures take kinship bonds as the fundamental source of social structure and social order", with the dominant categories of gender, marital status and parental status often intersecting (Warren and Hackney 2000, 8). While the reactions I faced from my first house owner and middle-class Hindu neighbours were on account of my gender, marital and parental status, the intersection of religion was a deciding factor in determining the terms of my recognition in Dinhata.

Further, my driver, Maajid Khan, who had been an integral part of our family in Delhi for 15 years, was living with my mother and me in our apartment in Dinhata. I was not prepared to be questioned about Maajid Khan's constant presence as a man in my apartment. I had clearly not expected that frequent interaction with Muslim men could emerge as a social and cultural problem. I felt outraged at my powerlessness, with my house owner. Focusing on how mutuality changes the researcher and the researched, Crapanzano (2010, 72) has observed, "As fieldwork progresses, the balance between the two changes. At first, at least in exotic sites, the weight is on the unfamiliar, but with time the unfamiliar becomes familiar. And from an anthropological perspective, this familiarity, as necessary as it is ethnographically, is not without its dangers, ethnographically, for we risk losing track of what was once salient. Personally, I have found it far more difficult to render the familiar unfamiliar and yet maintain its familiarity than to render the unfamiliar familiar and yet maintain its unfamiliarity …. Throughout our fieldwork, we are constantly negotiating our respective identities and our understanding of the situation in which we find ourselves." My emotions towards my house owner and his family and their reactions to me led me to reflect on my location in the field and rethink my approach to the field. I considered why I was angry and what were the failures in my expectations of cooperation that I had of my house owner, not just as the person who had given his property to me on a rental basis but as a resident of Cooch Behar district, where enclave residents had been living a life without dignity. I reflected that my emotional proximity to India and West Bengal as a Bengali speaker played a role in how an unknown subdivisional town in the Cooch Behar borderlands had felt so familiar to me. It had been mentally closer to me as a place in India and West Bengal than in my experience.

Through my field encounters, I realized the aspects of the field that I had not quite considered before I started living in Dinhata. The state of West Bengal within which Cooch district is located is an administrative unit but not homogeneous as a place and space. I had been familiar with Kolkata, the capital city of West Bengal, in the early 1980s and 1990s, where I spent my childhood and my years of undergraduate study, but after that I had lived in Delhi for almost 20 years before I had moved to Geneva, Switzerland, and be back to graduate study. While these places socio-culturally informed me, they were also very different from Cooch Behar, as space and place. Even though Cooch Behar as a district is not homogeneous socio-culturally, the Hindu majority Mekhliganj subdivision being different socially from the Muslim majority Dinhata subdivision, my experiences and emotions enabled me to understand that one of the cultural elements that spatially constituted Cooch Behar district was social articulation of difference between Hindus and Muslims. The district in the last three decades since the late 1980s had become used to its landscape being dotted with camps of the Indian Border Security Force, with 300 kilometres of the international border with Bangladesh being fenced and surveillance of irregular transborder movement being a primary task of paramilitary forces deployed in the region. The India-Bangladesh border fence stands as a site of identifying the nation's "others", by the respective postcolonial states and the practices of identifying people in terms of their religion was a practice on both sides of the border and these practices of differentiating had also percolated into Cooch Behar's society.

I had to find another apartment in Dinhata town for the rest of my field stay, amidst many of my interlocutors questioning why I shifted to a new apartment after doing up the first one as I went through weeks of offering verbal explanations regarding my change in residence. As Jackson (1989, 2) has observed, "lived experience encompasses both the 'rage for order' and the impulse that drives us to unsettle or confound the fixed order of things." Lived experience as I found from my fieldwork enables the accommodation of shifting sense of selves as both subjects and objects, "as acting upon and being acted upon by the world, of living with and without certainty, of belonging and being estranged, *yet resists arresting any one of these modes of experience in order to make it foundational to a theory of knowledge*" (emphasis in the original). My emotions around feeling unsettled resulted from my own expectations of receiving support from my immediate field environment in Cooch Behar, from people like my Hindu house owner or the district administration, whom I had presumed to be favourably inclined to my study. My consideration of them as secondary to my core field relations of new citizens of the former enclaves needed a reconsideration. To study the experiences of new Indian citizens, it is essential to study how other citizens in Indian society feel about them and in the process inform their subjective and bodily experience of citizenship and not just objectively through their behaviours like participating in elections or visiting the offices of the district administration, among others. My disappointments in the field led me to not only look for meaningful ways to study new citizenship but also gain an understanding of how citizenship informs a citizen's body with social meaning. The embodied borderland space was constituted through difference and absence of acceptance and approval of those considered national "other" as they were social "others". I draw upon Csordas (1990, 5), who has theorized the body as "the existential ground of culture". One sees in the approach of my house owner the coming together of both mind and body generating a phenomenology of perception towards my visitors and me and a self-perception constituted through cultural differences with poor working-class Muslims. I decided to take forward my research on new citizens with the epistemological premise that national belonging is embedded in the socially informed body rather than the legal documentation of identity, with legal citizenship having limited traction if not backed by social acceptance and that social "othering" offers a normative counter to legal rights. It was only through the set of emotions that I experienced through the encounter with my first house owner that I found how I could investigate the substantive experience of legal documentation of national identity.

6.6 Encountering Suspicion: Responding with Epistemology

I had been continuously aware of my challenges resulting from gender, marital and parental status and had been consciously building a relationship with my interlocutors and my house owner's family by being open about my life and my purpose of conducting the study. I spent social time with them and shared about my life, interests and work on the former enclaves to build a relationship of trust. I was aware that my interlocutors from the enclaves were used to talking to journalists from Cooch Behar, various places in India and abroad as the former enclaves had received wide media coverage. Many national and international scholars had also studied the enclaves and visited them. However, mostly the new citizens had been used to short-term visits of scholars and journalists. Long-term fieldwork was a relatively new experience for my interlocutors in the former enclaves and so I had been focused on establishing a relational space so that they could open up comfortably. Scholars have considered how relationships between the researcher and the people studied develop, through changes in "the state of being" of the anthropologist, which as Davies (2010) points out "may either enable or inhibit the understanding that fieldwork aims to generate", a historical reflection on the structures of relationships between the societies studied and the anthropologist as a subject emerges as a very significant factor in terms of the approach to the field and the subjectivity of researcher emerges as epistemologically significant. My powerlessness as a field researcher led me to embody some vulnerabilities and uncertainties similar to those of my interlocutors of the former enclaves as borderland bodies. It was a reflection of how in these borderlands, bodies were socially located and how society segregated and differentiated them through minimizing interaction between differently identified bodies, in this case of middle-class Hindus and poor Muslims. In defining my field of study through interactions and intersubjectivity, my method of the study included my experiences as an observer. In this way I was able to make myself an experimental subject and treat my experiences as primary data. As Jackson (1989, 4) puts it, "Accordingly, we make ourselves experimental subjects and treat our experiences as primary data. Experience, in this sense, becomes a mode of experimentation, of testing and exploring the ways in which our experiences conjoin or connect us with others, rather than the ways they set us apart." My field experiences and emotions of feeling unsettled made me realize that understanding identity formation of the new Indian citizens of the former enclaves in the Cooch Behar borderlands involved analysing the embodied nature of their experience of 'difference'. It included how as distinct socio-culturally marginalised bodies, as erstwhile Bangladeshi nationals, they were being looked upon by fellow Indians and their responses to the differential treatment in this early phase of the reterritorialization of the former enclaves. The subjective and objective experience of difference of these new Indian citizens call for being understood within a single cultural frame of "otherness", that significantly result from the physically present regime of national security in these borderlands, with the paramilitary forces round the clock sieving the "Bangladeshi" from "Indian".

My assumptions of field integration in Dinhata received a further jolt as I was informed by my interlocutors that an Indian intelligence agent had been enquiring about me in the neighbourhood, about the villages that I was visiting and about the questions I was asking in my interviews. Few of my interlocutors had been probed on what they considered might be the real reasons behind me spending so much time in a small town like Dinhata. Over the years, since my fieldwork in 2016, I have been following the lives of my interlocutors in Cooch Behar, and from their experiences other than mine, I argue that suspicion and surveillance has become a cultural aspect of Cooch Behar's borderlands society, where one's loyalties (to the nation) are questioned not just by law enforcement authorities, but socially and politically. While partly the involvement of some borderlands people in facilitating informal transborder trade and the existence of transborder family ties play a role in the imagining of the very ambivalent category of "the suspect other", whose bodies are tracked by agencies active in the area, it also creates the ground for political allegiances for protection and safe passage. Such a culture materializes through the intertwining of civil populations who are collaborated informally and socially by the Indian Border Security Force, the intelligence agents of diverse agencies who report to the various institutions of the Indian Central Government and the West Bengal State Government, other than the West Bengal State Police. Intelligence data includes keeping an eye on new people in the area including a Non-Resident Indian researcher like me, being indirectly linked to concerns of state security. Ghosh (2019, 447), writing on the daily interactions between the civil and military in the Bangladesh-India borderlands based on ethnographic fieldwork in Cooch Behar, has proposed looking at this space through the simultaneity of porosity and closure, observing that "militarization materializes through polychromatic, unstable and chameleon like relations as the work of border security brings together the civil and the military in daily interactions". The intelligence agents are required to report on security issues on a daily basis and an individual agent as part of daily work reporting has to produce "intelligence data". Often the agents who are recruited by the Ministry of Home Affairs and other institutions of the Indian Central Government do not have vernacular language competency or the cultural knowledge of a place to interpret information on their own. In an interview with an intelligence agent, a tall Rajasthani man, that I conducted at Changrabanda Border Post, who did not reveal his name nor allowed recording of his interview, I was told that they are informed of all new people moving in and out of Cooch Behar district. Also, they have many informants among the civil populations, who provide them information regularly. In return for passing information about suspicious activities in the area, these people receive protection from the agents, who help them, if they find themselves in any sticky situation with the West Bengal State Police or the Border Security Force (BSF). The politics of intelligence information cultivates suspicion as a positive value among the civil population in Cooch Behar.

Malmström (2019, 124) has observed that suspicion towards the field researcher "exposes how the transmission of affect constantly flows among matter, space and place". With the researcher using "her or his own body as a mediator, the researcher body is constantly remade, something that might benefit the study, but sometimes at a very high cost in relation to the private self". To address some of the concerns with regard to my presence, my husband and son visited me in Dinhata during the Eid celebrations in early July 2016. They attended two Iftar parties organized at the former enclaves, Poaturkutir and Madhya Mashaldanga, in the Dinhata subdivision and interacted with my interlocutors. Many people came to my apartment during that time to meet my family, sometimes carrying fruits and vegetables they cultivated as a gesture of welcome. Pictures of our visit to the former enclaves were posted by several new citizens on social media. Through my experience of feeling unsettled about the field and its social relations, I managed to rework my field relations taking the support of my family's presence. As observed by Gadamar et al. (1975), the "ethnographic encounter" addresses the influence of pre-understanding and prejudice with which one enters the field and "the value they put on openness and closure" (Crapanzano 2010, 58). My field experiences enabled me to reflect on how my own social body as a researcher changed over my time in the field. As my interlocutors came to trust me with their emotions, sharing details of their social negotiations, I came to understand their experience of citizenship as embodied structures of thoughts, feelings and actions, not only in the context of historical relationships but in view of their present status as documented Indian citizens. It required me to understand their experiences amidst the ongoing reterritorialization process in terms of their social relationship with other fellow Indians, institutions including the district administration and the place and space of the Cooch Behar borderlands.

6.7 Conclusion: Field as Continuous Structure of Experience, Emotions and Learning

I found from my time in the field that unsettling experiences and breakdowns can play an important role as they bring the researcher's attention to those aspects and nuances of the phenomena being studied, to which one might otherwise not pay attention as they are not obvious and may be diffused, dormant, ambivalent yet significant aspects for study. In staying open to the indeterminate, contradictions and problems that unsettle and disturb us, new connections between concepts and the things they represent can be discovered in the particular experiences of the fieldworker. As field researchers make themselves experimental subjects and treat their experiences in course of the fieldwork as data, the researcher comes to recognize the emptiness of an understanding or truth as objective phenomenon that is without any experiential content. A major strength that the fieldworker develops is the capacity to describe the phenomena being studied and that is the consequence of understanding which is shaped through interactions, encounters and learning in the field. In addition, the emotions, experiences and learning in the field result in data emerging from the interplay of the field researcher with the object of study as it enables the study of phenomena not through the lens of a single experience but one which is shaped through changes occurring in the emotions experienced between field interlocutors and the researcher, over time in the field. As James ([2010] 1909) had espoused, such a position emphasizes the inclusion of the "transitive" as well as "substantive", conjunctions as well as disjunctions, thus bringing into analysis the immediate, active and ambiguous aspects of existence. I have demonstrated here that through an understanding of the subject of study informed by emotional experiences and learning through them, an edifice is formed for ideas and intellectual framings to be based, through a continuous structure of emotional experience developed over time. Finally, the openness to engaging with the field subjectively makes the field researcher tolerant during the field engagement and enables the fieldwork in being imbibed with humanism, balancing power between the field researcher and the interlocutors.

BIBLIOGRAPHY

Cons, J., 2014. Impasse and Opportunity: Reframing Postcolonial Territory at the India-Bangladesh Border. *South Asia Multidisciplinary Academic Journal*, (10).

Crapanzano, V., 2010. At the Heart of the Discipline. *Emotions in the field: The psychology and anthropology of fieldwork experience*, edited by J. Davies and D. Spencer, pp. 55–78.

Csordas, T.J., 1990. Embodiment as a Paradigm for Anthropology. *Ethos, 18*(1), pp. 5–47.

Davies, J., 2010. Introduction: Emotions in the field. *Emotions in the field: The psychology and anthropology of fieldwork experience*, edited by J. Davies and D. Spencer, pp. 1–31. Stanford University Press.

Devereux, G., 1967. *From anxiety to method in the behavioral sciences* (Vol. 3). Mouton: The Hague.

Devereux, G., 2014. *From anxiety to method in the behavioral sciences* (Vol. 3). Walter de Gruyter GmbH & Co KG.

Gadamar, H.G., Weinsheimer, J. and Marshall, D.G., 1975. trans. Truth and Method. London: Bloomsbury

Ghosh, S., 2019. Security Socialities: Gender, surveillance, and civil-military relations in India's eastern borderlands. *Comparative Studies of South Asia, Africa and the Middle East, 39*(3), pp. 439–450.

Jackson, M., 2010. From anxiety to method in anthropological fieldwork. *Emotions in the field: The psychology and anthropology of fieldwork experience*, pp. 35–54.

Jackson, M., 1989. Paths toward a clearing: Radical empiricism and ethnographic inquiry. Bloomington and Indianapolis: Indiana University Press

James, William, 2010. *The Meaning of Truth, A Sequel to 'Pragmatism'*. The Floating Press

Jones, R., 2009. Sovereignty and statelessness in the border enclaves of India and Bangladesh. *Political Geography, 28*(6), pp. 373–381.

Malmström, M.F., 2019. Infused with suspicion: The transformation of the anthropologist body. *Anthropology Now, 11*(1–2), pp. 116–125.

Shewly, H.J., 2013. Abandoned spaces and bare life in the enclaves of the India–Bangladesh border. *Political Geography, 32*, pp. 23–31.

Som, Sonel., 2022. Male Labour Out-Migration and Its Impact on Left-Behind Women: A Study on Rural Cooch Behar District, West Bengal. *Pratidhwani the Echo Volume-X, Issue-III*, pp. 112–121

Turner, V. 1985. *On the edge of the bush: Anthropology as experience*. University of Arizona Press.

Sen Mookerjee, A., 2017. Changes in Border Policy and Border Identities: Post LBA Transitions in the Former Bangladeshi Enclaves in Cooch Behar, India. *Refugee Watch, 49*, pp. 95–108

Malmström, M.F., 2019b. Infused with suspicion: The transformation of the anthropologist body. *Anthropology Now, 11*(1–2), pp. 116–125.

Van Schendel, W., 2002. Stateless in South Asia: the making of the India-Bangladesh enclaves. *The Journal of Asian Studies, 61*(1), pp. 115–147.

Warren, C.A. and Hackney, J.K., 2000. *Gender issues in ethnography* (No. 9). SAGE Publications, Incorporated.

Whyte, B.R., 2002. Waiting for the Esquimo: An historical and documentary study of the Cooch Behar enclaves of India and Bangladesh.

CHAPTER 7

Developing Relationships over Many Years: Under Investigated but Important Types of Interview-Based Research

Ian G. Baird

7.1 Introduction

There has been much written about interviewing for research purposes, both in geography (Booth et al. 1995; Baxter and Eyles 1997; Hay 2005; Crang and Cook 2007) and in other allied disciplines, such as anthropology (Briggs 2007; Skinner 2013), sociology (Hermanowicz 2002; Lamont and Swidler 2014), and education (Wesche et al. 2010; Hammersley 2006; Madge and O'Connor 2004). However, the vast majority of qualitative methods literature about interviewing is concerned with conducting relatively short interviews with people whom the interviewer only interacts with for relatively short periods of time. The focus is also typically on interviews that only include minimal follow-up at most. Indeed, most authors recommend that interviews be kept relatively short so as not to overburden or overwhelm interviewees (Crang and Cook 2007; Baxter and Eyles 1997). For many, especially students, this makes sense.

The qualitative methods literature related to interviewing includes many useful insights, but I have long been struck by the lack of detailed discussion about how multiple interviews over long periods—sometimes many years—can result in certain types of relationships developing that go well beyond what is typical. Although there has been an acknowledgement that longitudinal interviews sometimes do occur (Pain 2003; Limb and Dwyer 2001; Crang and

---

I. G. Baird (✉)
Department of Geography, University of Wisconsin-Madison, Madison, WI, USA
e-mail: ibaird@wisc.edu

© The Author(s), under exclusive license to Springer Nature Switzerland AG 2023
N. Uddin, A. Paul (eds.), *The Palgrave Handbook of Social Fieldwork*, https://doi.org/10.1007/978-3-031-13615-3_7

Cook 2007), such admissions typically do not come with much detail specifically addressing the topic. This chapter is designed to partially fill this gap. It is also intended to promote reflexivity and careful consideration of positionality within qualitative research, by discussing the messiness of long-term relations, in line with theoretical approaches drawn from feminist geography (see Rose 1997; Moss 2001).

In fact, a series of interviews often occur over time, frequently gradually transforming into protracted discussions, rather than simple sets of interviews. This is especially the case for oral history projects (Atkinson 2012; Read 2018). Moreover, these discussions/interviews can, in my experience, go on for many hours. The relationships that develop over long periods and multiple encounters are never the same as each other—as context is crucial—but they almost inevitably inform and affect the types of questions and responses associated with them. For example, the interviewee often comes to know much about the interviewer, which alters the relationship. In addition, over time, relationships between interviewers and interviewees often lead to increasing candour and a sense of shared analysis of whatever is being studied. Indeed, I have interviewed a number of people whom I later developed deeper relationships with, with important implications for follow-up interviews and my own analysis of the research.

In this chapter, I consider methodological issues associated with long-term interview-based relationships, including the implications of these sorts of relationships, as they develop through many interviews conducted periodically over long periods. To do this, I present five divergent personal examples of these sort of interactions, one each from Laos, Thailand, Cambodia, the United States, and Canada, which provide varying opportunities for considering some advantages and disadvantages of this method. While getting close to research subjects has its potential disadvantages, such becoming too close to informants (Crang and Cook 2007), I contend that the benefits of such relationships often outweigh the disadvantages.

In what follows, I begin by briefly reviewing the literature on interviewing, including relevant readings for thinking about long-term and serial interview-based relationships. I then present five examples of long-term interview-based relationships I have personally developed with interviewees in recent years. I then discuss the nature of these relationships before providing concluding remarks.

7.2 Interviewing

Interviewing is undoubtedly the most important qualitative research method used in geography (Hitchings and Latham 2019a; Crang and Cook 2007). Hammersley (2006, 9) noted that ethnography is often heavily reliant on interviews, since standard interviews are frequently intertwined with other ethnographic methods, such as participant observation (Hitchings and Latham 2019b; Davies and Dwyer 2007), diary interviews (Latham 2003), photo-elicitation interviews (Harper 2002, 2003), mobile interviews (Finlay and Bowman 2017; Weiderhold 2015), the use of questionnaires (Winchester 1999), and others. Indeed, there are a wide range of possibilities. There are various methods that can usefully serve to supplement and enrich standard interviews (Dowling et al. 2015, 2017a). Thus, the boundaries between interviews and other ethnographic experiences are appropriately blurred, and outside of the most formal interviews, interviews are often best included as part of ethnography, especially considering that interviews are often conducted in informal and ad hoc ways, when time or circumstances allow (Hitchings and Latham 2019b).

There has been much written about various aspects of one-on-one interviewing. For example, Elwood and Martin (2000) considered how the places where interviews are conducted affect the discussions that emerge, and Sin (2003) specifically considered the socio-spatial construction of interview data. Cochrane (1998) and Hughes (1999) examined the nuanced skills needed to effectively conduct interviews in the corporate world, and various scholars, including Herod (1999), Mullings (1999), England (2001), and Oglesby (2010), have written about the art of interviewing elites, including considering notions of who are insiders and who are not. Beaverstock and Boardwell (2000) have investigated how issues of commonality between interviewers and interviewees affect the types of interactions that occur during interviews, while Jansson (2010) and Han (2010) examined the dynamics associated with interviewing people with views very opposed to their own. Lisa Tillmann-Healy (2003) discussed "friendship as method", and Ellis et al. (1997) considered a similar method, referred to as "interactive interviewing", both of which examine relationship development between researchers and research subjects. Dunn (2000) provided important insights regarding listening strategies during interviews, and Baxter and Eyles (1997) discussed the issue of rigor in interviewing. Oinas (1999) interrogated the issue of the anticipation of roles and the clashing of speech genres when conducting corporate interviews, and McKay (2002) considered how the exchange of life stories between interviewers and interviewees frequently plays out.

Some researchers consider interviews to be more like performances of constructed narratives than simply one-to-one reflections of daily life (Bennett 2000), and because of this, they advocate supplementing interviews with other emergent methods, such as diaries, mobile interviews, audio and video recordings of daily events, time and geocoded reflections (Dowling et al. 2015). Baxter and Eyles (1997) have critiqued the lack of transparency in many published studies that rely heavily on interviews, while Turner (2013) has interrogated the lack of transparency frequently associated with the use of research assistants when conducting interviews.

Apart from one-on-one interviews, much has also been written about group interviews (Holbrook and Jackson 1996; Miller et al. 1998; Crang 2001, 2002), including focus groups that draw on the tradition of conducting group interviews to determine market preferences (Crang and Cook 2007). Valentine

(1999), for example, explored how responses were different when interviewing couples together and separately.

Online interviewing has also received considerable attention (Dwyer and Davies 2010). Madge and O'Connor (2002, 2004), for example, investigated both individual and group online interviews, and Hine (2000) considered the nuances associated with "virtual interviews". Pickerill (2007) also examined the combination of online/onsite research methods, including interviews and participant observation. Speaking of my own experiences, sometimes the relationships that have developed using interviews have been via telephone discussions or online interactions, at least partially and sometimes primarily.

There are a wide range of ways to approach interviews (Hitchings and Latham 2020).

Berger and Malkinson (2000), for example, rejected the idea of conducting particular interviews, because they were deemed to potentially be too disruptive to those interviewed, with this empathy being linked to friendship. This link with method as friendship gets us closer to thinking about long-term relations and interviewing. There is also increasing recognition that some people do not like to or refuse to be interviewed (Hitchings and Latham 2020), and that ethnographic refusal, or the denial of interview methods more generally, is acceptable.

Obviously one important factor with regards to interviews is language ability, as it is much less likely that a close relationship will develop between a researcher and interviewee if an interpreter is used or if the interviewer does not have a good grasp of the language being used (Watson 2004). In some cases, cross-cultural differences can also make it difficult for close relations to develop (Wesche et al. 2010).

Although there has recently been an emphasis on not over relying on words, discourses, and representations, and paying more attention to practices (Delyser and Sui 2014) and affect (Hitchings 2012), interviewing is still a vital and vibrant research method (Crang 2005), one that has the potential to be applied in a wide variety of ways, depending on circumstances. The main thing to remember is—as Hitchings (2012) points out—that interview-based research can reveal far more than simply what the words tell us.

Interviews often combine both long-term observations and repeated interactions (Beazley 1998; Crang 2002; Tillmann-Healy 2003; Crang and Cook 2007). Crang and Cook (2007) wrote that, "The main difference between a series of multiple interviews with the same people and a range of single interviews with many more is that after repeated visits with the same person over a period of time, the relatively formal interviewing style discussed above can dissolve". The idea of "long-term interview relationships" require careful consideration, in relation to the types of relationships that emerge during different types of research experiences. Sometimes a relationship develops through only standard research interviews, but they also frequently emerge when interviews are intertwined with other types of research and non-research-oriented interactions. Thus, the definition of "long-term interview relationships" should not only refer to one particular type of narrowly defined interaction. Rather, the wide variety of ways that interviewers and interviewees interact over long periods of time need to be more explicitly acknowledged, including those that span a few years, or even longer, over which time relationships typically change and morph to varying degrees. However, oral history (Charlton et al. 2008; Giles-Vernick 2006; Ritchie 2003) or life history (Atkinson 2012) research is somewhat of an exception, as these approaches often require series of lengthy interviews (Ritchie 2003), which can help reduce biases associated with single interviews, as they allow for cross-checking and verifying information between interviews (Read 2018). Read also claims that serial interviews are appropriate for investigating ill-defined and complex topics, as they help get over the flattened complexity often associated with single interviews.

Crang and Cook (2007) mention that sometimes, important information can only be accessed through developing long-term relationships. This is especially true when engaging in intricate, political, or sensitive topics, leading interviewees to not fully trust interviewers, or to not disclose important information. Crang and Cook (2007) and Read (2018) mentioned some advantages of serial interviews, the main ones being that they increase the depth of discussions, reduce bias, and more adequately address ill-defined and complex issues. However, formalized interview series are also still sometimes warranted, even if they tend to be more rigid (Crang and Cook 2007).

Crang (2005) and others have made the point that interviews are co-constructions of knowledge, and Green and Baird (2016) have shown how interviews can, through focusing on certain aspects and not others, greatly affect the understandings of the circumstances by interviewees, legitimizing some issues and jettisoning others. Thus, they are not only vehicles for learning but can sometimes be powerful tools for affecting peoples' understandings of particular situations and circumstances.

Reporting on interviews through presenting excerpts is one of the key challenges of various kinds of interviews (Dowling et al. 2017b), particularly ones that are based on long-term relations. For example, Turner (2016) expressed concern that excerpts from qualitative interviews do not do justice to the non-verbal and non-individual textures of the worlds they derive from.

I now turn to introducing five examples of long-term relationships that I have personally developed based partially or largely on interviews, even if I am unlikely to be able to fully represent the depth of experience that can emerge through these long-term relationships.

7.3 Khamsone (Attapeu Province, Southern Laos)

Sone, an ethnic Brao man who has lived all his life in Phou Vong District, Attapeu Province, southern Laos, is the first person I would like to write about, in relation to long-term relationships and interviewing. I first met him in the early 2000s, when he was deputy head of the *Neo Lao Sang Xat* or the Lao Front for National Construction (LFNC) office of Phou Vong. At the time, I was the executive director of a non-government organization (NGO), the Global Association for People and the Environment (GAPE), which was based in Pakse, Champasak Province. However, one of our employees, Mr. Khamphanh, was Brao, and I was conducting my Master's and then PhD research with the Brao (Baird 2008, 2009). Therefore, we decided to develop some small development projects with the Brao in Phou Vong. One of those was to support Brao language local radio, and Sone headed up the project from the Phou Vong side, since he had received some training regarding minority language radio broadcasting elsewhere in Laos prior to us meeting.

We came to know each other fairly well, and whenever I stayed at the district centre, I put up a mosquito net and laid out a grass mat and slept at his house. He also sometimes travelled in the field with us. At this time, our relationship was mainly associated with my NGO's support for the radio project. Later, he also helped facilitate access to some of my fieldwork sites for my PhD research. I came to understand that he was interested in research himself, and that he had studied various aspects of Brao society, culture, history, and language. So, we talked a lot about our respective research interests. Sometimes we spoke in Brao; sometimes in Lao. However, at that time, I did not really consider him to be a research subject, and I did not conduct oral history with him. He was more of a colleague or friend with some converging interests. Here is where ideas about friendship as method becomes important (Tillman-Healy 2003).

However, beginning in 2013, I started collaborating on a project about large-scale land concessions, with my geographical focus being northeastern Cambodia and southern Laos, including in Phou Vong District, Attapeu Province, where the Hoang Anh Gia Lai (HAGL) company, a large Vietnamese agribusiness company, had been developing large-scale plantations—mainly rubber plantations—in the area since the early 2010s. By this time, Sone had resigned from his position with the government and was working full-time for HAGL. He was particularly responsible for managing domestic labour in Phou Vong for the company, and was being paid relatively well for his services. Part of the reason that they hired him was because he had been a government official in the district, and knew all the important officials there. He is also a member of Laos' only political party, the Lao People's Revolutionary Party, and therefore had some political influence with the local government.

At the time, I wanted to learn about HAGL's operations, and during the first year of my research project, I managed to meet him, and interview him about HAGL's operations in Laos. He is a talkative and inquisitive person—now in his 50s—and prides himself of being knowledgeable of local circumstances, since he is well connected. He thus became one of my key informant with regard to HAGL, and each year between 2013 and 2018, I visited him at his house in Phou Vong. He was generally more positive about the company than many of my other informants, but he provided crucial information about HAGL and its operations. I know him pretty well, and we get along well. Therefore, he was willing to update me each year about the ups and downs of different aspects of HAGL's operations in Phou Vong, and more generally, and sometimes more broadly in other parts of Laos and Vietnam as well.

This sort of research subject, someone who I met and came to know under one context, and later became a research subject in a different context, is not the type of research informant who is typically discussed in texts about interview methods (Crang and Cook 2007; Dowling et al. 2017b). I tended to interact with him in informal ways during discussions at an outdoor table near his house. The history between us, our past experiences together, and familiarity made him an excellent interviewee, but not a typical one. He knew I was doing research, but was willing to provide information to me that I am sure he would have been wary to have provided to others. He provided important material used in a number of journal articles (Baird and Fox 2015; Baird et al. 2019; Baird 2020b).

7.4 Khamphouy Sisavatdy

I first met Khamphouy Sisavatdy at his son and daughter-in-law's house in Beaverton, Oregon in 2008. Already in his early 70s at the time, Maha Phouy—as he is often referred to—since he received a high level of education as a Buddhist monk when he was a young man, before leaving monkhood and entering politics in the early 1970s, was happy to meet me.

In 1972, he was, to the surprise of many, elected as a member of the National Assembly in his home province of Sithandone, in the far south of Laos. Later, in 1975, when Laos became a communist country, he was one of the first to flee to Thailand as a political refugee. Soon, he became politically active, including producing newsletters strongly criticizing the new government in Laos. However, he ran into problems organizing politically on Thai soil, and the Thais came to believe he was a threat to national sovereignty. He was arrested and beaten up, and in 1976 he was compelled to become a political refugee in the United States.

Initially settling in Washington State, Maha Phouy soon became involved in anti-Lao communist politics, collaborating with other former refugees from Laos similarly bitter about the takeover of Laos. Although Maha Phouy had a wife and nine children, he became a full-time politician, even though doing so did not generate much income for supporting his family. After he racked up a huge telephone bill phoning long distance all around the United States to politically organize in the early 1980s, his phone was cut-off, and in a pre-internet era, he changed his political organizing strategy to driving around the United States to meet other Lao people with similar political views to him. He identifies himself to be politically "far right", and once told me that he considered former US President Ronald Reagan to be "like a father", since he supported anti-communist "freedom fighters", which included some of his political allies.

From the first time we met, I considered him to be a research subject, and I interviewed him, since he had accumulated a huge amount of knowledge about the history of anti-communist Lao politics in the United States but also in Europe, Australia, Canada, Thailand, and Laos between 1975 and the late 2000s. I initially stayed a few days at his son's house, interviewing him for most of the waking hours that I was there. Later, once I returned home to Victoria, B.C., Canada, and later when I moved to Madison, Wisconsin in 2010, we talked frequently on the phone. I also visited him a few times in Seattle and in Portland. We have come to know each other well. I still interview him and take notes each time we speak, but the interviews have become more like discussions over time. Sometimes he interviewed me about things that I knew about Laos that were of interest to me. From the time we first met, Maha Phouy was the Prime Minister of the Royal Lao Government in Exile (RLGE), an anti-communist Lao government in-exile. Therefore, he sometimes spoke to me as an interview subject, sometimes as a friend, and sometimes as an active politician. Early on, he was not entirely truthful with me, especially about the size of the military force he had influence over on the Laos-Thailand border, but over time our discussions became increasingly frank and honest, something that those who do oral history research have also noticed (Atkinson 2012). While Maha Phouy initially made some claims about his group's military power in Laos, later he was more honest about the actual circumstances. Apart from providing valuable information to me about the history of anti-communist Lao politics, my research topic when we talked, he also helped introduce me to countless other Lao political activists in the United States, Canada, and France. He became much more than an interview subject; he became an intellectual colleague and a gatekeeper who helped me make contact with others.

Again, my relationship with Maha Phouy does not fit the typical interviewer-interviewee relationship, and even today, we often talk on the telephone, and I frequently phone him when I have research questions. He has contributed important information included in articles and book chapters I have written (Baird 2012, 2016, 2018), and which will end up in the book I plan to eventually write about anti-Lao communist politics after 1975. My long-term interview-based relationship has developed in ways that are not well represented in the literature, and are somewhat different than what is typical for oral history research.

7.5 Bou Thang

I first met Bou Thang in the mid-2000s when I was conducting PhD research about the ethnic Brao people of northeastern Cambodia and southern Laos. Bou Thang was himself half ethnic Lao and half ethnic Tampuon, an Austroasiatic language-speaking ethnic group found only in northeastern Cambodia. He joined the Khmer Issarak, or Free Khmer, and briefly fought against French colonialism in April 1954. Soon after, when the French were defeated at Dien Bien Phu, in northern Vietnam, and France gave up Indochina and withdrew from the region, he walked to North Vietnam to receive advanced military training, becoming a communist "Khmer Hanoi". He stayed in

Vietnam for almost 16 years, until he walked along the Ho Chi Minh Trail from North Vietnam to northeastern Cambodia, where he became a military and political leader of the Khmer Rouge in northeastern Cambodia. However, in 1975, he rebelled, along with many other ethnic minorities from northeastern Cambodia, mostly ethnic Brao. He fled from Cambodia and became a political refugee in the Central Highlands of Vietnam. The anti-Khmer Rouge rebels he led were allowed to establish a new sub-district that became known as Gia Poc Commune, Sa Thay District, Gialai-Kontum Province, where he became a key leader. He also gradually replaced Bun Mi as the leader of the ethnic minority dissidents (Baird 2020a).

In late 1978, the government of Vietnam made the difficult decision to fully attack the Khmer Rouge, together with the pro-communist United Front for National Salvation of Kampuchea (UFNSK), which Bou Thang had emerged as the leader of. The goal was to remove Pol Pot and the Khmer Rouge from power in Cambodia, and he was leading the northeastern Cambodia faction of the resistance against the Khmer Rouge. Once the Vietnamese had gained control of most of the country, and the Khmer Rouge had mainly fled to regroup along the Cambodia-Thailand border, Bou Thang was elevated to the highest political body in the country, the Politburo of the Central Committee of the People's Revolutionary Party of Kampuchea (PRPK). He also chaired the central propaganda committee of the PRPK. He was particularly responsible for disseminating political theory. Then, in 1982, he was appointed as Minister of Defense of the People's Republic of Kampuchea (PRK), a position he held until 1985. He continued to hold senior positions in Cambodia, including being deputy Prime Minister between 1982 and 1992. Later, he became the Member of the National Assembly representing his home province of Ratanakiri, and after that he became a Senator.

When I first met Bou Thang at his house in Phnom Penh, he was friendly and quite happy to talk with me in Lao language, and occasionally Brao as well. However, as a senior long-time politician—probably the most senior politician in any country that I had ever met—he was initially guarded in answering important questions about the history of Cambodian politics after 1979. Sometimes he would side-step important questions, as might be expected since he was a deft politician. Sometimes he would laugh away questions and not answer. Sometimes he would frankly tell me that he would not answer certain questions that he considered to be politically sensitive. For example, he did not want to talk about the reason why Pen Sovan, the first prime minister of Vietnam-occupied Kampuchea, had been imprisoned in Vietnam in the early 1980s. Initially, he also did not allow me to scan any of his personal photographs. He was friendly but wary.

However, after our first meeting, we generally met once or twice a year for many years. Sometimes we met at his house in Phnom Penh. In other cases, we met at his house in Ban Lung, the capital of Ratanakiri Province, in northeastern Cambodia. Our meetings often went on for many hours. They were not short like what Crang and Cook (2007) have described, but I did take detailed notes when interviewing. Over time, we came to know each other well, and he increasingly supported my research. He even helped alleviate the concerns of some people I interviewed in northeastern Cambodia, and who later erroneously believed that I was a spy working for the Central Intelligence Agency (CIA) of the United States. Bou Thang, thus, took on a crucial role as a sort of senior gatekeeper (see Crang and Cook 2007). He also started speaking more freely with me, and his responses became increasingly open. He eventually allowed me to scan his personal photograph collection, but only after I knew him for a few years, and at one of our last meetings, he even spoke with me openly about Pen Sovan's demise. He also spoke about many other sensitive issues—including Vietnam and the border—that he would have certainly avoided responding to when we first met. Eventually, he accepted me as his de facto biographer, although we never entered any formal agreement, since he did not think of things like that, and I wanted to maintain my academic freedom. He later refused to sign a form giving me permission to use his photos in my recent book, *Rise of the Brao: Ethnic Minorities in Northeastern Cambodia during Vietnamese Occupation* (2020a). However, he verbally made it clear to my PhD student, W. Nathan Green, and I that he was happy for me to use his photographs in my book. He retired in 2017 and died in September 2019, at the age of 82 (Pech 2019), just months before the book that features him was published.

7.6 CHAO PANGKEO NAKHONE CHAMPASSAK

I first heard of Chao Pangkeo, a prominent member of the House of Champassak royal family, when I started conducting serious research about Champassak royals when I visited France in June 2009. However, I did not speak with him until I first phoned him on August 20, 2011, when I was in Thailand. Chao Pangkeo was initially friendly on the phone, but he was also wary of me, and refused to meet me in person, fearing the risk of possible assassination by security agents sent by the Lao PDR government. He would answer a few questions on the phone, but would not say much or talk for long. Every summer when I arrived in Thailand, I would phone him and try to arrange to meet, but he did not agree for a few years. At one point, he even lied to me that he could not meet because he was about to cross over from Thailand into Laos to attend his mother's funeral in Vientiane, since she had recently died in Laos. In fact, as a long-time opponent of the Lao communist government, he dared not return to his home country of Laos, even up to now. He did, however, introduce me to other members of his family, who he sent to meet me, including Chao Prasopsak (Tat) Na Champassak, who also became an important informant.

Finally, however, after failing to meet Chao Pangkeo for five years, he had a change of heart and decided to meet me in person. We met for the first time on September 19, 2016, at my hotel in Ubon Ratchathani. He insisted on meeting at a public place, but one without too many people around, so he would feel safe and we could talk. When we first met, he agreed to speak with me about the history of the House of Champassak, but told me outright that he would not talk with me about the anti-Lao communist insurgency, and his involvement in that insurgency during the 1970s and 1980s. He was very cautious, as his cousin, Chao Sinsamouth (Ke) had been assassinated by a gunman in Ubon Ratchathani in 2010 (Baird 2020c).

However, after we met a few times, always in Ubon Ratchathani when I visited northeastern Thailand, he gradually opened up, and before long he was not only providing useful information about the House of Champassak but also about the insurgency that he originally told me he would not talk with me about. He even let me scan a large number of photographs related to the insurgency that he collected over the years. Most recently, since I started writing a book about the Champassak royal family and sovereignty (Baird 2020c), I have been speaking with Pangkeo frequently via messenger on Facebook in order to ask him questions related to all kinds of details relevant for my book. While I have always taken notes when we have met or spoken via messenger, our interactions have changed dramatically over the years, from him being initially highly suspicious of me and unwilling to meet me in person in 2011, to having very frank discussions about important issues related to his family and the insurgency in 2020. Once again, we can see how the relationship, and the nature of our interactions, have changed and evolved greatly over the last number of years, and how the consequences of these relationships can vary considerably.

7.7 Kazue Sameshima

I first spoke with Kazue Sameshima, an elderly Japanese Canadian woman presently living in Lethbridge, Alberta, on the phone in April 15, 2018. She was 92 years old at the time, and her husband, another Japanese Canadian, had recently passed away at the age of 102. I was particularly interested in speaking with her because she spent most of her childhood years, in the 1930s, living in Nanaimo, British Columbia, Canada.

It was not easy for me to connect with her. Initially, I met her brother's wife, Audrey Shimozawa, who used to live in Nanaimo with her husband beginning in the 1960s up until the 2000s, when he passed away. She now lives at the Nikkei House in Burnaby, British Columbia. I interviewed her, and she also helped translate during another interview I did with an elderly Japanese Canadian woman staying at the Nikkei House. At some point, she must have realized that her sister-in-law in Lethbridge, the oldest sister of her husband, would likely have a lot of information about Nanaimo in the 1930s and early 1940s of interest to me. However, I later learned that Kazue told Audrey that she was not interested in talking with me, rebuffing Audrey's attempt to connect us and act as a de facto gatekeeper.

However, Kazue had a change of heart after I posted a photo of the Japanese Canadian community in Nanaimo before World War II in front of the Japanese school there in the Japanese Canadian newsletter, the *Nikkei Voice*, which she is on the mailing list for. When she saw the photograph, she was particularly touched because it included her mother. Therefore, she changed her mind and picked up the telephone and contacted me.

As with others already discussed, my relationship with Kazue Sameshima gradually developed, even though we have yet to meet in person. Initially, she answered my questions in a more distant way. However, over time, she became increasingly frank, and my interviews of her came to resemble informal conversations more than formal interviews, although I always took notes when we spoke, and she knew I was doing that. She told me that over time she came to look forward to my calls and our discussions, and to miss me when I did not phone her for an extended period. I do not want to exaggerate our relationship, but we have clearly become closer and closer as time has gone on, and my research about the Japanese Canadian community in Nanaimo has deepened through my many discussions with her. Since then, we have had over 20 extended interview telephone conversations. She contributed important information included in Baird et al. (2019), and more information provided by her will eventually end up in the book I intend to write about the Japanese Canadian community in Nanaimo, B.C.

7.8 Conclusion: Reflections on Long-term Relationship-based Interviews

In the above sections, I have provided some information about five people whom I have developed long-term interview-based relationships with. However, they are not the only ones who I have developed longer-term research relationships with. Others include Chao Keuakoun Na Champassak, an important member of the Champassak royal house in France; Chao Prasobsak (Tat) Na Champassak, who I mentioned above; and Chao Singto Na Champassak, another important Champassak royal and historian who lived in Metz, France, not far from the border with Germany. I have also developed a close relationship with Sahai Sou (Nhia Ja Sae Xiong), an ethnic Hmong former Communist Party of Thailand leader in Nan Province, northern Thailand. Yoep Vanson, an ethnic Brao man from Ratanakiri Province, northeastern Cambodia, is another person who I have developed a close relationship with over many years of collaborating on various research projects, and there are more. All these relationships have varied, although they have become normal for me, and I suspect that there are many others—some still lurking in the shadows—who have adopted similar approaches to engaging with long-term interview-based research, especially those who work on oral history of various type. However, more needs to be written about these sorts of interview-based relationships, especially outside of oral history.

While there has been much usefully written about interview methods, there has been surprisingly little written about the complex, messy and often unorthodox long-term interview-based relationships, this is actually more common than is typically acknowledged, and deserves much more attention than it has so-far received, both in oral history but also in other fields. In particular, this chapter demonstrates that interviewing can often occur over many years, and in a range of different contexts and formats, thus blurring the lines between researcher and research subjects in important and sometimes unexpected ways, including ways that are rarely imagined or described by those who write about qualitative research methods. There is not a particular way that long-term relationships between interviewers and interviewees tend to develop—as the diversity of examples above demonstrate—and these relationships are always contingent on a wide range of factors. We need to acknowledge and embrace the inherent messiness of these sorts of research encounters. Everything from the topic of interest to the researcher, to the nature of past interactions, to the context of when and where the interviewer and interviewee meet, and many more factors, far more than it is possible to outline in detail here, are potentially important for determining how different interview experiences play out. These sorts of relationship are especially useful when investigating politically sensitive topics, or other topics that require detailed understandings of the people involved.

We need to make more space for interviewing based on long-term relationship-building to be better recognized as a legitimate, indeed a necessary method, for investigating a range of different topics in an array of variable contexts, ones that can only really be properly studied through multiple interactions over potentially many years.

Acknowledgements I would like to sincerely thank those people who have allowed me to interview them and develop relationships with in a wide range of contexts over the years. Lynett Uttal also provided some useful suggestions.

References

Atkinson, R. 2012. The life story interview as a mutually equitable relationship. In J.F. Gubrium, J.A. Holstein, A.B. Marvasti, and K.D. McKinney, Eds., *The Sage handbook of interview research: The complexity of the craft*, 2nd ed., 115–129. Thousand Oaks, CA: Sage.

Baird, Ian G. 2020a. *Rise of the Brao: ethnic minorities in northeastern Cambodia during Vietnamese occupation*. Madison, WI: University of Wisconsin Press.

Baird, Ian G. 2020b. Problems for the plantations: challenges for large-scale land concessions in Laos and Cambodia. *Journal of Agrarian Change* 20(3): 387–407.

Baird, Ian G. 2020c (In Preparation). *Champassak Royalty and Sovereignty*.

Baird, Ian G. 2019. Developing an anti-racism methodology: considering Japanese and white Canadian fishermen relations in Nanaimo, B.C., Canada. *Canadian Ethnic Studies* 51(2): 107–130.

Baird, Ian G. 2018. Party, state, and the control of information in the Lao People's Democratic Republic: Secrecy, falsification and denial. *Journal of Contemporary Asia* 48(5): 739–760.

Baird, Ian G. 2016. An anticommunist monk and violence: Achan Chanh Ly. In Jeffrey Samuels, Justin Thomas McDaniel, and Mark Michael Rowe, eds. *Figures of Buddhist modernity in Asia*, 112–114. Honolulu: University of Hawai'i Press.

Baird, Ian G. 2009. *Dipterocarpus wood resin tenure, management and trade: practices of the Brao in northeast Cambodia.* Saarbrücken, Germany: Verlag Dr. Müller.

Baird, Ian G. 2012. Lao Buddhist monks and their involvement in political and militant resistance to the Lao People's Democratic Republic government since 1975. *Journal of Asian Studies* 71(3): 655–677.

Baird, Ian G. 2008. Various forms of colonialism: The social and spatial reorganisation of the Brao in southern Laos and northeastern Cambodia. Ph.D. Dissertation, Vancouver: University of British Columbia.

Baird, Ian G. and Jefferson Fox. 2015. How land concessions affect places elsewhere: telecoupling, political ecology, and large-scale plantations in southern Laos and northeastern Cambodia. *Land* 4(2): 436–453.

Baird, Ian G., William Noseworthy, Nghiem Phuong Tuyen, Le Thu Ha, and Jefferson Fox. 2019. Land grabs and labour: Vietnamese workers on rubber plantations in southern Laos. *Singapore Journal of Tropical Geography* 40: 50–70.

Baxter, Jamie and John Eyles. 1997. Evaluating qualitative research in social geography: establishing 'rigour' in interview analysis. *Transactions of the Institute of British Geographers* 22: 505–525.

Beaverstock, J. and J. Boardwell. 2000. Negotiating globalization, transnational corporations and global city financial centres in transient migration studies. *Applied Geography* 20: 277–304.

Beazley, H. 1998. Subcultures of resistance: street children's conception and use of space in Indonesia. *Malaysian Journal of Tropical Geography* 29: 11–22.

Bennett, K. 2000. Inter/viewing and inter/subjectivities: powerful performances. In A. Hughes, C. Morris, and S. Seymour, eds., *Ethnography and rural research*, 120–135. Cheltenham: Countryside and Community Press.

Berger, R., and R. Malkinson. 2000. 'Therapeutizing' research: the positive impact of research on participants. *Smith College Studies in Social Work* 70: 307–314.

Booth, Wayne C., Gregory G. Colomb, Joseph M. Williams, Joseph Bizup, and William T. FitzGerald. 1995. *The craft of research*. Chicago: University of Chicago Press.

Briggs, Charles L. 2007. Anthropology, interviewing, and communicability in contemporary society. *Current Anthropology* 48(4): 551–580.

Charlton, T.L., L.E. Myers, and R. Sharpless, Eds. 2008. *Handbook of oral history.* Lanham, MD: AltaMira Press.

Cochrane, A. 1998. Illusions of power: interviewing local élites. *Environment and Planning A* 30: 2121–2132.

Crang, Mike. 2001. Filed work: making sense of group interviews. In M. Limb and C. Dwyer, *Qualitative methodologies for geographers: issues and debates*, 215–233. London: Arnold.

Crang, Mike. 2002. Qualitative methods: the new orthodoxy? *Progress in Human Geography* 26(5): 647–655.

Crang, Mike. 2005. Qualitative methods: there is nothing outside the text? *Progress in Human Geography* 29(2): 225–233.

Crang, Mike and Ian Cook. 2007. *Doing ethnographies.* Los Angeles, London, New Delhi and Singapore: Sage.

Davies, Gail and Claire Dwyer. 2007. Qualitative methods: are you enchanted or are you alienated? *Progress in Human Geography* 31(2): 257–266.

Delyser, Dydia and Daniel Sui. 2014. Crossing the qualitative quantitative chasm III: enduring methods, open geography, participatory research, and the fourth paradigm. *Progress in Human Geography* 38(2): 294–307.
Dowling, Robyn, Kate Lloyd, and Sandra Suchet-Pearson. 2015. Qualitative methods 1: enriching the interview. *Progress in Human Geography* 40(5): 679–686.
Dowling, Robyn, Kate Lloyd, and Sandra Suchet-Pearson. 2017a. Qualitative methods II: 'More-than-human' methodologies and/in praxis. *Progress in Human Geography* 41(6): 823–831.
Dowling, Robyn, Kate Lloyd, and Sandra Suchet-Pearson. 2017b. Qualitative methods III: experimenting, picturing, sensing. *Progress in Human Geography* 42(5): 779–788.
Dunn, K. 2000. Interviewing. In Iain Hay, ed., *Qualitative research methods in human geography*, 50–82. Oxford and Melbourne: Oxford University Press.
Dwyer, Claire and Gail Davies. 2010. Qualitative methods III: animating archives, artful interventions and online environments. *Progress in Human Geography* 34(1): 88–97.
Ellis, C., C. E. Kiesinger, and L. M. Tillmann-Healy. 1997. Interactive interviewing: talking about emotional experience. In R. Hertz, ed., *Reflexivity & voice*, 119–149, Thousand Oaks, CA: Sage.
Elwood, S. and D. Martin. 2000. 'Placing' interviews: location and scales of power in qualitative research. *Professional Geographer* 52: 649–657.
England, K. 2001. Interviewing elites: cautionary tales about researching women managers in Canada's banking industry. In Pamela Moss, ed., *Feminist geography in practice: research and methods*, 200–213. Oxford: Blackwell.
Finlay, J. and J. Bowman. 2017. Geographies on the move: a practical and theoretical approach to the mobile interview. *The Professional Geographer* 69: 263–274.
Giles-Vernick, T. 2006. Oral histories: oral histories as methods and sources. In E. Perecman and S.R. Curran, Eds., *A handbook for social science field research: Essays and bibliographic sources on research design and methods*, 85–95. Thousand Oaks, CA: Sage.
Green, W. Nathan and Ian G. Baird. 2016. Capitalizing on compensation: hydropower resettlement and the commodification and decommodification of nature-society relations in southern Laos. *Annals of the American Association of Geographers* 106(4): 853–873.
Hammersley, M. 2006. Ethnography-problems and prospects. *Ethnography and Education* 1: 3–14.
Han, Ju Hui Judy. 2010. Neither friends nor foes: thoughts on ethnographic distance. *Geoforum* 41: 11–14.
Harper, D. 2002. Talking about pictures: a case for photo elicitation. *Visual Studies* 17: 13–26.
Harper, D. 2003. Framing photographic ethnography: a case study. *Ethnography* 4: 241–266.
Hay, Iain, ed. 2005. *Qualitative methodologies for human geographers*, 2nd edition. Oxford: Oxford University Press.
Hermanowicz, J. C. 2002. The great interview: 25 strategies for studying people in bed. *Qualitative Sociology* 25(4): 479–499.
Herod, Andrew. 1999. Reflections on interviewing foreign elites: praxis positionality, validity, and the cult of the insider. *Geoforum* 30: 313–327.
Hine, C. 2000. *Virtual ethnography*. London: Sage.
Hitchings, R. 2012. People can talk about their practices. *Area* 44(1): 61–67.

Hitchings, Richard and Alan Latham. 2019a. Qualitative methods I: on current conventions in interview research. *Progress in Human Geography* 44(2): 389–398.
Hitchings, Richard and Alan Latham. 2019b. Qualitative methods II: on the presentation of 'geographical ethnography'. *Progress in Human Geography* 44(5): 972–980.
Hitchings, Richard and Alan Latham 2020. Qualitative methods III: on different ways of describing our work. *Progress in Human Geography* (published online).
Holbrook, B. and P. Jackson. 1996: Shopping around: focus group research in north London. *Area* 28: 136–142.
Hughes, A. 1999. Constructing economic geographies from corporate interviews: insights from a crosscountry comparison of retailer-supplier relationships. *Geoforum* 30: 363–374.
Jansson, David. 2010. The head vs. the gut: Emotions, positionality, and the challenges of fieldwork with a Southern nationalist movement. *Geoforum* 41: 19–22.
Lamont, Michèle, and Ann Swidler. 2014. Methodological pluralism and the possibilities and limits of interviewing. *Qualitative Sociology* 37(2): 153–171.
Latham, A. 2003. Research, performance, and doing human geography: some reflections on the diary photograph, diary-interview method. *Environment and Planning A* 35: 1993–2018.
Limb, M. and C. Dwyer., eds. 2001. *Qualitative methodologies for geographers: issues and debates.* London: Arnold.
Madge, C. and H. O'Connor. 2002. On-line with e-mums: exploring the Internet as a medium for research. *Area* 34: 92–102.
Madge, C. and H. O'Connor. 2004. Online methods in geography educational research. *Journal of Geography in Higher Education* 28: 143–152.
McKay, D. 2002. Negotiating positionings: exchanging life stories in research interviews. In Pamela Moss, ed., *Feminist geography in practice: research and methods*, 187–199. Oxford: Blackwell.
Miller, D., P. Jackson, N. Thrift, B. Holbrook, and M. Rowlands. 1998. *Shopping, place and identity.* London: Routledge.
Moss, Pamela, ed. 2001. *Feminist geography in practice: research and methods.* Oxford: Blackwell.
Mullings, B. 1999. Insider or outsider, both or neither: some dilemmas of interviewing in a crosscultural setting. *Geoforum* 30: 337–350.
Oglesby, Elizabeth. 2010. Interviewing landed elites in post-war Guatemala. *Geoforum* 41: 23–25.
Oinas, P. 1999. Activity-specificity in organizational learning: implications for analysing the role of proximity. *Learning and Regional Development: Theoretical Issues and Empirical Evidence* 49(4): 363–372.
Pain, Rachel. 2003. Social geography: on action oriented research. *Progress in Human Geography* 27(5): 649–657.
Pech, Sotheary. 2019. Senior CPP member General Bou Thang dies. *Khmer Times*, September 13.
Pickerill, J. 2007. 'Autonomy online': indymedia and practices of alter-globalization. *Environment and Planning A* 39: 2668–2684.
Read, Benjamin A. 2018. Serial interviews: When and why to talk to someone more than once. *International Journal of Qualitative Methods* 17: 1–10.
Ritchie, Donald A. 2003. *Doing oral history: a practical guide*, 2nd ed. Oxford: Oxford University Press.

Rose, Gillian. 1997. Situating knowledges: positionality, reflexivities and other tactics. *Progress in Human Geography* 21(3): 305–320.
Sin, Chih Hoong. 2003. Interviewing in 'place': the socio-spatial construction of interview data. *Area* 35(3): 305–312.
Skinner, Jonathan, ed. 2013. *The interview: an ethnographic approach*. London and New York: Bloomsbury Academic.
Tillmann-Healy, Lisa M. 2003. Friendship as method. *Qualitative Inquiry* 9: 729–749.
Turner, Sarah. 2013. The silenced research assistant speaks her mind. In Sarah Turner, ed., *Red stamps and gold stars: fieldwork dilemmas in upland Southeast Asia*. Vancouver: University of British Columbia.
Turner, J. 2016. Voicing concerns: (re)considering modes of presentation. *GeoHumanities* 2(2): 542–551.
Valentine, G. 1999. Doing household research: interviewing couples together and apart. *Area* 31: 67–74.
Watson, Elizabeth E. 2004. 'What a dolt one is': language learning and fieldwork in geography. *Area* 36(1): 59–68.
Weiderhold, Anna. 2015. Conducting fieldwork at and away from home: shifting researcher positionality with mobile interviewing methods. *Progress in Human Geography* 15(5): 600–615.
Wesche, Sonia, Niem Tu Huynh, Erin Nelson, and Leela Ramachandran. 2010. Challenges and opportunities in cross-cultural geographic inquiry. *Journal of Geography in Higher Education* 34(1): 59–75.
Winchester, H. 1999. Interviews and questionnaires as mixed methods in population geography: the case of lone fathers in Newcastle, Australia. *Professional Geographer* 51: 60–67.

CHAPTER 8

Sick in the Field: Illness and Interbeing Encounters in Anthropological Fieldwork

Olea Morris

8.1 Introduction

All I knew, very suddenly upon waking up, was that something felt different. My forearm was covered in scratches, light bruises, and mosquito bites—normal, given my ongoing fieldwork working in agroecological farms and gardens in Mexico. What worried me most, however, was that my arm seemed to have doubled in size overnight, the skin inflamed and tight against my muscles. I was exhausted and dreaded dragging myself from the modest dormitory to the communal dining room for breakfast, let alone climbing the mountain path with the shepherds with whom I was conducting research. I tried to think back, retracing my steps through the pastures and parcels I had traversed the previous days, cataloguing the animals, plants, and people I had been in contact with. "What could have caused a reaction like this?", I asked myself. A second thought followed quickly, more worrisome to me as a student on a tight schedule and even tighter budget—"would I be able to carry out fieldwork like this?".

Getting sick—among a multitude of other unpleasant experiences—is an undeniable reality of carrying out fieldwork in social science research. Experiencing illness can be both physically and mentally debilitating, which in turn can have effects on data collection and the ability to participate in fieldwork settings. These experiences are often framed as anecdotal or circumstantial to the principal aims of the fieldwork experience; interestingly, to the extent

O. Morris (✉)
Department of Environmental Sciences and Policy, Central European University, Budapest, Hungary
e-mail: morris_olea@phd.ceu.edu

© The Author(s), under exclusive license to Springer Nature Switzerland AG 2023
N. Uddin, A. Paul (eds.), *The Palgrave Handbook of Social Fieldwork*,
https://doi.org/10.1007/978-3-031-13615-3_8

that illness is often planned for (and hopefully, mitigated or avoided altogether), it is also largely regarded as a nuisance or unintentional disruption to fieldwork research. In an account of their fieldwork research in Mexico, for example, anthropologist Laura Nader (1986) reflects on how bouts with malaria and hepatitis were initially mistaken as the result of the exhaustion or stress of her fieldwork practice and describes grappling with the guilt of not being able to gather "enough" data. Amy Pollard's (2009) piece "Field of Screams", which describes the self-reported anthropological fieldwork experiences of UK doctoral students, describes illnesses that were ignored or minimized, with the apparent aim of "proving" oneself as a capable researcher by enduring difficult periods of field research. Even though illness and intellectual or methodological rigour have little bearing on one another, these and other unfortunate circumstances still figure heavily into researchers' expectations for and evaluations of themselves and their work.

At the same time, it must be acknowledged that illness is just as much a part of the fieldwork landscape as any other condition common to the human experience. In one sense, fieldwork quite literally produces conditions for contracting illness—anthropological fieldwork brings about not only exposure to and encounters with new people but also to other environments, other species, and other pathogens. When understood this way—as particular kinds of embodied, interspecies relationships—getting sick is representative of the sorts of relationships to which anthropologists are becoming increasingly attuned. An obvious concern, however, is when those encounters get too close for comfort.

In this chapter, I reflect on the role that illness plays in shaping fieldwork experiences by engaging narratively with two distinct periods of illness I faced during my dissertation fieldwork research in Mexico. In doing so, I attempt to not only account for the direct impacts of these illnesses on my research and data collection but also how these illnesses became crucial touchstones in my experience both as a researcher and as an individual. In both instances, getting sick was directly brought about by the conditions of my fieldwork, which I had envisioned as a multi-sited ethnographic study of different intentional communities (known as *ecoaldeas*, or ecovillages) that had emerged throughout the country in recent years. The research involved not only engagements with human interlocutors but also with the plants, animals, insects, and microorganisms that resided in the community. These exploratory ventures into the world of nonhuman social relations yielded interesting data, unexpected encounters, and rich vignettes that ultimately allowed me to understand my research questions in new ways. These encounters also, at times, made me sick.

First, I briefly explore the ways that illness narratives have become implicated in the construction of anthropological knowledge, specifically focusing on researchers' personal experiences with illness in the field. Taking multispecies ethnographic approaches as a starting point for exploring such instances, I engage narratively with my own experiences of illness in the field, discussing these embodied experiences as kinds of interspecies encounters. In my discussion of my fieldwork experiences, I draw on ongoing discussions from anthropology that have highlighted the ways in which nonhuman beings are entangled with human social lives (Ogden et al. 2013). The instances I discuss below—an allergic reaction to a plant, and a gastrointestinal illness caused by an unknown microbial source—were unique instances brought about by the convergence of particular actors and circumstances in my field sites, in ways that were not always linear and predictable. For example, though I had prepared myself for potential illness brought about by proximity to livestock, following animals through pastures and fields brought about unexpected encounters with predatory insects or toxic plants. These examples speak to each other both because they illustrate how illness can be differently construed by distinct communities, as well as illustrate differences between the phenomena of experiencing illness alone and collectively. Finally, I highlight the ways in which these illnesses affected my research project from a methodological perspective—not only in the ways that such instances prevented or altered possibilities for data collection but also in how my illness was interpreted and responded to by my interlocutors.

8.2 Methodological Implications of Illness in Anthropological Research

Understandings of health and illness are socially and culturally produced and have long been the focus of anthropological research (c.f. Young 1982; Langdon and Wiik 2010). While a review of the methodological approaches used by medical anthropologists is beyond the scope of this piece (and indeed beyond my own area of expertise), my particular focus here is on the role of narrative in framing and understanding the experience and resultant significance of illness. As Hahn (1995) points out, "what counts as sickness" is deeply perceptual, linked to an individual's subjective experience and values, both on their own and in relation to society. Moreover, narratives of illness not only concern physical symptoms or sensations but also reveal particular understandings of patterns of causation (Garro and Mattingly 2000). Until relatively recently, exploring the construction of illness narratives (like much of anthropological inquiry) has understandably been directed outwards—towards interlocutors or "informants"—rather than towards anthropologists themselves.

In recent years, there has been a shift in the way that anthropologists' personal and embodied experiences are implicated in the production of knowledge. In particular, feminist geography has contributed substantially to the understanding that knowledge is "partial and situated" (Haraway 1988), and concepts of embodiment have been important for understanding knowledge as socially and politically constructed, rather than neutral and value-free (Jokinen and Caretta 2016). As researchers have become more transparent about the potential pitfalls and difficulties in carrying out qualitative fieldwork, the ways in which researchers' own embodied experiences are brought to bear on their research have become more visible (Parr 2001; Ahmed 2004; Billo and

Hiemstra 2013). Because methods germane to social science disciplines (including participant observation or interviewing) are by their nature interactive and discursive, the role and positionality of the researcher in shaping the outcomes of that discourse have been a key concern, and indeed an object of study in its own right (c.f. Kleinman and Copp 1993, Ingold 2004, Bondi 2005, Moser 2008, Punch 2012). Consequently, elucidating the ways that researchers are positioned at their research sites and their interlocutors has become an important consideration in analysing the results of social research. However, Davies and Spencer (2010) argue that such a focus has "left comparatively un-investigated the researcher's *states of being* during fieldwork and how these states might enable or inhibit the understanding that fieldwork aims to generate" (See also Punch 2012: 1). Evidently, there remains further ground to explore in how researchers themselves influence the results of their study.

In this respect, multispecies ethnography offers a useful perspective for understanding the ways in which embodied, ephemeral experiences like illness are implicated in the construction of social science research. As Ogden et al. discuss, multispecies ethnography involves strategies that are "attuned to life's emergence within a shifting assemblage of agentive beings" (2013: 6). Such approaches are well-suited to understanding illness, a state of being with fuzzy boundaries and which necessarily implicates other beings, both human and nonhuman (Nading 2013, Rock 2016). To describe experiences of illness as "personal" leave unacknowledged the encounters with other bodies—insects, plants, animals, microbes—that preceded or directly resulted in both the onset of illness, not to mention potential treatment or other forms of mitigation. Treating the human body less as a "skin-bounded, bio-mechanical organism" (Lock and Farquhar 2007) and rather as kinds of "super-organisms" (Lorimer 2016)—a multispecies assemblage of bacteria, fungi, and other nearly invisible beings—has created further space for understanding illness as forms of embodied "entanglements" between and among different beings (Rock 2016). Such approaches, however, introduce significant methodological considerations. Although the human body has been likened to a "tool" in ethnographic research (Parr 1998; Spry 2006; Paterson 2009), bodies are unlike other kinds of tools in that they cannot also be partitioned and selectively engaged at will by the researcher; indeed, they are necessarily implicated (at times, unwittingly or unwillingly) in the process of carrying out research.

Experiencing periods of illness while carrying out ethnographic research is a recurrent theme in accounts of fieldwork. While often downplayed, in the final, polished versions of ethnographic accounts, such circumstances seem to be the norm rather than the exception (Pollard 2009). As Punch (2012) observes, however, even "mundane" research topics and sites can require the engagement of a range of "intellectual, practical, and emotional challenges" (2012: 89). Fieldwork is often physically demanding; depending on the research questions at hand, participant observation can include strenuous physical labour or travelling long distances. These everyday realities are not inconsequential or extraneous to "real" data collection, but are woven into a researchers' embodied experience (Billo and Hiemstra 2013). Fieldwork has largely been constructed as an activity for those who can navigate these challenges with deft and ease, and has largely been constructed around able bodies (Jokinen and Caretta 2016).

Naturally, experiencing illness in the field influences the ways in which researchers go about collecting data. Experiencing the symptoms of illness are disruptive of our day-to-day lives, whether this involves active participant observation, physical labour, or even note taking. As the emergence of the COVID-19 pandemic has illustrated, widespread illness can result in barriers that discourage or foreclose entirely activities that are considered to be fundamental for carrying out fieldwork research—including travel, sharing food, or living and working in close proximity with interlocutors. At the same time, the emergence of crises tied to health—either of an individual or of a broader community—can reveal new understandings tied to experience with adversity. In an essay detailing her experiences both as a wife and later as a widow at her field site in Romania, anthropologist Diane Freedman (1986) discussed how the death of her spouse influenced the tone of her relationships with community members and resulted in newfound understandings of death and grief that became apparent through these relationships. Similarly, Punch (2012) writes that their experience with illness gave them an enhanced sense of admiration for their interlocutors. In disrupting socially established norms, crises like illness create circumstances where community members can develop new relationships and lines of rapport and solidarity through shared experience. In this sense, such experiences not only foreclose possibilities in carrying out fieldwork but also reveal them.

In the following narratives, drawn from my own fieldwork experience in Mexico over the course of approximately a year, I engage with how the experience of illness as an embodied phenomenon took on methodological meaning. Following Paterson's (2009) inquiry "how can we write meaningfully about those everyday embodied experiences … that cannot arise without the physicality of the body?" (2009: 766), I reflect on both the difficulties of recording one's own sensory experiences while also recognizing the ways that these experiences open new avenues for understanding.

8.3 *"Mala Mujer"* and Toxic Encounters

The morning I awoke with the swollen arm had occurred relatively early into one of my first fieldwork stays, in a mountainous region near the coast of the Gulf of Mexico.[1] At the time, I had been carrying out fieldwork for my dissertation research in a kind of intentional community in Mexico known as an *ecoaldea* (ecovillage), a small community that had been established with the goal of living life more simply and sustainably. The arrangement I had struck with the community leaders involved my exchanging my labour for a place to

---

[1] Identifying geographical characteristics are intentionally omitted.

stay and a few meals, which suited the nature of my project well. Consequently, much of my research involved following the people who cared for the community's livestock, or worked in the bakery, gardens, or dairy located on site. Though the work had been exhausting, I knew from my previous experience in agricultural settings that this was to be expected. The depth of my exhaustion, however, and the slow emergence of itchy welts on other parts of my arm, gave me pause for reconsideration.

At the suggestion of Juana,[2] a woman who prepared most of our communal meals, I undertook a consultation with her husband Giorgio, the community's resident medical professional. The source of the man's training was hazy at best—though he had evidently undergone training at a hospital facility in a nearby urban centre, he confessed disillusionment with and distrust of conventional medicine, expressing an affinity instead for a more "holistic practice". Despite the fact that I bore significant reservations about the credibility of the man, the stories I had read of other anthropologists' exploits and my own expectations for my fieldwork surfaced in my mind. I had learned in my earliest training as an anthropologist. I said yes.

Surprisingly, the consultation seemed to focus less on the state of my skin, and more on the state of my brain. Giorgio placed two magnetic disks on my palms and asked me to reflect on the cause of my emotional pain, which he identified without hesitation as the source of my skin ailment. Despite my scepticism, I found myself nodding in genuine agreement as he explained that the mind-body connection could produce ailments that seemed to appear out of nowhere. After all, I had been stressed trying to build working relationships with the other community members, and exhausted by the intensity of the daily workload—maybe it was psychosomatic, after all. While I attempted to observe the encounter from outside myself, constructing a mental catalogue for writing in my fieldnotes later, my desire to alleviate my symptoms had evidently shifted me out of "researcher" mode and into "patient" mode. Giorgio documented the session on a legal pad and asked me about how I was feeling and whether I had strained any personal or familial relationships lately—was there someone I had wronged? Someone who had wronged me? Despite my exhaustion, I was slightly amused by the self-recognition—the interviewer had become the interviewee. With the advice that I address my illness with prolonged daily meditation sessions, I was eventually dismissed. I left feeling tired, but relieved—by the end of our session, the itching of the welts had seemed to subside, my arm seemingly deflated. Maybe it was all in my head, I surmised.

Over the next few days, however, it became evident that my symptoms were not only still present but had returned with a vengeance. Large painful hives the size of tea saucers enveloped every part of my body, disappearing and appearing in unpredictable ways. My lips and eyelids swelled, then subsided, then swelled again, distorting my features to the point that I elicited gasps from the women I shared a room with when they saw me the next morning. Unable

---

[2] All names in this work are pseudonyms.

to eat and exhausted, I slept away days on a thin mat on the concrete floors of the communal house. As the days strung together into a full week, I realized I would be missing a special workshop at another community nearby, and fretted about how to make up for perceived lack of data. I wasn't able to join in the fields where I normally worked, and wondered how the sheep I had been helping care for were doing. I wrote nothing down for days, listening to a well-worn playlist and summoning strength for the next meal time.

The experience of the illness itself not only weakened me physically but also cultivated stress around my ability to successfully conduct research with my interlocutors. Despite my best intentions, my illness also strained relationships which had just begun to be formed. Some residents became frustrated with my demeanour, mistaking my lack of engagement (and appetite) for impoliteness. In turn, I grew somewhat agitated with some community residents, who seemed to downplay or ignore my symptoms. The lack of seriousness with which my illness was regarded was confirmed, I thought, by the offerings of inappropriate medications and palliatives that I received from my interlocutors—including tubes of mentholated cream designed for alleviating muscle soreness, clay-based cosmetic masks, and low-dose anti-histamine pills.

My illness, which I had come to realize was an allergic reaction to something (but what?) seemed to be a visceral confirmation of my inalienable otherness, both to me and my interlocutors. I had worked hard in my first weeks staying on the farm, putting in extra hours in the pastures in the hopes of building a rapport with residents, several of whom were inclined to view Americans like myself as rather lazy or ill-equipped to carry out physical labour. Worried that my illness would seemingly confirm this, I attempted to distance myself from my body, "walking off" the sickness at the suggestion of several. One young woman related that she was sure my illness was the sign of a long-term condition, noting that other foreigners who had visited Mexico often experienced such illnesses and did not experience respite until returning to their home country. "It's *mala mujer* ("bad woman"), for sure", one shepherd told me, referring to the colloquial name for plants in the *Cnidoscolus* genus that can cause a painful sting when touched. I protested that I had encountered the plant before, and never had such an intense reaction—it couldn't possibly be the source. He and two other young men concurred, however, that my reaction was all the worse because I wasn't a local—"we all grew up around here, that's why it doesn't hurt us as bad. You're not from around here, so [the toxin] is really powerful, you're just not used to it yet", they told me. I ignored the fact that the men were not only "not locals" themselves but were not even from Mexico (but were instead from another Central American country). I took the remark, though delivered good-naturedly, to highlight the extremity of my otherness.

Still, I hesitated to go to the hospital in the nearby town—partially because I doubted the cause of my symptoms, and partially because of the indifferent reaction of many community residents. Seeking medical care would have required the aid of other community residents, and those who controlled access to the community's vehicles had expressed strong doubts that the regional clinic would be able to help me—"they can't do more for you there than we can do for you here", a community leader told me. Confidently, Giorgio and two other residents who worked with me in the community reaffirmed poor health stemmed from a deep-seated emotional or psychological source, and that the hospital would not be able to do much more for me than the community could. This concurrence about my mental state shook me, even as I watched the hives continuing to spread. Were they right? I asked myself. Eventually, at the urging of a visiting volunteer from France, two community residents agreed to deliver me to a hospital; I learned later, however, that this decision was largely a last ditch effort to appease my nervous condition—visiting a hospital, they had reasoned, would at least be a powerful placebo. Days later, having visited the hospital twice, receiving multiple intravenous antihistamine infusions, I returned to the community to carry out the remaining weeks of fieldwork.

The day I returned from the hospital was also the last day I worked in the fields with the sheep. Though I hadn't realized it at the time, I had traded my visits to the hospital for the trust of several key interlocutors. Unluckily, the onset of my illness had coincided with several deaths in the flock—just the week before, I had helped cremate a young ewe found lifeless in the pen, joined by her lamb the following morning. The shepherds I worked closely with explained that sheep were particularly sensitive creatures, and often succumbed to gastrointestinal parasites. Still, an air of mystery pervaded the deaths—the shepherds had even summoned a veterinarian from a nearby city, who had commented the flock looked to be in poor health, but it was difficult to say why.

At a meeting with one of the main community organizers, the link between my illness and the poor health of the sheep was made clear to me. The way my illness was interpreted back to me gave me reason for pause—it was not my illness that was causing my lack of energy, bad mood, and sleeplessness, it was explained to me, but instead the other way around. The hives and the sores, while perhaps instigated by the exposure to the plant, reflected a much more grave illness—namely, a roiling, inner emotional world that needed tending to. I assented to a reassignment to the kitchen—"I'd be happy to do whatever it is you need", I offered weakly—however, the energetic consequences of my illness were reinforced once more, as the community resident replied, "it's not what *I* want, but rather what *they* want", he said. It took me a moment to realize the dissenters he referred to were, in fact, sheep.

In seeking out sheep as nonhuman research companions, I had unwittingly been brought into relationships with the plant that I had reacted to. Had I also unwittingly transferred my illness to them, a sublimation of "bad energy" that in turn had consequences in the physical world? The residents of the community that worked largely with livestock animals seemed to agree that sheep were sensitive beings, even more so than pigs, cows, or even goats. Following shepherds who had monitored the health of the sheep, I had watched them check the whites of the sheep's eyes for signs of anaemia and administered preparations meant to fortify immune systems. I had observed that several individuals in the herd seemed to be struggling with the presence of intestinal parasites, which was presumed to be related to changes in the weather or in the nutritive capacities of the pastures. Now I also contended with the presumption (despite my protestations) that my own energetic transferences could be at fault.

While shifting the locus of my daily work activities foreclosed some possible lines of research inquiry (namely, following sheep in the pastures directly), it also worked to salvage some of the relationships that had frayed during my illness. Sheep continued to die—at least one, while I was still in residence—but my involvement was no longer a possibility, and the death was attributed to anaemia brought about by intestinal parasites. While removing myself from an area I had hoped to explore more in-depth was initially disappointing, my vantage point from outside the pastures proved to be fruitful in its own right in that I could understand how shepherds responded to sheep death barring the possibility of my own illness. Grappling with the implications of my body and how it responded to my field site, however, turned out to be a recurrent theme in my other research sites as well.

8.4 Stomach Bugs and "Co-miseration" in the Field

Months later, my experience with the mystery plant was bookended by another bout of illness—this time, presumably caused by a mystery microbe.[3] I had recently arrived at another research site at a small community in the state of Yucatan, where I was enthusiastic about visiting old acquaintances and observing a youth festival organized around environmental issues. The spread of the mysterious affliction began slowly. First, one of the most active community residents, often on the move organizing workshops or special activities for the children in town, withdrew for several days, complaining of stomach pains. Each morning, it seemed, a different community resident would arrive at the communal breakfast table in the morning complaining of a poor night's sleep and a bad case of stomach upset. Over several days, the community's collective symptoms only intensified, evidenced by the uncharacteristic amount of food leftover from mealtimes and the enlargement of queues for the ecological "composting" toilets in the morning.

Besides the discrete effects produced by the illness—residents were unable to muster energy for daily activities, for example, or interpersonal disputes arose—diagnosing the source of the illness highlighted deeper perspectival differences between community residents. In one instance, a rift was created between a long-time resident, who advocated that visitors and other residents undergo testing for intestinal parasites. Another resident, who stressed that

---

[3] Though neither myself nor other community members received a positive diagnosis, symptoms strongly suggested *Giardiasis*, an infection caused by *Giardia*, a protozoan parasite, or an infection caused by *H. pylori*, a bacteria.

that the illness reflected a flagging commitment to personal hygiene, resented the insistence on the possibility of intestinal parasites, as it might have suggested design flaws in the water filtration system he had helped rig up.

Despite the urgent morning reminders to be mindful of cleanliness in common areas, sickness—largely characterized by stomach pains, gastrointestinal distress, and extreme malaise—seemed to spread more and more quickly. In our morning circles, other long-time residents communicated the need to maintain proper hygiene protocols in the communal kitchen and dining area. However, no measures taken seemed to have a noticeable effect on the rapidity of new cases emerging. The tell-tale symptom that seemed to be shared by all those affected was a sulphurous burp (smelling and tasting of rotten eggs), and residents and volunteers had begun reporting their symptoms with growing frequency at the communal breakfast table. The cause, however, was largely unknown—the water used for drinking and cooking was purchased already filtered and bottled in a nearby town, and extra precautions had been taken in sanitizing communal spaces.

When I myself became sick, it presented clear challenges to carrying out fieldwork. Although some days I was able to gather the energy to complete chores within the community, very little of my time and focus was left in the end to dedicate to field notes. Extreme physical exhaustion made participating in any activities or carrying out interviews difficult. Similar to Nader's (1986) account, seeking treatment for an illness while in the field produced its own set of anxieties about whether or not one is collecting "enough" data—nor was I entirely sure that what I was experiencing was illness at first. Sleeping in a tent slowly creeping with mould, waking before dawn to prepare communal meals, and the long bus rides in changing field sites had partly convinced me that the performance of such physical feats were necessary in transforming myself into a capable field researcher. Despite the fact that I still took time to write field notes, I felt guilt in the perception that my waning energy was preventing me from taking part in even more activities or building even more rapport. Part of my anxiety stemmed from logistical considerations—I had timed my visit to coincide with the second annual festival that the ecovillage community had organized for the youth of the local town. Navigating the flurry of activity in preparing for and holding the festival would have proved challenging under normal circumstances; as some afternoons I was largely incapable of moving from a hammock, recording the festival in any great detail became nearly impossible.

At the same time, I found myself grappling with the implications of my presence as a researcher on the community I was working with. Although I was not the only foreigner or visitor in the community, I could also not deny the effects of my presence on the community's permanent residents, now tasked with caring for a fleet of ailing volunteers instead of finishing work in the garden or ongoing construction of a small communal house. The material consequences produced by multiple individual experiences of illness challenged the existing systems of the ecovillage community. Collectively, our production of plastic waste increased significantly, as we discarded plastic sheets in which our antiparasite pills were encased. Fuel was needed to transport more and more visitors to the closest town where they could receive medical care if needed, and to transport back the tanks of natural gas that were used to boil water for sanitizing surfaces and consumption. While perhaps the illness would have emerged regardless of my presence or that of the other volunteers and visitors, it was undeniable that my presence placed an additional burden of my care on the more permanent residents of the community.

Reflecting on my fieldnotes from this time, I can see that what I was writing was reflected through a lens of illness. What I was able to write was imprinted by the spectre of exhaustion—I recorded events that had happened in the course of the day without additional reflection and with minimal description. Instead, my focus drifted inwards towards my own bodily experience. Fieldnotes focused heavily on my symptoms—exhaustion, dehydration, lack of appetite, extreme nausea—and alternatively reflected hopefulness that I would recover quickly and a resignedness to my condition. As I was too ill to participate in the ongoing festival in town, along with a number of my interlocutors, the quality of the data that I was recording seemed minuscule compared to the "more important" events (I assumed) I was missing out on. Dealing with my illness shifted my daily relations from one set of interspecies relations to another—instead of tending to seedlings in the greenhouse or observing the new beehive divisions, I instead swatted away flies and listened to the sounds of birds from the hammock.

On the other hand, I was able to get direct experiential knowledge of what many of my interlocutors were experiencing. The experience of "commiserating" with my interlocutors (quite literally, "suffering with" them), brought us closer, as we passed around indigestion tablets and prepared pots of weak tea for each other. Webs of dependency shifted as those who had recovered or were least affected became responsible for those who were debilitated, taking over chores and shifts in the kitchen or making trips to neighbouring towns for additional supplies and medicine. Unable to participate much at all in the festival preparations, which were now in full swing in the neighbouring town, the community residents that remained in our forest outpost began to rely more closely on each other for both practical and social needs. Often, there was nothing much to do except talk with one another. The experience of being ill in a communal setting was markedly different from when I had been ill on my own. For one, the questions that I asked myself were also being grappled with by the community at large. Was the illness caused by something I ate, something I drank, something I came into contact with—had I been unintentionally prolonging my state by interacting with contaminated substances? Was recovering simply a matter of putting up with the symptoms and "getting on with it", in the spirit of building goodwill with my collaborators, or would it require more drastic measures—a trip to the city, testing at the local clinic, a round of antibiotics?

Grappling with the proper way to address the outbreak of an unknown illness produced divergent speculations amongst community members, divergences with tangible social consequences. For example, some community members felt that all residents and visitors should undertake their courses of anti-parasitic medications as a matter of precaution, in case the illness was spread through human contact. Others refused, because such a treatment was a drastic approach, and one they would not undertake lightly (that is, without confirmation that pharmaceuticals were the only effective course of action). This refusal frustrated other residents, who understood their non-compliance in taking preventative courses of medication to be misguided at best, and selfish at worst. When two frequent visitors to the community travelled together to the nearby regional capital of Mérida to undergo testing for parasites and returned with a negative diagnosis, those who had resisted taking antibiotics in the first place expressed a sense of vindication, much to the annoyance of those who had initially proposed parasites as the cause of the illness.

As was apparent to visitors who arrived at the community perfectly healthy only to contract whatever afflicted us, it was the very act of creating a community that had produced the conditions that allowed the disease to spread. Bound by similar constraints—short attention spans and tempers, low energy levels and appetites—empathy flourished among the residents that had effectively been quarantined together, away from the ongoing festival preparations. Although I was unable to participate in the activity I had planned (recording the work of festival participants and volunteers), I had a front-row seat for the daily minutiae of community illness and recovery (rationing toilet paper, preparing easy to digest foods, settling interpersonal squabbles). While the interpersonal conflicts that sprung up around the cause of the illness initially seemed inconsequential to me, in retrospect I understand these events as the cascading activations of defence mechanisms. That so many people might be ill, despite measures to clean communal areas or inform residents of potential risks. It was seen as a threat by some founding members of the community, who had overestimated their epidemiological capacities.

These gaps faced by my interlocutors—between expectation and reality, or "known" and "unknown" factors influencing the health of the community—instigated significant shifts in community life which formed the basis of my experience there. When I eventually left several weeks later, it was a different community I was leaving—some residents had left the project, a result of interpersonal conflicts revealed by our collective sickness, while others had organized stronger protocols for preventing similar circumstances in the future. Though my symptoms dissipated gradually after departure, I also carried with me the intermingled memories of bird calls, languid afternoon chats, and the smell of rotten eggs.

8.5 Conclusion/Discussion

As anthropologist Tim Ingold rightly observes, knowledge is not "out there, waiting to be discovered", but is rather "grown in the forge of our relations with others" (2014: 391). With this in mind, interrogating how researchers are personally entangled with their interlocutors—both human and nonhuman—has significant bearing on data collection. Illness, among other unplanned circumstances that arise in the course of carrying out field research, is more common of an occurrence than many fieldwork accounts seem to reflect; experiencing "negative" states, such as loneliness, depression, anxiety, or illness are far more the norm than the exception (c.f. Pollard 2009, Billo and Hiemstra 2013). While certain levels of physical fitness and/or wellness are indeed useful resources for some forms of data collection, conflating wellness with objectivity is a slippery slope. Carrying forward the metaphor of the body of the researcher as a "tool" for ethnographic research, is it possible—given the porousness and susceptibility of the human body—to understand how such a tool might be "calibrated"?

Through this narrative engagement with my own fieldwork experiences, I suggest that illness—like other states of being that researchers might encounter—presents its range of possibilities for further (auto) ethnographic inquiry. The experiences detailed above were not extraneous to my fieldwork experiences but represented formative points in my research process as a whole, as well as the communities with which I worked. Both experiences of illness discussed above revealed broader patterns of relating that I might not have otherwise noticed—for example, gaps in communication between residents, latent biases, assumptions, or diverse knowledge systems implicated in framing and treating illness. Often these discussions reflected broader issues with which the community was grappling, and which I became privy to through these events. Experiencing illness as a collective phenomenon, rather than as an individual experience, had important ramifications for my rapport with my interlocutors as well as my capacity to collect information. As a participant in community life that had (like many of my interlocutors) fallen ill, my experience unwittingly became part of the broader base of evidence from which larger conclusions were drawn.

As fields in the social sciences delve more into the sensorial dimensions of methodological practice, it will become increasingly important to situate researchers' biases and individual experiences about the research aims. At the same time, embracing how activities like data collection might be constrained by the very real states which researchers occupy from time to time provides an understanding of disciplinary blind spots. It must be pointed out, after all, that in seeking to trace entanglements of human and nonhuman social relations, entangling oneself even further is to be expected. While I certainly don't suggest intentionally following in my footsteps, a growing genre of fieldwork accounts suggests that grappling with adversity in fieldwork is a frequent eventuality. Rather, I offer that treating illness and other "negative experiences" with sensitive ethnographic attention can reveal new avenues of investigation, and perhaps space for imaginative exploration in methodological strategy.

References

Ahmed, S. 2004. Collective feelings: Or, the impressions left by others. *Theory, Culture & Society* 21(2), pp. 25–42.

Billo, E. and Hiemstra, N. 2013. Mediating messiness: expanding ideas of flexibility, reflexivity, and embodiment in fieldwork. *Gender, Place & Culture* 20(3), pp. 313–328.

Bondi, L. 2005. The place of emotions in research: From partitioning emotion and reason to the emotional dynamics of research relationships. *Emotional Geographies*, pp. 231–246.

Davies, J. and Spencer, D. 2010. *Emotions in the field: The psychology and anthropology of fieldwork experience*. Stanford University Press.

Freedman, D. 1986. Wife, widow, woman: Roles of an anthropologist in a Transylvanian village. In: *Women in the field: Anthropological experiences*. Los Angeles: University of California Press, pp. 335–358.

Garro, L.C. and Mattingly, C. 2000. *Narrative and the Cultural Construction of Illness and Healing*. Los Angeles: University of California Press.

Hahn, R. 1995. *Sickness and Healing: An Anthropological Perspective*. Yale University Press.

Haraway, D. 1988. Situated Knowledges: The Science Question in Feminism and the Privilege of Partial Perspective. *Feminist Studies* 14(3), pp. 575–599.

Ingold, T. 2004. Culture on the ground: The world perceived through the feet. *Journal of Material Culture* 9(3), pp. 315–340.

Ingold, T. 2014. That's Enough about Ethnography. *Hau: Journal of Ethnographic Theory* 4(1), pp. 383–395.

Jokinen, J.C. and Caretta, M.A. 2016. When bodies do not fit: an analysis of postgraduate fieldwork. *Gender, Place & Culture* 23(12), pp. 1665–1676.

Kleinman, S. and Copp, M.A. 1993. *Emotions and fieldwork*. Newbury Park, CA: Sage Publications.

Langdon, E.J. and Wiik, F.B. 2010. Anthropology, health and illness: an introduction to the concept of culture applied to the health sciences. *Revista latino-americana de enfermagem* 18(3), pp. 459–466.

Lock, M.M. and Farquhar, J. 2007. *Beyond the body proper: Reading the anthropology of material life*. Duke University Press.

Lorimer, J. 2016. Gut Buddies: Multispecies Studies and the Microbiome. *Environmental Humanities* 8(1), pp. 57–76.

Moser, S. 2008. Personality: a new positionality? *Area* 40(3), pp. 383–392.

Nader, L. 1986. From anguish to exultation. In: *Women in the field: Anthropological experiences*. Los Angeles: University of California Press, pp. 97–116.

Nading, A.M. 2013. Humans, animals, and health: From ecology to entanglement. *Environment and Society* 4(1), pp. 60–78.

Ogden, L.A. et al. 2013. Animals, plants, people, and things: A review of multispecies ethnography. *Environment and Society* 4(1), pp. 5–24.

Parr, H. 1998. Mental health, ethnography and the body. *Area* 30(1), pp. 28–37.

Parr, H. 2001. Feeling, reading, and making bodies in space. *Geographical Review* 91(1–2), pp. 158–167.

Paterson, M. 2009. Haptic geographies: ethnography, haptic knowledges and sensuous dispositions. *Progress in Human Geography* 33(6), pp. 766–788.

Pollard, A. 2009. Field of screams: difficulty and ethnographic fieldwork. *Anthropology Matters* 11(2).

Punch, S. 2012. Hidden struggles of fieldwork: Exploring the role and use of field diaries. *Emotion, Space and Society* 5(2), pp. 86–93.

Rock, M. 2016. Multi-Species Entanglements, Anthropology, and Environmental Health Justice. In *Routledge Handbook of Environmental Anthropology*, pp. 356–369. Routledge.

Spry, T. 2006. A "Performative-I" Copresence: Embodying the Ethnographic Turn in Performance and the Performative Turn in Ethnography. *Text and Performance Quarterly* 26(4), pp. 339–346.

Young, A. 1982. The anthropologies of illness and sickness. *Annual Review of Anthropology* 11(1), pp. 257–285.

PART III

Bio-ethics, Fieldwork Practices, and Ground Reality

CHAPTER 9

At the Organ Bazaar of Bangladesh: In Search of Kidney Sellers

Monir Moniruzzaman

9.1 THE SETTING

The trade in live human organs, such as kidneys, livers, and corneas, has risen in Bangladesh, since cadaveric donation does not exist in that country to date. Its kidney market has expanded for more than two decades, while the liver trade has emerged in the last few years. The government of Bangladesh enacted the *Organ Transplant Act 1999*, which imposes a ban on trading body parts and publishing related classified ads. The act explicitly states that anyone violating this law could be imprisoned for a minimum of three years to a maximum of seven years and/or penalized with a minimum fine of 300,000 Taka (US$4300; Bangladesh Gazette 1999). Nonetheless, organ trade is openly defied by the Bengali media, which regularly publish newspaper advertisements seeking vital organs and any other transplantable parts of the human body. The recipients are domestic and diasporic residents (Bangladeshi-born foreign nationals) who solicit organ sellers in Bangladesh and then obtain transplant surgeries in Bangladesh as well as in India, Pakistan, Singapore, and Thailand. The sellers are poor rickshaw pullers, petty farmers, and slum dwellers who sell

---

The chapter was first published in an, D. Siegel, R. de Wildt (eds.), *Ethical Concerns in Research on Human Trafficking: Studies of Organized Crime* 13, (https://doi.org/10.1007/978-3-319-21521-1_14). The chapter has been reprinted here with slight modification with the permission of the author and publisher.

M. Moniruzzaman (✉)
Department of Anthropology, Michigan State University, East Lansing, MI, USA
e-mail: monir@msu.edu

© The Author(s), under exclusive license to Springer Nature Switzerland AG 2023
N. Uddin, A. Paul (eds.), *The Palgrave Handbook of Social Fieldwork*, https://doi.org/10.1007/978-3-031-13615-3_9

their body parts to get out of poverty and pay off microcredit loans. Amid this trading, a number of organ brokers have expanded their networks from local to national to international levels. Some medical specialists also benefit from this illegal exchange. The quoted price of a kidney is 100,000 Taka (US$1300); a liver lobe is 300,000 Taka (US$4000) in Bangladesh, where 50 million people live on less than US$1.25 a day (United Nations 2011).[1]

> I did not tell the story to anybody, not even to my wife. How could I? Selling a kidney is the most humiliating thing a person can do. You are the only person whom I trusted. It took enormous courage to come and talk with you. I was worried, however very relieved after sharing it with you—Nozrul, a 27-year-old kidney seller, following the interview.

In doing my ethnographic research on the illicit organ market, spanning more than a decade, I faced tremendous difficulties, particularly in gaining access to organ sellers, an extremely hidden population of Bangladesh (Moniruzzaman 2010, 2012, 2013, 2014a, 2014b). Many sellers did not disclose their actions to or even share their stories with their own family members, as selling body parts is considered an outlawed and repulsive act. In addition, sellers reside in every part of that country, so they are unknown to each other; as a result, I was unable to employ snowball sampling in locating them. When all avenues were exhausted, I gained the trust of Dalal, a major organ broker in Bangladesh, who helped me connect with 33 kidney sellers (30 males and 3 females) during my year-long fieldwork in 2004–2005. My new methodological grounding, that is, employing an organ broker to find organ sellers, raises major ethical challenges, however: Should Dalal be my key informant when he was involved in illegal activities and potentially exploiting others? To what extent should he be involved in my research? Why did he decide to support my research? Should I financially reimburse him for his support? In this chapter, I outline in detail how I gained access to 33 kidney sellers by employing an organ broker as my key informant. Relevant ethical issues, such as challenges and risks as well as roles and responsibilities of the researcher in conducting fieldwork on an illicit practice, will also be explored. As my research would not have been possible without the organ broker's support, I demonstrate that a key informant technique is beneficial in gaining access to hidden populations.

9.2 Fieldwork on Hidden Populations

Hidden populations are defined as groups of people who reside outside of mainstream society and who are often involved in clandestine activities (Watters and Biernacki 1989). Their activities frequently go unrecorded and remain concealed due to illegality. It is therefore challenging to contact and conduct research with hidden populations. Despite many difficulties, ethnographic

---

[1] All monetary values are presented in US dollars, as US$1 is equivalent to 75 Taka.

fieldwork has been carried out on these groups because they reveal a deeper understanding of outlawed but ordinary practices in our society. Several terminologies have been used to classify these groups, such as "underground," "subterranean," "informal," "clandestine," "concealed," "unofficial," "submerged" and, most commonly, "hidden."

Hidden populations can include drug users, unseen sex workers, homosexuals, carriers of infectious diseases (HIV/AIDS or tuberculosis), illegal migrants, alcoholics, school dropouts, unmarried pregnant teens, runaways, abused women and children, sexual abusers and paedophiles, street youths, gang members, criminals, and organ traffickers (Singer 1999). Among these hidden groups, some are more invisible than others. For example, organ traffickers are often more concealed than sex workers, and criminals are more concealed than alcoholics. Even within a particular hidden group, some subgroups are more hidden than others. For example, men who receive money for having sex with men are frequently more invisible than paid female prostitutes. The invisibility of hidden populations varies depending on the illegality, concealment, and stigmatization of their actions. Merrill Singer (1999) therefore points out four types of hidden populations: highly accessible, semi-hidden, hidden, and quite invisible in terms of research accessibility (p. 130). Each of these groups presents different challenges for researchers wishing to study hidden populations.

Ethnography—in particular "street ethnography"—is especially important in studying hidden populations (Weppner 1977). Ethnographers have unique tools to explore hidden populations as well as collect first-hand, insightful, and in-depth information through fieldwork. Ethnographers' natural inquisitiveness, wandering around, casual approach, techniques of rapport building, and grounded knowledge through participant observation as well as their long-standing fieldwork experience in noninstitutional settings offer a unique perspective to study hidden populations. As Singer (1999) notes,

> Ethnography takes the researcher out of the academia or institute suite and into the street (or other settings) where members of the target population live out their lives. Through rapport building, concern with the subject's point of view, and long-term presence in the field, ethnographers often are able to gain access to places, events, and information that might be hard for other methodologies to achieve. (p. 150)

Ethnographic fieldwork is imperative to explore the unseen lives of hidden populations.

One of the classic pieces of ethnographic fieldwork among hidden populations was carried out by William F. Whyte in 1937. In Street Corner Society, Whyte noted how a social worker in a local settlement house hooked him up with Doc, a street gang leader. After Whyte established rapport with Doc, Doc agreed to give Whyte access to his community. As a result, Whyte carried out interviews with the corner-boy gang as well as its members of a community of poor inner-city Italian immigrants who were otherwise unseen to those outside it (Whyte 1981). By a similar token, Philippe Bourgois gained trust of Primo, the manager of a crack house, and befriended street-level drug dealers, addicts, and thieves in order to study the crack culture in New York City's Spanish Harlem (Bourgois 1995). Thomas Ward approached his Salvadoran friends and acquaintances, who served as his initial inroads to the study of a street gang in Los Angeles, and arranged for him to meet active gang members, either in their homes or in local restaurants (Ward 2013). The common thread of these ethnographies is that a key informant, who is often a central figure of the outlawed groups, supported the researchers to gain access to hidden populations.

Laud Humphreys used a different, rather intrusive, approach that is often called "going native" to examine the sexual practices among homosexuals. In Tearoom Trade, Humphreys describes how he "hung out" in public washrooms and studied the men who were engaged in sex with other men. Unconventionally, Humphreys recorded the men's car license plate numbers and obtained their home addresses from the Department of Motor Vehicles. He visited their homes, introduced himself as a researcher, and obtained private data (Humphreys 1975). His ethnography was challenged as he "snooped around," "spied on," violated privacy and freedom, and took advantage of some powerless people to pursue his research (Hoffman 1975; Warwick 1975). In an even greater level of "going native," Ralph Bolton himself participated in casual sex with gay men to study their private sexual practices in bars, saunas, parks, streets, and private rooms in Brussels (Bolton 1992, 1995). Bolton's "sexual ethnography" is subject to serious criticism, as he used sex as a technique to diminish the distance between himself and his field subjects (Beusch 2007). These studies offer highly inaccessible data from different enclaves of hidden populations but raise serious ethical concerns to conducting underground fieldwork.

Since the mid-1990s, ethnographic studies on illicit organ trafficking have provided invaluable insights about methodological approaches to hidden populations. Nancy Scheper-Hughes (2004) addresses how she investigated covert and criminal networks of organ trafficking in various global settings. As she notes, the flow of organs follows the modern route of capital: from south to north, from Third to First World, from poor to rich, from black and brown to white, and from female to male (Scheper-Hughes 2000). To collect the data, Scheper-Hughes conducted "undercover" research in numerous sites—from the impoverished shantytowns of the Third World to the privileged and technologically sophisticated medical centres of the First World. Her multisited ethnography recruited graduate students, field assistants, human rights workers, private detectives, political journalists, documentary filmmakers, and "fixers," a class of paid research "intermediaries" long used in media reporting (Scheper-Hughes 2004, p. 32). Scheper-Hughes' research leads the way to map out global organ trafficking; however, it is subject to several criticisms. For example, in some field sites, she posed as a patient (or the relative of a patient) looking to purchase or otherwise broker a kidney (Interlandi 2009). Sometimes she visited transplant units and hospital wards, posting as a patient's friend or family member looking for another part of the hospital. At times, she introduced herself as Dr. Scheper-Hughes, while leaving it vague as to what kind of "doctor" she was (Scheper-Hughes 2004, p. 44). Her unorthodox approaches pose an ethical question: Should researchers conceal their identities and introduce themselves as potential end users to conduct "undercover fieldwork"? In addition, Scheper-Hughes collaborated with investigative reporters and documentary journalists, stating that she had no other option except to team up with them. I was unable to identify from her meagre description the procedures of recruiting respondents, such as sellers, buyers, dealers, and doctors (I assumed that it was done through fixers, but I did not find out about her transactions with fixers), how she approached her respondents to participate in interviews, and whether she faced any difficulties in dealing with friends and fixers (Scheper-Hughes 2004, pp. 42–43). Further, Scheper-Hughes noted that she reported some of her findings to criminal investigators from the U.S. Food and Drug Administration (FDA), the U.S. Attorney's Office in New York, Federal Bureau of Investigation (FBI) special agents, and the State Department's Visa Fraud Division. She stated, however, that she provided information only about the traffickers and surgeons and not about the people who had been trafficked. Neither was I able to identify how Scheper-Hughes guaranteed confidentiality, promised to protect identities, and obtained informed consent, nor was I certain whether she disclosed some of the organ recipients' names to government officials. Her research techniques raise another challenge: Should researchers report their respondents' actions and disclose their identities to law enforcement agencies if respondents are involved in an illegal activity? Furthermore, Scheper-Hughes noted paying a kidney seller US$20 for an interview (Scheper-Hughes 2004, p. 47); however, she did not disclose her payments, if any, to other participants, such as sellers, recipients, brokers, and doctors. As Scheper-Hughes herself noted that she was not fully comfortable with what she has taken on—not to mention the fact that her methods make some of her colleagues uneasy (Scheper-Hughes 2004, p. 41)—I did not follow her approaches to an "undercover ethnography" but rather focused on ethically grounded and methodologically sound fieldwork on domestic organ trafficking, particularly on kidney sellers of Bangladesh.

As there was no formal set of procedures to follow and the methods of hidden populations were problematic, limited, and unclear, I could not formulate a codified approach to organ trafficking before going into the field. Based on preliminary field trips in Dhaka, the capital of Bangladesh, I gathered that it would be extremely difficult to gain access to organ sellers and conduct fieldwork in the black market of human organs. Yet, I was able to interview 33 kidney sellers who had already sold their body parts and whose surgeries had been performed within and outside of Bangladesh. In the following section, I outline my means and methods of finding kidney sellers during my year-long fieldwork in Bangladesh. My ethnographic fieldwork exemplifies how I advanced and applied an ethical but effective approach to studying the hidden populations.

9.3 In Search of Kidney Sellers

Access to kidney sellers was the most arduous task in undertaking this research. In the first three months of a year-long fieldwork, all of my initial attempts were in vain. The turning point of my research occurred when I met a transplant recipient and he connected me with his kidney seller. Following this interview, I was unsuccessful in finding any other organ sellers for a while. After trying all feasible means, I finally employed an organ broker as a key informant and a kidney seller as a research assistant. With their support, I located, contacted, and interviewed a total of 33 kidney sellers in Bangladesh.

Going Nowhere

At the beginning of my fieldwork, I asked a range of local Bangladeshis for advice on finding organ sellers. Suggestions included contacting doctors, recipients, newspaper advertisers, lawyers, and slum dwellers, some of whom might be able to locate kidney sellers. However, all of these approaches turned out to be unsuccessful. First, I attempted to search kidney sellers through local health professionals affiliated with major transplant centres in Bangladesh. In October 2004, I attended a conference titled "The End State Renal Disease: A Global Issue," held in a hotel in Dhaka. In this meeting, local nephrologists and urologists repeatedly claimed that the lack of infrastructure hinders the establishment of a successful kidney transplant program in Bangladesh. They highlighted that kidney transplants from commercial donors/unrelated sellers are performed in other countries, but not in Bangladesh.

Through connections I made at the conference, I then met with the chief nephrologist working in a leading transplant hospital of Bangladesh. When I asked him if he could help me to connect with kidney sellers, he handed me a copy of the Organ Transplant Act which stated that trading kidneys is "strictly illegal" and noted that transplants from non-family members are not operated in Bangladesh. At the end of our meeting, I sought his permission to conduct interviews in his hospital. After several bureaucratic encounters, I finally obtained his verbal consent to carry out my research there. However, the permission did not ensure my access to nephrologists, urologists, and postgraduate trainees performing transplants in that hospital. In most cases, transplant specialists' lack of availability was attributed to their busy schedule, aloofness, and attitude. During brief encounters, they typically denied the existence of illegal organ transplant in Bangladesh. Surprisingly, I then noticed two posted advertisements for kidney sales in the hallway of the hospital (one ad was on a wall next to the elevator, and the other was in the doctors' seminar room) (Fig. 9.1).[2]

---

[2] During the fieldwork, several advertisements for selling kidneys were posted in this hospital. All of the advertisements were soon removed because of my physical presence.

9 AT THE ORGAN BAZAAR OF BANGLADESH: IN SEARCH OF KIDNEY SELLERS   145

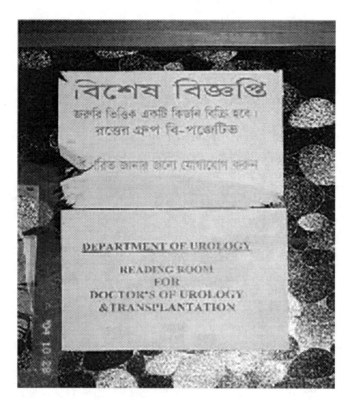

Fig. 9.1 Advertisement for selling kidneys posted on the entrance door of the doctors' seminar room in a leading transplant hospital in Dhaka, October 28, 2004. (Translation: *SPECIAL ANNOUNCE-MENT One kidney will be sold urgently. Blood group B+ . Contact me to discuss in detail. Tel:*)

The transplant specialists explained to me that kidney classifieds are periodically posted in Bangladesh but all unrelated (and therefore illegal) transplants are performed outside the country. A nephrologist added that many of his clients were transplant recipients who had purchased kidneys from local Bangladeshis, travelled to India for transplants, and then returned to Bangladesh for postoperative care. I asked him if he could put me in touch with some of these recipients, but no meetings ever materialized. I suspected that the doctors were reluctant to discuss organ trafficking with an outside researcher due to its illegality.

Second, I approached transplant recipients, whose operations were performed both in Bangladesh and India, in attempts to find kidney sellers. I interviewed a few recipients who had been admitted to that hospital for postoperative complications. These recipients typically discussed the inadequate organ infrastructure, poor health-care services, the high cost of surgery, and postoperative complexities involved in organ transplants in Bangladesh. When asked where the kidney came from, recipients claimed to have obtained kidneys from family members yet often avoided revealing the donors' identities. After I gained the trust of one particular recipient, he disclosed that he had purchased the kidney from a college student, but did not reveal the seller's identity. I also contacted some would-be recipients who were in the process of arranging transplants. The potential recipients similarly stated that they would be receiving kidneys from family members. One patient and her donor seemed unrelated to me, but both of them claimed to be close relatives by showing me an official certificate of their kinship. All of my attempts to locate kidney sellers through doctors and recipients thus failed.

Third, I searched organ classifieds published regularly in Bengali national newspapers to locate kidney sellers.[3] As I had previously experienced, recipients were not interested in connecting me with their donors/sellers; therefore, I focused solely on the sellers' ads. From these collected ads, I attempted to contact several sellers through their telephone numbers. However, only six phone numbers were in service, and I was unable to communicate with any of them. In one instance, a sister of the potential seller told me that her brother had not been in touch with the family for the last two months; I assumed that the seller went to India for the surgery. In other cases, the people did not answer my phone calls, or the phone service had been switched to a new customer.

Fourth, I contacted journalists and lawyers who specialized in medical crime. This process did not prove successful in obtaining any useful information for finding kidney sellers. One lawyer referred to newspaper coverage that reported that Bangladeshi children are smuggled to other countries for organ harvesting (Khayer and Badal 2004). However, he could not validate the claim, and the newspaper coverage seemed sensationalistic.

Lastly, I thought that slum dwellers and drug addicts could have been involved in selling kidneys, but I chose not to contact them. I realized that finding kidney sellers within this very broad group would be greatly challenging and time consuming. Indeed, it was frustrating not to be able to locate a kidney seller in three months despite my efforts to follow the leads I had been given.

The Turning Point

The turning point in my fieldwork came when a fellow anthropologist introduced me to Kamal Chowdhury, a transplant recipient. With his support, I was able to interview Manik Miah, his vendor.[4] Kamal is a 43-year-old university professor who had bought a kidney from Manik, a 32-year-old slum dweller,

---

[3] So far, I have collected 1288 organ classifieds published in five national Bengali newspapers between 2000 and 2008.

[4] To conceal the respondents' identities, all names used in this text are pseudonyms. I am also careful to avoid describing the personal information, interview details, and any other factors that could reveal their identities.

who had to sell his kidney to repay his debts. Their operations were performed in a renowned and luxurious hospital in India in January 2004. After the operation, Kamal flew to Australia to obtain better organ care, and Manik travelled back to Dhaka to pay off his debt.

Kamal agreed to facilitate my research largely because he himself was a researcher and had strong opinions on his life-saving medical procedure. In our first meeting, which lasted over 3 h, Kamal discussed the inadequacies of kidney transplant infrastructure and the poor health-care service in Bangladesh. He compared it with his transplant experience in India and postoperative care in Australia. We met again in a coffee shop the next week. In the 7 h that followed, Kamal described how he began his search for a kidney by posting ads in three major Bengali newspapers. He received phone calls from about 90 potential sellers. Based on blood group and initial screening, he selected 30 sellers for a tissue-typing test. Only six were then selected, based on the matching tissues. As tissue typing is often erroneous in Bangladesh, Kamal invited these six sellers to a major diagnostic centre in India, where the tissue-typing results were re-examined and verified yet again.[5] Kamal finally selected Manik Miah as their tissues matched closely, and Manik had asked for less money for his kidney than the other sellers had.[6] On the basis of this single encounter, I was able to gain access to a kidney seller, as Kamal connected me with Manik. Manik wished to discuss the issue in a concealed setting, so we chose to carry out the interview in my apartment in Dhaka. In a conversation lasting over 8 h, Manik revealed his experiences of selling his kidney. He emphasized that finding a buyer is the most difficult job for a kidney seller as the tissues seldom match. Manik sought a buyer for over eight months, competed with other sellers, and finally managed to sell his kidney. He received 120,000 Taka (US$1700) for the kidney, plus 15,000 Taka (US$111) for three months of living expenses. He spent most of the money to pay off his debt, which was compounded due to high interest rates. He also managed to purchase a television and some clothing for his family. When the money nearly ran out, Manik started a clerical job in a medical college at a monthly salary of 3500 Taka (US$50), which was arranged by Kamal. Unfortunately, he lost his job within a year and became a cell phone vendor, earning as little as 1500 Taka (US$22) per month. Currently, Manik is living without debt but with only one kidney.

Since I was eager to find additional informants, I tried to approach other kidney sellers by applying a snowball-sampling method through Manik, but this approach did not prove to be productive. The sellers usually tried to conceal their identities if they ever met with each other. I also asked the recipient

---

[5] Kamal, as did other recipients, noted to me that the human leukocyte antigen (HLA) test and other medical diagnostic tests are often inaccurate in Bangladesh. The recipients would have all preferred to re-examine the result of the HLA test in India but could not afford the travel expenses.
[6] Kamal told me that his tissue was matched as nearly perfect with that of Johra, another potential seller. However, he noted that Johra was "greedy" because she asked for three times more money for her kidney. It was difficult for Kamal to select Manik over Johra, but he opted for "needy" over "greedy," as he stated.

Kamal about the other sellers who contacted him through his newspaper ads. Unfortunately, Kamal no longer had that information, and many sellers did not disclose their identities. Kamal noted that the only way I could find kidney sellers was through organ brokers, who were connected with the sellers like a spiderweb. Kamal offered me the telephone numbers of four major organ brokers in Bangladesh. Of them, I was able to establish rapport with Dalal, who had delivered three prospective sellers to Kamal before his transplant.

A Novel Approach

While a key informant technique can be effective in gaining access to a hidden population, it can also be ethically and methodologically problematic. For example, searching kidney sellers through an organ broker posed several challenges: To what extent should Dalal participate as a key informant? How should he be approached, persuaded, and compensated? Why would he support research that might reveal, restrict or ruin his illicit business? After exhausting all the avenues to finding kidney sellers and even considering changing my research focus, I decided to approach Dalal and explore the possibilities of finding organ sellers, as Whyte had done through Doc, a street gang leader.

Over the phone, I told Dalal that I was a Bangladeshi citizen currently residing in Canada. At that point, I did not mention my research to Dalal, as my previous experiences had taught me that he might not be interested in discussing this illegal business with a researcher. Instead, I stated that I wanted to meet him in person to discuss kidney transplants in Bangladesh. Dalal asked me how I had obtained his phone number; I told him that I had received it from his client, the transplant recipient Kamal. Dalal wrote down my residence address and said he would visit my apartment when he was in my neighbourhood. One late morning, Dalal phoned me and knocked on my door. In our first brief meeting, I openly introduced myself, informed Dalal about my research and its progress since its inception, and asked for his support to find organ sellers. Dalal confirmed that he was connected with numerous kidney sellers but chose to ponder the entire issue and notify me of his decision later.

Both my insider and outsider insights influenced the dealings with Dalal. My familiarity with the local culture aided me in determining my initial approach while my fluency in Bengali provided an easy medium for sharing our thoughts without any confusion. My identity as halfy (half-Bangladeshi, half-Canadian; see Abu-Lughod 1991) and the distinctiveness as bedeshi (foreigner) of my partner, who accompanied me in the fieldwork, played an essential role in acquiring his trust. My personal connection and professional affiliation as a university professor in Bangladesh reassured Dalal that I was not an undercover police officer or journalist, but a "harmless" researcher. As Dalal and I were born in the same region of Bangladesh, our local ties may also have influenced his support for the research.

Dalal agreed to support the research when I contacted him a week later. But the question remains: Why did he do so? It may have been that his broker business is secure, as his clients were senior state officials, political leaders, police officers, and lawyers who could help him resolve any potential legal troubles. He may also have thought that my research would help to expand his business outside of Bangladesh as he often insisted on including his name and photo in my publications. I refused his requests, pointing out the potential legal and ethical risks involved. Dalal also assumed that he would receive lofty monetary benefits, but after bargaining, I agreed to reimburse him 500 Taka (about US$7) for his transportation and communication costs to locate each seller. As Dalal explained to me that he would need to travel to other places and make phone calls to contact the sellers, I decided to compensate these reasonable expenses considering that the payment would not create undue pressure on him to take part in the study. However, I was in constant negotiation with Dalal as he contacted the sellers in Dhaka but fabricated stories about their origins to exaggerate his transportation costs.

Dalal entered the organ market as a kidney seller after losing his job in the mid-1990s. He came to know about kidney vending through newspaper advertisements. He collected several organ classifieds and contacted the advertisers, all of whom were potential recipients. They examined his tissue-typing tests; after several attempts, he managed to match his tissues with a recipient. Eventually, Dalal and the recipient travelled to a private hospital in southern India for the surgery. As the recipient declined to pay him before the operation, Dalal returned to Bangladesh without selling his kidney. Within a month of visiting the Indian hospital, Dalal met other Bangladeshi recipients and sellers who also flocked there for kidney transplants. He realized that if he could start an organ-brokering business by collecting tissue-typing reports from them, it would be "handy for everybody," as he expressed it. Dalal approached Bangladeshi organ recipients in the hospital and shared his idea. With their support, Dalal commenced his business after returning to Bangladesh. In less than five months, he was able to match the tissues of his first client, and the operation was successfully performed in India. Dalal claimed that he received 10,000 Taka (US$143) from the recipient and did not ask for any money from the seller, which became a typical "business policy" he continued to follow. At the time of my interview, Dalal said he had collected more than 500 tissue-typing reports from both recipients and sellers and had arranged 97 transplants that were performed in Bangladesh and abroad.

The meeting that followed with Dalal seeded my research to explore this extremely hidden population in Bangladesh. Dalal and I outlined three possible approaches to connecting with kidney sellers: first, phoning the sellers who were still in touch with Dalal; second, visiting the sellers whose dwelling addresses were available to Dalal; and third, contacting Dalal's recipient-clients, some of whom could still be maintaining the relationship with their sellers. We both agreed that Dalal should approach the kidney sellers as sellers might not disclose their activities to an unknown researcher.

Dalal immediately made arrangements for me to meet Shamsu, a 30-year-old kidney seller who lived in Natore, a north-western town in Bangladesh.

Shamsu had sold his kidney to a Bangladeshi-born American citizen living in New York. The operation was performed in southern India in July 2003. With the support of Dalal, I had interviewed four more kidney sellers within a month. All of them were male, and their ages ranged from 27 to 41 years. Their professions varied, from barbers to street vendors to commercial artists. All of their recipients resided in Bangladesh, except a female Bangladeshi migrant, who was living in Italy. Of these cases, three transplants were performed in India, and the remaining one was in Bangladesh.

A New Lead

My fieldwork faced challenges when Dalal decided to go on a business trip to India for two months.[7] Due to time constraints and financial concerns, I asked Dalal to provide me with some kidney sellers' contact information. After persistent attempts, I collected nearly 30 sellers' and recipients' contact addresses and phone numbers from him. Dalal demanded a payment for providing me with the leads, but I refused to pay, stating that my ethical consideration regarding his payment was limited to reimbursing his expenses for locating each seller: for example, transportation and communication costs. I explained to him that I was not authorized to pay finders' fees.

Soon after, I realized that Dalal had provided me with sellers who were difficult to reach. At first, I attempted to contact the sellers through their telephone numbers. Unfortunately, many of these were no longer in service. I was successful in locating one seller and scheduled an interview with him. However, this seller did not meet with me, despite several attempts on my part to reschedule our meeting by phone. In addition, I found out that some of the addresses that Dalal had given me were incomplete or incorrect. Some sellers resided in remote parts of Bangladesh, but I could not go to them in person, as transportation was extremely inaccessible there. However, I contacted several recipients from Dalal's list over the phone. These recipients expressed concern about my phone calls and asked how I had obtained their contact numbers. Using Dalal's name as a reference did not help them to trust me.

I was stuck again. I reviewed Dalal's list and saw that I could successfully contact several sellers through their residence addresses, including some of those who were remotely located. However, I realized that if I approached them directly, I might not instil full trust and gain access to their hidden lives. It was only then that I realized that a kidney seller might establish trust between the sellers and recipients and me.

After careful thought, I contacted Shamsu (the first interviewed seller through Dalal) and employed him as a research assistant. Shamsu had extensive knowledge of the kidney trade as he had travelled to India twice: once to sell his kidney and once to accompany his brother who was attempting to sell his

---

[7] On average, Dalal travelled to India twice a year with his recipient-clients, who paid for his transportation, accommodation, and compensation for arranging kidney transplants in India.

kidney. Shamsu and I discussed ethical protocols, upcoming tasks, and the payment of 1500 Taka (US$20) for locating each seller as he had to travel to distant places, stay in hotels, and spend money on a cell phone.

Based on Dalal's list, Shamsu and I deduced that most sellers lived in the northern part of Bangladesh. To locate sellers, Shamsu agreed to travel to Natore, Dinajpur, Rajshahi, Ishwardi, and Mymensingh, some northern towns (see Fig. 9.2). When Shamsu met sellers at their homes, he usually invited them to go to a tea stall and a vacant property afterwards. At first, Shamsu identified himself as a kidney seller, then introduced my research to them, and finally

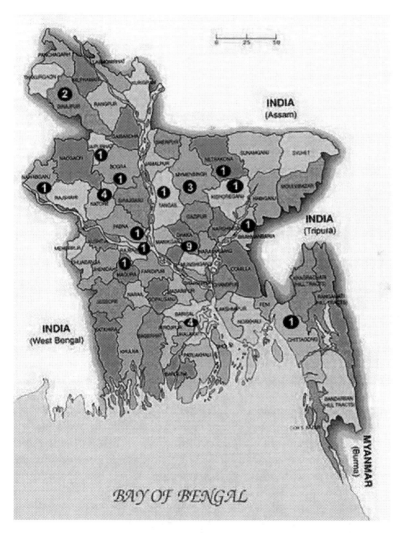

Fig. 9.2 Interviewed sellers on the map of Bangladesh. The numbers represent their regional locations. (Map source: www.dcdhaka.gov.bd/bangladesh_map.jpg)

asked for an interview. He gained most of the sellers' trust simply because he was a seller as well; they were able to share their sorrows, sufferings, and scars. At the end, Shamsu called me from his cell phone, and I talked with each seller in detail. I explained to them the research project, informed them of the ethical principles, obtained their consent and scheduled their interview. Only one seller refused to meet with me, while another seller set up an interview but did not show up. Following my instructions, Shamsu also contacted several transplant recipients residing in Dhaka, but they did not reveal their sellers' identities. Only one recipient agreed to introduce his seller. He later approached me and I successfully interviewed the seller.

With the support of Shamsu, I entered into the lives of seven more kidney sellers in the next two months. Of them, only one was female: a 37-year-old divorced woman, who was living with her two children and selling fruit on the streets of Mymensingh. The other six sellers were all males, aged between 25 and 42 years and had diverse occupational backgrounds, from farmers and butchers to day labourers.

The Final Cut

After interviews with 13 kidney sellers so far, I discovered that a man named Batpar Azam was the key broker operating the organ trafficking networks in Bangladesh. Many sellers went to Batpar and concurrently kept in touch with Dalal to maximize their chances of matching tissues with potential buyers. I obtained Batpar's telephone number from an interviewed seller, who warned me that Batpar was a dangerous thug who would do anything to protect his business. My connection with the local elite and familiarity with the culture, however, led me to believe that Dhaka was a safe place for me, so I decided to pursue my goal. In February 2005, I called Batpar and said that I would like to meet with him instead of talking over the phone in order to discuss kidney transplants. Batpar proposed an evening meeting, but I changed it to early afternoon to minimize my risks in dealing with this kingpin in his private office, located in a dilapidated building in old Dhaka.

Conducting fieldwork in a black market can be risky and challenging. I still remember that afternoon, walking through dark alleys in old Dhaka to meet with Batpar. My bedeshi partner accompanied me, as meeting with Batpar could risk my life. I also informed a friend about the meeting location and time and asked him to call the police if we did not return by that evening. When we arrived at Batpar's office, we noticed that the solid door was closed and that no sign was posted on it. I called his cell phone, and a man opened the door and showed us the way to the boss' personal room. Batpar was sitting on a black leather chair and encircled by three bodyguards and four ordinary men, who were most likely organ sellers. His office assistant served us tea, as Batpar was busy with his clients on the phone. When Batpar finally greeted us, I introduced us at length; I told him that I was neither a journalist nor an undercover police officer hiding my identity in an attempt to reveal his business. After guaranteeing confidentiality, I explained my research project and sought his support in search of organ sellers. With a cold face and calm voice, Batpar looked straight at me and asked: Who had informed you that I could be involved in such a nasty business? He utterly denied his organ brokering and warned us that we were playing with fire. As we did not have any power to challenge him, I naively thought that he might be cautious about discussing his business in front of other people, so I hastily handed him my address and phone number, hoping that he would help me at a later time. After leaving the office, we felt relieved to return to lively Dhaka.

Batpar never contacted me. I quickly realized that it was an inept mistake to give Batpar my residential address. On numerous occasions, I noticed that someone was following me in my neighbourhood; I was frightened by possible attacks by Batpar and constantly looked behind me. Sometimes I walked faster towards a crowd, sometimes I entered a store, while at other times I avoided going out at night. Yet, I did not report my risks to local police as they were widely known for corruption and could have created bureaucratic obstacles to my research. Despite this threat to my safety, I still wished to interview Batpar's clients in order to obtain deeper insights about organ-trafficking networks in Bangladesh. I asked both Shamsu and Dalal about the possibility of interviewing Batpar's clients in confidence.

Often, sellers did not receive the full payment from Batpar, so I learned (from Shamsu and Dalal) that if we were able to find them, they would be willing to share their experiences with me. I decided to strictly protect these sellers' identities, so they would not face danger from Batpar. Shamsu had met a few sellers who had sold their kidneys through Batpar during his transplant in India, while Dalal had come across some of Batpar's clients for brokering business, but neither of them had contact addresses for the sellers in question. Based on Dalal's advice, Shamsu tried to contact one of Batpar's clients in Dhaka. After several attempts, Shamsu was successful, but the man refused to discuss his selling experience with a researcher. It was a long time before I met some of the sellers who had sold their kidneys through Batpar.

Dalal had already arrived back in town by then. He arranged for me to meet with nine more kidney sellers, all of whom were his clients. All the sellers interviewed were men who lived in various parts of Bangladesh, including Dhaka, Barisal, Khulna, Bagerhat, and Rajbari districts. Six sellers went to India for the surgery, while three had the surgery performed in a prominent hospital in Dhaka. Dalal was disappointed with the amount of his reimbursement, so I agreed to raise it from 500 Taka (US$7) to 750 Taka (US$10). I considered this amount to be acceptable and appropriate to local standards, and so Dalal's travel and phone expenses, as well as his time and inconvenience, were compensated.

The research gained momentum when Shamsu bumped into Sodrul, a 22-year-old college student who had sold his kidney through Batpar. When I received Sham-su's phone call, I met with Sodrul right away in front of the Dhaka public library. The three of us sat down in a busy tea stall; I explained my research to Sodrul, guaranteed his anonymity (of course to Batpar), and convinced him to meet again for a detailed interview. I scheduled Sodrul's interview in my apartment in order to ensure our safety and to respect confidentiality. In an interview lasting over 9 h, Sodrul revealed how Batpar, a predatory organ broker, profoundly exploited the kidney sellers. Batpar usually transported four or five sellers at a time to India, where they lived in a bachelor apartment, which he continually rented for that purpose. Batpar charged the kidney recipients up to 700,000 Taka (US$10,000) and paid the poor sellers as little as 50,000 Taka (US$700). Like many other sellers, Sodrul failed to collect his entire payment from Batpar. The poor sellers never attempted to challenge Batpar as he was a rich businessman and well connected with the powerful class of kidney buyers. Sodrul mentioned to me that he might have contact information for some kidney sellers who went to India with him. He promised to connect me with these sellers, but he never picked up my phone calls afterwards. Perhaps Sodrul was afraid to play with Batpar's business.

My research was advancing when Dalal hooked me up with a 48-year-old transplant recipient who had purchased a kidney through Batpar. During the interview, the recipient stated that he was still connected with his seller, Dildar, a 32-year-old rickshaw puller from Bhairab Bazar in the central part of Bangladesh. When the seller Dildar visited his recipient in Dhaka, he phoned me; I promised to protect his identity and convinced him to proceed with an interview in my apartment. During the interview, Dildar described in depth the process and experience of selling a kidney through Batpar. Dildar was still angry, as he did not receive full payment from Batpar, even after he phoned the broker 30 times and visited his office nearly 10 times. Dildar and Sodrul, who had sold their kidneys through Batpar, told similar stories. Auspiciously, Dildar provided me with the contact address of the four other kidney sellers with whom he stayed in Batpar's apartment in India. I arranged interviews with three of these sellers shortly afterwards; the snowball-sampling method was successful, and phone calls were effective for these cases. Upon guaranteeing confidentiality and anonymity, these sellers and I met in my apartment and discussed the murky business of Batpar and documented the exploitative nature of the kidney trafficking of Bangladesh.

I wished to interview other sellers, but my fieldwork was close to an end. After several failed attempts, I managed to locate and interview two female kidney sellers, Hena Begum and Nergis Begum, two sisters-in-law who lived in Pirozpur, a southern town in Bangladesh. They disclosed that their husbands had asked them to sell their kidneys; after snatching their wives' kidney payments, the men started businesses and bought cell phones for themselves. I also interviewed three more kidney sellers, whose surgeries were performed in Pakistan (both recipient and seller were Bangladeshis, but the surgery was performed in Pakistan), Singapore (the recipient was a Bangladeshi-born US resident living in New York, the seller was from Bangladesh, and the surgery was performed in a prestigious hospital in Singapore), and Thailand (both the recipient and seller were from Bangladesh, but the surgery was performed in a renowned hospital in Thailand). During these interviews, one seller stated that he initially went to India for the surgery, but his recipient died before the surgery, so the seller matched his tissues with a new recipient and the surgery was performed in Thailand. These sellers revealed how their recipients evaded the legal system, passed the hospital committee verification, and engaged in transplant tourism in various transnational places. Finally, I interviewed another seller who sold his kidney directly to the recipient through newspaper ads; no broker mediated the trade. I was privileged to document the extremely inaccessible data, rich narratives, medical records, legal papers, and graphic images from 33 kidney sellers in Bangladesh.

9.4 Conclusion: Reflections

Following the late Pierre Bourdieu's call for "an engaged and militant intellectual," Nancy Scheper-Hughes has embraced a dual vision of anthropology as a disciplinary field, a traditional field of study, and a forced field—a site of political struggle and resistance (Scheper-Hughes 1992, 1995, 2004). Scheper-Hughes' moral reflexivity towards an engaged anthropology is grounded in epistemologically challenged and politically committed engagement that "stands-on-its-own-feet." To achieve such clarity, Scheper-Hughes departed from traditional anthropological discourse: She deliberately "loosened up" her methodological techniques, collaborated with several journalists and fixers, reported some of her findings to law enforcement agencies, and released names and photos of her respondents in publications. While I strongly support Scheper-Hughes' call for a "militant anthropology," I somewhat differ from her methods of multisited ethnography, undercover fieldwork, and loyalties to research subjects. My argument is that ethnographers should be truthful to their interview subjects, minimize their risks, and commit to the change by relentlessly exposing exploitation without revealing their identities. This not only crystallizes the ethical integrity of engaged ethnographers but also upholds professional responsibility, unlike to journalistic reporting, which is often labelled as "quick and dirty research."

Scheper-Hughes explores a multisited ethnography to map out global organ trafficking, while I delve into the domestic organ trade and its actors, processes, and experiences that intersect in the local, transnational, and global setting. The quintessence of Scheper-Hughes' multisited ethnography was "to follow the bodies"—what George Marcus formerly described as "follow the things" (Marcus 1995). One of the critiques of this approach is that following things leads followers away from the unique perspectives of the locals, who experience things removed from particular cultures (see the sapphire trade in Madagascar; Walsh 2004). I therefore contextualize the assemblages of the transplant economy, local processes of organ trade, and cultural meanings of damaged bodies rather than capturing fleeting glimpses of transplant tourism from a large number of global settings.

Unlike Scheper-Hughes' "undercover ethnography," I did not pose as an organ buyer to quickly gain access to transplant traffickers, but rather I upheld ethical integrity, promoted methodological innovation, and minimized my respondents' risks, amid facing serious challenges to locating kidney sellers in Bangladesh. Throughout my field notes, transcripts, and publications, I used pseudonyms and released photographs of my respondents without revealing their faces in order to protect their identities and minimize any harm to them (unlike Scheper-Hughes and mainstream media reports). I did not report my research findings to a law enforcement authority, and if the local police were ever to ask me to unmask my respondents, I decided to fulfil my ethical obligations to protect their anonymity. Of note, the Bangladeshi police busted an organ racket in 2011, and major brokers (including Batpar and Dalal) were arrested immediately; however, a local journalist, not I, served as the whistleblower. In my fieldwork, I was truthful to the participants, outlined my research objectives completely, and obtained proper informed consent. When some participants presumed that they would receive financial benefits from me, I clarified that there is no direct benefit for their involvement (except the reimbursement of travel expenses and work hours) and then asked for their voluntary participation in the study. The respondents willingly participated in my research because they wished to expose the violence, exploitation, and suffering incurred in this unethical trade. Some sellers were relieved to share their stories with me as they could not reveal it to anyone, not even to their own families, as selling body parts is considered an unethical and outlawed practice (as expressed by seller Nozrul, quoted at the beginning of this chapter).

Scheper-Hughes advanced a radical approach by endorsing that we ought to expose gross exploitation by any means, even if it evades professional ethical standards. Such a moral position raises thorny ethical challenges, such as the following: In the process of seeking justice, should researchers report their respondents' illicit acts to law enforcement agencies while the respondents are not informed that their participation could bring harm to themselves or others? Do the perceived benefits of legal intervention outweigh harms to the study populations, researchers' obligation against sham practices, and an emergence of overall mistrust towards the professions? While a number of anthropologists faced serious challenges to study hidden populations, they were truthful and loyal to their study subjects (see Nordstrom and Robben 1995; Green 1995; Bourgois 2003). Scheper-Hughes' large-scale research indeed brings justice to the world, but it has been criticized for breaching privacy, withholding information, and imposing harm on the subjects (see Schrag 2010; Gledhill 2000).

Scheper-Hughes felt the urgency to research, reveal, and report her data to a broadly concerned public as quickly as possible so that measures could be taken to curb gross human rights violations and correct abuses that undermine transplant medicine as a humane practice (Scheper-Hughes 2004, p. 42). However, one may extend similar reasoning to a range of other extraneous situations. For example, when researchers carry out clinical trials with trivial deception, they may consider that they promoted it for the sake of humanity, as the new drug could save million lives (Elliott and Abadie 2008); or when medical students perform pelvic examinations on anaesthetized patients, they may justify that it has been practiced for professional benefits, without any harm done to the patients (Wall and Brown 2004); or if physicians exaggerate the severity of their patients' conditions to insurance companies, they may argue that they play (if game) the system to ensure medical treatments for poor patients (Bloche 2000). Such reasons often exist for short-term or personal gain; however, dodging a system has damaging impacts on the profession and on the public, in the long term. They also shadow the distinction between institutional regulations of research versus self-governing modalities of practice. So too, they beg a question: To what extent can an ethnographer breach standard practices of ethical enforcement and professional tenets in the struggle to do fieldwork in underground settings?

In this chapter, I illustrated how a researcher can conduct challenging fieldwork without compromising his or her ethical integrity and professional responsibility.

As ethnographic fieldwork on illicit practices, particularly on organ markets, has its own problems and perils, the pivotal issue the researcher faces is how to gain access to and conduct fieldwork with hidden populations. I therefore described in detail my approaches to locating, contacting, and interviewing 33 kidney sellers—an extremely hidden population of Bangladesh. When all of my conventional means and methods (i.e. snowball sampling) of finding kidney sellers were barred, I appointed a broker as my key informant and a seller as my research assistant, and with their indispensable support, I successfully interviewed the invisible vendors from various parts of Bangladesh. As my collaboration with an organ broker could be ethically problematic, especially when he was involved in illicit activities and was potentially exploiting others, I embodied a fine balance between efficacy and ethics as well as delays and dangers, in conducting fieldwork in a black market. My ethical neutrality and negotiation, along with my identity and familiarity with local culture, aided me in gaining the key informants' trust and collaboration. I embraced the view that ethical integrity, professional transparency, and long-term involvement are essential for building rapports with research participants, retaining their friendship, and accessing their hidden lives in order to gather rich, reliable, and retrospect narratives from the field.

Although my ethnographic research stemmed from various methods, open-ended interviews remained the key methods for collecting data. As sellers resided in every part of Bangladesh and often asked for a confidential place to meet, I arranged their interviews in my apartment in Dhaka. On average, the sellers travelled 7 h to visit me; I met them at the bus or train station, invited them to my apartment, and shared meals with them. Each interview lasted about 10 h, starting in the morning and ending in the evening. At the beginning of my interview, I outlined to them the ethical guidelines of the Ethics Review Board at the University of Toronto, explained the nature and scope of my research, guaranteed strict confidentiality, ensured that they could withdraw their participation at any time, discussed their reimbursement, and obtained their voluntary consent. At the end of the interview, I accompanied the sellers to the bus or train station and compensated them with one day's salary plus their transportation cost, which ranged between 750 Taka (US$10) and 1000 Taka (US$15). I tried to record their interview using an audiotape, but I realized that the seller was uncomfortable with this (i.e. he was not spontaneous about recording his illicit action on tape), so I handwrote all the interviews, which constitute about 1500 pages of field notes.

Unstructured, narrative-based interviews allowed me to establish a casual relationship with kidney sellers and gave them the opportunity to talk. My responsibility was to guide the conversation according to the purpose of the study. I developed an informal way of exchanging ideas followed by a thematic arrangement of their interviews. First, I enquired about the socioeconomic conditions of the sellers, such as name, age, education, occupation, income, religion, and family composition, to initiate conversation and generate a preliminary rapport with them. Second, I focused on the processes of selling kidneys, such as when they became aware of kidney selling, why and how they sold their kidneys, and what are the health, social, and economic ramifications of selling a kidney. Third, I expanded the critical issues of organ commerce, such as who benefits from the organ trade, what roles the government should play to curb this practice, and whether a market of human organs should be regulated or banned. The thematic interviews aided me in generating preliminary rapport with the sellers, gathering deeply moving narratives from them, and exploring their critical understanding of organ commerce in Bangladesh.

My fieldwork not only recruited 33 kidney sellers but also included other research subjects, such as organ brokers, transplant recipients (and their families), medical specialists, state officials, political leaders, police officers, legal advisors, social workers, media reporters, documentary filmmakers, university researchers, Kidney Patient Welfare Association advisors, and Bangladesh Private Body Donation advocates, who shed light on organ trafficking during their interviews. I also used the participant observation method to collect in-depth data from them, while I spent time in transplant units, as doctors were on rounds, nurses were on duty, patients were prepared for surgery, family members were preparing meals in the kitchen or photocopying false documents in nearby stores, and brokers promised would-be recipients to find sellers. I also used case study methods by closely following three transplant surgeries (both recipients and sellers were interviewed and cross-checked in depth) to gain insights into organ trafficking in Bangladesh. In addition, I collected 1288 organ classifieds published in five national Bengali newspapers between 2000 and 2008. I also gathered other supporting documents, such as forged passports, notary certificates, medical reports, written agreements, bodily photos, personal notes, and Bengali publications to enrich my data.

One of the major drawbacks of my fieldwork was that I could not use the participant observation method to document the processes of selling kidneys, but rather collected interview narratives from kidney sellers to examine the organ trade. My fieldwork is also limited in terms of gender representation, as I interviewed 30 male kidney sellers, but only 3 females; as a man in the predominantly Muslim society and facing challenges for finding kidney sellers, I was certainly fortunate to interview this handful of female sellers. Despite these limitations, the account of my fieldwork is noteworthy in how it expands, examines, and compares ethnographic approaches to hidden populations. As I proved, the key informant technique could be ethically appropriate and methodologically effective in gaining access to hidden populations.

References

Abu-Lughod, L. (1991). Writing against culture. In R. Fox (Ed.), *Recapturing anthropology* (pp. 137–62). Santa Fe: School of American Research Press.

Bangladesh Gazette. (1999). *Transplantation of human body parts act (In Bengali, Manobdehe Anga-Protongo Shongjojoner Bidhar Korar Uddeshe Pronito Ayen) Additional volume*. Dhaka: The Parliament of Bangladesh.

Beusch, D. (2007). Textual interaction as sexual interaction: Sexuality and/in the online interview. *Sociological Research Online, 12*(5), 1–14. www.socresonline.org.uk/12/5/14.html. Accessed 3 Aug 2015.

Bloche, G. (2000). Fidelity and deceit at the bedside. *Journal of American Medical Association, 283*, 1881–1884.

Bolton, R. (1992). Mapping terra incognita: Sex research for AIDS prevention—an urgent agenda for the 1990's. In G. Herdt, & S. Lindenbaum (Eds.), *The time of AIDS: Social analysis, theory, and method* (pp. 124–58). Newbury Park: Sage Publications.

Bolton, R. (1995). Tricks, friends, and lovers: Erotic encounters in the field. In D. Kulick, & M. Willson (Eds.), *Taboo: Sex, identity, and erotic subjectivity in anthropological fieldwork* (pp. 140–67). London: Routledge.

Bourgois, P. (1995). *In search of respect: selling crack in El Barrio*. New York: Cambridge University Press.

Bourgois, P. (2003). *In search of respect: selling crack in El Barrio (Second updated edition)*. New York: Cambridge University Press.

Elliott, C., & Abadie, R. (2008). Exploiting a research underclass in phase 1 clinical trials. *New England Journal of Medicine, 358*, 2316–2317.

Gledhill, J. (2000). *Power and its disguises: Anthropological perspectives on politics* (2nd ed.). London: Pluto Press.

Green, L. (1995). *Fear as a way of life: Mayan windows in rural Guatemala*. New York: Columbia University Press.

Hoffman, N. (1975). Sociological snoopers and journalistic moralizer: Part I. In L. Humphrey (Ed.) *Tearoom trade: Impersonal sex in public places* (pp. 177–180, Enlarged edition). New York: Aldine de Gruyter.

Humphreys, L. (1975). *Tearoom trade: Impersonal sex in public places (Enlarged edition)*. New York: Aldine de Gruyter.

Interlandi, J. (2009). Not just urban legend. *Newsweek*.

Khayer, A. & Badal, H. (2004). Teenagers are smuggled for their organs, while drugs including fencidil are coming (In Bengali, Kidneysoho Anga Protanger Jonno Kishore-Kishore Pachar Hocche Asche Fencidil Soho Madokdrobbo). *The Daily Ittefaq*.

Marcus, G. (1995). Ethnography in/of the world system: The emergence of the multi-sited ethnography. *Annual Review of Anthropology, 24,* 95–117.

Moniruzzaman, M. (2010). "Living cadavers" in Bangladesh: Ethics of the human organ bazaar (Unpublished doctoral dissertation). University of Toronto, Toronto.

Moniruzzaman, M. (2012). "Living cadavers" in Bangladesh: Bioviolence in the human organ bazaar. *Medical Anthropology Quarterly, 26*(1), 69–91.

Moniruzzaman, M. (2013). Parts and labor: The commodification of human body. In A. Quayson, & G. Daswani (Eds.), *A companion to diaspora and transnationalism* (pp. 455–472). Malden: Wiley-Blackwell.

Moniruzzaman, M. (2014a). Domestic organ trafficking: Between biosecurity and bioviolence. In N. Chen & L. Sharp (Eds.), *Biosecurity and vulnerability* (pp. 195–215). Santa Fe: School of American Research.

Moniruzzaman, M. (2014b). Regulated organ market: Reality versus rhetoric. *The American Journal of Bioethics, 14*(10), 33–35.

Nordstrom, C., & Robben, A. (Eds). (1995). *Fieldwork under fire: Contemporary studies of violence and survival.* Berkeley: University of California Press.

Scheper-Hughes, N (1992). *Death without weeping: The violence of everyday life in Brazil.* Berkeley: University of California Press.

Scheper-Hughes, N.(1995). The primacy of the ethical: Proposition for a militant anthropology. *Current Anthropology, 36*(3), 409–20.

Scheper-Hughes, N. (2000). The global traffic in human organs. *Current Anthropology, 41*(2), 191–224.

Scheper-Hughes, N. (2004). Parts unknown: Undercover ethnography of the organs-trafficking underworld. *Ethnography, 5*(1), 29–73.

Schrag, Z. (2010). *Ethical imperialism: Institutional review boards and the social sciences, 1965–2009.* Baltimore: The Johns Hopkins University Press.

Singer, M. (1999). Studying hidden populations. In J. Schensul, M. LeCompte, R. Trotter, E. Cromley, & M. Singer (Eds.), *Mapping social networks, spatial data, & hidden populations* (pp. 125–92). United Kingdom: Altamira Press.

United Nations. (2011). Bangladesh: Country profile: International human development indicators. http://hdrstats.undp.org/en/countries/profiles/BGD.html. Accessed 22 Feb 2014.

Wall, L., & Brown, D. (2004). Ethical issues arising from the performance of pelvic examinations by medical students on anesthetized patients. *American Journal of Obstetrics and Gynecology, 190,* 319–23.

Walsh, A. (2004). In the wake of things: Speculating in and about sapphires in northern Madagascar. *American Anthropologist, 106*(2), 225–237.

Ward, T. (2013). *Gangsters without borders: An ethnography of a Salvadoran street gang.* Oxford: Oxford University Press.

Warwick, D. (1975). Tearoom trade: Means and ends in social research. In L. Humphreys (Ed.), *Tearoom trade: Impersonal sex in public places* (pp. 191–211). New York: Aldine de Gruyter.

Watters, J., & Biernacki, P. (1989). Target sampling: Options for the study of hidden populations. *Social Problems, 36,* 416–30.

Weppner, R. (1977). Street ethnography: Problems and prospects. In R. Weppner (Ed.), *Street ethnography: Selected studies of crime and drug use in natural settings* (pp. 21–51). Beverly Hills: Sage.

Whyte, W. (1981). *Street corner society: The social structure of an Italian slum (Third edition, revised and expanded).* Chicago: University of Chicago Press.

CHAPTER 10

"Can we talk about surrogacy?" Legal Precariousness and Qualitative Research in the Biomedical Context

Pragna Paramita Mondal

10.1 Introduction

Methodological questions in social science research have always been central to an understanding of the analytical frameworks that define a research problem. However, the relationship between research and the choice of methodology to address, conduct or represent it suffers from the problem of sequentiality—of setting precedence in terms of mapping the epistemological scope of the research question or in selecting the methodological structure that should facilitate the study. The question is one of assessing what comes first or which aspect determines the process and outcome of the research, as it is also about ascertaining if what we know can be independent of how we know it (Fierke 2004). This chapter deals with similar methodological concerns that were experienced as part of an intensive multi-sited field research on Indian surrogacy in the cities of Kolkata, Mumbai, Pune, Anand and Howrah between 2014 and 2017. The phased nature of the field research and the academic, interpretive exercise that followed it necessitated consistent methodological improvisations and involved a good deal of theoretical disengagement and re-engagement in keeping with the changing narratives that emerged on the field. The discussion would thus offer an insight into the challenges and processes of accumulating diversified qualitative data from the principal stakeholders in

P. P. Mondal (✉)
Narajole Raj College, Paschim Medinipur, West Bengal, India

Women's Studies Research Centre, University of Calcutta, Kolkata, West Bengal, India

© The Author(s), under exclusive license to Springer Nature Switzerland AG 2023
N. Uddin, A. Paul (eds.), *The Palgrave Handbook of Social Fieldwork*, https://doi.org/10.1007/978-3-031-13615-3_10

three different phases as the surrogacy law in India was constantly undergoing radical shifts and was transitioning from a commercial to a kin-based altruistic model. Family creation through assisted reproductive technology (ART) has more or less been a contested issue, but the insistence on the feasibility or appropriateness of using the surrogacy services of poor Indian women with socio-economic vulnerabilities changed the entire discourse of artificial reproduction in the country. Consequently, it added to the moral contingency and legal precariousness of surrogacy procedures following the periodic evolution of its legislative mandate in India. This had immense significance in the context of research accessibility and data collection on surrogacy as perceptions of confidentiality and legal immunity were reconfigured given the transformative guidelines.

The chapter is developed as per the following outline: the methodological shift from the mixed to the qualitative framework supporting the core ideas behind this study is first explained; the idea of 'precarity' and the alternative risk theorization in surrogacy research is then introduced. The aspects of bias and interdisciplinarity and the mediations of these concepts in this research are then discussed. The institutional dimensions of qualitative research in terms of securing ethical clearance for initiating research in human subjects and its disciplinary implications on the methods of executing the fieldwork are then focused upon. Emphasis is also placed on the conceptualization of participant subjectivity and 'informed consent' as part of the research design and its ramification in the fields of biomedicine, social sciences and feminist legal theory as being layered, subjective and incomplete. The next segment describes the experience of field research in the subsequent phases and highlights the aspects of trust-building and anonymity, the use of specific tools for data gathering, sorting and analysis, the intricacies of pooling respondents in varied region-specific contexts, and the alterations in methodology and strategies that impacted the outcome of the research. The conclusion provides a closure to the issues that this chapter raised and indicates future directions for researchers in health sociology and bioethics.

10.2   Methodological Background: From Mixed Method to the Qualitative Framework

Two fundamental nodes of thought need to be explained here before an actual delineation of methodological output in the given context is even attempted. In social science research, the appropriation of value-free or value-loaded approaches or the proportions of data mediation (Phillips and Hardy 2002) diversely relate back to a reflection upon the merits of quantification as compared to the advantages of qualitative reporting and analysis of data (Fierke 2004). The initial consideration in the present research also focused on the degree and relevance of quantification and the measures of impact assessment through the use of mixed methods that any probe on ART policy in a developing country could possibly be based on. Preliminary visits to the field and the feedback from stakeholders, however, revealed a huge gap in the attitudes and sensibilities of the respondents and my expectations as an investigator concerned with a specific research problem. Interesting observations in the field pointed to the multidimensionality of the issue and provided reasonable grounds to gravitate towards a qualitative framework of enquiry and analysis. While diversity in representation remained a research priority, the search for a statistical reference point and the reliance on a content analysis approach based on numerical robustness and replication of patterns within the sample group seemed redundant and inadequate.

The choice of the qualitative technique also presented its own set of problems so far as the theoretical anchorage of the study was concerned. My primary endeavour in questioning commercial surrogacy was focused on exploring, in moralistic terms, the reconceptualization of motherhood as a form of public activity bordering on the prospect of an economic enterprise. My principal assumptions were directed at being able to unpack narratives of vulnerability or victimhood from potential surrogates and to locate how ethical and relational structures were reconstituted in favour of those who exert power and control in an otherwise unequal exchange. But after the pilot testing and through the first few months of the field visit, I was most certainly intrigued by an awareness of the tangible economic instinct of these surrogate mothers, of their consciousness that benignly hovered over as some form of economic surrealism amid all the debates on the exploitation of maternal assets and discussions on the problematic of the female body. This inevitably led to the realization that the choice of an overarching, deterministic framework—such as the ramifications of female labour under forces of globalization—may not alone be able to fully capture the complexity of this exchange. It remained to be asked therefore if this economic instinct transpired into definite notions of empowerment and agency and to understand issues of governance and legality in this particular market and also to dig into its possible implications on public policy in health and biomedicine.

This change in approach not only pertained to an estimation of the relevant theoretical structure of the study but also enunciated the primacy and proliferation of 'discourse' as we find it in qualitative research. Discourse analysis in social science has more or less based itself on an exploration of the contexts within systems of language and is directed to understanding the embeddedness of knowledge in patterns of power relations and identity construction (Laffey and Weldes 2004; Crawford 2004). Discourse thus functions in creating a network of meaning with references to the social practices that produce it (Herrera and Braumoeller 2004). This study did not visibly incorporate the tools and techniques available in discourse-analytical theory in terms of linguistic deconstructivism but focused rather on the situatedness of the experiences of the respondents and decoded the attitudes and states of being that they revealed as part of their submissions during the interviews. Besides, for the last 20 years or so, discourse analysis in healthcare research has come to be regarded as an effective means of locating inequities and challenges within organizational spaces in health management (Garneau 2019; Buus 2005; Eines et al. 2019). The present study was thus designed to contribute to this area of enquiry in healthcare research by aligning its verbal resource-based qualitative data, that addresses a biomedical question, with the principles (if not the modes) of critical discourse analysis. Consequently, the study incorporates the voices of stakeholders from different Indian cities to ensure that the proliferation of discourses on reproductive policies and individual choices is adequately represented as a means to understand the 'situatedness' and diversity of their experiences.

10.3 Addressing Precarity and Risk in the Field

To account for the degree of precariousness that came to be associated with this research, it is necessary to provide a background to the socio-legal context of surrogacy in India. The aspect of precarity can of course be explained in terms of the moral hazards and the risk management issues that informed the process of research and data accumulation in surrogacy. In doing so, this chapter introduces 'precariousness' as an additional concern in the literature on risk expectancy in qualitative social research. It is often presumed in social scientific enquiry that the risk is unevenly faced by the participant/s alone and is not shared by the researcher undertaking the study. Lee-Treweek and Linkogle point out the lack of risk assessment so far as the academic and research staff is concerned and indicate very aptly that, "notions about academic work as a pen-pushing, middle-class pursuit contribute to the under-recognition of the risks of social research" (Lee-Treweek and Linkogle 2000). The institutional focus as shaped by the approach of the research ethics committee is also more accommodating of the risk incumbency of research participants and does not usually acknowledge the potential for physical or psychological harm that researchers are exposed to while conducting sensitive research (McCosker et al. 2001; Mauthner et al. 2002; Dickson-Swift et al. 2008; Bloor et al. 2010). When this field research commenced in early 2014, a partial ban on commercial surrogacy in India had already been implemented through the prohibition of foreign homosexual and live-in couples and single individuals as eligible commissioning parents (Rajadhyaksha 2013). In January 2013, the Union Home Ministry announced that only foreign heterosexual couples who have been married for two years may be allowed to avail of cross-border surrogacy in India and such surrogacy procedures will have to be conducted based on a special 'surrogacy visa' and not the regular tourist visa to ensure that the child is allowed to enter the country of the commissioning parents. However, the media scrutiny and public censure had already begun to shape and influence the general attitudes on surrogacy and the projection was mostly on the negative side. The issue of the exploitation of poor Indian women was never kept at bay and the transnational scope of surrogacy at that point made the debate more lopsided and morally aggressive. The provision of assisted reproduction thus began shifting gradually from the scientific and bioethical argument to a more politicized gender conformity argument that was reflected in the affidavit filed by the new government in the Supreme Court in 2015. This affidavit expressed the government's intention to prevent commercialism and to introduce altruistic surrogacy for married Indian couples only as a measure to protect the dignity of Indian surrogates. To prevent cross-border surrogacy the Department of Health Research, under the guidance of the Health and Family Welfare Ministry, also issued a directive to prevent the import of embryos into India except for research purposes (Sen 2015; Seetharaman 2015). This mobilization by the government eventually ended in the formal ban on commercial surrogacy through the Surrogacy (Regulation) Bill, 2016 (GOI 2016) which had been introduced in the Parliament in multiple versions subsequently and was awaiting modification and approval to become the Surrogacy (Regulation) Act, 2021 (GOI 2021).

The 'precariousness' that this research proposes to address originates at this exact point of legal and provisional reorganization that was taking place within the legislative premises and that prompted the stakeholders to recognize the limits of publicizing their interests and defend themselves against a pervasive public trial. There was the possibility of facing legal crackdown or procedural backlashes due to the public reporting of facts and the misrepresentation of liabilities that could emerge thereof; infertility clinics along with the surrogates and commissioning parents were thus largely dismissive of the idea of research participation and the prospect of getting people to 'talk' became increasingly challenging. In Kolkata in the initial months, approaching the clinics with a proof of intent, proper research credentials and the documentation secured from my university and supervisor to support my research purpose could not favourably convince the clinic directors to provide surrogates or commissioning parents for interviews. The service providers and other participants had become extremely sensitive to the risks associated with public articulation and this constraint intensified my struggles in keeping up with the expectations of the institutional research committee (RC). The fertility clinics were my primary research sites and could supposedly facilitate my efforts and put me in touch with surrogates, commissioning parents and surrogacy agents. But my inability to get hold of a single surrogate or commissioning parent in the first couple of months of my field visit provoked the scepticism of the research committee (during the work-in-progress seminar) regarding the potential and feasibility of my research in building up a persuasive qualitative enquiry. This caused enormous psychological pressure as I started questioning the very foundations of my research and my moral qualification as a social researcher. It was this precarity in executing the initial research design that led me to alter my empirical approach and search for new methods in carving out an interactive space in the field.

So what contributed to this precarity that I was forced to deal with as a persistent condition in my field research? In most notes on methodology, the procedure of gaining access is not adequately defined "giving the impression that access was unproblematic" (Grant 2017). The literature points to the problems of maintaining access on the field, especially during the negotiation phase and the layered nature of access at the macro, meso and micro levels (Blix and Wettergren 2015; Bondy 2013; Hammersley and Atkinson 2007; Molloy 2015; Grant 2017) also indicates the hazards of handling "gatekeepers" (Rashid 2007; Whyte 1943) to conduct interviews with select cohorts—the 'hard-to-reach' groups—in sensitive research. There are also references to the significant amount of identity and emotion work that characterizes the researcher's navigation across individuals and resources within organizational spaces on the field. While identity work addresses the insider-outsider divide and is based on a projection of shared or non-contrasting identity (Wagle and Cantaffa 2008) and notional affiliation with research subjects, emotion work involves a balance between emotional responsiveness and plausible objective neutrality on the field and motivates reflection on accumulated data outside the field (Dickinson-Swift et al. 2009).

The precarity in my research was not merely pivoted around problems of access and identity or emotional work but also centred on the clinics' assessment of my research subjectivity and their analysis of my intentions regarding the use of the sensitive data that I would procure as part of the fieldwork. It was thus not only my research integrity but also my ethics and responsibility in handling confidential information that was being mapped out by the 'gatekeepers'. For instance, in the first couple of months, my visits to the fertility clinics in Kolkata would involve long periods of waiting past the appointed hour (sometimes up to almost 5 to 7 hours a day) to meet clinic directors, infertility specialists and embryologists associated with the clinics and would invariably end up in the receptionist or the appointment manager informing me of the cancellation of the meeting on that day on account of some prior commitment. It was like a necessary ordeal or rite of passage that marked my initiation into reproductive ethnography where my conviction, patience and endurance were all put to test. Almost all infertility clinics had CCTV installations and I was certainly under surveillance inside their premises in presence of the groups of patients awaiting their turns to meet the doctor(s); these were indeed my study groups, my potential respondents that were sitting in communicable proximity. But the onus was on me to show professional restraint in not randomly approaching them with interview schedules or tracking them outside the clinics on my own by guile or in haste; this gesture helped communicate an informal code of ethics and my respect for privacy in the recruitment of subjects in the eyes of both the clinics and the patients and facilitated their 'opening up' in the later phase. Because surveillance in the pre-interaction phase appeared to be a major concern, a lateral reference might also be made here to a perceived profiling exercise supposedly attempted by a reputed hospital in Western India. There on my flight to the field, my co-passenger, who happened to be a native of the hospital town itself, under the pretext of having an informal conversation, kept badgering me with questions about my probable journalistic affiliation and my material expectations from the ongoing research. These unaccounted hazards would mostly remain undocumented in methodological journals of researchers because of the circumstantial nature of the experience and the lack of evidentiary support to outline such anonymized threats. These encounters may sometimes be more pronounced as reported by Rashid in her research on urban slums in Bangladesh (Rashid 2007) but do in no way justify the use of deception "while dealing with sensitive aspects of subjects' behaviour" (Clarke 1996) or in administering protocols in hostile or closeted spaces. Precariousness, in this sense, is also constituted by the pressures of bearing admissible conduct and speech while on the field and the anxiety of getting implicated in lapses that erupt out of unpredicted situations and incautious behaviour during interaction with participants, especially because of the huge legal costs involved in the subject of research.

10.4 Rethinking Approaches to the Study: Bias and Interdisciplinarity

It has been observed that qualitative research is "iterative rather than linear" and that "a good qualitative researcher moves back and forth between design and implementation to ensure congruence" (Morse et al. 2002) in the processes leading to analysis. While reordering the outline of my fieldwork, therefore, the first issue that I addressed from my previous approach was that of bias. The concept of bias is derived from quantitative research where it signifies a deliberate manipulation or distortion of the results as an expression of the researcher's agenda or beliefs. In the qualitative paradigm, bias is often reflected in the formulation of research questions or in the manner of the interpretation and representation of viewpoints that the researcher undertakes. Thorne writes of the crisis in objectivity that a qualitative study deals with and Galdas echoes her concern to suggest that although "it may be more difficult to quantify the impact of qualitative research, we should resist the temptation to reach for a positivist tape measure to solve this problem. To do so will lead us to become apologists for the subjectivity that is the very strength of interpretive work" (Thorne 2009; Galdas 2017). My reflection on the subjectivity resonating in my presentation of the problem in the initial encounters with the clinics led me to the realization that in the preliminary stages it might be pre-emptive to incorporate a dominant subjective note into the modes of enquiry (before it was convincingly formed) because that would only amount to an articulation of bias. The fact remains that I had been to the field to learn and understand the questions myself as much as I wanted to enlighten others about the research or share my perspectives on the state of Indian surrogacy. But my own positionality on the issue was bound to change and evolve in the process and so an overtly subjective probe or a value-driven gaze at the beginning of the fieldwork only contradicted my real motives and misplaced the focus of my research in the view of my respondents.

Consequently, as the fieldwork advanced, I rephrased some of the critical questions asked to the participants to release their defensive attitudes and elicit more confident and open responses. To give an example, in my first interview with an infertility specialist in a clinic in Behala (Kolkata), I asked the following question: *"In light of the ongoing debate on injustices faced by surrogates in our country, do you think that as a service provider you're able to do enough to safeguard their interests?"* (personal interview, 2014). This interrogation was quite opinionated and direct and was certainly not reflective of how I came to understand the idea of individual and reproductive justice in surrogacy at a later phase of my research. But this question had much agitated my respondent and had pumped into him a sense of urgency to defend his ethical role as a facilitator in surrogacy and to spell out the limitation of his legal liabilities in the procedure. The information that the question meant to generate was thus lost in the mutual management of biases and in neutralizing the moral overtone of the statement. In subsequent interviews, therefore, I rephrased this question to convey the right tenor of this enquiry to my respondent: *"It is often thought that the surrogates are incapable of safeguarding their interests in this procedure because of their social vulnerability. Has your experience been any different in this regard and how do you personally look after the interests of the surrogates who work for this clinic?"* (personal interviews). This and similar modifications proved to be very effective because they communicated neither a vindication nor an invalidation of the clinic's role in my estimation and sourced the narratives that respondents felt an urge to share: the moral open-endedness of the questions liberated them to come out with stories that they valued and considered to be an important part of their experiences.

The other concern that I had to sort out through the different stages of the fieldwork was the aspect of interdisciplinarity that my work on surrogacy was meant to encompass. This interdisciplinarity was not only the basis of my research training and my approach to engaging in a field-oriented study of women in surrogacy but it also related to the gap that I tried to address within the literature on Indian surrogacy. The existing studies on surrogacy in India that were rooted in some form of ethnography or field research delved into issues in the sociology of labour (Pande 2014; Rudrappa 2016), cultural and medical anthropology and transnational studies (Majumdar 2017; Deomampo 2017), colonial-feminist encounters (Vora 2009), psychological well-being (Lamba 2017), law and bioethics (Nadimpally and Marwah 2014; Nadimpally 2015; Mitra 2018) and reproductive bio-markets (Saravanan 2018). My research ventured into areas that had not so far been explored, such as the economic sociology of surrogacy in terms of its market modalities, or fields such as reproductive policy studies, contract and transaction cost economics, ethics and behavioural economics, consumption studies, neoliberal rationality in reproductive healthcare management and the insurance literature. This task was easier said than done, for interdisciplinarity was not a coherent practice that could be preordained but an approach that needed to mature and develop over time. The usual caveat on interdisciplinary methods states that because of "the extent to which different disciplines have their way of doing things; [through] deeply embedded ontological, epistemological, and methodological assumptions; and different specialized languages...[some] of these differences might be incommensurable" (MacCleave 2006). The nature of the data sought through interviews and the range of the enquiry thus continued to change and grow in newer directions and that added largely to the richness and potential of the research. The interdisciplinary tool was also useful in explaining my positionality as a researcher because some of my respondents were curious enough to ask me how my research would contribute to a field that specifically concerned doctors, medicine and medical technology. Faced with such queries, I could reasonably convince them about why it was essential to focus on the social dimension of surrogacy and to incorporate the voices of people on the ground to explain the legal, economic and cultural repercussions of the policy outline. The interdisciplinary setting thus helped me to get my respondents involved in processes of communication that were more experiential and polyphonic and not mechanical or discipline-bound. While the narratives on the field continued to build, the aspects of theoretical intervention or the points of critical analysis gradually shaped up and streamlined the mandate of the study. The interdisciplinary approach was therefore, in a way, quite compatible with the multidimensionality of this issue and had a positive impact on constructing the pluralistic lens that I needed to be equipped with to answer certain fundamental research questions.

10.5 Securing Ethical Clearance and Understanding 'Informed Consent' in My Work

Although the role of the Human Research Ethics Committee has been discussed in the qualitative research literature mostly in terms of its commitment to preserving participants' rights (Beauchamp and Childress 1994; Dickson-Swift et al. 2005) and to approve the ethical codes of the proposed study, I would discuss my experience in securing institutional ethical clearance for slightly different reasons. This is primarily to draw attention to the fact that within local research practices, the concept of seeking institutional clearance in bioethical research did not apply much to the humanities or the social scientific disciplines, but rather concerned the clinical and applied sciences. As such when I submitted my research proposal and protocols for scrutiny and approval by the University Ethics Committee, I had to undergo a procedure that my departmental research peers in the social sciences had never engaged with. Other than the apparent disciplinary divide, there was also a spatial and contextual difference as the Institutional Bioethics Committee for Humans functioned at the Science College campus of the university and lay outside my familiar operational ambit.

During my defence at the meeting convened by the Committee, the members were genuinely receptive and accommodating in listening to my views on the research. However, two issues were significantly emphasized in their statements: the first related to my understanding of the legal ambiguity around surrogacy in India and my consideration of the possible need for the psychological rehabilitation of the surrogates; and the second concerned my method of data collection and interviewing by seeking voluntary informed consent from participants. On the first account, the committee strictly recommended that my research should not stand in violation of "the law of the land" (the surrogacy law to be precise) and should adhere to the ICMR Guidelines. I must admit that at that moment I did not quite fully understand the import of this cautionary premise because since its inception the surrogacy law in India had been quite dynamic and it was still constantly changing and evolving. It was thus my obligation as a social researcher to explore the contrasted legal provisioning on surrogacy and to analyse how these contradictions affected the experiences of stakeholders. Nonetheless, I assured the committee that my research practices were completely transparent and socially driven and were not designed to solicit legal entanglements of any kind. Upon examination of my research questions and schedules, they seemed to be adequately satisfied in that regard. Their second concern about the method of 'consent taking', however, was a bit difficult to explain because in applied psychology or clinical biology, consent is usually secured in the written format. So the efficacy of the oral consent to share personal narratives and the conditions of evoking it as a form of an implicit social contract between the participants and the researcher provoked a host of critical questions. The matter was eventually settled through my explication of how securing oral consent before qualitative interviews were standard practice in social sciences research. It also subscribed to ethical parameters because not attesting their consent in the written form gives participants the right to protect their identity and autonomy in sensitive research.

Following this deliberation, the Committee provided the approval necessary for the research to continue. But the question regarding the complexity of 'informed consent' remained with me and signalled a conceptual fallacy that frames our basic understanding of participant subjectivity in qualitative research. Literature suggests that biomedical advancements challenge how informed consent can be exercised so much so that in certain cases it gets reduced to a mere "medico-legal orthodoxy" (Hewer 2019; Caulfield 2007). The construction of informed consent that should reflect the voluntary will, capacity and autonomous consideration of 'salient' information by the participants may be seriously undermined by their lack of scientific literacy (Beauchamp and Childress 2013; Sisti and Stramondo 2015). The feminist legal theory thus questions the liberal subjecthood that presumably produces the informed consent and points out that its disembodied, rational and asocial nature is always constrained and constituted by dependency principles (Azétsop and Rennie 2010; Mackenzie and Stoljar 2000). There is also a Foucauldian resonance in the analysis of the consenting subject as representing a self that has been groomed to embody social norms and internalize the disciplinary regimen of the clinic and thereby enact a consent that is not concomitantly an articulation of authentic autonomy (Ells 2003).

This layering and incompleteness of consent were manifested in the ways my respondents revealed narratives about their expectations and experiences of the medical intervention that they had voluntarily allowed to be performed upon them. Their consent regarding the IVF procedure operated at a functional level: they knew that it was bound to be effectively modified and was subject to amplification as per the outcome of particular protocols at the different stages of the treatment. As far as their consent to research participation was concerned, they felt that my conversational approach was in no way incisive or invasive and the discursivization helped them in many ways to relate to the liberating aspect of their experiences. Many commissioning parents emphasized the social value of their research participation and expressed their satisfaction over the fact that their narrativization of reality as part of my research initiative would help many others afflicted with infertility. However, this ease was mostly inspired by a verbal enactment of queries—handing them out questionnaires for filling in their responses did not appeal to them much and was received as a mechanical and distant approach to the significance of their life stories. On most occasions, I did not read out the consent form in strictly formalistic terms but communicated to my respondents the essence of it before seeking their permission to proceed. I would of course very emphatically pronounce the part which stated that they had every right to withdraw from the interview or to not answer any question that they found awkward or chose not to accommodate as part of the research.

Written documents, papers and schedules that I used to carry along into the field initially proved to be a genuine hindrance while getting people in the conversational groove. Memorizing the schedule did not always help because people had their ways of ordering, arranging and presenting information that would not match the sequencing of questions on the schedule in many instances. In many cases, the (mostly) illiterate surrogates felt somewhat anxious to witness my attempts to shuffle through printed pages, which is reminiscent of Ounanian's experience of administering survey questionnaires and vignettes to participants within the fishing community; she puts it very aptly when she says that, "…I had vastly overestimated the population's comfort reading and responding to written questions. The room was silent. It was as though I was administering an exam. I felt guilty…" (Ounanian 2021). The surrogates' earliest encounter with the printed document in this procedure had been in the form of the legal contract of which they had a gross and problematic understanding but which also acted as the source of power that the law and the clinic had over them. They shared a relation of reverence and awe with the written word and therefore my initial attempts to write down all their responses on the printed schedule at the moment of articulation (with the eye contact disrupted for certain lengths of time) interrupted their narrative and affected their manner of speech. It was discouraging to some surrogates and made them uncomfortable and intimidated: *"kagoje ki shob likhe nichchhe"* ("she's getting things written on paper")—would be their embarrassing reaction. The replication of the power dynamics between the researcher and the participant is not something to be emulated and should best be avoided for the sake of the ethical exchange and dissemination of information. Interestingly, this power relationship has both physical and psychological dimensions associated with it, and thus I switched over to conscious minimalism while getting equipped with the qualitative research paraphernalia during field visits. I carried only a notebook that contained all the handwritten questions for me to glance over and in which I took brief notes during interviews and later recorded the details of the conversations and also passages reflecting my participant observation in the specific situations. As mentioned earlier in this chapter, I had to spend considerable amounts of time in and around the clinics or other locations waiting for the interviews to happen, often on a one-to-one basis. This gave me ample opportunity to sort and translate the data and preserve it for effective analytical use.

10.6   Outline of the Fieldwork

Initially, my field research was confined to West Bengal, and it was only after the drafting of the Surrogacy (Regulation) Bill, of 2016 that I decided to visit other cities in India to make the study more prolific and interesting. The data on surrogacy was collected through primary research in four Indian cities in three phases and over a period of four years starting from February 2014 to November 2017. It was part of a conscious decision to go out into the field between intervals and to interview the principal stakeholders at different points in time as major amendments to the ART (Regulation) Draft Bill were being announced over these four years. The research was multi-sited and involved different clinics and hospitals in different cities of India. This was sought primarily to generate diversity in sampling and to explore the varied nature of the industry in different regions of the country. Infertility and surrogacy have mostly been sensitive areas to explore, especially in the Indian context. However, due to public and legal censure, it had turned overtly sensationalized in the last few years. Consequently, it had become increasingly difficult to crack the market, build trust and convince the clinics to participate in the research. The clinics had suddenly grown more cautious and suspicious of approaches from researchers or journalists as they were apprehensive of legal backlash and media trials. Therefore, the choice of cities, clinics and samples in this field research was based on convenience, availability and access. Of course, the response of doctors, professionals, surrogates and other parties to the research varied across states and that made the study all the more comprehensive and challenging.

The preliminary part of the field research began with the preparation of the list of providers of IVF and commercial surrogacy in Kolkata through extensive Internet browsing. In the initial couple of months, most of these clinics and IVF centres were approached either in person or through telephone calls. Efforts were made to explain to them the real purpose of the study and to seek appointments with doctors and IVF specialists. After repeated attempts to persuade the clinics to participate in the research, only three centres—one in

North Kolkata and two from South Kolkata—responded. Each of these institutes supported the research in different capacities and it was possible to eventually conduct 15 interviews (5 surrogates, 6 doctors, 3 commissioning parents and 1 lawyer) in the first phase of 2014. In the second phase, three more clinics in Kolkata and Howrah consented to participation and interviews were thus held throughout 2015 and 2016. Repeated visits to these clinics and other locations following a snowball sampling method ensured 43 interviews (27 surrogates, 3 doctors, 9 commissioning parents, 2 agents and 2 coordinators) in the second phase. The third phase that fetched 39 more interviews (19 surrogates, 16 doctors, 1 commissioning parent, 1 agent and 3 coordinators) focused on other cities in India and initial contact with these clinics was made either in person or via email. A long list of clinics and hospitals in Pune and Mumbai was drawn and request e-mails were sent out after researching their websites. A few clinics in Mumbai welcomed the research and provided dates for interviews immediately. But some clinics did not respond to the mails and some mails even failed to get delivered. Communication with the two major hospitals in Pune seeking appointments for interviews was attempted over the telephone but did not materialize. The meeting with the doctors in these hospitals, therefore, happened only after visiting them in person with proper credentials and relevant questions. The third phase also included a field visit to a reputed hospital in Anand (Gujarat) that made global headlines due to its unprecedented success in providing large-scale, state-of-the-art surrogacy services in India to national as well as international clients. This hospital was cordial enough to host my queries, and the time of the visit was fixed through correspondence over e-mail and telephone.

10.7 Tools Used

To facilitate data collection separate sets of semi-structured questionnaires were prepared for infertile couples, surrogates, providers, and lawyers in English, Bengali and Hindi. A consent form (including the declaration of purpose and the statement of anonymity/confidentiality) was affixed at the beginning of the questionnaires prepared for the commissioning parents and surrogate mothers. These questionnaires were subsequently used as guides while conducting interviews within the clinics and at other sites to encourage conversational ease among respondents and to gravitate towards an ethnographic rather than a quantitative mode of data collection. Questions in vernacular were administered mostly to the surrogates and the commissioning parents. All the interviews were conducted physically at the clinics or the surrogacy dorms or some other location as per the availability and convenience of the interviewees. For the respondents who refused to be identified in person, interviews were conducted over the phone. In the first phase, the respondents had no issues with recording interviews on electronic devices or through the cellular call recording system. But in the two subsequent phases, the research environment had turned highly constrained and respondents were no longer willing to allow audio footage of interviews to be retained. These interviews, therefore, were diligently covered through field notes. Throughout the entire research, emphasis was laid on conducting in-depth interviews within the allocated time frame to form a qualitative understanding of the different issues involved.

Although the research relied on the ethnographic format, there were certain deviations from traditional ethnographic methods based on endogenous conditions within the research site. It was not possible to stay with the surrogates that I interviewed and to conduct participant observation at a more proximal level. In that respect, I was forced to assume the role of a commuter researcher (Musante 2015) and travel in and out of the field subject to the availability of participants. The extended periods of waiting at the clinics however facilitated icebreaking and resulted in passive participation while observing modes of behaviour, practices and institutional norms as an 'outsider' (Spradley 1980). It also opened up chances of interaction with staff and participants on a relatively informal note and was useful in pooling responses around issues that would have otherwise gone unnoticed. Excepting the providers, the majority of the commissioning parents and a few surrogates, it was mostly not possible to revisit participants and to do follow up interviews over time. In Bengal, the clinics managed multiple cases of surrogacy around the year but they did not encourage having interview sessions with surrogates beyond the first meeting in consideration of externalities and adverse social repercussions. They disallowed keeping in touch with participants or over-familiarizing with them on grounds of professionalism, confidentiality and as a means to protect the interests and identities of all parties concerned. This study had thus not set out to trace the trajectory of the surrogates' experiences of surrogacy and to represent conclusive narratives based on their evolution of opinions. Some cases could be flagged where a few surrogates were undergoing the procedure for the second time and could reflect on their specific experiences in the past. However, throughout the study, I mostly encountered surrogates and commissioning parents who were at different stages of the procedure at the time of the interview. To fulfil the research objectives, my questions were thus focused on their fundamental thoughts about choices and risk assumptions, their individual rationales and the broad social, legal, and medical spectrum of their transactional experience in surrogacy. As this model of interaction and data gathering had effectively worked for me in the first two phases, I continued with this approach in the third phase while extending this research in Maharashtra and Gujarat. The interviews with surrogates would be under an hour, and those with the commissioning parents and the providers would last for long and would mostly require two sessions or more.

10.8 Data Analysis

The preservation of the data was a greater concern because it was the quality and the usability of the data that would determine the viability of the analysis at a later stage of the research. The interviews in Bengal were conducted in Bengali and Hindi. In Maharashtra and Gujarat, interviews with service providers were conducted in English, and those with surrogates were all in Hindi. Due to my proficiency in all three languages, I had no problems taking notes at the time of the interviews and later translating responses that were originally delivered in vernacular languages. Most of the translations were done with the closest possible association to the actual words spoken by the respondents. Besides, participants had their distinct modes of speech and their ways of choosing words and phrases and emphasizing details while sharing their stories. These effective articulations and typified expressions were more or less replicated in the translated versions of the transcripts so that their resonances and significations could be retained. Because anonymity of the respondents was a necessary precondition while accommodating their voices in the research, I had reckoned that using pseudonyms for each participant would be more appropriate. However, most of the commissioning parents and surrogates who did not wish to share their names were clueless when asked to suggest a name of their choice, sometimes dismissing it as a redundancy. My initial attempts at involving respondents in selecting their pseudonyms suggested that they deemed the exercise as unrealistic and mechanical and not in the spirit of the gravity that their articulations conveyed. To me, assigning names to the participants on my own appeared to be rather arbitrary. It was equivalent to exertion of my authority over the nomenclature and the representative merit of the participants which, I felt, would amount to a reconstruction of their identity and a partial loss of agency. It was on this consideration that I decided to use coded combinations (with letter and number) to identify the respondents and went ahead with profiling different participants and marking their responses on the interview transcripts accordingly.

As explained earlier in the chapter, this study focused on the interdisciplinary framework of analysis, and the motivations for exploring the different aspects of surrogacy were derived from the terms of the trade that the responses of stakeholders revealed. The surrogates' profiles were sorted following the general, economic and childbirth histories that they had shared and the specific experiences of surrogacy that they narrated. The data on commissioning parents were also sorted based on the personal, social and psychological information that they disclosed concerning the surrogacy procedures. Since a rich bulk of data was gathered as a result of the multi-sited research, extensive reading of various interdisciplinary literature indicated ways in which this data could best be represented. Thus developed the different threads of analysis and excerpts from interviews with surrogates, commissioning parents, doctors, coordinators and agents were interspersed with the discussions to add corroborative value to the principal contentions.

10.9 Regional Diversity

One of the primary reasons for extending the fieldwork to multiple cities was to capture the diversity of precepts and practices in surrogacy in different parts of the country. Out of the other major Indian cities where the surrogacy industry flourished, I chose to focus on those in Western India, that is, Mumbai and Pune, because ethnographic work in these places had not so far been conducted. Besides, cases of celebrity surrogacy were mostly concentrated in Mumbai, and the doctors in Kolkata suggested during their interviews in the first two phases of my research that the surrogacy market in Mumbai functioned more or less as an organized sector hosting strong international preference. New Delhi was another hotspot of surrogacy within the country, but several studies by researchers and NGOs had already been based there. Anand in Gujarat was picked as the final destination because it had pioneered in cases of transnational surrogacy since the early 2000s and had also featured in the Oprah Winfrey show due to its remarkable number of successful cases. Pande's ethnographic work in Anand was conducted at a time when the prohibitive legislation on Indian surrogacy had not been remotely suggested (Pande 2014). It was thus imperative to find out how this hospital and the surrogates associated with it fared in the wake of the critical sanctions that were being placed upon surrogacy within the country. In retrospect, it can be very convincingly claimed that the study had greatly benefited from the multi-locational inputs that unfolded the Indian surrogacy market in all its variations.

As far as the client composition is concerned, the providers in Kolkata and Howrah mostly catered to the middle and upper-middle classes with a significantly low number of cases in cross-border surrogacy. The surrogacy industry in Bengal was thus more localized, and the levels of awareness among the surrogates regarding the financial and legal prospects of the procedure varied widely. The clinics and hospitals that I had visited in Mumbai and Pune almost had a corporatized structure and were designed to receive both domestic and international clients. Their degree of preparedness while sharing information during interviews and their professional approach to protecting the interests of all parties concerned were reflected in the way they had standardized the terms of the trade. This corporatization could have hurt the agency claimed by the surrogates, but the ones that were interviewed seemed to have a strong sense of moral and civic subjecthood and were very secure in articulating their expectations from the procedure. It was indeed this professional set-up that also made the providers more approachable and accessible: hospitals and clinics that participated in the research processed my requests for interviews and acted upon the correspondences with a sense of urgency. The hospital in Anand was a self-sustaining enterprise, and the surrogacy sector that it managed had almost assumed a cooperative structure with strong linkages and active networks among the women who arrived there to become surrogates. Because of the collective nature of their involvement in the surrogacy process (that their cohabitation in the surrogacy dorm made possible), the women possessed greater informational literacy and had a better perception of bargaining goals and limits. Giving research access in this hospital was also considered on formalized grounds as the providers were more inclined to live up to an image of responsibility and social commitment. This attitude and time-bound approach on the part of the providers facilitated my primary research in these cities to a great extent. Of course, the references to my previous fieldwork in Bengal and the appropriateness of my personal and research conduct helped to overcome the institutional barriers and convince the 'gatekeepers' in this sector to share information and participants for the study.

10.10 Conclusion

This chapter has been an exploration of how my qualitative research has sought to overcome the limitations that operational constraints have otherwise generated in the documentation of surrogacy in India. The methodological insights presented in the chapter relate to questions of access, research subjectivity, bias, the harm principle, informed consent and ethical negotiations in conducting social research on biomedical subjects and are conspicuously based on my first-hand experience of the 'learning by doing' process. I have thus tried to communicate to future researchers attempting field-oriented studies in medical anthropology and the health humanities as to what techniques could be adopted to penetrate legally hazardous or socially bounded research sites through effective trust-building and appropriate navigation skills. This chapter does not intend to extrapolate the methodological findings of this research to derive generalizable axioms on qualitative research designs in the field of bioethics and the sociology of healthcare. The strategies explained here are not meant to act as a deterrent to future researchers investigating similar fields. What it tries to achieve is to relate to the ground realities of research and to show that, in the face of legislative inconsistencies and procedural instabilities, researchers need to take cognizance of the moral hazards that they are bound to encounter on the part of the different actors in the field. The other aim that this chapter sets out to accomplish is to deliver an understanding of why interdisciplinarity could function as a useful analytical tool in interpreting contentious issues on the socio-legality of the reproductive policy discourse as has been played out in the Global South. The discussion thus proffers certain recommendations on the future directions of conducting social-scientific enquiry in the fields of biomedicine, law and reproductive health.

References

Azétsop, Jacquineau, and Stuart Rennie. "Principlism, Medical Individualism, and Health Promotion in Resource-Poor Countries: Can Autonomy-Based Bioethics Promote Social Justice and Population Health?." *Philosophy, Ethics, and Humanities in Medicine 5 (1)*, 2010: 1.

Beauchamp, T. L., and J. F. Childress. *Principles of biomedical ethics (3rd ed.)*. Oxford, UK: Oxford University Press, 1994.

Beauchamp, Tom L., and James F. Childress. *Principles of Biomedical Ethics, 7th ed.* New York: OUP USA, 2013.

Blix, S. B., and A. Wettergren. "The emotional labour of gaining and maintaining access to the field." *Qualitative Research, 15*, 2015: 688–704.

Bloor, Michael, Ben Fincham, and Helen Sampson. "Unprepared for the Worst: Risks of Harm for Qualitative Researchers." *Methodological Innovations Online 5(1)*, 2010: 45–55.

Bondy, C. "How did I get here? The social process of accessing field sites." *Qualitative Research, 13*, 2013: 578–590.

Buus, N. "Nursing scholars appropriating new methods: The use of discourse analysis in scholarly nursing journals 1996-2003." *Nursing Inquiry, 12(1)*, 2005: 27–33.

Caulfield, Timothy. "Biobanks and Blanket Consent: The Proper Place of the Public Good and Public Perception Rationales." *King's Law Journal 18 (2)*, 2007: 209–226.

Clarke, L. "Covert participant observation in a secure forensic unit." *Nursing Times, 92(48)*, 1996: 37–40.

Crawford, Neta C. "Understanding Discourse: A Method of Ethical Argument Analysis." *Qualitative Methods: Springer 2004 Newsletter*. Harvard University, 2004. 22–25.

Deomampo, Daisy. *Transnational Surrogacy Race, Kinship, and Commercial Surrogacy in India*. New York: New York University Press, 2017.

Dickinson-Swift, V., E. L. James, S. Kippen, and P. Liamputtong. "Researching sensitive topics: Qualitative research as emotion work." *Qualitative Research, 9*, 2009: 61–79.

Dickson-Swift, V., E. James, and S. Kippen. "Do university ethics committees adequately protect public health researchers?" *Australian and New Zealand Journal of Public Health, 29(6)*, 2005: 576–582.

Dickson-Swift, Virginia, Erica L. James, Sandra Kippen, and Pranee Liamputtong. "Risk to Researchers in Qualitative Research on Sensitive Topics: Issues and Strategies." *Qualitative Health Research Volume 18 Number 1*, 2008: 133–144.

Eines, Trude Fløystad, Elin Angelo, and Solfrid Vatne. "Discourse analysis of health providers' experiences using service design." *Nursing Open, Volume 6, Issue 1*, 2019: 84–92.

Ells, Carolyn. "Foucault, Feminism, and Informed Choice." *Journal of Medical Humanities 24 (3/4)*, 2003: 213–228.

Fierke, Karin. "World or Worlds? The Analysis of Content and Discourse." *Qualitative Methods: Spring 2004 Newsletter*. Harvard University, 2004. 36–39.

Galdas, P. Revisiting Bias in Qualitative Research: Reflections on Its Relationship With Funding and Impact. *International Journal of Qualitative Methods Volume 16*: 1–2. 2017.

Garneau, Amélie Blanchet, Annette J. Browne, and Colleen Varcoe. "Understanding competing discourses as a basis for promoting equity in primary health care." *BMC Health Services Research volume 19, Article number: 764*, 2019.

GOI. "The Surrogacy (Regulation) Bill 2016." *www.prsindia.org*. 2016. https://www.prsindia.org/sites/default/files/bill_files/Surrogacy%20%28Regulation%29%20Bill%2C%202016.pdf.

GOI. "The Surrogacy (Regulation) Act, 2021." https://egazette.nic.in/WriteReadData/2021/232118.pdf.

Grant, Aimee. "I Don't Want You Sitting Next to Me": The Macro, Meso, and Micro of Gaining and Maintaining Access to Government Organizations During Ethnographic Fieldwork." *International Journal of Qualitative Methods, Volume 16: 1–11*, 2017.

Hammersley, M., and P. Atkinson. *Ethnography: Principles in practice*. New York, NY: Routledge, 2007.

Herrera, Yoshiko M., and Bear F. Braumoeller. "Symposium: Discourse and Content Analysis." *Qualitative Methods, Spring 2004 Newsletter*. Harvard University, 2004. 15–19.

Hewer, Rebecca. "Vulnerability and the Consenting Subject: Reimagining Informed Consent in Embryo Donation." *Feminist Legal Studies, 27*, 2019: 287–310.

Laffey, Mark, and Jutta Weldes. "Methodological Reflections on Discourse Analysis." *Qualitative Methods, Spring 2004 Newsletter*. Harvard University, 2004. 28–30.

Lamba, Nishtha. "Psychological Well-Being, Maternal-Foetal Bonding and Experiences of Indian Surrogates." *Department of Psychology, Centre for Family Research, University of Cambridge Repository*. September 2017. https://www.repository.cam.ac.uk/bitstream/handle/1810/271335/Lamba-2018-PhD.pdf?sequence=5 (accessed May 1, 2021).

Lee-Treweek, G., and S. Linkogle. *Danger in the field: Risk and ethics in social research*. London: Routledge, 2000.

MacCleave, A. "Incommensurability in cross-disciplinary research: A call for cultural negotiation." *International Journal of Qualitative Methods, 5*, 2006 : 40–54.

Mackenzie, Catriona, and Natalie Stoljar. *Relational Autonomy: Feminist Perspectives on Automomy, Agency, and the Social Self*. Cary: Oxford University Press, Incorporated, 2000.

Majumdar, Anindita. *Transnational Commercial Surrogacy and the (Un)Making of Kin in India*. New Delhi: Oxford University Press, 2017.

Mauthner, M., M. Birch, J. Jessop, and T. Miller. *Ethics in Qualitative Research*. Thousand Oaks, CA: Sage, 2002.

McCosker, H., A. Barnard, and R Gerber. "Undertaking Sensitive Research: Issues and Strategies for Meeting the Safety Needs of All Participants." *Forum: Qualitative Social, 2(1)*. February 28, 2001. https://www.qualitative-research.net/index.php/fqs/article/view/983 (accessed May 1, 2021).

Mitra, Sayani. "Cross-Border Reproflows: Comparing the Cases of India, Germany, and Israel." In *Cross-Cultural Comparisons on Surrogacy and Egg Donation Interdisciplinary Perspectives from India, Germany and Israel*, by Sayani Mitra, Silke Schicktanz and Tulsi (eds) Patel, 83–102. Cham: Palgrave Macmillan, 2018.

Molloy, C. (2015). "Getting by or getting in? Grappling with access and affect in qualitative research projects involving vulnerable human subjects." *Qualitative Inquiry, 21* (467–476), 2015: 467–476.

Morse, Janice M., Michael Barrett, Maria Mayan, Karin Olson, and Jude Spiers. "Verification Strategies for Establishing Reliability and Validity in Qualitative Research." *International Journal of Qualitative Methods, 1(2)*, 2002: 13–22.

Musante, Kathleen. "Participant Observation." In *Handbook of Methods in Cultural Anthropology, 2nd Ed.*, by H. Russell Bernard, Clarence C. Gravlee and (eds.), 251–292. New York: Rowman & Littlefield, 2015.

Nadimpally, Sarojini, and V. Marwah (eds). *Reconfiguring Reproduction: Feminist Health Perspectives on Assisted Reproductive Technologies*. New Delhi: Zubaan, 2014.

Nadimpally, Sarojini. "For Motherhood and for Market: Commercial Surrogacy in India." In *New Cannibal Markets: Globalization and Commodification of the Human Body*, by Jean-Daniel Rainhorn, El Boudamoussi and eds., 105–122. Paris: Editions de la Maison des sciences de l'homme, 2015.

Ounanian, Kristen. "Naked Methodology: Baring It All for a Realistic Account of Marine Social Science." In *Researching People and the Sea Methodologies and Traditions*, by Madeleine Gustavsson, Carole S. White, Jeremy Phillipson, Kristen Ounanian and (eds.), 23–45. Cham: Palgrave Macmillan, 2021.

Pande, Amrita. *Wombs in Labor: Transnational Commercial Surrogacy in India.* New York: Columbia University Press, 2014.

Phillips, N, and Hardy, C. *Discourse analysis: Investigating processes of social construction.* Thousand Oaks, CA: Sage Publications, 2002.

Rajadhyaksha, Madhavi. "No surrogacy visa for gay foreigners." *The Times of India.* January 18, 2013. https://timesofindia.indiatimes.com/india/No-surrogacy-visa-for-gay-foreigners/articleshow/18066771.cms (accessed May 1, 2021).

Rashid, S. F. "Accessing married adolescent women: The realities of ethnographic research in an urban slum environment in Dhaka, Bangladesh." *Field Methods, 19*, 2007: 369–383.

Rudrappa, Sharmila. *Discounted Life: The Price of Global Surrogacy in India.* New Delhi: Orient Blackswan, 2016.

Saravanan, Sheela. *A Transnational Feminist View of Surrogacy Biomarkets in India.* Springer Singapore, 2018.

Seetharaman, G. "Ban on surrogacy for foreigners: How govt's recent decision will push a booming industry into black market." *The Economic Times.* November 8, 2015. https://economictimes.indiatimes.com/news/politics-and-nation/ban-on-surrogacy-for-foreigners-how-govts-recent-decision-will-push-a-booming-industry-into-black-market/articleshow/49703554.cms (accessed May 1, 2021).

Sen, Shreeja. "Against commercial surrogacy: Govt tells Supreme Court." *Livemint.* October 28, 2015. https://www.livemint.com/Politics/vItqt0Dp5TyNzKKXyGpsqN/Govt-plans-to-ban-booming-surrogacy-service-to-foreigners.html (accessed May 1, 2021).

Sisti, Dominic, and Joseph Stramondo. "Competence, Voluntariness, and Oppressive Socialization: A Feminist Critique of the Threshold Elements of Informed Consent." *IJFAB: International Journal of Feminist Approaches to Bioethics 8 (1)*, 2015: 67–85.

Spradley, James P. *Participant Observation.* Toronto: Thomson Learning, 1980.

Thorne, S. "The role of qualitative research within an evidence-based context: Can metasynthesis be the answer?" *International Journal of Nursing Studies, 46*, 2009: 569–575.

Vora, Kalindi. "Indian transnational surrogacy and the commodification of vital energy." *Subjectivity, Volume 28, Issue 1*, 2009: 266–278.

Wagle, T., and D. T. Cantaffa. "Working our hyphens exploring identity relations in qualitative research." *Qualitative Inquiry, 14*, 2008: 135–159.

Whyte, W. F. *Street Corner Society: The social structure of an Italian slum.* Chicago, IL: University of Chicago Press, 1943.

CHAPTER 11

Qualitative 'Fieldwork' in Health Geographic Research: Self-reports from Bangladesh

Alak Paul

11.1 INTRODUCTION

Health geographers have been most active in the analysis of smaller unit areas (Andrews et al. 2007) and they have turned to narratives as a way to engage with the everyday, situated experiences of people in place (e.g. Kearns 1997; Parr 1998). Curtis (2004) thinks that the geography of health is focused on the ways that the health of populations is differentiated between places and the range of factors that explain these differences. Many recent works in the branch of health geography have suggested that a shift from medical geography to the geography of health is more than a change in title. It also represents an epistemological shift that questions the grounds upon which medical geographical knowledge is based (Brown and Duncan 2002; Gesler and Kearns 2002). Pearce (2003) thinks that there has been a major change in the nature of research undertaken by geographers with an interest in health. In other words, distinctions are often made between medical and health geography, with medical geography dominated by biomedical models favouring intensive quantitative methods, whereas health geography relies more on socio-ecological models and often employs more extensive qualitative approaches (Mayer 2000; Gesler 2006). In recent years, health/medical geographers have challenged the dominance of a bio-medical discourse and have demonstrated the inherently social and political nature of health and health care (Wilton 1999), a growing new

A. Paul (✉)
Department of Geography and Environmental Studies, University of Chittagong, Chittagong, Bangladesh
Paul.alak@cu.ac.bd

© The Author(s), under exclusive license to Springer Nature Switzerland AG 2023
N. Uddin, A. Paul (eds.), *The Palgrave Handbook of Social Fieldwork*, https://doi.org/10.1007/978-3-031-13615-3_11

geographical research feature of qualitative methodology. Traditionally, medical geographers represent a strong quantitative emphasis along with statistical hypotheses on disease incidence or prevalence spatially which provide clues to disease aetiology. These changes of emphases have been accompanied and facilitated by methodological shifts from quantitative to qualitative which, in Kearns' (1995) emphasis, is 'recasting of the subjects of research as persons rather than as patients' (p. 252); using participant observation, in-depth interviews, focus groups, storytelling and autobiography as methods (Kearns 1995, 1997). Wilton (1999) stated that 'in health geography, qualitative research may involve talking with people who are dealing with poor health, with the social stigma attached to certain conditions and who are otherwise in potentially vulnerable situations' (p. 262). He also gave importance (1999) to recognising the direct involvement in people's lives that qualitative research implies (Cohen et al. 2015; Kaley et al. 2019). Qualitative research aims to understand how the lived experiences and meanings associated with health risk are influenced by different social, cultural and economic contexts (Rhodes 1995) through everyday interaction and experience (Rhodes and Quirk 1996). Qualitative research thus proceeds on the assumption that it is possible to gain an insight into the factors producing social behaviour, primarily through engaging with participants themselves (Agar 1980). Qualitative health research aims to answer 'what', 'how' or 'why' questions about social aspects of health, illness and health care (Green and Thorogood 2004).

Geographers have worked on infectious diseases such as cholera, malaria, influenza, measles and hepatitis for a long time (e.g. Learmonth 1952; May 1958; Stamp 1964; Pyle 1969; Cliff and Haggett 1988; Thomas 1992) and are now making contributions to the geography of HIV/AIDS in the contemporary period (Paul 2009). The global epidemic of HIV/AIDS has come under scrutiny since the 1980s and, particularly, from the beginning of the 1990s. As a topic of research, it has a strong pull because of the heavy toll of morbidity and mortality, and also because of the intellectual challenge of understanding its epidemiology. Analysis of the geographic distribution and migration of HIV is an established field of study where mapping is the main element to show the origin of the virus and its diffusion over space. All of the quantitative-based works have determined that HIV/AIDS has tended to cluster in certain areas, and infection, diffusion and overlap can be expected between different population subgroups, even those who have not traditionally been at risk. The quantitative research designs of most HIV-prevention studies do not measure accurately the intimate practices of vulnerable people (Bourgois et al. 2003). Most research studies, particularly those of an epidemiological or quantitative slant, are unable to describe how risk behaviour is understood (Rhodes 1995). Instead, the advent of AIDS brought about major shifts in the substantive interests of qualitative researchers, as well as methodological innovations more generally on risk behaviour (Lambert et al. 1995; Wiebel 1996). Qualitative understandings of the social context of risk behaviour are paramount in understanding HIV infection, and HIV-related risk behaviour, as a product of the particular 'risk environments' in which they occur (Rhodes et al. 2001). In addition, qualitative research techniques are now a commonly used and accepted means of social inquiry, particularly the case among 'hidden' or 'hard-to-reach' populations—such as sex workers or drug users—where there exist practical and methodological difficulties in the use of large-scale quantitative surveys and representative sampling designs (Aviles et al. 2000). However, qualitative research approaches are increasingly recognized for their importance in the geography of health and health care (Curtis et al. 2000). In developing the 'new geographies of HIV/AIDS' which are alternatives to the quantitative approach, many authors (i.e. Downing 2008; Ghosh et al. 2009; Kuhanen 2010; Schatz et al. 2011; Seckinelgin 2012; Tobin et al. 2013; Lewis 2016; Collins et al. 2016; Paul 2020) highlighted different issues, including place, vulnerability, stigmatization, marginalization, etc., through in-depth narratives.

The author was involved with the everyday life of the marginalized and stigmatized people in HIV/AIDS discourse during his doctoral research using a qualitative approach. The chapter presents a self-reported description developed by him regarding his research subjects, support and surrounding environments during his 'fieldwork' in the arena of health geographic study. Here, the present researcher discusses how he planned his research settings; managed his diversified participants both individual and group; developed suitable contacts through 'snowballing' or peers; earned trust using 'body language' and friendly attitude; shown interest to listen to their 'sad stories' through in-depth interview, group discussion, case study, participant observation, etc. Apart from different experiences on survey planning and data collection experiences, problems faced in the 'fieldwork' and overall limitations of the qualitative research have also been described in the following sections.

11.2 Research Planning and Experiences

I received a scholarship from the British government in 2005 for pursuing my PhD in the Department of Geography, University of Durham, UK. I chose a topic on HIV/AIDS in Bangladesh for my doctoral research, which seems to be very sensitive in nature. When I approached the research subject to both supervisors in a presentation at the begining, they were hesitant about its expected outcomes because of the stigmatized environment, poor availability of related literature, and marginalized people in HIV discourse in Bangladesh. Meanwhile, I found many interesting pieces of literature, especially from the African context that built my epistemological, ontological and methodological clarity about my proposed research. I received high attention for my presentation organized for the post-graduate students named 'Geographical Imagination' both in the University of Durham and the University of New Castle, UK. I explained in detail to my audiences, including my supervisors about my study objectives, study location, expected field plan and design. Being a part of PhD research in health geography, I came to Bangladesh in

2006 from the UK and spent more than seven months an extensive 'fieldwork' using qualitative methods. I never faced or interviewed any sex workers or drug users or HIV infected people who are almost treated as 'banned' in the Bangladeshi society and never thought to visit any brothel or drug user's den in my life before this fieldwork. I chose to work in Jessore and Khulna districts which are considered geographically significant for HIV/AIDS research. I visited many stigmatized places like brothels and talked with those who are marginalized in the Bangladeshi conservative society. I also found many vulnerable communities (especially transport workers) who can be considered as 'risk-bridging' people in the HIV/AIDS literature to see the situation and know the condition of this health threat through this study.

As the HIV/AIDS issue is stigmatized in Bangladesh, the selection of specific interviewees and focus group discussion participants was very carefully planned. I stayed in the field for more than seven months for this research. Different socially marginalized communities and vulnerable groups were considered as research participants in order to understand their exposure to health risks, their coping strategies and their 'lifeworlds'. However, I also managed to develop contact with local civil society participants and officials of national and international agencies to elicit their views about the issues, plans and future policies on HIV/AIDS in Bangladesh. In many cases, I obtained NGO permission from the head office for accessing their office and stakeholders at the local level. What kind of security measures did I take due to the fact that it was a challenging job? I thought carefully about personal safety. Before starting fieldwork, I had regular communication with local civil administration high officials including, District Commissioners and high police officials of the study areas since I worked with some groups who are usually termed 'dangerous' by local people. Many locals advised me to keep in regular contact with the police to avoid potential danger or harassment from drug users, sex workers or others. The police high officials reassured me and I was given relevant mobile telephone numbers for emergency contact. Moreover, I developed good relationships with local influential journalists and local university and college teachers as well for references. In most cases, I visited these people personally after getting an appointment by mobile phone. Before starting data collection, I checked the question themes to make a few interviews and group discussions with these mentioned groups as a part of a pilot study. Then I modified the question themes accordingly. Moreover, I kept in regular contact with my supervisors during fieldwork as some of the question themes needed to be changed. By making an appointment scheduled, I regularly communicated with the NGO peer educators and other sources who had good relationships with project participants.

11.3 Problems Faced During Fieldwork

As my research issue is considered 'sensitive' and I worked with some socially marginalized and vulnerable people, I faced a number of problems during fieldwork, as described below.

1. I faced abusive language during a few interviews at a Jessore brothel and was forced to leave the place due to an interruption from an influential woman. For example, I was interviewing a '*chemri*' (bonded sex worker) when suddenly a lady approached and shouted rude language at both of us, and I was compelled to stop the interview at an incomplete stage.
2. Some respondents assumed that I came from a daily newspaper, so they were very cautious. At Fultola brothel, one girl willingly allowed some photos to be taken by my assistant, but the next day, when we arrived, she asked me not to publish the pictures in any local daily newspaper. She became confused and shouted at us to delete her pictures. I became very concerned to see her sudden outburst, but some local NGO workers solved the problem on our behalf.
3. In Jessore and Khulna, some Local Civil Society (LCS) participants missed appointments several times, which hampered my schedule. Most of the time, when I phoned to confirm the schedule, they cancelled the appointment and gave me another time. Also, during the interviews with LCS people, many of them received phone calls, which interrupted the flow of conversation.
4. A few addict interviewees were selected by NGO workers who then refused to talk to me. A few even denied their drug addiction. NGO workers explained that this was because people felt scared, but it did waste time.
5. I requested an NGO to organize a programme to show me its operation in the field. But unfortunately the NGO was unwilling to agree to this. They gave some poor excuses for not organizing this, but I think they wanted to avoid seeing me conceal this area of their weakness.
6. When I was talking with addicted respondents beside the road or in a residential area, it was common for local people to interrupt or become curious to listen. Sometimes these onlookers stubbornly refused to move on. Sometimes they tried to blame the addicts as an anti-social element and even asked me to arrest them, which ultimately interrupted the conversation.
7. There were a few technical problems with data collection. For example, on some occasions at the start of an FGD or interview, the digital voice recorder failed to operate properly, and I was required to make written notes.
8. One addict respondent sought money from me for heroin. When I refused, he became angry and told me that he would go to sell his blood and refused then to continue his conversation with me.

9. I introduced myself to one street girl near Khulna railway station and started to talk to her sitting on the footpath. When we were talking, many people on the street were looking at me strangely and may have considered me to be a punter. When we had just started our interview, I discovered that the girl was feeling shy about responding. Her husband was sitting beside her and he gave me advice not to ask any questions which might bother or embarrass him. I was confused to hear that the woman's age was 35, but her so-called husband was 22. The woman was clearly not free to talk with me about risky behaviours and I felt threatened by her husband, so I decided to stop the interview, giving the excuse that it was a noisy environment.

11.4   Diversified Participants

I talked with different people during my fieldwork. In the beginning, I interviewed some people who are treated as vulnerable to HIV infection in the HIV literature in Jessore and Khulna. They are commercial sex workers (including hotel, residence, floating, brothel and street-based); drug users (including heroin smokers and intravenous drug users); transport workers (including Indian and Bangladeshi truckers and rickshaw pullers); and female slum dwellers and people living with HIV (PLWH). At the later stage, I talked with some local known people in both places, for example, journalists, NGO personnel, local government officials, international agency people, teachers, physicians, local elected representatives and religious persons who can be considered knowledgeable and local elite. Finally, I managed to work with key personnel and policy planners for HIV in Dhaka, including Bangladeshi NGO high officials, international agency officials and members of funding organizations. Regarding the sampling issue, I used the purposive sampling method and 'snowballing' technique mostly to select my diversified participants as these strategies work well on sensitive topics. Apart from specific marginalized and vulnerable people, I also interviewed their family members to understand the social context and family opinions. In order to know and understand addicts' attitudes and behaviour, I undertook interviews with mothers and wives. In order to follow up on case verification for the addicts, I went to some of their houses and met with their family members, whilst keeping confidentiality or making a phone call to inquire about the addict's present condition. In most cases, family members, particularly wives, did not want to admit to their husbands' heroin addictions due to the social stigma, but a few wives confessed and told me about their troubles with their addicted husbands. I also met with some recovering addicts' family members and, in a few cases, I used the opportunity of having both parties present to question the former addict and the rest of the family together about their experiences. In addition, I met with a recovering addict who was the former local representative. I also arranged a few interviews with family members of PLWH, and, in this regard, I selected an NGO worker (not as Local Civil Society: LCS people) who deals with PLWH and knows their emotional world. I decided to talk with her to assess the PLWH's different demands from the NGOs. Some NGO outreach workers (former CSWs and DUs) who give support to their peers, helped to assess all of my respondents' information authenticity. I interviewed them to get their ideas about how NGO accessibility can improve. In a few brothels, I was privileged to meet some customers along with their sex partners. I asked some questions related to HIV to understand their knowledge. Finally, I undertook a few interviews with local healers in Benapole, and I also visited CSW's children's house to get an idea about their lives.

11.5 Finding and Selecting Suitable Participants

I was very cautious about the selection of my research participants and FGD member as the issue of HIV is a sensitive matter. Apart from my own searching of the respondents, I found some local NGOs that are working with vulnerable groups in Jessore and Khulna. When I approached them by telling them my research objectives, they showed their interest to help me by getting access to their stakeholders directly. These NGOs also introduced me to their peer educators, who worked at the field level, so that they could help me to find street drug users and sex workers and transport workers in the 'open field' like steamer terminals, tea stalls, transport terminals, residential streets, beside the highway or in rickshaw garages. I visited these different places on my own with my research associates. For example, I found a heroin addict at a drug selling point in Jessore where I introduced myself and wanted to talk about his miseries. We started our conversation sitting beside a coconut tree. I managed a few contacts and addresses of heroin addicts from him and approached them later on using the snowball technique. This is how I managed to develop relationships with some members of the marginalized community and find more participants from these groups. Snowballing technique was less effective for Indian truckers because nobody trusted me or wanted to speak about their personal lives in front of another friend. In that case, I took help from some NGO peer educators who involve in HIV prevention programs with the truckers. These NGO workers approached them, especially Indian transport workers who have spare time to talk with me in the afternoon session. In most cases, they thought that I came from any intelligence branch, as most of them feared. After telling the research aim to them, I sat beside the truck in the terminal area for the interview or FGD. In most cases, I didn't ask their name which helped them to talk freely with me. When they trusted me, the foreign truckers were quite reluctant to speak about their sexual life. Some truckers considered and believed me as a physician, though I clearly stated my educational qualifications before the interview. I took help from the interpreter for the Hindi-speaking Indian drivers in Benapole terminal, Jessore. Other than 'open field', I managed many interviews in the closed rooms of NGOs for interviewing drug users, brothel-based sex workers and people living with HIV. Some NGOs even have their offices in the brothel where I interviewed and organized FGDs with girls. For

HIV infected people, I also took help from the NGO offices for talking with these many stigmatized people. Only in a few cases, I visited their house for talking and getting the impressions about them from their other family members. Organizing FGD with sex workers and drug users in the 'open' environment was difficult in many cases rather than in a 'close' setting. In the closed environment, all participants were very attentive in replying to my questions and queries. But all respondents, especially street drug users felt a threat by the local people while I was talking to them. Although I took the NGO's help in many aspects, they had no influence on my research participants. From an ethical point of view, I always assured my interviewees that I was not an NGO official, so they could easily share their views and I found this to be beneficial. In addition, many other prominent local people in both study areas and policy planners in Dhaka gave interviews in their offices.

11.6 Earning Interviewees' Trust

Regarding my interview approach, I told everyone about my PhD project and my objectives in detail, at the beginning. When they agreed to participate, I started my interviews or group discussions. Some felt embarrassed or were afraid to talk with a stranger. When I met them in an 'open field' (street corner or transport terminals or abandoned house, etc.) or in a closed room, such as an NGO office, I found some to be very nervous. I tried to make them feel relaxed at first by asking 'ice-breaker' questions and engaging in normal small talk. In the FGD format, at first, I introduced myself to my participants (who ranged in number from five to eight), and then I explained my research topic—but not in elaborate detail, otherwise, they might think it was a problem for them. Finally, I gave them an assurance of anonymity. Fortunately, in most cases, my interviewees felt reassured because it was not so much a formal interview as a normal conversation, and I found them to be easy, relaxed and flexible. I did not always finish my question schedule because interviewees wanted to continue their life stories or history of their suffering. If the participant stopped contributing at any point, then I usually asked another question derived from his or her previous conversation. When I could not find anything special, I changed my interview style and asked them some 'light' questions. Sometimes I asked the same question twice at different times in order to assess the authenticity of the answer. In the event of a discrepancy, I tried to help them recall their previous answer to work out what the truth was. However, when I asked participants to talk about facts, a few were worried about confidentiality. In these cases, I gave categorical assurances about anonymity. To see the group dynamics and participants' psychology, the whole research team including my assistants observed each discussion which was held in brothels, NGO offices or in field sites, and in each discussion, I played the role of moderator to facilitate the conversation.

During each interview, I needed to earn the trust of the interviewee to get information. I came to understand that many marginalized people, particularly sex working girls, often do not want to share their emotions and feelings even with NGO peers. On reflection, I feel privileged because I think that I was able to explore many of their 'lifeworlds', although it is difficult to draw firm conclusions from an hour-long interview. Many people tried to assess 'up to which level they would trust me', then some of them told me real facts since they considered me to be trustworthy. I adopted no authoritarian or patronising attitudes in my approach to them. Many addicts and TWs thought me to be a detective police officer at the beginning. Sometimes my attempts at consolation also induced them to share stories of their suffering in the 'banned life' or stigmatized life of a hidden sex worker, drug user or PLWH. During my interviews, I was sympathetic; good behaviour and simplicity, and sometimes some emotional expressions, also influenced them to share their untold stories. It is difficult to say what should be the real academic query style for these marginalized groups, but I found that if I could understand their sorrows and if they could see it in my eyes, they would tell their facts. I never showed any aggressive or hostile attitudes in my questions and did not ask about any issues that they might consider disrespectful. I never tried to exploit these people in any way. I always tried to keep myself as quiet as possible, which helped them to trust me rapidly. I showed all of my respondents a high level of respect. If they received phone calls during the interview, I advised them to receive the call. I never asked them to switch off their phones because many of them received calls from paying customers. On the other hand, some girls were annoyed to receive calls during the interview and switched off their phones willingly. Some wanted to continue talking with me after more than an hour had passed, so I reminded them of the time so that they would not suffer by losing customers. Sometimes I wondered why they were so interested in giving up their time to talk with me. I think that one reason is 'sharing'. They cannot share their life with anyone because they have no trustworthy friends. They considered me a friend, which also helped my research findings. One hotel girl, who shared her life story with me without hesitation, told me that there are some issues of life which she did not share even with her husband. She said, "*I feel very happy that I could share many of my sufferings with you. There are some things which I don't talk about with my husband because he might get angry or be sad to hear my feelings. Now I feel light from my heart after sharing many things with you, but I don't know what you think of me.*"

11.7 Emotional Involvement

The fieldwork was by no means all plain sailing. Although I had some bad experiences with these 'inaccessible' communities, I had a lot of good experiences, including the willingness of people generally to talk and share their life stories with me. I will mention a few of these here. When I heard about the sorrows or discrimination in the family of the PLWH or marginalized people, I felt very sad and sympathized with them. For example, one of the PLWHs appealed to me to arrange the marriage of her daughter after her death. When one of the PLWH participants was crying, I tried to give her some consolation. I emphasized keeping her confidence and reminded her to trust in God. I hinted to her that some good opportunities might come up in the future. Another PLWH was telling me about her husband's love affair with tearful emotion—which was a really emotional moment for me. In addition, I visited a baby having HIV in a hospital when he has been suffering from some opportunistic infections. I took some fruit and chocolate for him. I encouraged his father and advised him not to be anxious. They were all asking me to do more for their welfare in future. Many PLWH invited me to visit their house or village. One of them was so enthusiastic that she had been waiting for me to call her as an interviewee. She said, "*I was waiting for your interview call. I thought that as I cannot speak Bengali language* [she is a foreigner] *you will not call me. But I was very willingly interested to hear from you.*" Now I feel that I can also play a positive role in their welfare. Moreover, as many drug addicts considered me an NGO high official, they requested me to admit them into an NGO treatment centre after the interview. They were telling me that they wanted to be cured. I approached an NGO on behalf of a few addicts and finally, they got the chance of being admitted into the treatment centre. However, other respondents made jokes with me and asked about personal issues, such as my marital status, religion and home address. One participant told me that I did not look like a university teacher because I looked very 'young' in their eyes. One sought a job from me and another thought that I would give them a prize on the basis of their knowledge of HIV after the interview. In an FGD session with addicts, they wanted to sing a song on drug addiction and its vulnerability. I was encouraged to hear it as it was a melodious song which described the vulnerability of addiction. In addition, I asked almost everybody what they understood about my study or research. However, regarding the issue of positionality, many respondents asked questions about their risk behaviour after the interview or FGD when they became close to me. These participants thought that I was a practising medical doctor and wanted to learn from me about health risks. They also anticipated that they could obtain prescriptions for medication from me. In most cases, I tried to give answers to their questions and so increase their awareness of HIV risk. I advised those participants who showed me their physical problems to visit a doctor immediately. I believe that my research helped many vulnerable people to get involved with safe practices—particularly in terms of needle sharing and condom use.

11.8 Experiences in Data Collection

I used in-depth interviews, focus group discussions, participant observation and naturalistic observation. I used a digital voice recorder for recording data and a written diary was used on an everyday basis. Observation reports from research assistants and photographs were also used in the research. The research assistants received a week of intensive training before the data collection started. I also collected secondary materials like published books, annual reports, NGO working maps and documents, and posters and leaflets. The following experiences are reproduced to illustrate my data collection points and approaches.

In-Depth interviews: An in-depth interview is a one-to-one research encounter in which a respondent answers the questions of a researcher. In this study, different questions were asked of individuals to elicit their understanding of the issues of HIV risk. As a technique of in-depth interview, I approached some brothel girls (in *Maruary Mandir*, Jessore; *Fultala* and *Baniashanta* of Khulna) when they had finished their 'business' with the customer. Most non-brothel girls were anxious about recording the interviews. For drug users, I found many addicts who either had already taken drugs or were waiting to take drugs. Most of them gave their in-depth interview in the open. I did not observe any fear or shyness about giving interviews with the addicts. Transport workers showed their reluctance to be interviewed concerning their risky behaviour. I found most truckers for interviewing—including Indians—in the terminal areas of Benapole land port. In the case of PLWH, I found them through different NGOs and interviewed them in the NGO office. Many gave long interviews and with much emotion. On the other hand, some respondents replied only briefly to my questions. Interviews with slum dwellers, rickshaw pullers, and local healers were undertaken at convenient times and places for them.

Focus group discussion: The group situation can also stimulate people in making explicit their views, perceptions, motives and reasons. The FGD method was adopted in this research since the study of HIV issues in marginalized communities was complex and was thought to benefit from participants interacting with each other. It was really difficult to organize and conduct group discussions with the sex workers and addicts, but I was able to organise 30 focus groups in total. I found the people in many FGDs to be different with many interesting issues with their group dynamics. For example, with addicts, I was required to mix with them in different ways and to listen to their emotions with more attention. Sometimes I observed that when I was listening to one addict's voice or opinion, the others wanted to speak against that. Some participants thought that I would give them money for heroin or would provide opportunities for treatment. Different individual characters like addicts in a group discussion are very difficult to manage. In an FGD with brothel sex workers, I found that the girls wanted to withdraw from the discussion after a while. Apart from their 'business' time limitation, the main reason behind this is that some of the girls do not wish to discuss their life stories or other issues in front of their colleagues. In the FGD, some of them seemed to be very vocal and others very quiet. When I tried to break their silence, sometimes I could but sometimes they laughed. Sometimes they carried their baby along and when the baby cried, they were forced to leave the session. However, although addicts were very willing to speak or discuss sexual matters in a group format, many TWs were embarrassed to speak about sexual issues. Among FGD participants, many transport and addicts wanted to show me or talk to me individually about their sexual infections.

Participant observation: In participant observation, the researcher seeks to observe events and the behaviour of people by taking part in the activity themselves. As an observer, I adopted many dynamics during my fieldwork. I visited drug addicts' treatment and rehabilitation centres and drop-in centres of NGOs as a participant-observer to see how people are living life or passing their time. And sometimes I asked their opinions about life there.

Case-1: Participant observation in a commercial drug treatment centre gave me many different experiences during fieldwork in Jessore. This is a treatment centre where I did not find a doctor or any trained person for the addicted patients. It seemed like a prison to me, where I found few living rooms and one toilet and bathroom for all the patients. After getting permission to observe activities, I stayed there for one day and tried to talk to and follow their everyday life or daily routines. I took my food with the patients.

Case-2: I decided to visit an addicts' rehabilitation centre, though they didn't allow me to do so at the outset. I stayed in that centre for the whole day from morning to evening. My assistant and I tried to follow the addicted people's life skill training by observing and talking with them through the use of a voice recorder, camera and diary writing. I held an FGD with a few patients and a few recovering addicts in the rehab centre during their leisure time or in between two sessions.

Case-3: I also visited an NGO treatment centre for addicts where I was allowed to see the patients' activities and talk with them about the nature and cause of their addiction and also how they sought remedies from the treatment centre.

Case-4: I visited an HIV positive house in Khulna in order to see her life with other family members. I took my lunch with the all-family members to show my integrity. I stayed with them for more than six hours and inquired about different issues, particularly whether HIV is affecting their everyday and social life in any way. I brought sweets and some energy drinks for them.

Naturalistic observation: As a naturalistic observer, I visited some parts of the India-Bangladesh border which are considered to be a 'trafficking zone' and drug smuggling point. During that trip, I took a local man with me to show me how the trafficking of women takes place. He showed me some points of the border where 'syndicate' people from both countries work together for human and drug trafficking. In that land port area, I saw many issues of the truckers, including Indians. In order to see the addicts in both my data collection areas, I visited many places which are known as drug selling points. Most are located beside the transport terminals and slum areas where population mobility is high. In addition, I also visited drug-taking points to see how addicts take their drugs and to understand how long they take them and their reactions after taking the drugs. In the case of sex workers, I visited places in both towns, Jessore and Khulna, where the floating, street-based sex workers can be found. I saw many girls in places, such as busy street corners and beside the cinema, waiting until midnight looking for customers. At all the brothels I visited, I found potential customers waiting in the street outside the brothel entrance.

11.9 Limitations of the Study

A number of limitations during data collection have been identified in this study. **First**, some of the participants arranged by NGO people for my research were motivated by NGO peers. When NGOs brought participants into the office, sometimes peers shared my research interest with the participants, which seemed to me to be one of my research limitations. Participants considered that I was there to evaluate their HIV knowledge so when I asked a question they irrelevantly replied that they 'know everything about HIV'. To some extent, dependency on NGOs for choosing the participants from the field hampered the standard of my requirements. **Second**, during the first few interviews, I missed some opportunities to explore more important themes from the respondents because of my excitement. During data collection, I became very emotional after listening to the suffering of the respondents, which to some extent stopped the flow of the interview or hampered my attempts to acquire the best information. However, I did not fully understand their (CSW and DU) language, tone and eye contact, though I learned the meaning of their language after a certain time. **Third**, in FGDs, sometimes I was uncomfortable asking the respondents difficult questions regarding their sexual behaviours. Sometimes I asked them questions which irritated them, causing some hesitation for both of us. My observation is that people feel embarrassed discussing sexual matters. When I asked any relevant questions to them, they replied very briefly, rather than as I expected. I was required to ask many questions to understand their level of risk. They sometimes felt shy and embarrassed. **Fourth**, I had some preconceived notions from the surveillance report of the Bangladesh government that most potential drug users would be injecting drug users (IDU). But in both of my field areas, I found that most drug users were actually heroin smokers. I did not find many IDUs, which hampered my understanding of their health risks. **Fifth**, for key personnel interviews, I tried to question the highest-ranked officials, but in some cases, I experienced that they were reluctant to keep the appointment and referred me to other officials. This also happened at the field level, where government officials avoided this responsibility. In some cases, high officials told me many issues only when I switched off my recorder. They talked about 'sensitive' matters of government as well as their own organization which they insisted had to be 'off the record'. **Sixth**, the data on health risks, particularly sexual activities and drug habits were collected through self-reports in interviews which are always a matter of validity and reliability and recall problems despite the researcher's efforts. **Seventh**, as the present study is a qualitative study and the data collected are exploratory and thematic in nature, there are no quantitative comparisons. This might have contributed to missing some more positive ideas in the research because the qualitative approach has some limits on the generality of the findings.

11.10 Concluding Remarks

Like other diseases, geographers are now making contributions to the geography of HIV/AIDS in the contemporary period. Traditionally, medical geographers highlight a strong quantitative emphasis on disease incidence spatially, on the other side, health geographers aim to understand the meanings of health risk associated with different social, cultural and economic contexts mainly using a qualitative approach. The author was involved with the everyday life of the marginalized and stigmatized people in the HIV/AIDS discourse during his doctoral research. Here, qualitative data were used to understand the interactions between health risk, stigma, place and policy. In addition, the qualitative methods in this study examine how people lead their 'everyday lives' when they are marginalized or stigmatized in the society in the context of HIV vulnerability following in-depth interviews, focus group discussions and participant observation. The chapter presents a self-reported description of his respondents, supports and surrounding environments during his 'fieldwork' through a qualitative approach in the arena of health geography.

Acknowledgements This chapter is based on the author's doctoral study conducted at the Department of Geography, University of Durham, the UK in 2009. The author is very grateful to Emeritus Professor Dr Peter J Atkins and Dr Christine E Dunn of the above department for their supervision during the PhD program. The author is also grateful to the authority of ORSAS/UK and the Doctoral fellowship program of Durham University for their financial awards.

References

Agar, M. (1980) *The professional stranger: an informal introduction to ethnography*, Academic Press, New York

Andrews, G. J., Cutchin, M., McCracken, K., Phillips, D. R. and Wiles, J. (2007) Geographical gerontology: the constitution of a discipline, *Social Science and Medicine*, 65 (1), 151–168

Aviles, N. R., Barnard, M., Rhodes, T. et al (2000) Qualitative research on the health risks associated with drug injecting: needle and syringe sharing, In EMCDDA (ed) *Understanding and responding to drug use: the role of Qualitative Research*, Scientific monograph series, No. 4, Luxembourg

Bourgois, P., Lettiere, M. and Quesada, J. (2003) Social misery and the sanctions of substance abuse: confronting HIV risk among homeless heroin addicts in San Francisco, In J. D. Orcutt and D. R. Rudi (eds) *Drugs, alcohol and social problems*, Rowman & Littlefield Publishers, New York, pp. 257–278

Brown, T. and Duncan, C. (2002) Placing geographies of public health, *Area*, 34 (4), 361–369

Cliff, A. D. and Haggett, P. (1988) *Atlas of disease distributions: analytic approaches to epidemiological data*, Blackwell, New York

Cohen, A. T., Goto, S., Schreiber, K. and Torp-Pedersen, C. (2015) Why do we need observational studies of everyday patients in the real-life setting? *European Heart Journal Supplements*, 17 (Suppl-D), pp D2–D8

Collins, A. B., Parashar, S., Closson, K., Turje, R. B., Strike, C. and McNeil, R. (2016) Navigating identity, territorial stigma, and HIV care services in Vancouver, Canada: a qualitative study, *Health & Place*, 40 (July): 169–177

Curtis, S. (2004) *Health and inequality: geographical perspectives*, Sage, London

Curtis, S., Gesler, W., Smith, G. and Washburn, S. (2000) Approaches to sampling and case selection in qualitative research: examples in the geography of health, *Social Science and Medicine*, 50 (7–8), 1001–1014

Downing Jr, Martin J. (2008) The role of home in HIV/AIDS: a visual approach to understanding human-environment interactions in the context of long-term illness, *Health & Place*, 14 (2): 313–322

Gesler, W. M. (2006) Geography of health and healthcare, In B. Warf (ed.) *Encyclopedia of human geography*, Sage, Thousand Oaks, CA, pp. 205–206

Gesler, W. M. and Kearns, R. A. (2002) *Culture/Place/Health*, Routledge, London

Ghosh, J., Wadhwa, V. and Kalipeni, E. (2009) Vulnerability to HIV/AIDS among women of reproductive age in the slums of Delhi and Hyderabad, India, *Social Science & Medicine*, 68 (4): 638–642

Green, J. and Thorogood, N. (2004) *Qualitative methods for health research*, Sage, London

Kaley, A., Hatton, C. and Milligan, C. (2019) Health geography and the 'performative' turn: making space for the audio-visual in ethnographic health research, *Health and Place*, 60 (November), 102210

Kearns, R. A. (1995) Medical geography: making space for difference, *Progress in Human Geography*, 19 (2), 251–259

Kearns, R. A. (1997) Narrative and metaphor in health geographies, *Progress in Human Geography*, 21 (2), 269–277

Kuhanen, J. (2010) Sexualised space, sexual networking & the emergence of AIDS in Rakai, Uganda, *Health & Place*, 16(2): 226–235

Lambert, E. Y., Ashery, R. S. and Needle, R. H. (eds) (1995) *Qualitative methods in drug abuse and HIV research*, National Institute on Drug Abuse, Monograph 157, Rockville

Learmonth, A. T. A. (1952) The medical geography of India: an approach to the problem, In K. Kuriyan (ed) *The Indian geographical society*, The silver jubilee volume, Indian Geographical Society, Madras, 201–202

Lewis, N. M. (2016) Urban encounters and sexual health among gay and bisexual immigrant men: perspectives from the settlement and aids service sectors, *Geographical Review*, 106(2): 235–256

May, J. M. (1958) *The ecology of human disease*, MD Publication, New York

Mayer, J. D. (2000) Health geography, In R. J. Johnston et al (eds) *The dictionary of human geography*, Blackwell, MA

Parr, H. (1998) The politics of methodology in 'post-medical geography': mental health research and the interview, *Health & Place*, 4 (4), 341–353

Paul, A. (2009) Geographies of HIV/AIDS in Bangladesh: vulnerability, stigma and place, Durham theses, Durham University. (http://etheses.dur.ac.uk/1348/)

Paul, A. (2020) *HIV/AIDS in Bangladesh: stigmatized people, policy and place*, Springer, London

Pearce, J. (2003) Editorial: emerging new research in the geography of health and impairment, *Health & Place*, 9 (2), 107–108

Pyle, G. F. (1969) The diffusion of cholera in the United States in the nineteenth century, *Geographical Analysis*, 1, 59–75

Rhodes, T. (1995) Theorizing and researching 'risk': notes on the social relations of risk in heroin users' lifestyles, In P. Aggleton, P. Davies and G. Hart (eds) *AIDS: safety, sexuality and risk*, Taylor & Francis, London

Rhodes, T. and Quirk, A. (1996) Heroin, risk and sexual safety, In T. Rhodes and R. Hartnoll (eds) *AIDS, drugs and prevention: perspectives on individual and community action*, Routledge, London

Rhodes, T., Barnard, M., Fountain, J. et al (2001) *Injecting drug use, risk behaviour and qualitative research in the time of AIDS*, EMCDDA, July, Luxembourg

Schatz, E., Madhavan, S. and Williams, J. (2011) Female-headed households contending with AIDS-related hardship in rural South Africa, *Health & Place*, 17(2): 598–605

Seckinelgin, H. (2012) The global governance of success in HIV/AIDS policy: emergency action, everyday lives and Sen's capabilities, *Health & Place*, 18(3): 453–460

Stamp, L. D. (1964) *The geography of life and death*, Cornell University Press, Ithaca, NY

Thomas, R. W. (1992) *Geo medical systems: intervention and control*, Routledge, London

Tobin, K. E., Cutchin, M. C., Latkin, A. and Takahashi, L. M. (2013) Social geographies of African American men who have sex with men (MSM): a qualitative exploration of the social, spatial and temporal context of HIV risk in Baltimore, Maryland, *Health & Place*, 22 (July): 1–6

Wiebel, W. (1996) Ethnographic contributions to AIDS prevention strategies, In T. Rhodes and R. Hartnoll (eds) *AIDS, drugs and prevention: perspectives on individual and community action*, Routledge, London

Wilton, R. D. (1999) Qualitative health research: negotiating life with HIV/AIDS, *The Professional Geographer*, 51 (2), 254–264

CHAPTER 12

Adolescent Drug Use in Connecticut Private High Schools: Zero Tolerance, Contextual Peer Influence, and Deterrence Effectiveness

Minjune Song

12.1 Introduction

Criminological deterrence, the concept of deterring criminals and non-criminals from committing crimes, is central to the criminal justice system. Deterrence theory also has a place in school discipline, notably in the form of school zero-tolerance policies. In general, zero-tolerance policies prohibit people in authority from exercising discretion on a case-by-case basis, instead of mandating severe and certain punishments regardless of individual circumstances. Recent research on the negative consequences of zero-tolerance policies has caused the media and the federal government to regard zero tolerance in an increasingly critical light. A 2008 Zero Tolerance Task Force report by the American Psychological Association (APA) indicates that the use of zero-tolerance policies often fails to improve school discipline and is instead associated with higher rates of school dropout and failure to graduate (APA Zero Tolerance Task Force 2008). In addition, in 2014, the U.S. Department of Education and Department of Justice Civil Rights Data Collection briefing encourages educators to reduce their reliance on zero-tolerance punishments like suspensions and expulsions when creating safer learning environments (U.S. Department of Education Office for Civil Rights 2014). In the era of heightened educator accountability, it is appropriate to thoroughly evaluate whether zero-tolerance policies indeed contribute to furthering educational

M. Song (✉)
Groton, CT, USA

© The Author(s), under exclusive license to Springer Nature Switzerland AG 2023
N. Uddin, A. Paul (eds.), *The Palgrave Handbook of Social Fieldwork*, https://doi.org/10.1007/978-3-031-13615-3_12

goals. This paper extends the debate on zero-tolerance policy by examining the relationship between zero-tolerance policies and student drug use in three different peer contexts.

The punitive and exclusionary nature of zero-tolerance policies has been linked to detrimental consequences for punished students. Recent research has found that zero-tolerance policies result in the suspension of Black students at three times the rate of White students (U.S. Department of Education Office for Civil Rights 2014). At least one study provides evidence that zero tolerance aggravates already existing racial inequalities in rates of student suspension and expulsion (Hoffman 2014). In the field of exclusionary discipline, studies have found the rates of suspensions and expulsions to be closely correlated with increased delinquency, lower academic achievement, and higher school dropout rates (Raffaele Mendez 2003; Martinez 2009). While research so far has demonstrated the negative outcomes of zero-tolerance policies' exclusionary nature, relatively little research evaluates the deterrence effect (if any) of such policies.

Studies so far have found drug use to be a sizable contributor to student suspension: nearly 15% of all suspensions are a result of illegal drug abuse. Despite nearly 98% of schools nationwide have written drug and alcohol policies, only a small number of studies measure the effectiveness of school zero-tolerance policy in deterring collective student drug use (APA Zero Tolerance Task Force 2008; Curran 2016). If indeed zero tolerance generally deters students from using drugs, the harms of zero-tolerance policies may be offset by their overall benefits.

However, emerging research on adolescent brain function and social behaviour offers results that are contradictory to the core philosophy of zero tolerance. Under the bioecological model, adolescents perceive rewards more strongly around peers and lack impulse control because of changes in the brain's maturation process (Bronfenbrenner and Morris 2006; Steinberg 2008). Studies have also shown that adolescents in tight, intimate peer groups are more likely to hold delinquent views at odds with social norms. It has been well established that peer pressure has a strong influence on adolescents, in general surpassing parental moderation (Dorius et al. 2004). Peer interaction is an everyday occurrence for adolescents both in and out of school. The effectiveness of zero tolerance cannot be accurately measured without considering the contextual factor of the peer influence that is so highly prevalent in real-world scenarios. Steinberg's findings on adolescent behaviour especially suggest the possibility that adolescents may prioritize rewards from peer interactions over a punishment deterrent in decision making. Under these frameworks, the zero-tolerance policy and its deterring effects may not apply to adolescent age groups.

Fundamentally, this study aims to assess the influence that the severity and likelihood of punishment in zero-tolerance policies have on licit and illicit adolescent drug use. The study addresses two questions: (1) Does a correlation between student drug use and punishment severity and likelihood exist? and

(2) Do contextual factors like peer influence have a stronger correlation with adolescent drug use compared to zero-tolerance policies? This study aims to lay the groundwork for future research by juxtaposing the deterrence effects of zero-tolerance policies with the influence of a contextual factor on adolescent drug abuse, challenging researchers and educators to reconceptualize the reaches of peer influence and the limits of punitive and exclusionary discipline.

12.2 Literature Review

Adolescent Drug Abuse

Adolescent drug abuse remains a deeply ingrained problem in schools and communities nationwide. National use of tobacco, alcohol, marijuana, and other illicit drugs has stabilized and is on a downward trend, but new emergencies like vapable nicotine and marijuana gained significant traction among adolescents. 35.7% of 12th graders, 28.8% of 10th graders, and 11.8% of 8th graders reported having used marijuana in the past year (U.S. Department of Health and Human Services 2019). The use of regular cigarettes has continued to decline, with 5.7% of adolescents reporting using cigarettes regularly compared to 7.6% and 13.6% in 2017 and 2014, respectively. Vaping products, however, have gained alarming popularity, appearing to replace traditional tobacco products for a younger audience. One in four 12th graders has reported vaping nicotine in the past month, and 8.1% of 12th graders noted that they vaped because they are "hooked." In 2018, only 3.6% of adolescents vaped because they were addicted to nicotine (U.S. Department of Health and Human Services 2019).

The growing prevalence of adolescent vaping poses a formidable threat to public health and educational performance given that early and frequent substance use in adolescents predicts lower academic achievement, lower engagement in school, and earlier contact with the criminal justice system. In a study of Canadian youth, the rates of tobacco, alcohol, and marijuana use were found to be strongly associated with proximity measures that predicted poor education (Pathammavong et al. 2011). Research has also shown adolescent drug use to be associated with truancy, a precursor to delinquency (Ellickson et al. 2004). Research has also shown student academic performance in school to be strongly negatively linked with marijuana use. When ranked from highest academic achievement to lowest academic achievement, students who did not use marijuana ranked the highest, and students who used marijuana both regularly and in school ranked the lowest (Finn 2012).

In addition, adolescent drug abuse disproportionately affects youth in areas marked by underemployment and non-traditional family structures. Past research has found that high poverty and high unemployment were community indicators strongly associated with higher adolescent drug use (Hoffmann 2002). Areas afflicted with poverty and unemployment may be unable to organize and influence the behaviour of their residents, failing to prevent adolescent drug use at the community level (Elliott et al. 1996). Children from single-parent families and step-parent families used drugs at a significantly higher rate than children from families with both a biological mother and a biological father, implying that children from non-mother-family structures may lack the necessary parental support at home (Hoffmann 2002). Evidence from studies on a smaller scale also suggests adolescents marginalized from school or society often use drugs as part of their counter-school identity (Fletcher et al. 2009). One study raises the point that adolescent drug abuse may take the form of creative resistance, in this case in the form of "mellow resistance" against a confirmative school environment (Fletcher et al. 2009). Concerns that adolescent drug abuse stems from deeper systemic inequalities like race or social class exist, and there is consensus in research that structural change in school and the broader society must take place to create an environment more conducive to high performance for all students.

Exclusionary Discipline

In schools, exclusionary discipline is a type of severe discipline that punishes students by excluding them from school grounds. Exclusionary discipline takes two forms: suspensions and expulsions. While the length of exclusion may vary by school, a "suspension" generally refers to a shorter period of exclusion (within ten days), while an "expulsion" refers to a longer period of exclusion that may span the semester or the academic year. Evidence shows that the use of exclusionary discipline for students increases as they progress from grade to grade, peaking at around age 15 (Arcia 2006). While research finds that suspensions do not diminish student misbehaviour (Raffaele Mendez 2003), increased suspensions are strongly correlated with lower academic achievement (Arcia 2006). Furthermore, the suspension rates in students have also been correlated with earlier encounters with the juvenile justice system (Costenbader and Markson 1998). Past research focuses more on the immediate association between suspension and problem behaviours, often failing to identify a causal relationship. Previous research has also been limited in that it often does not explicitly evaluate the role that school exclusionary policies play in overall student misbehaviour. As exclusionary discipline is widely applied in school policies like zero tolerance, studying the effects of exclusionary discipline on general misbehaviour levels would be significant given how widely such discipline is implemented.

Zero-Tolerance Policy

Zero-tolerance policies entered schools in the United States in 1994 when the Guns Free School Act (GFSA) mandated that states receiving federal funding implement state laws that required the year-long exclusion of any students who brought a firearm onto school grounds. In the twenty-first century, nearly all schools embraced the federal initiative by adopting a zero-tolerance policy for major infractions beyond firearm offenses. Principles nationwide defined a zero-tolerance policy as "a school or district policy that mandates predetermined consequences or punishments for specific offenses" (U.S. Commissioner of Education Statistics 1998). The OCR defines zero-tolerance policies as follows (APA Zero Tolerance Task Force 2008):

> [a] commonly accepted definition of a 'zero-tolerance policy' is one that 'mandates the application of predetermined consequences, most often severe and punitive in nature, that are intended to be applied regardless of the gravity of behavior, mitigating circumstances, or situational context'

The 2008 APA Zero Tolerance Task Force notes there is a significant lack of research focusing explicitly on zero-tolerance policy and its effects on overall student misbehaviour (APA Zero Tolerance Task Force 2008). Curran's study that focuses on zero-tolerance policies finds little to no change in principal perceptions of problems (an increase in problem perception for assault) after conducting a longitudinal study of problem perceptions before and after the passing of the GFSA (Curran 2016).

Despite existing literature criticizing the use of exclusionary policies like zero tolerance (Morrison and Skiba 2001; Maag 2001), the 1996 National Center for Education Statistics report found 87 to 88% of principals nationwide to have put zero-tolerance policies in place for alcohol and drug use, respectively (U.S. Commissioner of Education Statistics 1998). Adolescent drug abuse is a multi-faceted problem that stretches beyond school policy and impacts other stakeholders like the administration, students, and the wider community. While much academic literature condemns zero tolerance and exclusions for alienating students and aggravating delinquent behaviour, suspensions and expulsions packaged into zero-tolerance policy remain the favourite "treatment" for adolescent drug abuse (U.S. Commissioner of Education Statistics 1998). Zero tolerance as studied in this paper refers exclusively to school zero-tolerance policies. While zero-tolerance often has associations with severe or confirmative school environments that take a zero-tolerance approach, this study limits itself to zero-tolerance policies per se and their effectiveness in reducing drug use to peer context factors.

Competing Theories on Zero Tolerance

Two competing theories prominent in the relevant academic literature, the theory of deterrence and the theory of adolescent risk-taking, serve as the framework and basis of this study. The criminological theory of deterrence is the theoretical foundation of zero-tolerance policies. The principles of deterrence theory rest on a set of presumptions that humans act based on decisions that hold the greatest advantage of benefits to cost (Bentham et al. 1982; Zimring et al. 1976). In deterrence theory, humans are rational enough to consider the outcomes of their actions and will be influenced by those outcomes when making decisions (Kennedy 2010). The principles of deterrence theory state that humans are self-interested, rational, and reasoning. Several hypotheses on deterrence theory have been offered based on these presumptions (Gibbs 1968):

1. The greater the certainty of legal punishment, the lower the crime rate.
2. The greater the severity of legal punishment, the lower the crime rate.
3. The greater the celebrity of legal punishment, the lower the crime rate.

The certainty and severity of punishments following an infraction are factors believed to prevent people from committing crimes, and laws more strongly associated with the three factors above are believed to output a lower crime rate (Beccaria 2009; Nagin 1998). Deterrence theory has had some effect in deterring youths in the juvenile justice system from committing crimes (Pauwels et al. 2011), while its effect on school misbehaviour has been less studied.

Alternatively, the adolescent risk-taking theory used in this study draws from social behavioural and neurobiological research that considers adolescent behavioural outcomes in the context of characteristics of the maturing adolescent brain. Social behavioural studies, in turn, draw work from bioecological theory and social learning theory. Bioecological theory suggests that adolescents are influenced strongly by contextual factors surrounding their development (Bronfenbrenner and Morris 2006), while social learning theory maintains that deviant impulses are inherent in adolescents: social controls from family or other social institutions act to stop adolescents from acting on deviant impulses (Hirschi 1969). Studies following the social learning framework found intimate and small peer group environments to allow adolescents to observe, participate, and reinforce deviant behaviours, including drug use (Reed and Rountree 1997).

In studies that utilized neuro scanning to study adolescent risk-taking, evidence suggests that neurobiological characteristics of the adolescents are correlated with an inordinate focus on rewards rather than a consequence of actions (Gardner and Steinberg 2005). Steinberg suggests that neurological changes in dopamine pathways and oxytocin receptors act to heighten adolescents' desire for rewards in the presence of peers (Steinberg 2008). In addition, Steinberg (2008) also demonstrates that adolescents lack well-developed impulsive behaviour control functions in the prefrontal cortex, underdevelopment that may contribute to their disproportionate focus on rewards. Evidence also suggests that through positive experiences of peer-involved marijuana use, adolescents develop positive cognitive associations with the use of marijuana, expecting similar positive social responses when they use marijuana in the future (Petraitis et al. 1995).

While evidence suggests that adolescents are capable of rational thinking not unlike that of adults, the competing theories about adolescent risk-taking seem to suggest peer influence may warp decision-making at the fundamental levels of the adolescent brain. In a realistic school environment where adolescents interact robustly with peers in and out of classrooms, the theory of deterrence may not hold.

12.3 Results

Subsection A: Methods

Data Sample
Data for the analysis was obtained through an online survey distributed to high school students via email. Students completed a 15-question questionnaire regarding their drug use and their perceptions of school drug and alcohol policy; their names remained anonymous to encourage honest responses. Of the 54 student respondents, 50 attended a high school in Connecticut in the 2019–2020 school year.

Out of 50 respondents, 22 respondents were 11th graders (juniors), 13 were 10th graders (sophomores), 10 were 9th graders (freshmen), and 5 were 12th graders (seniors). 35 students (69.2%) were boarding students who lived on-campus during the school year, while 15 students were day students who did not live on campus.

Connecticut is a state with the second-highest per capita income in the U.S. (U.S. Census Bureau, 2010–2014), and a state particularly renowned for its abundance of private schools, and for having the third-highest educational performance in the nation (Education Week 2018). Past research has shown that children from families with higher disposable incomes and children attending more conformist and academically intensive schools are often more prone to drug abuse (Luthar et al. 2018). Due to the dominance of boarding school students in the sample, this study hypothesized that the conflict between peer influence and school policy would be prominently displayed in the results.

Measure: Rates of Drug Use
Students answered a total of four drug use questions, two on licit drug use (any form of tobacco/nicotine use, alcohol, non-prescribed prescription drugs, inhalants/hallucinogens purchased legally), and two on illicit drug use (non-prescribed marijuana, LSD/mushrooms, any form of opiates, cocaine, MDMA variants, other substances illegal in the state of Connecticut) on a past school month and a projected future school month. Expected drug use was measured by asking students what their expected rate of licit/illicit drug use would be in a future school month. For all questions, students were asked to rate their drug use on a scale of 0 to 4 (0 = none, 1 = once a month or less, 2 = two to four times a month, 3 = two to three times a week, 4 = four times a week or more).

Measure: Peer Influence
This study posed questions to specifically measure the effect peer contexts had on student drug use. The degree of influence peers had on students in each peer context was measured by three aspects: the proportion of student's friends who approved of drug use; the proportion of student's friends who regularly

used drugs; the proportion of student's time spent around friends who regularly used drugs.

To measure what proportion of respondent's friends approved of drug use, students were asked to rate their friends' approval of drug use on a scale of 0 to 10 (0 = none, 1–2 = almost none, 3–4 = fewer than half, 5 = half of them, 6–7 = more than half, 8–9 = nearly all, 10 = all). To measure what proportion of a respondent's friends used drugs, students were asked to indicate the proportion of their friends who regularly used drugs on a scale of 0 to 10 (0 = none, 1–2 = almost none, 3–4 = fewer than half, 5 = half of them, 6–7 = more than half, 8–9 = nearly all, 10 = all). To measure how much time students spent around friends who used drugs, students were asked to report the proportion of free time that they spent around friends who regularly used drugs on a scale of 0 to 10 (0 = none, 1 = 2 almost none, 3–4 = fewer than half, 5 = half, 6–7 = more than half, 8–9 = nearly all, 10 = all).

Measure: Perceived Punishment of Policy
Under the principles of criminological deterrence theory, three hypotheses exist the greater the certainty of punishment, the lower the crime rate; the greater the severity of punishment, the lower the crime rate; the greater the swiftness of punishment, the lower the crime rate. Questions were accordingly devised to measure student perceptions of punishment severity and punishment likelihood for breaking a school drug and alcohol policy. The swiftness of policy delivery is not explicitly specified by schools unlike punishment severity, nor can students gauge the celebrity of punishments unless they have been punished: thus, this study does not measure student perception of punishment swiftness. By quantifying how students perceive the school policy, this study aims to see if the "crime rate" (student drug use) is dependent on student perceptions of punishment severity and likelihood.

To measure the severity of drug and alcohol policy punishments, students were asked to rate their perceived severity of punishment consequences on a scale of 0 to 10 (0 = no punishment, 1–2 = not severe enough, 3–4 = not on the severe side, 5 = just right, 6–7 = on the severe side, 8–9 = more severe than necessary, 10 = extremely severe). Student perceptions of punishment severity are not objective: therefore, broad definitions reflecting how students personally feel about the punishment were used to measure severity. To measure the likelihood of receiving a punishment, students were asked to rate the perceived risk of getting caught using drugs at school on a scale of 0 to 10 (0 = no risk of getting caught, 1–2 = minimal risk of getting caught, 3–4 = not likely to be caught, 5 = fifty/fifty risk of getting caught, 6–7 = likely to be caught, 8–9 = very high risk of getting caught, 10 = certainly caught). It is important to measure certainty concerning the perceived risk of getting caught: if students perceive punishments to be severe but chances of detection to be low, the zero-tolerance policy may not deter students from using drugs.

Subsection B: Results

Licit and illicit adolescent drug use varied widely by age and by boarding status, affirming trends in national surveys where adolescent drug use increased along grade lines and peaked among 11th and 12th graders. Around 90% of freshmen students did not use licit or illicit drugs four or more times in one week (heavily), and 40% of freshmen did not use any licit or illicit drugs. Sophomores had higher rates of drug usage, yet 61.5% of sophomores did not use any drugs during school months: 15.4% used both licit and illicit drugs heavily. By contrast, juniors and seniors had high concentrations of students who used drugs heavily. Only about one-fifth of junior and senior respondents said they did not use both licit and illicit drugs in the past school month. Less than half, 40.7%, of juniors and seniors used either a licit or illicit drug heavily. Among this age group, more respondents used both licit and illicit drugs heavily (25.9%) than those who did not use drugs at all.

A divisive contrast in drug use between students who live on campus (boarding students) and students who live at home (day students) indicates that adolescents living on campus use drugs more frequently. Twenty per cent of day students did not use both licit and illicit drugs, and none used both licit and illicit drugs heavily. On the other hand, only one in eight boarding juniors did not use either a licit or an illicit drug during school months. Being a freshman or sophomore boarding student meant most would not use licit or illicit drugs at all: out of the 14 boarding students who did not use both licit and illicit drugs, 11 were freshman or sophomores. Of the total 9 respondents out of 50 who used both licit and illicit drugs heavily, 7 were boarding juniors.

Major Trends 1

In this section, two hypotheses were proposed to explain major correlations between the expected frequency of licit and illicit drug use and the three peer context factors. In Table 12.1, drug use trends from *past use* to *expected use*

Table 12.1 Expected frequency of past and licit and illicit drug use

	Past use				Expected use			
	Licit		Illicit		Licit		Illicit	
Variable	n	% (n=50)	n	% (n=50)	n	% change from past (n=50)	n	% change from past (n=50)
None	21	42	23	46	16	-10	19	-8
Once a month or less	6	12	8	16	10	+8	10	+4
2–4 times a month	6	12	3	6	8	+4	7	+8
2–3 times a week	5	10	5	10	6	+2	6	+2
4 or more times a week	12	24	11	22	10	-4	8	-6

Table 12.2 Correlation between licit drug use and peer context factors

Expected use	Proportion of friends who regularly use drugs (0–10)				
	0	1–3	4–6	7–9	10
% distribution					
None ($n = 16$)	25	50	18.8	6.3	
Once a month or less ($n = 10$)			30	60	10
2–4 times a month ($n = 8$)		25	25	50	
2–3 times a week ($n = 6$)			16.7	83.3	
4 times a week or more ($n = 10$)			10	70	20
	Proportion of friends who approve drug use (0–10)				
	0	1–3	4–6	7–9	10
% distribution					
None	6.25	25	56.25	12.5	
Once a month or less			10	40	50
2–4 times a month			50	25	25
2–3 times a week				83.3	16.7
4 times a week or more				60	40
	Proportion of free time spent with peers who regularly use drugs (0–10)				
	0	1–3	4–6	7–9	10
% distribution					
None	25	56.25	18.75		
Once a month or less		20	20	50	10
2–4 times a month		50	12.5	25	12.5
2–3 times a week		16.7	33.3	50	
4 times a week or more				60	40

indicate a shift in students who previously used little or no drugs expecting to increase their frequency of drug use. By this study's goal to identify how school policy punishment severity and likelihood and peer context factors influence student drug use, *expected drug use* results will be utilized as an independent variable for Tables 12.2, 12.3, 12.4, and 12.5 to measure the effect variables have in determining future adolescent drug use patterns.

Hypothesis:

- The hypothesis states there will be a positive correlation between the frequency of licit and illicit student drug use and peer context factors. The hypothesis will stand if peer context factors increase with student drug use frequency. The hypothesis follows the general presumption that adolescents value their social standing among peers strongly and that peer context factors will override deterrence from adults and school. Major findings from the literature that may support the hypothesis are as follows: adolescents who use drugs socially develop positive cognitive definitions of drug use; adolescents in intimate peer groups develop deviant behaviours like drug use via observation, practice, and reinforcement; adolescents disproportionately focus on rewards rather than risks in the presence of peers; and adolescent brains lack impulsive control functions.

Table 12.3 Correlation between expected frequency of illicit drug use and peer context factors

Expected use % distribution	Proportion of friends who regularly use drugs (0–10)				
	0	1–3	4–6	7–9	10
None ($n = 19$)	21.05	42.11	21.05	15.79	
Once a month or less ($n = 10$)		10	20	70	
2–4 times a month ($n = 7$)		14.29	28.57	57.14	
2–3 times a week ($n = 6$)			16.67	66.67	16.67
4 times a week or more ($n = 8$)			12.5	62.5	25

	Proportion of friends who approve drug use (0–10)				
% distribution	0	1–3	4–6	7–9	10
None		26.32	47.37	15.79	10.53
Once a month or less			30	40	30
2–4 times a month			28.57	71.43	
2–3 times a week				66.7	3.33
4 times a week or more				37.5	62.5

	Proportion of free time spent with peers who regularly use drugs (0–10)				
	0	1–3	4–6	7–9	10
% distribution					
None	21.05	47.37	10.53	15.79	5.26
Once a month or less		30	40	30	
2–4 times a month		28.57	14.29	57.14	
2–3 times a week		33.3	16.67	33.3	16.67
4 times a week or more				50	50

Table 12.4 Correlation between expected frequency of licit drug use and punishment severity and likelihood

Expected use % distribution	Perception of punishment severity				
	0	1–3	4–6	7–9	10
None ($n = 16$)		6.25	31.25	62.5	
Once a month or less ($n = 10$)			20	80	
2–4 times a month ($n = 8$)		37.5	12.5	50	
2–3 times a week ($n = 6$)				50	50
4 times a week or more ($n = 10$)			30	40	30

	Perception of punishment likelihood				
	0	1–3	4–6	7–9	10
% distribution					
None		37.5	37.5	25	
Once a month or less		20	30	50	
2–4 times a month	25	37.5		37.5	
2–3 times a week		16.67	50	16.67	16.67
4 times a week or more		10	60	20	10

Table 12.5 Correlation between expected frequency of illicit drug use and punishment severity and likelihood

	Perception of punishment severity				
Expected use	0	1–3	4–6	7–9	10
% distribution					
None (n = 19)		5.26	31.58	63.16	
Once a month or less (n = 10)			10	90	
2–4 times a month (n = 7)		42.86		42.86	14.29
2–3 times a week (n = 6)			33.3	33.3	33.3
4 times a week or more (n = 8)			25	37.5	37.5
	Perception of punishment likelihood				
	0	1–3	4–6	7–9	10
% distribution					
None		36.84	36.84	26.32	
Once a month or less		10	20	70	
2–4 times a month	28.57	28.57	42.86		
2–3 times a week		33.3	33.3	16.67	16.67
4 times a week or more		12.5	50	25	12.5

Null hypothesis:

- The null hypothesis states that there will be a negative correlation between the frequency of licit and illicit student drug use and peer context factors. If peer influence decreases when the frequency of drug use increases, the null hypothesis will be true. If found to be true, the null hypothesis would contradict the findings of a large body of literature that estimate peer influence to significantly affect adolescent drug use. Significant evidence from the literature supporting the null hypothesis may be summarized as follows: adolescents possess a capacity to think rationally equal to adults and will be deterred by severe and certain policies with similar effects; as high parental monitoring is found to counter peer influences promoting drug use, high school monitoring can achieve effects similar to those of peer influence. Furthermore, there is also the possibility that findings supporting the hypothesis are lacking in scope and do not apply to this sample.

In Table 12.2, a moderate to strong positive correlation was found linking the frequency of licit student drug use and the three peer context factors. A statistically significant, moderate positive correlation existed between the expected frequency of licit drug use and the proportion of friends who approved of drug use, r (50) = 0.529, p < 0.001. No respondents stated that all their friends disapproved of drug use. Students who expected not to use any licit drugs were split between having almost no friends who approved of drug use (31.25%) and having half or more than half of their friends approve of drug use (68.75%). Compared to other groups, students who expected not to use licit drugs were more likely to have none, almost none or fewer than half of their friends approve of drug use. Also, students who *expected to use* licit drugs, regardless of frequency, did not have friends whom nearly all or all disapproved of drug use.

A statistically significant, moderate positive correlation was found between the expected frequency of licit drug use and the proportion of friends who regularly used drugs, r (50) = 0.629, p < 0.001. All students who did not expect to use licit drugs said that none of their friends regularly used drugs, but a small fraction (6%) of them said nearly all their friends regularly used drugs. Students who did not have peers who regularly used drugs as friends could be found only in respondents who expected not to use licit drugs (25%). In contrast, none of the students who expected to use licit drugs 2–3 times a week, or 4 times a week or more, had friends all of whom did not regularly use drugs.

Finally, a statistically significant, strong positive correlation existed between the expected frequency of licit drug use and the proportion of free time spent around friends who regularly used drugs, r (50) = 0.718, p < 0.001. Students who expected to use licit drugs 4 times a week or more almost exclusively spent their free time around peers who regularly used drugs: 60% more than half to nearly all, 40% all. More than half of those who did not expect to use licit drugs spent almost none of their free time around peers who regularly used drugs (56.25%), and a quarter never spent time around peers who regularly used drugs. The pattern of spending more time around drug-using peers the more frequently one expected to use drugs was evident among students who expected to use drugs once a month, 2–4 times a week, or 2–3 times a week. Nevertheless, only a fraction of these students extended to either extreme of spending almost no time around drug-using peers or spending all their free time around drug-using peers.

The observed trends in Table 12.2, both positive and statistically significant, contradict the null hypothesis. There was a moderate to strong positive correlation between peer context factors and expected licit drug use. Results from Table 12.2 support the hypothesis, showing a statistically significant positive correlation between an increase in peer context factors and a decrease in expected licit drug use across the board.

A weak to moderate positive correlation was shown to exist between the expected frequency of illicit drug use and the three peer context factors. A statistically significant, yet weak positive correlation was shown between the expected frequency of illicit drug use and the proportion of friends who approved of drug use, r (50) = 0.472, p < 0.001. In contrast to Table 12.2, there were no students who expected not to use drugs, yet reported that all of their friends disapproved of illicit drug use: in fact, 10.53% of them had friends whom all approved of drug use. A large portion of students who reported higher rates of expected illicit drug use had a high proportion of friends who approved of drug use: 33.3% of students who expected to use illicit drugs 2–3 times a week and 62.5% of respondents who expected to use 4 times or more a week said all of their friends approved of illicit drug use.

A statistically significant, moderate positive correlation was found between the expected frequency of illicit drug use and the proportion of friends who regularly used drugs, r (50) = 0.609, p < 0.001. Here, only students who expected to use illicit drugs 2–3 times a week and 4 times a week or more had friends who all regularly used drugs, 16.67%, and 25%, respectively. As in the trends from Table 12.2, most students who did not expect to use drugs had no or nearly no friends who regularly used drugs, 21.05%, and 42.11%, respectively. Interestingly, 70% of students who expected to use illicit drugs once a month said that nearly all their friends regularly used drugs. No group other than students who did not expect to use illicit drugs said that they had no friends who regularly used drugs.

In addition, a statistically significant, moderate positive correlation existed between the expected frequency of illicit drug use and the proportion of free time spent around friends who regularly used drugs, r (50) = 0.621, p < 0.001. Students who expected to use illicit drugs 4 times a week or more reported spending their free time almost exclusively around peers who regularly used drugs. Students who did not expect to use illicit drugs 4 times a week or more but still used illicit drugs were split between spending little time around drugs using friends and spending nearly all of their time around peers who regularly used drugs.

Associations found in Table 12.3, being positive and statistically significant, further undermine the null hypothesis. There was a moderate positive correlation between peer context factors and expected illicit drug use. Results from Table 12.3 support the hypothesis, demonstrating a statistically significant positive correlation between an increase in peer context factors and a decrease in expected illicit drug use.

Major Trends 2
Much as in the previous section, this section proposes two hypotheses for Tables 12.4 and 12.5 that may explain the correlations between the expected frequency of licit and illicit drug use and the perception of punishment severity and likelihood.

Hypothesis

- The hypothesis posits that the deterrence theory is ineffective in producing a deterrence effect in the studied sample. The hypothesis states there will either be a positive correlation or no correlation between adolescent drug use and severity and the likelihood of punishment. The hypothesis will hold if the frequency of drug use increases with an increasing perception of punishment severity and likelihood, or if no trend exists. The hypothesis is supported by the following findings in the literature: there is a lack of social control in place to inhibit adolescents' inherent deviant impulses; adolescents' ability to make rational decisions is impaired by their lack of brain impulse controls; adolescents disproportionately focus on rewards rather than risks in the presence of peers; and adolescents use drugs as a creative choice of resistance against the school in line with their counter-school identity.

Null hypothesis

- The null hypothesis assumes that policies under the theory of deterrence are effective in deterring drug use generally in the studied sample. The null hypothesis states that a negative correlation between adolescent drug use and both severity and likelihood of punishment will exist. The null hypothesis will stand if the frequency of drug use decreases with an increasing perception of punishment severity and likelihood. The null hypothesis is assumed to be true when consistent with the principles of the theory of deterrence: humans are self-interested beings that will make rational decisions for the best-benefit outcome; the more severe the punishment, the lesser the crime rate; the more certain the punishment, the lesser the crime rate. Some evidence from the literature suggests adolescents are capable of rational thinking with similar capabilities to adults. Therefore the desired rational deterrence effect of policies following the deterrence theory will support the null hypothesis.

For both punishment severity and likelihood variables, a positive (albeit very weak correlation) existed between perceptions of punishment severity and likelihood and expected frequency of licit drug use. There existed a statistically insignificant, very weak positive correlation between the expected frequency of licit drug use and perception of punishment severity, $r(50) = 0.202$. No students, regardless of their expected licit drug use, found that their school policy punishment had zero severity. All students replied that their school policy punishment was on the severe side, more severe than necessary, or extremely severe. All students who expected to use licit drugs 2–3 times a week replied that their school policy punishment was more severe than necessary or extremely severe (50%, 50%); 30% of students who used licit drugs 4 or more times a week rated their school policy punishment to be "10," as in extremely severe.

Furthermore, there existed a statistically insignificant, very weak positive correlation between the expected frequency of student licit drug use and student perception of punishment likelihood, $r(50) = 0.106$. Ten per cent of students who expected to use licit drugs 4 or more times a week believed they would certainly be caught, while 25% of students who expected to use licit drugs 2–4 times a month believed there was zero chance of them getting caught. Students who did not expect to use licit drugs were split evenly between believing the punishment was not severe enough and on the severe side, 37.5%, and 37.5%, respectively. Only 16.67% and 10% of students who expected to use licit drugs 2–3 times a week and 4 times a week or more, respectively, marked their chances of being caught as certain (10).

The associations demonstrated in Table 12.4, being positive and statistically insignificant, reject the null hypothesis. There was no discernible correlation between an increase in perceptions of punishment severity and likelihood and a decrease in the expected frequency of licit drug use. A very weak argument could be made that the expected frequency of licit drug use is positively correlated with punishment severity and likelihood, but the two relevant correlations fail the statistical significance test (p > 0.05). Results from Table 12.4 support the hypothesis, as no statistically significant correlation exists between an increase in both punishment severity and likelihood and a decrease in the expected frequency of licit drug use.

Consistent with Table 12.4, in Table 12.5, the correlation between expected frequency of illicit drug use and perceptions of punishment severity and likelihood was positive and very weak. There existed a statistically insignificant, very weak positive correlation between the frequency of student expected illicit drug use and student perception of punishment severity, r (50) = 0.133. As in Table 12.4, no students out of 50 perceived the punishment to have zero severity, and the students who expected to use illicit drugs largely believed the punishment was more severe than necessary or extremely severe.

In addition, there existed a statistically insignificant, very weak positive correlation between the expected frequency of student illicit drug use and student perception of punishment likelihood, r (50) = 0.044. There was virtually no correlation between the expected frequency of illicit drug use and student perception of punishment likelihood. 37.5% of students who expected to use illicit drugs 4 or more times a week believed they were at a very high or at a certain risk of getting caught. Interestingly, 70% of students who expected to use illicit drugs once a month also believed that they were at a very high risk of getting caught: the largest distribution of students among any other group to perceive the likelihood of punishment to be very high.

The correlations demonstrated in Table 12.5, being positive and statistically insignificant, contradict the null hypothesis. There was no strong negative association between student illicit drug use and student perception of punishment severity and likelihood that the null hypothesis assumed. A weak argument could be made that the expected frequency of illicit drug use is positively correlated with punishment severity and likelihood: however, the two relevant correlations fail the statistical significance test (p > 0.05). Instead, analysis of Table 12.5 supports the hypothesis as no statistically significant correlation exists between an increase in punishment severity and likelihood and a decrease in the expected frequency of illicit drug use.

12.4 Discussion

This study does not find increasing severity and likelihood of school drug and alcohol policy punishments to be linked with a decrease in student drug use: on the contrary, students who used drugs most heavily seemed to perceive punishment severity and likelihood to be slightly higher. Instead, this study finds compelling evidence that the frequency of student drug use is closely associated with student exposure to contextual peer influence factors. In this section, the findings from the results will be discussed in greater detail and placed in still more explicit relation to previous research.

Generally, adolescent drug use was found to be highly dependent on grade level and day or boarding status. Students were more likely to use licit or illicit drugs as their grade level increased, and students in the junior grade level were found to use drugs most frequently. The 2019 national MTF survey corroborates the increase in drug use along grade lines: 25.5% of 12th graders vaped nicotine in the previous month, followed by 10th graders at 19.9% and 8th graders at 9.6% (U.S. Department of Health and Human Services 2019). Boarding students were found to use drugs more frequently in the previous month compared to today students. No day students who used drugs were able to use both licit and illicit drugs as heavily as boarding students of the same grade, suggesting that boarding students were less inhibited by social controls like parents and that high accessibility to peers might increase drug use. The absence or inadequacy of parental monitoring has been associated with an increase in adolescent drug use (Dorius et al. 2004). Due to the significant physical barriers placed between boarding students and their parents, adolescents may not act out of conformity because they feel no need to conform to appease their parents (Dorius et al. 2004). In a similar light, for some adolescents, conformity to school might be less important than conformity to parents. Combined with the lack of parental monitoring and connection that has proven to reduce peer influence, adolescents living in dormitories with or alongside peers have more opportunities to engage in intimate peer groups where deviant behaviour is observed, practised, and reinforced (Hirschi 1969). Consequently, lower rates of drug use among day students may be symptomatic of their physical distance from parents and peers.

Of the two major trends, this study identified, *major trend 1* affirmed the hypothesis since a moderate to strong positive correlation was shown between adolescent drug use and peer context factors. A moderate positive correlation was found between the expected frequency of student licit and illicit drug use and proportion of student friends who regularly used drugs and the proportion of student friends who approved of drug use. The positive correlation between the expected frequency of student licit drug use and the proportion of free time spent with peers who regularly used drugs was the strongest ($r = 0.718$); the same correlation for illicit drug use was slightly weaker ($r = 0.621$). Social learning theory provides supporting evidence for this association, with findings backing the theory establishing that intimate peer groups create an environment where social deviances like drug use are observed, practised, and reinforced (Hirschi 1969; Reed and Rountree 1997). Adolescents whose friends largely use drugs and advocate drug use may be exposed more frequently to situations where social drug use is rewarded and celebrated among peers: the more complete this echo chamber, the higher the proportion of their friends approve of drug use. Steinberg (2008) claims adolescents in the presence of peers are especially susceptible to focusing on rewards rather than risks, suggesting a higher score on the peer context factors indicate higher exposure to circumstances where rational thinking is suppressed. Furthermore, Steinberg (2008) also finds adolescents to have underdeveloped brain regions that moderate impulse control, raising the possibility that impulsive decision-making may further aggravate adolescents' narrow focus on rewards. While the causality of these correlations cannot be conclusively demonstrated, findings from the adolescent risk-taking theory and neurobiological research provide compelling evidence suggesting the role of peer context factors in facilitating adolescent drug use.

The link between the proportion of student friends who approve of drug use and the frequency of drug use is especially concerning. Adolescents value the opinions of peers and their social standing among peers more than any other age group, and the general approval of drug use among friends may take priority over the disapproval of drug use by school or the broader society. Past research found adolescents who used marijuana in social circumstances developed positive cognitive definitions of marijuana and future social marijuana use. Popular peer approval of drugs might, in a similar way, cause adolescents to define drug use positively and expect positive outcomes in future social drug-using sessions. In this study, illicit drugs were approved by a larger proportion of peers across the independent variable when compared to proportions of peers who approved licit drugs. The recent decriminalization and legalization of marijuana in many states (though not legalized in Connecticut) is thought to have contributed to the disparity between licit drug approval and illicit drug approval.

Major trend 2 positively (but weakly) correlated punishment severity and likelihood with the expected frequency of student drug use. All correlations were statistically insignificant and suggested a weak trend: no correlations were found across the board. The direct relationship between zero-tolerance policies and problem behaviours remains significantly understudied. However, Curran (2016) provides evidence from a nationwide review of zero tolerance that finds zero-tolerance policies do not reduce perceptions of problem behaviour among school principals. Contrary to popular presumptions, students who used licit and illicit drugs heavily said they viewed school policies to be highly severe and punishment to be highly certain. Student perceptions of punishment severity and likelihood did not vary widely by their expected frequency of drug use. If perceptions of punishment had been universal and not varied individually, stronger correlations may have been found, yet even such assumptions cannot explain why students who used drugs 2–3 times a week or 4 times a week or more perceived their school policy punishment to be more severe and likely than any other group.

There is the possibility that some students were deterred by the high severity and likelihood of punishment, and only groups of students are "immune" to the consequences of continued heavy drug use (while fully aware of the stakes). Past studies on student counter-school culture confirmed the occurrence of these immune student groups, discovering that students marginalized from school used drugs as a creative means of "mellow resistance" against the school (Fletcher et al. 2009). Indeed, some students in this study may use drugs because they genuinely disrespect the school's highly punitive punishments for infractions. However, it might equally be the case that a zero-tolerance policy with harsh punishments is not effective at reducing problem behaviour. Being suspended or expelled might not be the best-benefit outcome for adolescents in the long run, but in the context of peer influence, results from this study suggest immediate social rewards take precedence over school consequences, regardless of severity or likelihood.

There are several limitations to this study. First, using cross-sectional data that is not longitudinal or derived from a controlled setting, this study does not demonstrate causality behind correlations. The correlations themselves show peer context factors to increase with the frequency of student drug use but soliciting peer context factors as a direct cause of an increase or decrease in student drug use frequency would require a longitudinal approach.

Second, the sample size is limited to 50 students. There is a chance that anomalies have skewed the results of the observed trends somewhat. The sample group is also geographically specific: respondents are largely private school students bound to the state of Connecticut (other states might hold substances differently accountable), and findings from this study may not be recreated in alternate regions and demographics.

Third, grade level remains a strong predictor of student drug use, as does boarding students or day-student status. More accurate results surrounding peer contexts and punishment severity and likelihood could be drawn if future studies separate data by grade level or occupational status. The separation of data, inherently requiring a larger data pool, may account for such preconditioned trends that may skew results.

Finally, all data was gathered through a student self-reported survey. While accurate and honest measures of student drug use are difficult to collect without student cooperation, school punishment severity and likelihood could be ascertained without relying on student perceptions. There are a few reasons why student perceptions may be an inaccurate measure of punishment severity or likelihood: misconceptions about school policy, personal experiences with the school disciplinary system, or exaggerating perceptions. A more systematic approach would be taken to rate school policy and its punishments on some standard metric, through questioning administrators or by self-conducting policy analysis. This effort, again, would require a large-scale study with a broader state-wide or national scope.

12.5 Conclusion

Despite growing evidence that condemns the negative effects of punitive and exclusionary discipline, Zero-tolerance policies remain an integral part of school discipline. A few studies have attempted to estimate the efficiency of zero tolerance in reducing problem behaviours. However, the general deterring effect of zero tolerance has been refuted by at least one study (Curran 2016), and the results from this paper corroborate those results. This paper elaborates on a body of literature that questions the efficiency of zero tolerance in reducing problem behaviour, focusing on studies that find contextual factors like peers and adolescent neurobiological characteristics that directly challenge the theory of deterrence. This paper aimed to determine if factors that predicted peer influence held stronger authority over adolescent drug use compared to policies that follow deterrence theory.

As a whole, the results of this study suggest perceptions of punishment to be unrelated to adolescent drug use but finds factors that predict student interaction with drug-using or drug-approving peers to be strongly correlated with drug use. Student drug use could be predicted quite accurately from their interaction with drug-using or drug-approving peers: while perceptions of school drug and alcohol policy punishments varied randomly with no strong pattern among students. Despite strong evidence that peers hold powerful control over adolescent behaviour, prior research failed to investigate the extent to which peers determine deviant behaviour like drug abuse. This study endorses the possibility that peer influence supersedes deterring measures, at least in terms of adolescent drug use.

Results from this study provide initial evidence that contextual factors, peer influence or otherwise, might override principles of deterrence theory in drug and alcohol discipline. Such evidence provides crucial grounds for practices revising deterrence theory, like zero tolerance, with consideration of the persuasive influence of peer adolescents, and the limits of rational deterrence in adolescents. In this way, results of this study encourage future researchers in zero-tolerance discipline and adolescent drug abuse to broaden the scope of their inquiry and include various real-world contextual factors that mitigate the effectiveness of school discipline.

REFERENCES

American Psychological Association Zero Tolerance Task Force. (2008, December 1). Are Zero Tolerance Policies Effective in the Schools? An Evidentiary Review and Recommendations. https://www.apa.org/pubs/info/reports/zero-tolerance.pdf. https://doi.org/10.1037/0003-066X.63.9.852

Arcia, E. (2006). Achievement and Enrollment Status of Suspended Students: Outcomes in a Large, Multicultural School District. *Education and Urban Society, 38*(3), 359. https://doi.org/10.1177/0013124506286947

Beccaria, C. (2009). *On Crimes and Punishments.* Seven Treasures.

Bentham, J., Burns, J. H., & Hart, H. L. A. (1982). *An Introduction to the Principles of Morals and Legislation.* Methuen.

Bronfenbrenner, U., & Morris, P. A. (2006). The Bioecological Model of Human Development. In W. Damon & R. M. Lerner (Eds.), *Handbook of Child Psychology: Theoretical Models of Human Development* (pp. 793–828). John Wiley & Sons Inc.

Costenbader, V., & Markson, S. (1998). School Suspension: A Study with Secondary School Students. *Journal of School Psychology, 36,* 59–82. https://doi.org/10.1016/S0022-4405(97)00050-2

Curran, F. (2016). Estimating the Effect of State Zero Tolerance Laws on Exclusionary Discipline, Racial Discipline Gaps, and Student Behavior. *Educational Evaluation and Policy Analysis, 38*(4), 658–660. Retrieved August 1, 2020, from www.jstor.org/stable/44984559

Dorius, C., Bahr, S., Hoffmann, J., & Harmon, E. (2004). Parenting Practices as Moderators of the Relationship between Peers and Adolescent Marijuana Use. *Journal of Marriage and Family, 66*(1), 163–178. Retrieved August 1, 2020, from www.jstor.org/stable/3599873

Education Week. (2018, September 5). Connecticut Earns a B on State Report Card, Ranks Third in Nation. *Editorial Projects in Education, 37*(17).

Ellickson, P. L., Tucker, J. S., Klein, D. J., & Saner, H. (2004). Antecedents and Outcomes of Marijuana Use Initiation during Adolescence. *Preventive Medicine, 39*(5), 976–984. https://doi.org/10.1016/j.ypmed.2004.04.013

Elliott, D. S., Wilson, W. J., Huizinga, D., Sampson, R. J., Elliott, A., & Rankin, B. (1996). The Effects of Neighborhood Disadvantage on Adolescent Development. *Journal of Research in Crime and Delinquency, 33*(4), 389–426. https://doi.org/10.1177/0022427896033004002

Finn, K. (2012). Marijuana Use at School and Achievement-Linked Behaviors. *The High School Journal, 95*(3), 3–13. https://doi.org/10.1353/hsj.2012.0005

Fletcher, A., Bonell, C., & Rhodes, T. (2009). New Counter-School Cultures: Female Students' Drug Use at a High-Achieving Secondary School. *British Journal of Sociology of Education, 30*(5), 549–562. Retrieved August 1, 2020, from www.jstor.org/stable/40375481

Gardner, M., & Steinberg, L. (2005). Peer Influence on Risk Taking, Risk Preference, and Risky Decision Making in Adolescence and Adulthood: An Experimental Study. *Developmental Psychology, 41*, 625–635. https://doi.org/10.1037/0012-1649.41.4.625

Gibbs, J. P. (1968). Crime, Punishment and Deterrence. *Southwestern Social Science Quarterly, 48*, 515–530.

Hirschi, T. (1969). *Causes of Delinquency.* Berkeley: University of California Press.

Hoffman, S. (2014) Zero Benefit: Estimating the Effect of Zero Tolerance Discipline Policies on Racial Disparities in School Discipline. *Educational Policy, 28*, 65–100. https://doi.org/10.1177/0895904812453999

Hoffmann, J. (2002). The Community Context of Family Structure and Adolescent Drug Use. *Journal of Marriage and Family, 64*(2), 314–330. Retrieved August 1, 2020, from www.jstor.org/stable/3600106

Kennedy, D. M. (2010). *Deterrence and Crime Prevention.* Routledge.

Luthar, S. S., Small, P. J., & Ciciolla, L. (2018). Adolescents from Upper Middle Class Communities: Substance Misuse and Addiction across Early Adulthood. *Development and Psychopathology, 30*(1), 315–335. https://doi.org/10.1017/S0954579417000645

Maag, J. W. (2001). Reward by Punishment: Reflections on the Disuse of Positive Reinforcement in Schools. *The Council for Exceptional Children, 67*(2), 173–186. https://doi.org/10.1177/001440290106700203

Martinez, S. (2009). A System Gone Berserk: How Are Zero-tolerance Policies Really Affecting Schools? *Preventing School Failure, 53*(4), 153–158. https://doi.org/10.3200/psfl.53.3.153-158

Morrison, G. M., & Skiba, R. (2001). Predicting Violence from School Misbehavior: Promises and Perils. *Psychology in the Schools, 38*(2), 173–184. https://doi.org/10.1002/pits.1008

Nagin, D. (1998). Criminal Deterrence Research at the Outset of the Twenty-First Century. *Crime and Justice, 23*, 1–42. Retrieved August 1, 2020, from www.jstor.org/stable/1147539

Pathammavong, R., Leatherdale, S. T., Ahmed, R., Griffith, J., Nowatzki, J., & Manske, S. (2011). Examining the Link between Education Related Outcomes and Student Health Risk Behaviours among Canadian Youth: Data from the 2006 National Youth Smoking Survey. *Canadian Journal of Education, 34*(1), 215–247. Retrieved August 1, 2020, from www.jstor.org/stable/canajeducrevucan.34.1.215

Pauwels, L., Weerman, F., Bruinsma, G., & Bernasco, W. (2011). Perceived Sanction Risk, Individual Propensity and Adolescent Offending: Assessing Key Findings from the Deterrence Literature in a Dutch Sample. *European Journal of Criminology, 8*(5), 386–400. https://doi.org/10.1177/1477370811415762

Petraitis, J., Flay, B. R., & Miller, T. Q. (1995). Reviewing Theories of Adolescent Substance Use: Organizing Pieces in the Puzzle. *Psychological Bulletin, 117*, 67–86. https://doi.org/10.1037/0033-2909.117.1.67

Raffaele Mendez, L. M. (2003). Predictors of Suspension and Negative School Outcomes: A Longitudinal Investigation. *New Directions for Youth Development, 99*, 19–35. https://doi.org/10.1002/yd.52

Reed, M. D., & Rountree, P. W. (1997). Peer Pressure and Adolescent Substance Abuse. *Journal of Quantitative Criminology, 13*, 143–180. Retrieved August 1, 2020, from www.jstor.org/stable/23366028

Steinberg L. (2008). A Social Neuroscience Perspective on Adolescent Risk-Taking. *Developmental Review: DR, 28*(1), 78–106. https://doi.org/10.1016/j.dr.2007.08.002

U.S. Commissioner of Education Statistics. (1998, March 18). Violence and Discipline Problems in U.S. Public Schools: 1996–97. *National Center for Education Statistics.* https://nces.ed.gov/pressrelease/violence.asp

U.S. Department of Education Office for Civil Rights. (2014). *Civil Rights Data Collection—Data Snapshot: School Discipline* (Issue Brief No. 1). http://ocrdata.ed.gov/Downloads/CRDC-School-Discipline-Snapshot.pdf

U.S. Department of Health and Human Services. (2019, December 18). Monitoring the Future 2019 Survey Results: Overall Findings. *National Institute on Drug Abuse.* https://www.drugabuse.gov/drug-topics/trends-statistics/infographics/monitoring-future-2019-survey-results-overall-findings.

Zimring, F. E., Hawkins, G. J., & Gorenberg, J. (1976). *Deterrence: The Legal Threat in Crime Control.* University of Chicago Press.

CHAPTER 13

Dilemmas and Challenges in Qualitative Fieldwork with Climate-Vulnerable Communities

Md. Masud-All-Kamal, S. M. Monirul Hassan, and Nasir Uddin

13.1 Introduction

Doing research with vulnerable communities always involves different kinds of challenges, including emotional attachments vs professional detachment, objective analysis vs subjective interpretation and mere collection of data vs doing something for them. Research sets out to address research questions related to a particular social phenomenon. In the research process, both researchers and the studied population play a vital role to find an authentic and credible answer to the posed research questions. The relationship between the researcher and the research participants has long been debated, and it has led to the emergence of diverse philosophies or epistemologies (Uddin 2011; Jakimow 2020). Epistemology refers to a theory of knowledge that provides researchers with a philosophical background to choose what kinds of knowledge are legitimate and adequate to understand a social milieu, human behaviours or actions (Gray 2014). Epistemological positioning is important as it directs the relationship between researchers and research subjects. At the same

---

Md. Masud-All-Kamal (✉) • S. M. Monirul Hassan
Department of Sociology, University of Chittagong, Chattogram, Bangladesh
e-mail: masud.kamal@cu.ac.bd; monirul.hassan@cu.ac.bd

N. Uddin
Department of Anthropology, University of Chittagong, Chattogram, Bangladesh
e-mail: nasir.anthro@cu.ac.bd

© The Author(s), under exclusive license to Springer Nature Switzerland AG 2023
N. Uddin, A. Paul (eds.), *The Palgrave Handbook of Social Fieldwork*, https://doi.org/10.1007/978-3-031-13615-3_13

time, it illuminates the authenticity and validity of the quality of information through the application of different techniques of data collection. The role of researchers is vital to conducting credible qualitative research because human beings are the instrument of research, whereas quantitative research is contingent upon the use of standardised data collection instruments and statistical procedures (Patton 2002; Creswell 2014). The qualitative approach is often regarded as subjective because of the reflections of the researcher's attitudes, personal characteristics and social positions in the research process (Sultana 2007). The nature of relationships between researchers and the people studied is an important determinant of knowledge production in qualitative research.

Qualitative researchers do not play the 'god-trick' by separating themselves from the research subjects. They are actively present in the research process and influence the outcomes of studied phenomena. Researchers co-construct the knowledge in collaboration with the participants which is widely known as a "joint product" (Uddin 2011). The outputs of qualitative research, therefore, become a collective effort and joint venture to some extent. The validity and reliability of qualitative research, however, have long been questioned by the adherents of objective epistemology. In response, qualitative researchers tend to focus on the nature of the influence of subjective and intersubjective factors over the research process and pay particular attention to the outcomes to increase rigour and trustworthiness. By so doing, a researcher does not pretend to be emotionless and get detached from research participants, rather they become variously involved in their social, collective and personal lives. Nonetheless, researchers deliberately rely on research ethics to determine the level of relationship and the degree of engagement of the researcher with the research participants.

Though ethics is a relative phenomenon and it largely depends on the researcher's personal, political and ideological composition, research ethics follows a set of guidelines for doing research. Ethics in social research is divided into two types: procedural ethics and ethics in practice. Procedural ethics refers to institutional ethical standards that a researcher commits to maintain through seeking formal approval, whereas ethics in practice involves contextual and unanticipated ethical issues that a researcher faces during the fieldwork period (Guillemin and Gillam 2004). Community-based qualitative research is guided by procedural ethical principles, that is, respect for participants, beneficence and justice (Orb et al. 2001). The overarching focus of these ethical principles is to avoid harm as well as maximise benefits for participants. At the same time, a social researcher needs to be careful whether she/he becomes emotionally involved and extremely sympathetic to the vulnerable people which might hamper the objectivity of the research. Ethical review boards instruct researchers to maintain confidentiality, anonymity and honesty in research involving people. Institutional ethical codes and guidelines, however, seem insufficient to address ethical dilemmas and challenges faced by researchers (Sampson 2019). Researchers, therefore, use 'ethics in practice' to overcome ethical issues that they face while conducting fieldwork with vulnerable communities.

Qualitative research is socially and culturally contextual, and so knowledge is produced through the interactions between the researchers and participants in a specific time and place (Dodgson 2019). The settings of research shape the research process and practice. We conduct community-based research with rural communities vulnerable to multiple climatic and non-climatic factors. These communities are vulnerable to natural hazards, and the relationships within these communities are hierarchical, class-based and gendered (Masud-All-Kamal et al. 2021). Researchers, therefore, encounter unique ethical challenges in conducting research with at-risk communities. Yet, these unexpected dilemmas often remain unaccounted and unaddressed. Readers always see the research content and the findings of the research, but what kind of ethical and practical changes the researchers go through during the fieldwork often remain undisclosed.

A prolonged engagement is essential in qualitative research to understand the research settings and to gain mutual trust between researchers and participants (Lincoln and Guba 1985). Apart from the repeated engagement and re-engagement with the object of study in different contents on various occasions, a researcher immerses into the social milieu under scrutiny maintaining guidelines set by the human research ethics committees. A researcher has a responsibility to comply and follow the code of ethics, but prolonged engagement places a researcher in ethical dilemmas such as the establishment of honest and open interaction, voluntary consent and beneficence (Shaw 2003). In addition, research involving vulnerable populations (e.g. poor, underprivileged and marginalised groups) leads to certain ethical issues, including conflict of procedural and contextual ethics, identification of participants' problems and the researcher's inability to support participants (Mura 2015). These issues often put qualitative researchers into dilemmas and various forms of challenges. Insufficient attention has, however, been paid to reflect upon ethical dilemmas and challenges faced by researchers during fieldwork. This chapter seeks to fill up this gap by providing a detailed account of the ethical dilemmas that we encountered during fieldwork with vulnerable populations in coastal zones of Bangladesh. In doing so, we reflect on our fieldwork experiences with the climate-vulnerable coastal communities. In the next section, we are going to describe the context of this analysis and then shed light on ethical dilemmas and challenges in qualitative fieldwork.

13.2 Context: Researching with Climate-Vulnerable People and Communities

We have been working with coastal communities in Bangladesh for more than a decade. These communities are considered vulnerable because they are exposed to multiple natural hazards such as cyclones, storm surges and floods. These extreme events tend to trigger a disaster for the coastal communities. In future, these communities are likely to face more intense and frequent climatic shocks as Bangladesh is considered one of the most vulnerable countries to adverse global environmental change. However, not all people in a given community will be equally affected, meaning that the people who live on the margin of society are likely to be more affected (IPCC 2022). In the scholarship on climate change and disaster management, such marginalised sections of a community are considered 'vulnerable'.

In the current understanding of social sciences, vulnerability is considered a product of social, economic and political conditions. The concept of vulnerability in climate change and disaster research was drawn from biomedical research. The meaning of vulnerability in biomedical research, however, differs considerably. In climate change/disaster literature, vulnerability is defined as the "state of susceptibility to harm from exposure to stresses associated with environmental and social changes and from the absence of capacity to adapt" (Adger 2006, p. 268). In this view, vulnerable people have less capacity in terms of access to resources, power and networks. A combination of factors such as class, gender, age and health status determines the vulnerability of coastal people in Bangladesh (Ferreira et al. 2015). To enhance the capacities of vulnerable people of coastal communities, government, and non-governmental organisations (NGOs) have implemented a wide range of interventions. In the past, these responses, however, were focused on relief operations and infrastructure development in the wake of disasters. More specifically, a substantial amount of resources have been distributed in the aftermath of events that created a 'relief-centric' disaster management culture. There has been a shift in the risk management approach that focuses on capacity building and risk mitigation, but people's perceptions about external interventions did not change (Masud-All-Kamal and Nursey-Bray 2022). Such perceptions have important implications for researchers who work with coastal people and communities in Bangladesh.

In our research, we mainly focus on understanding the underlying causes of coastal people's vulnerability to climate change and extremes, and strategies to address them. In so doing, we conduct community-based research using interviews, observations, key information methods, case studies and group discussions. We usually collect data from all segments of the local community, yet the focus remains on the most vulnerable section of communities. The vulnerability of these groups is produced through the interaction of different social markers, including class, age, status and gender (Sultana 2014). Scholars interested in adaptation and disaster research conduct fieldwork with 'vulnerable people', but participants of such projects are unlikely to get any special protection. As people and communities in Bangladesh are most often open and curious to participate in research, both local and international researchers can easily build relationships with the participants and collect data. In particular, international researchers often receive an overwhelming reception while doing fieldwork as Bangladeshi people are widely known as hospitable to foreigners. That is why, many international scholars praised local people and communities (see Paprocki 2021). In qualitative fieldwork, interactions with participants often take a long time and are intense. We listen to participants' life histories which often make us upset, sad and anxious. Long engagement with participants and life histories, therefore, put us in ethical and moral dilemmas. The idea of this chapter stems from our long-term fieldwork experiences with vulnerable people and communities. In this chapter, therefore, we reflect on these dilemmas and challenges that we faced during fieldwork with vulnerable communities in coastal Bangladesh. In that sense, this is a very personal experience that has deep and intensive academic, epistemic and professional relevance because personal experience in qualitative research is the most valuable 'data' (Uddin 2022).

13.3 Dilemmas and Challenges in Qualitative Fieldwork

Fieldwork seems like an isolated and lonely journey for a researcher, but it involves numerous personal, moral and political issues along the way. Dilemmas and challenges in fieldwork depend on the settings of social research as well as the researcher's ethical stance and positionality. In the following section, we reflect on our experiences of conducting fieldwork with coastal communities. We are not going to share a particular fieldwork experience, rather we, as long-term research collaborators, reflect on ethical issues that we often encountered in qualitative field research with climate-vulnerable people living in different coastal areas.

Psychological and Emotional Burden on the Researcher

The focus of our research is to understand how societal structure and culture shape the most vulnerable population to deal with natural hazards and vice versa. These individuals often consider themselves peripheral, marginalised, excluded, deprived, poor or extremely poor. We, as qualitative researchers, ask our respondents to share their personal and collective accounts concerning vulnerability and adaptation to environmental changes and disasters in their local settings and everyday experience. These accounts or life histories consist of a description of their helplessness, struggle, hope and despair. The vulnerability of the respondents is often underpinned by hierarchical societal structure and power relations. A common aspect of their life histories is a description of how social institutions and locally powerful people undermine their adaptive capacity to climate variability and extremes. These accounts touch our hearts and cross our minds. Observing and listening to such distressing life histories of research participants are emotionally wrenching, but as researchers, we record their narratives and use them for our purpose only. We as academic researchers use them and their stories as the raw materials of our research project, and later publish them for our professional upliftment. But we literally cannot do anything to reduce participants' pains, sorrows and vulnerability. We manage our emotions, show our empathy and leave the respondents behind.

Although we complete a project, the life histories of research participants remain with us and sometimes haunt us. As Stahlke (2018) observes, researchers who work with vulnerable people and communities are at emotional and psychological risks. But researchers do not know how they can deal with these stresses. It is mainly because vulnerability is fundamentally contextual and is grounded in specific social, cultural, economic, historical and political settings.

Another cause of emotional burden arises from the dilemma of whether we should 'help' our respondents if they ask (Ferdoush 2021). We experienced that some respondents, who trusted us and became friendly, asked for help. Most of the cases they request us to connect them with the local government offices or NGOs, or provide information so that they can access cash or in-kind resources available for the poor. Some reciprocity (e.g. babysitting, sharing snacks) with participants is not uncommon in ethnographic research in the global south, but the demands of some respondents go beyond such reciprocity. Respondents tend to think that we are 'educated', affluent, have a better economic background and networks with local organisations—so we can influence the local organisation or persons holding power and authority in favour of them. We, however, know that we have very little capacity to help them out. Researchers build careers by reading the lives of respondents, recording their narratives and translating them into the text to produce academic pieces, but when it comes to 'giving back', a researcher can offer very little apart from knowledge. Researchers tend to offer 'false hopes' just to convince the participants so that they can get reliable information. Thus, our role as researchers does not allow us to meet their demands which give us imposter and helpless feelings.

The vulnerable population tends to go through a wide range of stresses, that is, financial crisis, sickness, deprivation or injustice. As qualitative researchers, we spend a substantial amount of time with respondents and often observe the distressing situation and various forms of crises in their local settings. Certainly, experiencing such conditions of respondents makes us sympathetic to them and sometimes hurts us, yet we do not know how to respond in such situations. As the following example illustrates:

> *Rani (pseudonym) played a vital role to complete our fieldwork in Cox's Bazar. She was initially a respondent who later became our local collaborator. She introduced us to many other respondents. At a stage of the fieldwork, we went to visit her home and found her mother was severely ill and needed immediate hospital care. She did not have enough money and connections to avail hospital care for her mother. Several times she expressed her concern about her mother's condition and indicated whether we could help her. We felt very sad but could not help her as there were time and resource constraints. We selfishly used her as a gatekeeper and completed our research project. When we came back after completing the fieldwork, we started to realize that we failed to perform our moral obligation to help her. We still feel that we left her in the middle of nowhere. This incident still haunts us.*

It is admittable that we could help Rani so that she could provide medical treatment to her mother, and it was seemingly not a 'big break' in the code of conduct in qualitative research, but it could create precedence for 'help' in the locality. As a consequence of such 'help', many others could come forward to seek help, and if we did otherwise, it would have a huge negative impact on our research. Every action of a researcher in qualitative fieldwork has various forms of chain effects. Although we become sympathetic to people in crisis, we maintain professional codes to deal with the participants. Personal and professional identities are always in contestation in social research (Denzin 1997).

Institutional ethical guidelines do not cover how a researcher should respond to participants' demands in this situation. But, can a researcher deny such responsibility towards the respondents? Although we feel a moral obligation to give back to the respondents, our research plan does not encourage such action. We know that a small help can bring meaningful differences to participants' lives in vulnerable communities, but we are not in a position to fulfil our moral obligations. Of course, what moral obligations mean for a researcher is also a problematic idea in social sciences (Wolfe 1989), but we refer it here as helping those participants in need and vulnerable situations.

In addition, institutional codes of ethics do not guide the researchers to act or react in any form if they observe an incident of injustice done to a participant by individuals or organisations (Orb et al. 2000). In our fieldwork, for example, we were interviewing a marginalised section of two coastal communities to explore their perceptions of an NGO-initiated climate adaptation program, and participants were complaining about unfair selection of project beneficiaries and distribution of project resources and corruption. We were listening to them and taking notes as part of our research but not as a complaint against NGOs' activities. It was observed that such interventions had various unintended consequences (e.g. conflict) over communities. Respondents blamed a field staff of the project implementing NGO. We were in a dilemma about how we should respond to this situation. We, as researchers, listened to and recorded their narratives and remained silent about the injustice done to the communities. To have successful completion of fieldwork, we maintained good relationships with staff members of NGOs and left the 'field'. It was our professional task to know the facts and record them as part of local dynamics but not to redress the facts and we did it very professionally. Despite full professional dealings, we felt a kind of moral dilemma for not taking a stand in favour of participants. Rather, we maintained good relations with both research participants and NGO workers.

One of the key reasons to conduct fieldwork for academic research is to write articles and reports, and in most cases, it is for professional advancement and promotion in the career. Advancing a career is a key objective for doing fieldwork with individuals and communities. In this sense, fieldwork is driven by self-interest from the position of researchers. Therefore, researchers move from one project to another, but our participants remain in the same state for ages in most cases as there is hardly any direct benefit they receive from a research project. That means, we extract information from the participants for our benefit. As observed by Jakimow (2020, p. 155), "research is good if the information it produces helps the people who give it, but this research has only helped the researchers." She emphasises that research should be designed in a way so that both researchers and the participants can mutually be benefitted. Jakimow seems right but in most cases, researchers benefit most and the participants get less or nothing. We agree with Ferdoush's (2021, p. 76) assertation that "denying responsibility toward the participants and communities we study must be deemed unethical." This is a growing concern in social science that how the participants could be directly benefitted from the research since they provide the fundamentals of research what we call 'data'. Research ethics, therefore, need to highlight how researchers can perform their responsibility and redress injustice in social research with vulnerable people and communities. This consideration should start from the beginning of fieldwork, which may help a researcher to establish his/her identity in the studied communities. This is crucial to be successful in community-based fieldwork. But, at the same time, researchers should have adequate consciousness of different categories of research particularly the differences between academic research and action research since action research most often is done to solve the problem and help the community on the ground (see for more detail, Craig 2009).

Dilemmas Associated with Establishing Our Identity as a Researcher

In fieldwork, we often struggle to establish our identity in studied communities. Researchers' positioning is always a big issue in qualitative research since building rapport with the participants is very significant to undertaking good quality research (Uddin 2011). Although we introduce ourselves as researchers to the potential respondents, they tend to have different perceptions about our roles and activities. The perceptions are often shaped by their previous experience and encounter with 'outsiders'. The coastal communities in Bangladesh have experienced several disasters triggered by tropical cyclones and storm surges. In response, external organisations, especially NGOs, have operated relief and recovery programs targeting the most vulnerable section of local communities. Although we introduce ourselves as academics and professional researchers, or *gobeshok* in Bangla, respondents do not understand our positions and roles, rather they seem to perceive us as '*NGOwalas*' (staff members of an NGO), who often visit them for enlisting and providing some supports. For example, at the initial stage of the fieldwork, we interviewed a woman from a southeast coastal community in Bangladesh. She provided us with insightful information. While we were interviewing other women, she saw us visiting her community regularly. One day, while we were leaving one of her neighbours' homes after an interview, she approached and commented:

> *Why are you spending so much time surveying so many women? Give us whatever you want to give. Others (indicating NGO professionals) do not spend so much time—*

they do a quick survey and later support us (in-kind or cash). What kind of NGOs are you working for? Talking too much but giving nothing!

This statement reflects that perpetual relief operations and the transfer of resources shaped their perspectives towards researchers. The participants often expect that they will receive something after the interview and survey. Despite our conscious efforts to establish ourselves as researchers, we could not change respondents' perceptions about our roles and activities. Though the participants were not non-cooperative as such, their vulnerable conditions make them understand that outsiders are NGO workers visiting the locality to help them. This perception has important implications for qualitative fieldwork and research outcomes.

Such a perception is also partly shaped by their unfamiliarity with the term *gobeshok* (researcher). The educated respondents seem to understand the meaning of the term and the activities of a social researcher, while the most vulnerable section of rural coastal communities with little formal education and knowledge about the world of research does not understand the role of a *gobeshok*. Some participants pretend as if they understand the purpose of the interviews, but in reality, they may have inadequate and different understandings of research and researchers. This sometimes puts us in a dilemma whether they trust us and truly express their opinion. Thus, trust and mistrust work together in social settings, but the researchers must render themselves trustable to the participants because quality data depends on the depth of relations between the researchers and the participants in a given context.

The principal purpose of performing fieldwork is to record knowledge and experiences from participants about the study at hand. As such, researchers possess detailed information about the study and fieldwork sites but do not share all information. They only disclose personal and research related information using their discretion to achieve maximum cooperation and information from participants (Bravo-Moreno 2003). In the rapport-building process, researchers follow various tactics including self-disclosure, making friendships, transparent to the participants and finding commonalities to obtain data needed for a study (Karnieli-Miller et al. 2009). These are actions without which a researcher may not gain expected insights and information from participants, but researchers fall into ethical dilemmas. We know that these relationships are temporary, purposeful, goal-oriented and unequal. This often raises the question: are we deceiving the participants? Procedural ethics does not guide a researcher in the rapport-building process. Researchers use their cultural understanding and personal experiences to build relationships with respondents that facilitate the timely completion of fieldwork. Of course, it is admittable that how a researcher can build rapport largely depends on the personal quality, professional integrity and academic training of the researcher (Denzin 1997).

In community-based research, respondents tend to ask about the purpose of data collection and the benefits they will get. They often want to see some immediate outcomes of the research from which they expect to be benefitted. For example, when we explained to the respondents that we were researching climate/disaster risk management, they asked us to lobby for building strong embankments that would protect them from storm surges and flooding. Similarly, during recent fieldwork with an island community that experienced river erosion and flooding, our respondents often asked:

> *We are river eroded people. We lost our land in the river and moved our houses many times. We see many people come and collect information. But we don't become benefited. Would your data collection and reporting help to protect us from river erosion?*

We could not provide them with any straightforward answers to that question. At the same time, we could not give any 'false hopes' to them. We explained our roles and tasks as social researcher. We made our position clear that we cannot offer any direct benefits to communities that are vulnerbale to climate change. Theoretically and practically, the impetus for choosing a topic for academic research comes from researchers' interests, potential funding opportunities and apparent knowledge gaps. For this reason, we hardly consider community priorities and needs. Although the community members participate in research, they feel disconnected from the objectives of a study. Thus, inadequate participation in community-based research project may result in ethical challenges as intensive community participation could produce a more valid and significant result in qualitative research.

Dilemmas Associated with Potential Risks to Research Collaborators and Respondents

We work at a university and live in urban areas. We know little about remote coastal communities; we therefore initially contact local NGOs to get access to the targeted communities. NGOs in Bangladesh are good facilitators to initiate fieldwork as they have a wider network with local communities. Keeping this notion in mind, we plan to get in touch with NGOs working in the coastal areas which work with/on vulnerable communities. When we first contact NGOs, they assign a staff member who plays a gatekeeping role in our research. He was very knowledgeable and aware of the social and physical settings of the locality. Therefore, the gatekeeper provides important information about various study sites and local communities. The staff member also accompanies and introduces us to some prospective participants in the early stage of fieldwork which was very helpful for us to get acquittance with the local community. However, the influence of gatekeepers, to some extent could be called research assistants at the beginning, is not always positive. They tend to convince us to select particular study sites, communities, groups and people which are convenient to them rather than the interest of the research focus. NGOs tend to introduce us to the community members who are their beneficiaries and have a positive attitude towards their activities because NGO workers always tend to provide an affirmative picture of what they are doing in the community. In some cases, we found that NGOs become suspicious about our research and its outcomes if we select the participants on our own beyond their prescription. They think that if we select participants by our choice, they may provide negative information about their activities. As we are aware of the influence of gatekeepers on making initial contacts with community members, selecting research participants and collecting data, we devise different strategies to avoid gatekeepers' 'biases' and 'influence'. In a project, for example, we spent a substantial amount of time observing the relationship dynamics between NGOs and community members as well as the details of relations even among community members. Although this strategy was frustrating for the gatekeepers, we were able to avoid gatekeepers' influences on the data collection process. It was also a serious ethical dilemma that we were guided by a prescribed instruction which could lead us to a wrong understanding of the community sentiments, perceptions and everyday struggles and whether NGOs played a vital role in the (re)production of various forms of vulnerabilities. Nevertheless, we could get rid of such misconceptions very intelligently.

We try to find someone within the studied communities who can facilitate us throughout the fieldwork as the data collection process of qualitative research needs a long period. We intentionally select a research collaborator from the marginalised section of local communities so that they may accept us and agree to participate in our research. The very local collaborator became a new gateway for us to get an insight into the community we studied. Our experience reflects that the marginalised section of communities is not homogenous, rather they are divided and compete to access the essential resources. Therefore, selecting a local research collaborator is always crucial which can influence the fieldwork process and research outcomes. It is admittable that a research assistant, whom we term here as a research collaborator, always influences the research in one way or another which is historically evident in many qualitative research experiences. Although sometimes it is very helpful, sometimes it misdirects (see for details, Tang and Gube 2022).

For instance, in a project, the lead author selected a 'poor woman' called Kulsum (pseudonym) as a local collaborator for six-month-long fieldwork. The project sought to explore women's experiences in participating in an NGO-initiated climate adaptation program. A staff member of a local NGO introduced the researcher to this woman, who maintained a good connection with different NGOs as well as within communities, particularly with other 'poor women'. Kulsum took the initiative to connect the researcher with other women who participated in the NGO's adaptation project. When the interviews started, the researcher realised that some potential respondents, who initially agreed to be interviewed, declined later on because of a 'not so good relationship' with Kulsum. As observed, in some cases the tension between Kulsum and other females turned into an open dispute. Locally influential people also did not like her role and they indirectly expressed their disappointment during interviews. Indicating Kulsum, one of the locally influential interviewees commented, "you will not get correct information from that woman." Other respondents also seemed unhappy and expressed their anger as Kulsum was breaking social norms on many occasions. However, Kulsum explained that some community leaders were anxious and criticised her leadership role in different NGO-initiated groups. This reflects a long-standing conflict between traditional leaders and perpetual clients of NGOs to dominate the power structure of rural communities.

As per our experience, local research collaborators and respondents may not only face psychological but also physical risks to some extent. We have observed that there is a high level of distrust and disagreement among different sections of coastal communities, particularly those who have faced recurrent disasters (Masud-All-Kamal et al. 2021). Widespread mismanagement and corruption in relief and rehabilitation programs largely contribute to weakening community social capital in disaster-prone areas (Mahmud and Prowse 2012; Islam et al. 2017; Aase 2020). Although we follow standard ethical guidelines to protect our participants in such communities, there is always a risk of physical harm only because of their participation and 'giving information' to us which might go against them. More specifically, as local political elites are involved in corruption, sometimes they become afraid of the fact that the respondents may reveal their misdeeds. Our collaborators and respondents therefore may become the target of repression when the researcher/s leave(s) study areas. Undoubtedly, they take such risks for the sake of the research itself. But sometimes we ignore the physical risks that our research collaborators and respondents are likely to face by participating in disaster/climate change-related research projects. This kind of academic genre also poses a moral dilemma to the researcher because we collect information for our research, but we put our informants at risk of physical assaults and various forms of repression. We, the researchers, take the information but do not take the responsibility of the informants who face risks for giving the information. This is also a big ethical question.

The rural societies in Bangladesh are class-based, hierarchical and tied through a unique form of social capital (Masud-All-Kamal et al. 2021). We were aware of such relational dynamics and their effects on our collaborators and participants. We used different strategies to minimise the risks of our local research collaborators and participants. Such measures, however, seem insufficient to address risks faced by them during and after fieldwork. They are likely to encounter increased psychological, emotional and physical risks after completing the fieldwork. As Jakimow (2020) points out, research collaborators and participants may face multiple risks in sensitive research that are hardly addressed in the existing research ethics. Although we leave our collaborators, participants and respondents behind, we cannot stop thinking about their potential risks. As qualitative researchers, we find this experience disturbing and frustrating which makes us helpless. We thought about it twice and thrice but found no satisfactory answers which put us in an ethical dilemma.

13.4 Concluding Remarks

Our analysis demonstrates that qualitative researchers who work with climate-vulnerable people face several unique and subtle ethical dilemmas and moral challenges. The ethical challenges arise from relationships with participants, miscommunication between researchers and respondents, and relational dynamics between researchers and collaborators. As the relationship between researchers and participants becomes close in qualitative fieldwork, respondents disclose their distressing conditions and seek help. Researchers feel moral responsibilities of 'giving back' or helping 'vulnerable' people, but they have little option as the research plan focuses on completing fieldwork and data collection in a specific time rather than helping people in vulnerable conditions. As a result, researchers would feel discomfort and guilty for not giving back to the research participants and not doing something that directly benefits them. Vulnerable people in disaster-prone communities face a wide range of economic, social and environmental challenges, whereas the researchers are busy with 'self-centred and egoistic' exercises (Gonda et al. 2021) and 'research leading activities'. To conduct ethically sound research, we need to be mindful of the extractive nature of fieldwork and engaged in reciprocity by helping people in need. Such consciousness and act could reduce researchers' feelings of guilt and contribute to changing the lives of vulnerable communities and the people in need.

Professional associations and universities uphold procedural codes of social research and protocols of fieldwork. The primary goal of ethical review committees is to protect research participation from physical, social and psychological harm. In turn, researchers become aware of the need to ensure participants' autonomy, privacy, confidentiality and justice (Gallagher et al. 1995). While researchers maintain these ethical guidelines, they may face some contextual ethical challenges. The formalised principles of ethics do not focus on dilemmas that arise from the context of the research. However, the researchers minimise some of these dilemmas based on their experiences. If researchers become aware of local perceptions and perspectives about research, researchers and common research terminologies (e.g. *gobeshona*) they may avoid discomfort and confusion.

Research with vulnerable people and communities is complex as their vulnerabilities are intertwined with various social, economic, political and cultural factors. Relationships among community members tend to be hierarchical, distrustful and competitive. The selection of local collaborators is also critical as it influences the perceptions of respondents and the rapport-building process. For instance, if a local research collaborator is chosen from a wealthy and locally powerful family, respondents from marginalised sections of communities may not trust the researchers. Lack of community trust may enhance ethical dilemmas and moral obligations which in turn can jeopardise the intended outcomes of fieldwork in qualitative research. Incongruent with Marshall and Rotimi (2001), we suggest that researchers need to focus on developing a mechanism to build a solid foundation of community trust during the design and implementation of research protocols to minimise ethical dilemmas and challenges. It could altogether reconfirm the strength, quality and validity of data as well as it could reduce the degree of ethical dilemmas.

The unpredictable nature of qualitative research causes diverse ethical challenges. As Orb et al. (2001) point out, despite maintaining ethical codes and guidelines in qualitative research with at-risk communities, ethical dilemmas are apparent. Ethics committees and researchers need to be aware of the unexpected ethical dilemmas and their unintended consequences on researchers' well-being. It is important to have some effective strategies in place to deal with them. We suggest broadening ethical measures to minimise researchers' dilemmas and challenges. In addition to that, informal support networks with colleagues trusted friends and family members can minimise ethical dilemmas that arise from fieldwork with climate-vulnerable communities.

REFERENCES

Aase, M. (2020). Listing for change? Exploring the politics of relief lists in Bangladesh after Cyclone Sidr. *Disasters*, *44*(4), 666–686.

Adger, W. N. (2006). Vulnerability. *Global Environmental Change*, *16*(3), 268–281.

Bravo-Moreno, A. (2003). Power games between the researcher and the participant in the social inquiry. *The Qualitative Report*, *8*(4), 624–639.

Craig, D. V. (2009). *Action research essentials*. Jossey Bass, USA.

Creswell, J. W. (2014). *Research design: Qualitative, quantitative, and mixed methods approach*. Sage Publications, Thousand Oaks, CA.

Denzin, N. (1997). *Interpretive ethnography: Ethnographic practice for the 21st century*. SAGE, Thousand Oaks, London and Delhi.

Dodgson, J. E. (2019). Reflexivity in qualitative research. *Journal of Human Lactation*, *35*(2), 220–222.

Ferdoush, M. A. (2021). To "help" or not to "help" the participant: A global South ethnographer's dilemma in the global South. *Geoforum*, *124*, 75–78.

Ferreira, R. J., Buttell, F., & Ferreira, S. (2015). Ethical considerations for conducting disaster research with vulnerable populations. *Journal of Social Work Values and Ethics*, *12*(1), 29–40.

Gallagher, B., Creighton, S., & Gibbons, J. (1995). Ethical dilemmas in social research: No easy solutions. *The British Journal of Social Work*, *25*(3), 295–311.

Gonda, N., Leder, S., González-Hidalgo, M., Chiwona-Karltun, L., Stiernström, A., Hajdu, F., Fischer, K., Asztalos Morell, I., Kadfak, A., & Arvidsson, A. (2021). Critical reflexivity in political ecology research: How can the Covid-19 pandemic transform us into better researchers? *Frontiers in Human Dynamics*, *3*, 1–16.

Gray, D. E. (2014) *Doing research in the real world*. Sage Publications, London.

Guillemin, M., & Gillam, L. (2004). Ethics, reflexivity, and "ethically important moments" in research. *Qualitative Inquiry*, *10*(2), 261–280.

IPCC. (2022). *Climate Change 2022: Impacts, Adaptation, and Vulnerability*. Contribution of Working Group II to the Sixth Assessment Report of the Intergovernmental Panel on Climate Change [H.-O. Pörtner, D.C. Roberts, M. Tignor, E.S. Poloczanska, K. Mintenbeck, A. Alegría, M. Craig, S. Langsdorf,

S. Löschke, V. Möller, A. Okem, B. Rama (eds.)]. Cambridge University Press, New York.

Islam, R., Walkerden, G., & Amati, M. (2017). Households' experience of local government during recovery from cyclones in coastal Bangladesh: Resilience, equity, and corruption. *Natural Hazards*, *85*(1), 361–378.

Jakimow, T. (2020). Risking the self: Vulnerability and its uses in research. In Wadds, P., Apoifis, N., Schmeidl, S. and Spurway, K. (eds.) *Navigating fieldwork in the social sciences* (pp. 147–161). Palgrave Macmillan, Cham.

Karnieli-Miller, O., Strier, R., & Pessach, L. (2009). Power relations in qualitative research. *Qualitative Health Research*, *19*(2), 279–289.

Lincoln, Y. S., & Guba, E. G. (1985). *Naturalistic inquiry*. Sage Publications, Thousand Oaks, CA.

Mahmud, T., & Prowse, M. (2012). Corruption in cyclone preparedness and relief efforts in coastal Bangladesh: Lessons for climate adaptation?. *Global Environmental Change*, *22*(4), 933–943.

Marshall, P. A., & Rotimi, C. (2001). Ethical challenges in community-based research. *The American Journal of the Medical Sciences*, *322*(5), 241–245.

Masud-All-Kamal, M., & Nursey-Bray, M. (2022). Best intentions and local realities: Challenges to building social capital through planned adaptation: Evidence from rural communities in Bangladesh. *Climate and Development*, *14*(9), 794–803.

Masud-All-Kamal, M., Nursey-Bray, M., & Hassan, S. M. (2021). Current research in environmental sustainability. *Current Research in Environmental Sustainability*, *3*, 100091.

Mura, P. (2015). "To participate or not to participate?" A reflective account. *Current Issues in Tourism*, *18*(1), 83–98.

Orb, A., Eisenhauer, L., & Wynaden, D. (2001). Ethics in qualitative research. *Journal of Nursing Scholarship*, *33*(1), 93–96.

Paprocki, K. (2021). *Threatening dystopias: The global politics of climate change adaptation in Bangladesh*. Cornell University Press, Ithaca.

Patton, M. Q. (2002) *Qualitative research and evaluation methods*, Sage Publications, Thousand Oaks, CA.

Sampson, H. (2019). 'Fluid fields' and the dynamics of risk in social research. *Qualitative Research*, *19*(2), 131–147.

Shaw, I. (2003). Ethics in qualitative research and evaluation. *Journal of Social Work*, *3*(1), 9–29.

Stahlke, S. (2018). Expanding on notions of ethical risks to qualitative researchers. *International Journal of Qualitative Methods*, *17*(1), 1–9.

Sultana, F. (2007) Reflexivity, positionality and participatory ethics: Negotiating fieldwork dilemmas in international research. *ACME: An International Journal for Critical Geographies*, *6*(3), 374–385. https://doi.org/10.1016/j.ijedudev.2008.02.004.

Sultana, F. (2014). Gendering climate change: Geographical insights. *The Professional Geographer*, *66*(3), 372–381.

Tang, N. & Gube, J. (2022). Research assistants as knowledge co-producer: Reflection beyond fieldwork. In *Facilitating community research for social change: Case studies in qualitative, art-based and virtual research*, edited by Burkholder, C, Aledejebi, F, & Schwab-Cartas, J (pp. 146–160). Routledge, London.

Uddin, N. (2011). Decolonising ethnography in the field: *An anthropological account*. *International Journal of Social Research Methodology*, *14*(6), 455–467.

Uddin, N. (2022). Research on Rohingya refugees: Methodological challenges and textual inadequacy. In Uddin, N. (ed.), *Voices of the Rohingya people* (pp. 27–52). Palgrave Macmillan, Cham.

Wolfe, A. (1989). *Whose keeper? Social and moral obligation.* The University of California Press, Berkeley.

PART IV

Gendered Fieldwork and Gender in Social Research

CHAPTER 14

Risks and Challenges in Fieldwork on Gender-Based Violence: Gendered Identity, Social Taboo and Culture

Nahid Rezwana

14.1 Introduction

Gender-based violence (GBV) is a very common human rights issue in all societies irrespective of location, place, culture and religion. Despite long-term consequences on a survivor's health and well-being (Hossain and McAlpine, 2017), GBV is mostly kept hidden within the family, remains underreported and rarely gets proper attention from the respective authority. Recently, a range of research is being conducted for a better understanding of the causes and consequences of GBV and to highlight its importance in enhancing social development; however, this area of research always raises a particular set of risks and challenges for the researcher and respondents (Jewkes et al. 2000). Researching GBV includes victims, survivors, perpetrators and observers, and requires special attention to ethical issues as well as to the safety of the researched and the researcher due to its sensitive nature. The present chapter focuses on the latter; risks and challenges faced by a researcher when conducting fieldwork on gender-based violence. Based on several empirical research located in remote regions of Bangladesh, it presents how researchers overcome these challenges and conduct their fieldwork while being concerned about their insecurity. It is expected that these practical experiences will be helpful for future researchers

---

N. Rezwana (✉)
Geography and Environment, University of Dhaka, Dhaka, Bangladesh
e-mail: nahid.rezwana@du.ac.bd

© The Author(s), under exclusive license to Springer Nature Switzerland AG 2023
N. Uddin, A. Paul (eds.), *The Palgrave Handbook of Social Fieldwork*,
https://doi.org/10.1007/978-3-031-13615-3_14

237

in taking proper decisions when overcoming these challenges and conducting the study while keeping them safe in a risky environment.

14.2 Fieldwork Risk and Challenges in GBV Research: World Perspective

Working on sensitive topics in a threatening environment is not new for social researchers. There is a growing interest in sensitive topics like gender-based violence, which 'introduces challenges not usually found when dealing with other social or research topics' (Fraga 2016, p 77). Gender-based violence (GBV) is defined as 'violence against a person because of that person's gender or violence that affects persons of a particular gender disproportionately' (European Commission 2020). GBV can be of various forms: physical, sexual and psychological, and results in physical, sexual, psychological and economic harm. Although GBV can take place against both men and women, women and girls are the main victims of GBV irrespective of geographical locations, economic conditions and culture. Violence against women and girls is a global issue that affects one in three women in their lifetime (The World Bank 2019). Domestic violence, sex-based harassment, female genital mutilation (FGM), forced marriage and online violence are examples of violence against women. Researching GBV requires an in-depth understanding of the context and often includes qualitative methods such as Focus Group Discussions (FGD), observations, Key Informants Interviews (KII), especially in-depth interviews with female survivors, local representatives, health professionals, activists and even sometimes interviewing males who may be perpetrators themselves, and inquiring about their opinions on any violent behaviour towards women. Interview methodology is very useful because of its capacity to give voice to GBV survivors (Reinharz and Chase 2002 in Campbell et al. 2009). However, these methods and area of research entail a particular set of risks and concerns for the researcher, especially while staying in the study area in a threatening environment (Robson and McCartan, 2016). Jewkes and her team elaborately presented the problems that surveyors experienced when collecting data on GBV in Southern African countries and their strategies for overcoming the challenges and risks (Jewkes et al. 2000). Their paper recommends paying attention and taking proper measures for the interviewer's safety to avoid any unwanted circumstances and risks when conducting fieldwork on GBV. Dicksonswift and her team's research also revealed similar results in Australia. Interviewing 30 Australian public health researchers has shown that researchers confront several physical and emotional risks when conducting qualitative research on sensitive issues (Dickson-swift et al. 2008). One of them explained how she felt intimidated when a participant behaved improperly during the interview at his home. She sensed risk and was upset when she left the area. Jewkes mentioned in her paper that investigators received anonymous death threats while studying a gang rape on a university campus in Canada (Jewkes et al. 2000). Several other studies also revealed different types of physical risk for the researchers or social workers, especially women working at the field level (Domenelli 2013; Rezwana 2018).

Domenelli (2013) described in her paper the physical risk female aid workers (students) faced in Sri Lanka during the 2004 Indian Ocean Tsunami. One of them described how she faced sexual abuse during the daily journey by bus and its strong mental impact on her. Gender identity became a strong factor for female researchers or aid workers. Similar experiences were also described by the female aid workers who were working in the coastal region of Bangladesh after cyclone Sidr. They were discriminated against by male aid workers and the residents in continuing their daily basic routine, for example, taking baths, going to the toilet, etc. They were criticized and charged for taking help from their male colleagues to secure their safety when having to take baths in an open pond during the early morning. They had to leave the area to avoid further humiliation without completing their plans of relief distribution and help (Rezwana, 2018).

Besides, GBV research has mental health impacts on the researchers. The characteristics of qualitative approaches, playing a dual role as both an insider and an outsider, and maintaining reflexivity (Cui, 2015) may lead 'to power relations and researcher vulnerability which manifested in tangible ways' (Raheim et al. 2016, p 1). The qualitative researcher's perspective is a paradoxical one (Maykut, P., & Morehouse, R. 1994 in Dwyer and Buckle 2009) and may require sharing the researcher's personal information when gaining the trust of the participants and residents of the study area. However, this disclosure might place them in a vulnerable position (Raheim et al 2016), especially in ethnographic studies in which longer stays are entailed.

The physical risk and challenges along with the mental impacts increase the risk of the researchers' conducting fieldwork on sensitive topics. However, risk assessment in research is historically limited to the examination of risks to participants. Recently, researchers' risks in the fields are getting attention. The Social Research Association (SRA) in the UK has developed 'A Code of Practice for the Safety of Social Researchers' that focuses on the physical and psychological safety of social researchers (Dickson-swift et al. 2008). WHO (World Health Organization) recommended ensuring female researcher's safety in 'Putting Women First: Ethical and Safety Recommendations for Research on Domestic Violence Against Women' published in 2001 (WHO 2001). Boynton (2005) in her book also elaborately discussed the researcher's safety, based on her experience when studying prostitution. She analysed 'risk assessment for researchers', which is very helpful for researchers to get prepared for their safety, especially researchers who are working on sensitive issues (Boynton 2005 in Robson and McCartan 2016). There is some other research, which has also highlighted the danger faced by the researchers, along with recommendations based on practical experiences of the fieldwork in a risky environment (Campbell et al. 2009; Dickson-Swift et al. 2008; Jewkes et al. 2000).

Proper attention in assessing researchers' risks, and making plans to ensure their safety while designing research projects are the most common recommendations mentioned in previous papers. Among the plans, training on safety and preparation, along with proper guidance and supervision, is a must for the GBV researcher before conducting fieldwork (Dickson-Swift et al. 2008). Fraga (2016) advised substantial investment in interviewers' training so that they can handle unusual or unprecedented circumstances while conducting interviews. Interviewers should know their exit plan for emergencies before starting fieldwork in a difficult environment. Considering researcher's safety and acquiring preparation before the fieldwork not only saves them from the physical and mental health impacts of challenging fieldwork regarding violence but also saves them from fear that can affect the quality of their data collection (Robson and McCartan 2016) and ensure the satisfaction of the participants as positive experiences (Jansen et al. 2004). However, despite its high importance, the number of studies on researcher's safety during fieldwork on sensitive topics is not enough, especially among the researchers located in developing countries. More studies and academic papers are needed, as 'it is essential to ensure that women are not placed at risk as a result of the research' (Jewkes et al. 2000 p 94). Considering the importance, the present research discusses the challenges and risks of GBV research that was located in the disaster-prone regions of Bangladesh. Based on practical experiences, it mentions recommendations on how to combat such challenges and thus ensure the researcher's safety in difficult circumstances that arise during fieldwork.

14.3 Methodological Challenges of Fieldwork on Gender-Based Violence

Gender-based violence is a sensitive topic to study. Different types of methodological challenges arise during the fieldwork even in well-planned research. Though there is a commonality among GBV research in applying qualitative methods, such as interviewing, FGD and observations, the challenges are contextually unique for each research. Geographical location, culture, social attitude and especially gender perception among the studied social workers are factors that increase challenges and risks for the researcher, which are elaborately described in the following paragraphs.

Social Taboo and GBV: Challenges in Snowballing Process and Interviews

Gender-based violence or violence against women and girls (VAWG) is a global pandemic (The world Bank 2019) but is still very commonly less discussed, kept within the family and society. In most cases, it becomes very difficult to find the right person for the Key Informant Interview (KII) who will disclose the GBV condition of the village. It is a social taboo to talk about gender-based violence. An example from recent research will be helpful to explain the situation. The research was located in a flood-prone village of Rangpur, Bangladesh, to find out the GBV conditions during disasters (Table 14.1, RN4). Secondary data analysis was conducted at the preliminary stage of the research, and it showed that Rangpur ranked the second-highest division in Bangladesh in regards to physical violence against women (55.3% of women) (BBS 2016). However, it became difficult to get the real condition of the village from the first few key informant interviews, conducted with the local businessman, housewife, educated residents and madrasa teacher. The gatekeeper also was not clear with his opinion. All of them strongly mentioned the presence of VAWG such as 'child marriage', which is mostly forced marriage against girls but other violence against women such as wife-beating, dowry violence, sexual harassment and rapes remained under the curtain. The snowballing process to reach GBV victims could not be started with the help of these interviews.

According to the researcher,

'I can feel something is wrong in this village, I talked with them (key informants)… they are not opening up, even the key contact… only mentioning the problems but no other specific information…for days I have been here…walking, talking and returning to my hotel… but there has been no mentionable result…'. (Fieldwork, 2019)

After two visits to the village (six working days), one key informant (a female school teacher) opened up about the problems. She described the real

Table 14.1 Overview of the studies

Research number (RN)	Location and year	Sample size	Methodology and methods	Major topics
RN 1	Barguna, Bangladesh, 2012–2015	In-depth interviews -30 KII- 13 FGD-4	In-depth interviews, KII, FGD observation	Disasters and access to health care, gendered analysis
RN 2	Barguna, Bangladesh, 2017	In-depth interviews -37 KII- 8	In-depth interviews, KII, observation	Gender-based violence during disasters
RN 3	Bhola, Bangladesh, 2018	House survey - 93 In-depth interviews (case study) - 4 KII- 7	Household survey, in-depth interviews, case studies, KII, observation	River bank erosion and its impact on people's life
RN 4	Rangpur, Bangladesh, 2019	House survey - 204 In-depth interviews (case study) - 18 KII- 5	House survey, in-depth interviews, KII, observation	Gender-based violence in floods [1]

conditions of GBV in the village. Later, the study found other participants for the KII, who mentioned the GBV conditions elaborately. However, without her (school teacher) help, it was difficult to start the snowballing process and find out the address of the victims in this village. The final finding of this study shows that the GBV condition is alarming in this village, which increases in high numbers during the floods.

Challenge: Gender-Based Violence as the Study Topic

Based on research experiences, the present study reveals that the researcher has to be prepared with a demo topic to meet the unwanted curiosity of residents during the fieldwork on GBV. It is a very common picture in rural areas that residents ask team members about the research whenever they are seen in the village; maybe on the pathways, at the tea stalls or even while sitting in any house. From the first day, residents become very interested in the research and the team members. Sometimes it becomes risky for the future of the study if locals know the topic is on GBV or VAGW (Jewkes et al. 2000). Residents, especially male members, try to protect the information on GBV, thinking that disclosing those to the research team may destroy the image of the village, women's personal information may be exposed to the outer world, or they do not want outsiders to know the real situations of violence against women in this village, and sometimes, they do not think this is an important topic to be researched on. Fraga (2016) mentioned in her paper that admitting to rape cases might result in death in some countries. So, the research team has to prepare a topic which looks common, more important to the residents, and at the same time related to GBV, such as 'Problems of women in disasters' or 'Health problems of women'. These topics are very familiar among the rural residents of Bangladesh. Male members of society always welcome teams who work on health issues. This strategy helped the research on the flood-prone village in Rangpur in 2019 (Table 14.1 RN). While taking an interview of a domestic violence (wife-beating) victim at a quiet and safe place of the house, her husband appeared, which was unusual. He came to check on the interviewers, the subject matter and the environment of the interview. The research team quickly changed the topic after seeing him. They introduced themselves to the husband and discussed the problems of women in a flood-prone village with him. After he was assured and happy, he left for work so the researchers could continue the interview.

An interviewer in Barguna, the southernmost coastal district of Bangladesh, also faced such a challenge. Barguna was one of the severely affected coastal districts during Cyclone Sidr in 2007. A study was conducted on the impacts of the cyclone on GBV conditions (Table 14.1 RN2). During the fieldwork, an interview was scheduled to meet with a domestic violence victim. The interview was going well for the first few minutes but later the interviewer had to stop and change the topic of the interview several times when the victim's family member (mother-in-law) started spying on them and had become suspicious. That interview was not completed as the victim did not want to continue in the fear of future abuse from her in-laws and husband.

Challenge: Finding GBV Victims

Finding victims is a major challenge for the researcher in GBV studies. According to Fraga (2016), data on non-fatal violent injury is typically restricted to the hospital or support service records whereas unreported violence remains undetected. If victims do not willingly want to talk about their experiences, it becomes a challenge to identify and measure violence. During the study in Rangpur, the research team identified a domestic violence victim from the snowballing process (Table 14.1 RN4). The victim also primarily agreed to share her experiences. However, later, during the interview, she refused the allegation of wife-beating against her husband. Instead, she was justifying his actions, as it was her fault that she could not hold her temper during a child's tantrum. The interview was not successful.

In another case, an interview with a rape victim was scheduled in Barguna. She was gang-raped after Cyclone Sidr and her case was published in a newspaper. The whole neighbourhood knew the fact. She was contacted beforehand to get her consent if she would like to participate in the interview on GBV. It was a long way to reach her house and the full team (two female interviewers and one male field investigator) had to visit the area due to the insecurity of the interviewers. It was costly and time-consuming. During the interview, the respondent denied the fact that she was attacked after cyclone Sidr. She did not talk about the incident and did not continue the interview. Following the ethical codes, the research team left the area without conducting the interview.

Longer Time Needed to Complete the Fieldwork

GBV research mostly follows the qualitative research strategy and design, which are 'ongoing', and 'are grounded in the practice, process and context of the research itself'. They cannot produce a 'once-and-for-all' blueprint for the research (Mason 2002, p 24–25). However, they still have to prepare a design in the form of a research proposal with a Gantt chart to gain funding or approval from the funders, supervisors, or research gatekeepers, and for their (research team) own use.

Practical experiences regarding GBV research show that it becomes difficult to follow the research plan, as 'sampling and fieldwork will be dependent on having negotiated access' (Mason 2002, p 44). As discussed in the last sections, some of the attempts to conduct interviews with GBV victims might be unsuccessful. In that case, the study needs more time to select new respondents and continue the investigation. Besides this, building trust and getting access to the selected society also takes time as it is dependent on the local culture and social expectations of the studied society. Research in three regions of Bangladesh: Barguna in the south-western region, Bhola in the south-eastern region and

Rangpur in the northern region (Table 14.1), show the differences between the regions regarding the acceptance of the GBV research team by the residents and the GBV survivors. In Barguna, GBV victims and survivors eagerly participated in the interviews and shared their experiences. They mentioned their pleasure in getting the opportunity to share their experiences with someone who wants to know their pain, struggle and recovery stories. Whereas in Rangpur, it was very difficult to get information on GBV as most victims or survivors did not want to talk clearly about their experiences. Building trust was difficult in Rangpur. In Bhola, women were found to be conservative and hesitant in sharing their personal experiences.

Again, interviewer training is essential for the GBV research (Fraga 2016); however, training lessons cannot be applicable at all times, especially when facing unusual or unexpected circumstances that can arise in the field. So, the investigator has to take a pause, invest more time to understand local cultures and plan to get more familiar with the residents. Time needs to be spent according to the amount that is necessary for ensuring successful interviews and the good quality of the data collected.

The Gender Identity of the Interviewer/Researcher and Challenges

The gender identity of the interviewer may become a strong factor in data availability on GBV in Bangladesh. According to Fraga (2016), though the gender of the interviewer might not have any influence on data availability, Jansen et al. (2016) and other researchers recommended the recruitment of female interviewers for the study on violence against women (Jansen et.al. 2004). Experience of GBV studies in Bangladesh (Table 14.1) also reveals that female interviewers are highly needed when getting data on violence against women. Female victims and survivors feel comfortable and secure with female interviewers/researchers. They believe that only a woman can understand the pain of another woman (Table 14.1 RN1). Besides, religious belief works as a factor for the women who follow '*Parda*' rules and regulations. They do not want to talk with unknown males, especially on a sensitive topic (Table 14.1 RN 3). Again, the head of the family, who is mostly male, prefers female investigators in his house to talk with the female members of the family (elaborately discussed in section 4).

On the other hand, male victims also do not prefer to talk with female interviewers and even, sometimes with unknown male interviewers. In Barguna (Table 14.1 RN 2), male victims of domestic and sexual violence only talked with the male interviewer among the team members who were well known to them. These experiences show that studies on GBV need to select interviewers according to the objectives. However, it is not always possible to get the required investigator. Moreover, female investigators face more problems while working at the field level (mentioned in the following sections) which becomes a great challenge for the GBV study.

14.4 Risk and Challenges of the Researcher at the Individual Level

Along with the methodological challenges, GBV researchers experience risk and challenges at the personal level, which are described in the following sections:

The Personal Safety of the Female Researcher and Chaperon

GBV research includes working with the victims, survivors, perpetrators or bystanders, and allies, and in a difficult environment, which might become risky and violent for the research teams too. The researcher may feel threatened by harassment and sexual abuse as the present study reveals, after having analysed the experiences of the four researchers located in remote locations in Bangladesh. Similar experiences were mentioned in Swift's paper on Australian GBV researchers and Jewkes's paper on the African region (Swift et al 2008 and Jewkes et al. 2000). They recommended emphasizing the researcher's safety during fieldwork on GBV. The researcher of this present study also planned for the safety measures at the earlier stage of the research on GBV. It became a vital issue for the researcher to allocate the local contact and secure the chaperon and her accommodation in the study area. In Barguna, the researcher took help from her relatives to find a safe rented flat as her accommodation and to select the chaperon, who was a local male and also a distant relative (Table 14.1 RN 1) of the researcher. During the Rangpur study, she had taken help from her husband, who accompanied her during the fieldwork. The reasons for this plan are described in the following points:

a. Local travel, interviewing and risk:

Travelling from one location to another to meet the respondents for interviews becomes challenging and risky for a female researcher, especially one who is an outsider in the study area. The present study found that the female researcher's presence created curiosity in small towns and villages. Lonely roads, remotely located houses and offices became very risky for her to conduct interviews. The researcher faced staring, catcalling, abusive words and even threats when she had to move alone from one place to another. On one occasion, a local perpetrator threatened her, being alone while shopping in an overcrowded bazaar in Barguna. She had managed to escape that day but later had to engage a chaperon (a known male) who accompanied her to every single location that she needed to visit during her stay in Barguna (Table 14.1 RN 1). Her movement became easier and safer.

b. Accommodation, workstation and risk:

Qualitative, especially ethnographic, research requires staying in the study area for a relatively long period. The researcher needs to find safe accommodation for her and/or her team. Previous studies reveal that residents become very curious to know who the new tenants are and what their purposes for staying are. This consequently increases the risk of theft, burglary and even sexual harassment. In a study, the researcher revealed that her stay created a huge amount of curiosity in the neighbourhood, which resulted in verbal abuse. She had to take the help of the local authority to ensure her safety. Especially, local suspicion fumes if a female researcher stays alone. Along with accommodation, she needs to fix a workstation (the place where FGDs and KII are arranged) which is safe and work-friendly. In Bhola, the researcher took an NGO rest house during the fieldwork, and in Rangpur, a local relative's house as the workstation.

Humiliation and Being Underrated as a Female Researcher

'Gender, age and marital status are all aspects of a researcher's identity that can limit access to informants or situations' (Flowedew and Martin 2005, p125). The present chapter reveals that a female researcher can be taken lightly by the residents. They, especially, male members of the studied society did not take the research and the female researcher seriously and treated it with the attitude of, 'women are working for women's problems', 'this is not a serious problem', and 'it's on women's health'. Humiliation is found to be present in their conversations. This perception created problems when getting the interview schedule with local key informants in some cases and sometimes also, their attentive replies. It has been found that they become reluctant in explaining their opinions and sometimes did not want to complete their answers. However, the residents expect that female investigators should interview women. The Head of the family or gatekeepers does not want to allow male interviewers to talk with the female members. In some cases, local women even do not come in front of the male investigators (Table 14.1 RN 2 and RN 3).

Trust Building and Culture: Gender, Education, Occupation and Position of the Researcher

'Did you come here alone, staying alone?' is the most common question asked to the researcher while conducting fieldwork in remote locations of Bangladesh. It is a very sensitive issue in rural areas of Bangladesh. It is considered a sign of a 'good woman', who moves with a chaperon, especially with her family or guardians. The present chapter reveals that the researcher could build trust easily when she was with her family in the study area and got access to the local women's life without any challenge. The researcher was with her in-laws during her long stay in Barguna and with her husband in Rangpur (Table 14.1 RN1 and RN4). Respondents showed appreciation for her decisions; taking chaperons with her and fulfilling her familial duties. She was welcomed into the house;

in the living rooms and kitchen. Respondents eagerly participated in interviews and became involved in discussions. However, this arrangement was not possible for all research and all occasions. In those cases, curiosity and hesitation among the residents were found at the first site (Table 14.1 RN 3).

However, maintaining the local dress code, a smiling face and the use of appropriate greetings help to reduce the challenges in gaining trust (Flowerdew and Martin 2005, p125). Besides, having higher education, good jobs and positions; being a faculty member of the university, postgraduate student and researcher position also helped the researcher in trust building with the residents and conducting fieldwork (Table 14.1).

Opening Up and Exposure To-Mental and Physical Risk

Trust building with residents also demands sharing personal information and opening up about the researcher's life. Longer fieldwork, staying in the study area and attending several functions exposes the researcher's information to a wider audience (Table 14.1 RN 1). This personal disclosure may increase the risk of the researcher's mental stress, being judged by the residents and excessive self-analysis (Raheim et al. 2016). Besides, physical threats are also created when the researcher's personal information falls into the wrong hands. During a field visit, a man collected the phone number of the researcher and started to call her without a valid reason (Table 14.1 RN 3). She had to take action against him. Besides this, the researcher felt intimidated and threatened in several other cases as the residents of the study areas called or visited her after completing the research.

However, these mental pressures have a very strong impact on the researcher and her research plan. The researcher may have to decide to shorten her stay or change the plan to save her from these risks.

14.5 How to Cope with the Risk and Challenges in GBV Research Fieldwork

The present chapter demonstrates that researchers experience several types of risk and challenges during the fieldwork on a sensitive topic like GBV. Based on these experiences, recommendations have been made to help future researchers in planning their fieldwork with more awareness and preparation against risk and challenges in GBV research. The recommendations are mentioned as follows:

Taking Time to Find the Perfect Key Informants

Being a social taboo, it may become difficult to find participants who eagerly talk about the GBV conditions in his/her area. GBV is mostly kept concealed within the family and local society and is rarely shared with an unknown person. The researcher has to keep trying to find the perfect key informant. The researcher, as an outsider, needs the perfect person from the local society to help her. With the key informant's reference along with the gatekeeper's help, trust building between the residents and the research team becomes easier and quicker. Without their help, it would be difficult to reach GBV victims and collect rich data.

Being Prepared with a Second Topic to Avoid Unwanted Circumstances

Researchers working on violence against men/women may face unwanted or threatening circumstances during the fieldwork. It is recommended that the researcher should prepare with a second topic, which allows her/him to meet the curiosity of the residents who are not related to/involved in the study. Previous studies show that while victims/survivors of GBV eagerly want to share their experiences, their oppressors or families do not want them to participate and inform others. Therefore, the researcher should prepare a second topic and a questionnaire to show when confronted during interviews. This might help to protect researchers and the participants from further harassment.

Patience as a Solution for Successful Interviews in a Challenging Environment

Conservative social attitudes, unfriendly behaviour and non-cooperation sometimes create delays in fieldwork on gender-based violence. Getting access to a new society and building trust needs patience. Researchers should spend more time in the study area and get familiar with the local people. He/she should attend invitations, talk with the locals doing daily shopping and visit local gatherings (water collection points, shared ponds, etc.) for a deeper understanding of local cultures. More discussions with residents might be needed to reach the perfect respondents and the researcher has to patiently find the right person for the in-depth interviews.

Planning for a Flexible Time Frame and Additional Budget

Uncertainty is very common in GBV research, especially in fieldwork. Many challenges arise when choosing respondents and interviewing them. In some cases, selected respondents might not participate in the interview or want to leave without completing it. In these cases, a researcher should leave the area without conducting interviews. They might need to find new respondents or set new interview schedules, which will require extra budget and time. A flexible time frame and additional budget should be planned for the GBV research to combat these challenges of uncertainty in the fields.

Trust Building and Female Investigators

The present study reveals that female investigators and researchers are more welcomed by the studied society. They get easier access to the houses and women's private life. GBV victims or survivors, who are mostly women, believe them and are comfortable sharing their experiences. Employing female investigators is essential to study GBV to overcome the fieldwork challenges successfully.

Researcher's Safety: Chaperon, Safe Accommodation and Working Station

The present study recommends that GBV researchers should select chaperons, and fix their accommodation and workstation at the planning stage of the research to ensure safety during the fieldwork. In this case, analysing secondary data on the GBV conditions and a pilot survey before finalizing the study area will be helpful. The chaperon should be well known or at least with good references so that he is reliable and safe. However, if the investigators plan to visit in pairs, then male chaperons could be chosen from the study area. Reference is one of the mandatory criteria when choosing chaperons.

Accommodation and workstation should be chosen carefully considering local culture and context. The researcher should be fully aware of the social expectations. They should follow and respect local culture to get easy access to the society.

Misunderstandings are common when interviewing in different cultures and contexts, so paying attention when choosing dress, language, greetings and words during the interviews is very important. Violence against women is a very sensitive topic, so the researcher should be attentive and compassionate while talking to the victims. They have to be welcoming, friendly and patient when gaining the trust of the respondents and collecting good quality data.

Training to Protect the Unwanted Circumstances

Training on 'emergencies and safety' is essential for the research/investigation team before commencing the fieldwork. They should have proper knowledge about the study area: location of the basic facilities, for example, hospitals, clinics, dispensaries, police stations, bus stations, food corners, etc.; local maps will be helpful in this regard. All members should have local contact numbers and emergency numbers, and the team should know each other's mobile numbers.

Before entering a house, office or any infrastructure, the investigator should be well informed about the exits of the house and confirm the presence of the participants. The chaperon or team members should travel in pairs. Overcrowded places such as bazaars, streets and any demonstration should be avoided. Above all, the researcher/investigator has to know when they should stop interviewing or leave the study area to keep them safe from any unwanted circumstances.

14.6 Conclusion

Research on gender-based violence or violence against women often focuses on context-based analysis along with an understanding of the inter-relationship of local culture, tradition and gender perceptions. This type of research needs intensive fieldwork, with the application of qualitative research methods. However, the sensitive nature of the topic, while being a social taboo, and one's gendered identity increase the risk and challenges for the researcher working on gender-based violence. The present chapter highlights the practical experiences of four researchers when describing the risk and challenges (methodological and individual levels) researchers faced while conducting a field study in remote locations of Bangladesh. It describes how researchers overcame them with several strategies and patience. It is expected that this paper will be helpful for future researchers in understanding the risk that arises during the fieldwork and the need to take measures to ensure the researcher's safety in research, especially on a sensitive topic like gender-based violence or violence against women.

References

BBS (2016). Report on violence against women (VAW) survey 2015. Bangladesh: Bangladesh Bureau of Statistics.

Boynton, P. M. (2005). *The research companion: A practical guide for the social and health sciences.* UK: Psychology Press.

Campbell, R., Adams, A. E., Wasco, S. M., Ahrens, C. E., & Sefl, T. (2009). Training interviewers for research on sexual violence: A qualitative study of rape survivors' recommendations for interview practice. *Violence against women, 15*(5), 595-617.

Cui, K. (2015). The insider–outsider role of a Chinese researcher doing fieldwork in China: The implications of cultural context. *Qualitative Social Work, 14*(3), 356-369.

Dickson-Swift, V., James, E. L., Kippen, S., & Liamputtong, P. (2008). Risk to researchers in qualitative research on sensitive topics: Issues and strategies. *Qualitative Health Research, 18*(1), 133-144.

Dominelli, L. (2013). Gendering climate change: Implications for debates, policies and practices. In M. Alston and K. Whittenbury (eds.).*Research, action and policy: Addressing the gendered impacts of climate change* (pp. 77-93). Dordrecht: Springer.

Dwyer, S. C., & Buckle, J. L. (2009). The space between: On being an insider-outsider in qualitative research. *International journal of qualitative methods, 8*(1), 54-63.

European Commission (2020). What is gender-based violence? www. ec.europa.eu. accessed on 27/10/2020.

Flowerdew, R., & Martin, D. (Eds.). (2005). *Methods in human geography: a guide for students doing a research project.* UK: Pearson Education.

Fraga, S. (2016). Methodological and ethical challenges in violence research. *Porto Biomedical Journal, 1*(2), 77-80.

Hossain, M. and McAlpine, A. (2017). *Gender Based Violence Research Methodologies in Humanitarian Settings: An Evidence Review and Recommendations.* Cardiff: Elhra.

Jansen, H. A., Watts, C., Ellsberg, M., Heise, L., & Garcia-Moreno, C. (2004). Interviewer training in the WHO multi-country study on women's health and domestic violence. *Violence against women, 10*(7), 831-849.

Jewkes, R., Watts, C., Abrahams, N., Penn-Kekana, L., & Garcia-Moreno, C. (2000). Ethical and methodological issues in conducting research on gender-based violence in Southern Africa. *Reproductive health matters, 8*(15), 93-103.

Maykut, P., & Morehouse, R. (1994). *Beginning qualitative researchers: A philosophical and practical guide.* Washington, DC: Falmer.

Mason, J. (2002). Qualitative researching, Sage Publications Limited, UK.

Råheim, M., Magnussen, L. H., Sekse, R. J. T., Lunde, Å., Jacobsen, T., & Blystad, A. (2016). Researcher–researched relationship in qualitative research: Shifts in positions and researcher vulnerability. *International journal of qualitative studies on health and well-being, 11*(1), 30996.

Reinharz, S., & Chase, S. W. (2002). Interviewing women. In J. F. Gubrium & J. A. Holstein (Eds.), *Handbook of interview research: Context and method* (pp. 221-238). Thousand Oaks, CA: Sage.

Rezwana, N. (2018). *Disasters, gender and access to healthcare: women in Coastal Bangladesh.* UK: Routledge.

Robson, C., & McCartan, K. (2016). Real-world *research.* USA: John Wiley & Sons.

The World Bank (2019) 'Gender-based violence (Violence against women and girl)', www.worldbank.org., accessed on 29/10/2020.

WHO (2001). *Putting Women's Safety First: Ethical and Safety Recommendations for Research on Domestic Violence Against Women.* WHO/EIP/GPE/99.2. WHO, Geneva.

CHAPTER 15

Rethinking Ethnographic Research as 'Gendered and En-casted Labour': Reflections from a Non-metropolitan City of West Bengal, India

Ekata Bakshi

15.1 Introduction: The Promise of Feminist Ethnography and Oral History

The methodological imperatives of feminist ethnography, especially feminist oral history, come from feminist standpoint theory. Sangster (1994) argues, "(a)s feminists, we hoped to use oral history to empower women by creating revised history '*for* women', emerging from actual lived experiences of women" (p. 11). The assumption here is that the particular material and social position of women produce "a unique epistemological vision which might be slowly unveiled by the narrator and the historian" (ibid.). However, as Sangster (1994) soon goes on to argue, this aim of empowerment through research is elusive given the hierarchical structures within which academic/social research is embedded. The problem here is twofold: firstly, the access gained to other women's testimonies is done in the professional capacity of the researcher and for professional ends; and secondly, the interpretative frames of the researcher and the people studied regarding the same action might be at variance. Since the feminist researcher has an overt political understanding; it might be the case that a feminist perspective may contradict the self-image of the respondents. They might reject the feminist perspective. Similar concerns are raised

E. Bakshi (✉)
Centre for Women's Studies, Jawaharlal Nehru University, New Delhi, India

© The Author(s), under exclusive license to Springer Nature Switzerland AG 2023
N. Uddin, A. Paul (eds.), *The Palgrave Handbook of Social Fieldwork*,
https://doi.org/10.1007/978-3-031-13615-3_15

by Boreland (1998) too. Yet, in the text produced it is the case that the researcher's perceptions are likely to gain precedence. This is because, in the ultimate analysis, she is the owner of the work and has the legitimacy to produce such work as a professional. To use her words, "(I)t is the privilege that allows us to interpret, and it is our responsibility as historians to convey their insights using our own" (Sangster 1994, p. 12).[1]

The central question for feminist oral history/ethnography then becomes how to, in such cases, carry out such interpretative tasks ethically, given our own frames of understanding may be at variance with that of our respondents. The question is further complicated by the fact that such interpretative understanding is mired in our own social locations. In other words, our feminisms too are a product of our social locations. Understandably, this question assumes added significance when the researcher and the researched not only belong to different groups but also groups that are placed at different levels of hierarchy in the social order. The question then posed differently becomes—given the power relations between the researcher and the researched are so unequal— who has the right to write whose history? But then, if we cannot write across boundaries, are we to limit ourselves to autobiographies? (Alcoff 1991–1992; Sangster 1994) As has been argued by Sangster (1994), Abu-Lughod (1990), it is precisely at this juncture, in the asking of these questions, that the feminist critique of anthropology, and particularly of ethnography as a method (as well as an end product), comes to coincide with the post-structuralist critique of anthropology.[2] In other words, ethnography is a constructed account by the researcher of the constructed narrative of the respondent. To post-structuralist anthropologists, then, the answer to destabilizing the authority of the author was to collaborate with the respondents to write poly-vocal texts.[3] Both Sangster (1994) and Abu-Lughod (1990) argue this is nothing but obfuscation of the institutionalized power relations between the researcher and the researched, rather than any direct attempt to dismantle them. Abu-Lughod (1990) further argues that the absence of textual innovation among feminist researchers is in part due to concerns about maintaining professional rigour in male-dominated academia. Feminists, Abu-Lughod (1990) and Sangster (1994) opine, have tried to emphasize the reality of oppressive structures by

---

[1] For a detailed discussion of the institutionalized inequality even in feminist research see Ann Oakley (1981), Susan Geiger (1990), Judith Stacey (1988).

[2] "Post-structuralist anthropology argues 'all ethnographies are situated and none are simply objective representations of reality' and are mired in asymmetrical power relations" (Abu-Lughod 1990, p. 11). For details, *Writing Culture—The Poetics and Politics of Ethnography* (1986) edited by James Clifford and George. E Marcus.

[3] Boreland's (1998) monograph can be seen as a primary example of similar experiments by feminists.

adhering to conventional forms, lest such assertion is lost in the narratives about multiple realities and the lack of an authoritative subject.[4]

The 'critical' in critical feminist ethnography, which has challenged conventional ethnographic notions, has then come from elsewhere—in the inability to write about a singular experience of being a woman. It has questioned what it means to write about women's experiences when there is no singular reality of experiencing the world as a woman. At the heart of these contestations is the category of experience. The link between knowledge and experience is the foundational category for second-wave feminism, linking the personal and the political. The shared experiences of women become the basis for the political claims of second-wave feminism. Yet, soon this monolithic category of women's experience came to be questioned, and it had to be acknowledged that women were differently placed across lines of class, caste, race, sexuality and so on so much so that these divisions came to threaten the category of woman itself (Abu-Lughod 1990).

15.2 The Indian Context[5]

Indian feminist works emerging from the 1970s and, especially, 1980s onwards were quick to point out the inherent colonialism of feminist perspectives and sort to chart out a distinct path for post-colonial South Asian feminism that spoke to and from the experiences of the women in the sub-continent.[6] Smita (2017) argues that the dominant feminist movement failed to acknowledge that Dalit women form a different category than women from other castes and communities. The women's movement in India though attempted a sophisticated analysis of the inter-relations between class and gender, never "addressed the problem of the Dalit women as fundamental caste-based Indian reality" (ibid., p. 3). It was only in the 1990s, that the Dalit feminist critiques posed serious challenges to established feminist canons, its curricular protocols and its

---

[4] Abu-Lughod (1990) also points out that textual innovation has often led to consolidation of elitism and privilege by emphasizing the dependence on literary and philosophical abstractions rather than democratizing the process. Also see Nancy Hartsock (1987) for a detailed discussion on how destabilization of authorial authority and any claims to a stable reality have coincided with the rise of assertions of marginalized groups to claim a voice in academia.

[5] Following Sen-Chaudhuri (2016), I use the word Indian not to denote any unique constellation, let alone of women. I simply use the word to denote the debates that have animated the discussions on feminism and the category 'Women' in the politico-geographical context marked as India.

[6] One of the most earliest and powerful attempts in this direction was the now seminal essay, 'Under the Western Eyes' By Chadra T. Mohanty (1988). For a brief overview of the trajectory of South Asian feminism see 'Recasting Women: Essays in Colonial History' edited by Kumkum Sangari and Sudesh Vaid (1989), Discrepant Dislocations by Mary John (1996) and 'South Asian Feminisms' edited by Ania Loomba and Ritty E. Lukose (2012).

alliances with brahminical power and privilege (Sharmila Rege 2006).[7] The Dalit feminist critique also, however, pointed out the patriarchal biases of Dalit politics spurring Gopal Guru (1995) to argue that Dalit women need to talk differently.

The Dalit feminist standpoint subsequently came to explicate how the intersecting regimes of class, caste and gender have come to marginalize Dalit women and paved the way for important and critical disruptions to both the Dalit movement and feminist movement (Rege 2006; Patil 2017). The Dalit feminist critique has given rise to what Rege (2006) calls the oppositional Dalit feminist pedagogies which are built on a "complex, relational understanding of social location, experience and history … In such curricular models, narratives of (D)alit women's historical experience become crucial to thinking and theorising not because they present an unmediated version of 'truth' but because they destabilise received truth and locate debate in complexities and contradictions of historical life" (Rege 2006, p. 95). To Patil (2017) thus, to see Dalit feminist assertions merely as identity-based assertions is misleading. The Dalit feminist critiques should rather be understood as a critique that "question(s) the limited materialist determinants of brahminic knowledge producers/systems that cut across the spectrum of political ideologies" (p. 38). She (2013) adds, "Dalit feminist thought has the epistemic vantage location to challenge the authenticity of knowledge that is generated for the emancipation of the oppressed through pointing out the caste-cum-class privilege of the dominant intelligentsia and Brahmanic institutional histories" (p. 43). She, however, warns against the "Indian versions of de-classing which appropriates the epistemological priorities of (D)alits and (D)alit women" (ibid.). Following Patil (2017) I try to understand how the *savarna*[8] feminists engage with the question of caste and gender? Should she or should she not engage in an academic understanding of the life worlds of Dalit women while embarking on such a project? If she does how does she do so without appropriating her epistemic privilege?

---

[7] Some of the notable examples of theorizing caste by Savarna feminists are—'Conceptualising Brahmanical Patriarchy in Early India- Gender, Caste, Class and State' (2013) and 'Gendering Caste: Through a Feminist Lens' (2002) by Uma Chakravarti, *The Caste Question: Dalits and Politics in Modern India* by Anupama Rao (2009), 'The Gender of Caste: Representing Dalits in Print' by Charu Gupta (2018).

[8] *Savarna* is the epithet collectively used to denote castes that fall within the Varna order, as opposed to the Dalits who do not. The use of the term *Savarna* feminism/feminist theory here however, mainly refers to the academic works produced by women belonging to the first the groups in the *varna* order.

15.3 The Savarna Feminist Researching the Dalit Women

The decades of feminist disavowal of caste as an analytical category while theorizing about gender relations and exclusive theorizing from a *savarna* point of view has made the *savarna* feminists'. recent interest in caste a suspect. The question quite simply put, is, whether the *savarna* feminist engagement with caste, is an attempt to salvage the progressive credentials of feminism, that has increasingly become tarnished by the strengthening anti-caste movement in the country in the post-Mandal moment? Is it an attempt on her part to score progressive brownie points within academia for the advancement of her own career? A more important question is, however, why to study caste should the *savarna* woman essentially have to study her other than the Dalit woman and claim to assume her stand-point? The moral charge of the argument here is beyond refute. It is impossible to deny that in a society where access to education has been strictly regulated along caste lines, even seventy years after the formal proclamation of equality via the adoption of the constitution, for *savarna* women to write on behalf of Dalit women, turning them into data is to further rob of them of the ownership over their own experiences. In the absence of institutional access to education, often the only means (no less potent) left to Dalit women is to directly build on their experience to further their political claims. The question here then alludes to larger questions about the exploitative character of academic enterprise and its connections with politics which is beyond the scope of this paper.[9] I shall then return to this question, in the end, posing it differently.

If one were to, however, even grudgingly accept that academics could have some critical role beyond agendas of pure self-aggrandizement and that even *savarna* feminists within the ranks of academia, potentially have a possibility of engaging critically engaging with the category of caste; then probably a guilt-laden refusal to engage with the experiences of Dalit women and merely focusing on oneself might not be the answer. If they study only their own groups and remain caste-blind in studying their own population, it will remain equally problematic and status-quo. Conversely, it is also true that studying Dalit women in itself is nowhere progressive, and it could quite end up being the obverse.[10] If at all *savarna* feminist academics choose to engage with the experiences of Dalit/ Bahujan women how does one do that ethically and critically? Sen Chaudhuri (2016) points out that the obverse of silencing cannot be "'retrieving' the marginalized voices presuming her experiences ... (to be) given." Intrinsic to the negotiation that studying the complex 'lives of others' require, is 'self-reflection'. This self-reflection to quote Abu-Lughod (1990)

---

[9] At this point, I do not mean to abandon this question altogether but only the moral framing of the question.

[10] For a related discussion regarding white women and women of colour see 'The Problem of Speaking for Others' by Linda Alcoff (1991–1992).

involves, "acknowledg(ing) how our own culture, class position and political world view shapes the oral histories we collect, for an interview is a historical document created by the agency of both the interviewer and the interviewee." If acknowledging is not understood to be merely stating, the question is what this active acknowledgement means?

Sen-Chaudhuri (2016) argues that only by understanding how upper-caste women and Dalit women are simultaneously produced by the logic of caste, that is, an analysis that is attentive to both difference and relationality, can feminism break away from essentializing Dalit women. Argued in this manner then Savrana woman/researcher simply by deciding to study her 'Other' the Dalit woman has no access to a readymade anti-caste standpoint that they can inhabit and thereby challenge the existing dominant feminist cannons. Making sense and writing about the experiences of others as well as oneself is intrinsically related to how these categories and the experiences of each category are defined and analysed. It requires us to pay as much attention to the experiences of the researched as that of the researchers. How does one then analyse oral histories relationally? The partial answer I argue is to trace the shared conditions that shape these experiences and the condition narrativising such experiences—conditions both material and discursive. I shall elaborate on these by drawing upon four instances from my fieldwork. But before proceeding further, let me briefly introduce my field.

15.4　Partition-Induced Refugee-Hood, Gender and Caste in Asansol, West Bengal: A Brief Overview

Despite not having a clearly formulated refugee-policy, India has been the recipient of one of the largest number of forcibly displaced population on account of the Partition of the colonial empire on the basis of religion. After the Partition, along the Eastern border the 'Refugee' emerged as the 'new proletariat' and the principle subject of Left politics in West Bengal, and it was believed that the complete state apathy and the abject conditions of living did away with the customary boundaries of caste and gender paving the way for a progressive refugee politics. Refugee narratives as available through cultural texts like films, literary fiction, and memoirs and autobiographies (especially post 1990s) have led to further sedimentation of such sentiments by constantly emphasising their heroic struggles and their victim status. These narratives, however, were largely male, upper caste, upper class and metropolitan (Calcutta)-centric and glossed over the possible differential experiences. Feminist rewriting of the Partition in Bengal tried to subvert the male narratives about the trauma of the Partition by claiming it as a watershed moment for women's emancipation that provided for a newfound legitimacy to women's presence in paid labour. The assumed homogeneity of the category 'women', however, once again, explained away the differences produced by regional and caste locations which more often than not, were overlapping.

Migrants belonging to ex-untouchable groups, who were predominantly rural, were rehabilitated to Asansol-Durgapur industrial complex in West Bengal to support its industrial development by providing cheap labour.[11] It must be mentioned here that the first phase of immigration started from East Bengal after the religious riots in Noakhali and Tippera of now Bangladesh and continued till 1949. The refugees of this phase were mainly upper and upper-middle classes consisting of the *bhadraloks*[12] or the landowners, merchants and professional classes. The second phase of migration started around 1950 and consisted mainly of the *chotoloks* or the agricultural labourers and people involved in menial services, closely mirroring caste-based divisions. The *bhadralok* refugees found it humiliating to take shelter in the government camps. They had cultural capital in the form of education and social capital in the form of family networks in Calcutta. They could establish themselves somehow on the fringes of the local economy and despite multiple hardships were able to overcome the travails of displacement in the next four-five decades. The *chotolok* refugees left last because of their dependence on the rural economy and were the worst victims of communal conflicts. They did not on crossing the border possess much economic, social or cultural capital that could help them rehabilitate themselves. They relied largely on the government for help. The government sent them to transit camps setup in various areas of West Bengal and later, after 1956, dispersed them off to various locations to provide developmental labour. While, it has been commonly understood that rehabilitation within West Bengal was favourable to the camp refugees, the same cannot be said about Asansol given the large number of deserters in the early days. Yet, lack of better options forced many to stay back in Asansol. Some other refugees from ex-untouchable groups also came to Asansol later in search of jobs. The flow refugees in Asansol cannot be limited to definite temporal periods or official statistics alone. Refugees with multiple antecedent trajectories have come to Asansol at different points of time, especially in the period immediately before the Bangladesh war, but even after, as recently as 2018. It is difficult to separate the refugees from various time-periods in water tight compartments given the ties of sociality and kinship between various groups. However, for the purpose of this research I have focused mainly on families of refugees who crossed over in the 1970s.

On coming to Asansol, though *bhadralok* refugees could largely find employment in white-collar professions, the refugees from ex-untouchable backgrounds could find employment mostly as blue-collar workers, both in the formal and informal sector. I argue that despite being highly exploited, the male refugees in the formal sector and more infrequently in the informal sector

---

[11] Industrial development in this region from the colonial period had developed in a highly en-casted manner.

[12] Bhadraloks—They were the upper caste distinguished by education and non-manual labour. They drew their source of sustenance from their position as landlords in the British Zamindari system and this income helped them get access to capital, education, professional opportunities and a refined life style (Bose 2006).

gained limited stability and mobility as blue collar labourers. This was, however, undone by general economic down turn of the city due to multiple industrial closures that begun from mid-1980s and too up speed in the 1990s. Existing injunctions against women joining blue collar work, concerns about physical safety in the hostile city-space and the exploitative nature of the work offered to them, had forced the women of these families to refrain from taking up paid work. They had to take up extremely underpaid informal work when threatened with economic exigencies, especially in the case of industrial closures. Their institutionalized exclusion from education and other prevailing socio-economic conditions have ensured that the same pattern is repeated over generations inhibiting the possibility of physical and socio-economic mobility, except for in marriage. My project then aimed at studying how the condition of refugee-hood had affected the lives of these women and I located my research in a refugee colony in Asansol that was set up with government help. It must be pointed out here that women in my research did not identify themselves as a 'Dalit or Bahujan woman', that is reclaiming their marginality in a specific political way for seeking visibility and political valence. The stories that follow are then a product of a mediated interaction and connived intimacy between the women of refugee families from ex-untouchable groups and me a young middle-class researcher who appeared at their doorstep on a sultry August evening with certain political frames and do not claim to narrate any essential truth about the lives of these women.

This attempt, though now somewhat systematic, has evolved through many stumbling blocks which have helped me think through some of my ways of doing oral history. A deeply perplexing moment in the research was reading silences. Often when I walked up to lower caste women in the refugee colony and asked them to tell me about their life stories, there were two typical responses I received. "I have nothing to say" and "I am not a refugee. My parents came from Bangladesh but I have no memory of Bangladesh." Everybody though warmed up to conversations about *kochursaag* and *maach* and added little snippets about how life in erstwhile East Bengal used to be. Most also told me that they had heard from their parents, refugees who had come there hard and struggled a lot. "*Baba maar mukhe shunechi prochur kashto koreche jara refugee hoyeeshechilo*", was the popular refrain. It was difficult for me to read these responses but over time, I realized the refusal to narrate could be read as both a resistance to the perceivably upper-caste researcher suddenly invading the homes of people lower in the social and economic hierarchy. As I strained my ears on the streets and eavesdropped on practically any conversation, I realized that while they did not tell me stories, they were telling that to each other all the time. I realized that many of the second- and third-generation refugees, despite being aware of the fact that the event of displacement has affected and still affects their socio-economic and political conditions, do not want to use the term refugee for themselves because of the stigmatized connotations of the term. This is especially relevant in recent times when the categories of insider and outsider have become so pronounced in national politics. Yet some others simply did not want to tell their stories because they did not want to remember the past. "*Oshob katha bole ar ki hobe, kashta korechi korte hoy*" (What is the point in recounting such stories, I struggled because one had to).

15.5   Woman to Woman?: The Savarna Researcher and the Dalit-Bahujan Respondents

Given this context, let me analyse three instances to put forward my methodological observations that have been steered by the experiences of this fieldwork. The first instance is from my interview with D.R., who was a first-generation migrant herself and had crossed the border sometime around the Bangladesh war. At the time of the interview, she was aged somewhere between 45 and 50. She had lost her mother early in her life and on crossing the border, after a brief stay with her brother's family, she was married off. Her husband worked as a cook for the police mess. But he was given to heavy drinking, and on most days, he remained absent from work. He did not contribute much to the family's finances and was also violent towards her. D.R mentioned that on one of the days after she had become a mother and she had nothing to feed her infant son, she decided she had to go out to work. She had no capital to start anything, so finally, she decided to gather a few colocasia leaves and went to the nearby market to start working as a vegetable vendor. Thus began her working life which continued till the time of the interview.

After briefly narrating her life story to me, when she tried summing up her life to me, she said:

My life has been full of *kashta* … everybody says in this colony, nobody else has done as much *kashta* as me … With a lot of *kashta* I have today been able to bring a little stability to my *sangshar*.

Yes, I will never be able to get over this *kashta* … as long as I live this will eat into me, yet, if my son is not being able to manage, can I just watch him suffer being a mother … being a mother can I just sit at home and eat?

I am there, therefore I am selling vegetables, now if I am not there, will she (meaning her daughter-in-law) go to sell vegetables? Will my son let her go? No … Have I not taught my son that? … He will not ask the women of his house to go and work … he will never do such a thing as her husband.

The question before me was how to read her statements, given that the feminist re-writing of the Partition in Bengal argues that it was a watershed moment in the gendered history of Bengal. The feminist narrative has argued that the Partition by legitimizing women's public presence, especially in the context of paid work and political participation, paved the way for gendered emancipation. Yet, the main register through which D.R speaks of her life is that of *kashta*. *Kashta*, here I argue can be roughly translated to have three related meanings. In the first utterance, *kashta* denotes a generalized pain or trauma that marks her entire life. In the second instance, *kashta* is enduring difficulties. Here *kashta* is joined with the verb *kora* or doing to denote an active engagement with the difficulties of life. In the third instance, *kashta* is still used to denote an active engagement, but an engagement that also can be read as resistance, even though in a limited sense. She argues that, by doing a lot of *kashta*, she has been able to find some stability for her *sangshar*,[13] the unsaid implication is against all odds.

Given the way D.R situates her life and her experiences of work in it, is it enough to say they experienced work differently and hence it needs to be understood as a different self-contained world? Conversely, do we read her responses in relation to the dominant feminist canon of work and empowerment in a way that denotes her lack or an inability to embody this radical feminist subjectivity? By denoting her experiences through the lens of *kashta*, is she mirroring the *bhadralok* ideals of domesticity,[14] that is the logic that women ideally should remain confined to the domestic space, and the reversion of the same is essentially traumatic? Is this then her attempt to gain social respectability, by projecting herself in the language of idealized femininity, a kind of respectability that otherwise remains unattainable to her because of her association with paid physical labour, an attempt at Sanskritization? I submit that none of these frames is adequate to make sense of her responses. It is important to note here that her responses can be understood in the manner stated above, only when we assume the following:

1. That paid work has an inherently feminist potential to empower women.
2. That work is a source of identity, beyond being a means to fulfil material needs of survival.
3. The family and the domestic is the principal site of exploitation for women and the possibility of participation in the public has the potential to subvert such exploitation.

A look at the history of gendered and en-casted labour in Bengal, especially in the colonial period, however, reveals a different story Chatterjee (1993) argues that in the nineteenth century, Bengal witnessed a gradual cheapening of women's labour. There was also labour surplus and cheapening of labour in the agrarian sector which forced marginal and small peasants to depend more on the labour of women and children to be able to provide for the family. However, at the same time, since female labour became cheap, it did not amount to making a significant contribution to running the household. The middle peasant and traders were now able to withdraw their women from the field of paid labour due to cheapening of agricultural labour in general. The

---

[13] Yet, another perplexing term here is *sangshar*. *Sangshar*, merely does not denote family (meaning family members), but the world of material and social relations that sustain the family unit.

[14] For details see 'The Nationalist Resolution of the Women's Question' and Hindu Wife , Hindu Nation.

involvement in paid labour then separated the lower caste/ class women from their upper-caste counterparts. There was a stress on the women's nurturing capacity and her role as the mother and the wife within the home and women located outside the logic of domesticity came to be known as deviant. She also confirms that only widows and lower caste women took up paid employment outside the home besides a small number of women who did so to supplement household incomes. These women who joined as domestic help or entered the lowest rungs of factory workers were understood to be prostitutes. It was the loss of traditional occupations which forced women to take up prostitution or work as domestic help (Chatterjee 1993). The claim that the working women population of Bengal is constituted mainly of lower caste women has also been supported by Tanika Sarkar (1989) and Nirmala Banerjee (1989). Sarkar (1989) further adds that such women were found in very few occupations including domestic service, agricultural labour and sometimes as workers in very few organized industries. Thus, the idea of domesticity was particular to upper-caste women and a product of a specific set of historical conditions. The lower caste women on the other hand continued to work in non-domestic spaces. These spaces did not offer them any necessary empowerment but they were rather exploited economically and physically in such settings. The narrative of being withdrawn from non-domestic spaces and seeking a return to the same albeit in transformed ways is then very specific to the construction of the *Bhadra mahila*.[15]

Thus, when the middle-class Savarna researcher walked in with her own set of assumptions about work and the construction of identity, equating all kinds of paid work with a disregard for the historically determined socio-economic conditions for different kinds of work, women engaged in that D.R's experience of work began to sound 'different'— something she struggled to come to terms with. It was not that I was not aware of the differential conditions of work that women faced. My earlier work had precisely dealt with the same, but even with this acknowledgement, the a-priori assumption that paid work despite all the difficulties it presented had an agentive role was difficult to shake off. Implicitly then I had assumed the historically particular experience of the *Bhadra mahila*, of having been confined to the domestic space and struggling to carve out a space beyond it, to be universal because of my own caste position. For D.R marriage was a promise of a life where her needs could be taken care of, without her having to face the degrading conditions of work that she would otherwise have to sustain herself. Her hopes surrounding marriage were, however, not met and she had to work as a vegetable vendor to provide for herself and her family. Her work did not provide her anything beyond the means for survival. Moreover, going out to work also meant she had to shoulder both the difficult conditions and work hours outside and at home. It also

---

[15] For details see 'The Nationalist Resolution of the Women's Question' by Partha Chatterjee (1989).

meant having to face the stigma of being involved in informal work.[16] The domestic sphere in her expectations was then more of a space of protection and security rather than the space of extreme exploitation; a hope that unfortunately was not met.

Now let me turn to the second instance. The response I discuss here is from S.D. S.D was a second-generation migrant. While she was the only daughter, she had two brothers. She belonged to an OBC family. Her father had come to Asansol, from a refugee camp, to be settled in a refugee colony. He had found some stability as an industrial worker in the Senraleigh Cycle factory, but soon that stability was threatened by industrial closure. S.D was pulled out of education and married soon after. But her husband, who was a truck driver, passed away soon. Her father and brother tried helping her financially and even bought her a plot of land near their house and helped her build her house. After her husband's death, she had no other option than to take up the job of a domestic worker.

> I would want that since my daughter is getting the education she would work in a sector related to education ... maybe something related to the computer or work in a call centre ... It would be so satisfying to watch her carry a bag, wearing a *churidar* or a *saree*, like educated respectable people she too would look respectable ... this cannot happen if you are a cook at somebody's house ... it does not look good.

She stressed that she could never accept her status as a domestic worker yet had to do the job out of sheer necessity.

> There is a reason why I say so. We are not accustomed to doing such work, in our kind of environment, the environment of our house, and that of our neighbourhood nobody works in such professions. In our kind of environment, everyone is engaged in some kind of a non-domestic profession such as some kind of regular service or business. The men sometimes work in other people's shops but in our kind of environment, women do not work outside ... Now times have changed if the boys and girls get educated and work that is a different matter altogether ... but none of us has the 'mentality' of working at other people's houses.

While S.D recounted her story, the middle-class *savarna* researcher found herself feeling discomforted and feebly interjecting at regular intervals that all kinds of work were respectable including her work, that is that of being a domestic worker. While, there is nothing wrong with this apparently feminist observation, what it translated into at that moment, even though unintentionally, was that I, the middle-class *savarna* researcher, was able to respect her and her work more than her. Yet, while listening to the whole recording there was

---

[16] See Tuhina Ganguli (2013) for a detailed discussion on the difference between *chakri* (formal work) and *kaaj* (informal work) that took shape in colonial Bengal and its relationship to caste status and stigma.

no suggestion that she was ashamed of herself. S.D took pride in being a single mother who had raised two daughters. She recounted the sacrifices she had made for her daughters with great detail and her satisfaction in the fact that they had yielded the desired results. The term she used for her work was "*mene nite parina*" which translates as 'I cannot accept'. Now it was I and my limited feminist frames of feminist subjectivity and self-respect that read this non-acceptance as that of oneself rather than the conditions which forced S.D to take up work she did not want to, that is, work in other people's houses. That is, through this statement she rejects the conditions that did not allow her to take up the kind of work she wanted herself or her to take up—the kind of work that was related to education and the kind of work that allowed her to dress in a certain fashion. The aspiration she describes in detail is in the first part of her quote. Ganguli (2013) has pointed out in her work on colonial Bengal, how precisely these two markers, that is, the relationship of work with education and dressing were a deeply en-casted phenomenon. Thus, what we find in S.D's responses is rather a rejection of resentment towards caste-ordained work, even though she is forced to do it. Her aspirations for her daughters then represent her deeply political desire for a different future.[17]

Now, let me point out the third instance. During the course of my fieldwork, I became particularly close to M.P and his family. On a particular morning when I was travelling with M.P's college-going daughter M.P.2 on a shared *toto* (e-rickshaw) after having spent the night at their place, she suddenly pointed out to me a girl on the road who was wearing a sleeveless dress. "What do you think about wearing a sleeveless dress?" she asked. She was quick to add, "Doesn't it seem vulgar to you, wearing a sleeveless dress?" I, caught between the imperative to uphold my feminist sensibilities and not upsetting and alienating her, for quite selfish reasons, had only feebly managed to say, "I do not wear sleeveless clothes usually, but I do think it's a matter of choice for people who wear it … after all how much can you get to know about the person from her clothes?" What this incident and a few other pieces of information I picked up over the next few days forced me to reflect on was the notion of respectability and its en-casted and gendered implications. On the face of it, M.P.2's admonition of sleeveless dresses can be read as an emulation of respectable standards of dressing to claim respectability. But what the information I picked up forced me to reflect was on the motivations behind the desire to claim respectability in a particular way and what the lack of the same implied.

The area I was visiting was infamous for being a hub of disreputable women who allegedly engaged in sexual labour. A.P and M.P's house quite literally was at the farthest end of where the zone of respectable inhabitants ended and the zone of disreputable began. On multiple occasions, M.P.2 had hinted at how they were different from the rest of the people of their neighbourhood, the implications of which I was yet to understand. As the self-identified feminist

---

[17] For a detailed discussion around similar questions see "The 'dirt' in Dirty Picture: Caste, gender and Silk Smitha" by Jenny Rowena (2012).

and educated researcher, it became evident to me later that I had taken my respondents to be a homogenous block of cultural and caste others whose lifeworlds I had gone to explore and, therefore, I was at best indifferent and at worst mildly offended at these attempts at differentiation. I had been warned by M.P and A.P to not go alone to the areas beyond their house to meet my respondents or share my details, especially with random new acquaintances, especially males. I did heed these warnings but as dos and don'ts of fieldwork without reflecting much on their meanings until much later. However, in the evenings that followed at a tea stall where I sat chatting with male respondents, discussing factory closure or buying savouries at a local shop, I became increasingly aware and discomforted by the male gaze, and I felt myself desperately clutching to my upper-caste, upper-class, English speaking self's privilege to ward off any possibility of sexual advances. It is then that the insistence on difference and maintaining respectability began to make sense to me.

A.P had told me the area was infamous not only for licentious practices but also for the prevalence of sexual crimes, including rapes. On the face of it, it might be ascribed to the depravity of the men of that area but my ethnographic insights into Asansol point out that sexual harassment and abuse are prevalent in almost all parts of the city equally including middle-class and upper-caste neighbourhoods. Therefore, an increased number of sexual abuses in an area could arguably be only an indicator of the increased vulnerability of the women of the area rather than the increased depravity of the men. Further, as pointed out by Sarkar (1991), the logic of respectability that governed the political landscape of Bengal during the left rule, and possibly even after, made it impossible to recognize crimes against women whose respectability was already suspected. Having questionable respectability thus could be understood as a vicious circle, where disrepute and increased vulnerability to sexual violence reinforced one another. Given that acute poverty might have in some cases pushed some of the women in these areas into sex work, it is possible that such a reputation made them easier prey to sexual violence. Further, when sexual favours, not infrequently forcefully obtained are part of the experience of work in the informal sector, it is possible that the boundaries between sex work and sexual harassment became blurred in many cases. It is easily understandable that women in this area, largely SC and OBC women, were more vulnerable to sexual violence with impunity.

When viewed in this light it becomes understandable why, as observed by Twamley and Siddharth (2019), the precarious attachment to a respectable reputation made the respondents take to "*defensive* positions … constantly negotiating with the researcher and the others (in) their positioning as a respectable and not a faltu (loose) woman" (italics mine). To reaffirm a fragile sense of respectability is then simultaneously to avoid falling prey to sexual violence and avoid being stigmatized. Reaffirming respectability through dress, speech and distancing oneself from those of questionable repute can be read as attempts to resist such possibilities of sexual harassment/violence from taking shape. The *aggressive, radical* (as opposed to the defensive) position of wearing whatever one wants then comes from having a relatively secure position vis-à-vis respectability, not in the least affirmed by one's caste status, and hence comparatively greater immunity to threats of sexual violence. The very simple fact that I had the economic means to book an e-rickshaw entirely to myself, that is, convert the public transport to a private one temporarily, whenever I felt the slightest threat as opposed to M.P 2, whose daily allowance permitted her to travel in the shared modes, made our experiences of public transport greatly different. It is perhaps not incidental that my privilege was directly related to being able to buy relatively subsidized labour of M.P.2's father, who was an e-rickshaw driver.

What do then these observations mean for the ethical question involving the saving of the woman researching the experiences of life and labour of those from whose continued exploitation (especially in terms of labour) her research work benefits? I have no absolute answer. But the partial answer I submit begins from this very acknowledgement. With this acknowledgement, it becomes evident that the frames of interpretation and the understanding of feminism the researcher carries come from her caste and class privilege.[18] This privilege then limits the possibility of interpretation that the researcher is capable of.[18] To return to Sangster (1994), I argue that the aim of feminist research even in this case remains one of interpretation and analysis. Yet here, propose instead of bringing in feminist frames to analyse the lives of 'Others' what might be more useful and ethical is to understand and analyse feminist frames in light of their observations. It might be useful to question why certain assumptions of feminism and what it means to be a feminist do not speak to the lives and realities of some women. This then helps us understand how caste positions limit the possibilities of feminist imagination and praxis and contributes toward developing feminist subjectivity that simultaneously strives to be anti-caste. Subadra (2020) observes that the order of dominant feminist practices has been interpreting Dalit Bahujan women through its frames and preoccupations. "The line you laid, built from the wisdom gained from your experiences, your interpretations, your directions—we're supposed to follow." My methodological submission is a step in reversing that order. I, following Sangster, argue that it is still important to locate the lived experiences of women through a historical, contextual understanding of social, economic and political conditions. I, however, add that it can only be done comparatively. Understanding what conditions shape the lived experience of the respondents is not enough in itself. It is important to locate what conditions shape the worldview of the feminist researcher. In other words, in the case of interpretation, it is important to trace what conditions allow for a certain subjectivity to develop and be claimed as feminist. To give an example, I argue, following the methodological framework I suggest, while analysing paid work it is important to analyse what conditions enable the experience of paid work to become

---

[18] For a discussion on how privilege arrests interpretative abilities see "White Ignorance" by Charles. W. Mills (2007) and "Epistemologies of Ignorance" by Linda Alcoff (1991).

emancipatory for certain women. The corollary question is what conditions prevent it from being so for some other groups of women.

I argue it's possible to deconstruct the dominant feminist subjectivity by trying to listen as closely as possible. In this framework, listening does not translate to empathy. Following Serpell (2019), I further argue that to be able to understand one's complicity in structures of oppression and deconstruct, it is not required to step into the shoes of the oppressed, that is, assume her standpoint. It is both an impossibility and a vulgar need on the part of the privileged to do so. Instead, I argue that from a position of exteriority[19] it is possible to engage seriously with the 'Other's' narrative to essentially question the dominant frames. This process of deconstruction is, however, essentially incomplete because it is impossible to deconstruct privilege completely while simultaneously using it to conduct the research work. Yet, to the extent, it is employed to demystify the process of research, and its outcomes and is used to broaden the scope of feminist praxis, it could be useful. Such an attempt is inherently open to critique and even criticism, engaging with which can only help the process of deconstruction further. To turn away from such criticism by simply not engaging with the 'Other' can be another form of asserting *savarna* self-righteousness, then accepting the possibility of going wrong and learning from it.

References

Abu-Lughod, Lila. (1990). 'Can There Be a Feminist Ethnography?. In *Women & Performance: a journal of feminist theory*, 5 (1): 7–27.

Alcoff, Linda. (1991–1992). "The Problem of Speaking for Others." *Cultural Critique*, No. 20 (Winter), pp. 5–32

Ann, Oakley. (1981). "Interviewing women: a contradiction in terms." In *Doing Feminist Research* edited By H. Roberts, pages 30–61. London, Boston & Henley: Routledge & Kegan Paul.

Banerjee, Nirmala. (1989). 'Working Women In Colonial Bengal: Modernization and Marginalization'in Recasting Women – Essays in Indian Colonial History, eds., K Sangri and S Vaid, Rutgers University Press, New Jersey, pp. 269-301.

Boreland, Kathrine. (1998). "'That's not what I said': Interpretive conflict in oral narrative research." In *The OralHistory Reader* edited by Robert Perks & Alistair Thomson (pp. 320–332). London, New York: Routledge.

Bose, Pablo. (2006). Dilemmas of Diaspora: Partition, Refugees, and the Politics of "Home". *Refuge: Canada's Journal on Refugees*, 23 (1): 58–68.

Chakravarti, Uma. (2013). *Conceptualising Brahmanical Patriarchy in Early India: Gender, Caste, Class and State*. Critical Quest.

Chakravarti, Uma. (2002). '*Gendering Caste: Through a Feminist Lens*. New Delhi: SAGE.

---

[19] Here I do not use the term exterior(ity) and interio(rity) in the way Sangster (1994) uses them, that is, in terms of the life worlds of the respondents. I simply use it to denote the relative position of the researcher to the respondent.

Chatterjee, Partha. (1989). "The Nationalist Resolution of the Women's Question." In *Recasting Women: Essays in Colonial History*, edited by Kumkum Sangari and Sudesh Vaid, pages 233–253. New Delhi: Kali for Women.

Chatterjee, Ratnabali. (1993). 'Prostitution in Nineteenth Century Bengal: Construction of Class and Gender'. *Social Scientist*, 21 (9/11): 159-172. Available from JSTOR [15 June, 2015].

Sen-Chaudhuri, Ritu. (2016). *The Caste Gender System: A Necessary Analytic of Experience?* TISS Working Paper-09. India: Tata Institute of Social Science.

Clifford, James & Marcus, George, ed. 1986. *Writing Culture: The Poetics and Politics of Ethnography*. California: The University of California Press.

Ganguli, Tuhiana. 2013. "Conceptualizing Work/Employment in India: A Study of Chakri in Colonial Bengal (19th–20th centuries)." *Australian Journal of Historical Studies* 24(1): 172–197

Guru, Gopal. (1995). Dalit Women Talk Differently. *Economic and Political Weekly*, 30(41/42): 2548–2550. http://www.jstor.org/stable/4403327

Gupta, Charu. (2018). *The Gender of Caste: Representing Dalits in Print*. Washington: Washington University Press.

John, Mary. (1996) *Discrepant Dislocations: Feminism, Theory, and Postcolonial Histories*. Berkeley and Los Angeles: The University of California Press.

Hartsock, Nancy. 1987. "Rethinking Modernism: Minority vs. Majority Theories." *Cultural Critique* 7(2): 187–206.

Loomba, Ania and Lukose, Ritty eds. (2012) *South Asian Feminisms*. Durham and London: Duke University Press.

Mills, Charles. (2007). "White Ignorance." In *Race and Epistemologies of Ignorance* edited by Shannon Sullivan, Nancy Tuana, pages: 11–38. New York: The State University Press of New York.

Mohanty, Chanmdra. (1988). "Feminist Encounter: Locating the politics of encounter." In *Social Postmodernism: Beyond Identity Politics* edited by Londa Nicholson & Steven Seidman. Cambridge: The Cambridge University Press.

Rao, Anupama (2009). *The Caste Question: Dalits and Politics in Modern India*. Berkeley, Los Angeles and London: University of California Press.

Passerini, Luisa. (1989). 'Women's Personal Narratives: Myths, Experiences and Emotions'. In Interpreting Women's Lives: Feminist Theory and Personal Narratives, edited by The Personal Narratives Group, pp. 189–198, Bloomington, Indianapolis, Indiana University Press.

Patil, Smita, M. (2017a). *Caste and Gender in India*, Asia Leadership Fellow Programme. Available at https://www.academia.edu/60987706/CASTE_AND_GENDER_DEBATES_IN_INDIA.

——— (2017b). "Revitalising Dalit Feminism: Towards Reflexive, Anti-caste Agency of Mang, Mahar Women in Maharashtra". *Economic and Political Weekly*, 48 (18): 37–44.

Sharmila Rege, (2006). *Writing Caste, Writing Gender*. Zubaan, New Delhi.

Rowena, Jenny (2012). "The 'dirt' in Dirty Picture: Caste, gender and Silk Smitha" available at http://www.dalitweb.org (Access on May 22. 2022).

Sangari, Kumkum and Vaid, Sudesh, eds. (1989) *Recasting Women: Essays in Indian Colonial History*. New Jersey: Rutgers University Press.

Sangster, Joan. 1994. "Telling our stories: feminist debates and the use of oral history." *Women's History Review* 3(1): 5–28.

Sarkar, Tanika. (1989). 'Politics and women in Bengal-the Condition and meaning of participation, in Women in Colonial India, eds J Krishnamurty. Oxford University Press, New York, pp. 231–241.

Sarkar, Tanika. (1991). 'Reflections on Birati Rape Cases: Gender Ideology in Bengal', *Economic and Political Weekly*, 26(5): 215–218. Available from JSTOR [15 June, 2015]

Serpell, Namwali. (2019). "The Banality of Empathy". The New York Review. Available from: https://www.nybooks.com/online/2019/03/02/the-banality-of-empathy/

Stacey, Judith. (1988). 'Can There Be a Feminist Ethnography?' In Women's Studies International Forum, 11 (1): 21–27.

Subadra, Jupka. (2020). Patriarchy, Feminism and the Bahujan Women, *Savri*. Available from: https://www.dalitweb.org/?p=4041

Susan Geiger. 1990. "Women and African Nationalism." *Journal of Women's History*, 2 (1): 227–244.

Twamley, Kathrine and Siddharth, Juhi. (2019). "Negotiating Respectability: Comparing the experiences of poor and middle-class young urban women in India." Modern Asian Studies, 53 (5): 1646–1674. Cambridge University Press.

CHAPTER 16

Capturing the Uncaptured: Photovoice as a Method for Women's Empowerment in Domestic Violence

Zuriatunfadzliah Sahdan

16.1 Introduction

Domestic violence is the most prevalent form of violence against women worldwide, which kills, tortures, and harms them psychologically, physically, sexually, and economically. It is one of the most fundamental violations of human rights, denying women equality, security, dignity, and their right to enjoy freedom (UNICEF 2000). The World Health Organization (WHO 2021) reports that 1 in 3, or approximately 736 million women in the world experience physical and/or sexual violence by their husbands/intimate partners. This number has largely remained the same and has not changed since the last decade WHO (2021). Yet, domestic violence is "a concealed and ignored form of violence against women" (UNICEF 2000). As the real statistics are hard to obtain, not least because of underreporting, the term 'domestic violence' itself hides the reality of its cruelty and effect. Hammer (2002) rejects the term 'domestic violence' as it suggests the violence is something that is easy to overcome and subtle in nature; other terms used today to highlight this issue—'conjugal violence', 'spouse abuse', and 'intimate partner violence'—all erase the reality of domestic violence as gender-based violence (Hammer 2002).

Z. Sahdan (✉)
Department of Geography and Environment, Universiti Pendidikan Sultan Idris, Tanjong Malim, Perak, Malaysia
e-mail: zuriatun@fsk.upsi.edu.my

© The Author(s), under exclusive license to Springer Nature Switzerland AG 2023
N. Uddin, A. Paul (eds.), *The Palgrave Handbook of Social Fieldwork*, https://doi.org/10.1007/978-3-031-13615-3_16

In society, the important terms that are often used to understand the cause and effects of gender-based violence, such as patriarchy and trauma, are not well understood in the community itself. Domestic violence is not understood as a crime; it even becomes normal and is understood as a normal fight between husband and wife. Society plays a role in causing gender-based violence to last and continue to be hidden. In a situation where women are trapped and abused, society focuses on women's submission which is related to gender roles. Women, who often receive advice to fix the situation, are blamed for causing their partners to abuse them.

According to Wang (1999), photovoice is a tool that can be applied to women's health research. Photovoice is a methodology whereby participants are given the opportunity to photograph their everyday lives, create narratives about the photos, and dialogue with each other in order to make meaning of their collective experience. The idea of this photographic technique is grounded in feminist theory. This is well suited for providing a voice to women and allowing women to carry out programmes by and with women in order to honour their intelligence and first-hand experiences. Visual reflections of oneself can help participants with family-based interpersonal violence experiences capture moments that played a role in their social relationships while providing an outlet for their perceptions regarding current and past relationships (Harrison 2002).

This chapter sets forth to explain the pictures and narratives that women capture in photovoice regarding domestic violence that have not been captured in society. It also explains what pictures cannot be captured by women but opens a discussion that can be captured in this study. The synergy between participants and researchers in Participatory Action Research (PAR) allows important information to be included for social awareness. Drawing examples from field experience in Malaysia, the contributions of photovoice as a PAR strategy for empowering abused women are described.

16.2 Overview of the Project

In Malaysia, the main issue is a misrepresentation of domestic violence experience, which triggers undesirable responses from the community and formal interventions regarding the issue. Therefore, my research examined the complexities of space and the everyday lives of women in domestic violence and the ways in which interventions might be made. The decision to use photovoice is to realise that domestic violence is something that society usually finds difficult to share with the public. Aspects of daily life as an intimate partner are often associated with shame in the household as opposed to crime. Photovoice is a method in my study to obtain other different and in-depth qualitative data forms if there are many aspects verbally undisclosed during interviews and storytelling. According to Latham applying Pred's (1989 in Crang 2005, p. 233) experiments, researchers may "use pictures, text and time diaries to convey a sense of practising places." Rose (2003 in Crang 2005) also highlights that the visual and the verbal are interrelated and speak to different ways of knowing rather than just being treated as different kinds of evidence.

The women survivors participating in this research project were recruited through Women's Aid Organisation (WAO), a Malaysian non-governmental organisation located in a large urban area, provides shelter to abused women and their children. There are only six refuge centres for domestic violence victims in this country (Putit 2008). The WAO was the first refuge ever built in Malaysia in 1982. Taking into account its experience in assisting abused women and its openness to research, I chose the WAO refuge as the study site and got a positive response from them. Through the internship programme, I engaged with a group of women who live in the shelter located in the study area. Ten participants were recruited on a voluntary basis. All were married, aged between 21 and 41 at the time of the research, and residents at the WAO refuge. All were of Malaysian nationality and defined their ethnicity as either Malay (four Muslim participants) or Indian (five Hindu and one Christian participant). The participants were from varied socio-economic backgrounds, generally well-educated and had held good jobs. All but two were mothers.

During the fieldwork, the staff in the shelter introduced me to the survivors as an intern. This position created a barrier between me and them. This is because interns in WAO are often stereotyped as 'feminist', middle class, from overseas universities, and prefer to use English as the first language. Most women (regardless of ethnicity) at that moment were rather awkward about starting a conversation with me. Then, the management of the shelter gave me a task assignment to facilitate engagement with the volunteers, and I was asked to teach them computing. The process of building rapport was easier once participants recognised me as a volunteer, as it made it easier for them to approach me and for us to get to know each other.

As a Malay-Muslim woman, I am an outsider to the Indian participants, especially in terms of culture and religion. Besides, being a wife to a non-abusive husband, means I have different experiences from all of the women. However, some of the Islamic values that have been instigated in me since childhood, such as avoiding pride, have shaped my character, and this has helped me to connect with and understand my interviewees. Pride is an egoistic trait that includes characteristics such as being self-conceited, looking down upon, and underestimating others, as well as being censorious or fault-finding. Among the causes contributing to this characteristic are property, position, knowledge, and lineage. Avoiding pride is important because some survivors feel inferior when they are communicating with other survivors, who claim that their case is 'not that bad', and this can be worse when they are communicating with other women who have never experienced domestic violence. In addition, the researcher's empathy is a key requirement to gaining the trust of survivors. According to Herman (1997), in any relationship that exists after separation from a perpetrator, in every encounter, trust becomes the ultimate question. Traumatised women, once free, often share their stories with one another (ibid, 1997). For women, there are limited numbers of roles that reflect their life in captivity: one can only be a perpetrator, ally, passive witness, or rescuer. Some women choose to keep their problems a secret, even from social workers:

> So, we can trust no one, so for any decision, you take … suit yourselves. It's your life, you know how to deal with it, what is better for you, that's it. You don't need to listen to anyone, ignore them (Chumy).

Lieya: Why did you hide about this thing?
Harini: I couldn't recall whether I had told someone about this or not. Yesterday, I let it fall during a conversation with Meena (another survivor), and then she pushed me to inform the social workers.
Lieya: So if you don't let that slip, no one will know until now?
Harini: You know, in this world, I only trust God and myself.
Lieya: But they (social workers) want to help you.
Harini: She nodded.
Lieya: So last two years, you didn't see a doctor after giving birth?
Harini: It's hard for me to go out. When I checked my body with my husband, he knew that I have the disease (breast cancer); he said it's not his business so why does he need to bother?
Lieya: But do you feel any pain?
Harini: Yes. But if I told him I'm hurting, he would press my breast until my tears flowing down my cheek. It was so painful.

Many of the survivors admitted that they started sharing stories once they trusted me because I showed them empathy. Usha, like other women in this study, tended to define most people she encountered as passive witnesses whom she felt often manipulated her. Experiences of 'sudden outbursts' led her to have trust issues with other people, leaving her with feelings of shame and of being manipulated. She has internalised this by thinking that her mind had stopped functioning and that she has become mentally ill due to the psychological pressure. As in Tamas' (2012 in Coddington 2016, p. 4) account, trauma studies are thick with survivor testimony, to the point where survivors 'feel pressured to give voice to unspeakable events again and again':

Usha: We cannot tell (our story). But our mind is not working, I'd experienced that. You know, I become psycho, "even when I don't know a person, I'll still tell them my whole life story". After that, I'm wondering why I'm humiliating myself. "No, they don't understand, it's useless! They ask a bit, but I'll tell you everything! Why do we want to tell them? If we tell them, can they do anything for our life? After what I've done, I do this stupid thing. Then I realise, they may just mock me, after knowing what I've been suffering.
Lieya: For fun?
Usha: Yes, Lieya!

Chumy: Some people have that kind of character. Because you care, you can accept what we tell you, you can understand, even if you're not in our shoes, you can feel us. But for some people, they use that for their own advantage. So they just smile at you, but behind, they'll tell others about us and our issues. There are people like this, we tell them stories, but they cause us problems. In fact, we want to vent out our feelings, but they abuse that.

According to Haraway (1991, p. 193), positioning is 'the key practice grounding knowledge' because 'position' marks the kind of power that enables a certain kind of knowledge. Therefore, I asked the participants about their purpose in sharing their stories with me. According to them, I am a researcher, so they trusted that I have no bad intentions when I wanted to listen to their story. Other people may manipulate their story and use it to look down on them, but I was trusted. I gained this trust by always making myself accessible to them when I was in the shelter. I mingled with them when they were taking care of their children, or while cooking, having lunch, and afternoon tea. Most of them start the day quite late because they could not sleep due to the effects of psychological abuse. They never asked for anything from me, they just needed a listener who can understand them. However, they also realised that I was just there only for a while, but that I would, in fact, continue to think of them.

There are also some ethical considerations in the use of photovoice, such as the risk of privacy invasion. Prior to the photovoice project, I explained to the participants the objectives of the project, which are to gather material through which to discuss and provoke conversation about domestic violence, and I also described the specific methodological techniques that would be used to minimise participants' risks and to maximise benefits to them. Because the photographs in the photovoice exercise would be shared with others, I reminded them to not take pictures of faces or places that others could identify. I then obtained signed permission from the participants to release the photos, so that their photos could be posted or used in the exhibition, digital stories, or the website. Those who agreed to be participants were required to sign an approval form, thus giving their permission to the researcher and WAO to use their photovoice pictures and to record their storytelling about the pictures. Each participant was given materials including a disposable camera labelled with their own name, a copy of the template question, and a photo ownership sharing agreement form. The template question only serves as a guide to the participants in identifying meaningful photos to them. In general, the participants had total control to determine which image to take.

Once I got back the cameras, I sent the films to be processed. Upon completion, I asked the participants to choose the best six photos that represent the experiences, they wanted to share. Participants completed a reflection sheet for each selected photo to explain and justify their choice. The reflection sheet contains such questions as a brief description of the photo, why you want to share this photo, what's the story behind this photo, how does this photo relate to your life, the life of people in your community, or both. I then manually analysed 35 photos, reflection sheets, and storytelling about photovoice. All the data from the field research are in the Malay language.

16.3 Empowering Aspects for Abused Women

Photovoice in this study aims to empower the women survivors through the settings and the results (as it will be discussed in the next section). The settings include who is in charge in terms of framing the content, the extent to which the participants' leadership is respected and how researchers are involved to ensure that the content they want to deliver were achieved. As Zimmerman (1995) adds, when we are working to enhance empowerment outcomes, we should provide settings that facilitate shared leadership, skill development, growth of group identity, and participation. Therefore, it involves active engagement by all the women and researchers in the research process as well as the implementation of a process that results in social action and social change (Bradbury and Reason 2003).

PAR is the core of photovoice concerned with the democratisation of knowledge development as a component of social justice (Liebenberg 2018). Photovoice conveys the realistic views of abused women in accordance with the atrocities of domestic violence and the form of assistance available in Malaysia, which they have accessed and identified its direction. Content generated from photovoice is from research participants' own intention to empower other women through their experience in domestic violence:

Chumy: I don't really mind if I get money or not. But I just want to share my experience.
Mariam: I can share out these strong feelings.
Chumy: Maybe some people will listen once I share my story. If they can't understand, it's ok. Because, if others can gain awareness from my experience, they may be able to change their behaviour or lifestyle.
Mariam: Even if we can't give money (to the abused women), we can also help from that aspect.
Chumy: If I know someone outside who's suffering the same fate, this is the chance for me (to be an activist).

16.4 Capturing the Uncaptured

The result of this study is twofold. First, photovoice captured the uncaptured understanding of domestic violence in the community. The women provide visual narratives for domestic violence explanations that are often misunderstood or become norms by the patriarchal society, such as women provoked their husband's violence and women don't want to leave an abusive relationship for good. Through photos, they are voicing their real experiences that other women and society should become aware of. Second, photovoice opens the discussion of domestic violence from the uncaptured pictures. Most participants gave their ideas about the pictures they would take or planned to take, but some could not fulfil them, sometimes because the necessary items were not available, lack of time, no sense of violent space, or missed certain moments that represented abused experience, confidentiality issues, and not able to capture certain things due to trauma. Nevertheless, the women shared with me the domestic violence narratives for all the photos they could not capture. The following section explains narratives and photographs in photovoice that provided a rich understanding of participants' views on the theme.

16.5 Unprovoked and Deliberately Severe Physical Abuse

Physical injury is the benchmark for laws and public understanding on domestic violence. However, public understanding of physical abuse is not exact. For instance, news headlines in Malaysia as shown below give the justification that domestic violence stems from wife provocation:

> Nagging about financial issues, wife hit with shoes (Kamal 2016)
> Get a thrashing, evicted, divorced: nagging punishment (Ibrahim and Raja Rahim 2015)
> The wife was beaten because she refused to 'be together' (Wahid 2017)
> A husband hit his wife, because of not cleaning the chicken well (Mohd Najib 2017)

These reports give the impression that the wives influence their husbands' behaviours through certain actions or words on their part. The idea that women provoked their husband's violence is explicitly stated; wives hit due to nagging (Kamal 2016; Ibrahim and Raja Rahim 2015), refusing sex (Wahid 2017), and incompetence with the house chores (Mohd Najib 2017). This principal sides with perpetrators, as suggested by Jones (2000), Stark (2007), and Pain (2015); the blame is placed on those suffering from it.

Photovoice in this study directs attention back to the perpetrator's abusive behaviours through physical abuse description. Physical abuse from husbands is usually driven by the thought that the wife deserves to be badly treated. Hennessy (2012) stated that perpetrators' intention is driven by an evil intention to inflict damage on the women that they perceive as targets. In cases where the target of domestic abuse remains resilient, the perpetrator will often seek to exert his possession through physical violence and harm. The abuse of the female victim by the perpetrator continues until the latter is satisfied, without considering the effect of the abuse on those targeted with it. As Harini recounted:

He would think by himself, contemplating all questions, and answered them by himself. Then suddenly, his anger was fully redirected to me. Whenever he could reach an object (weapon), it was used to bash me. These are photos (Figs. 16.1, 16.2, 16.3 and 16.4) of the items that used to beat me (Harini).

Fig. 16.1 "The Items That Used to Beat Me" Shot by Harini

Fig. 16.2 "The Items That Used to Beat Me" Shot by Harini

Fig. 16.3 "The Items That Used to Beat Me" Shot by Harini

Fig. 16.4 "The Items That Used to Beat Me" Shot by Harini

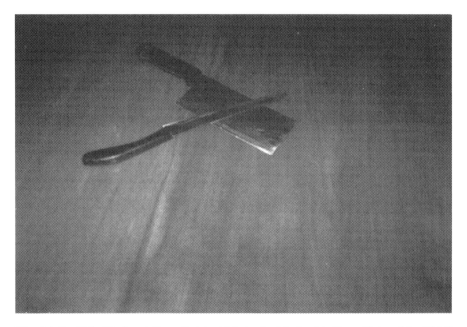

Fig. 16.5 "My Husband Once Stabbed Me in the Neck with Sharp Knives Like This" Shot by Rekha

Women's photos inform the public that domestic violence is indeed a crime and that women are at risk of being murdered. Like Rekha, when she reached the shelter, her neck was filled with the effects of a knife stabbed by her husband in several attempts to kill her. According to Rekha:

> My husband always threatened me by showing me sharp knives like this (Fig. 16.5). We cannot remain silent if such an incident occurs.

Lieya: How many times has your husband cut your neck?
Rekha: Two or three times already. Look, here there is a scar, here there is also (the scars of her neck).
Lieya: Different knives and different times?
Rekha: Yes. But the initial scar is not gone.
Lieya: The wound is deep?
Rekha: Yes.

Rekha wants to take other pictures but suffers from chronic trauma and can only take one picture of knives. She opened the discussion on some of the things that triggered her trauma, which is the picture of the fan and broom:

Rekha: Actually, I want to take pictures of many brooms.
Lieya: What does a broom mean?

Rekha: He hit me.
Lieya: With a broom?
Rekha: Yes. When I wanted to sweep the house, I remembered he hit me.
Lieya: What about the fan?
Rekha: He scared me, bring my son like this (put his son towards the fan). Because he asked me… money.
Lieya: Asking for money?
Rekha: Yes, ask for money.

These findings are significant because provocation is always used by perpetrators as their excuse to evade legal sanctions. Although the physical injury is the benchmark for domestic violence laws in Malaysia, in this way, perpetrators can still get away with the crime. According to Mohd Yusoff (2010), if the act of abuse (physical) is caused by a sudden loss of temper, this can be a mitigating factor that frees those perpetrators from being charged. For instance, if it can be argued that the offence is due to provocation by the wife, the perpetrator can be excused for hitting or harming her.

However, the findings of this study clearly show that the abuse is rarely a consequence of a sudden loss of temper or a one-off incident but is understood as a product of a long-term process of possession that shapes the perpetrators' physical abuse pattern. It is not caused by provocation but can occur anytime and can be life-threatening for the women. It casts light on the appalling and unacceptable violence towards women and resists excusing this by ascribing blame to women.

16.6   Entrapped at Home

Why abused women don't leave?—This is a common question asked of abused women. This is difficult to understand by the community (see Sahdan 2018) because some survivors live with abusers for up to decades. For example, in this study, the longest period the women stay with the abusers was 20 years. In the WAO record, there are women who have lived with abusers longer than that period. As Warrington (2001) argues there are many reasons why they live with abusers. Fear is often the main reason for survivors to remain in an abusive relationship; this fear is rational and justified (Pain 2012). The women in this research have left their relationships because of the fear of abuse, which gets worse from day to day while they are in captivity. Nevertheless, there is often a pattern of repeatedly going back to their perpetrators because the violence is unceasing and escalates after a few leaving attempts as Pain's (2012) research shows in a different context.

Through photovoice analysis, survivors illustrate their experience of being confined in a house controlled by abusers. Home is the main site for domestic violence (Pain 2012). As Herman (1997, p. 74) argues, "aman's home is his castle; rarely is it understood that the same home may be a prison for women and children whereas often unseen." Across different cultures, home is regarded as a 'private' space. For abused women, this specialisation of privacy creates the conditions for intimate captivity, which has both physical and psychological dimensions. Through photovoice analysis, a survivor illustrates her life in captivity as being like a mouse being trapped within the four walls of a mousetrap (Fig. 16.6). She describes the trap as symbolising the space of their house:

As her husband asserted, this space of violence is secret to the public:

He (husband) said, whatever happens in these four walls, don't you dare to tell other people (Ashna).

Harini added her photovoice (Fig. 16.7):

I want to share this photo because it shows an enclosed and dark space. This depicts my life, which is constrained in the house (Harini).

Fig. 16.6 "Life at Home like a Mousetrap" Shot by Ashna

Fig. 16.7 "A Restricted Life, Locked Inside the Doors of Violence" Shot by Harini

Shalini describes her feelings of being trapped behind the prison-like barrier via a photovoice (Fig. 16.8):

> I shared the picture when I stayed with my husband; I felt entrapped in this place, unable to go out the house freely, locked inside the house. The true story is—some of the women in this world experience this kind of life. We have to pass this door, which was tightly closed. My husband always locked me inside. He did not only lock the door, he also restricted my freedom.

These physical barriers are associated with survivors' feeling of being in solitary confinement via their photovoice analysis; I felt entrapped in this place, unable to go out of the house freely, locked inside the house, locked inside the doors of violence. The space is locked, tightly closed, and secluded. It is also under the control of violent husbands. The survivors affirmed that this kind of life is real for some women.

All of the participants in this study report feeling that they were trapped, physically and psychologically, both within and beyond the home. They are physically confined in a house that is locked, tightly closed, and secluded. In some cases, the house is also equipped with surveillance systems that create prison-like barriers: CCTV and spotlights, and the women feel watched and guarded by their abusers as if they were in prison. The spaces of surveillance

Fig. 16.8 "He Tightly Closed the Door and My Freedom" Shot by Shalini

shape the survivors' psychological state as constantly being watched, without freedom, and thus feeling controlled and terrorised by their abusers.

A common outcome where intimate captivity makes abused women feel stupid and blame themselves for the fear and pain suffered by them and other family members affected by the violence. The perpetrator keeps repeating that the abused woman should know better because it is her behaviour that dictates his reaction. For Ashna, a small character such as a mouse is representing herself being confined by her husband. In planning her photovoice, Shalini attempts to describe this situation and how it made her feel like a candle burning itself out:

Shalini: Actually, I want to have a picture of a candle.
Lieya: A picture of a candle?
Shalini: A candle that is burning itself out... (melting).
Usha: Suicide.
Shalini: It's not suicide!
Usha: Finishing herself off.
Shalini: (Ignoring Usha's opinion).
Mariam: Sacrificing ourselves.
Shalini: Yes, sacrificing ourselves like a candle.

Despite similar experiences, there is a difference of opinion between Shalini and Usha. Shalini and Usha had both been convinced by their perpetrators to protect their children and to protect their family members from being threatened. Usha had the experience of being trapped in intimate captivity for 20 years, which she desperately wanted to leave. She felt that there was only one way out for her to protect her children, which was to commit suicide. Shalini, however, had no suicidal thoughts in mind, even though she was similarly trapped in an abusive relationship. However, she suffered from chronic fear and severe psychological depression, which she illustrates as a form of self-destruction, like a candle burning out.

Although self-harm is perceived as a passive response. Many scholars point out that self-harm, in most cases, is not carried out with the intent to end life (Deiter and Pearlman 1998; Stengel 1964). However, some victims feel that suicide is the only way out; they are entrapped in prison, with a sense of being possessed, unable to flee, and enduring abuse that gets more severe, beyond what they can handle. As argued by Stark (2007) and Flitcraft and Stark (1995), it is the sense of entrapment for such women that may lead to them committing suicide: the feeling of being trapped and caged by perpetrators' tactics of possession (Humphreys and Thiara 2003).

16.7 Prolonged Violence and Entrapment

Women who successfully escape are usually considered to have left violence for good. In fact, violence is present even after leaving through chronic trauma and perpetrator threats if they can contact survivors. Photovoice conveys a flashback experience and opens a discussion of the sense of traumatised person. A flashback of abuse is a sudden, vivid memory of a traumatic event, accompanied by terror. This ensures past trauma intrudes in survivors' everyday lives (Matsakis 1996). Flashback stand to occur among people who have endured situations that involve intense chronic moments, or a loss of pervasive security and lack of safety (ibid., 1996). Abused women may replay the scene of traumatic abuse, smell it, and hear its sounds. Some women, for example, Usha, say that their sense of terror is heightened by the flashbacks of stalking and incarceration, with the perpetrators seeming to appear in places such as doors or windows. Usha also conveyed this in her photovoice, in which her images and accompanying descriptions show her feeling of being constantly watched or haunted by her husband:

> I feel my husband's shadow in places such as in these photographs (Figs. 16.9 and 16.10). It seems like he is standing there, whispering my name... Usha... Usha... Usha...

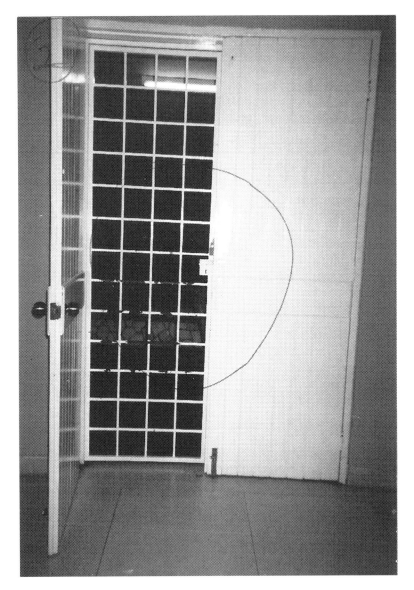

Fig. 16.9 "I Feel My Husband's Shadow Here" Shot by Usha

Usha added:

My husband kept intimidating me like that, in the house that I lived in before. This shows the nature of a man who does not trust his own wife and keeps eyeing her from windows and doors. How frightening to live with a husband like him.

Shalini also experienced flashbacks of stalking (see Fig. 16.11):

Fig. 16.10 "I Feel My Husband's Shadow Here" Shot by Usha

Fig. 16.11 "I Feel the Silhouette of My Husband" Shot by Shalini

I'll be scared witless when I see open windows. I feel the shadow of my husband, he's standing, peering at me.

In contrast to Usha and Shalini's flashbacks of stalking when they look at open windows, Harini comes across traumatic incidents in her confined space (see Fig. 16.10):

My husband locked me in the house. When I see window frills, I'll think of past violent incidents (Harini).

There are some types of space that trigger trauma, but the sense of space is not the same. As stated by Ashna:

Ashna: He hit me again. He said arghh...I'm angry, I do not know why I cannot control. He locked me in the toilet for three hours, he suddenly came hit me, then he locked me back, he left.
Lieya: What are you doing in the toilet?
Ashna: I feel calm sitting in the toilet. The day I sat there (toilet in the shelter) I thought (want to take a picture). But this toilet is not scary, it is not visibly similar.

Ashna decided not to take a picture of the toilet that reminded her of the violent space but the atmosphere of the space did not produce an accurate picture of her experience. In fact, many survivors were very particular in capturing the pictures, by which they have thought on how to give meaning to a message they want to convey. The meaning meant by women is from the sense of space, objects, and situations that closely remind them of life in domestic violence.

16.8 The Reality of Being a "Survivor"

The term survivor is someone who has successfully survived the violence. The community and study participants also assumed that they would be able to free themselves from domestic violence after getting help at the shelter. The photovoice analysis in this section shows their hopes as a survivor after getting help and getting out of the shelter or known as 'rebuilding'.

The majority of other interviewees also gave their opinion about 'regaining the world they have lost' and want to achieve better economic, career, and education positions. They want to prove their success by living independently from their perpetrator, in-laws, and their own family who looked down on them when they were in an abusive relationship. According to Rekha, this is a stage she had to go through for her to move on, as depicted in her photovoice (see Fig. 16.12) as a multi-layered tree, which represents an increasingly advanced life. For her, it is important to upgrade herself, and to protect her son, particularly by providing him with a good education:

16 CAPTURING THE UNCAPTURED: PHOTOVOICE AS A METHOD FOR WOMEN'S... 289

Fig. 16.12 "An Increasingly Advanced Life" Shot by Rekha

In the future, I want to rise to a higher position like this tree (Fig. 16.12). Going up layer by layer. Yeah, I should make progress little by little. To protect my son. To give him a good education, to raise him up, I need to move forward. Then, I can push on for my son.

Nevertheless, evidence from my research suggests that survivors coming out of the shelter very often return to their perpetrators, live in their family's house known to the perpetrators, and have to hand over the children to their perpetrators because they are unable to take care of the kids on their own, or have to be separated from their children because they lose child custody or children are simply taken by perpetrators. Others live alone in trauma and fear after leaving the shelter. A situation that provides the conditions of stable recovery is very hard to obtain. Herman (1992) suggests that the task of establishing a safe environment cannot be done by one person; instead, it requires societal support.

In Malaysia, resettlement services for domestic violence cases are not yet established, so temporary shelters are the only efficient short-term intervention for abused women. After three months of protection at the shelter ends, women are advised to live independently. Because other formal interventions are less effective, the majority of women face difficulties living independently and freeing themselves from violence. This is due to issues such as having no financial support, no safe shelter, and no reliable childcare.

In general, women who have children with their perpetrators find it hard to live independently without family assistance. Pressure from the family puts women at risk once they are out of the shelter, not only because of being tracked by the perpetrators but also because it can reduce the possibility of getting help from others, such as colleagues and employers, who had been trying to save them before. Women's action in returning to the high-risk situation causes the community to judge them as being passive and ineffective in decision-making. Chumy visualises this complexity like a forest through her photovoice (Fig. 16.13):

> Now I'm confused of what should I do for my future. The decision that I make will determine whether my life will turn bright or ugly. After this, I need to decide by following my own gut.

Harini tells the story of the difficulty of her daughter and herself to separate from each other for the purpose of earning a better income during the rebuilding process.

Harini: Yesterday I took a picture of Ally (her daughter), she was playing with Alice (a social worker). I wanted to show that this picture has a story.
Lieya: Look, Ally doesn't want to let go of Alice's legs, when Alice pulls her she wants to bite.
Harini: The story is like this, her mother said she doesn't want to leave her child, but she has no choice. The child said, "I don't want to let you go, mum, I don't want to".

Therefore, it seems clear that the photographic images and narratives are not only a reflection of self but also are reflections of what the participants

Fig. 16.13 "My Confusion and Uncertain Future" Shot by Chumy

choose to capture, record, and share (Harrison 2002). These self-defined 'truths' participants generate have the potential to help them move forward into a life that is not characterised by interpersonal violence.

16.9 Conclusion

This chapter has explained the impact of photovoice on abused women through pictures they can take or not in this study. Capturable pictures provide visual and narrative explanations of various things that need to be conveyed to the community. The understanding that domestic violence is simply synonymous with physical abuse due to female provocation has been broken down through photovoice. The women in this study showed that physical abuse can occur at any time without provocation and can lead to death. Women in this study have also answered the question of why they are not easily leaving an abusive relationship through a powerful message from photos and its explanation about confined life with their abuser. This kind of life shows that the captivity that prevents them from leaving is not only in the form of physical incarceration but also includes psychological barriers. This is a reflection of survivors of domestic violence through their real experiences of domestic violence. Therefore, the photos and narratives presented by the women in this study not only give them space to voice out their unheard voices but also convey those voices to other women who may be able to change the direction of their lives.

REFERENCES

Bradbury, H. and Reason, P. (2003) 'Action Research: An Opportunity for Revitalizing Research Purpose and Practices', *Qualitative Social Work*, 2(2), p155–175. https://doi.org/10.1177/1473325003002002003.

Coddington, K. (2016) 'Contagious trauma: Reframing the spatial mobility of trauma within advocacy work', *Emotion, Space and Society*, xxx, p1–8.

Crang, M. (2005) 'Qualitative methods (part 3): there is nothing outside the text?', *Progress in Human Geography*, 29(2), p225–233.

Deiter, P. and Pearlman, L. (1998). 'Responding to Self-injurious Behavior' in P. Kleespies (ed.) *Emergencies in Mental Health Practice: Evaluation and Management*. New York: The Guilford Press, pp. 235–257.

Flitcraft, A. and Stark, E. (1995) 'Killing the Beast Within: Woman Battering and Female Suicidality', *International Journal of Health Services: SAGE Journals*, 25(1), p43–64.

Hammer, R. (2002) *Antifeminism and Family Terrorism: A Critical Feminist Perspective*. Lanham, MD: Rowman and Littlefield.

Haraway, D. (1991) 'Situated Knowledges: the science question in feminisms and the privilege of partial perspective' in Haraway, D. *Simians, Cyborgs and Women: the reinvention of nature*. London: Free Association Books.

Harrison, B. (2002) 'Seeing health and illness worlds-using visual methodologies in a sociology of health and illness: A methodological review', *Sociology of Health and Illness*, 24, p856–872.

Hennessy, D. (2012) *How he gets into her head: The mind of the intimate abuser*. Cork, Ireland: Atrium.

Herman, J. (1997) *Trauma and Recovery: The Aftermath of Violence from Domestic Abuse to Political Terror*. New York: Basic Books.

Herman, J. L. (1992) 'Complex PTSD: A syndrome in survivors of prolonged and repeated trauma', *Journal of Traumatic Stress*, 5(3), p377–391.

Humphreys, C. and Thiara, R. (2003) 'Domestic violence and mental health: 'I call it symptoms of abuse', *British Journal of Social Work*, 33, p209–226.

Ibrahim, M., & Raja Rahim, R. (2015) 'Dibelasah, Diusir, Dicerai; BalasanMembebel', *Harian Metro Online*. Available at: https://www.hmetro.com.my

Jones, A. (2000) *Next Time She'll Be Dead: Battering and How to Stop It*. Boston: Beacon Press.

Kamal, K. M. (2016) 'SuamiDitahandalam Kes PukulIsteri', *Sinar Online*. Available at: http://www.sinarharian.com.my

Liebenberg, L. (2018) 'Thinking Critically About Photovoice: Achieving Empowerment and Social Change', *International Journal of Qualitative Methods*. https://doi.org/10.1177/1609406918757631.

Matsakis, A. (1996) *I Can't Get over It: A Handbook for Trauma Survivors*. Oakland, CA: New Harbinger.

Mohd Najib, K. (2017) 'Pukulisteriangkarabasuhayam', *Sinar Online*. Available at: http://www.sinarharian.com.my

Mohd Yusoff, J. (2010) *JenayahKeganasanRumahTangga*. Kuala Lumpur: Penerbit Universiti Malaya.

Pain, R. (2015) 'Intimate war', *Political Geography*, 44, p64–73.

Pain, R. (2012) *Bringing terrorism home: connecting domestic violence and global terrorism*. Durham University.

Putit, Z. (2008) *Domestic Violence: Refuge Provision in Malaysia*. Unpublished PhD thesis, University of Bristol.

Sahdan, Z. (2018) *Demonic Possession: Spatial and Cultural Accounts of Domestic Violence in Malaysia*. Unpublished PhD thesis, Durham University.

Stark, E. (2007) *Coercive Control: the entrapment of women in personal life*. United States: Oxford University Press.

Stengel, E. (1964) *Suicide and Attempted Suicide*. Oxford: Penguin Books.

UNICEF Innocent Research Centre. (2000). Domestic Violence Against Women and Girls. Italy

Wahid, A. (2017) 'IsteriDipukul Kerana Enggan Bersama',*Sinar Online*. Available at: http://www.sinarharian.com.my

Warrington, M. (2001) 'I must get out: the geographies of domestic violence', *Transactions of the Institute of British Geographers*, 26(3), p365–382. https://doi.org/10.1111/1475-5661.00028.

Wang, C. (1999) 'Photovoice: a participatory action research strategy applied to women's health', *Journal of women's health*, 8 (2),p185-92.

World Health Organization. (2021) Devastatingly pervasive: 1 in 3 women globally experience violence. https://www.who.int/news/item/09-03-2021-devastatingly-pervasive-1-in-3-women-globally-experience-violence (accessed December 2021).

Zimmerman, Marc A. (1995) 'Psychological empowerment: Issues and illustrations, *American Journal of Community Psychology*, 23(5), p581–599.

CHAPTER 17

Fieldwork with Opposite Gender: Exploring the Agency of Left-Behind Women of Migrant Households in Rural Bangladesh

Main Uddin

17.1　Introduction

One afternoon in April 2017, when I was walking along the village road near Rashunia bazaar, a leader of Rashidpur village stopped me on the way and asked why my female research assistant and I were talking about very private and sensitive issues with the left-behind wives of migrants. Some women complained to him that we talked about sensitive and unnecessary topics like sexuality. At the beginning of the fieldwork in January 2017, when we got to know him, we told him about the objective of our research in detail. So, he knew what we were exploring in the fieldwork. Hearing the complaint, I explained the details to him again. I assured him that while writing the report we would use pseudonyms and not share the information with anyone in the village or elsewhere by mentioning their names. I told him that we respect the norms and values of his society. We also respect the privacy and dignity of the informants. We are grateful to the informants and the villagers for their cordial support. After that, he calmed down and suggested that we should not ask about privacy issues because the informants do not benefit from these discussions. Instead, if we disclose the information to anyone, they may be at risk of tarnishing their image. I assured him he would not worry.

M. Uddin (✉)
Department of Anthropology, Jagannath University, Dhaka, Bangladesh

Department of Social and Cultural Anthropology, Tallinn University, Tallinn, Estonia
e-mail: mainuddin@anp.jnu.ac.bd; mainjnu@tlu.ee

© The Author(s), under exclusive license to Springer Nature Switzerland AG 2023
N. Uddin, A. Paul (eds.), *The Palgrave Handbook of Social Fieldwork*,
https://doi.org/10.1007/978-3-031-13615-3_17

These conversations exemplify the troublesome experiences I gathered while conducting ethnographic fieldwork with the opposite gender in a traditional Muslim society in rural Bangladesh. This article is the combination of such experiences and my strategies to manage the situations during the whole period of fieldwork. The gender identity of the researcher significantly influences the interaction between the researcher and the researched (Kane and Macaulay 1993). According to feminist experts, the researcher's gender identity and social status are important to build rapport with community people (Gilbert 2008). Women and men have different personalities because their life experiences are different (Maynard 1994). Thus, the main focus of traditional feminist research was to match their gender identity with the participants (Finch 1984; Oakley 1981). Feminist researchers have also shown how the ethnicity of the researcher affects the relationship between the researcher and the participants and the findings of cultural research (Collins 1991; Phoenix 1994). American ethnographer Michalowski (1997) mentioned that his interaction with the informants was greatly influenced by his American identity while conducting fieldwork in Cuba. He argued that gender identity, age and ethnicity of the researcher are important in ethnographic fieldwork (p. 504).

Al-Makhamreh and Lewando-Hundt (2008) showed that the gender identity of the researchers influences the way they conduct research and the kind of information they collect (Orrico 2015). It is observed that men and women researchers have different experiences in the field (Belur 2014; Bruni 2006; Roberts and Sanders 2005; Soni-Sinha 2008). Historically, women researchers have done research on women's issues (Berliner and Falen 2008). However, this methodological awareness of female researchers is challenged when male researchers work on the lives of women and bring different experiences and new dimensions (Maynard 1994).

Experiences of Female Ethnographers

Falen (2008) viewed that of all research methods, ethnography may be the most successful or disappointing based on gender identity and the rapport between the researcher and the participants. Hanson and Richard (2020) interviewed female researchers who had conducted research with male respondents in other cultures. The authors highlighted the experiences of the young female researchers in the field where local informants sought sexual favours, made unwanted contacts, forcefully entered rooms and abused researchers in various ways. They further showed that when female researchers want to develop friendships with male participants during ethnographic research, the participants may misinterpret their behaviour as sexual.

Gurney (1985) said that the obstacles that the women researchers face can be termed 'sexual hustling' because women have to face various sexual proposals and deceptive behaviours in the field. In this regard, Lumsden (2009) viewed that her gatekeeper once expressed sexual interest in her which made her uncomfortable in the field. Similarly, Orrico (2015) said that at the beginning of her fieldwork, a male artist saw her nail polish and praised her with a sexual overtones. She had encountered this type of 'romantic' desire many times (p. 479). Likewise, Pini (2005) said that when she asked a man if he could give an interview, the man replied, "I always have time for a beautiful woman." In another case, while she was walking, a man was joking in a way he wanted to do something with her behind a closed door (p. 206). Pini wrote in her observation notes how annoying and uncomfortable she was in the field. She was not treated as an educated, intellectual and upper-class woman; rather, she was treated as a 'sex object.'

Despite a variety of vulnerabilities, while compared to male researchers, experts say that female researchers are more flexible or possibly more 'bisexual' in the field than men (Gregory 1984; Brandes 1987). Abu-Lughod (1986: 23) claims that she enjoyed more privileges when working with males in Bedouin society. Similarly, Nader (1970: 114) enjoyed greater advantages than men when working with men and women in Mexico and Lebanon. Winchester (1996) worked with single fathers and showed that female researchers could more conveniently narrate men's stories by listening to them as good listeners. Karla and Steven (2020) showed that women can understand the experiences, thoughts and feelings of men through feminist research methods. Women anthropologists can easily understand the real experiences of women informants because of their sexuality (Falen 2008). Sampson and Thomas (2003) said that female researchers are better listeners than male researchers when the respondents share emotional stories (p. 177). Women have more empathy and less anger than men (Brody and Hall 2000: 344). Similarly, Davis (1996: 60) said that most psychologists have shown that empathy is more important in the identity of women than in men. Kosygina (2005) viewed it from the perspective of the participants and argued that local women are more open and spontaneous with female researchers in disclosing information about their personal lives. She again argued that female researchers can obtain information differently from male researchers (p. 11).

Experiences of Male Ethnographers

The experiences of male ethnographers are quite different from female ethnographers. During fieldwork in Yemen, Caton (1990: 23–24) noticed that it was impossible to gather information on women and their poetry. Similarly, Abu-Lughod (1986: 23), while researching Bedouin women in Egypt, showed that male researchers could never enter and study Bedouin women. Male researchers have limited access to female world. McKeganey and Bloor (1991) said that they had access to the men's quarters and social areas. But their access to women's areas such as kitchen, TV rooms, lounges or corridors was restricted (p. 200). Gregory (1984) viewed that it is very difficult or in some cases impossible for male researchers to investigate the daily activities, pregnancy difficulties, childbirth experiences, child-rearing and changes in routines of women. Similarly, it is often impossible to gather information on various sensitive topics such as sexual activities and various health problems (p. 319). He argued that female researchers do not have to deal with the same problems as men when they conduct fieldwork with the opposite gender. They are now able to overcome various obstacles and collect information from men. On the contrary, male researchers have not yet been able to overcome the barriers of working with women. He again said that sometimes female researchers disguise themselves to collect information from men. They can gather information from both men and women (p. 322). But male researchers cannot disguise themselves for which are unable to collect sufficient information from women. They consider it a threat to their masculine self-esteem. Male researchers have to recognize these facts while trying to gather sensitive information about women's world (p. 323).

Importance of Both Gender

Opinions of both gender are important for a fully understanding of the social issues in ethnographic research. Gatrell (2006) conducted fieldwork on motherhood among working women. Initially, she started to work with women excluding men. But soon after starting the fieldwork, she realized that father's views are also important for a complete picture (p. 242). Falen (2008) discussed about the gender of the researcher and viewed that he could not talk to women until engaging a local female research assistant while conducting fieldwork in an exotic environment in Benin (165). He shared his experiences as an anthropologist while doing fieldwork with female respondents and said that there are many examples where the gender identity of the researcher affected the process of the fieldwork. Sometimes, it is believed that male researchers are not fit to study female's issues (p. 164). However, Falen further informed that after engaging an assistant, he gradually began to participate in some interviews with the assistant, and later when he had developed a trust worthy rapport, he could talk to women alone. Once, he had such a trustworthy rapport with some men and women of the community that he negotiated quarrels between husband and wife in some cases (p. 169). He said that although many women talked to him about social, economic, religious or political issues, he could not talk to them about their private or sexual issues (p. 169). So, it is clear that not only participants from both gender are significant but also researchers from both gender are important in order to have a complete picture from both ends.

Falen (2008: 172) said that male anthropologists should contribute to the anthropology of gender. Many scholars have described men's interest in seeing women's perspectives and men's role in feminist movement (Philips 1987).

Experiences Written in Textbooks

The literature on the experiences of conducting research with the opposite gender is very important, particularly in ethnographic research. But, McKeganey and Bloor (1991) showed that almost all the writings about the impact of gender on the research process in the social sciences are written by women researchers. There is a lack of reports from male researchers (p. 195). Taking into consideration the silence of male researchers, it seems that their research process is not influenced by their gender identity. When we review the literature on the influence of gender identity on the researchers, we find very few writings from male researchers. Gurney (1985) showed that female researchers also do not disclose their violent and bad experiences in the field, fearing that this may hamper their dignity in the family and society (p. 44). If a female researcher receives a sexual proposal, it is clear that the problem is due to her gender identity (p. 45). Gurney again said that sexual harassment is more when a male or a female researcher goes to the field alone to talk with the opposite gender (p. 46). Against such a background, the present study details a comprehensive account of my personal engagement with left-behind women of migrant men in various challenging social situations. It also highlights my strategies applied in the field to manage the situation for successful completion of the research. Thus, the study contributes to feminism by exploring a range of gendered aspects of social and cultural life in rural Bangladesh.

17.2   Research Setting and Research Methodology

Together with a female research assistant, I conducted the ethnographic fieldwork mainly from January to December 2017, at Rashidpur, a migrant village in Rashunia Union Parishad, under Sirajdikhan Upazila, Munshiganj district, Bangladesh. I again conducted fieldwork in the village intermittently from September 2021 to March 2022 after the covid-19 pandemic situation. In fact, since the beginning of the fieldwork in 2017, I have been maintaining regular contact with many villagers by phone, Facebook or other social media.

The village is an hour's bus ride to the south from Dhaka, the capital city. It is located in a lowland area. Commuting to and from the village is very difficult as it does not have road connections with the adjacent villages from three sides. There is a cement road on the southern side of the village. The villagers use this road as their main path to commute to other villages. Recently, a few shops including grocery, tea stall, garage for auto rickshaws and stationary shops have been established on both side of the road, making the area a small bazaar and the main meeting place for villagers. The bazaar sits daily in the morning to sell vegetables, fish, meat and other raw commodities. There is very little or no constructed road to commute from one homestead to another within the village; there are only unpaved paths to go from one homestead to another. As a result, the homesteads become separated from each other during monsoon as if they are scattered islands in the water. Therefore, the boat is the only means of their communication during monsoon.

The villagers worked mainly as agricultural labourers, growing paddy and jute inland, fishing and plying boats in marshy land until 1975, when the Indian government built the Farakka barrage to drain water from the Ganges. After the barrage was built, silt gradually accumulated under water, affecting agriculture, fisheries and livelihood in the Rashidpur area and throughout the riverine areas of Bangladesh (Matin et al. 2014). As a result, typical occupations such as jute cultivation and catching fish in marshy land have now disappeared.

Currently, the main agricultural activities of the people of Rashidpur are cultivating potatoes and paddy. However, many villagers complained that cultivation does not produce as much money as it costs. As a result, many villagers have lost interest in cultivation. Furthermore, most of the villagers lacked adequate agricultural land or schooling for which they were looking for an alternative to earn their living. But, because of their low education and the prevalence of corruption in the employment process in the country, managing good jobs or doing a profitable business is challenging in Bangladesh (Bal 2013). Therefore, the people considered migration as a better alternative. Hence, they started going abroad in the early 1980s. At present, remittance has become the primary source of earning for many villagers. It has brought a significant change in the lifestyle and housing condition of the villagers as the houses have been transformed from thatched to corrugated tin, or sometimes to brick buildings.

Remittance has become a part of rural life in Bangladesh. It has transformed not only the socio-economic condition of Rashidpur and the surrounding villages but also the country as a whole. About ten million Bangladeshi people are working abroad, with Saudi Arabia, the United Arab Emirates, Oman, Malaysia and Singapore being the top five destinations (World Migration Report 2018). These migrants are considered "sojourners" (Gardner 1995) because they do not settle down in their destination countries, but rather travel back and forth for many years, accumulating enough capital to pursue a profitable business after returning home. Currently, remittances account for 5.4 percent of the national GDP (World Bank Group, April 2019) of Bangladesh. So, remittance is regarded as the governing wheel of the country's national economy (Lewis 2011).

We conducted the study applying participant observation as the main method along with a variety of other anthropological techniques such as census, key informant interview (KII), in-depth interview, life story interview, informal group discussion and observation of male and female migrants, returned migrant and aspirant migrant households. We also spoke with village leaders, religious leaders, traders, primary school teachers, service holders, drivers, masons, rickshaw pullers, agricultural labourers and others to get a full picture of the village's gendered social transformation. The fieldwork consists of approximately 200 individual and group discussions lasting from half an hour to several hours depending on situation.

The village has 1404 people divided into 307 households. There are 110 migrant households; from these 133 (127 men and 6 women) have migrated to various countries, mostly to the Middle East, Southeast Asia and East Asia. There are 55 returned migrants living in 48 households in the village. Rashidpur is predominantly a Muslim village. There are only six Hindu households, four of which have migrants abroad.

The present study was conducted in a patriarchal Muslim society in rural Bangladesh where the interaction between male and female is minimal (Dannecker 2005). This social milieu is challenging for male researchers for conducting ethnographic research with female informants. It is really hard to talk to female informants about their opinion regarding any issue. Even if a way to communicate with women is discovered, many women may not express themselves in front of an outsider due to the norms of a patriarchal society (Keesing 1985). In this respect, England (1994) warns that "ethnographic fieldwork may expose the investigated to increased danger and maybe more invasive and possibly oppressive than more conventional methods" and that "manipulation and probably betrayal is inherent to research work." Finally, if the aspect of the study with women shows aspects of women's disadvantage, it can be sensitive. Considering these, I was concerned about my rapport and interaction with women, particularly with those who are alone due to the absence of their husbands. To overcome these, I engaged a female research assistant, having a background in anthropology and gender, to work with me in the field. Initially, she collected confidential information from women while I spoke with men to learn about their perspectives on women's issues. In several cases where the situation allowed, she spoke with men while I spoke with women alone or in groups. We conversed with the same male or female informants on many occasions, particularly in the group discussions.

Research Ethics and Data Analysis

This chapter is part of my doctoral study when I conducted fieldwork with the opposite gender in a rural setting in Bangladesh. During fieldwork, we were especially concerned about ethical issues. Before starting the interviews, we informed the participants clearly about the objective of the study and took their consent for collecting expected data and information. We did not record the conversation as we realized that people do not speak about their innermost feelings when they know the conversation is being recorded. We also did not use the camera without the villagers' permission to ensure their privacy. The discussions and group discussions of the fieldwork were informal and open-ended. After the fieldwork, I read the scattered and messy interview notes, field notes and observation notes several times to code them according to the purpose of the study. Then, I expanded the codes and categorized them for writing the report according to the central theme of the study. Complete anonymity is important to guarantee the well-being of the participants (Wilson 2019). So, I used pseudonyms to ensure the well-being of the informants and the villagers.

17.3 Glimpses of the Experiences of Ethnographic Fieldwork in Bangladesh

There are only a few ethnographic studies that highlighted the experiences of the researcher with opposite gender particularly in migration studies in Bangladesh. Gardner's (1995) ethnographic research in a migrant village in Sylhet, Bangladesh, is the pioneer study that explained migration by linking the local and global perspectives, which was not seen in other migration studies in Bangladesh before it. While discussing gender relations, she showed that the absence of men brings significant changes in the role of women as they can move in public places wearing *burqa* (veil). Similarly, Dannecker conducted qualitative research with migrant women in Dhaka and linked the rural-urban migration of women from the village to Dhaka city with the development of the garment industry. She demonstrated that though women migrate from rural areas and get their first job with the help of kin, they develop a network for additional new jobs, residence, and survival or resistance. As a result, a unique and special transformation occurs in household structure and gender relations because of this recent economic activity (Dannecker 2002). Bal and Roos conducted a study on the construction of migration desire among the educated, middle-class youth in Dhaka, Bangladesh, and showed that the local, socio-economic and political insecurities made the youth yearn for 'safe' places to fulfil their dream (Bal and Roos 2014).

Raitapuro and Bal conducted intensive research on the culture of migration among the Garo indigenous community at Birishiri in Netrokona, Bangladesh, and showed that mobility plays a vital role in everyday life and the future aspirations of young individuals. They pointed out that successful migrants build a home, buy land and invest in small businesses, which also influence the non-migrants in the village. As a result, young Garos have developed future dreams which can no longer be fulfilled in the villages (Raitapuro and Bal 2016).

Similarly, Rashid (2013), in her ethnographic study on two Gulf migrant villages in Cumilla, Bangladesh, argues that although women can negotiate household decision-making and can move in public places in the absence of their men, they do not necessarily enjoy the decision-making power, autonomy and freedom. Instead, they like to follow social norms and stay under male protection. Therefore, they feel more secure and empowered when they stay with their husbands. As a result, the impact of male migration on stay-behind women in rural Bangladesh lacks insights with regard to ethnographic details (Rashid 2013).

Gardner (1995), Dannecker (2002) and Raitapuro and Bal (2016) talked to the participants of other gender while conducting ethnographic research with the members of migrant households, but they did not highlight their research experiences with the opposite gender. Uddin (2011) is somewhat exceptional in this regard. He is a Bangladeshi Bengali researcher who conducted ethnographic fieldwork with the indigenous people in the Chittagong Hill Tracts.

He showed that as a male researcher, he faced many kinds of criticism. Being a male researcher, it was difficult for him to collect information from women. He was in a difficult situation how to explain women's experiences in a hilly culture where women's economic contribution is significant in the household and society, which is opposite to the mainstream society of Bangladesh.

17.4 Challenges and Coping Strategies in the Field

Hanson and Richard (2020) stated that researchers encounter a variety of challenges, vulnerabilities and experiences in the field, particularly while conducting research with other gender. During fieldwork, it is not only the female researchers who are concerned about harassment or sexual violence but also the male researchers when they work with women in the field (Pascoe 2007; Grenz 2005). Gregory (1984) showed that both male and female researchers may be harassed while working with the opposite gender. So, they need to apply various strategies to manage the situation. Researchers should write down their challenges and strategies so that future researchers are well prepared. My fieldwork experience at Rashidpur shows that just as the researchers observe the people in the research area, so do the people on the movements and interactions of the researchers. So, the researchers need to adopt various strategies for collecting expected information, especially when conducting ethnographic research. For example, if a male researcher talks to a left-behind young wife of a migrant household for a long time in an empty house, the neighbours may not take it positively. They may spread a rumour against the woman and the researcher, or they may come and ask them what they are talking about or they may call her migrant husband over a phone call or complain to other male members of her household, which may create an embarrassing situation for the researcher and the wife. The woman may be insulted by the household members of her in-laws, including her husband. Therefore, the researchers need to gather information by keeping family and social norms in mind, so that no one can consider their discussion negatively.

One afternoon, I talked to Sumi (32), the left-behind wife of a migrant household, sitting in the front room of her house while two of her under 5/6-year-old children were playing on the ground. After a while, we saw three enthusiastic women of different ages were standing outside the house and listening to our discussion. They were curious to know what we were discussing about. At one point, they entered the house and asked what we were talking about. I told them the details of my research. Then they sat next to my informant and started participating in the discussion. They stayed until the discussion was over and gave their opinions about different issues. As a result, I could not finish the discussion that day. So, I went to her house another day and talked with her, sitting on a chair under a mango tree in the open corner of her homestead. That day, when I was coming back after the discussion, a man from a neighbouring homestead stopped me on the way and asked what I was talking about with the woman in such a separate place. I told him the details of my study. I have encountered many such embarrassing experiences when discussing with women inside the household. So, later, keeping this in mind, I tried to discuss with women sitting in the open yard or an open space of the homestead instead of sitting in a room of their house. I did it so that nobody could listen to our discussion from the other side of the fence/wall, or if anybody comes, we can see from far.

The findings also show that when a male researcher talks to a woman, sometimes enthusiastic neighbours come and sit next to the woman and start sharing their opinions. In such cases, neither the researcher nor the informant can tell them to leave. If they are asked to go away, they may be upset and spread rumours against the researcher and the informant. So, the researcher and the informant have to continue the discussion. One afternoon in December 2017, I talked to Rekha (42), the wife of a migrant in Malaysia, sitting on a chair under a tree in a corner of her husband's homestead. Before talking about her issues, I told her that if anybody comes to listen to our discussion, we will change our topic and continue our discussion on a different topic so that she/he cannot doubt our conversation. I told her that it is safe not only for my information but also for her privacy. However, when we were talking about her personal issues, at one point, we saw that two women were moving towards us. Then, we technically changed our discussion to a general topic of the village. The women came to us, and when they saw that we were talking about unimportant matters, they went away. After that, we moved the discussion to the previous topic. This strategy was important to avoid challenges and outside interference when discussing personal matters.

The people of the society keep the researcher men and the informant women in surveillance all the time. When the researcher leaves after a discussion, family members or neighbours want to know from the informant what the researcher was talking about. They may also ask if the researcher wanted to know any secret. The family members may consider it a matter of threat if there is anything disgraceful in the discussion and if the researcher shares with anybody else in the society. One afternoon in April 2017, I conducted a long interview with Sharifa (30), the wife of a migrant and the mother of three children. When I went to talk to her again three days later, she informed me that her uncle-in-law (husband's father's brother) had asked her what about I had talked to her the day before. The wife replied to him that we were talking about many issues of migration and there was nothing harmful. At that point, I asked her why she did not say the right things in detail. She replied that it would be very difficult for her to positively convince him by telling everything in detail. So, she thought it was safe to answer briefly.

The researchers and the informants are observed differently by people in the community based on age, gender, marital status, family status, dress code and body language. They don't like to see a male researcher and a young female informant talking in a particular place for a long time. So, female informants may find it unsafe to talk to an outside researcher. In such cases, some women feel comfortable talking with a male researcher keeping one or two of their minor children around so that other people do not suspect their discussion. It is a strategy of the rural women to desexualize their interaction with outsider men in the household or the public spheres (Dannecker 2005). The women of Rashidpur village did this in many cases when I talked to them in separate places. However, women's gender identity is not a big issue when talking to older women. Nonetheless, the older women also prefer to speak to the researcher keeping their younger grandchildren around them instead of talking alone. It is a common strategy of the village women in Rashidpur when dealing with outsider men in public or at home. I also would feel comfortable to talk to women if they had young children with them during the discussion. One afternoon in December 2021, I talked to Marjina (50), a mother of a migrant, sitting on a stool in her backyard where her two grandchildren were playing beside her. We talked a lot about women's household management and their interaction with outside men. I was not much worried when talking to her because of her age. Neighbouring women were also not much concerned about our interaction and discussion.

However, when I talked to women counterparts of migrant men, I was careful about the norms and values of the society and of the position of women in the household of their husbands and in the community. So, in most of the cases, I did not take the personal history of the young wives who live in *ekloge* (extended/joint) households with their in-laws. Instead, I took the personal history of young wives only in a few cases where the marriage took place between relatives, or in the same village or where the wives had friendly and informal relation with their in-laws. Mainly, I talked to some liberal young wives of *bhinno* (nuclear) households, particularly those who were middle-aged or older with grown-up children. However, although I talked to some liberal women in separate places, I could not directly ask anything about their extramarital affairs or their feelings of loneliness because these are private and secret affairs associated with shame. However, I got some indication that they want to share their agony and loneliness if they get a trustworthy person. If the person is an outsider, it is better for them as there is no fear of spreading anything in the locality.

Fonow and Cook (1991: 715) argued that because of the outsider status of the ethnographer, people do not see any harm in believing and faithfully sharing their personal information which they would not share with an insider. Similarly, Bucerius (2013) showed that insider status is not necessary for building trustworthy relationships during research. Whether an ethnographer can gain trust from people depends on the level of their relationships (p. 691). She argued that a trusted outsider can better understand the deeper information. However, when it comes to gathering sensitive information from other gender, the researchers must consider not only their own safety but also of the women who live in the household of their in-laws. So, my female research assistant, Laila gathered sensitive information from women in most of the cases while I talked to men to know their opinion on women's issues. I collected sensitive information mainly from male respondents with whom I had friendly and informal relationships. I could only verify this information through indirect and general discussions with women by maintaining a respectful and trustworthy relationship.

When I talked to men, the scenario was different. If the researcher can build a trustworthy rapport, sometimes male respondents may spontaneously talk about extramarital relations. I found a few men who were willing to speak about extramarital and sexual issues of other women. However, they say it in such a way that I cannot recognize the women. Usually, they talk about women of other village or their relatives whom I do not know. Even if they talk about the women of the same village, they do not disclose the women's identities. For example, one moonlit night in April 2017, Miraj (35), a returned migrant, was accompanying me when I was walking through the path of the village field. He shared cases of several extramarital affairs in Rashidpur and surrounding villages. I had heard many of such cases from a few men. However, they try to avoid telling stories of their own. Laila also has similar experiences with women who share the stories of others instead of their own.

People observe not only our interaction with the villagers but also between us. They notice the pattern of our interaction when we move in the village and in the locality. Sometimes, we did not see anyone while walking along the village road or doing anything in the village or the area, but later we heard from the villagers that they knew where we had sat and with whom we had talked to and so on. This indicates that people had eyes on us and our doings. As a result, we had to be extra careful in the field, especially when talking to respondents of other gender.

We wore modest clothes and were careful when interacting with the villagers. I also used to pray in the village mosque. There are two mosques and four shrines in the village. The authority of each shrine arranges *Orosh* (a gathering of followers in front of a shrine on the death anniversary of a pir or knowledgeable Islamic leaders) every year. Not only the men and women of the village but also the relatives of surrounding villages attend the programmes that continue until late night. I attended two *Orosh* held at night and participated in the activities with the villagers to build a trustworthy and informal relationship with them. This way, I finished the fieldwork by encountering different challenges and applying various strategies.

17.5 Female Agency and Male Researcher

Exploring female agency by the male researcher is a challenging endeavour especially in a patriarchal Muslim society like rural Bangladesh. I was always wary not only of the reaction of the community people but also of the women of the village when talking to them individually in separate places. For that reason, I took a long time to understand the situation and to find out the liberal families where I can talk to women. Initially, Laila and I conducted a census moving from door to door to be introduced to the villagers and let them know the objective of my research. Then, we spent a lot of time chatting with villagers in tea shops, at home, on the streets or in the fields to eliminate their doubts about us. Laila accompanied me most of the time while chatting with the villagers to motivate them that men and women can talk together. During the whole period of fieldwork, I used to be enthusiastic to talk to the villagers wherever I met them to build up an informal and trustworthy relationship. This was not my natural behavior in my practical life to make friendship with everyone around. But I did it in the field for building a rapport for collecting indepth information and for my safety in the field. This way, I maintained good relations with the village leaders, *imam* (leader) of mosque, *khadem* (caretaker) of shrines, *kobiraj* (local healers who treat by herbs), Union Parishad members, grocers, tea shopkeepers, entrepreneurs, primary school teachers, service holders, drivers, masons, rickshaw pullers, agricultural labourers and the like to create a friendly environment in the village so that they do not say anything on my face even if they see me talking to women in separate places. I always waited for a trustworthy and congenial relationship before having individual discussion with the wives of the migrants.

Initially, Laila talked to women alone, while I talked to men to understand their opinion on various issues of male-female interaction in the household and the public places. Our objective was to motivate the villagers to create a favourable environment for the research and to select the women and men for individual discussions. At one point, I began to accompany Laila when she talked to women. Later, I too started to talk to women individually in separate places where situation allowed. Laila followed the same technique before talking to men individually in separate places. In many cases, we talked to the same men or women to avoid risk and to collect the detailed data. We also talked together with the villagers in many group discussions.

Exploring Agency

I observe that for women of Rashidpur village it is not a problem talking to outsider men. Although women themselves are migrants in the households of their in-laws, they may be willing to talk to an outsider or a researcher if they find him reliable. They are mainly worried about the people of their surroundings and the norms and values of their family and society. They also fear that if the person is not trustworthy and if he shares their secret and private issues with someone else, it may damage their dignity and personal image. Young women also may share issues with an outsider if the person is trustworthy and reliable. I observe that, except for some exceptions, **purdah** (veil) or religious issues are not the obstacles to talking to an outsider man or a researcher. Their main concern is their social circumstances and the values of a patriarchal society. For this reason, I found that women spontaneously talk to outsider men if there are male members or their husbands available at home. In a few cases I saw that women are willing to talk to me but their circumstances did not allow them.

The findings of the study show that the agency of women develops through experiences of taking over responsibilities in various family and social matters. I heard from several women that if they get the opportunity to manage households alone and interact with others and move outside, they can learn many things which, in turn, will increase their confidence. On the other hand, women who are not used to talking to outsider men are not confident to talk to a stranger or a male researcher. Women of traditionally rich and extended/joint migrant households may be powerful in society because of the male support they get (Gardner 1995). But their agency may not be strong because they do not get to manage households or move outside alone to interact with others on various occasions. On the contrary, women of nuclear migrant households manage households and take over various responsibilities for which they need to interact with others in the public sphere.

When I asked about the practices of agency many women spontaneously shared that they enjoy their participation in household decisions, moving into the public sphere and interacting with others. They want to express their opinion if they get a chance. They love to talk about their potentiality and capacity to manage household or outside issues. The women who go to the bazaar, bank, doctor or urban area share their experiences with others. They also can advise others if anybody needs support for any reason. If the wife can manage the family well in the absence of men, their husbands can also be relaxed abroad. As a result, the opportunity to express agency is very important for women in Rashidpur village.

17.6   Conclusion

This chapter aimed to explore the difficulties a male researcher faces while conducting an ethnographic study with left-behind women of migrant households in a majority Muslim society in rural Bangladesh where the interaction between male and female is not common. The interaction between male and female is especially difficult when strangers want to talk to village women individually in separate places. The ethnographic fieldwork of this study was conducted in such a social milieu to explore the agency of women.

Rural women of Bangladesh are typically seen as housewives who stay at home and take care of children, while men work outside to earn the livelihood of the household members. However, the migration of men abroad leaving their wives in the village brings various social and psychological changes in their family life including marital relations. To conduct ethnographic research in such an environment, I hired one of my female anthropology students to work as my assistant in the field. She conducted most of the individual discussions with women while I talked to men to understand their views about women's issues. I also talked to many women of different ages individually in separate places considering the situation and the sociability of the women.

The findings of the study show that, in many cases, the agency of women is not the barrier in Rashidpur village to talk to outsider men. Their main concern is about the people around them and the gender codes of the society while talking to a male researcher or outsider men. They also fear that if the researcher or the outsider man shares their private issues with others in their society, they will be humiliated. I found that, with some exceptions, *purdah* (veil) or religious ideology is not the main barrier to talk to an outsider or a researcher. Their main concern is their social milieu and the gender codes of the patriarchal society. I saw that, in some cases, women are willing to share their personal issues with outsider men if the person is trustworthy and reliable. They are willing to talk about their potential and capacity to manage a household or outside affairs. Women who have experiences of visiting the bazaar, bank, doctor or urban area, are more willing to share their experiences with others. They also may suggest others if anybody needs support. If the wives are capable of managing the household well in the absence of men, their husbands can also be relaxed abroad. As a result, the opportunity to express agency is significant for women. In conclusion, this study provides a new methodological approach in anthropological studies, which will help future studies in Bangladesh or abroad.

References

Abu-Lughod, L. 1986. *Veiled sentiments*. Berkeley: University of California Press.

Al-Makhamreh, S.S. & Lewando-Hundt, G. 2008. Researching 'at Home' as an Insider/Outsider: Gender and Culture in an Ethnographic Study of Social Work Practice in an Arab Society. *Qualitative Social Work*, 7(1) 9–23. https://doi.org/10.1177/1473325007086413.

Bal E. 2013. Yearning for Faraway Places: The Construction of Migration Desires among Young and Educated Bangladeshis in Dhaka. *Identities: Global Studies in Culture and Power* 21(3):275–289. DOI: https://doi.org/10.1080/1070289X.2013.833512.

Bal, E. and Roos, W. 2014 Introduction: Aspiring Migrants. Local Crises and the Imagination of Futures 'Away from Home'. *Identities: Global Studies in Culture and Power*. https://doi.org/10.1080/1070289X.2014.858628.

Belur J. 2014. Status, gender and geography: power negotiations in police research. *Qualitative Research* 14(2): 184–200. https://doi.org/10.1177/1468794112468474.

Berliner, D. and Falen, D. J. 2008. 'Introduction to special section on men doing anthropology of women', *Men and masculinities*. Sage Publications Sage CA: Los Angeles, CA, 11(2), pp. 135–144. https://doi.org/10.1177/1097184X08315090.

Brandes, Stanley. 1987. Sex roles and anthropological research in rural Andalusia. *Women's Studies* 13:357–72.

Brody, L. R., & Hall, J. A. 2000. Gender, Emotion, and Expression. In M. Lewis, & J. M. Haviland-Jones (Eds.), *Handbook of Emotions: Part IV: Social/Personality Issues* (2nd ed., pp. 325–414). New York, NY: Guilford Press.

Bruni A 2006. Have you got a boyfriend or are you single? On the importance of being 'straight' in organizational research. *Gender, Work, and Organization* 13(3): 299–316. https://doi.org/10.1111/j.1468-0432.2006.00309.x.

Bucerius S.M. 2013. Being a Trusted Outsider: Gender, Ethnicity and Inequality in Ethnographic Research. *Journal of Contemporary Ethnography*, 42 (6) 790–721. https://doi.org/10.1177/0891241613497747.

Caton, S. 1990. *Peaks of Yemen I summon*. Berkeley: University of California Press.

Collins, P. H. 1991. *Black Feminist Thought: Knowledge, Consciousness and the Politics of Empowerment*. New York: Routledge.

Dannecker, P. 2002. *Between Conformity and Resistance: Women Garment Workers in Bangladesh*. Dhaka: University Press Ltd.

Dannecker, P. 2005. Transnational Migration and the Transformation of Gender Relations: The Case of Bangladeshi Labour Migrants. *Current Sociology*, July 2005, Vol (534): 655–674 SAGE Publications. https://doi.org/10.1177/0011392105052720.

Davis, M. H. 1996. *Empathy: A Social Psychological Approach*. Boulder: Westview Press.

England, K. V. L. 1994. Getting Personal: Reflexivity, Positionality, and Feminist Research, *The Professional Geographer*, 46:1, 80–89, https://doi.org/10.1111/j.0033-0124.1994.00080.x.

Falen, D. J. 2008. The "Other" gender? Reflections of Fieldwork in Benin, 11(2), 164–173. https://doi.org/10.1177/1097184X08315094.

Finch, J. 1984. 'It's great to have someone to talk to: The ethics and politics of interviewing women, *Social Researching: Politics, Problems, Practice*, London: Routledge and Kegan Paul.

Fonow, M. and Cook, J. 1991. *Beyond Methodology*. Bloomington: Indiana University Press.

Gardner, K. 1995. *Global migrants, local lives: Travel and transformation in rural Bangladesh: Travel and transformation in rural Bangladesh*. Clarendon Press.

Gatrell, C. 2006. Interviewing Fathers: Feminist Dilemmas in Fieldwork, *Journal of Gender Studies*, 15:3, 237–251, https://doi.org/10.1080/09589230600862059.

Gilbert, N. 2008. *Researching Social Life*. Los Angeles, CA: Sage.

Gregory, J. R. 1984. 'The myth of the male ethnographer and the woman's world', *American Anthropologist*. Wiley Online Library, 86(2), pp. 316–327.

Grenz, Sabine. 2005. "Intersections of Sex and Power in Research on Prostitution." *Signs: Journal of Women in Culture and Society* 30 (4): 2091–2113.

Gurney, J. N. 1985. 'Not One of the Guys: The Female Researcher in a Male-Dominated Setting', *Qualitative Sociology* 8: 42–60.

Hanson, R. & Richards, P. 2020. Harassed: Gender, Bodies, and Ethnographic Research, *Social Forces*, Volume 98, Issue 4, June 2020, Pages 1–3, https://doi.org/10.1093/sf/soz166.

Kane, E. W. and Macaulay, L. J. 1993. 'Interviewer gender and gender attitudes', *Public opinion quarterly*. Oxford University Press, 57(1), pp. 1–28.

Karla, E. & Steven, R. 2020. 'Balancing generosity and critique: reflections on interviewing young men and implications for research methodologies and ethics', *Qualitative Research*, 20(6), 767–783, https://doi.org/10.1177/1468794120904881.

Keesing, R. M. 1985. Kwaio Women Speak: The Micro-politics of Autobiography in a Solomon Island Society, *American Anthropologist*, 87(1) 27–39.

Kosygina, L. 2005. 'Doing Gender in Research: Reflection on Experience in Field', *The Qualitative Report* 10(1): 87–95.

Lewis D. 2011. *Bangladesh: Politics, Economy and Civil Society*. Cambridge University Press.

Lumsden, K. 2009. Don't ask a woman to do another woman's job: gendered interactions and the emotional ethnographer. *Sociology* 43(3): 497–513.

Matin, M.A., Ismal, M. M., and Siddique, A. 14–16 Feb, 2014. *Fresh Water Corridor in Southwest Region of Bangladesh and Impact of SLR*. Proceedings of the 2nd International Conference on Civil Engineering for Sustainable Development (ICCESD-2014), 14~16 February 2014, KUET, Khulna, Bangladesh.

Maynard, M. 1994. Methods, practice and epistemology: the debate about feminism and research. In Maynard M and Purvis J (eds) *Researching Women's Lives from a Feminist Perspective*.

McKeganey, N., and Bloor, M. 1991. Spotting the invisible man: The influence of male gender on fieldwork relations. *The British Journal of Sociology* 42 (2): 195–210.

Michalowski R.J. 1997. Ethnography and anxiety: fieldwork and reflexivity in the vortex of U.S.-Cuban relations. In: Hertz R (ed.) *Reflexivity and Voice*. Thousand Oaks, CA: Sage, 45–69.

Nader, Laura. 1970. From anguish to exultation. In Golde P. (ed), *Women in the field*, 97–116. Chicago: Aldine Publishing.

Oakley, Ann. 1981. "Interviewing Women: A Contradiction in Terms." In Roberts H. (ed), *Doing Feminist Research*, 30–61. London: Routledge.

Orrico, L. A. 2015. 'Doing Intimacy' in a public market: how the gendered experience of ethnography reveals situated social dynamics, *Qualitative Research*, 5(4) 473–488. https://doi.org/10.1177/1468794114543403.

Pascoe, C. 2007. *Dude, You're a Fag*. Berkeley: University of California Press.

Philips, Susan. 1987. The new gender scholarship. *Signs* 13 (1): 192–95.

Phoenix A 1994. Practising feminist research: the intersection of gender and 'race' in the research process. In: Maynard M and Purvis J (eds) *Researching Women's Lives from a Feminist Perspective*. New York: Taylor and Francis, 49–71.

Pini, B. 2005. Interviewing men: gender and the collection and interpretation of qualitative data. *Journal of Sociology* 41(2): 427–442.

Rashid SR 2013. Bangladeshi Women's Experiences of Their Men's Migration: Rethinking Power, Agency and Subordination. *Asian Survey* 53(5):883–908. https://doi.org/10.1525/as.2013.53.5.883.

Raitapuro, M. & Bal, E. 2016. Talking about mobility: Garos aspiring migration and mobility in an 'insecure' Bangladesh. *South Asian History and Culture*, Vol. 7, No. 4: 386–400. https://doi.org/10.1080/19472498.2016.1223723.

Rebecca, H. & Richards, P. 2020. Harassed: Gender, Bodies, and Ethnographic Research, *Social Forces*, Volume 98, Issue 4, June 2020, Pages 1–3, https://doi.org/10.1093/sf/soz166.

Roberts JM and Sanders T 2005. Before, during and after: realism, reflexivity and ethnography. *The Sociological Review* 53: 294–313. https://doi.org/10.1111/j.1467-954X.2005.00515.x.

Sampson, H. and Thomas, M. 2003. "Lone Researchers at Sea. Gender, Risk and Responsibility." *Qualitative Research* 3:165–89.

Soni-Sinha U 2008. Dynamics of the 'field': multiple standpoints, narrative and shifting positionality in multisited research. *Qualitative Research* 8(4): 515–537. https://doi.org/10.1177/1468794108093898.

Uddin, M. 2011. Decolonising ethnography in the field: an anthropological account, *International Journal of Social Research Methodology*, 14:6, 455–467, https://doi.org/10.1080/13645579.2011.611382.

Wilson, E. 2019. Community-based Participatory Action Research. In Liamputtong P (eds.) *Handbook of Research Methods in Health Social Sciences.* Springer, pp. 285–298.

Winchester, H.P.M. 1996. 'Ethical Issues in Interviewing as a Research Method in Human Geography', *Australian Geographer* 2(1): 117–31.

World Migration Report 2018. International Organization for Migration (IOM): The UN Migration Agency.

World Bank Group. April 2019. Migration and remittances: Recent development and outlook.

PART V

Theoretical and Epistemic Challenges in the Field

CHAPTER 18

Between an Activist and Academic: Contested (Re)positioning of Ethnographers in Refugee Research

Nasir Uddin

18.1 INTRODUCTION

An unsettled contestation between activist standpoint and academic positioning has long been an issue of powerful debate in social research (see, Grey 2013; Flood et al. 2013; Choudry 2020; Leal et al. 2021). It brings certain fundamental methodological questions in social search on board including subjectivity versus objectivity, emic versus etic, outsider versus insider, native versus foreigner, 'self' versus 'others' and so on. Ethnographers frequently struggle to uphold a sensible equilibrium of a dichotomized positioning between attachment versus detachment, association versus disassociation and engagements versus disengagement with the object of study while doing fieldwork (see Uddin 2011). It turns more critical when it comes to the question of refugee research since refugees are often depicted with various negative connotations by the host society (Uddin 2012), but the researchers tend to stand by the refugees due to perceived vulnerable conditions of refugeehood (Uddin 2022b). This contested representation takes shape and is articulated amidst the dynamics of refugee management. For example, many human rights organizations, refugee rights activists and different rights bodies often help the refugees living in the place of migration in very inhuman conditions with poor housing, inadequate food and water supply, unhealthy sanitation, and the lack of many

---

N. Uddin (✉)
Department of Anthropology, University of Chittagong, Chittagong, Bangladesh
e-mail: nasir.anthro@cu.ac.bd

© The Author(s), under exclusive license to Springer Nature Switzerland AG 2023
N. Uddin, A. Paul (eds.), *The Palgrave Handbook of Social Fieldwork*, https://doi.org/10.1007/978-3-031-13615-3_18

everyday essentials, whilst the host community depicts refugees living in "rajar hale" (living like a king/queen) and receiving more than what they need to be supplied by the national and international aid agencies working in the refugee camps. When a researcher stands for the refugee rights, they become more an activist than an academic in the eyes of the host society. When a researcher, on the other hand, does mere research without paying attention to the sufferings, needs and struggles, the refugees look upon them as meaningless academic. Given the context, the chapter, with my decade-long experience of research on/with the Rohingya refugees, presents the contestation of activist and academic (re)positioning in refugee research, because an academic cannot "blame the victims" (Said 1988) on the one hand and cannot ignore the sufferings of the host society (Barman 2020) on the other hand. The chapter illuminates the ways how an ethnographer could make an intelligent balance between being politically sensitive without being an activist and being deeply committed to the object of study by maintaining a maximum degree of academic neutrality. Though objectivity and neutrality are relative ideas and subjectively loaded concepts (Clifford 1986), an ethnographer with training, ethical ground, moral standard and a strong sense of commitment can maximize the degree of academic objectivity to minimize the gap between activism and academia.

18.2 Academic and Activist: Conceptual Contestation

Academics work in academia, particularly in academic institutions, and conduct academic research with the broader idea of finding the objective truth and discovering value-free knowledge (Briggs 2005). Though objective knowledge itself is a problematic proposition, academics often involve in academic research to produce objective knowledge to contribute to the existing scholarship. The outcome of academic knowledge helps people understand a particular topic better than what is commonly known among the public. Besides, academic research helps policymakers redress a particular problem with the policy recommendation made by academics. Most often, academics conduct academic research and produce scholarly publications for their personal and professional accomplishment (see Masud-Al-Kamal and Uddin 2022 [this volume]). Since the researcher's personal, political and ideological positioning reflects in the findings of the research (Uddin 2011), 'producing objective truth' has become an issue of subjective discourse. Therefore, what an academic does in the name of finding an objective truth is no more beyond question and debate (Clifford 1986). Nonetheless, academics are expected to be more objective than subjective to the object of research.

On the contrary, activists are those who work for a particular issue in terms of rights and entitlement, and hence they are more politically motivated and subjective in their objective (see Croteau et al. 2005). Activists work on various issues and set different demands to meet the respective issues. Activists deal with the issue with a preset agenda and predetermined goals, which are largely subjectively designed. Activism is fundamentally a political activity which is done to achieve a certain goal in favour of the people concerned. Therefore, activism is more subjective than objective since it has little space for objectivity and neutrality. It is absolutely focused and target-oriented and intimately affiliated with the rights and entitlements of the people involved (see O'Donnell 2018). Therefore, an activist cannot be an unbiased academic and thereby judgemental. Academics are objectives, but activists are subjective. Academics find the result from the ground after conducting research, but activists know the result even before starting their activities because they start the activities with the preset outcome.

Considering the philosophical, ontological, political and practical aspects, it is clear that academics are more objective and neutral than activists. It does not essentially mean that an academic cannot be an activist and an activist cannot be an academic (see O'Donnell 2018). Rather, ethnographers who are popularly called pro-people academics and scholars are always passionate and compassionate towards the people they study. Ethnographers uphold a strong sense of commitment to their informants, respondents and participants (see Graeber 2009). Nonetheless, they always consciously maintain a distance between activism and academia. They intelligently balance objective goals and subjective minds (Uddin 2011). Yet, it becomes very difficult in refugee research which I will explain here with some very personal experiences of doing long-term research among the Rohingya refugees living in Bangladesh.

18.3 Methodology Applied: Beyond Orthodox Ethnographic Rituals

When I write about my research methodology on/with/among the Rohingya people, I always try to provide readers with a feeling that my whole life is entwined with the transforming Rohingya crisis and its various associated issues, particularly in Bangladesh. My research on Rohingya does not essentially follow the 'typical ethnographic genre' (see Fetteraman 2009) or an 'ordinary empirical social research' (Hammersley and Atkinson 2019) like going to the field, spending some reasonable period among the people, taking part in their everyday life, if necessary learning their language, trying to understand them from their point of view what Bronislaw Malinowski called "native points of view",[1] coming back from the field, writing down the field report and publishing it in the form of a book, journal article or another form of the academic piece to present 'research findings' before an academic audience (see Gobo 2000). Of course, I was doing this sort of 'typical ethnographic research' twenty years ago. Now, my methodology is completely different due to my multifaceted engagement with the Rohingya people and the Rohingya refugee issue. I firmly admit that I also do 'typical rituals' of ethnographic fieldwork in one sense like gathering information by applying orthodox ethnographic

[1] Understanding a particular culture from their point of view is widely known as the "native point of view" in anthropology. For details, see Malinowski (2015 [1922]).

techniques of data collection (Gobo 2000), such as doing participant observations, applying unstructured interviews, using key informants, organizing focused group discussions (FGDs), doing case studies, recording life histories, applying genealogical method and practising multi-sited ethnography (see Falzon 2012), but I did much more than what a typical ethnographer does for an intensive, comprehensive and ethnographic research. It is because I have deep engagement, intensive observation, decades-long affiliation and active participation in/with Rohingya people in many ways for many years. In fact, there are five ways how I have been involved in Rohingya research which have theoretically and ontologically become part of the methodology in my research. Firstly, I was born and brought up in Cox's Bazar where the Rohingya people have been living as refugees for more than four decades. The first Rohingya influx took place in 1978 when temporary refugee camps were built to shelter them in Ukhia and Teknaf (see Uddin 2020a). The camps are now 50 minutes' travel distance from my residence in Cox's Bazar. As I had been living in Cox's Bazar as a local resident in close proximity to the Rohingya refugees since my childhood, I was fortunate enough to have the opportunity to closely observe the Rohingya life, their struggle for everyday essentials, their fights for survival, their everyday dealings with the local people, 'local states' (see Sharma and Gupta 2006; Uddin 2020a), and their crisis of social integration. Such scopes of observation in an intimate contact provided me with a deep academic insight and analytical strength to understand the transforming Rohingya crises over the years. Secondly, I started my professionally typical academic research on the Rohingya refugees—particularly focusing on their crisis of social integration in the host society—soon after I got an appointment as faculty of anthropology at the University of Chittagong in 2000. I have written elsewhere that "my training in Anthropology at the University of Dhaka shaped my outlook in being open to a bottom-up approach, which gave me different insights, unlike the popular narratives regarding Rohingyas in Bangladesh. Besides, my experience of doing research in Japan, the United Kingdom, Germany, the Netherlands, and India as well as my research engagement with colleagues of many universities from the United States of America, Canada, Japan, India, Germany, and the United Kingdom on the triplicate relations of the state, marginality and the people of cultural difference gave me a deep analytical scholarship and a solid theoretical foundation to understand the evolving relations between the state and the Rohingyas" (Uddin 2020a). Thirdly, I did conventional ethnographic fieldwork on both registered Rohingya refugees and unregistered Rohingyas[2] for a long period, starting from 2000 to 2003, and again from 2008 to 2022. I also did fieldwork on the local host community to understand their changing attitudes towards the Rohingya refugees and the dynamics of 'hosting' the

---

[2] Before the 2017 influx, the Rohingya refugees were divided into two categories: registered and unregistered. Registered refugees were living in two officially registered camps, Nayapara in Teknaf and Kutupalong in Ukhia. And unregistered refugees used to live in two makeshift camps: Taal in Ukhia and Leda in Teknaf.

Rohingya refugees in their locality (see Uddin 2012). I wrote in my other book chapter that "Of many villages co-habited by unregistered Rohingyas and local Bengalis in Teknaf and Ukhia, I selected two, *Vasan Para*[3] (pseudonym) of Teknaf and *Pasan Para*[4] (pseudonym) of Ukhia.[5] ... I also visited the *Kutupalong* and *Nayapara* refugee camps and the *Taal* located in Ukhia and *Leda* located in Teknaf makeshift camps many times between 1997 and 2017 before the recent massive influx took place. Apart from these, I recorded hundreds of case studies, life histories, genealogies, and personal narratives during this long period of my engagements with the Rohingya research. I interviewed hundreds of Rohingyas in 1992, 2012, 2015, 2016, and 2017 following the new influx" (Uddin 2022a). Fourthly, I got the opportunity to interview many diaspora Rohingya communities, diaspora Rohingya leaders and activists both in person and through email. I visited Penang in Malaysia,[6] Heidelberg in Germany,[7] Waterloo-Kitchenware area in Canada,[8] New York in the USA[9] and Bradford in England.[10] I had a long discussion with many Rohingya diaspora political activists about the Rohingya past, their critical present and uncertain future. This kind of interaction with the Rohingya diaspora activists and community leaders gave me a different insight into the vision and mission of their lives at home and abroad. Fifthly, I have recorded 500 narratives of Rohingya

---

[3] Vasan Para means mobile village. The Rohingyas first come to Teknaf after crossing the Naf River. They stay in Teknaf for a short period and move to another place, particularly to Ukhia. Since the Rohingyas use the space of Teknaf as their transit to move to another place, I metaphorically name my research site in Teknaf as a mobile village or Vasan Para.

[4] Pasan Para literarily means cruel village. Rohingya people cross the border and take initial shelter in Teknaf. After few days/weeks/months, many of them move from Teknaf to Ukhia. After they arrive in Ukhia, the Rohingya people try to stay for longer term as they do not have any alternative place to go in general. Therefore, they usually settle down in Ukhia. Since they stay for longer period of time, they get in touch with the local people and sometimes get involved in various forms of conflict of interest. Local people also blame the Rohingya people for their different types of problems and miseries, what the Rohingyas consider as the 'cruel' behaviour to them. Considering the Rohingya perspective, I metaphorically use the pseudonym of my research site in Ukhia as Pasan Para. Though it is a simple village name, it contains some sort of reality.

[5] As a local resident of Cox's Bazar, both villages are familiar to me: three of my relatives live there and therefore I had easy access to the villagers.

[6] I interviewed Rohingya refugees living in Penang in Malaysia in 2018.

[7] I interviewed a few Rohingya people in Germany in 2013 when I was a Visiting Fellow at the South Asian Institute, Heidelberg University. They had shifted there from Thailand and then migrated to Thailand in 2012. I recorded their experience of migration from Rakhine State to Thailand and from Thailand to Germany.

[8] I met the diaspora Rohingyas living in Waterloo-Kitchenware in 2012 and 2017. I met as many as twenty Rohingyas there, discussed with them many issues and interviewed them. I also met some Rohingyas in Toronto in 2017 and interviewed them on the massive campaign against Rohingyas that took place from August 2017.

[9] I met some Rohingya diaspora in New York in 2015 and 2019, and conducted some sessions of unstructured interviews. Some of them are well-established in New York but hold strong sense of belongingness to the Rohingya people living in Myanmar and Bangladesh.

[10] I interviewed Rohingya diaspora living in Bradford in London in 2014 and 2018. I met many Rohingya activists and online bloggers in London in 2018.

genocide survivors which are now the great testimonies of genocide, ethnocide, domicide, ethnic cleansing and the crimes against humanity executed by the Myanmar security forces in collaboration with some vigilantes in 2017. I have written two books and a couple of book chapters, as well as a couple of journal articles based on my experience in ethnographic fieldwork among the Rohingya refugees living in Bangladesh. This chapter is solely based on my long-term engagement in Rohingya research. I quite often write op-eds for the rights of the Rohingya people and Rohingya refugees in different national (see Uddin 2020b) and international (see Uddin 2018) media outlets which seem, to some extent, an activist's works. I also appear on the different TV channels to advocate in favour of the rights of Rohingya refugees, which is also a kind of activism. But I am quite aware of the political and ideological differences between activists and academics. Therefore, I feel a kind of moral challenge and ethical disconfirm as an ethnographic researcher in the matrix of academic and activist positioning (see Love 2012). I found that the ethical, moral and ontological challenges I faced are not only my solitary problem but a general problem of refugee research in social sciences. The dialectics and contestation between academic and activist positioning within the larger canvas of trust and mistrust, subjectivity and objectivity, sympathy and empathy, insider and outsider, and emotional attachment and professional detachment have always been issues of serious methodological challenges in social sciences (Uddin 2011). They are more vivid and sensitive in the research of refugees in the host societies. I will try to touch upon these challenges based on my experience of researching the Rohingya refugees.

It is also to be mentioned here that soon after the major influx started on August 25, 2017, I moved to Teknaf from Chittagong and witnessed the tide of traumatized people who rushed to cross the border in Bangladesh. Within a week, I formed a team of ten trained research assistants who were fresh graduates of anthropology at the University of Chittagong. They were well capable of documenting oral testimonies and traumatized narratives. All of them were from the Chittagonian region and hence could speak in Rohingya dialects. Some of them could speak and understand the Rohingya language better than many Rohingyas did. Every day each research assistant recorded two narratives of Rohingya genocide survivors in detail from either Teknaf or Ukhia. They started recording at the beginning of September and completed their recording at the beginning of October. Each research assistant recorded 50 narratives of traumatized Rohingya genocide survivors. Altogether, I received 500 vivid narratives[11] of first-hand eyewitnesses of genocide, majority of whom were victims since they went through extreme forms of atrocities perpetrated by Myanmar security forces, some ethnic extremists and some Buddhist fundamentalists. I personally and very intimately supervised the recording process, and in most cases, I was present with them in person while interviewing the

[11] My book *Voices of the Rohingya: A Case of Genocide, Ethnocide and Subhuman Life* (Switzerland: Palgrave Macmillan, 2022) has a good number of narratives I recorded in September–October 2017.

victims. Apart from the recording done by my research assistants, I personally recorded more than 100 traumatized and vivid narratives of Rohingya genocide survivors. Their narratives were recorded following five central questions: (1) How were their lives, livings and settlement in the Rakhine state? (2) Why did they flee to Rakhine or what forced them to cross the border? (3) How did they cross the border or what are the channels they followed to come to Bangladesh? (4) What are their current conditions in Bangladesh refugee camps? (5) What is their future plan and aspiration for the coming days? This chapter presents the experience of recording these traumatized narratives which put me in serious methodological changes as far as the code of ethics in ethnographic research is concerned. More specifically, the chapter attempts to relate my personal experience to the broader spectrum of refugee research across the globe to address the ethical challenges, epistemological questions and ontological debates regarding the research of vulnerable categories of people. These records motivated me to be an activist to work for the justice of the Rohingya people, because all those narratives were loaded with plenty of terrible atrocities. As a human being, it was very difficult not to be emotionally biased, but I had to maintain academic professionalism. That is the fundamental reason why Stahlke said that researchers who work with vulnerable people and communities are at emotional and psychological risks (see Stahlke 2018). So, there is always an academic and activist conflict in my understanding, my interpretation, my writing and my analysis as far as the Rohingya research is concerned.

18.4 Epistemological and Methodological Challenges in the Field

Apart from academic and activist issues, research on the Rohingya refugees is always challenging because it is very difficult to know what happened in the Rakhine state. In 1978 and 1991–1992, the media was not strong enough and the Internet connectivity was not as good as it is today, so the outsiders could not easily know what happened to Rohingya people in the Rakhine state. In 2012, 2016 and 2017, media became more proficient and the Internet facilities were drastically enhanced so that people outside Myanmar could know many things that happened to the Rohingya people in the Rakhine state. Nonetheless, the original sources of information the researchers received are the narratives of the Rohingya people, but we have very little scope to justify, verify and cross-check their statements. Therefore, it is a big methodological challenge in Rohingya research that I have explained in detail in my other writing (see Uddin 2022b). In my recent book, I have written that there are four ways to receive information about the Rohingya experience in the Rakhine state. "Firstly, researchers and media receive information from Myanmar which is strongly filtered and sponsored (in fact censored!) by the state. Myanmar's media reports are heavily controlled by the state and hence seriously lack authenticity…Secondly, researchers and media have some drone footage and satellite images of affected areas of the Rakhine state captured, after the genocidal attacks were over, by the Guardian, the Amnesty International and Human Right Watch (HRW), and so on, which … clearly about what kind of massacre and domicide took place in August 2017. … (3) Thirdly, we have some amazing photographs and video footage taken and shot from the Bangladesh border standing on the bank of the Naf River on the Bangladesh side. The photographs and footages show some houses burning with wild-flam of fire and sky-going smoke which give some glimpses about domicide … (4) Fourthly, the direct interview of the genocide survivors, provide some genuine first-hand experiences of victims to present the relatively real picture of what was happened to Rohingya lives in the Rakhine state…[But] I must admit that there is little scope to verify and cross-check the narratives of Rohingya genocide survivors whether their statements and experience uphold real facts or facts with slight fiction" (Uddin 2022b: 48–51). I have used Rohingya narrative in my many writings as "victims' statements" as the most valid and solid source of information because Rohingya people either witnessed or personally went through the genocidal actions that took place in 2017 in the Rakhine state. This kind of methodological question also sometimes relates to the issues of activists and academics. For example, from an academic point of view, it seems that the narratives of the Rohingya should somehow be justified for their validity, but from an activist point of view Rohingyas are the victims and victims' narratives are good enough to draw a conclusion. Therefore, in every aspect of doing research on the Rohingya refugees, a conscious sense of contestation between academic and activist positioning always puts me in a dilemma of ethical concerns.

18.5 Moral Challenges in Dealing with Refugees

I wrote in my book, "It was 25 September 2017, just one month after the military crackdown started … in Rakhine State … I was travelling by a compressed natural gas (CNG) scooter from Kutupalong to Balukhali when I saw hundreds of Rohingyas, mainly women and children, sitting on both sides of the road. At a certain point during my journey, I got off my scooter and spoke to some of those women … At first, they thought that I had brought some relief aids for them, as they were sitting there hoping to receive food. Therefore, their interest in me was met with disappointment when they came to know why I stopped speaking to them. In fact, I had a strong feeling that it was not an appropriate time for a researcher to conduct fieldwork and ask questions… Survival appeared to be a necessity for them and it was important for me to be empathetic to their plight since I see myself as a pro-people scholar and humanistic ethnographer" (Uddin 2020a: 01). Research on the Rohingya refugees always involves this sort of dilemma whenever and wherever I meet them. Whenever I visit the Rohingya camps in Ukhia and Teknaf, the Rohingya refugees always expect something material from me. This is not mainly because they are greedy, but they know that I am compassionate to them as I know their conditions in

Bangladesh better than others. And they believe that I could really do something better for them. Particularly, they expect some support in the form of money, food, clothes and everyday essentials. Few of those who have known me for a long time try to avoid me based on their long-term experience in dealing with me since I only 'talk, and ask questions but give nothing.' Those who don't know me come to me very overwhelmingly thinking of me as a member of some NGOs or any NU organization who sometimes visits the camp to make a list of people in need of material support. They come to me, willingly talk to me and overwhelmingly respond to my questions, but they become frustrated and hopeless at one point knowing that I am a researcher and have to talk to them to know them and their everyday life, 'giving nothing in return'. One day, one of my respondents, named Jalal Uddin (22), directly asked me, "you are doing research. Talking to us. Gossip with us. Sometimes, you express your kindness and sympathy for us. You ask too many questions and we respond to you very cordially, sincerely and honestly. You are taking notes of what you need. You will go back and use our information for your personal benefit. You will sell us in the market and you will be benefitted for sure. But what will we get from it? What is the price of the time that we are investing for you? What is the value of the time we are spending for you? How can we directly benefit from your research? You people are simply using us. We are being used as the raw materials for your business. Please don't mind. Have I told anything wrong?" Jalal works for an NGO in the camp. He passed HSC in Maungdaw town in the Rakhine state. He crossed the border in 2017. He now lives in Kutupalong Rohingya refugee camps. He is very critical of refugee 'researchers' in the camp since he thinks that researchers are doing nothing for the refugees and using them as "raw materials" in their research for their personal and professional benefits. Though I have a good relationship with him because he reads my op-ed in Bangla and English national dailies and watches 'talk shows' on the private TV channels where I always stand for the Rohingya rights, I couldn't respond to his question very convincingly. And I am sure that many researchers across the world face similar experiences while doing fieldwork in protracted refugee situations. Now, the question is what indeed researchers could do for the refugees? All researchers are not activists, don't work for their rights and don't move for their material needs. According to the research ethics in social sciences, researchers are advised to remain careful about 'not to do harm', 'not to disclose privacy', 'not to put the participants in danger', 'not to make any derogatory remarks', 'be committed to the object of study' and so forth (see Love 2012). Whether researchers could really do anything that could directly benefit the participants is a big question in social research. Particularly, a researcher who studies refugees in a protracted situation feels that refugees experience various kinds of challenges in their everyday life including the shortage of everyday essentials, insufficient medical facilities, lack of proper sanitation, inadequate water supply, state of insecurity, a threat of forced eviction and so forth. In the case of Rohingya research, I also faced similar claims from the participants. But, I hardly did anything to resolve their various problems, which sometimes made me helpless before the participants. One of my Rohingya informants, Hasan Mian (52), told me one day, "You are doing research which is good to know our conditions from your end. But, from our end, knowing us is not enough since we need support and help to redress the practical problems that we are experiencing in our everyday life. We have come here to save our lives from the genocidal attack in the Rakhine state. We are passing our lives in the camps in critical situations since Bangladesh doesn't want to host us anymore. Myanmar is not willing to take us back to the Rakhine state. In fact, we are leading our lives with an extreme sense of uncertainty. So, what's the benefit of giving information to you and other researchers working on us? We need indeed practical and effective support." Hasan Mian crossed the border in 2017 and had settled down in Kutupalong Rohingya refugee camps. He has six family members but lives in the same small tent built of plastic sheets and bamboo. During the rainy season, the house's plastic-made roofs transport water from outside to inside. During the dry season, his family suffers from an acute shortage of drinking water, and his wife and daughters have to bring drinking water in pitchers, far from the place where they live in. He requested me to set a tube well for them, but how I could do that. I requested an NGO working there to set up a tube well, but it didn't work out. Then Hasan Mia, along with many others, said in a later interview, "you are just doing research but doing nothing for us. Even you could not keep a small request to set up a tube well. What can you really do for us? You are just using us for your personal benefits." This was an embarrassing situation for me at that time, and I had to face similar situation many times, on many occasions. How could I make them understand that I am a professional academic to do academic research and not an activist who can bring a solution to their numerous problems. Many requested me to find some places for the refugees so that they can escape the protracted camp situation. Many requested me to help in admission for some Rohingya youths in different local schools and colleges. Many requested me to help them get out of the refugee camps in Ukhia and Teknaf. Many requested me to help them get jobs in NGOs or in the locality. Many requested me to help them to go to Malaysia or any Middle East countries. Many asked me to request different NGOs to give them more food, health facilities and better housing. I received various types of requests during my fieldwork but could hardly meet any. On principle and ethical grounds, I could not help them get out of the camp, get a job which is not permitted for them, manage admission for Rohingya students to the local schools and college and get access to go out of the country. But refugees demand a lot to get themselves out of their refugee life since they live in a very protracted situation. Therefore, researching refugees is always morally challenging and ethically concerning because researchers can hardly do anything to help them beyond the local and international laws as well as the code of ethics of social research. Sampson observes that institutional ethical codes and guidelines, however, seem insufficient to address ethical dilemmas and challenges faced by researchers (see Sampson 2019). However, a refugee researcher upholds a strong sense of feelings for their demands, deep attachment to their pains, profound affection for their everyday struggle and a passionate mind for their everyday needs. Denzin is of opinion that personal and professional identities are always in contestation in social research (see Denzin 1997). Despite having all these in my mind, I cannot be an activist to openly work for them and fight for them to resolve their problems. I, time and again, tried to convince them, explaining that academic research at some point is taken into consideration in framing policies at the national and international levels, which will benefit them in the long run. Besides, I also tried to clarify my position that I often visit many countries to give talks and lectures on the recurrent Rohingya crisis where I speak on behalf of them and represent them with my research and research findings. In these various ways, I implicitly work for them. But they need immediate material benefits, which I cannot provide as an academic researcher. I am sure many researchers across the world face similar dilemmas while conducting research on the refugees, and I have had similar moral challenges in researching the Rohingya refugees.

18.6 Ethical Discomfort in Dealing with the Host Society

During my fieldwork, I often spend time with the local people and the host community, particularly in Ukhia and Teknaf. Before entering the Kutupalong refugee camps, I use to spend some time in Kutupalong Bazar and sit in nearby tea stalls or restaurants. Similarly, before entering the Balukhali refugee camps, I use to spend time at Paan Bazar, the entry gate of Balukhali camps, and sit at some tea stalls and restaurants. When I visited Nayapara and Leda camps, I would often spend some time at tea stalls or restaurants at the main road entry gate of the roads towards the refugee camps. Most of the time, while taking tea, I used to talk to the local people in the restaurants and tea stalls and tried to know their sentiment, mentality and approach towards the Rohingya refugees living in the 34 refugee camps set up in Ukhia and Teknaf. Since many of them know me very well as I have been visiting their restaurants and tea stalls for many years, they openly discuss everything with me without any conscious filtering and any self-censorship. Besides, when I travel by CNG scooter and rickshaw, which is the local transportation, and meet the local people of many layers at different spots and occasions, I always try to learn their changing 'sense of hosting' and 'degree of relations' with the Rohingya refugees living inside and outside the refugee camps in Ukhia and Teknaf. Surprisingly, the local people seem invariably seriously annoyed, extremely angry, deeply disappointed and totally disturbed with the massive presence of the Rohingya refugees in Ukhia and Teknaf. I noticed this just after the arrival of the massive influx of Rohingyas refugees in 2017. What I found in 1991–1992, and even in 2012, is now completely missing in the sense of hosting the refugees in Ukhia and Teknaf. Particularly, after the massive influx in 2017, the local people of Ukhia and Teknaf seem completely fed up with the Rohingya presence in Bangladesh. It is undeniable that the massive Rohingya presence has seriously affected the lives of the local people and the local settings in many ways in their everyday course of life. Abus Salam (56), a local restaurant owner at Paan Bazar, once explained[12] to me, "Brother, don't take it any other way, Rohingya people are not human beings in the true sense. The plate with which you offer food for them, they will make a hole after they finish eating. They are the most ungrateful people in the world. They are our guests as we have sheltered them to save their lives, but now the way they behave as if they are the owners of this territory. In fact, they have destroyed our lives. They have damaged our forests and jungles. They have devastated our infrastructure. They have captured our local job market. They have spoiled the law-and-order situation in Ukhia and Teknaf. Robbery and stealing have become everyday incidents in our locality. Even killing people has become a regular news item in Ukhia and Teknaf. Yaba business, arms trafficking, drug smuggling and 'what not' have become a common phenomenon in our lives as everywhere you will find Rohingya involvements." He continued, "Hundreds of NGOs and INGOs are working in the camps providing the best living standard, good quality medical services and adequate food facilities to them while the local communities, like us, remain outside of any sort of support and help. The local communities are just witnesses of their activities as if guests are well-taken care of with 'biriyani' whilst the hosts remain in starvation." The way he was making this statement was full of anger, annoyance and disturbance which I had not seen in him before 2017. I have known Abdus Salam for more than two decades. Twenty years ago, he seemed very sympathetic and compassionate to the Rohingya people because he had a strong feeling for them out of his sense of Muslim brotherhood and fellow-feeling for them as the people living in a close neighbourhood. But, the feeling has been completely altered and U-turned during this period. I must admit here that the massive Rohingya presence hurts the local economy, ecology, politics, security and resources. Given the context, being a Bengali doing research on the Rohingya refugee and having deep sympathy for them becomes a critical issue, which puts me in a serious moral challenge in the eye of the host community. I know that Rohingya refugees are the victims of the system and the state's atrocity in Myanmar. They have come to Bangladesh to save their lives from genocidal attacks. No Rohingya crossed the border willingly leaving their lives, livings, properties, family and "home" in Myanmar. So, I cannot "blame the victims" on principle and ethical grounds. At the same time, I cannot ignore the suffering of the local people and the adverse impacts on the local infrastructure, economy and resources. However, many local Bengalis seriously criticized my position as if I am doing "dalali" (broker), advocating in favour of Rohingya refugees taking a stand against 'my

---

[12] I was in November 2019 when I was visiting the Balukhali refugee camps. I interviewed him in November 2019 at his restaurant located at Paan Bazar, Balukhali, Ukhia, Cox's Bazar.

own community'. One day in Kutupalong Bazar at a tea stall, Abdul Gafur[13] (52) attacked me, "Don't mind, brother! I have been observing you for a long time that you have been doing research on the Rohingya refugees. In fact, you are doing good business with the Rohingya. You people don't want the Rohingya to go back to Myanmar. If they go back to Myanmar, your business will be stopped and your earning source will be closed. Many NGOs are also working against Rohingya repatriation. So, you people are the collaborators of the groups who are working against the Rohingya repatriation. Actually, you are doing it against the interest of your own country and own community." Abdul Gafur was very harsh to me and I received similar criticism from many local Bengalis living in Ukhia and Teknaf. This sort of criticism puts me in a serious ethical dilemma and moral discomfort while researching on Rohingya refugees. Not only that, I sometimes write, as I mentioned before, for the rights of Rohingya people and publish in different national and international media outlets. I also advocate for their repatriation, but I always demand that it should be voluntary and dignified with legal recognition and social safety. Many colleagues in my university, the University of Chittagong, where I work as a faculty of anthropology, even strongly criticize my position, saying that "Rohingya refugees have brought a big scope for you to do both research and business. If they go back, your business will be finished. That's the reason why you don't want them to return." This is the way how I face various forms of moral challenges and ethical discomfort while dealing with the host community about Rohingya research. In fact, this does happen not only in my case but any researcher from the host community working on the refugee might face the same criticism because the host community is not willing to host the refugees anymore. Besides, it is undeniable that the host community has to bear some costs for hosting the refugees in their locality everywhere in the world (Omata and Weaver 2015). Therefore, any researcher from the host community working on the refugees might be brought under a similar question which puts them in dilemma related to moral concerns and ethical challenges. The local community believes that I am an activist who works for the rights of the Rohingya refugees and against the interest of the local community. But I am a professional academic who holds a strong sense of commitment to the object of study. This is the way how academic and activist positioning always puts me in a moral challenge and an ethical dilemma as far as the Rohingya refugee research is concerned.

---

[13] Abdul Gafur is a local resident who is a business person-cum-politician. He is one of the leading vocals who talk about Rohingya repatriation. He sometimes leads the movement against Rohingya presence in Ukhia and Teknaf.

18.7 Conclusion

Refugee research deserves special attention, sharp sensitivity and great care from social researchers because refugees are usually forcibly displaced from their country of origin/residence and take refuge in the country of migration. Nevertheless, special attention and cordial care as such should not be in an extreme form which could be turned into an activist positioning. Since there is always a contestation between academics and activists in their roles, positions, interpretations and analysis (Briggs 2005; Grey 2013; O'Donnell 2018), refugee researchers should be careful between emotional attachment and professional detachment. It is widely known that the activist position is always subjectively grounded, and hence objective understanding is rarely found in the subjective analysis. Therefore, despite having deep sympathy for the object of study, academics should maintain a deliberate balance between academic and activist positioning in doing fieldwork and writing their findings. I do not mean that an academic cannot be an activist or an activist cannot be an academic, but maintaining an intelligent balance between the two is essential to conducting good quality research and producing relatively objective findings. It is more applicable in refugee research, because refugees are structurally a vulnerable group of people and a politically marginalized category which, in turn, put the researchers into different forms of moral challenges and ethical dilemmas.

References

Barman, B.C. (2020). "Impact of Refugees on Host Developing Countries." Das, S.K. and Chowdhary, N. (Ed.) *Refugee Crises and Third-World Economies*, Emerald Publishing Limited, Bingley, pp. 103–111.

Briggs, Senga. (2005). "Changing roles and competencies of academics." *Academic Learning in Higher Education* 6(3): 256–268

Choudry, Aziz. (2020). "Reflections on academia, activism, and the politics of knowledge and learning." *The International Journal of Human Rights* 24(1): 28–45.

Clifford, James. (1986). "Partial Truth". In Clifford, J., and Marcus, G.E., eds. *Writing Culture: Poetic and Politics of Ethnography*, pages; 01–26. Berkeley, CA: California University Press.

Croteau David, Hoynes, & Ryan Charlotte (eds). (2005). *Rhyming Hope and History: Activists, Academics, and Social Movement Scholarship*. Minneapolis & London: The University of Minnesota Press.

Denzin, N. (1997). *Interpretive Ethnography: Ethnographic Practice for the 21st Century*. Thousand Oaks, London and Delhi: SAGE

Fetteraman, David. (2009). *Ethnography: Step-by-Step*. London & New York: Routledge.

Falzon, Mark-Anthony. (2012). *Multisited Ethnography: Theory, Practice and Locality in Contemporary Research*. London & New York: Routledge.

Flood, Michael, Martin Brian, & Dreher Tanji. (2013). "Combining academia and activism Common obstacles and useful tools." *Australian Universities' Review* 55(1): 17–26.

Graeber, David. (2009). *Direction Action: An Ethnography*. UK: AK Press.

Grey, Sandra. (2013). "Activist Academics: What Future?" *Policy Futures in Education* 11(6): 700–711.

Gobo, Giampietro. (2000). *Doing Ethnography* (translated by Adrian Belton). Los Angeles, London, Delhi & Singapore: SAGE.

Hammersley, Martyn & Atkinson, Paul. (2019) [fourth edition]. *Ethnography: Principles in Practice.* London & New York: Routledge.

Leal, Debora, Strohmayer Angelika & Krüger Max. (2021). "On Activism and Academia: Reflecting Together and Sharing Experiences Among Critical Friends." A conference paper presented on *CHI '21: CHI Conference on Human Factors in Computing Systems,* May 8–13, 2021, Yokohama, Japan.

Love, Kevin (ed.). (2012). *Ethics in Social Research.* UK: The Emerald Group Publishing Ltd.

Malinowski, Bronislaw. (2015 [1922]). *Argonauts of the Western Pacific.* London & New York: Routledge.

Masud-Al-Kamal, Hassan Monir & Uddin, Nasir. (2022) [this volume]. "Researchers' dilemmas and challenges in qualitative fieldwork with climate-vulnerable communities." In Nasir Uddin and Alak Paul edited *Palgrave Handbook of Social Fieldwork.* USA: Palgrave Macmillan.

O'Donnell, Katherine. (2018). "Academics Becoming Activists: Reflections on Some Ethical Issues of the Justice for Magdalenes Campaign" In Pilar Villar-Argáiz edited *Irishness on the Margins: Minority and Dissident Identities,* Pages: 77–100. Cham: Palgrave Macmillan.

Omata, Naohiko & Weaver, Nian. (2015). *Assessing the economic impacts of hosting refugees Conceptual, methodological and ethical gaps.* Working Paper Series-111, Refugee Studies Centre (RSC), The Oxford University. Available at: https://www.alnap.org/system/files/content/resource/files/main/wp111-economic-impacts-of-refugees-on-hosts.pdf (Accessed on March 22, 2022)

Said, Edward. (1988). *Blaming the Victims: Spurious Scholarship and the Palestine Question.* London: Verso.

Sampson, H. (2019). 'Fluid fields' and the dynamics of risk in social research. *Qualitative Research,* 19(2), 131–147.

Sharma, A., & Gupta, A. (Eds.). (2006). *The Anthropology of the State: A Reader.* USA, US & Australia: Blackwell Publishing.

Stahlke, S. (2018). "Expanding on notions of ethical risks to qualitative researchers." *International Journal of Qualitative Methods* 17(1): 1–9.

Uddin, Nasir. (2011). "Decolonising Ethnography in the Field: An anthropological Account." *International Journal of Social Research Methodology,* 14(6), 455–467.

Uddin, Nasir. (2012). "Of Hosting and Hurting: Crises in Co-Existence with Rohingya Refugees in Bangladesh." In N. Uddin (Ed.). *To Host or To Hurt: Counter-Narratives on Rohingya Refugee Issue in Bangladesh,* pp. 83–98. Dhaka: Institute of Culture and Development Research, (ICDR).

Uddin, Nasir. (2018). "Ongoing Rohingya repatriation efforts are doomed to failure", *Al-Jazeera,* August 25, 2018. Available at: https://www.aljazeera.com/opinions/2018/11/22/ongoing-rohingya-repatriation-efforts-are-doomed-to-failure (Accessed on March 12, 2022)

Uddin, Nasir. (2020a.) *The Rohingya: An Ethnography of 'Subhuman' Life.* Delhi: The Oxford University Press.

Uddin, Nasir. (2020b). "Three years on what's next for Rohingya refugees in Bangladesh?" *The Daily Star,* August 25, 2020. Available at: https://www.thedailystar.net/opinion/news/three-years-whats-next-rohingya-refugees-bangladesh-1950253 (Accessed on March 12, 2022)

Uddin, Nasir. (2022a). *Voices of the Rohingya: A Case of Genocide, Ethnocide and Subhuman Life*. Switzerland: Palgrave Macmillan.

Uddin, Nasir. (2022b). "Research on Rohingya Refugees: Methodological Challenges and Textual Inadequacy." In Nasir Uddin *Voices of the Rohingya: A Case of Genocide, Ethnocide and Subhuman Life*, pages: 27–51. Switzerland: Palgrave Macmillan.

CHAPTER 19

Moving Research Methods to the Field: Challenges and Lessons Learnt Across African Contexts

Deo-Gracias Houndolo

19.1　Introduction

Data are essential to support any credible research, and when primary or secondary data are collected, simulated, or compiled, they are used to generate evidence. Hence, the quality of evidence produced through research is primarily dependent on the quality of the data used (AfriAlliance, 2008). Thus, it is critical to care about data quality and take necessary measures in that respect. Many factors can affect data quality, and they include how well and consistent the research methods and design were implemented in the field. In empirical research, it is not hard to realize how challenging it can be to remain faithful to methodological requirements in the field. This happens as the field itself is characterized by a set of uncertainties and challenges, namely the socio-cultural, demographic, agro-ecological, and climatic environment of the unit of observations from which data will be collected. The field is also characterized by defiers, never takers, always takers, and compliers. In the field, there are also persistent historical tensions, conflicts, norms, poor infrastructures, and so forth. Nevertheless, and no matter how challenging the field can be, any mismanagement or a failure to steadily and rigorously implement research methods can compromise study designs, alter data quality, affect the credibility of findings, and change or ruin the course of any research. In that regard, it is

---

D.-G. Houndolo (✉)
International Institute of Social Studies-Erasmus University Rotterdam, The Hague, The Netherlands

© The Author(s), under exclusive license to Springer Nature Switzerland AG 2023
N. Uddin, A. Paul (eds.), *The Palgrave Handbook of Social Fieldwork*, https://doi.org/10.1007/978-3-031-13615-3_19

necessary to know about the best practices in moving research to the field, the challenges that may occur, and how to mitigate them. That prepares researchers, young professionals, and practitioners to anticipate effectively possible unplanned shocks in the field.

As a policy impact evaluation researcher, with around 20 years of exposure to research designs and implementation in African contexts, I note how high the risk of failure may be in moving research methods into the field. Failure of field research would definitely affect the evidence and policy recommendations that would be made from such studies, and ultimately mislead policymakers whose decisions are informed by research evidence. Hence, the experiences and lessons learnt from different African contexts in general, and Francophone Africa in particular, are documented in this chapter as a contribution to research quality, to strengthen potential impacts that research evidence would have on policy. This paper is also meant to enrich the existing literature in that respect.

This chapter is structured around five main parts. The first part presents the background, motivation, methodology, and data used. The second part covers challenges and trade-off during fieldwork preparation. In the third part, details are provided on the process of moving research to the field and the challenges and lessons learnt at each key moment. The fourth part contains the characteristics of post-field work activities and how to effectively manage its challenges. The fifth part consists of presenting the issues and possible solutions in addressing the challenges that are specific to enumeration, baseline, and endline in the context of panel data collection or not.

19.2 Methodology and Data

Content analysis and deductive logical reasoning are used to process data from different sources, contexts, and times in this chapter. This allowed generating the findings that apply to each of the three main phases of field research: the preparatory phase, fieldwork with boots on the ground and the post-fieldwork phase.

Focusing on each phase, I extract data from enumerator training reports, pre-test and pilot phase reports, survey reports, daily reports prepared by enumerators in the field explaining the challenges they face, the adjustments with the initial methodologies, my personal field notes, direct observations, formal and informal discussions with policymakers, local authorities, respondents to data collection instruments, peers, and other actors who also play a role in field works.

With respect to the types of studies and contexts, I substantially draw data from process evaluations, performance evaluations, and impact evaluation studies designed and conducted in different African contexts (Benin, Burkina-Faso, Cameroun, Democratic Republic of Congo, Ivory Coast, Kenya, Niger, Nigeria, Rwanda, South Africa, Tchad, Togo, Senegal, etc.). In the context of those studies, the following types of surveys were conducted: listing, baseline, midline, and endline; including panel data surveys design.

In terms of sectors covered, the data used in this paper emerged from researches designed or undertaken in different development sectors, namely agriculture, water, sanitation, humanitarian assistance, rural development, gender, land titling, food security, social inclusion, peacebuilding, education, entrepreneurship, and so forth.

In those studies, I played either a direct role in the design or implementation, or an indirect role as a reviewer or a technical advisor. In that respect, the data that informed this paper come from different perspectives that I had while playing the following roles: principal investigator, technical advisor, senior manager, researcher, field coordinator, data quality back-checker, and enumerator.

19.3 Fieldwork Preparation

As far as best practices are concerned, to collect primary data and more specifically during impact evaluation research, it is essential to do a listing of stakeholders and run their analysis to know the parties, directly and indirectly, involved in your study, and their roles and interests considering the scope and timeline of the study. In doing so, one would work with different types of stakeholders: the funding organizations (bilateral and multilateral partners, governments, foundations, etc.), the commissioners (governments, NGOs, foundations), the organization in charge of the study, the data collection firm, the implementing organization, and the intermediary and other partners including (local authorities, potential respondent, technical committees, civil society organizations, etc.). Fieldwork preparation may be categorized into institutional preparation and stakeholder's engagement, technical preparation, and logistic and operational preparation.

In general, fieldwork preparation requires a research team that is at the centre of managing the ecosystem of actors. In that respect, it will develop, lead, and manage the institutional preparation and stakeholders engagement. During that phase, the team would make sure it complies with administrative and legal requirements in the intervention areas and country, but also towards its partners, namely subcontractors (survey firm on the ground) and personnel, and ensure that everyone is in line with legal requirements. Some of these aspects are covered in Mike Gibson, Ben Morse (2020) and in Preparing for data collection (n.d.).

19.4 Institutional Preparation and Stakeholder Engagement

One of the most challenging moments during the institutional preparation and stakeholders engagement is to submit the application and get the approval for data collection. In some cases, this takes the form of an IRB procedure. In other cases, it is a statistical visa that is issued by a committee set up for this matter. In certain countries, there is only a regular body to issue such approval or clearance for data collection, and it is only set up for health research. Hence, it becomes quite an issue to get an official IRB when the research is carried out in other sectors like education, agriculture, and development in general. This process can delay the start of research and its implementation. When survey instruments, sample size, and sample composition are required to obtain the approval of data collection, it adds to the risk of delay, and the sooner the procedure starts the better the outcome. In many African contexts, National Institute of Statistics issue data collection authorization, which can help reduce huddle. However, conflict of interests occurs in some cases as the National Institutes of Statistics also bid and work as data collection service provider. This may lead to a situation where a data collection firm that won a bid over the National Institute of Statistics is supposed to get data collection authorization from its rival. In such a delicate context, early engagement and communication help.

Another serious challenge occurs when the methodology proposed by the research team is not known to the members of the committee in charge of approving the fieldwork. The committee may then be reluctant or oppose the authorization for fieldwork unless the research team complies with requirements that may even distort their methodology (e.g. a requirement by the committee not to use money while that is a core characteristic of the methodology proposed by the research team). Such tension is common in research that involves an application of "game theory" or "behavioral economics", and data collection methods that involve financial transactions in the field. When such challenges emerge, they may lead to a serious delay before the fieldwork is approved and could start. In case the data to be collected are sensitive to season variations and other climate factors, this delay may negatively affect the whole planning. In some extreme cases, research team are denied approval for data collection, which causes considerable problems. Negotiation plays a key role in any of the above cases and helps to ease tension; hence, it pays off to take the necessary time to explain the methodological details of the concerned research and convince authorities to get approval for fieldwork.

It also happens that research teams negotiate or get conditional approval to start collection while in parallel they provide further documentation and details to answer comments and questions, and they address the requirements of the data collection visa approval committee.

In rare circumstances, the research is postponed or simply abandoned due to a lack of approval from the local authorities to go to the field and collect data.

Engagement with stakeholders plays a key role in the successful institutional preparation of field work. In that respect, mapping the stakeholders gives an overview of who they are, and documenting their roles and interests and the interactions in the system the research will operate allows to develop contacts and build alliances in the field. This approach is particularly important and effective as it helps the research team to be aware early enough of changes in legislation, rules, and policies with respect to research and data in the country of intervention. It also helps to learn about similar interventions that may contaminate the design in place. It also gives the research teams and their partners (including survey firms) the necessary edge during potential future negotiations. In this process of engagement, it is worth being critical and safeguarding against partnerships that may compromise research independence, create conflicts of interest, and eventually affect data quality, reporting, or publication bias.

19.5 Technical Preparations

Technical preparations to move research to the field are essentially about sampling design, development of data collection instruments, programming survey instruments, compliance of the research design with ethical norms, finalization of mapping and any other GIS materials.

During the preparation phase, knowing all the details about the research sample is necessary to precisely locate the units in the field. But it is one of the most sensitive and difficult steps in moving research to the field. The challenge is even greater in contexts where there are very limited secondary data on the population units (individuals, households, businesses, electricity production units, etc.). Research in African rural areas is particularly concerned with these challenges.

In case there is a strong technical capacity within the research team, remote sensing helps to constitute an initial sampling frame, but it remains limited. In case it is not possible to use alternative sampling technics when there is a lack of data, an enumeration survey becomes one of the most credible solutions.

Enumeration of sample units may be conducted either as a separate phase from the actual fieldwork or implemented right before data collection starts and as the first step. The decision, however, depends on the sample size, the time frame available, the resources available to the team, and the weight and complexity of the sampling design. For example, when research uses a weighted sample with stratification across a large area inhabited by a population relatively dense with irregular or non-systematic housing structures on the ground, it is less advisable to integrate enumeration within the fieldwork for data collection. Actually, when settlement is complex and not regular, the sampling approach may be well designed and still impossible to apply in the field. For example, planning to do systematic random sampling with a specific step (1:10 households) may become challenging, if not impossible, to implement when housing settlement is non-systematic and irregular.

To prevent sampling complications in the field, it is worth learning and considering ground realities during the design phase. If resources allow, a field visit pays off and contributes to designing a good sampling approach that can be implemented.

Data collection instruments constitute another important element of fieldwork technical preparation that comes with challenges and adjustments and teaches lots of lessons. Instruments include survey questionnaires, interview guidelines, checklists, and so forth. In this section, the focus will be on questionnaires and interview guidelines.

The main challenge with questionnaires is their length, clarity of questions asked, and the risk of endless changes that happen during the preparation phase with respect to their structure, composition, and format. While basic rules such as limiting a questionnaire length to less than two hours (for face-to-face survey) are known to most research teams, in practice it is usual and common to design questionnaires that require between 3 to 6 hours, with several rounds of discussions planned with respondents. Such a situation happens when several parties are interested in the research, provide funding, and list specific questions or domains to cover. This leads to having too many research questions, which increases the length and duration of data collection in the field. Similar reasons explain the length of interview guidelines.

To avoid the consequences of long data collection instruments such as too much missing data, half-filled questionnaires, high refusal rate, and poor data quality, it is necessary to run proper pre-tests during the preparation phase and learn the lessons. Moreover, it is important to take action after the pre-test and pilot phase and do necessary questionnaire pruning, reduce the length of instruments, and use "focused instruments" for data collection.

In some cases, it is required to translate survey instruments into other languages, namely local languages. The main challenge is in the consistency of terminologies that may vary by area or region for the same language. This kind of situation occurs quite often with African languages. While those variations are useful to know about and discuss with local language experts, good training of field staff helps successfully manage those situations.

Data collection in modern days uses either partially or entirely computer-assisted personalized interviews. They require programming the instruments in ways that allow using a smartphone for data collection. As a new technology, the availability and accessibility of strong technical capacities are limited and can become a challenge in some cases. This requires an adjustment to rely on remote expertise.

The complexity of the questionnaire and how respondents are selected may make programming much more complex than it appears. For that reason, "keep it simple!" is the main adjustment that seems to work. In the same vein, it is recommended to work with programming teams that are available, flexible, and dedicate due time to the assignment. Spending the necessary and required time to complete strong programming, including alpha and beta testing, and all the preparatory test is the way to avoid frustration, delays, and problems with data once in the field and subsequently. No compromise should be made at this stage to justify persistent bugs or non-compliance with the flow of the data collection instrument.

Remote sensing and GIS data play a central role in some cases. It requires technical capacities and skills in using GPS devices and GIS software (ArcView, ArcMap) and mobile applications (Google Map, Locus Map Pro, etc.).

Common challenges in that respect start when the study sampling design depends on the geographical data of the sample units. Such initial GPS coordinates can be collected during the enumeration phase, to inform sampling. Sometimes, secondary data are available and can also be considered, but it matters to make sure they are up to date. This requires a field visit mission and may take considerable time and could be labour-intensive.

19.6 Operational and Logistical Preparation

This phase of fieldwork preparation requires designing the organigram of the field staff, conducting a pre-test of data collection instruments, arranging a field visit to build contacts on the ground, and organizing the recruitment of field staff (enumerators and supervisors) and their training including a pilot survey.

Field staff recruitment is essential to manage things well, as high-quality and motivated field staff weigh considerably in the success of research in the field. In that respect, it is recommended to advertise the different positions to reach as many potential candidates as possible. This process pushes the research team to think in advance about the details of the assignments for each position to ensure successful fieldwork. The selection process requires to have a team that uses clear procedures and criteria to decide on the best candidates. Considering there is always a risk of drop-out, it makes sense to pre-select a few more candidates than required to compensate for any attrition. The actual number depends on the likelihood that people drop out before the fieldwork. That itself depends on the context including the employment rate in the research area, the payment rate, the incentives proposed by the research team, the duration of the fieldwork as longer fieldwork may be correlated with attrition, and the general context of data collection in the country which corresponds to check if there are other fieldworks taking place in the same period.

Managing the recruitment process to get the best candidate is always better. Note that best candidates do not necessarily mean the most educated, but it entails capable and motivated candidates who show interest in the assignment, grab well the methodology and survey administration procedure proposed by the research team, and who can make "smart" comments and contributions based on their experience and knowledge of the context, to improve the process instruments.

In some instances, research teams may not have enough time to go through the aforementioned process. In another context, they have an existing pool of field staff they trained well and have a conclusive work experience with. In those circumstances, field staff recruitment procedures are shortened, and the research team simply relies on its existing network.

It commonly happens that the field staff recruitment process is parallel to the pre-test of the survey instrument. In that respect, a small team of highly experienced enumerators is pulled together to revise, scrutinize, and improve the questionnaire with respect to its content and structure. The same applies to any other data collection instruments for the fieldwork. This may lead to important decisions on reformulation, cutting off or adding new questions, and so forth. This is particularly intensive when it is the first time that the instruments will be tested; otherwise, a pre-test may be less disruptive to the instruments and procedure prepared by the research team.

The second moment of a pre-test is the pre-test fieldwork and its challenges. In general, it is organized in an area or with observation units that are not in the fieldwork sample. It lasts a few days but requires good preparation and the right attitude to learn lessons that will inform the final strategy for the actual fieldwork. In that process, the management of respondents' expectations is probably one of the most important aspects to consider.

Data collected during a pre-test should be taken seriously and managed with due diligence as they will be analysed to assess the duration of the questionnaire, quality of the formulation of questions, clarity of question, and the understanding of respondents. It is also an important phase to assess programming issues and quality. A pre-test is the best opportunity to learn about the limitations and what to fix with respect to the data collection instruments, programming, GIS data, introduction procedure in the field, behaviour of respondents, and so forth. A pre-test that is well done is such an enriching phase before moving research to the field.

19.7 Moving Research to the Field: Process, Challenges, and Adjustments

Following the preparatory phase, when fieldwork is launched, the main objective is to collect data, and moreover quality data in a specific period. Though there are several persons with different roles involved in the field, everyone needs to work as an effective team.

Fieldworks are organized in social settings that function with their rules and norms that need to be acknowledged, respected, and accounted for. In other words, fieldwork should not disturb significantly how a community functions. Moving research methods to the field should be like harvesting in a forest without disturbing ''much'' of the ecosystem in place.

The process can be subdivided into the following key steps: inception phase, data collection phase, and closing phase.

19.8 Inception Phase in the Field

The inception phase in the field starts with travel to the study area where the data will be collected. The common problems that may then emerge during the journey include someone in the field staff forgetting to take an important document or medicine; the driver leaving his driving license and the police stopping the car, or the car breaking down unexpectedly. In case those problems are addressed, upon arrival on the site, it is highly advised to organize a formal meeting with local authorities to inform them about the mission objectives, the members, the target groups, and the duration. In sensitive security or political context, it is common to organize a different meeting with each of the key authorities, respecting the local hierarchy. This can go from the governor down to the chief of the village, from the mayor to the local police station.

During the inception phase, it may happen that some of the high profile local authorities are not informed of the mission in their area. In those instances, when the team arrives in the field, they are denied access to households and the authorities may refuse to welcome the members. Sometimes, the authorities are away when the field team arrives and none of their staff can authorize the mission to start fieldwork. Such a situation may block the process and prevent data collection to start. The first implication is the waste of time that could run up to a few days, which was not anticipated and/or budgeted for.

In other instances, misperception of local authorities who suspect the mission as a political manoeuver can create a tension that delays data collection starts. It also happens that rumours and misinformation about the mission negatively impact the perception of local authorities. For example, knowing that there is a gender-based session in the questionnaire where women will be interviewed alone and individually may be tricky to communicate and may cause problems. It also happens that due to existing conflicts among communities in the area caused by the object of the data collection, authorities oppose the fieldwork (e.g. during the implementation of a land titling programme, some communities may have had conflictual relationships and any fieldwork on the topic may revive those conflicts). Resolving these issues and being able to conduct the fieldwork may also take days in some cases. In some other instances, when someone dies in a community and people are mourning it is not allowed, or it is not possible to devote time for something else (including a questionnaire survey) other than the funerals. This may prevent any data collection to start on the planned day and cause days of delays.

These challenges culminate in a few hours to a few days of delay in starting data collection. In consequence, it becomes necessary to adjust the timeline. Adjusting the fieldwork timeline is quite a challenge as it affects key budget lines including housing, the salary of the enumerators, car rental, fuel, and availability of enumerators. In that respect, some enumerators would not be able to stay till the end of the fieldwork as they may have left their other job for a specific duration.

Addressing those challenges is not straightforward, and a case-by-case analysis could be the way to sort them out. The main lesson to manage the inception phase of fieldwork is good preparation. In that respect, it is essential to send an official letter to authorities at different levels and inform them about the mission, its objective, and the likely time it will take place. Always keep proof that such information letters were sent, and communicate this to all team members in the field.

It is necessary to have a budget line that allows facing unpredicted situations with the cost increase. This should, however, not justify poor planning and anticipation. As far as the budget adjustment is concerned, when it is really not possible to fully cover the idle time spent by the staff in the field while dealing with the above challenges, it is essential to compensate them in monetary terms to some extent. It also helps to reflect on such possibilities and how they will be managed in the contract.

19.9 DATA COLLECTION PHASE

During the inception phase in the field, the focus is more on coping with the general environment and context on the ground. However, actual data collection entails an engagement with the units of observation, respondents, and their environment. Requesting a guide is a common practice in areas that are not familiar to enumerators.

It starts with an informal presentation of the objectives, the expectation that the enumerators have vis-a-vis the unit of observation, the potential respondents, and approximate duration and anything else that is particular to the mission or potentially unusual to the respondents. This may include the use of a GPS device, recording a conversation, taking pictures, video recording, weighting children, and so forth. During this process, enumerators seek an informal approval, and it is only after that the respondent allows the actual questionnaire survey and data collection. Upon approval of the respondent to administer the questionnaire, data collection runs generally smoothly. Nevertheless, a change in the respondent's expectations with respect to the duration, the types of questions, and other non-obvious reasons may lead to a refusal of the respondent to continue or answer some questions. Sometimes, logistical constraints like no Internet signal, no signal to save GPS data, and low smartphone battery may affect the course of data collection. Unexpected changes in the respondent's environment like the sudden death of a family member or an emergency in the household are all reasons that impede smooth data collection. Though the following factors are manageable, they also negatively impact data collection: poor management of the field staff, enumerators getting sick, frustration between team members, and accidents.

19.10 CHALLENGES IN MANAGING EXPECTATIONS

During data collection, there is a dynamic equilibrium that needs to be managed between the expectation of respondents with respect to the question asked, the duration of the survey, and the conditions required by enumerators. For example, it happens that asking sensitive questions like intra-household violence, feeding pattern, and social inclusion may create a shock and make respondents reluctant to answer that specific question, and in worst-case scenario leading to a refusal to continue the survey. In such an unexpected situation, being supportive could be a different way to adjust to the situation and limit the risk of closing the survey and missing the data that are not yet collected. One could show compassion, explain the possibility to skip that question, and take the necessary time for the respondent to get back on track.

In other contexts, the duration of the survey is much longer than announced initially by the enumerator or longer than anticipated by the respondent who may cut it short. In such a situation, one may adjust by suggesting a pause and coming back later for a follow-up.

It also happens that respondents that are not yet surveyed become reluctant to participate based on their perceptions. This may be fed by what they hear from other respondents, the duration, questions asked, or other factors. In such cases, they may postpone the meeting endlessly or avoid the enumerator.

19.11 Challenges with Logistical Constraints and Adjustments in the Field

Paper-based surveys are less appealing nowadays in comparison to computer-assisted personalized interviews. However, both are still well used in the field and have their challenges. The most common challenges with paper-based surveys include the loss of questionnaires during transportation from the field to the "city". It also happens that enumerators get confused with questions skipping patterns and eventually mess up with missing data and/or collect unnecessary data that may be non-coherent. In those cases, it is difficult to identify and fix the problem in the field. A thorough check of data quality in the field is the only way out. More can be covered in Back Checks (n.d.); Data Quality Assurance Plan (n.d.); High Frequency Checks (n.d.). A high sense of responsibility of the control team help. In certain circumstances, namely during the rainy season, it happens that questionnaires get wet and the data collected may not be readable anymore. Similarly, the rain or dust on the questionnaire paper in some contexts prevents enumerators from using their pens to collect the data. Those factors can cause serious delays in the field and even affect the initial timeline. The adjustments to those issues may include drying out the paper-based questionnaire and using a pencil to take notes when a pen is not an option anymore.

As far as computer-assisted personalized interviews (CAPI) is concerned, programming bugs are the most common challenges during data collection. In several instances, they slow down fieldwork and may cause several days of delay unless the team programming is dedicated and fully available during the first days to fix any problem; otherwise, the adjustment can become chaotic.

For other common problems like Internet failure and a lack of signal to capture and save GPS coordinate waypoints or tracking, working with an offline set-up can help and is proven to be much better; otherwise, little can be done in those cases which results in data inaccuracy. In some contexts, namely in remote areas, the lack of electricity or unexpected electricity power cut may lead to no battery for most electronic devices, including data collection tablets. The way to adjust is to include power banks in the fieldwork material. When that option is not possible and devices run out of energy, an executive decision could be to pursue the data collection using paper-based questionnaires that would be printed in anticipation. The data will then be entered electronically later when the electricity problems are fixed.

In line with material and logistics challenges, in some rare cases, enumerators go on strike in the field and oppose continuing data collection and submitting the questionnaires and data collected. When that happens in the field, negotiation and mediation to settle the issues as quickly as possible help to adjust and avoid any deepening of crises in the field. Such a challenge occurs when enumerators' payment, transportation, or lodging conditions are not well planned or clearly communicated from the start. This leads to frustration and reaction in the field, negatively affecting data collection. Such a challenge may also happen at the end of the fieldwork.

19.12 Challenges Due to Changes in Respondent's Environment

Data collection takes place generally in households, businesses, health centres, and so forth. Those environments have their own dynamics that influence ongoing activities, including data collection. In that respect, sometimes during a survey, a household member may get sick to the extent that the respondent prefers to stop, cancel, or refuse to continue the discussion. In those circumstances, enumerators can only be supportive and sympathize. A successful adjustment would be to arrange another meeting to continue the survey when possible. However, when data collection is planned in a way that allows only one day in the community, this challenge is critical and difficult to adjust to. This may result in missing data and the replacement of respondents as an adjustment measure.

In some other circumstances, a whole village or community is affected by a death or funeral that could prevent data collection to start or continue. Similarly, other events like weddings, religious or cultural rituals, agricultural harvesting ceremonies, and political events may disturb the data collection plan. The most effective adjustments to those challenges include changing the initial data collection plan or travel itinerary and revisiting the concerned area when that is feasible. However, in case this occurs at the end of the data collection period, making necessary endeavours to collect the data at a mutually agreed time with the respondents or requesting the support of local opinion leaders is a credible option that helps.

Even though harvesting may not be a clear factor of the respondent's environment, data collection organized during the peak of harvesting or other farm or business activities may be disturbed considerably if appropriate measures are not taken. Such circumstances can be managed by adjusting to the respondent's availability including working at night and going to the respondent's farmland or business place if it does not compromise the quality of data that will be collected. This has proven effective and helped manage data collection effectively in many settings. Additional details can be found in World Bank Group (2017).

19.13 Challenges and Adjustments in Managing Field Staff

Effective management of field staff is one of the most critical aspects of data collection. It is so because it affects all the dimensions of the system on the ground. While everyone agrees with the importance of field staff management, during the implementation, several challenges appear. In that respect, coordination issues start quickly and manifest through enumerators, supervisors, and back-checkers not complying with the methodological rules or defying instructions. Any time there is such a trend, it is quite a threat to data collection in general and to data quality. It helps to quickly analyse the context, identify the main issues and actors, and address the problem (Gideon, 2012; AfriAlliance, 2008). It helps sometimes to have one-on-one discussions, remind the staff of the rules, and take appropriate decisions including hard ones. In case this does not help, one may explore the possibility to switch team members, between different groups if possible.

Health issues among field staff are an important challenge in some cases. When a staff is aware of the illness but does not report that before the field, it may deteriorate in the field and cause serious problems. In any case, going straight to a hospital helps, but a hospital may not always be nearby. Hence, having an emergency pharmacy box helps and is a sensible solution for some illnesses. One example is when an enumerator faints due to epilepsy crises. In that case, managing the emergency is the first objective. But afterwards, it may make sense to send the staff off the field for proper treatment. This may result in a delay to complete the fieldwork on time. The solution becomes a replacement of the sick staff or an intensification and increase of workload for the rest of the team.

19.14 Management Post-fieldwork: Challenge and Adjustments

When data collection in the field is over, a new phase of management starts. It consists of accessing hard copies of filled questionnaires and keying in data when a paper-based survey is conducted. In the case of computer-assisted personalized interviews, the process is about accessing raw data, cleaning data, closing normally the fieldwork, and moving on with data analyses.

This process is sensitive and requires a close and attentive involvement of the research team working with the survey firm (if applicable) and the enumerators (when necessary). The main points of attention include data coherence, the scope of missing data, the accuracy of unique identifiers of observations, and the accuracy of GIS data, notably geographical coordinates, refusal rate, and missing observation (United Nations, 2005). When everything has gone well in the field, this process of data quality check and constitution of a clean database takes a few days. Unfortunately, that rarely happens. The following challenges occur and are quite common. In some instances, enumerators go on strike at end of the fieldwork, which is different from the situation where they go on strike during data collection, protesting against low payment, not being paid as per their contract, or asking for better financial treatment. Such a situation could be caused by an extension of data collection duration without financial compensation to enumerators, a much longer duration of questionnaire administration in comparison to the version used during the training. This may happen as a result of additional questions, change in the structure of a questionnaire, adding more respondents to the questions, requesting enumerators to collect GIS tracking data instead of waypoints data as initially planned, and so forth.

In those conditions, enumerators may hold up paper-based questionnaires, or tablets with data not uploaded on the server, and in some extreme cases, or they vanish and remain silent to any call and endeavour to contact them. The best adjustment to such challenging issues is to prevent this from happening. But when it happens, the negotiation power is on the enumerator's side, and the cost may be high for the survey firm (when it is applicable) and the research team.

In other circumstances where paper-based questionnaires are used, at the end of the fieldwork, the questionnaires that are filled are compiled in remote areas, stored in boxes, and sent to the research team or the survey firm via bus companies, taxies, and other local means that are not necessarily safe and secured. In those cases, it happens that the questionnaires are lost, and therefore all the data collected that is not keyed-in. Similarly, the boxes could be mishandled, and water could be poured on them, destroying some pages of the questionnaires. This leads to data loss. When such things happen, there is little one can do to revert. If the data loss is too much, the sad solution left is to reorganize the survey again or give up the research.

When all the challenges are dealt with and the research team accesses the raw data, a data quality check is the following step. It is quite a straightforward process when the right expertise is involved. The result may indicate inaccuracy of the data for specific modules or sessions of the questionnaire; the non-response rate for a critical module (e.g. household composition roster), or high missing observations for a sensitive module (e.g. gender). At other times, GPS coordinates are not saved in the right format, and after their projection, some observation units are off-map and/or outside the survey area. These circumstances affect data quality and may lead to severe and costly decisions like returning to the field to double-check the validity of the data collected or re-administer the modules with poor data. When the data cleaning process reveals serious issues with the questionnaires of specific enumerators, their data may be deleted, and other enumerators sent back to the units in the field to collect the data again. When such decisions are made and implemented, they delay research and increase the overall costs. Sometimes, they affect the relationships between data collection firms /intuitions (e.g. National Institute of Statistics) and research teams. When those challenges occur, it is advisable that both parties make a compromise and take their responsibilities.

19.15 Challenges and Adjustments Vary by the Type of Fieldwork Implemented

One of the main and most critical factors that affect any fieldwork is to locate sample units accurately. In that respect, preparation norms, challenges, and lessons learnt vary if one is conducting an enumeration, a baseline survey, a follow-up survey, and an endline or a long-term assessment survey.

For most researchers in an African context, constructing a sample frame is very challenging, in particular for baseline studies, as there are very few data sets disaggregated (at individual or household or another cluster level) that are up to date and accessible. To some extent, national population or housing censuses are used to extract necessary data for the sampling frame. However, those data are either not up to date, are incomplete, or do not provide the level of detail needed by the research team. Hence, other secondary data sources that are credible and representative (e.g. DHS survey) are considered. However, they rarely satisfy the requirement of research teams. This leads to opting for enumeration surveys during the preparation phase.

While such a decision is optimal, it is conditional on the availability of an enumeration budget. When financial resources are limited and the research team happens to discover the lack of data and data sources to construct a sampling frame, fieldwork can be delayed and eventually affects study design and quality.

As far as sampling unit selection is concerned, three cases may be listed. The first situation is when a sampling frame exists and the units are drawn, and the survey is carried. The second one is when there is no sampling frame and the units are selected during the fieldwork, which assumes no enumeration survey took place before the fieldwork was launched. This happens when financial resources are limited and there are few details on the target population during the preparation phase. This happens typically for baseline surveys. The third situation is when an initial sample was already surveyed, and a follow-up survey is organized and required going back to the same units. This situation occurs when the research team is building panel data. It is typical for follow-up surveys, online surveys, and long-term assessment surveys.

As far as panel data are concerned, the initial and subsequent training of enumerators needs to be of a high standard. Quality-check procedures must be well developed and known to all field staff members. This is particularly important to deter enumerators from loose effort or not following methodological requirements. While training on panel data collection is demanding, it becomes more sensitive when there is a possibility for replacement under certain conditions.

Replacement in the sampling approach is another sensitive factor that requires much attention and training to avoid jeopardizing the research methodology and design. To ensure a successful and consistent implementation of the procedure, during the training phase it is recommended to sensitize enumerators on the consequences of doing random replacement and not following the procedure in place, and notably share the consequences of random decisions on the validity of the research design and the findings that would emerge from the data.

One of the most critical lessons learnt throughout all processes of moving research to the field is that the management must be flexible but firmly objective-focused, and "no panic" is the right attitude during a hard time in the field.

References

AfriAlliance. 2008. "The Handbook on Data Collection". https://afrialliance.org/files/downloads/2019-03/AfriAlliance_Handbook_on_data_collection_2018_ENG.pdf

Back Checks. n.d. DIME, Wiki. https://dimewiki.worldbank.org/wiki/Back_Checks

Data Quality Assurance Plan. n.d. DIME, Wiki. https://dimewiki.worldbank.org/wiki/Data_Quality_Assurance_Plan

Gideon, L., 2012. *Handbook of survey methodology for the social sciences*. New York: Springer.

High Frequency Checks. n.d. DIME, Wiki. https://dimewiki.worldbank.org/wiki/High_Frequency_Checks

Mike Gibson, Ben Morse, 2020. "Data quality checks". Abdul Latif Jameel Poverty Action Lab. https://www.povertyactionlab.org/resource/data-quality-checks

Preparing for data collection. n.d. UNICEF. https://mics.unicef.org/files?job=W1siZiIsIjIwMTUvMDQvMDMvMDYvNDIvNDgvODI3L2NoYXAwNS5wZGYiXV0&sha=6c9b323f32ae9785

United Nations. Statistical Division and National Household Survey Capability Programme, 2005. *Household Surveys in Developing and Transition Countries* (Vol. 96). Chapter X, page 189. United Nations Publications.

World Bank Group, 2017. "Monitoring Data Quality in Real Time". https://merltech.org/wp-content/uploads/2017/02/Doing-Data-Better-Real-Time-Data-Quality-Monitoring-MJones.pdf

CHAPTER 20

Entry, Access, Bans and Returns: Reflections on Positionality in Field Research on Central Asia's Ethnic Minorities

Matteo Fumagalli

20.1 Introduction

During the summer of 2003, the world was still trying to come to terms with the SARS pandemic.[1] In the middle of my doctoral research, I landed at Tashkent International Airport in Uzbekistan for an extended period of research in Central Asia. I was expecting some degree of health measures, though the toughness and racial profiling that took place startled me considerably. Representatives of the local health authorities stepped briefly on board the cabin to make an announcement, singling out the only passenger whose name suggested Chinese heritage. Asked to identify himself, he was then ordered off the plane and was taken away from the aircraft. Apart from the rather questionable health rationale of singling out a single individual in a 200+ passenger aircraft or the officials' display of power (which I, helplessly, witnessed), that experience served as a stark reminder of how my initial preconceptions of being

---

[1] Compared to Covid-19, SARS was much more regionally confined, with impact on public health and travel mostly restricted to countries in Asia.

M. Fumagalli (✉)
School of International Relations, University of St Andrews, St Andrews, UK
e-mail: matteo.fumagalli@st-andrews.ac.uk

© The Author(s), under exclusive license to Springer Nature Switzerland AG 2023
N. Uddin, A. Paul (eds.), *The Palgrave Handbook of Social Fieldwork*, https://doi.org/10.1007/978-3-031-13615-3_20

a rather powerless young researcher did not make me, in fact, powerless. Quite the contrary, my EU passport and citizenship endowed me with clear privileges, including that of not being regarded as a walking health risk. The authorities eventually checked my temperature and let me go.

Several years on, like many other fellow researchers, I had to take a break from fieldwork owing to the restrictions introduced during the Covid-19 pandemic. Being separated from family and living in different countries in Europe and Asia was a far bigger concern, but over time I came to realise I was also missing the excitement and the opportunities of fieldwork.

Travelling during a pandemic is of course different compared to what it was before, and all that we used to take for granted. Being able to move and travel internationally is another source of privilege for scholars of the Global North, made even more evident by access to vaccines (in general) and the 'right' vaccines (those internationally recognised), boosters and the vaccination status papers. Some countries, as they tried to protect themselves from the social and economic effects of the pandemic, found themselves unable to keep their borders hermetically shut for a long time. Uzbekistan was one of those countries, and by late August 2021, the authorities had announced restrictions on entry, for those holding citizenship of certain countries and with a certain vaccination status: not just double-vaccination but vaccination with Western-produced vaccines.[2] Previously mandatory requirements for quarantine and self-isolation were lifted. And so, I set out for an additional round of fieldwork in Uzbekistan, as I needed some data for completing a manuscript.

Building on the insights of feminist scholarship (England 1994; Fujii 2010, 2017; Mohanty 1988; Nencel 2014) as well as reflexive accounts in anthropology (Chattopadhyay 2013), sociology (Adams 1999; Tewksbury and Gagné 1997; Wackenhut 2018; Wood 2006) and geography (Chacko 2004; Megoran 2007, 2017; Ryan and Tynen 2020; Sultana 2007), and a small but growing body of literature in political science and international relations (Bliesemann de Guevara and Bøås 2021; Mac Ginty et al. 2021; Barnes 2022; Krystalli 2021; Markowitz 2016; Heathershaw and Mullojonov 2021; Fumagalli and Rymarenko 2022), in this chapter I seek to reflexively consider issues of positionality, focusing especially on privilege and (self-)representation. I try and tease out how my own multiple identities, roles and status evolved in terms of their effects on research participants, 'the field' and the process of knowledge production. What resulted is very much 'situated knowledge'. The main message I seek to convey in this chapter is that just like Lee Ann Fujii crucially observed, positionality is not static, but rather 'fluid and relational' (Fujii 2010). My relationship with and effect on participants changed not only over time, which is understandable, but also within the same country or locale. The

---

[2] Vaccination with Russian-produced Sputnik and Chinese-made Sinovac or Sinopharm has come with greater restrictions to international travel compared to vaccination with western vaccines such as Moderna and Pfizer.

'field' (or rather the fields) changed over time, shifting from 'scientific closure' (Markowitz 2016) to varying degrees of illiberalism (Koch 2013).

This chapter is structured as follows. In the next two sections I briefly sketch out those features of post-Soviet Central Asia that are more relevant to my research and introduce my research on ethnic minorities. Next, I turn to the multi- and interdisciplinary scholarly conversations on reflexivity and researcher positionality, focusing particularly on the challenges arising from conducting field research in authoritarian, illiberal and post-conflict environments, and this is most relevant to my own work. The remainder of the chapter focuses on three case studies. The first is about my initial attempt to carry out research on the Tajik minority in Uzbekistan in 2001, which ultimately did not take off. The second vignette is from a multi-site and multi-year comparative ethnography on Uzbek identity transformation and ethnopolitics in Uzbekistan, Kyrgyzstan and Tajikistan. The third and last vignette is about the Central Asian Koreans, also known as Koryo Saram, in Kyrgyzstan and Uzbekistan. My reflections on situated knowledge and my process of knowledge production were also shaped by some of the affiliations I had before entering the field and in the field itself. Some of these were tremendously useful in 'opening doors', as some came with various types of resources. At times, the very same affiliations at other times contributed to me being abruptly forced out of the field, sometimes for protracted periods of time.

Ultimately, though, as exciting as it often is, field research is also another form of foreign intervention and extractive activity (Barnes 2022; Malejacq and Mukhopadhyay 2017). This is especially, though by no means exclusively, the case of research on and with communities in environments heavily surveilled by the state. There, Barnes notes, inquiry 'can be a form of invasion we must also recognise the inherently extractive nature of our research and should tread with caution sensitivity and respect when entering marginalised spacers or studying or documenting life there'. To minimise the negative impacts of our action, it helps to practise what Soedirgo and Glas (2020) call 'active reflexivity'. To be clear, this chapter does not intend to be an attempt to display how ethical a researcher I am, nor is this a contest for moral superiority (Krystalli 2021). We all make mistakes, face blunders and failures and hopefully learn lessons that could be valuable in the future. Just as Kappler noted (Kappler 2021), the objective here is to share the origins (my positionality and multiple identities) as they shaped the knowledge I produced in the process, and make those structures and their impact explicit.

20.2 Central Asia: An Evolving and Diverse Context

In 1991, the Central Asian republics of Kazakhstan, Kyrgyzstan, Tajikistan, Turkmenistan and Uzbekistan were 'catapulted' to independence (Olcott 1992), as Soviet rule unravelled. While the drivers of the Soviet collapse are manifold and are discussed extensively elsewhere (Brown 2010), one important aspect was the role of nationalism and the tidal waves of nationalist mobilisation that emerged and grew in intensity and frequency in 1990 and 1991. The relaxation of control by the Communist Party of the Soviet Union and the launch of perestroika and glasnost under Gorbachev led to processes of cultural revival across the Soviet state. Grievances, often framed around national issues, could be aired, and organisations were formed to channel and represent them, challenging the incumbent authorities in the non-Russian peripheries as well as in the 'centre'.[3] As Beissinger observed (2003), what appeared 'seemingly impossible' up until 1990 and 1991, in the early months of 1991 had turned into 'seemingly inevitable'. Did the Soviet Union implode (also) because of centrifugal pressures? Was it a case of implosion from the centre as Russia pushed for breaking away from the USSR? What role, if any, did the republics and the nationalities in the periphery play in this process? There was considerable variation both in terms of the levels of nationalist mobilisation, and the impact these processes had on the disintegration of the Soviet state (Hale 2000; Beissinger 2003; Khalid 2021).

The Soviet collapse and the independence of fifteen successor states led to several simultaneous and daunting challenges for the new states and societies, ranging from the building of new state institutions, the formation and consolidation of new identities and the restructuring of economies in light of the collapse of the command economy.

Nationalism emerged as an important theme in post-Soviet, and - more broadly - post-communist scholarship. As local archives became accessible to international scholars, attention focused on the national-territorial delimitation in 1924–1936, which gave the Soviet Union and later the post-Soviet space its current boundaries (Haugen 2003). The territorialisation of identities and ethno-federalism were important processes in making Soviet nations and transforming pre-existing identities (Hirsch 2005). As regards more contemporary issues, scholars scrutinised the transformation and salience of national identity in the new states, with nationalism used as a source of legitimacy for the new elites, particularly in Central Asia where pro-independence movements in the late Soviet period were small in number and of negligible impact (Cummings 2012).

Identities were fluid and overlapping, and, in many ways, despite Soviet attempts to categorise and impose exclusive categorises, they remained so (Schoeberlein 1994; Finke 2014). The very notions of nations, ethnicity, majorities and minorities, and diasporas were fluid and contested. Borders had been drawn according to different, at times mutually conflicting, logics in Soviet times, and the Soviet collapse left millions of people stranded on the 'wrong' side of the border. Because of how borders were drawn (on debates see Hirsch 2000, 2005; Haugen 2003; Megoran 2017 about Central Asia), the

---

[3] Although the opposition centre/periphery has been framed as around the language of anti-Russian opposition reality on the ground was more complex, with Russian communities in the periphery too and non-Russians living in the Russian Socialist Soviet Federative Republic. The conflict was more political than ethnic.

making of ethnonational majorities also engendered the creation of new minorities, whose 'minority status' was as much demographic as political (in terms of diminished status). The mismatch between ethnic and political boundaries was of limited practical consequences in Soviet times. Whether one community found itself on one or the other side of the border became suddenly consequential when the Soviet Union fell apart in December 1991. Entire communities, over seventy million Soviet citizens, or one in four, found themselves, overnight, *at home abroad*.

20.3 My Research: Understanding Communities at a Cusp

One of my longest-standing research interests revolves around the study of ethnic minorities, particularly the processes of identity transformation and the politicisation of identities in the aftermath of the Soviet collapse. Identity transformation was not a process distinctive to minority groups of course. Majorities in those states and the co-ethnics in neighbouring stages were undergoing similar experiences. Under pressure from competing nationalisms, and with limited opportunities to articulate grievances and demands in authoritarian and illiberal settings, ethnic minority groups turned out to be *communities at a cusp*, not part of the new communities in the new states and not regarded as 'their own' from their co-ethnics across the border. I was also interested in the debates inside those communities themselves, without assuming that shared ethnicity would be the only type of identity for people or that shared ethnicity would shape preferences singly.

Post-Soviet Central Asia was then the main site for my research. Central Asia—just like the rest of the Soviet space—was home to large numbers of ethnic minorities. Some were settler minorities (Russians, Ukrainians, Belarusians), others were descendants of deported people in the 1930s and 1940s (Koreans, Chechens, Germans, Crimean Tatars, Meskhetian Turks, among others), some others were indigenous, but their minority and the cross-border location was a direct consequence of the national delimitation of the early decades of Soviet rule. Although the largest minority group in Central Asia were the Russians (or Russified settler communities as Melvin called them to better capture their heterogeneous nature, Melvin 1995), the largest indigenous group in the region were the Uzbeks, amounting to roughly 50% of the Central Asia population, with around three million of them settled alongside Uzbekistan's borders, but on 'the other side', in the neighbouring republics (Fumagalli 2007a).

Often portrayed as dangerous (Lubin and Rubin 1999), Central Asia, and particularly the Ferghana Valley where I spent most of my time in the field, appeared 'anything but' (for a critique of these 'discourses of danger' see Heathershaw and Megoran 2011 and Megoran 2000; Reeves 2005). Having spent some time in the region in 1998 and 2001, before starting my doctoral research, I had developed a hunch that alongside some well-established grievances, which might have—if unaddressed—sparked conflict and violence, I thought that there was a more complex and nuanced story to tell. What sparked my curiosity was that the 'diasporization' of such communities was not due to people moving across borders, but rather, post-Soviet collapse, the movement of borders across settlements. People did not move. Borders did.

How did people adjust to being at home abroad? What sort of relationships would they develop with the state of residence? Would they see this as their homeland? Would the states regard them as loyal citizens or potential fifth columns? How would the kin state relate towards their co-ethnics on the other side of the border? These were some of the questions driving my enquiry. I found the work of sociologist Rogers Brubaker (1995) on cross-border minorities in post-war Europe particularly insightful. Brubaker called this set of relationships between the competing nationalisms of the host state, the minority group and the external homeland a 'triadic nexus'. I found in my research that each of these players was, in fact, a complex and evolving contentious field. In other words, there was as much going on between the players and within them (Fumagalli 2007a, 2007b). They 'did not speak with one voice' (Gorenburg 2003).

Although my research interests have also shifted and broadened over the years, I conducted most of my ethnographic fieldwork on ethnic Uzbek minorities in Kyrgyzstan, from 2003 onwards, with the latest visit in 2019, and in Tajikistan, particularly in the 2003–2012 period. I carried out research visits to Uzbekistan between 2002 and 2006. There was a ten-year hiatus between 2007 and 2017, during which I could not enter the country (I expand on this later in the chapter). I have resumed carrying out research in Uzbekistan in 2018, with my most recent visit in October 2021.

Although the region remains, as a whole, an area of illiberalism, in some post-conflict environments (e.g. Tajikistan and southern Kyrgyzstan), there was a considerable variation in terms of the spaces left available for minority groups to express themselves, and for researchers—local and international—to conduct ethical and meaningful research on the topic. There was considerable variation in terms of political outcomes and dynamics for my case studies to be methodologically meaningful (Fumagalli 2006).

20.4 Positionality, Self-representation and Reflexivity in Field Research

As Scott et al. observed, 'fieldwork can be one of the most exciting parts of the process of social research' (2006, 28). Fieldwork is as challenging as it is exciting, as it 'also involves the negotiation of complex relations, interests, situations and logistics'. These 'range from application for research visas, request for official data, the negotiation of relationships with local host institutions and gatekeepers' (Scott et al. 2006, 28). Reflexive accounts of the role and positions of the researcher and their relations with the field have long been present in anthropological (Chattopadhyay 2013), sociological (Wackenhut 2018) and geographical (England 1994; O'Loughlin and Toal 2019; Zhao 2017) scholarship. Political science has slowly but steadily caught up. The handbooks by Bliesemann de Guevara and Bøås (2021) and Mac Ginty et al. (2021) are excellent cases in point, as they both contain numerous valuable reflections on the role and impact of academics conducting fieldwork in this field. Beyond research in violent settings (conflict and post-conflict), another strand of literature has paid close attention to the challenges of carrying out research in authoritarian and/or illiberal settings (Koch 2013; Clark and Cavatorta 2018).

Crucial in all these conversations is the concept of researcher positionality. Positionality can be defined as 'the relative position of individual vis-à-vis others, or how an individual is situated in society in terms of class, caste, gender, ethnic identity, sexual orientation and so forth' (Sirnate 2014, 399).

Thus, Sirnate argues, positionality is 'often a proxy for relations of power. Some people are more equal than others' (Sirnate 2014, 399). When researchers enter the field, 'they bring a set of competing identities, which interact with the identities of people in the field, creating several social and ethical dynamics that often inform the research project' (Sirnate 2014, 399).

Who we are, in essence, affects and impacts on research participants and the research process. Positionality is not just about who we are as researchers. Importantly, as Njeri shows, it 'refers to how researchers explore their situatedness and their multiple and shifting identities and how these identities inform research processes' (Njeri 2021, 386). Positionality, Njeri argues, 'is thus determined by where one stands about 'the other'' (Njeri 2021, 386).

Thus, attending to one's positionality also means acknowledging on one's privilege (or types of privileges) and showing awareness of how this shapes the research process. Privilege, inevitably, takes multiple forms and is shaped by the many intersectional identities we hold as researchers (Kappler 2021; Chacko 2004). As Kappler notes (2021, 425), 'privilege is not a one-dimensional thing: it can open many spaces, but close others', and what is needed is a 'differentiated recognition of privilege' and the disadvantages we encounter in the field (2021, 430). What follows, Kappler contends, is the 'ability to be able to conduct extended field research may also be an expression of privilege' (2021, 431), such as funding or the kind of institutional affiliation we carry.

The intertwined nature of our identities, roles and affiliations (with institutions in the field and those 'back home') raises the question of how we present—or represent—ourselves and how we are perceived: the question of assumed and presumed identities (Tewksbury and Gagné 1997), something especially challenging when drawing boundaries between researcher, activist or advocacy, becomes difficult and the lines blurred. Though the issue of self-representation can play out in several different contexts, the challenges are especially evident in the case of research on ethnic minorities. In her work in upland Southeast Asia, Turner (2010) conducted research on geographically dispersed and politically fragmented minority populations, undertaking research fraught with specific challenges, dilemmas and negotiation. Thus, positionality involves the recognition that all knowledge is produced in specific contexts or circumstances and that this situated knowledge is marked by its origins (Turner 2010). If one's positionality is 'inclusive of one's race, class, gender, age, sexuality, disability and life experiences' (Turner 2010, 126), reflexivity refers to the constant awareness, assessment and reassessment by the researcher of the researcher's contribution, influence or shaping of intersubjective research and the consequent research findings (Sirnate 2014, 806).

20.5 Reflexivity in Post-Soviet Studies Scholarship

Under Soviet rule, Central Asia used to be off-limits to international scholars, and to visitors more generally, with very few exceptions. One of the rare examples of extensive ethnographic work on identity issues was the research by Schoeberlein on Tajik, Uzbek and Samarkandi identities in the late 1980s (Schoeberlein 1994).

The reflexive accounts of fieldwork in the region, while relatively few in number, generate several important insights valuable to both experienced and relatively new researchers. Though the situations and some of the challenges are peculiar/distinctive to the post-Soviet context, many speak to broader issues relevant to researchers focusing on the Global South too. First, as many authoritarian countries tend to regulate the possibility of conducting research by restricting entry (through visas), it is perhaps not surprising that this also attracted considerable attention in the literature. Markowitz takes a holistic approach to the question, as he discusses both the question of entry/denied entry and the fact that even after entry researchers face enormous constraints accessing archives or speaking to relevant informants (Markowitz 2016). Authoritarianism in Uzbekistan impacted scholarly research in several ways, including 'the inaccessibility of archives, data access and availability' (Markowitz 2016, 895). Markowitz's experience was the experience of many, including myself, as we saw Uzbekistan drift towards closure in the mid-2000s. The closure meant denied entry (no visa being granted), but also other issues including the harassment of friends and collaborators, defied exit (until recently Uzbekistani citizens were required to have an exit visa to leave the country even for short periods). Many 'Uzbekistan experts' relocated, not just metaphorically, to neighbouring Kyrgyzstan, which was until recently home to a much more open political environment.

Scholars have reported serious challenges to the personal safety of local and international partners when conducting research in Tajikistan in the 2010s (Heathershaw and Mullojonov 2021), although others seem to have been able to continue field research (Kluczewska and Lottholz 2021). Even Kyrgyzstan has become an increasingly unsafe and challenging environment to navigate for both local and international scholars (Bekmurzaev et al. 2018). Overall, Heathershaw and Mullojonov note that there is a fundamental problem of 'whether to conduct research at all is that of how one is politically and ethically positioned once at work' (Heathershaw and Mullojonov 2021, 102). Dilemmas involve trade-offs 'between access and impartiality; permission, official approval and surveillance', and the choices 'between consent and overt versus covert approaches' (Heathershaw and Mullojonov 2021, 102).

Beyond just Central Asia and across the whole post-Soviet space, the dilemmas of entry have more recently confronted scholars working on Crimea and Ukraine more generally (Knott 2019; Wolff 2021; Fumagalli and Rymarenko 2022; O'Loughlin and Toal 2019). Ukraine had long been a relatively open and welcoming country for scholars, and Crimea itself had attracted considerable interest over the years (Sasse 2007; Hale 2018). As examined in greater detail elsewhere (Fumagalli and Rymarenko 2022), conducting fieldwork in Crimea has, until recently at least (following Russia's invasion of Ukraine in 2022), not been as hazardous as in the Donetsk and Luhansk People's Republics in the Donbas, where scholars have resorted to collecting data in other ways (Wolff 2021). Violence in Crimea was limited at the time of Russia's annexation in 2014; although the political and research environment has closed in recent years, dissident voices have left, are repressed or are self-censored. Crimea's political environment was in flux when I carried out field research in the region (Fumagalli and Rymarenko 2022). The question of entry into Crimea was and still is at the same time an ethical, logistical and ultimately also a legal challenge. Entering Crimea by air via Russia is currently illegal by Ukrainian law, although this is the only feasible way for non-Crimean residents to access the region. At the same time, the very fact that being in Crimea would enable us to observe Fujii's 'meta-data' (Fujii 2010) tilted the balance in favour of a visit. This was neither an endorsement of Russia's annexation nor an invitation to others to uncritically make a similar choice. It was a personal decision, involving serious trade-offs, and was taken after a lengthy and serious reflection.

Another question confronting researchers is the issue of (self-)representation, as discussed in Adams' account of her role as a 'mascot researcher' during her field research on culture and identity in Uzbekistan (Adams 1999), raising the question of how academics should introduce themselves and their research to the participants, and what is regarded as possible, legitimate or even desirable to say in a context when one's role is presented as that of a guest, with the expectations and responsibility—and privileges—that this status entails. Overall, what follows from a growing awareness of one's positionality is the explicit discussion of the impact of one's research (or intervention) on the data generated and knowledge produced. This is especially visible in Megoran's reflection on his research on the Uzbekistan-Kyrgyzstan border (Megoran 2017). As Megoran insightfully pointed out, 'who we are as individuals influence the data we gather and the knowledge we produce' (2017, 29–30), making 'the awareness of how we place ourselves and how we are placed' (2017, 29–30) imperative. As Fujii emphasised about her work in post-genocide Rwanda (Fujii 2010), field research, even in dangerous settings, can generate those 'spoken and unspoken thoughts and feelings such as rumours, body movements, silences, so material that is not clearly articulated in their stories and interviews' (Fujii 2010, 231), that we would otherwise miss by working from afar: the 'meta-data'. Fieldwork is often essential but requires careful reflection on the ethics thereof, prior to, during and even after field research is concluded (Knott 2019).

20.6 Case Studies

As Barnes noted about his research in the favelas of Rio de Janeiro in Brazil, it was also important for me to recognise my position of considerable power and privilege as a researcher tied to prestigious universities in the Global North (Barnes 2022, 9). In the 1990s, and even the early 2000s, it was still relatively uncommon for Central Asians to meet someone from Italy. What slightly complicated matters were that I wasn't even living in Italy, I was based in the UK (and later Hungary before returning to Britain), and I was not even just 'there' for tourism, but rather for research. Despite the relatively uncommon sight of Italians in the region (this was soon to change as the number of Italian scholars working in Central Asia grew exponentially!), the encounters never felt distant or dry, as there were issues that would relate and bond us. Italy was a 'known quantity' in Soviet times, but not perceived or construed as a threat to the Soviet order, although of course Italy and the USSR were on different sides during the Cold War. This allowed for the Italian language and culture to be widely studied at schools and universities, and for Italian films and music festivals to be screened on Soviet TVs or broadcast on radios. This contributed to making me 'legible' locally. The fact that this reminded many (well, those that could remember Soviet times at least) of times past, brought up ill-defined sentiments of nostalgia. That helped me in the sense that we could relate, through songs, singers or music bands we could all remember or actors in TV series. As a white male researcher affiliated to universities in the Global North, I always felt fairly autonomous in my movements and research in the region (with the occasional flashback of Adams' mascot researcher). Just like Barnes in his work in Brazil (Barnes 2022), although I was not able to reflect on how my ethnicity was viewed in the field or how it affected my research, I was aware that if I was at times indistinguishable, it was because I also could come across as Russian or more generally belonging to a Slavic communities, of whom there are still considerable numbers in the region.

Case 1: The Tajiks of Uzbekistan (Entry, Access and Exit)

After an initial summer trip in 1998 to get a 'feel of the place', I came to realise that I wanted to research identity transformation in post-Soviet Central Asia further. The city that most appealed to me for this was Samarkand, the over 2500-year-old historical city in Uzbekistan. I then set out to study Uzbek and Tajik languages as I completed my MA and before starting my PhD in the UK. It was a challenging summer, and not just because of the over 40 degree

Celsius. I usually spent four hours a day studying Uzbek at Samarkand State University and two hours Tajik at the Institute of Foreign Languages. Through my then teacher of the Tajik language, I was introduced to the local Tajik intellectual community which included journalists, poets, writers and a diverse cultural community. I started to attend the meetings at one of the centres and meeting points behind the Registan, Samarkand's main architectural landmark. My visits there became a regular, almost daily event. I was introduced to how local Tajiks maintained ties with co-ethnics in Tajikistan, Afghanistan and Persian speakers in Iran. I became familiar with the newspapers, printed in Dushanbe but smuggled across the other Central Asian borders (*Tojikoni Dunyo*), or the challenges of broadcasting and printing newspapers in the Tajik language in Uzbekistan (*Ovozi Samarqand*). While on the one hand, I was experiencing the vibrancies and struggles of what being Tajik meant in the early post-Soviet years, I also became acutely aware of the difficulties the members of the local Tajik community were confronted with in their daily lives. If by the end of the summer I had become acutely aware of how much importance many Samarkandis attached to their Tajik heritage, it was in a shared car journey to the capital Tashkent, where we were supposed to have a meeting at the local Iranian embassy, that the challenges of coping and survival were laid bare. Back then, whenever passing administrative, inter-regional (*viloyat*) boundaries, cars were stopped and the passengers were asked for their documents by the local police. At some point, I was the one holding everyone's documents, and we all started, with curiosity, to go through each other's passport pages. Many post-Soviet passports to this day have an entry (the fifth line, *pyataya grafa*) which indicates the passport holder's ethnicity. All my fellow passengers, whom I came to know over the summer of 2001 as extremely proud of their Tajik identity, had Uzbek in that line. Expressing one's own Tajikness has become challenging in Uzbekistan, particularly under the rule of first President Islam Karimov (himself of mixed Tajik-Uzbek heritage, as so many people from Samarkand are). Just like Markowitz observed, the 2000s were an era of growing challenges for scholarly research, and it became evident that this was not a topic that the authorities liked anyone, especially foreigners, to go around and ask questions about. I could still enter Uzbekistan for a few more years before being banned, but researching minority groups in Uzbekistan became more and more challenging for me, and for my research participants, some of whom had left for Iran, Tajikistan, Russia or elsewhere in Europe. The story I was starting to learn was about coping, survival and adaptation, but carrying out research in Uzbekistan, at least on these issues, was no longer possible, and thus I changed my focus. I exited the field and tried to move on, regrettably and culpable, feeling ashamed I was not able to tell the story of Samarkand's Tajiks.

Case 2: Uzbekistan and Uzbeks abroad (Entry, Access, Ban and Return)

In the early 2000s, on of my main identites in the region was that of a student, but as I started my PhD, my identity changed somewhat, as in local parlance (Russian) I became an '*aspirant*' (a doctoral student). What still had to be clarified was what would a foreign PhD student from a UK university do locally, what sort of data would I collect and what would be done with those. Everyone could understand what a student is and does, but ... research on ethnic minorities? What for and for whom? Starting from the late autumn of 2002, I was out to conduct a comparative multi-site ethnography on Uzbek identity and communities in Uzbekistan, Kyrgyzstan and Tajikistan.[4] Tajikistan was still a post-civil war country when I began to visit in 2003. Kyrgyzstan had experienced a bloody conflict between Uzbeks and Kyrgyz in June 1990, and another one in June 2010, so the country was, depending on the visit, a post-conflict environment or very much a conflict-active one. Entry to Uzbekistan has been typically challenging for most of the post-Soviet period, particularly from the mid-2000s onwards, including for research purposes. If an earlier entry had been facilitated by local tourist organisations (in 1998) and the university in Samarkand (2001), in 2003 my multi-entry research visa—I needed to travel extensively across the region—was arranged by the local Soros Foundation (formally, the Open Society Institute-Assistance Foundation) in Tashkent. The processes, because of the then status of the organisation in the country, contributed to opening doors and made my position legible and recognisable among local researchers and institutions. Little did I know at the time that the situation would change dramatically in less than a year when, in the wave of the colour revolutions across the post-Soviet space, Uzbekistan's president at the time would crack down on local civil society, NGOs and international organisations. US philanthropist George Soros began a bogeyman for post-Soviet authoritarian leaders. The Soros Foundation in Uzbekistan was closed, and some of its leading figures had to swiftly relocate abroad to escape repression. Karimov's crackdown on civil and political liberties was relentless, as evidenced by the Andijan massacre of 2005. In the meantime, I had moved from Western Europe to East-Central Europe. I began working at Central European University, then in Budapest, Hungary, in 2007. CEU was also founded and funded by George Soros. The Open Society Institute (OSI, later Open Society Foundations, or OSF) was also based in Budapest, and I began active and fruitful cooperation with its International Higher Education Support Program (HESP). My institutional affiliations (with the 'Soros network') meant that my entry to some post-Soviet countries started to become restricted, if unevenly so. I continued to be able to enter Russia and even Turkmenistan, but I could no longer receive an Uzbekistani visa. This lead to a re-orientation of my

---

[4] Over three million Uzbeks live in Afghanistan but do not share a Soviet legacy with the other Central Asian Uzbeks.

research to countries such as Kyrgyzstan and Tajikistan where it was still possible to conduct scholarly research. Having moved—and returned —to a UK university, and arguably thanks to a less controlled research environment in the country since late 2016 under a new country leadership, meant that I have been able to return to Uzbekistan in 2018.

My initial encounter with Tajikistan as a research environment was shaped by the time I had spent in Uzbekistan. I spent a few weeks conducting research in Tashkent, during which I listed to Uzbekistani TV and read local media. I had visited Uzbekistan before entering Tajikistan and had spent considerable time there. Over time, I had come to absorb the Uzbekistan state narrative according to which Tajikistan represented Uzbekistan's anti-model, its significant other, the place of chaos and turmoil, from where violence and insecurity could spill over into the island of stability, 'Fortress Uzbekistan'. This was relevant as in the summer of 2003 I was about to move to Uzbekistan's smaller and mountainous neighbour to its east, for a long period of research on the local Uzbek minority. I had learnt to be critical of state media, but still the image of the country construed and propagated in Uzbekistan was overwhelmingly negative, and ultimately my views were shaped by such narratives. So, with some trepidation, I set out on my car trip from Tashkent to the Tajik border. Inter-state relations had been poor for some time, and the border was frequently closed, often at a short notice. The Oybek border post had the reputation of being relatively 'easier' to cross compared to others and was open to third-party national, though Tajik citizens had long struggled to get into Uzbekistan. I had established contacts in Tajikistan, who had arranged my research visa and had arranged to pick up me on the Tajik side, so that we would head to Khujand, Tajikistan's second-largest city and the main city in the northern Sughd region. Although the experience was relatively smooth—especially compared to my expectations—I was repeatedly asked by the Uzbek border guards whether I was certain I wanted to visit Tajikistan, whether I was aware of the dangers and that Tajikistan 'was not like Uzbekistan' (the subtext was that while the latter was stable and comparatively wealthier/better off, Tajikistan represented the very opposite of the country I was leaving). A few weeks later, returning through the very same route and passing by the same border posts I was subject to rather lengthy health measures, set in place to prevent the spill-over of SARS into Uzbekistan. Whilst health precautions were non-existent on both the Uzbek and Tajik sides on the way out, on the way back into Uzbekistan the thoroughness of the checks was extensive. I did not object to the controls and the health measures per se, of course, but the message was that Fortress Uzbekistan and its people had to be protected and that Tajikistan was the source—or one of the sources—from where threats were coming. While these were usually articulated in terms of security threats (terrorism), it turns out that health security was another source of threats.

Being able to move and travel internationally is another source of privilege for scholars of the Global North, as many of us were once again starkly reminded during the Covid-19 pandemic. Some developing countries, as they tried to protect themselves from the social and economic effects of the pandemic, found themselves unable to keep their borders hermetically shut for a long time. Uzbekistan was one of those, and by late August 2021, the authorities had announced restrictions on entry, for those holding citizenship of certain countries holding 'full vaccination status' (Pfizer, AstraZeneca and Moderna being regarded as the 'accepted vaccines') would be allowed into the country without the need to quarantine. Previously mandatory requirements for quarantine and self-isolation were lifted. And so in October 2021, I set out for an additional round of fieldwork in Uzbekistan, as I needed some data for completing a manuscript as the country had introduced new policies in that area in recent years, and so I wanted to speak to well-placed informants, whom I could not otherwise reach from a distance. Anyway, as the Uzbekistani authorities boasted that the country would compensate anyone catching covid with about $3000, I took my Covid-19 PCR test and boarded the Tashkent-bound Uzbekistan Airways flight from London. Travel is a privilege afforded to academics of the Global North, and one that has often been taken for granted. Till Covid-19 and the restrictions to international travel that ensued served as a stark reminder that this is, in fact, a privilege and one that people can easily be stripped off, and it is an excellent illustration of the point that 'we inherently benefit from the structures in which we conduct research' (Kappler 2021, 421).

Case 3: Central Asia's Koryo Saram (Entry, Access and Detours and Discoveries)

The third and final case study comes from my research on the Koryo Saram, or the ethnic Koreans living in Central Asia who are descendants of those ethnic Koreans settled in the Russian and Soviet Far East and later deported by Iosif Stalin to the region in 1937. Overall, the post-Soviet space is home to about half a million ethnic Koreans (Fumagalli 2021, 2022), of whom two-thirds live in Central Asia, primarily in Uzbekistan and Kazakhstan, with smaller communities in Kyrgyzstan.

Compared to the other cases, researching the conditions of the local Korean population was considerably less contentious as the community is much smaller and the challenges they may experience are comparatively less politically sensitive. Unlike the Uzbeks or Tajiks who lived geographically concentrated in areas adjacent to Uzbekistan and Tajikistan, the Koryo Saram are a highly heterogeneous and geographically dispersed population. Long regarded as the model Soviet nation (for its assimilation, they rapidly became linguistically and culturally Russified by the 1960s), the Koreans also adapted to life in post-Soviet Central Asia. Their life trajectories are marked by multiple mobilities and similarly multiple strategies of adaptation. It was relatively easier to speak to government officials and members of the community about the difficulties confronting the community, as Koreans were not regarded as the majority group's 'significant other'. Members of the local community, for example from local Korean cultural associations, as well as business people, religious figures, market sellers and students were all eager to share their views on a community that is constantly changing, so access has traditionally been fairly unproblematic. At some point in the 2010s, I held a large institutional grant by the Korea Foundation (one of South Korea's main funding institutions), which required frequent visits to partner universities in Central Asia, as the project revolved around setting up online education focused on Korean studies. I was concerned that being perceived as 'someone that comes with a Korea Foundation grant' would negatively influence my relationship with participants old and new, as my already existing privileges would be rendered even more evident by the presence of this grant, with the risk (perhaps always there) that I would be given the answers that people thought I wanted to hear, perhaps in anticipation of grants. I was not in the business of grant-making, but my travels were facilitated by an institutional grant at my previous institution. I was careful to get the boundaries between my role as an individual researcher interested in the conditions of local Koreans and ways in which the study of Korean studies could be promoted via the grant. Despite my best and conscious efforts to keep the two issues and my two identities separate (and I tried to keep contacts separate), it was not always possible. At times I benefitted from my more institutional position in rather accidental ways. In 2013, when setting up the online education consortium in Bishkek, Kyrgyzstan, I was having meetings with various administrators of Bishkek-based universities, including the American University of Central Asia (AUCA), one of my then home institution's sister organisations (also partly supported by George Soros). I was looking to diversify my partners locally for the project and was advised to contact some colleagues who had previously worked at AUCA but had long left to set up a smaller university (the International University of Central Asia, IUCA) in Tokmok, a town about a two-hour drive from the capital Bishkek. The meeting itself was productive and the inter-institutional partnership continued for the duration of the project, but what I found more interesting was the side stories and contact that emerged, thanks to the visit that was relevant to my other research on minority groups. These were also examples of Fujii's metadata (Fujii 2010), or situations I only became aware of because of my presence in the field. Trips driven by new grants and projects led me to uncover hitherto unheard stories of peaceful cooperation not just between different ethnic groups (itself nothing new), but between some rather conservative Muslim communities living in Tokmok and the overseas supporters of IUCA.

20.7 Conclusion

In this chapter, I have tried to reflect on how my various and evolving identities and positionalities shaped my research, including my relationship with the participants and 'the field' broadly conceived. I used examples from three case studies of relevant ethnic minority groups in Central Asia, offering some degree of variation in terms of access and entry, and the degree of openness and closure of the local research environment to discuss my positionality.

Three main reflections follow from the discussion above. First, while my research and the ability to conduct fieldwork broadly followed the contours of Central Asia's drift towards authoritarianism over the past there decades, the extent to which it did varied considerably, not just over time (as Markowitz 2016 noted and I also experienced in Uzbekistan), but also over space, locally. Although it often felt less contained to conduct research in Kyrgyzstan, especially when coming from some of its neighbours, at times it also felt as I were part of a mass-scale international intervention effort, particularly in the city of Osh. Other localities, such as Jalalabad (also in the south of Kyrgyzstan), experienced a significantly lower international presence, and local participants were eager to speak, often feeling that they had significantly reduced opportunities to do so compared to fellow citizens in Osh and Bishkek.

Second, and partly following from this, positionality, just like Fujii pointed out (Fujii 2017), is never fixed. Just like our own multiple identities, it is relational, fluid, situational and context-dependent and context-specific. The way I was received and perceived in Uzbekistan and the other Central Asian countries changed as a result of my institutional affiliations, and in some cases, the very same at times opened doors and at times contributed to closing them. Thirdly, as I was acutely reminded by the ten-year hiatus of fieldwork in Uzbekistan because of my work with and for Soros organisations, and more recently during the pandemic, access and being denied access are forms of privilege (Barnes 2022; Krystalli 2021). Travel is expensive. During the Covid-19 pandemic the requirements to take various types of tests, to be able to show proofs of one's own vaccination and, more generally, the uneven and inequitable distribution of vaccines globally all served as powerful reminders of the structures and hierarchies and inequalities that, as researchers, we share and at times benefit from.

To conclude, the cases of entry, access, bans and returns examined in this chapter speak to questions of power, hierarchies and inequalities, and the structures and systems that create, underpin and perpetuate them. While some of these issues and dilemmas may be unavoidable (Bliesemann de Guevara and Bøås 2021, 277), researchers 'need to consider carefully the power they may represent to others in terms of access to money, publications, jobs or even just access point to the outside world' (Bliesemann de Guevara and Bøås 2021, 277). As Krystalli notes, this is not a competition over moral superiority or to show who is the most ethical researcher (Krystalli 2021). Instead, sharing the dilemmas of assessing risks, making choices and showing which ones benefitted us and which ones did not are all part of an honest process of 'acknowledging imbalances between foreign and local researchers' (Kappler 2021; Njeri 2021).

References

Adams. L.L. 1999. The mascot researcher: Identity, power, and knowledge in fieldwork. *Journal of Contemporary Ethnography* 28, no. 4: 331–363.
Barnes. N. 2022. The logic of criminal territorial control: military intervention in Rio de Janeiro. *Comparative Political Studies* 55, no. 5: 789–831.

Beissinger, M. 2003. *Nationalist Mobilization and the Collapse of the Soviet State.* Cambridge: Cambridge University Press.

Bekmurzaev, N., P. Luttholz, and J. Meyer. 2018. 'Navigating the safety implications of Doing research and being researched in Kyrgyzstan: cooperation, networks, and framing. *Central Asian Survey* 31, no. 1: 100–118.

Bliesemann de Guevara, B. and M. Bøås. Eds. 2021. *Doing Fieldwork in Areas of International Intervention. A Guide to Research in Violent and Closed Contexts.* Bristol: Bristol University Press.

Brown, A. 2010. *Rise and Fall of Communism.* London: Vintage.

Brubaker, R. 1995. 'National minorities, nationalizing states and external national homelands in the new Europe.' *Daedalus* 124, no. 2:107–132.

Chacko, E. 2004. 'Positionality and praxis: fieldwork experiences in rural India.' *Journal of Tropical Geography* 25, no. 1: 51–63.

Chattopadhyay, S. 2013. 'Getting personal while narrating 'the field': a researcher's journey to the villages of the Narmada valley.' *Gender, place and culture* 20, no. 2: 137–159.

Clark, J.A. and F. Cavatorta, eds., 2018. *Political Science Research in the Middle East and North Africa Methodological and Ethical Challenges.* Oxford: Oxford University Press.

Cummings, S.N. 2012. *Understanding Central Asia: State and contested transformation.* London: Routledge.

England, K.V.L. 1994. 'Getting personal: reflexivity, positionality, and feminist research.' *Professional Geographer* 46, no. 1: 80–89.

Finke, P. 2014. *Variations on Uzbek identity. Strategic choices, cognitive schemas and political constraints in identification processes.* Oxford: Berghahn Books.

Fumagalli, Matteo. 2022. 'The Post-Soviet Koreans.' *Oxford Research Encyclopedia of Asian History.* https://doi.org/10.1093/acrefore/9780190277727.013.635

Fumagalli, M. and M. Rymarenko. 2022. *Krym…Rossiya…Navsegda?* Critical Junctures, Critical Antecedents, and the Paths not Taken in the Making of Crimea's Annexation. *Nationalities Papers.* https://doi.org/10.1017/nps.2021.75

Fumagalli, M. 2021. '"Identity through difference": liminal diasporism and generational change among the Koryo saram in Bishkek, Kyrgyzstan.' *European Journal of Korean Studies* 20, no. 2: 37–72, 3

Fumagalli, M. 2007a. 'Framing ethnic minority mobilisation in Central Asia: the cases of Uzbeks in Kyrgyzstan and Tajikistan.' *Europe-Asia Studies* 59, no. 4: 567–590.

Fumagalli, M. 2007b. 'Informal Ethnopolitics and Local Authority Figures in Osh, Kyrgyzstan.' *Ethnopolitics* 6, no. 2: 211–233.

Fumagalli, M. 2006. 'A Methodological Note on Researching Central Asia's Ethnic Minorities: Why Studying 'Non-Events' Matters'. *International Journal of Central Asian Studies* 11: 72–85.

Fumagalli, M. and A. Kemmerling. 2022. Development aid and domestic regional inequality: the case of Myanmar. Eurasian Geography and Economics, https://doi.org/10.1080/15387216.2022.2134167

Fujii, L.A. 2017. *Interview in social science research: a relational approach.* New York: Routledge.

Fujii, L.A. 2010. 'Shades of truth and lies: Interpreting testimonies of war and violence.' *Journal of Peace Research* 47, no. 2: 231–241.

Gorenburg, D.P. 2003. *Minority Ethnic Mobilization in the Russian Federation.* Cambridge: Cambridge University Press.

Hale, H.E. 2018. 'How Crimea Pays: Media, Rallying 'round the Flag' and Authoritarian Support. *Comparative Politics* 50, no. 3: 369–391.

Hale, H.E. 2000. 'The parade of sovereignties: testing theories of secession in the Soviet setting.' *British Journal of Political Science* 30, no. 1: 31–56.

Haugen, A. 2003. *The establishment of national republics in Central Asia.* Basingstoke: Palgrave.

Heathershaw, J. and P. Mullojonov. 2021. 'The politics and ethics of fieldwork in post-conflict environments: the dilemmas of a vocational approach.' In *Doing Fieldwork in Areas of International Intervention. A Guide to Research in Violent and Closed Contexts*, edited by B. Bliesemann de Guevara and M. Boas, 93–111. Bristol: Bristol University Press.

Heathershaw, J. and N. Megoran. 2011. 'Contesting danger: a new agenda for policy and scholarship on Central Asia.' *International Affairs* 87, no. 3: 589–612.

Hirsch, F. 2000. Towards an Empire of Nations: Border-Making and the Formation of Soviet National Identities. *Russian Review* 59, no. 2: 201–26.

Hirsch, F. 2005. Empire of nations. Ethnographic knowledge and the making of the Soviet Union. Ithaca, NY: Cornell University Press.

Kappler, S. 2021. 'Privilege.' In *The Companion to Peace and Conflict*, edited by R. Mac Ginty, R. Brett, and B. Vogel, 421–432. Cham: Springer.

Khalid, A. 2021. *Central Asia: a new history from the imperial conquests to the present.* Princeton, NJ: Princeton University Press.

Kluczewska, K. and P. Lottholz 2021. Recognizing the never quite absent: de facto usage, ethical issues, and applications of covert research in difficult research contexts. *Qualitative Research* 1–17.

Koch, N. 2013. Introduction—field methods in "closed contexts": undertaking research in authoritarian states and places.' *Area* 45, no. 4:390–395.

Knott, E. 2019. 'Beyond the field: ethics after fieldwork in politically dynamic contexts.' *Perspectives on Politics* 17, no. 1: 140–153.

Krystalli, R. 2021. 'Narrating victimhood: dilemmas and (in)dignities.' *International Feminist Journal of Politics* 23, no. 1: 125–146.

Lubin, N. and B.R. Rubin. 1999. *Calming the Ferghana Valley. Development and Dialogue in the Heart of Central Asia.* New York: Council on Foreign Relations.

Mac Ginty, R., Brett R. and B. Vogel, eds. 2021. *The Companion to Peace and Conflict Fieldwork.* Cham: Springer.

Malejacq, R. and D. Mukhopadhyay. 2017, 5 April. 'Yes, it's possible to do research in conflict zones. This is how.' *Monkey Cage*.

Markowitz, L.P. 2016. 'Scientific closure and research strategies in Uzbekistan.' *Social Science Quarterly* 97, no. 4: 894–908.

Megoran, N. 2000. 'Calming the Ferghana Valley experts.' *Central Asia Monitor* 5, no. 5: 20–25.

Megoran, N. 2007. 'On researching 'ethnic conflict': epistemology, politics and a Central Asian boundary dispute.' *Europe-Asia Studies* 59, no. 2: 253–277.

Megoran N. 2017. *Nationalism in Central Asia. A biography of the Uzbekistan-Kyrgyzstan boundary.* Pittsburgh, PA: University of Pittsburgh Press.

Melvin, N.J. 1995. *Russians beyond Russia.* London: Bloomsbury.

Mohanty, C.T. 1988. 'Under Western Eyes: Feminist Scholarship and Colonial Discourses.' *Feminist Review* 30: 61–88.

Nencel, L. 2014. 'Situating reflexivity: voices, positionalities and representations in feminist ethnographic texts.' *Women's Studies International Forum* 43: 75–83.

Njeri, S. 2021. 'Race, positionality and the research.' ' In *The Companion to Peace and Conflict*, edited by R. Mac Ginty, R. Brett, and B. Vogel, 381–394. Cham: Springer.
O'Loughlin, J. and G. Toal. 2019. "The Crimea Conundrum: Legitimacy and Public Opinion after Annexation." *Eurasian Geography and Economics* 60 (1): 6–27.
Olcott, M.B. 1992. Central Asia's catapult to independence. *Foreign Affairs* 71, no. 3: 108–130.
Reeves, M. 2005. 'Locating danger: *Konfliktologiia* and the search for fixity in the Ferghana Valley borderlands.' *Central Asian Survey* 24, no. 1: 67–81.
Ryan, C.M. and S. Tynen. 2020. 'Fieldwork under surveillance: Rethinking relations of trust, vulnerability, and state power. *Geographical Review* 110, nos. 1–2: 38–51.
Sasse, G. 2007. *The Crimea Question: Identity, Transition, and Conflict*. Cambridge: Harvard University Press.
Schoeberlein, J.S. 1994. '*Identity in Central Asia : construction and contention in the conceptions of "Özbek," "Tâjik, " "Muslim, " "Samarqandi" and other groups*'. PhD dissertation, Harvard University.
Scott, S., F. Miller, K. Lloyd. 2006. 'Doing fieldwork in development geography: research culture and research spaces in Vietnam.' *Geographical Research* 44, no. 1: 28–40.
Sirnate, V. 2014. 'Students versus the State: The Politics of Uranium Mining in Meghalaya.' *Economic and Political Weekly* 44, no. 47: 18–23.
Soedirgo, J. and Glas, A. 2020. Toward Active Reflexivity: Positionality and Practice in the Production of Knowledge. *PS: Political Science & Politics*, 53, no. 3: 527–531. doi:10.1017/S1049096519002233
Sultana, F. 2007. 'Reflexivity, Positionality and Participatory Ethics: Negotiating Fieldwork Dilemmas in International Research.' *ACME: An International E-Journal for Critical Geographies* 6, no. 3: 374–85.
Tewksbury, R. and P. Gagné. 1997. 'Assumed and Presumed Identities: Problems of Self-Presentation in Field Research.' *Sociological Spectrum* 17, no. 2: 127–55.
Turner, S. 2010 'Challenges and dilemmas: fieldwork with upland minorities in socialist Vietnam, Laos and southwest China.' *Asia Pacific Viewpoint* 51, no. 2: 121–134.
Wackenhut, A.F. 2018. 'Ethical considerations and dilemmas before, during and after fieldwork in less-democratic contexts: some reflections from post-uprising Egypt.' *American Sociologist*, 49: 242–257.
Wolff, S. 2021. 'Enhancing the robustness of causal claims based on case study research on conflict zones: Observations from fieldwork in Donbas.' *Nationalities Papers* 49, no. 3: 542–561.
Wood, E.J. 2006. 'The ethical challenges of field research in conflict zones.' *Qualitative Sociology* 29: 373–386.
Zhao, Y. 2017. Doing Fieldwork the Chinese Way: A Returning Researcher's Insider/Outsider Status in her Home Town. *Area* 49, no. 2: 185–191.

CHAPTER 21

Doing Ethnography on Sexuality Among Young Men in Dhaka, Bangladesh: How Has Reflexivity Helped?

Sayed Md Saikh Imtiaz

21.1 Introduction

Ethnographic research tries to obtain a holistic picture of the study subject. It emphasizes portraying the everyday experiences of individuals by observing and interviewing them (Bryman 2004; Fraenkel and Wallen 1990) and by taking part in their everyday interactions. The ethnographic study can include in-depth interviewing and continual and ongoing participant observation of a situation (Thomas 1993; Jacob 1987). In doing so, it attempts to capture the whole picture revealing how people describe, define and structure their world (Fraenkel and Wallen 1990). The role of the researcher, therefore, is very important when conducting research incorporating an ethnographic design.

Traditional ethnographers research in a manner as if they are invisible! This 'ideal role' of an ethnographer, with the tendency to produce 'objective' research, was criticized extensively in the 1970s and 80s as the "ethnographer did not have to examine critically the subjective bases of the questions she/he asked (and the ones she/he failed to ask), the kind of data she/he collected, and the theories she/he developed" (Spronk 2006). Problematizing the idea of 'objectivity', a group of researchers demand a more critical reflection on the researcher's role in the research process, regarding the formation of data and knowledge (Clifford and Marcus 1986). Practising ethnography demands that

---

S. Md. S. Imtiaz (✉)
Department of Women and Gender Studies, University of Dhaka, Dhaka, Bangladesh
e-mail: s.imtiaz@du.ac.bd

© The Author(s), under exclusive license to Springer Nature Switzerland AG 2023
N. Uddin, A. Paul (eds.), *The Palgrave Handbook of Social Fieldwork*,
https://doi.org/10.1007/978-3-031-13615-3_21

the ethnographer in the field gets to know people and participates in their daily routines while regularly excluding himself/herself to reflect by creating written records of others' lives (Emerson et al. 1995).

In ethnographic research, a researcher needs to know how she/he can become an instrument of primary data collection; what Bryman (2004) thinks of a researcher necessitates the identification of personal values, assumptions and biases at the outset of the study. Aslop (2002) proposes that conducting ethnographic research requires shifting one's notion of centre and periphery and coping with the complexity of multiple centres within multiple peripheries. However, some have also cautioned about the role of the researcher and argued that the researcher's contribution to the research setting should be useful and positive rather than detrimental (Locke et al. 1987). Thus, the researcher's relationship with the culture and study context, and how she/he situated herself/himself within the study context, is very important in ethnography.

Van Grinkel (1994) remarked, that the problem of the anthropologist researching 'home' is how to get out of her/his culture, while her/his colleagues working in a 'foreign culture' struggle to get in (Van Grinkel 1994, p. 12). This initiative to get 'in' or 'out' is a must, as only then can one understand the degrees of 'outsiderness' created between the 'native'/ 'non-native' ethnographer and the respondents by temporal, geographic, demographic, intellectual or emotional distance from the field. Moreover, one should also know the deliberate stance taken by the ethnographer during the study. Both of these issues are important as they can reveal the process of identity transformation to the reader, which thereby makes ethnographic sites prolific for the mingling, multiplying and disappearance of various self-identities: those of the ethnographer as well as the participants (Chawla 2006).

As this paper's intention is to discuss how I as an ethnographer have critically used 'reflexivity' to define my role in my research on sexual practice among men in Bangladesh, at first I introduced the basic understanding of reflexivity. The next section has focused on the problems and challenges in conducting ethnography on sex. Then I moved on to introduce the reader to the study settings and people, briefly stating the methodology. The following section has elaborated on how 'reflexivity' has helped to resolve different challenges in the fieldwork. The concluding section has summarized the arguments.

21.2 Defining Reflexivity: Being Critical of Positionality and Subjectivity

'Reflexivity' in the simplest sense could be defined as being critical to one's subjectivity and positionality in ethnography. Alvesson and Sköldberg (2009) defined reflexivity as 'attention to the complex relationship between processes of knowledge production and the various contexts of such processes, as well as the involvement of the knowledge producer' (Alvesson and Sköldberg 2009:

8). So to understand reflexivity, we should have a clear idea about positionality and subjectivity and how these may impact our research process.

Marcus (1998), who has defined reflexivity in terms of positionality, depicts reflexivity as the practice of positioning, stating that it 'locates the ethnographer his or her literal position about subjects'. A researcher's positionality may depend on hishe/her identity and context. On the other hand, a researcher's identity may depend on gender, class, education, sexual orientation, race, ethnicity, age, language, culture and so forth. The contextual aspect may include the research's relation with the research context. For example, a researcher who is conducting research in her/his own society and culture (native ethnographer) would surely face different challenges than her/his colleague who is researching in a different society than her/his own. All these issues define a researcher's positionality and influence not only the data collection process but also data analysing and writing initiatives. Positioning helps an ethnographer explore certain human phenomena better than others while offering explanations of how different types of insight can be facilitated and blocked by life circumstances.

Positionality compiles an ethnographic encounter and writing to become experiences of shared and multiple subjectivities (Angrosino 1998; Rosaldo 1989). Following Ortner (2005), subjectivity can be understood as the ensemble of modes of perception, affect, thought, desire, fear and so forth that animate acting subjects; she also indicates the cultural and social formations that shape, organize and provoke those modes of affect, thought and so on (Ibid., p. 31). She further states that subjectivity deals with the problem of domination and freedom between the subjection of the subject and the subject's agency. She considers subjectivity as "the basis of 'agency', a necessary part of understanding how people (try to) act on the world even as they are acted upon" (Ortner 2005, p. 34). Ortner gives more room to the agency as she thinks actors are bound but choosing, constrained but transforming, both strategically manipulating and unconscious of the frames within which they move (Ortner 1996).

As reflexivity may help a researcher to become aware of her/his biases or relative advantages because of his positionality and subjectivity, it can also help her/him to become a better 'instrument' in conducting ethnographic research and writing. Frederick Steier (1991, p. 3) argued that reflexivity involves an ethnographer being aware of her/his research activities, telling a story about herself/himself. Therefore, Steier (ibid., p. 4) thinks reflexivity helps a researcher to depart from linear understandings of subject-object relations and embed her/him with the research field embodying the research process.[1]

Typical ethnographic research employs three kinds of data collection: interviews, observation and documents. This, in turn, produces three kinds of data: quotations, descriptions and excerpts of documents, resulting in one product: narrative description. This narrative often includes charts, diagrams and

---

[1] Steier, F. 1991. Research and Reflexivity. London: Sage.

additional artefacts that help to tell 'the story' (Hammersley 1990). An ethnographer could surely make her/his 'stories' or ethnographic accounts reliable if she/he could give the readers a better understanding of how she/he becomes reflexive to overcome possible biases. However, for any ethnographic account of sexual practice, giving detailed accounts of positionality and subjectivity becomes very difficult for several reasons.

21.3 Reflexivity in Ethnography on Sexual Practice: Key Challenges

Reflexivity, more specifically critical reflexive approaches to sexuality have become a rich site of substantive inquiry and scholarly production in anthropology (Elliston 2005).[2] This scholarship has significantly contributed to "research methodology (including the dynamics of fieldwork), pedagogy, and problematics in the politics of representation, ethnographic and otherwise" (ibid., p. 21). As Eliston argued, there is no doubt that the 'reflexive turn' in the late 1980s (Clifford and Marcus 1986; Marcus and Fischer 1986) has given legitimacy to be reflexive about sex and sexuality as a mode of theorizing and foregrounding problems with the self/other binary (ibid., p. 22). However, Blackwood and Wieringa (1997) argued what constitutes sex varies dramatically across cultural and social contexts.[3] Therefore, in the case of Bangladesh, the understanding of sex and sexuality among young men requires special attention before moving into any further discussion.

In Bangladesh, generally talking about sex is interesting to young men as long as you do not ask about very personal, sensitive sexual practices. For example, a male informant Ashique (pseudonym) from the lower socio-economic background, 25 years of age, from Dhaka, from my first fieldwork in 2006, stated after three months of friendship with me:

> Open Sex is a taboo, and so is talking about sexuality openly, even though it's regarding HIV/AIDS. We are Muslims, but still being young men we have a lot of dirty little secrets. I know you do have also. But if I ask will you reveal that to me? I know you will not. No one wants to lose his prestige.

What kind of act is considered a sex act, and what kind of sexual practices one considers as personal and sensitive, however, varies dramatically from group to group, and even sometimes from person to person. To some young men it is somehow prestigious to speak about very intimate sexual practices, while to others it is shameful; certainly it depends on the context and people involved in such discussions. I think that the notion of how 'prestige' and 'shame' are constituted and how far these influence one's discursive openness regarding

---

[2] See Deborah Eliston, Critical Reflexivity andn Sexual Studies in Anthropology: Siting Sexuality in Research, Theory. Ethnography, and Pedagogy, Reviews in Anthropology, 34: 21–47, 2005.
[3] See also Boellstorff (2005), Carrillo (2002), Blackwood and Wieringa (1997).

sexuality should also be understood in the broader context of sexuality politics in any given context.

Here sexual politics should not be read as only the politics of identity construction; rather, far beyond that, it is a 'social mechanism' to govern the everyday life of a community and of an individual in 'socially and culturally acceptable'[4] ways. All of the young men in Dhaka, Bangladesh, with whom I was concerned as part of the study, expressed the same attitude as Asique (pseudonym) in individual interview sessions. It seemed that the norms and attitudes in public have not changed at all. There are many ways to read this attitude; one such way might be to take it as a 'hegemonic masculine' attitude of not surrendering to another; thus, the discussion of sexuality can start only if the parties involved in the discussion share the same masculine attitude and have had similar sexual experiences in the discussed case. There are hundreds of similar examples in both of my fieldworks from which I can infer that at least in the context of Dhaka, as far as sexual politics is involved, one cannot escape gender issues, and how masculinities and femininities are constructed and influence sexuality. The statement—that sexuality is not openly discussed—also partly reveals the mainstream attitude regarding sexuality; at least in public, talking about sexuality is not desirable. Asique's statement also possibly indicates the massive presence of 'dirty little secrets' among young men ("that all we have…").

Thus, this very brief statement might raise a set of questions in the mind of a conscious reader; why does the young man consider talking about sexuality even with another man, as taboo? Is it the socially acceptable and desirable way to respond to such a situation, or is it because the researcher has failed to establish a good rapport with the informant? If the former is correct, then how are such socially acceptable or desirable rules governed? Does the phrase 'we all have dirty little secrets' indicate a massive presence of 'undesirable' sexual practices among young men in general in the country? If so, what are they and how can they be explained in relation to Islam ("We are Muslims…") as a religion, gender issues and the sexual politics in the country as a whole? But to me, the most striking was the question posed by Asique: "We are Muslims, but still being young men we have a lot of dirty little secrets. I know you do have also. But if I ask will you reveal that to me? I know you will not."

This question and the corresponding answer by the questioner himself not only make me a part of the researched group but also confirms that my experiences and reactions are similar to those constituting that group—Muslim

---

[4] By *culture* I indicate a set of representations and principles which can be indicated that consciously organize the different aspects of social life, together with the set of 'positive' and 'negative' norms and the values that are connected with these ways of acting and thinking. Whereas by *society* one can understand a set of individuals and groups who interact on the basis of common rules and values which govern their acting and thinking, and who regard themselves as belonging to the same 'whole,' which they must reproduce as they pursue their own self-interest. Moreover this objective social whole, this community recognized as such, as well as this particular intersubjective culture, are already there in existence and active at the birth of each individual.

'heterosexual' young men in Dhaka with a lot of 'dirty little secrets.' Why does a young man with a different socio-economic background, and without knowing about any of my personal experiences, almost confirms my 'dirty little secrets'? This question also posits a very important methodological concern regarding my own subjectivity as a researcher. In fact, because of such complexities in a relationship in ethnography with the respondents, a researcher must be aware of his own positionality and subjectivity. There is no doubt that dealing with subjectivity and positionality also needs to be substantiated by corresponding data collection methods specifically when conducting research on sexual practices. Nevertheless, giving a 'thick description' of the subjective experiences to conduct the ethnographic fieldwork can ensure an alternative to the 'objectivity' of positivist research methodology while ensuring the reliability of the study.

21.4 Introducing the Study: Location, Actors and Methodology

The Study Location

The study was conducted in Dhaka, the capital city of Bangladesh, as part of two projects. The first one was my PhD research, while the second one was my postdoctoral research. Both of the studies have the main objective to understand the sexual practices of young Muslim heterosexual men. Dhaka has ranked the sixth most populous city in the world with a density of 23,234 people per square kilometer. Dhaka city, about 300 square kilometers, has seen a 3.39% increase in population from 2021. According to the latest population and housing census, preliminary report 1, 02, 78,882 people were living in Dhaka—1.5 times higher than 69,70,105 in 2011 (BBS 2022). Khaleda et al. (2017) observed that the urban land use/cover change results revealed that built-up land increased over 10 times (from about 11.6 to 118 km^2) between 1989 and 2014, and the simulated urban land use/cover changes indicated that built-up areas would increase to approximately 169.7 km^2 by 2030. According to the World Bank (2007, p. 17), its population was around 12 million in 2007. As the financial, commercial and entertainment core of the country, Dhaka accounts for up to 35% of the country's economy and generates one-third of the GDP (ibid.). This major beta city holds one-third of total employment in the country. As the capital of the country, Dhaka is basically a place where youth from all over the country come to look for their livelihoods. The youth community in Dhaka—the largest in the country—comprises different religious, economic, occupational, educational and social backgrounds.

It is literally impossible to conduct ethnographic work covering the whole city; however, to start the fieldwork I chose six different locations on the basis of their socio-economic and demographic characteristics. In time, I gradually visited the various sites of interest of the informants, which included different corners of the city, and even the country. In order to reach the educated young men from higher and middle socio-economic backgrounds, I chose two universities—Dhaka University and North South University. To include married 'educated' and 'illetterate' or less literate young men of higher and middle socio-economic background who are engaged in business, young men from the Old Town (Puran Dhaka) and Gulshan were targeted. The Old Town was the business heart of Dhaka in the last century, with the famous river port of the city. These days it has become the place of 'stock business,' from where different kinds of goods are supplied to all over the country, and most of the businesses here are owned by illiterate or less educated people. On the other hand, Gulshan is a relatively newly developed urban centre for the elite and educated.

People from lower socio-economic background were accessed from the Kamrangirchar and Satarkul (Badda). Although situated in two different corners of the city, they are mainly inhabited by lower socio-economic background people who are poor, illiterate and mostly live on daily earnings in *bastis* (shanty towns). As my rapport with the youth increased gradually and I got access to their sites of sexual interest, after a few months the whole city became the area of this study, due to the fact that their sites of interest regarding sexuality were located in other areas than where they stayed in most cases.

The Actors

The informants in this research are mostly 'heterosexual young men' aged 15–24 years.[5] However, for the purpose of the group discussions, both young men and women were included in some cases. These informants were chosen based on socio-economic and educational background. For the 'case study' and 'life history' phases, only young men were recruited. For these phases, informants were selected based on socio-economic background, age, education and marital status. These sub-divisions helped to make the research more focused from the beginning to grasp *intersection lines* of masculinities and sexual practices about economic status, education, age and marital status. The other actors included INGO, government and NGO officials of different levels. I also interviewed some elderly women and men who were the family members of the respondents to get a more in-depth understanding of different aspects of the young men's family life, and some female sex workers, male sex workers and *hijras* who were sexual partners of the young men, to get more information about their sexual life and also to triangulate the data I gathered.

---

[5] Young men are defined as between the ages of 15 and 24 following the UN definition made for International Youth Year, held around the world in 1985. See: https://www.un.org/en/global-issues/youth. Accessed 30 December 2021.

The Research Design

The core of the research design for this study is based on an ethnographic research tradition. Like any other ethnographic research (Bryman 2004; Fraenkel and Wallen 1990), this study intended to obtain a holistic picture of the sexual life of young men, with an emphasis on portraying the everyday experiences of individuals by observing and interviewing them. Following Thomas (1993) and Jacob (1987), in this study, I included in-depth interviewing and continual and ongoing participant observation of the young men's sexual practices while trying to capture the whole picture of their sexual practices as revealed and described by the young men to understand how they 'structure their world'. Moreover, I have combined several other methods, including group discussion (i.e. focus group discussions (FGDs) and participatory group discussion), informal interviews, in-depth interviews, case studies and life histories, together with discourse analysis, to produce the 'narrative description' of the lives of young men.

Data collection was completed in three phases. In the first phase, using FGDs, key informants were identified; in the second phase, these key informants were interviewed; using snowball sampling, more key informants were identified who were interviewed in the last phase using life history interviews to get more in-depth information. In all these three phases, participant observation was continuous. Though I discuss the different methods and tools used in this research below, the following Table 21.1 states a brief rationale for using different tools, which may help to understand the research design more thoroughly.

For participant observation, during the fieldwork, I repeatedly visited the research locations, initially located in the six different places of the city. At the beginning of the study, these visits were limited to the purpose of becoming familiar with the people and establishing rapport. I took participatory group discussions and FGDs as ways to establish rapport with the local people. With the help of a research assistant, I organized three group discussions at each site and gave preference to inviting young men who had more leisure time to spend with us. During the FGDs, I chose key respondents for the next phase to provide case studies. Initially, I had six key informants, one from each site, who assisted me in becoming involved with the local young men and conducting informal interviews to recruit more.

From these young men, I chose twenty informants for the case studies. While doing case studies, I built up an individual rapport with them that enabled me to take part in their daily activities as much as possible. These activities included going to 'sexual places' such as night-clubs and student dormitories, 'hanging out' in different places, watching movies, watching traditional dramas and so forth. Thus, the participant observation started with a much-generalized understanding of different locations (in Phase I), and gradually became more focused in relation to the study objectives following the individual (in Phase II). The observation was reversed in the life history phase (Phase III), where the focus shifted from the individual to the contextual.

Table 21.1 Fieldwork phases, purposes and rationale for using methods and tools

Phase	Methods/Tools	Purposes	Rationale for using the tool/s
Phase I Exploratory phase	FGDs Participatory group discussions Participant observation	To refine and correct the checklist for the interviews. To become familiar with the people and study locations. To recruit key informants.	Group discussions can help to generate a substantial amount of data within a very short period of time.
Phase II Case study phase	Case studies In-depth open-ended interviews Participant observation	To gather data following the checklists and add additional issues in the checklist for the next phase. To check the generalizing patterns of data emerging from the group discussions. To know better about the people and to establish rapport. To get in-depth information on data gathered during group discussions.	These tools can help to explore undefined domains in the formative conceptual model, identify new models, break down domains into component factors and sub-factors and obtain orienting information about the context and history of the study and study site.
Phase III Life history phase	Life history interviews (Participant observation)	To collect in-depth data. To get insights on the study topics.	This tool can help to understand one life across time, and how individual lives interact with the whole.[a]

[a] See Atkinson (1998) for a detailed discussion on life history interviews

Table 21.2 shows different dimensions of the participant observations in relation to the present study.

I used two different types of group discussions: participatory and focused. Participatory research is not a new concept, having emerged in the 1960s (Hardon 1998). Borrowing this concept to make the group discussions more participatory, I used a short video documentary titled *Our Boys* made by a Bangladeshi short film producer, in which the life history of a boy from middle socio-economic status was narrated. In most cases, I used my laptop to show the documentary, and afterwards I invited the viewers to discuss

Table 21.2 Dimensions of participant observations in relation to the present study

Dimensions	My position	Rationale
Role of the observer	Any of these four roles depending on the situation: Complete participant Participant as observer Observer as participant Complete observer	Ensure reliability, subjectivity, flexibility and adaptability in the research settings.
Portrayal of role to others	In between overt observations and covert observations.	Ensure subjectivity and adaptability. For example, in those cases where I needed informants to read and comment on the data, I had to inform them about the role, whereas in some cases informing them about the role simply increased the stigma and made the job of getting information on sexual practices more difficult.
Portrayal of study purpose to others	Partial or full explanations.	As above.
Duration of observation	Long-term multiple observations.	To come up with a holistic picture.
Focus of observation	Gradually from broad to narrow, then narrow to broad.	To understand how context shapes individual lives and how an individual places himself/herself in context or influences context.

masculinity—the theme of the short film—in relation to their own life.[6] Sometimes I also used a popular movie song that had some lyrics on masculinity to initiate discussion,[7] which gradually resulted in discussions on sexuality.

Where screening of the documentary was not possible, FGDs were conducted. Participatory group discussions were conducted with mixed types of people, whereas for FGDs groups were formed on the basis of economic status, age and educational background. The focus of the FGDs and participatory group discussions was to grasp their views on different forms of masculinities and processes of embodying different forms of masculinities and to identify 'hegemonic forms' and 'marginal forms,' ideal code of conduct (determined by society) for sexual practices, preferred codes of conduct for sexual practices with respect to socio-economic background and so forth. I chose those young

---

[6] Amader Chhelera (Our Boys), a documentary made by Manzare Hassin, is a short film where a pop group and a young artist, all from the newly emerging middle-class families of Dhaka, open up their lives to the director. Key topics of the discussion include duties and obligations, women and desire, confusions and contradictions, etc.

[7] See Chap. 4 for the lyrics of the song.

men as key informants who somehow shared their own feelings or came to discuss with me their concerns.

As the purpose of the case study is to study a single unit for the purpose of understanding a larger class of (similar) units (Gerring 2004), depending on the patterns of data, twenty key informants were chosen based on their sexual experience and socio-economic background.[8] While doing so, case study data were analysed repeatedly to find out what kind of generalizations were emerging out of the data. Alternatives of such generalizations or *grounded theories* were further investigated carefully against *formal theories*. During the interview sessions, a checklist was used, which was prepared on the basis of themes that emerged from the data collected earlier during FGDs; based on the findings of this phase, I edited the checklist and used it in the life history interviews.

Considering the fact that life history interviewing is very useful for gathering information on the subjective essence of one person's entire life (Atkinson 1998) and may help to understand single lives in detail and how the individual plays various roles in society (Cohler 1993; Gergen and Gergen 1993), I was very keen to refine the cases (informants) on the basis of their accounts to assess them in more depth across time. Here, decisive factors for selection were the regularities or irregularities of enacting certain kinds of masculinity and associated sexual practices throughout the life course.

I used critical discourse analysis (CDA) to analyse the 'intertextuality' and 'interdiscursively' (Fairclough 1992) surrounding the discourse of masculinities. A CDA approach "aims to show non-obvious ways in which language is involved in social relations of power and domination" (Fairclough 2001, p. 229) and refers "to textual traces of different discourses and ideologies contending and struggling for dominance" (Weiss and Wodak 2003, p. 15). For doing CDA on HIV/AIDS, sexuality and masculinity, I collected and analysed reports and advocacy materials (printed documents and audio-visual texts) on HIV/AIDS published by the Government of Bangladesh, NGOs and INGOs in Bangladesh, together with the data I collected from interviews.

21.5 Reflexivity in Action: How I Neturalize the Challenges to Study Sexual Practice

From the very beginning of this chapter, I was aware of the fact that though we all are bound to diverse 'social and cultural formations,' following Ortner (2005) having agency we also have the freedom to choose, transform and strategically manipulate these formations. The question is when do we want to do this consciously and why? Here, I mean that even when someone knows that her/his culture does not allow some activities or that society does not permit something, when does she/he want to 'break' the rule and how and why?

---

[8] I have interchangeably used the terms socio-economic background and class. In no way is my use of the term related to Marx, Weber, Bourdieu or any other theorists. Whenever I used the term class, I simply mean a person's position in the social strata in terms of income.

There might be many reasons for that, but one very important reason is the 'consciousness' about one's own desire (i.e. to become aware of the process through which society or culture disciplines her/his aptitude of desiring). In the present research, in being a researcher, my subjectivity and the subjectivities of my informants required an initial agreement on certain points about breaking the socially desired rules (i.e. not to speak about sexuality openly, not to reveal the 'dirty little secrets'). Reaching this destination was not easy. I had to adopt some anthropological research techniques as well to remain conscious about the rules of the social and cultural formations. Nonetheless, some other advantages and disadvantages about my subjective self also influenced the process.

My subjectivity—being a 'native,' (temporary) resident of 'sin city Amsterdam,'[9] a Bengali speaker, male, heterosexual, moderate Muslim, married, middle-class university teacher, non-*Dhakaia*,[10] cricketers, debater, television presenter, youth organizer—fashioned the course of the research in particular ways. I can also assume that the subjectivities of my informants, most of whom were young men, were also fashioned by several factors including their age, sexual preference, socio-economic background, co-curricular preferences, geographical origin (home district), occupation and so forth.

Adopting Anthropological Techniques: Becoming Conscious of My Subjectivity

To avoid or reduce bias in the research resulting from one's subjective positions, an anthropologist may adopt some strategies. Following Peskin (in LeCompte et al. 1999), I tried to identify my biases in terms of 'hot spots' and 'cold spots' before going to the field. Here, hot spots refer to those aspects of fieldwork towards which one is drawn, and therefore spends more time exploring, whereas cold spots are those that one tends to dislike or feel uncomfortable with, and therefore spends less time on. In terms of these spots, I identified several issues beforehand to be aware of during the fieldwork.

Firstly, being a heterosexual person I realized that I might spend more time with other heterosexuals, and might take a conservative position regarding the fluidity in heterosexual practices and thus might not explore issues that questioned heterosexuality. I thought it might also make me uncomfortable to spend time with people who practise same-sex sexual acts, or people who have different sexual identities (sex workers, transgendered, gay people, etc.). The reverse might also have been true. Thus, to avoid this bias, I always kept a

---

[9] This discursive construction of Amsterdam is quite well known among the upper-class young men in Dhaka. Referred by one of them, I also read about such constructions on the web. See, for example, http://movie-tv-episode-database.com/Documentary/Amsterdam-City-of-Sin-55444/. Accessed 27 October 2009 at 14:59 GMT; and also https://theman.today/amsterdam-city-of-sin-canals-and-bikes/. Accessed 30 December 2021 at 11:59.

[10] People who live in Dhaka for a generation are known as *Dhakaia*. For a detailed discussion see Chap. 3.

journal and assessed the transcriptions of interviews to evaluate the nature of my questions and also ensure time allocation to people with a different sexual orientation duly. During the selection of key informants, I also made a balance between heterosexual people with different sexual orientations and people with 'other sexualities.'

Secondly, having a middle-class socio-economic background, I considered that I might not feel comfortable around people from other socio-economic backgrounds. Thus, I chose my key informants in a manner so that they could represent people from all socio-economic levels.

Thirdly, being a university lecturer, I thought that I might want to avoid sexual sites, as spending time on these sites might hamper my 'prestige' and image as a 'good teacher.' This prestige issue might also compel me to avoid discussing sexuality openly with my respondents, some of whom might be my university students. My journal shows that initially during the data collection process, I avoided language that I considered 'slang.' Gradually, however, I realized that these slang words are codes through which a kind of friendship bond develops among the young people. For example, during the FGD session, a lot of young people from the lower class and middle class used the term *pasa mara*, which means 'fucking someone in the anus.' I felt so uncomfortable initially that I did not mention it in my questions, though I was referring to those sexual acts. Gradually I realized the rule; using such 'slang' comfortably resembled the degree of closeness that you have with your friends, and in my case with the other 'young men.'

Fourthly, being a Muslim, I might not want to identify Muslim people as practising sex that is forbidden in Islam, or at least in Islamic discourse in Bangladesh, and thus might want to spend more time with Muslims having 'acceptable sex' and/or with those among other religions or ethnic groups having 'deviant sex.' Thus, I always tried to read the transcripts carefully and coded accordingly to reduce any bias that might come out of my religious identity. In selecting case studies for life-history interviews, I also ensured a balance among the 'core Islamic' and 'moderate Islamic' (my emphasis) respondents; 'core Islamic' are those who read in religious schools (*Madrasas*), whereas 'moderate Islamic' are those who do not have any orientation in religious school. Nonetheless, I relied on the respondents' identification of their affiliation with such terminologies in most cases, which went beyond such simplified categorization.

While I was in the field, I regularly consulted my diary and tried to identify more 'hot spots' or 'cold spots,' and adopt techniques to overcome such biases. For example, after starting the fieldwork, I realized that I avoided interviewing HIV positive people and spent more time in upper-class 'parties' or 'night clubs'; thus I took necessary measures to overcome such issues. Furthermore, I discovered that my relations at home with my wife, or my 'expected role' as a 'husband,' was a big factor when conducting research on sexuality. In many instances, I avoided interacting with 'young girls' because my newly married wife did not like it, and on some occasions there were 'warlike situations' between us regarding the issue. Finally, we could get past this because she understood the importance of my work through her own work on female sexuality for the partial fulfilment of her own MSS (Master of Social Science) programme, and also possibly by then we had started to develop trust in each other.

Though these points were my initial guidelines to avoid bias in the field and were thought up before I commenced fieldwork, during the course of fieldwork itself I encountered a few other important issues and invented many other selves that I could not have imagined before. This invention of new selves stimulated me to adopt multiple roles as an ethnographer. Buford H. Junker (1960) described four theoretical social roles of a participant-observer: (1) complete participant, (2) participant as observer, (3) observer as a participant and (4) complete observer. According to Junker, a participant-observer may find her/his position and activities shifting through time from one to another of these roles, even as he continues observing the same human organization. In my case, adopting different roles in terms of multiple selves in different contexts helped me to establish rapport and collect more in-depth data; some of these I was completely aware of, while others occurred to my complete ignorance, only becoming apparent when I consulted my journal at the write-up stage.

'Home' Dilemma, 'Amsterdam' Factor and a Complete Participant in Sexuality Research

As has been mentioned earlier, whether 'native' or 'other', an anthropologist always faces certain difficulties. However, who is an 'authentic' observer, a 'native' or an 'other'/'foreigner' has been debated widely. In a sense, the conclusion does not go in favour of any of them, as now we are in a time when anthropologists can be viewed only in terms of "shifting identifications amid a field of interpenetrating communities and power relations" (Narayan 1993, p. 671). As Rosaldo (1989) has pointed out, "the lone ethnographer's guiding fiction of cultural compartments has crumbled," and added that the "so-called native does not 'inhabit' a world fully separate from the one ethnographers ' living in'" (Rosaldo 1989, p. 45).

In the case of Dhaka, understanding the complexity of being a 'native' requires minimum knowledge of the Bengali language. In Bengali, for example, the word 'home' has two meanings: one is a temporary residence, *bari*, and the other, *basa*, indicates a place of origin (i.e. the place where one has lived for generations or has permanent residence). In Dhaka, only the people known as *Kutti* are known as the original *Dhakaia*, as they have lived in this place for hundreds of years. These days, most of the people living in Dhaka have come from different regions of the country over just a few generations, in which case Dhaka is actually full of foreigners. During the FGD sessions, I found most of the young men were not *Dhakaia*, though some of their families had lived in the city for generations.

Thus, at a certain point, I agreed with most of the participants in the FGD sessions that we all are to some extent 'foreigners' in Dhaka. This 'foreign' origin helped to melt the ice, but then the respondents started to ask me about Amsterdam, a sin city in their eyes. To these young men, especially those from lower- and middle-class backgrounds, it is among such places in the world where men and women are always playing 'wild games.' They considered me among those 'sinners' who have experienced all the 'honey' of the 'wild.' Thus, my exposure to the 'Western lifestyle' created a distance between me and my informants—a distance of jealousy and experience. They gradually started to identify me as a *boropapi* or 'big sinner.' In most cases, as we sat together after dark when all of them were finishing their tasks over *cha* (tea), they requested me to talk about Amsterdam—how the girls looked, how little clothes they wear, how they 'fucked' their boyfriends all the time in public places and so forth. Gradually, this kind of discussion turned into discussions of female 'physiology' and 'anatomy.' Finally, after several weeks, these discussions started to end with the chronicle of their own experiences in *pokum fight* or penetrative sex.

During the FGD sessions, I found a lot of young men engaged in arguments using slang language. I gradually realized that these slang words were used only among friends, so when I became their friend, and also to harness our bond of friendship, I also started to use some of them myself. After a few months, some of them become my good friends, and after or before the individual interview sessions, sometimes we use to watch *garam* (hot) movies together or go to their sites of sexual interest.

The 'Amsterdam factor' (i.e. my short time living in Amsterdam for about a year) also helped me to enter into the 'private life' of the young people from the upper class. I gained access to the upper-class private clubs, as only I had had exposure to the 'sophisticated' Western life in Amsterdam. The club owners or party throwers realized I would not show a typical middle-class mentality and would understand them. Thus, it actually enhanced my status and raised me up to their level. Being a native middle-class teacher, I would otherwise never have had that opportunity. Being an 'Amsterdammer,' I could easily gain access to the gay networks in the city as well. This happened through a friend of mine, who introduced me to young men using the reference that I had 'lived in Amsterdam.' Later on, some young men from this gay group become a very vital source of information for the research, as the sexual partners of heterosexual young men.

My partial claim to be a complete participant can only be comprehended if one understands the local meaning of a sexual act among young men, as it covers a whole series of acts performed by an individual alone or between two or even several persons of the same and opposite sex, including sexual talking or using slang words. I realized the ways in which young people listened to my descriptions of Amsterdam and revealed their own stories, all of which were sexual acts. However, this did not mean that I became a complete participant, but at least it ensured that I performed the role of the participant as an observer, and this helped me to be an observer as a participant.

Watching 'Live Sex,' Participating in Private Clubs and Becoming a Complete Observer

In sexuality research, becoming a complete observer is as difficult as becoming a complete participant. Some of the young men with whom I worked for at least three years were my friends with whom I studied in the university for many years, while others were complete strangers to me. However, gradually I became closer to these young men and started receiving invitations to their 'private parties.' In the case of the young men from lower- or middle-class socio-economic backgrounds, these 'private parties' had several sexual arrangements ranging from watching 'sex films' to enjoying sex workers together, whereas in the upper classes, dancing, drinking and enjoying the company of 'free girls' were the norm. In most of these parties, I became an observer; maybe a complete observer or observer as a participant, though I did not have the opportunity to see penetrative sex before my eyes or participate.

Perhaps what made me a complete observer was the opportunity of becoming a 'hidden cam' movie watcher. Some of these movies are widely available in the markets and are made by local young men with their 'girlfriends' with hidden cameras, while others are taken only for friends from parties or private meetings with girls. While watching these movies with these young men, I used to listen to their conversations and tried to understand their code of conduct, desires for sex and so on. I also downloaded many of these movies on my laptop and listened to the conversations when possible to understand the meanings of sexual acts while watching 'live sex.' I did the same in private parties, seeing who came there and why. What is it that drives them to such clubs? What kinds of activities do they perform and why? How do they run the club and go for 'hangouts'? Whether participating in these private parties and watching 'raw' private *garam* movies makes me a complete participant is a debatable issue, but for sure these experiences helped me to become an observer as a participant.

21.6 Way Forward

Like any ethnographic research, there are three issues that were very much important in relation to the study: data analysis procedure, the issue of reliability or validity and ethical considerations. Like any other qualitative research following McCracken (1988), the data analysis procedure was a dynamic, intuitive and creative process of inductive reasoning. The objective was to determine the categories, relationships and assumptions that inform the respondents' view of the world in general, and of the topic in particular. Following Jacob (1987) throughout the data analysis process, I indexed or codeed the data using as many categories as possible to notice relevant phenomena. Following

Seidel and Kelle (1995), I collected as many examples as possible of those phenomena. This helped me to analyse the phenomena and find commonalities, differences, patterns and structures that could identify and describe patterns and themes from the perspective of the participant/s. Following Miles and Huberman (1994), I took help from both the 'grounded' approach originally advocated by Glaser and Strauss (1967), and a provisional starting list of codes based on the conceptual framework, list of research questions, checklists, problem areas and/or key variables that I as researcher brought to the study. During the data gathering process, I organized the data categorically and chronologically, reviewed it repeatedly and continually coded it. I also made a list of major ideas and chronicled these ideas for further investigation, as suggested by Merriam (1988). My field notes and diary entries were very helpful tools for reviewing these regularly. Being 'reflexive' and critical to my positionality and subjectivity in terms of hot spot and cold spot helped me to minimize the biases while addressing the issue of 'reliability'.

Though the issue of 'validity' or 'reliability' is a major concern in any qualitative research, as this markedly differs from 'positivist,' quantitative methodology, I think the reliability issue can be dealt with through reflexivity. In my attempt to ensure external validity, following Merriam (1988) I try to give rich, thick detailed descriptions wherever possible in the write-ups so that anyone interested in transferability has a solid framework for comparison. I also employed three techniques to ensure reliability in this study. First, I provide a detailed account of the focus of the study and made it clear to the respondents taking enough time, the researcher's role, the informants' position and basis for selection and the context from which data were gathered (Goetz and LeCompte 1984). Second, triangulation or multiple methods of data collection and analysis were used, which strengthen reliability as well as internal validity (Merriam 1988). Finally, data collection and analysis strategies were reported in detail in order to provide a clear and accurate picture of the methods used in the study. Moreover, all phases of the research process were subject to scrutiny by an external auditor (local supervisor) who was experienced in qualitative research methods.

Most authors who discuss qualitative research design address the importance of ethical considerations (Locke et al. 1987; Marshall and Rossman 1989; Merriam 1988; Spradley 1980). First and foremost, the researcher has an obligation to respect the rights, needs, values and desires of the informant/s. To an extent, ethnographic research is always obtrusive. Participant observation invades the life of the informant (Spradley 1980), and sensitive information is frequently revealed. This is of particular concern in this study, where the informants' positions and institutions were highly visible. I employed the following safeguards to protect the informants' rights: the research objectives (including a short description of how data would be used) were always articulated verbally and in writing so that they were clearly understood by the informants; written permission to proceed with the study as articulated was received from the informants where necessary; informants were informed of all data collection devices and activities; verbatim transcriptions and written interpretations and reports were made available to the informants; the informants' rights, interests and wishes were considered first when choices were made regarding reporting the data; and the final decision regarding informant anonymity rested with the informants themselves.

REFERENCES

Angrosino, M.V. 1998. *Opportunity house: Ethnographic stories of mental retardation.* Walnut Creek, CA: AltaMira.

Alvesson, M., and K. Skőldberg. 2009. *Reflexive Methodology: New Vistas for Qualitative Research* (2nd Edition). London, Sage. ISBN 978-1-84860-112-3.

Aslop, C.K. 2002. Home and away: Self—Reflexive Auto-/Ethnography. *Forum: Qualitative Social Research*, 3(3), [Online]. Available online at: http://www.qualitative-research.net/fqs-texte/3-02/3-02alsop-e.htm. Accessed 21 August 2004.

Atkinson, R. 1998. *The Life Story Interview.* Thousand Oaks, CA: Sage.

BBS. 2022. Population and Housing Census Preliminary Report. Dhaka: Ministry of Planning, Government of Bangladesh.

Blackwood, E. and Wieringa, S.E., eds. 1997. Female Desires: Same-Sex Relations and Transgender Practices Across Cultures. New York: Columbia University Press.

Boellstorff, T. 2005. The Gay Archipelago: Sexuality and Nation in Indonesia. Princeton, NJ: Princeton University Press.

Bryman, A. 2004. *Social Research Methods.* 2nd ed. New York: Oxford University Press Inc.

Carrillo, H. 2002. The Night is Young: Sexuality in Mexico in the Times of AIDS. Chicago, IL: University Chicago Press.

Chawla, D. 2006. Subjectivity and the "Native" Ethnographer: Researcher Eligibility in an Ethnographic Study of Urban Indian Women in Hindu Arranged Marriages. *International Journal of Qualitative Methods*, 5(4), [Online]. Available online at: http://www.ualberta.ca/~iiqm/backissues/5_4/HTML/chawla.htm. Accessed 8 April 2011.

Clifford, J. and Marcus, G.E., eds. 1986. *Writing Culture. The poetics and politics of ethnography.* Berkeley: University of California Press.

Cohler, B.J. 1993. Aging, morale, and meaning: The nexus of narrative. In: T.R. Cole, W.A. Achenbaum, P.L. Jakobi, and R. Kastenbaum, eds., *Voices and visions of aging: Toward a critical gerontology.* New York: Springer, pp. 107–133.

Elliston, D. 2005. Critical Reflexivity and Sexuality Studies in Anthropology: Siting Sexuality in Research, Theory, Ethnography and Pedagogy. *Reviews in Anthropology* 34: 21–47.

Emerson, R.M., Fretz, R.I., and Shaw, L.L. 1995. *Writing Ethnographic Fieldnotes.* Chicago: The University of Chicago Press.

Fairclough, N. 1992. *Discourse and Social Change.* Cambridge: Polity Press.

Fairclough, N. 2001. *Language and Power.* 2nd ed. London: Longman.

Fraenkel, J.R. and Wallen, N.E. 1990. *How to design and evaluate research in education.* New York: McGraw-Hill.

Gergen, M.M. and Gergen, K.J. 1993. Narratives of the Gendered Body in Popular Autobiography. In R. Josselson and A. Lieblich, eds., *The Narrative Study of Lives.* Newbury Park: Sage.

Gerring, J. 2004. What is a case study and what is it god for? *American Political Science Review*, Vol. 98(2), pp. 341–354.
Glaser, B., and Strauss, A. 1967. *The Discovery of Grounded Theory: Strategies for Qualitative Research*. Mill Valley, CA: Sociology Press.
Goetz, J.P. and LeCompte, M.D. 1984. *Ethnography and qualitative design in educational research*. San Diego, CA: Academic Press.
Hammersley, M. 1990. *Reading Ethnographic Research: A Critical Guide*. London: Longman.
Hardon, A., ed. 1998. *Beyond rhetoric: Participatory research on reproductive health*. Amsterdam: Het Spinhuis: Amsterdam.
Jacob, E. 1987. Qualitative research traditions: A review. *Review of Educational Research*, 57 (1), 1–50.
Junker, B.H. 1960. *Field Work. An Introduction to the Social Sciences* (With an Introduction by Everett C. Hughes). Chicago: University of Chicago Press.
Khaleda, S., Mowla, Q.A., Murayama, Y. 2017. Dhaka Metropolitan Area. In: Murayama, Y., Kamusoko, C., Yamashita, A., Estoque R. (eds) Urban Development in Asia and Africa. The Urban Book Series. Springer, Singapore. https://doi.org/10.1007/978-981-10-3241-7_10.
LeCompte, M.D., and Schensul, J.J. 1999. *Analyzing Ethnographic Data*, Book Five.
Locke, L.F., Spirduso, W.W., and Silverman, S.J. 1987. *Proposals that work*. 2nd ed. Beverly Hills, Sage.
Marcus, G. 1998. What comes (just) after "post"? The case of ethnography. In N. Denzin & Y. Lincoln (Eds.), *The landscape of qualitative research: Theories and issues* (pp. 383–406). Thousand Oaks, CA: Sage.
Marcus, G.E., and M.F. Fischer. 1986. *Anthropology as cultural critique: An experimental moment in the human sciences*. Chicago: University of Chicago Press.
Marshall, C., and Rossman, G.B. 1989. *Designing qualitative research*. Newbury Park: Sage.
McCracken, D.G. 1988. *The Long Interview (Qualitative Research Methods, Vol. 13)*. Newbury Park: Sage.
Merriam, S.B. 1988. *Case study research in education: A qualitative approach*. San Francisco: Jossey-Bass.
Miles M.B., and Huberman, A.M. 1994. *Qualitative Data Analysis*. London: Sage Publications, Inc.
Narayan, K. 1993. How native is the "native" anthropologist? *American Anthropologist*, 95, pp. 671–686.
Ortner, S.B. 1996. *Making Gender: The Politics and Erotics of Culture*. Boston, MA: Beacon Press.
Ortner, S.B. 2005. Subjectivity and cultural critique. *Anthropological Theory*, 5, pp. 31–52.
Rosaldo, R. 1989. *Culture and truth: The remaking of social analysis*. Boston: Beacon.
Seidel, J., and Kelle, U. 1995. Different Functions of Coding in the Analysis of Textual Data. In: U. Kelle, ed., *Computer-Aided Qualitative Data Analysis: Theory, Methods and Practice*. London: Sage.
Spradley, J.P. 1980. *Participant observation*. Fort Worth: Harcourt Brace.
Spronk, R. 2006. *Ambiguous Pleasure: Sexuality and New Self-definition in Nairobi*. Unpublished Ph.D. dissertation, University of Amsterdam, Amsterdam, The Netherlands.
Steier, F. 1991. Research and Reflexivity. London: Sage.

Thomas, J. 1993. *Doing Critical Ethnography*. Newbury Park, CA: Sage.
Van Grinkel, R. 1994. Writing Culture from Within Reflections on Endogenous Ethnography. *ETNOFOOR*, VII (1), pp. 5–23.
Weiss, G. and Wodak, R., eds. 2003. *Critical Discourse Analysis. Theory and Interdisciplinarity*. London: Palgrave Macmillan.
World Bank. 2007. *Dhaka: Improving Living Conditions for the Urban Poor*. Bangladesh Development Series, Paper No. 17. Dhaka: The World Bank Office.

PART VI

Nativity, Participant Selection, and Challenges in Archival Research

CHAPTER 22

A Native Anthropologist's Positionality of Being an Insider/Outsider: A Reflective Account of Doing Ethnographic Research in Nepal

Kapil Dahal

22.1 Introduction

The development of anthropology in Nepal can grossly be divided (Dahal 2016: pp. 20–21) into three different periods: (a) the rise of anthropology during 1811–1950,[1] (b) anthropological research carried out by professional anthropologists between 1951 and 1990,[2] and (c) from 1990 onwards.[3] Dahal has pointed out that anthropology was initiated in Nepal in the form of ethnographic research by Western scholars.

The establishment of the joint department of anthropology and sociology in Nepal in 1981 to provide postgraduate (MA) training in sociology/anthropology has played a critical role in the development of anthropology in Nepal.

---

[1] A period commonly considered as the pre-modernization era in Nepal, in which mainly the scholars from abroad carried out anthropological research or the research which can be regarded as anthropological.

[2] Delineating the timeline when Nepal was more opened up to the outside world, which paved the way for anthropologists from overseas to conduct studies in Nepal.

[3] During this period there is a rise and growth of native anthropologists, trained within Nepal, outside of or at academic institutions in both areas.

K. Dahal (✉)
Central Departmet of Anthropology, Tribhuvan University, Kirtipur, Nepal

© The Author(s), under exclusive license to Springer Nature Switzerland AG 2023
N. Uddin, A. Paul (eds.), *The Palgrave Handbook of Social Fieldwork*,
https://doi.org/10.1007/978-3-031-13615-3_22

Almost after four decades of joint operation, the discrete department was established with the realization that both the discipline can burgeon in their way of knowledge production through specialized teaching and research (Uprety and Pokharel 2016). Nevertheless, native anthropologists in Nepal have already begun to contribute to knowledge production in their specialized area or sub-discipline of anthropology.

The shift of Nepali anthropology in its priority from a romantic-orthodox approach to the one with an emphasis on social change and development-oriented teaching and research had also contributed to its expansion (Devkota 1994). Along with the flourishing of anthropological engagements in Nepali academia, Lama Tamang et al. (2016) have recognized the dream of Nepali anthropology and secured an idea of making the vibrant academic community who are likely to be contributing to studying and analysing Nepali society and culture which will be meaningful to local realities (p. 107). Dividing anthropologists on the generational line, these scholars state that anthropologists from the elder generation have pointed to the imperative of applied anthropology, whereas others aspire towards contributing to theory building.

Anthropologists researching in Nepal have contributed in its various subfields including examining the health, illness, healing practices, and health policies and planning (Justice 1986; Levitt 1993; Acharya 1994; Harper 2007; Kohrt and Worthman 2009; Pigg 2013; Dahal 2010, 2022). The aim of this paper is not to comprehend the anthropological research on health/illness in Nepal, but to bring forth some of them which can be linked in the debate of positionality of the researcher and its implication on the epistemological aspect of the study.

Moving through the background of anthropological research in Nepal, the introductory section of this article provides the foundation for its formation. In the next part, I would like to deal with the inside/outside debate in anthropology and how that shapes the process of ethnographic endeavours. Then, the different facets related to the positionality of the researcher and simultaneous process, contradictions, and evidence have been extensively analysed.

22.2 Inside/Outside Debate in Nepali Anthropology

Anthropology has been emphasizing the claim of representing the ideas, beliefs, practices, knowledge, norms, and values of the people anthropologist's study. Staying among the natives and following their way of life and repeatedly seeing their customs, ceremonies, and transactions, only then anthropologists can bring forth rich ethnographic data which Malinowski (2005) regards as 'full body and blood of actual native life' (p. 14). This kind of participant observation is a backbone and hallmark of anthropology through which anthropologists reach closer to the people and makes them able to bring forth the cultural ideas and practices which otherwise would deteriorate in the lap of history (Geertz 1973). Moreover, the kinds of ethnography Malinowski espoused and regarded as scientific ethnography did contribute to extending 'the conception of rational humanity, simultaneously questioning Western arrogance and demanding intellectual respect for "primitives"' (Grimshaw and Hart 1994: p. 234).

Anthropologists themselves began to criticize the undialectical objectivism of anthropology's claim to come up with the real voice of the studied population. Often referred to as a crisis in anthropological theory, it loudly came in the 1970s, and mainly through the poststructuralist and postmodernist influence in anthropology. Anthropologists also questioned the ethnocentric representation of natives by the foreigners, and the outsiders, mainly following the publication of *Writing Culture* (Clifford and Marcus 1986). Their advocacy was for a more fluid and two-sided approach, reorganizing subject-object relations beyond the imagination of the conventional approach and suggesting 'more egalitarian, reciprocal, and reflexive relations with the subjects and readers of ethnography' (Grimshaw and Hart 1994: p. 251).

The ramification of such debates in anthropology also reached into Nepali anthropology with some implications in assessing ethnographic studies carried out in Nepal. Along with Dahal (2016), Chhetri and Gurung (1999) have demarcated the inside/outside of Nepali anthropological growth based on the nationality of the anthropologists, whether the researcher is a foreigner or from within a country, a native. Uprety and Pokharel (2016) have also kept on the tradition of demarcating anthropologists based on their nationality, foreigners, and native anthropologists, both of whose contribution lies mainly in the areas of socio-cultural anthropology in Nepal. It is important to note what Shah (2004) argues about the selective nature of foreign scholars to carry out anthropological studies in Nepal. He states they are inclined to research a certain segment of Nepali society, picking up one or two ethnic/caste groups. This kind of approach does not help to see the way Nepali society is constituted. He chose and argues for community studies, to see these ethnic and caste groups as they are in their totality.

In line with such divisions, Lama Tamang et al. (2016) have also appreciated the contribution of anthropologists from outside of Nepal in comprehending Nepali society, history, polity, and culture. For them, limiting the debate only to the binary between foreign and native anthropology is not only insufficient but also irrelevant. Rather, the involvement of anthropologists from diverse national contexts also complements each other to comprehend Nepali society in a better way. They argue it is 'one way of…making our academic community more representative and inclusive' (p. 120). Nevertheless, they have observed two kinds of fallacies in the contribution of foreign anthropologists, 'romanticism and refusal to see Nepali society in its own terms' (pp. 109–110).

The above few selected literature substantiates that Nepali anthropology is largely inclined to categorize and thus dichotomize anthropological contribution based on the nationality of the anthropologists who have done anthropological research in Nepal. Against these backdrops, this chapter aims to carry forward such debate towards the representation of subjects in the anthropological study and their relation with the anthropologists doing research on them. In this process of engagement, this paper aims to engage with some of the questions. Is nationality the only category that makes local people relate themselves to the anthropologist researching them? What happens when a Nepali anthropologist conducts research in Nepal among other castes/ethnic groups? Also, what happens when they are of a different gender? Is being an insider/outsider a fixed entity? Are there any single criteria that make someone an insider/outsider in a research field? These are some of the questions the subsequent sections will deal with.

In her paper developed based on her subjective/academic experiences as a Muslim researcher and her reflections on reflexivity, positionality, and representation while carrying out her ethnographic research in a high-school setting with Muslim youth, Miled (2017) has highlighted the complexity of insider/outsider positionality and the intersection of religion, class, age, ethnicity, and gender in influencing her positionality in the field. Taking his 17-day-long medical anthropological research carried out in the central hill of Nepal as empirical evidence, Anderson (1984) argues that ethnographic research can be carried out even in a short period, provided that the multidisciplinary team comprises someone who can speak the local language. He has given primacy to the understanding of the local language, here Nepali, a lingua franca among the local people of the multilingual and multi-ethnic group. Interestingly, he points out that it is sufficient to have other team members who can assist the ethnographer to facilitate the conversation and understand the people.

22.3 Positionality: How It Is Co-constructed in My Field?

I carried out a multi-sited ethnographic study to generate information about health-seeking practices and to know about the health and well-being of Tarai Brahmin women in different periods during 2012 and 2015, in Lakhanpur, a pseudonym I gave to anonymize the identity of the research participants. I did not confine my research strategy only to the conventional community ethnography and its various rites of passage. I also followed the people related to health-seeking and their interactions with service providers at a health facility in the locality and also in the neighbouring towns and cities in India. Various forms of interaction, participation, and observation techniques were employed in this study to produce grounded information.

Social scientists have analysed the positionality of the researcher, and the nature of his relationship with the research participants influence the knowledge production process in qualitative research. Enosh and Ben-Ari (2010) would like to regard their relationship with the research participants as dialectical instead of confining it into a simplistic dichotomization of cooperation and conflict. And, they state that only this kind of relationship is crucial to information generation.

In my research, I have also found that the nature of the relationship between the researcher and the participants over the period passes through the dialectical upheavals and I would argue that, eventually, such a pattern contributes ultimately to the production of knowledge. In that sense, agreeing with Wolf (1996), I would argue that the relation between the researcher's positionalities and the research participants is fluid. The form of relatedness between the research partners and various spectrums between them, ultimately, at least for a reflective researcher, contributes to knowledge production.

In his article "Behind Many Masks," Berreman (2004) states that the field was a stratified village, its dwellers from top to bottom suspicious of the outside. More at the top than at the bottom, though, people tried to hide what was and to put it in front of others. When the author's high-caste assistant took sick leave and was replaced by a Moslem one, automatically untouchable (as a non-Brahmin) and impure, the bottom-level people became friendlier and more open, and even some high-caste folk felt more relaxed in the presence of a no-account type than they had when the assistant had been of a high caste like himself or herself. In this way, not only the kind of local people's relation with the ethnographer but the context of the field also affects the ethnographic process.

Adeagbo (2021) carried out her research among HIV-positive adolescent mothers living in Johannesburg. She demonstrates, contributing to the debate of positionality and the reflexivity of the researcher, reflections on research experiences and her positionality influenced the process and representation of this research. She further explores what impact 'sameness' based on 'race' and 'gender' has on the relationship between the researcher and the research participants and reflects that making sense of the effects of positionality is not an easy job. As an active ongoing process (Davies 2008), she asserts that reflexivity must be consciously sustained. Emotional reflexivity crucially promotes the reliability and credibility of qualitative research in addition to promoting the self-awareness of the ethnographer.

From the beginning, I was aware and prepared for the reality that my 'very presence alerts the situation I was going to study' (Berreman 2004: p. 161). Local people related to me sometimes as someone close to them and on a few other occasions as distant from them, often due to my multiple identities. Multiple identities, as Isabella Ng (2011) concludes from her experience, can be disturbing but also fruitful in conducting truly ethical and thorough research. She has reflected that in her fieldwork, her multiple identities helped her gain access and shift easily from one position to another to reach the insider stories of the people researched. While construing the distance as narrower, my research participants tried to relate themselves to me as a Brahmin researching the Brahmins. My host also introduced me to some of his neighbours and relatives as a hill Brahmin doing a study among the Brahmins of the Tarai.

In my previous study (Dahal 2013), I had experienced women research participants often distanced themselves from me as a male and as a person from a hill area. While trying to talk to women, they were hesitant to chat with me as a male, which is very common even with their male counterparts from their area. They were reluctant to share information with me about the etiology and experience of illness and their lived experience of themselves as a woman in Tarai. For them, it was not easy to comprehend why I wanted to know about their lived experience of womanhood, structural violence, and embodied experience of suffering. To manage this situation, I had sought the help of two local girls, who had recently completed their higher secondary education. The choice of having two research assistants was based not on the load of the research task but rather to create a conducive environment for these research assistants to work with a stranger male researcher in a highly gender-segregated patriarchal context.

My host advised me to have two research assistants instead of one. They assisted me in collecting ethnographic information using the elaborative checklist I had developed, facilitating me in carrying out in-depth interviews with women, translating questions to participants, and sometimes translating their responses as well. Their assistance was crucial, especially in collecting information with the young daughters-in-law. They talked to the women, who were also their relatives, neighbours, or kin. These research assistants played the role of second-layer key informants (Edwards 2010), as on some occasions, they led me on whom to meet, when to meet, and often asked the initial questions. They offered crucial information that helped to clarify cultural differences and to make me better understand whom I was interviewing.

The situation was different this time. I was no longer a stranger to many people. Even if the women had not met me earlier, I might have met their male family members, relatives either man or woman, or at least they had heard that I had recently already been into their locality. This has helped me a lot in negotiating access. It does not mean that the one-time negotiation worked all the time. I agree with Wolf (1996) that as the positionality of the researcher is fluid, the access negotiated at one level of interaction does not, and did not, always work at all times during the fieldwork. Every time, I had to be sensitive to my specific male, educated, hill identity while interacting with them. It was the case not only with the women but also while interacting with the men.

Engaging with ethnographic research from two different cultural contexts in the US and India, DeLuca and Maddox (2015) argue that '…reflection on the role of the self is a crucial task for researchers working to understand the lived realities of others' (p. 2). Discomfort is the basis of meaningful learning and discovery, which makes the ethnographer involved in a unique process of continual negotiation of himself with the research subjects. In this process, embodied self of the ethnographer becomes the constitutive element of the research along with the resultant 'feeling of guilt and privilege' (p. 13).

I have also felt that the typicality of my research topic has also positioned me in a particularly convenient situation to carry out this study. As my research topic is related to health, problematic health situations, and the healing trajectory of women, it has made me easier to enter into the setting, which otherwise would have been difficult for a man, an outsider to approach their life. The selection of the topic, at least seemingly, not a common everyday phenomenon of the women, made it easier for me to conduct a study about these women. Everyday matters of the women would have been difficult to deal with by the outsiders. Even though health and healing practices are embedded into their sociocultural whole, however, as it is perceived locally as related to the modern health care system and, at least seemingly, not a matter of everyday feminine domain. Such understanding provided me comfort zone to generate data in this domain. Likewise, my study also did not deal with any aspects of health considered taboo to discuss, such as sexuality and reproductive health.

Local males also sometimes tried to bring themselves closer to me, and sometimes they deliberately attempted to distance me from them. While trying to distance themselves from me, they represented my identity as the one from the hills. They were critical of the suppression of the Madheshi people by the hill Brahmin-Chhetri-dominated state machinery. Likewise, especially those who came to know about the hill culture tried to distance them from me based on the cultural differences that exist between the people of Tarai and the hill origin people. Often, they have different clothing patterns, food and food habit, crops and cereals grown in the area, housing patterns, and so on as the area of disjuncture between the two places and cultures.

When the level of rapport was at the initial stage, I felt uncomfortable about the way people were repeatedly distancing themselves from the hill origin people. Sometimes, such feelings kept on coming into my mind and I consistently attempted to acquire information from different segments of society. Later on, contrary to such negative cycles of feeling, their warm hospitality, friendliness, openness, initiation to invite me frequently to their home, assurance of safe and convenient stay in their locality, and willingness to share information on the matters very much private to them gradually weakened my doubts. Nevertheless, such cycles and counter-cycles perpetually came to me on different occasions. Such feelings, I would prefer to rephrase as realizations, have helped me to constantly think about the relevance of my questions, the level of rapport, my presence, and my negotiated self and be reflexive on the overall strategies of the research. In this way, I was both the subject and the object of the study procedure doing research as a researcher and I constantly observed my presence and actions and their impacts on the local people and their response to me.

When the level of rapport deepened, I felt that the way they distanced me is not due to shortcomings in my endeavours to gather relevant information. Rather, it reflected the way knowledge is constructed. Relating and contrasting similar and dissimilar things, Levi- Strauss' (McGee and Warms 1999) binary opposition, is a universal process of human cognition and comprehension which was also prevalent in the field setting. It is one of the dominant approaches of the local people to perceive phenomena in the framework of binary opposition.

Nevertheless, it does not mean that having the development of amicable relationships over the period was always a smooth process—it was dialectical (Enosh and Ben-Ari 2010) many times. Sometimes, because of their positionality in the local context, I could not win the confidence of some people, especially that of the two doctors, one each from Sitamadhi and Bairginia. The doctor, owner of probably one of the biggest clinics in Sitamadhi, did not allow me to carry out my study in his clinic with the logic that I have to carry out my study in Lakhanpur to know about their experience of cross-border medical travel; he also threatened me that I better not bother him in the functioning of his clinic. His wife, also a reputed doctor from the locality, had already permitted me to talk to the visiting Nepali patients, whereas he did not like that idea saying that that will hinder the normal functioning of the clinic and it will disturb the patients who have paid huge money for quality service at his clinic. The other one from the Bairginia did not allow me to meet his wife, who serves as a gynaecologist in the locality amidst the rumour that she is not a doctor but simply an experienced compounder.

The two obstructive circumstances emerged neither because I was unable to develop amicable relationships in the field nor because both the parties/doctors were hostile to the strangers. I think it was because of our differential interests, and I could not develop an adequate friendship with them. For me, getting information, at least the permission to visit the place and/or meet the people, was important to move forward with my research. On the other hand, considering their reality of explicit disclosure or not, of their situation, about which they were aware, they might have found my presence unwanted or even a threat to the way they were running their clinic. Realizing these divergent interests, I decided to give up the follow-up visits at these clinics. It was helpful for me in the sense I did not invite any more enmity in these localities and there were no obstructions to my research in these areas.

The way social relations evolved during the research process remarkably benefitted my act of knowing. Nevertheless, I have also realized that, in this process of knowing in this research, I was not the only knower and my research participants were mere knowee. Rather both sides happened to be the 'knowing subject' (Gunzenhauser 2006). I have felt that whenever they realized that some areas of their cultural whole could be strange, unfamiliar, and uncommon to me they used to ask me about the prevalence/absence of such traits in my culture, the one they have perceived. In this way, they facilitated my comprehension of the exotic, comparing it with the familiar. Their act of asking a question only at a certain point of conversation on specific aspects of my culture, for me, is their reflection of their awareness of their social and cultural contexts. Their reflection and my knowing went on simultaneously, making us, on both sides, the knowing subjects.

On the other hand, questions from the research participants on different occasions were an integral part of the study. Once while I was commuting in a horse cart, a college teacher asked me why I had chosen to know about the healing trajectories of Madheshi women. In another instance, a medical doctor from the local health facility asked me whether I had conducted a similar study about the healing trajectories of hill-origin women. I told him very politely that

I have not done any systematic study but, somehow, I am familiar with that at least in my locality in Gorkha.

From these experiences, I realized that in ethnographic research, it is not always given/granted who the knower is. The knowee can simultaneously posit herself/himself in the position of the knower. Nevertheless, it does not mean that my researcher/knower position was a problem in the field. Rather, I regard it as the way any form of human interaction takes place, including during ethnographic encounters.

As presented in the above discussions, the information I have acquired and interpreted is subjective. I would like to accept that the knowledge, whatever I have been able to produce, is a very much "positioned knowledge" (Kleinman 1995: p. 76), not only because of my evolving position, as discussed in the earlier part of this chapter, but also due to the position of the informants who provided their information from their respective social locations.

I would like to reflexively look at my presence in the field and how it has influenced the data, the process of data collection, and, ultimately, the knowledge gained. Being a hill-origin educated male Brahmin doing an ethnographic study among and about Tarai Brahmin women has affected these crucial aspects. However, it is not related to the convenience/inconvenience, completeness/incompleteness, or true and false aspects of data. Rather, it is the reflection upon the presence of a researcher in the study he had carried out. In this way, the knowledge I have produced has been very much shaped by my positionality. Nevertheless, I did not go into much detail as Guéguen and Martin (2017) did while looking at the compliance rate of interviewees when the interviewer wore glasses. They found that wearing glasses positively affects the compliance rate.

Arthur Kleinman (1995) regards that the knowledge and experience related to suffering, and I would add health, illness, and healing to the list is intersubjective, that is it is experienced by the individual, the subject, in his/her relation with the other members of the society. The subject's experience is not merely personal and thus psychological. Rather, it is constructed in his/her relation with others. The local women also understood and construed their self and knowledge in an intersubjective way. Intersubjectivity is not confined only among the local people but also when they happen to be in relation with an outsider such as an ethnographer.

Through intersubjective processes, the conventional positivist tradition of collecting ethnographic data by the researcher has been profoundly challenged. In a way this procedure is against the idea that data/social facts are "out there" and the job of the researcher is to simply collect them through the application of the appropriate methods. Rather, it has contributed, also being a part of the process of data collection, to the tradition of generation of data, not through the unilateral efforts of the researcher but with the active participation of the research participants. It does not mean that the role of the qualitative researcher has been curtailed as the knowledge is produced collaboratively. Rather, the researcher's job becomes further crucial to make the participants open up avenues of their life in a way they want.

Initially, the in-charge of the PHCC was reluctant for letting me conduct my study at his health facility. He never said that he would not allow me to study there; rather, he questioned why I am interested to carry out the study in this tiny health facility with limited staff, medical supplies, and equipment in this *dehat* (rural) setting. I attempted to convince him in different ways about my interest to carry out a study at this health facility.

As I have told others from the locality, I also told him in front of other staff that I chose this region considering the very limited anthropological study. I also added that my interest is not to learn about how big hospitals are run but to understand the health-seeking practices of women from this area and their interactions with the service providers in their locality. I further added that I came to the Tarai region as I am from a hill area and somehow familiar with the life and health situation of people from that area.

He was not much convinced with my reason for choosing the study population and area. The next day, the PHCC in-charge saw me in the local bazaar with my host, known as a reputed and friendly person in the locality. We took tea together in the nearby tea stalls. They talked about the recently held election of the school management committee. Nevertheless, that meeting was crucial for me to improve my rapport with the in-charge.

Once my rapport had been established, sufficient for the adequate access, I approached to talk with the local pharmacists. While talking to them, I got to know that some of them had already noticed me in the local bazaar and even know why I am there. Two pharmacists told me that they were aware of why I was there. Just to verify what they knew about my presence I asked them what they know about my visit. They told me that I was there the study women's health. I thought this level of understanding will be all right for me to carry forward my research.

Physical proximity had also played a crucial role for me to meet a pharmacist and develop rapport. Mr. Rohan Jha's pharmacy lies at the entrance of the trail towards the house of my host. He noticed me when I exit from the trail to the bazaar area. Likewise, the horse carts are also stationed in front of his pharmacy. I have seen him many times arguing with the cart rider to take away their carts. This spatial proximity had also helped me to interact with him. Later on, he became a very good friend of mine.

I had a mixed experience conducting research on hospitals (actually the private clinics) in India. Initially, I was not sure about how to get access to these clinics. I was wondering whether I need ethical clearance from any institutions to conduct such research. As I was not affiliated with any Indian academic institutions and not doing research entirely in India, I decided that it is not necessary to take permission from any institutions in India. I was also not sure whether they will permit me to research this topic. I convinced myself that I am simply following the Nepali patients, so I do not need to take any permission from any authorities in India. Nevertheless, I was sure that I had to take permission from each institution to conduct the study.

A few times, I had been to India, but in the other parts. However, I had not stayed anywhere in bordering towns overnight. I was a bit reluctant to visit there for a long time at once. I explored with the owner of the lodge at the district headquarters about the possible place to stay in these prospective towns. He was much familiar with most of the areas and told me about the potential places where I could stay. As the closest neighbouring city was within 15 minutes tempo ride from the district headquarters, I did not stay there overnight, but commuted every day.

Initially, I went to Sitamadhi to meet Dr. Jha, who was a relative of my host at Lakhanpur. I met him at his clinic. He inquired about my family and also about my study. He was glad to know that social scientists are researching medical issues. When I asked about the two prominent doctors whom many females from Lakhanpur visit. He knew both of them. He provided me with letters for each of them on his letterhead. This connection was quite crucial for me to have an initial approach at the clinic. Both the doctors welcomed me and were ready to provide me with any information that I may need. Initially, they thought that I was there to fill out some survey forms. However, later on, they were convinced with the iterative way I wanted to carry out my ethnographic study and let me observe the waiting room and interact with the patients.

I had experienced some constraints while carrying out a study about/at some clinics in India, including the threat from a politician doctor, whom I had approached first with the letter from that senior medical doctor. The letter was to his wife, also a gynaecologist. I was waiting to see the gynaecologist at her clinic after sending the request to her that I would like to see her. She called me shortly, and I told her about the purpose of the visit and also presented the letter the senior doctor had provided. She allowed me to stay in the waiting room and conduct the study.

I sat in a vacant chair in the corner of the room and began to observe and write something. When I was writing my field notes, one of the clerks came to me and inquired about whether or not I had met with madam (referring to the doctor). In response to my positive note, he told me that it will be better if I could meet doctor *saahib* (referring to her husband) as well. The politician doctor was not there at that time at the clinic. After about two hours, I was called by a giant person wearing a tie. I went to him. He took me into the room and asked me about why I was there and what I was writing. I got to know during the conversation that he was doctor *saahib*. I told him about my research and also about the prior meeting with his wife. Then, he began telling me that they do not have any problem with letting me talk to the patients but few patients have complained to him about my presence and about talking to people and/or writing in the waiting room. He further added that as an owner of the private clinic he had to listen to the voice of the patients, because that is why people opt to go to private clinics instead of public health facilities.

Considering his political power, I decided not to visit his clinic again, even though his wife at that time had sounded quite polite and willing to share data with me, who also mentioned that her natal family was also in the southern part of Nepal, not so far from my study site in Nepal. Nevertheless, the data acquired from that first visit were also crucial for me to peep into the world of private clinics, and the destinations of medical travel for the patients from the Nepali side of the border.

It is interesting to note how the doctor persuaded me not to research his place. Despite the permission from his wife, his unwillingness made me uncomfortable to go there again. So, the gendered power relation is not only there for the patients but also there for the female medical doctors. This doctor himself did not ultimately take responsibility to make me not study at his place but with the discourse of respecting the patients' voice and keeping his business intact.

The process of fieldwork, both in the community setting and in the institutional setting, was forward-looking, always preparing and anticipating to know new and more things. Never satisfied, always expecting more. Nevertheless, the data generation was also based on and built on the data at hand at a particular point in time. On the other hand, the analytical process was a bit different from that of the collection of data. It was a backward-looking process, reflecting upon and looking for linkages and patterns in the data.

22.4 Conclusions

The polemic division of a researcher's positionality based on his/her nationality, foreign or native, has been dominantly prevalent in anthropology, in Nepal and elsewhere. I argue that such a division based on nationality is not enough to understand the nature of relationships between the ethnographer and his research subjects. It is the perceived or real positionality of the researcher which makes him/her in the situation inside/outside in the field setting. However, these positions are dichotomous. Neither do they depend upon any fixed criteria nor operate in a one-dimensional way. Trigger et al. (2012) rightly point out that the distance and closeness experienced during the ethnographic fieldwork should not be regarded as fixity but rather need to be taken as a part of fluidity. Accepting the flow of their occurrence as "normal" would help the researcher in his efforts of generating in-depth, situational, and engaged knowledge. It is not the lack of trust, confidence, or even conflict but the positionality of the researcher as taken by the research participants that influences his relations with them.

As a hill-origin and urban educated man, I have gained access in a certain way to talk about the health situation of healing pathways of research subjects, the Tarai-origin women and those living in the rural locality. Expanding my understanding of their language and immersion into their culture as well as expanding my horizon of network among the local people helped me a lot to minimize the barriers at a level so that I could grasp their situation from their perspective. As Hill et al. (2010) have experienced, I constantly made reflexive analyses of my relationship with my research participants and how that shapes my positionality in the field and reshapes the knowledge arising from the research. In doing so, I have also presented here 'dilemmas of (my) self' (Chesney 2001) in the study process. My reflection portrays not only the hesitation and shyness of the research participants but also that of mine, whenever I had acted as 'the reluctant researcher' (Scott 1985).

Being reflexive of one's positionality does not handicap any researcher to generate rich information from the field. Since any representation is only partial and based on the specific limitations of the particular researcher's positionality and perspective (Boyd 2008), the researcher is expected to explicitly show his positionality so that the readers will comprehend the ethnography accordingly. Supposing that all-knowing occurs in relation, I fully buy the idea of Gunzenhauser (2006) that 'the quality of qualitative research depends upon the quality of relations established between the researcher and the knowing subjects' (p. 62).

Reflection on own positionality makes the ethnographer aware of and grasp the insights from revelatory moments (Trigger et al. 2012). The emotion, surprises, and sometimes even the discomforts experienced temporarily open up the ethnographer's horizon of thinking, revealing surprising insights to look at the data hand, approach the situation, and meaningfully engage with the natives in the field. Ethnographer's relation in the field is an outcome of the complex relationship between his positionality, research question, stock of knowledge of the people, and degree and dimensions of participation of the researcher in the process of unfolding social realm to the researcher and the level of acceptance of his presence in the community. This points out that knowledge and information produced from the field are not objective reality; rather, they are the outcome of the complex process of social construction.

References

Acharya, B. K. (1994). Nature cure and indigenous healing practices in Nepal: a medical anthropological perspective. In: Allen, M. (ed.) *Anthropology of Nepal: Peoples, Problems and Processes*. Kathmandu, Nepal, Mandala Books, pp. 234–244.

Adeagbo, M. J. (2021) An 'outsider within': considering positionality and reflexivity in research on HIV-positive adolescent mothers in South Africa. *Qualitative Research* 21(2), 181–194. https://doi.org/10.1177/1468794120922072.

Anderson, R. T. (1984) An orthopedic ethnography in rural Nepal. *Medical Anthropology* 8(1), 46–59. https://doi.org/10.1080/01459740.1984.9965888.

Berreman, G. D. (2004) Ethnography: method and product. In: Srivastav, V. K. (ed.) *Methodology and Fieldwork*. London, UK, Oxford University Press, pp. 158–190.

Boyd, D. (2008) Autoethnography as a tool for transformative learning about white privilege. *Journal of Transformative Education* 6(3), 212–225.

Chesney, M. (2001) Dilemmas of self in the method. *Qualitative Health Research* 11(1), 127–135.

Chhetri, R. B., & Gurung, O. (1999) Anthropology and sociology of Nepal: retrospect and prospects. In: Chhetri, R. B., & Gurung, O. P. (eds.) *Anthropology and sociology of Nepal: cultures, societies, ecology and development.* Kathmandu, Sociological and Anthropological Society of Nepal (SASON), pp. 1–9.

Clifford, J. & Marcus, G. E. (eds.) (1986) *Writing culture: the poetics and politics of ethnography: a School of American Research advanced seminar.* Berkeley, University of California Press.

Dahal, D. R. (2016) Anthropological tradition in Nepal: history and practices. In Pokharel, B., Rai, J., & Lama, M. S. (eds.) *Nepali anthropology: New direction and contributions.* Kathmandu, Nepal, Central Department of Anthropology, Tribhuvan University, pp. 19–42.

Dahal, K. B. (2013) Structural violence, body politic and women's health in Terai, Nepal.a final report submitted for HarkaGurung Research Fellowship (SIRF/HGRF/2011/A) to Social Inclusion Research Fund (SIRF) Secretariat, SNV Nepal, Kathmandu.

Dahal, K. B. (2010) Widowhood, life situation and suffering: a medical anthropological perspective. In: Chhetri, R. B., Pandey, T. R., & Uprety, L. P. (eds.) *Anthropology and Sociology of Nepal.* Kathmandu, Nepal, Central Department of Sociology/Anthropology, Tribhuvan University. pp. 305–330.

Davies, C. A. (2008) *Reflexive ethnography: a guide to researching selves and others.* London, Routledge.

DeLuca, J. R., & Maddox, C. B. (2015) Tales from the ethnographic field: navigating feelings of guilt and privilege in the research process. *Field Methods* 28(3), 284–299. https://doi.org/10.1177/1525822X15611375.

Devkota, P. L. (1994) Anthropological perspectives on grassroots development in Nepal. *Occasional Papers in Sociology and Anthropology* 4, 50–71.

Edwards, R. (2010) A critical examination of the use of interpreters in the qualitative research process. *Journal of Ethnic and Migration Studies* 24(1), 197–208. https://doi.org/10.1080/1369183X.1998.9976626.

Enosh, G., & Ben-Ari, A. (2010. Cooperation and conflict in qualitative research: a dialectical approach to knowledge production. *Qualitative Health Research* 20(1), 125–130.

Geertz, C. (1973) *The interpretation of cultures: selected essays.* New York, NY, Basic Books.

Grimshaw, A., & Hart, K. (1994) Anthropology and the crisis of the intellectuals. *Critique of Anthropology* 14(3), 227–261.

Guéguen, N., & Martin, A. (2017) Effect of interviewer's eyeglasses on compliance with a face-to-face survey request and perception of the interviewer. *Field Methods.*

Gunzenhauser, M. G. (2006) A moral epistemology of knowing subjects: theorizing a relational turn for qualitative research. *Qualitative Inquiry* 12(3), 621–647. https://doi.org/10.1177/1077800405282800.

Harper, I. (2007). Translating ethics: researching public health and medical practices in Nepal. *Social Science & Medicine* 65, 2235–2247.

Hill, P. S., Lee, V., &Jennaway, M. (2010) Researching reflexivity: negotiating identity and ambiguity in a cross-cultural research project. *Field Methods* 22(4), 319–339.

Justice, J. (1986) *Policies, plans and people: foreign aid and health development.* Berkeley, CA, University of California Press.

Kleinman, A. (1995) *Writing at the margin: discourse between anthropology and medicine.* Berkeley, CA, University of California Press.

Kohrt, B. A., &Worthman, C. M. (2009) Gender and anxiety in Nepal: the role of social support, stressful life events, and structural violence. *CNS Neuroscience & Therapeutics* 15(3), 237–248.

Lama Tamang, M. S., Dhakal, S., & Rai, J. (2016) Nepal school of anthropology: emerging issues and future directions. In: Pokharel, B., Rai, J., & Lama Tamang, M. S. (eds.) *Nepali anthropology: new direction and contributions*. Kathmandu, Nepal, Central Department of Anthropology, Tribhuvan University, pp. 107–126.

Levitt, M. J. (1993) A systematic study of birth and traditional birth attendants in Nepal. Nepal: John Snow Inc./USAID.

Malinowski, B. (2005) *Argonauts of the western Pacific: an account of native enterprise and adventure in the archipelagoes of Melanesian New Guinea [1922]*. London, Routledge.

McGee, R. J., & Warms, R. L. (1999) *Anthropological theory: an introductory history*. New York, McGraw Hill Companies Inc.

Miled, N., (2017) Muslim researcher researching Muslim youth: reflexive notes on critical ethnography, positionality and representation. *Ethnography and Education* 14(1), 1–15.

Ng, I. (2011) To whom does my voice belong? (re)negotiating multiple identities as a female ethnographer in two Hong Kong rural villages. *Gender, Technology and Development* 15(3), 437–456.

Pigg, S. L. (2013) On sitting and doing: ethnography as action in global health. *Social Science & Medicine* 99, 127–134.

Scott, J. C. (1985) *Weapons of the weak: everyday forms of peasant resistance*. New Haven, CT, Yale University Press.

Shah, S. (2004) *A project of memoreality: transnational development and local activism among rural women in Nepal*. Ph.D. Dissertation, Harvard University.

Trigger, D., Forsey, M., & Meurk, C. (2012) Revelatory moments in fieldwork. *Qualitative Research* 12(5), 513–527. https://doi.org/10.1177/1468794112446049.

Uprety, L. P., &Pokharel, B. (2016) Teaching anthropology in Nepal: a critique and a proposal. In: Pokharel, B., Rai, J., & Lama Tamang, M. S. (eds.) *Nepali anthropology: new direction and contributions*. Kathmandu, Nepal, Central Department of Anthropology, Tribhuvan University, pp. 43–92.

Wolf, D. (1996) Situating feminist dilemmas in fieldwork. In Wolf, D. (ed.) *Feminist dilemmas in fieldwork*. Oxford, UK, Westview Press, pp. 1–55.

CHAPTER 23

Recruitment of Participants from Vulnerable Groups for Social Research: Challenges and Solutions

Melati Nungsari

23.1 Introduction

Social research begins, fundamentally, with human participants. In many advanced economies, data are readily available on individuals, their lives, and a variety of socioeconomic variables that a researcher may be interested in. However, this generally is not true for both emerging and developing economies, as well as vulnerable populations in most countries. Thus, a researcher has to sometimes go "to the field" and collect data. This process is often complicated by geographical challenges, ethical considerations, funding capacity, and, perhaps most importantly, the recruitment of participants for the research project. In this chapter, I address the issue of participant recruitment and working with vulnerable groups for this purpose.

In my experience, the recruitment of participants is often the hardest step—significantly more complicated than the conceptualization of the research question and design, or even the analysis of the data collected. This problem is compounded even further when one works with hidden or vulnerable groups. Some questions that arise are the following: how do you find and "uncover" individuals from the groups you are interested in working with? How can you ensure that the research that you are conducting is ethical? How do you build

---

M. Nungsari (✉)
Asia School of Business, Kuala Lumpur, Malaysia

Massachusetts Institute of Technology, Boston, MA, USA
e-mail: melati@mit.edu

© The Author(s), under exclusive license to Springer Nature Switzerland AG 2023
N. Uddin, A. Paul (eds.), *The Palgrave Handbook of Social Fieldwork*,
https://doi.org/10.1007/978-3-031-13615-3_23

rapport and trust with individuals from a vulnerable community? How do you find individuals who do not want to be found to jumpstart research projects aimed at helping them? Once you've identified groups that you are interested in and if you are a researcher interested in making generalizable conclusions from your study, how can you ensure that sampling of participants was done correctly? If you are recruiting participants for a training programme, how can you ensure that most participants who start the programme also complete it? There is an entire universe of questions and problems surrounding the recruitment of participants, but I shall focus on the following aspect in detail: how to recruit participants and ensure their continuation in a research project. I will first discuss, as is most important when working with vulnerable populations, the ethical considerations that one must ruminate on. Then, I present some challenges for participant recruitment, as well as some proposed solutions. I end the chapter by summarizing and by reflecting on my multi-year experience as an economist in an emerging country.

23.2 Ethical Considerations

There are two main ethical considerations that a researcher should be aware of when collecting data in the field. The first is the power imbalance between the researcher and the participant, in particular, acknowledging that the researcher comes from an elite position as an observer, while the participant may be undergoing a significant amount of stress and trauma as they are being solicited as a participant. This power imbalance may cause the participant to decline to participate in the study, or worse, cause the participant to incorrectly report their situation and untruthfully answer any questions that are posed. I assert that the latter is more of a problem for any study than the former because the truthfulness and quality of the data from a research study influence almost the entire trajectory of the study going forward—the analysis of the data, the conclusions generated, and potential policy recommendations. Thus, one could argue that bad data are significantly worse than no data and that this is important to keep in mind when in the field. Collecting social data also takes a lot of time, and the researcher may be tempted to bypass any "pauses" or cut corners when it comes to data collection in the field, but this is unwise, particularly so when working with vulnerable populations. The most important fact to note is that field research typically requires individuals to build rapport—a process which can take upwards of years, even decades. In keeping in line with the fast-paced academic world, one may argue that an acceptable amount of rapport-building could be shortened to a span of a couple of months, but even so, one must acknowledge that there will still be a certain level of discomfort in participants to really, truly trust the researcher and that the answers that researchers receive will be biased. I would strongly recommend that researchers acknowledge this bias in their papers and reports, as well as acknowledge the fact that the data they collect are not the absolute truth, but rather reports of the truth. Zarowsky et al. (2013) have also suggested that "real work—at both intellectual and policy/political levels—lies in understanding and responding to the dynamics, meanings and power relations underlying actual instances and processes of vulnerability and harm". Particular attention should also be given to participants who are responding to issues which are considered "political" (Lancaster 2017).

In trying to reduce the power imbalance, a researcher must not only think about the invisible power imbalance between themselves and the participant, but also the time, venue, and method in which data are being collected. For example, due to the pandemic, many researchers have started conducting interviews via phone or video. These interviews, while effective at mitigating the risks of transmitting the virus, may be very costly for the participants due to poor Internet, phone data, or phone minutes access. Participants may also feel more vulnerable because they are revealing personal information (i.e. their phone number) to a researcher whom they do not fully know. The time that a researcher proposes for an interview or survey data collection may also be problematic—one should not assume that "normal" times (such as business hours during weekdays) are convenient for their research participants. Data collection should also be conducted at venues that are viewed as "neutral". To give an example of a non-neutral location, consider a study in which the researcher is trying to understand how workers in a particular company feel about their working conditions. Conducting said interviews at the actual physical location in which the company operates would be highly unwise, as participants cannot be expected to reveal the truth about what they feel.

The second ethical consideration is the issue of information and consent. Consent can either be informed consent (i.e. a participant is briefed on the study, and then verbally acknowledges that they understand and are willing to participate) or direct consent (in which a participant may be required to deal with signing a document stating their agreement to participate and their consent). Many researchers utilize informed consent when dealing with vulnerable groups, as problems surrounding privacy and illiteracy may be side-stepped. However, this may be problematic. Mkandawire-Valhmu et al. (2009), for example, have illuminated "the limitations of informed consent in research with vulnerable populations of women". Other authors such as (Aldridge 2014) have championed an "adaptive, more inclusive, and sometimes individualistic case-by-case" approach when conducting qualitative interviews in the field.

In alleviating issues surrounding the legitimacy of informed consent, we would like to propose, alongside many other authors, that researchers employ participatory methods in participant recruitment. Bradbury-Jones et al. (2018) found that "participatory spaces can recalibrate opportunities and attention given to marginalized and silenced groups", and that these ways allow "children and young people to develop skills and exercise political and moral agency". They further discuss how a participant-based approach may solve issues surrounding trying to advocate for political and social change. In a separate paper, I also found the same to be true—that social research with vulnerable groups must, at the core, begin with the participants and work its way to the issues and questions being explored and answered (Nungsari and Flanders 2020). A "top-down" approach to research in which the researcher proposes the questions to be answered by the participants, without taking their thoughts and ideas into consideration, will often fail. Participants should be treated as partners in the researcher's journey, and not as mere participants. This is particularly true since the researcher may be blinded by the theoretical or conceptual lens that they are employing, and may miss certain important issues or questions that are worth answering. The participants can, in many situations, help guide the research project towards more fruitful, impactful directions. In becoming a partner in the research process, the participant, in turn, not only provides their consent to participate in the study but also acts as a "manager" of their agency. In my personal experience in the field, "down-top", participatory studies tend to also progress faster, and more cohesively, than "top-down" ones.

The third ethical consideration is the issue of incentives for participating in the study. In general, scholars are split on the issue of whether or not to pay participants. On the one hand, payments of cash can induce a participant to join a study but may cause a bias in which the participant answers according to what they perceive the researcher wants to hear from them. Payments may also complicate the relationship of the participant with the researcher, because they may transform the role of a researcher from an "independent outsider" to a potential source of funds. However, one could also argue that a vulnerable person's time is valuable, and their mental energy in participating in a survey or interview should be valued. In many instances, a vulnerable person may also have to take time off from their paid work to participate in a study. They may also incur other costs that seem small to an outsider, such as increased phone bills, but still represent a significant burden on their income and expenditures for that period.

Another consideration would be the transference of dignity to a participant—whether or not the acceptance of the token of appreciation would be seen as a payment that cheapens their participation in the study. Economists have studied this issue in the context of markets that are considered undesirable or "repugnant"—for example, a mother cooking for her children during a festivity does not expect payment for her labour, although it is significant. Direct cash payment to said mother, in most families, would be viewed as repulsive, as though an act of love was "marketed", that is, placed in a capitalistic marketplace. Some vulnerable people may be interested in helping the researcher better their community and helping guide policies towards better outcomes for their own people. Hence, payment may be problematic.

Of course, a researcher can choose to provide non-monetary incentives to participants, such as food aid. In many developing economies, this is common. Instead of paying a participant cash, a researcher may also elect to provide a food basket consisting of typical food items consumed by the participant's community. However, this can also be problematic for three reasons. The first is that this assumes that the researcher knows, for a fact, exactly what the participant and their families consume daily. For example, granting food aid that includes chicken may offend a vegetarian participant. For a less extreme example, a participant may not consume the same products that the researcher does, and if the researcher does not understand this, many food items may go to waste. The second reason that this is problematic is that funders may expect a detailed report on the sourcing of items to be included in the food basket. It is also not uncommon for funders to dictate what exactly should be included in the food basket, which may pose additional problems for researchers. The final problem that may come up for researchers is the problem of logistics, particularly for a long-term study that includes many individuals. If an individual is given, for example, 5 kilograms of rice for each encounter, 6 individuals are interviewed in a day, and this study goes on for 6 months, the researcher will need to figure out a supply chain to buy, store, and distribute more than 5400 kilograms of rice! Such small details such as the disbursement of benefits should not be taken lightly as it does impact the mobility of the researcher throughout the research process.

Thus, in consideration of all these issues, we would suggest the following. The researcher could, through cash or an equivalent non-cash amount (such as in vouchers to buy groceries), demonstrate that they appreciate the time that the participant has spent with them. The amount and value of the incentives should not be deemed as "too high" to sway the opinion of the participant or to cause them to feel like they need to behave appropriately to express themselves. Rather, the incentive should be seen as a token of appreciation or compensation for the energy the participant has invested into the study. A clear benefit of cash incentives is also the issue of record-keeping—a researcher could simply keep an Excel spreadsheet documenting the alias of the participant and the date the incentive was given out—which is significantly easier to keep track of than, say, bundles of food packets. Cash or vouchers also is less paternalistic as it does not assume that the researcher knows about the habits and life of the participant, and returns agency to the participant to make their own consumption choices.

23.3 Recruiting Participants: Challenges

Traditionally, methods of participant recruitment in a study include the following: recruitment through personal networks (i.e. researcher's close contacts), recruitment through an organization (say, a non-governmental organization (NGO), international agency, or a government agency), or direct recruitment through community leaders. Each of these methods has its pros and cons, as we analyse below.

The first challenge is the issue of participation bias. In particular, researchers should be highly cognizant of the fact that the method they choose to recruit participants will influence the composition of participants in their study. Since researchers typically come from a place of privilege, the first method of recruitment as outlined above is arguable the most problematic. This is because, due to homophily, humans tend to surround themselves with individuals who are very similar to themselves. Thus, if one recruits from one's social network, it is highly likely that one will obtain very biased results. Drawing further conclusions and policy recommendations from these results will also be problematic as a consequence.

Two commonly used sampling methods for participants that relate to participation bias are snowball sampling and convenience sampling. In snowball sampling, a researcher sources a few participants to collect data from and subsequently asks each participant to recommend the next person to talk to. This is a very efficient way to obtain participants, as it takes away some burden from the researcher and places it on the participant to obtain more numbers. However, it is problematic for two main reasons, the main being that one can easily continue "circling" with a single network without ever leaving it, thus threatening the validity of the study's results. The second is that this method places too much burden on the vulnerable person, in many cases, as it forces them to reveal others within their network, something they may not be keen on doing. For example, consider a study surrounding the COVID-19 pandemic and compliance with public health measures, such as wearing face masks. A vulnerable person who is interviewed in this study may feel very uncomfortable about exposing one of their friends or loved ones to an external party, particularly also if they are aware of non-compliant behaviour in their community. A researcher should be aware of these issues with snowball sampling—it can be very problematic, though efficient. In inconvenience sampling, a researcher samples participants who are present (perhaps physically) in a particular location. This sampling method is supposed to be "easy" in the sense that it is convenient to ask a group of people what they think about if you're already speaking to one individual in the group. This sampling method is also very efficient—a researcher can expect to move to different localities and sample a large number of individuals rather quickly. However, it also runs into participant bias as individuals who tend to group, as mentioned above, are perhaps more similar to each other than average.

It's also important to note that when a researcher tries to recruit through an organization, the said organization will tend to recommend individuals close to it, and hence the picture obtained from the study may end-up being very unrepresentative of the actual situation. This is particularly true because "community contacts" tend to be "community leaders", who may be very different from the average individual in the community. Many studies recruit participants through community leaders (Sigel and Friesema 1965; Natale-Pereira et al. 2008; Chan et al. 2015), with the assumption being that the voice of the community leader represents the will of the community they belong to. This is the second challenge: to what extent can we study the entire population by studying only a few people at the "top", especially when there usually is no democratic process that governs the selection of leaders?

In my personal experience in the field, it is also very possible to accidentally exclude a large swath of the population by focusing on community leaders. This is true partly because of limited resources. Community leaders, or those who take the role of being the "go-to" person in their community, are often operating under very strict constraints. They must often choose which families and members to aid, and how to divide resources amongst a large group of people. Thus, it is unrealistic to expect that they cover a large portion of the group that they belong to. Consequently, if you are trying to understand an entire (large) population by speaking only to and recruiting a dozen or so community leaders, you will not be able to conclude very much.

The third challenge with recruiting participants through an organization is the amount of control that the researcher gives up to the organization in the research process. When recruitment of participants is done through an organization, the organization will typically have a say in who gets included, what is asked, and other parameters surrounding the study. This is very problematic, as the organization may itself end up "taking over" the researcher's study, steering it towards unplanned directions. This is not to say that partnering with an organization necessarily implies that a study will be flawed, but a researcher should be aware of the politics of working with particular organizations, especially if the particular organization is backed by funders with particular agendas.

The fourth challenge relates to retention—specifically, once a participant is recruited for a study that includes repeated interactions with the researcher, how can the researcher incentivize the participant to stay in the study, and not drop out? Drop-out rates are common in social studies, but particularly so with vulnerable groups. In my work with urban refugees (i.e. refugees who do not live in camps), it is very difficult to trace individuals or to do longer-term studies that look at the longitudinal effects of particular interventions. Studies that involve training programmes or educational workshops, with data collection being done pre- and post-training, are also tricky. We caution the researcher to be conservative in estimating how many participants they can carry through these sorts of programmes—in particular, to be ready and plan for very high attrition rates.

Another challenge that I would like to highlight concerns the nature of the study itself. As discussed in the ethics section, participants should be briefed on their participation in the study, and consent should be obtained. However, how does one explain a study to a vulnerable group without going into significant detail and contaminating the results of the study? For example, let us consider a study in which the researcher is trying to understand whether or not a certain government policy has impacted the participant in good ways or bad. If the researcher explains to the participant the true nature of the study, the participant may refuse to be included in the study for fear of persecution from the government. Conversely, a participant may decide to only focus on the negative effects, anchoring on the bad and not the good, and ignoring the positive effects of the particular policy on their lives. This is a general issue with social science research, but one that can be particularly difficult with vulnerable groups. For another example, consider a study that is trying to examine the impacts of the COVID-19 pandemic on a vulnerable population's mental health. If the researcher asks the vulnerable person directly about their mental health, due to the sensitivity of the question, they may receive very short, terse answers, or worse, untruthful answers. The researcher in this position will have no other choice but to report their findings, which may be completely off-base. The issue of soliciting information from participants to enrol them in studies is one that is very difficult to deal with. This is particularly difficult to do with children. Below, we highlight some possible solutions.

Finally, I would like to speak of a very important challenge to overcome in a social science study, namely, the underrepresentation of women as participants. In many vulnerable communities, the husband or a male household member is typically seen as the "leader"; in many situations, they are the ones who work, and thus are the ones who a researcher is most likely to encounter, and hence include as a participant. However, I argue that this is an issue for a study as it disregards or denigrates women. In some vulnerable societies, a researcher even has to get permission from the men to speak to the women in the society. In these settings, it could be potentially impossible to even understand the issue at hand from a female perspective, to the detriment of the study. Women oftentimes also serve as the main childcare provider in the family. This being, excluding women from studies typically also means that the perspective of children is also discarded. Thus, it is important to recognize this in studies, and researchers have an ethical and academic responsibility to ensure that the participation of women in studies, though significantly harder to get than the participation of men, must be encouraged.

23.4 Recruiting Participants: Solutions

How can a researcher overcome some of these biases? In a sense, many of the difficulties with recruiting participants from vulnerable populations stem from the very fact that the researcher is working with vulnerable populations—that is, the traits of the population itself—and therefore may be unavoidable. However, I argue that there are some ways in which a researcher can help mitigate some of these issues.

Social science researchers are interested in uncovering the truth surrounding a particular issue or question. In alleviating participation bias, a researcher could argue that a biased sample—perhaps if sourced from one's networks—explains one part of the absolute truth, and fully acknowledges this limitation in their work. In my experience, many researchers opt not to display the weaknesses in their studies in their write-up—a problem which is, to me, both unethical and cheapens the value of the research study. By pretending that one can explain more than one can, and by claiming that one has discovered the absolute truth, it allows for a very thin interpretation of the world that can easily be torn apart or seen through by the reader and other scholars. Thus, in presenting solutions to challenges, I first urge the reader to consider devoting a significant amount of time in their academic articles to discussing perhaps some of the weaknesses of their participant recruitment and acknowledge all the possible biases that may arise.

Aside from recruiting from one's networks, recruiting by using community leaders is by far the next easiest method of obtaining participants. However, as mentioned before, a researcher needs to be cautious about whether or not recruitment through a community leader maximizes the spread of recruitment, as well as recruits participants who may not agree with the opinions of the community leader. To alleviate this problem, we suggest the following: the researcher keeps a list of names of community leaders and continually adds to this list as time passes. By maximizing the number of "injection points" into a social network, the researcher can try and reduce the issue of community leader bias in their study. Additionally, the researcher can also do two-step recruitment in which they first recruit a set of community leaders, and then conduct snowball sampling with individuals identified by the community leaders as members of the community. This method may allow a researcher to intersect with different social networks than the initial one that they entered at the start of the study.

A researcher should also be aware of the politics between different community groups and leaders within a geographical location. For example, if one wants to study the population of all migrant workers in a city, one must be aware that the different groups of migrant workers—perhaps partitioned by countries of origin—are economic competitors in terms of job opportunities. Thus, if a researcher tries to source participants through one group of migrant workers and asks for contacts for another group, they are likely to hit a wall. Thus, political considerations revolving around the participants of the study must be taken into account as well.

One challenge that was brought up above was the issue of relinquishing control over the study and the recruitment of participants due to the preferences of funders. In addressing this particular challenge, I urge the researcher to be well-prepared in terms of plans presented to the funder, as well as long-term goals of the study, selection criteria for participants, and eventual outcomes of the study (be it academic publications or policy reports for popular consumption). The researcher also wants to put all of these expectations and foundational matters into paperwork—that is, agreeing from the very start on all aspects of the study to be funded, including how participants will be recruited, and the responsibility of the researcher to the funding body. Although contracting cannot completely resolve the issues related to this, it can certainly create a very real responsibility to stick to the plan, as well as impose mental, non-specific responsibilities and nudges towards allowing the researcher to be in control, and not the funding body. Thus, ironing out any differences in methodology and opinions before the actual start of the study can be beneficial for all parties involved in a particular research project.

A longer-term challenge that a researcher faces beyond that of participant recruitment is the retention of the participant in the research project, particularly also if the project is longitudinal or requires follow-up. To mitigate issues that may arise in this aspect, researchers should stagger follow-ups through the entire time of the study and particularly also stagger the giving of incentives. For example, if a study is expected to continue for a year, having a check-in with participants (which may just be a quick phone call) every two months, with incentives built into the check-in process, would be desirable. This is both to ensure that participants stick with the study and that the researcher knows what is going on with the participants and can anticipate if they are about the withdraw from the study.

Finally, to address the challenge of the under-representation of women and children, we encourage researchers to employ a variety of different methods of data collection when faced with these groups. A woman in a highly patriarchal community, for example, may be very uncomfortable and refuse to participate in a study that requires her to sit down for long periods for an interview or to answer a survey. However, in our experience, non-standard methods of data collection, such as the use of drawings, physical manoeuvring of objects such as candies and rocks to explain a situation or phenomenon, and retelling of personal experiences through music and plays, can sometimes work as well as the standard interviews and surveys. These methods are also incredibly successful in rapport-building, and can often be used to break the ice with participants and encourage them to open up to the researcher. Aside from ethnographic studies, which typically take time, these methods can be used at the beginning of a study to get to know participants better and to explore issues that the researcher may not even be aware of. It's also important to note that non-standard survey methods work well with children, a hyper-vulnerable group that many researchers have trouble accessing for a variety of reasons. Thus, I urge researchers to carefully consider a broad set of data collection tools when dealing with individuals and potential participants from vulnerable groups.

23.5 Conclusion

In the years that I have spent working closely with vulnerable groups, I have found that the needs of each group and study are so diverse—so much so that one can never expect to apply the same strategy for participant recruitment twice. However, this chapter has presented some common challenges that a researcher can experience while recruiting participants, alongside some commonly used solutions. I would like to end this chapter by encouraging researchers interested in social sciences to plan, plan, and plan some more. There is no such thing as being over-prepared to start a research study. All possible states of the world should be considered, and all options for completing the research study should be on the table.

REFERENCES

Aldridge, Jo. "Working with vulnerable groups in social research: dilemmas by default and design." *Qualitative Research* 14, no. 1 (2014): 112–130.

Bradbury-Jones, Caroline, Louise Isham, and Julie Taylor. "The complexities and contradictions in participatory research with vulnerable children and young people: A qualitative systematic review." *Social Science & Medicine* 215 (2018): 80–91.

Chan, Kim-Yin, Marilyn A. Uy, Oleksandr S. Chernyshenko, Moon-Ho Ringo Ho, and Yoke-Loo Sam. "Personality and entrepreneurial, professional and leadership motivations." *Personality and individual differences* 77 (2015): 161–166.

Lancaster, Kari. "Confidentiality, anonymity and power relations in elite interviewing: conducting qualitative policy research in a politicised domain." *International Journal of Social Research Methodology* 20, no. 1 (2017): 93–103.

Mkandawire-Valhmu, Lucy, Elizabeth Rice, and Mary Elizabeth Bathum. "Promoting an egalitarian approach to research with vulnerable populations of women." *Journal of advanced nursing* 65, no. 8 (2009): 1725–1734.

Nungsari, Melati, Sam Flanders, and Hui Yin Chuah. "Refugee Issues in Southeast Asia: Narrowing the Gaps between Theory, Policy, and Reality". *Refugee Review: Emerging Issues in Forced Migration – Perspectives from Research and Practice*, Vol 4, No 1(2020): 129–146.

Natale-Pereira, Ana, Jonnie Marks, Marielos Vega, Dawne Mouzon, Shawna V. Hudson, and Debbie Salas-Lopez. "Barriers and facilitators for colorectal cancer screening practices in the Latino community: perspectives from community leaders." *Cancer Control* 15, no. 2 (2008): 157–165.

Sigel, Roberta S., and H. Paul Friesema. "Urban community leaders' knowledge of public opinion." *Western Political Quarterly* 18, no. 4 (1965): 881–895.

Zarowsky, Christina, Slim Haddad, and Vinh-Kim Nguyen. "Beyond 'vulnerable groups': contexts and dynamics of vulnerability." *Global Health Promotion* 20, no. 1_suppl (2013): 3–9.

CHAPTER 24

Navigating Archival Readings of Rural Technology

Sanjukta Ghosh

24.1 Archiving the Plough

This research is set in the broad framework of colonial knowledge formation and dissemination in the early decades of twentieth-century India that was promoted through scientific institutions (Cohn 1996; Chatterjee 2003; Kumar 1995). Various categories of colonial scientific knowledge representing the ideas of state officials were accumulated through illustration projects such as surveys, settlements, maps and technical manuals among other forms of institutional and personal/amateur pursuits (Edney 1997; Grout 1990; Robb 1998). This article is concerned with the application of colonial science in India, using the example of the plough and the bullock cart as a means of technology transfer, the salience of which was evident in the diagrams and working drawings of farm and agricultural department reports since the late nineteenth and twentieth centuries. The recording and gathering of empirical information about indigenous and local rural conditions underlined colonial official enterprise towards agricultural development in this period. Scientific analysis evident in earlier instances of botanical, topographical and geographical surveys entailed observation, collection and illustration of samples, specimens and species, mapping and measurement of external boundaries and local landmarks, or charting imperial spaces of control. Officials were largely concerned with the definition of terms derived from local informants, and with incorporating these in the textual narrative in surveys, settlement reports and gazettes. But the

S. Ghosh (✉)
South Asia Institute, SOAS, The University of London, London, UK
e-mail: sg83@soas.ac.uk

© The Author(s), under exclusive license to Springer Nature Switzerland AG 2023
N. Uddin, A. Paul (eds.), *The Palgrave Handbook of Social Fieldwork*, https://doi.org/10.1007/978-3-031-13615-3_24

appointment of experts and professionals in the wake of institutional changes, such as the establishment of an Agricultural Department (1870), required practical investigations that considerably influenced both the collection and the classification of agricultural knowledge (Hodge 2007; Ludden 1994).

The British notion of progress and state responsibility for development was first deployed in the Indian agricultural economy, which remained an autonomous domain of scientific inquiry, open for progressive intervention (Ludden 1994). Wider socio-economic management by the state was instituted systematically from about the turn of the nineteenth century and as a result, defined the agrarian sphere. Scientific surveys were undertaken to identify, describe and explain the agrarian conditions (Chatterjee 2003; Robb 1998). Such professional specialisation of the experts replaced the earlier non-specific interests of orientalist scholars, amateur travellers and company surgeons. There were direct and practical interventions of British civil servants and experts to resolve local agricultural problems that were evident in the reports on farm experiments (Hodge 2007).

The usual picture is one of Western science forced on India, sometimes with disastrous consequences. Currently, it is doubted whether Indian agriculture was organised according to the rationale offered by colonial officials and agronomists. Recent research also points to colonial knowledge as a network of ideas that relied on exchange of ideas, sharing and dialogue to circumvent the Eurocentric approach in the current history of science. Western rationality and its counterpart scientific knowledge as key Enlightenment legacies decided the terms in which material and moral progress was assessed in colonial policy and practice. Scientific farm experiments provided a channel through which many ideas in the realm of technology penetrated India during the colonial period, but their absorption by the indigenous community was slow and responses were varied (Henry 1995; Macleod and Kumar 1995). The outcomes, however, depended also on Indians as agencies of change and upon other internal circumstances. Without denying instances of top-heavy interventions, this article using the various illustrations of the plough within the textual narrative of official reports presents the possibilities of scientific dialogue. The article focuses on the type of agricultural knowledge produced through farm-level experiments, interactions with local perspectives and the distinctions following such developments.

Illustrations demonstrated the colonial government's desire to collect and order indigenous knowledge so that the unfamiliar physical environment of India could be mapped accurately. The representation of scientific knowledge and experiments in the form of illustrations is most notable in the field of natural history. In India, official observation and recording through extensive field notes revealed the exotic perception of the tropical flora and the fauna. Mainly through drawings and paintings of the tropical environment, indigenous ways of life and artefacts were diligently depicted by a select group of artists, travellers and some scientific professionals such as naturalists, who tried to combine their amateur interests with their careers in civil service. The result was an eclectic mix of styles in object illustrations that stemmed from personal and amateur interests to more systematic categorisation, such as economic botany, which developed under the rubric of direct supervision from metropolitan scientific organisations (Kew, Royal Agricultural Society, Royal Society among others) and rural entrepreneurial interests (British manufacturers of the plough) (Goddard 1988; Kumar 1995; Arnold 2005).

Scientific visualisation in these early pursuits of object illustration had a looser interpretation and focused mainly on the direct comparison (flora, fauna, topographical details), showing the urge to maintain accuracy in scientific observation and research. In the case of technology transfers, such as the plough and the cartwheel, illustrations needed to be accurate and represent the object exact to its internal structure and exterior shape. Indigenous implements that were subject to survey, collection and used for purposes of engineering models belonged to this genre of scientific illustrations.

The extent to which illustrations as visual cultures represent 'reality' on paper has been one of the key issues in the communication of technical knowledge. Plough illustrations demonstrate a pursuit of empirical truth, but these were also informed by certain stereotypical archived images of the Indian peasant and their practices. The indigenous plough was visualised in a way that fitted neatly into the colonial imagination of traditional village life, and the wonder of the tropics, particularly in relation to the different depictions of animals, plants and birds in visual culture. The scientific depiction of the plough merged with the exotic impressions of tropical creatures such as the elephants and camels (Illustrated London News 1847). These impressions had very little bearing on real situations, where large animals could not be used to power ploughs for the small plots of the Indian peasants, as opposed to large-scale capitalist farms. Although some of these pictures show ploughs driven by the power of horses, elephants, camels or well-stocked herds of bullocks, many of these animals behind the plough only had experimental or sensational value.

In contrast to these exotic impressions, colonial officials took practical initiatives in the promotion of agricultural machinery to increase food supplies, at a pace in line with population growth, and were simultaneously motivated by trade (Boserup 1965). Hence, they were willing to experiment with labour-saving devices on farms. Most power-driven implements distributed by the colonial Agricultural Department represented top-heavy initiatives to improve production but without an adequate understanding of the small peasant's constraints. The labour-saving implements such as the tractors were put through trial in advance of any general demand that remained consistently low in rural areas with surplus labour. Many of these devices were essentially incongruent with the actual conditions of Indian agriculture too. Images of power-driven machinery figured prominently in farm journals, accompanying comparative notes of existing indigenous implements that were more suited to the tropical agroecological conditions.

Instead of focusing on exotic or imported species to improve crop production, everyday practicalities led plant breeders and farm scientists to look for improved implements appropriate to the tropical soil. For many British officials, the principal vehicle of positive changes in agriculture would be the peasant, as opposed to those who proposed universal and technocratic solutions to food production. Given the differences between the two approaches (actual and utopian conditions), new technology needed to be modified, because of changes in the official approach or adapted due to changes in the actual conditions of production. To reflect these changes in farm reports, illustrations were directed to produce positive results of technology transmission.

As an example of this ongoing debate on technology transfers, some farm reports carried numerous illustrations of the plough—a low-capital intensive technology, trials of which were systematically carried out as scientific experiments in Pusa—a colonial agricultural research institution that was set up in India modelled on the Rothamsted in Britain (Arnold 2005; Bayly 1996). The illustrations demonstrate the subject of scientific knowledge exchange in historical circumstances that facilitated a process of adaptive empiricism among the scientists and the indigenous agencies. The indigenous plough known variously as the 'nagar' was an object of illustration in this context.

II

The *nagar* was often portrayed as a primitive tool representing the rudimentary and aesthetic qualities of indigenous implements (Indian Council of Agricultural Research 1960). Gradually the aesthetic images of the plough were recast with the intimate and everyday practicalities to establish a new technical reality. These practicalities incorporated both environmental/agroecological factors and those concerning peasant practices. Illustrations of ploughing carried the physical details of soil, containing thick descriptions of how the plough turned on different soil—hard and rocky, lumpy, soft clay, dry, laterite, black and red soil—representing both scientific and travel imaginaries of unknown topographies such as the wild marshes, village waste lands, riverine tracts that were susceptible to undue and everyday vagaries of unpredictable monsoon, floods and drought (Fig. 24.1a, b).

By 1911, agriculturists had categorically justified the need for improving ploughing techniques to facilitate better irrigation, the sowing of mature seeds, and weeding in line with different soil conditions. Farm officials had developed an understanding of complex issues of soil aeration and furrow irrigation, and how changes in crop yield could be brought about by using ploughs that reached to greater depths in the soil rather than a few inches on the surface.

Two important conditions in relation to soil moisture—waterlogging and water loss that were deemed relevant for turning ploughs were factored into reconstructing the design of the *nagar*. The problem of waterlogging was related to the prevalent practices of ploughing and related to certain methods of ploughing. In India, as the plough bullock always turned to the left and never to the right, the ploughing was done from the outside to the middle on small plots, forming a hollow in the centre and a rim on the edges. This practice enhanced the possibilities of waterlogging and reduced crop yield. Hence,

24 NAVIGATING ARCHIVAL READINGS OF RURAL TECHNOLOGY   421

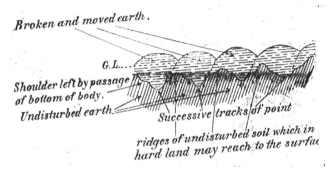

Fig. 24.1 (a) and (b) Negalu, dabbi naga, naga, light plough, Deccan harrow

to improve drainage, farm officials redesigned and encouraged the supply of left-handed mould-board ploughs with which the cultivators were left with no option but to turn the earth to the left while reaching the middle of the plot. The iron ploughs of the mould-board types worked much deeper and turned the soil upside down, refined and exposed it to the effects of the sun. Ploughing with these meant deep actions, which facilitated the growth of beneficent organisms, the effects of which contrasted with the wooden plough that had only pulverised the surface.

Environmental factors aside, officials complained regarding the 'indolence' of the 'native' peasant towards raising the productive capacity of the land, and their responses to the introduction of new or European methods of cultivation and land use. This article reads into the textual narrative accompanying plough illustrations that mediated a colonised image of 'inefficiency', while the actual illustrations were meant to represent the structure of the plough as mechanical art. The changing features in plough illustrations reveal not only the mechanical alterations of implements, but also the inter-relationship between imagination, praxis and the recording of key moments in technology transfers. While considering the processes of technological transfer, some British officials focused on existing peasant practices and their relevance to improving the plough. Farm journal prints contained evidence of early illustrations of rudimentary tools by government-commissioned indigenous artists that reveal the value attached to peasant practices and the need to take that stock of indigenous knowledge (Anon 1820). Most illustrations of Indian peasants working on tools showed operations on bullock-drawn ploughs, chopper or *dau*, wooden peg tooth harrows, wooden planks for pulverisation and smoothing, bullock carts and a range of hand tools such as *khurpi*, crowbar, spade, hoe, sickle, axe, and so on. Of these, the indigenous *hal* was illustrated as a versatile implement that was made and repaired by local craftsmen (Fig. 24.2a, b).

The method of ploughing depicted in the images clearly reveal that it was usual for peasants to 'scratch' the soil only three to four fingers deep with an ordinary spade known as *kodali* which could be used to plough their small plots of land varying in size (Fig. 24.3a, b). The type of labour pictured was mainly household labour: Several men pictured in the ploughing operation with the *nagar* show that it was essentially labour-intensive for specific crops, the results of which varied according to the soil composition. The *nagar* was used three or four times for the ordinary crops, the operation being dependent mostly on household labour without adding to the overall costs of production.

Illustrations of the *nagar* /plough focusing on certain structural elements were linked to practices of preparing the soil with varying degrees of success. The ordinary peasant combined his cultivation, ploughing and harrowing operations using his *nagar* plough and the beam that was commonly known as the *patela*. These were effective on light soils but failed to achieve the desired tilth on heavier soils containing variable proportions of clay or stones. On harder soils, particularly following the monsoon, the tearing action of the country plough simply turned the clay into hard lumps. The traditional method of passing the *patela* over only partially pulverised the soil (Fig. 24.4a, b, c).

24 NAVIGATING ARCHIVAL READINGS OF RURAL TECHNOLOGY   423

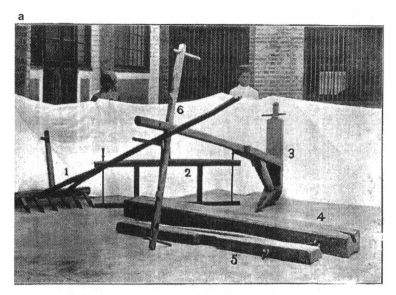

nplements—1 Dantal. 2 Chokiu (Double yoke). 3 Nangar (Sugarcane planting plough) nmar (large clod crusher). 5 Patiu (small clod crusher). 6 Zusari (single yoke).

Implements—1 Karpi or karabdi (Hoe). 2 Dariu. 3 Hal. 4 Single yoke for plough. 5 (harrow). 6 Phavdi. 7 Vakhelu (2 coultered drill). 8 Single yoke for hoes. 9 Tarfen tered drill). 10 Dhariu (scythe). 11 Karapdi (weeding hook).

Fig. 24.2 (a) Dantal, Chokiu, Nangar, Large clod crusher Patiu, Zusari and (b) Karpi, Dariu, Hal, Single yoke for the plough, Harrow, Phavdi, Vakhelu, Single yoke for hoes, Tarfen, Dhariu, Karapdi

Fig. 24.3 (a, b) Manual Power Tillage Implements

24 NAVIGATING ARCHIVAL READINGS OF RURAL TECHNOLOGY 425

tak—1 Negalu (heavy plough). 2 Dabbi Naga (Double yoke). 3 Naga (single yoke).
'anti (light plough)

IV

Deccan harrow.

Fig. 24.4 (a) Negalu, Dabbi Naga, Naga, Light Plough, Deccan Harrow and (**b**, **c**)

Fig. 24.4 (continued)

Despite these shortcomings, the practical applications of the *nagar* were seen to be environmentally appropriate. For colonial officials, the *nagar* was inefficient on harder clay soil for purposes of deep tillage, but it had its practical uses and was seen as a viable option to maintain soil fertility for the ordinary cultivators. Voelcker, the imperial agricultural chemist, reported that the *nagar* produced a fine and better tilth that was often suitable for the regional crops and retained moisture in the soil following a heavy monsoon (Voelcker 1893/1986). Experiments showed that the fine tilth produced by frequent ploughing with the *nagar* produced a surface that absorbed water better than that left by a furrow-turning plough after the rains. In the case of rice cultivation, for example, a digging and stirring plough like the *nagar* working through mud covered by several inches of water proved to be the best option. In the case of breaking up new land, the *nagar* had advantages like the tearing actions of a steam digger. Hence, the indigenous *nagar* was valuable and could produce satisfactory results to meet the immediate needs of the cultivators. Other indigenous implements that featured include a wooden roller or *lakkar* that was used to obtain a fine tilth proved equally inadequate and a labour-intensive method for breaking up clods (Hailey 1918). The benefits of other tools such as a wooden ladder or *moi*, for example, were measured in terms of effective retention of moisture in the soil ('Krishi Sampad'/Agricultural Resource 1910, 339). As the *moi* was very light in weight, it proved to be less effective in breaking clods for preparing the soil but served the purpose of puddling the fields that was very useful to the paddy cultivators.

With ongoing experiments, illustrations accompanying farm reports increasingly featured elaborate description of the 'country nagar plough'. These also included accounts of the 'value' of its usage followed by a comparison with modified or 'improved iron ploughs' which were introduced through a series of scientific experiments on government farms. As will already be evident, the Indian wooden plough was one of those agricultural implements that the British considered 'imperfect in the extreme'. Illustrating the difference between the two types, a common visual rhetoric deployed was to contrast the figures in terms of their building materials. Illustrations highlighting the difference between the wooden country and the 'efficient' iron plough implicitly codified the assumed difference between praxis and scientific knowledge (Fig. 24.5a, b).

The iron plough is displayed showing the functions of different parts, their use in relation to the type of soil, the direction of mechanical and human bodily motion, movement of the bullocks, depth of a dig, transformation of the soil surface, effects on the plant/crop and its subsequent yield changes. Illustrations of the country *nagar*, by contrast, are *only* (emphasis mine) focused on a piece of wood shod with an iron point constituting the share. It was fitted with a wooden pole and drawn by one to three pairs of bullocks. The country *nagar* had no mould-board for inverting the soil and no cutting parts to eradicate weeds. These were portrayed as mere 'grubbers' which stir up the soil, lacking the share of sufficient depth to penetrate the soil above three inches deep. Equally they found it difficult to plough the dry soil as the *nagar* had to be used several times to achieve any results (Sangawan 1989). These discrete differences evident in the illustrations of plough materials were gradually replaced by an interest in depicting the stages of revisions in plough models.

As adaptive empiricism stemmed from an understanding of peasant practices, modification of the existing *nagar* was adopted to improving agricultural production. Illustrations of the furrow technique constituted a strategic method of initiating a scientific dialogue between those in favour of iron

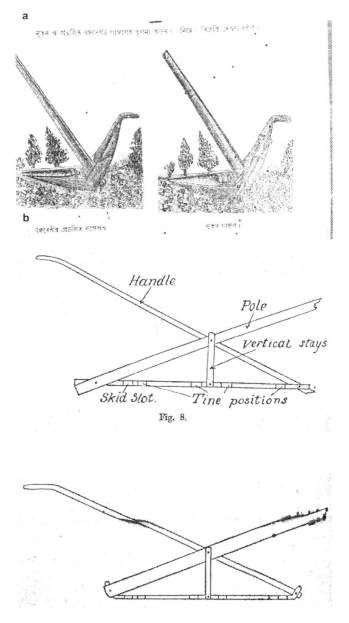

Fig. 24.5 (a, b)

ploughs and those who were used to the wooden ones. The main problem identified by British officials was the failure of the wooden share to invert or dig soil deep enough. Cultivators needed to re-plough and cross-plough to reach some depth and to invert the soil. Peasants commonly used a *nagar* to open a furrow shape with its depth and width varying according to the size of the plough, but usually did not exceed four inches in depth and six inches in width. An unploughed strip was always left between one furrow and the next. When the field was cross-ploughed, the remains of squares of unploughed ground required numerous ploughings (Yegna Narayan Aiyer 1953). Comparative experiments in Pusa showed that the furrows obtained with the mould-board types were distinctly different from those of the *nagar* plough. With a mould-board plough, the furrow was L-shaped and the furrow slice was rectangular in section, which ensured the complete ploughing of the field without leaving any unploughed ridges. Hence, illustrations showing the material differences between wooden and iron ploughs in relation to traction strengths were replaced by those that specifically showed functional modifications such as the angle of the share, its adjustability, the alignment of handle and body, depths of furrows and other changes that had a more immediate impact on agriculture (Indian Council of Agricultural Research 1960).

Illustrations of new plough designs were meant to show how these impacted estimates of agricultural input/output and crop productivity in novel ways (Mollison 1900; Godbole 1914; Henderson 1917). These substituted other diagrams and charts that showed the static variations in price indices, with the introduction or diffusion of new technology. Illustrations showing variations of plough technology promoted a combination of ecological knowledge and economics that was likely to increase soil and labour productivity, expose the value of innovations and agricultural experiments. Experiments on Pusa farm plots showed that the mould-board plough was easily run (Fig. 24.6a, b) with its share flat across the bottom of the furrow at an even depth. It was kept in a direction parallel to the last furrow at a distance generally measured at seven or eight inches from it. Like the prevalent local ploughs, the depth of furrows could be increased or decreased by hitching the bullocks either a little more forward or backwards, respectively. Several plough illustrations were drawn up to show the differences in furrow techniques, and their advantages were judiciously compared.

Illustrations of furrows were often printed separately from those of new plough designs in agricultural reports or journals. This separation implied a shift in the context of technological change too—from a commercial perspective in mechanical innovations to changes that bridged innovations with improved crop production. There were several diagrams of furrows showing changes in soil drainage, irrigation patterns and so on that emerged alongside narratives of plough technology. The assumption here was first to demonstrate the possibility that if better ploughs improved the quality of the furrow, then there might be fewer weeds, higher rates of seed germination and hence higher yields.

Second, the impact of plough design on farm inputs could be examined, by looking at the relationship between better ploughs and the chances of increased productivity from plough teams. In addition to exogenous factors such as soil quality and crop types, illustrations increasingly supported the hypothesis that the size of the plough team was primarily determined not solely by technology, but also by economic forces of joint agricultural labour.

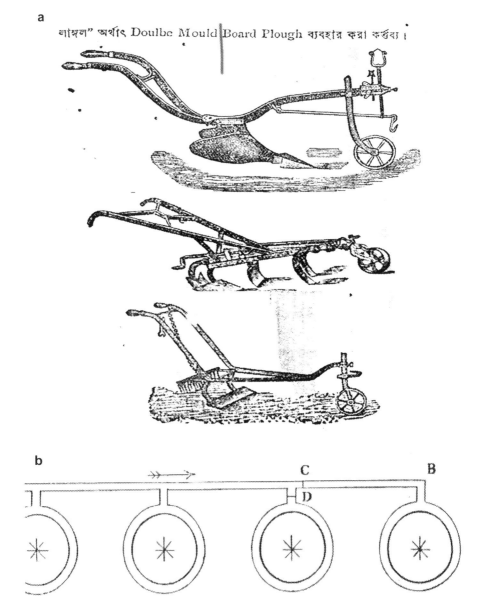

Fig. 24.6 (a, b) Double Mould Board Plough and Furrows Illustration

III

As improvements in technology were heterogeneous, incremental and poorly documented in colonial India, illustrations served the qualitative purpose of filling up some gaps in information about causality in technical changes and its corresponding relation to agricultural improvement. There were many ways in which a plough could be improved, but the level of each improvement seemed difficult to quantify. Farm officers had no direct information on the number of ploughs sold based on certain technological variables such as changes in the weight of a plough or the mechanical efficiency of each mould-board. Changes to the different plough characteristics could not be aggregated to measure the overall level of technological efficiency. Similarly, the impact of plough design on farm output could not be measured, except by speculating on certain non-technical probabilities.

Ploughs, therefore, represented complex agricultural technology that combined the energies derived from improved engineering, the uses of family/community labour and available draught animals that constituted an efficient plough team. Illustrations that were primarily focused on the engineering acumen and guile of plough designers/traders were used to pitch the function of a plough in complex environmental situations. It was illustrated as an implement used not only to break the variegated tropical soil but also to turn the soil in several angles for different productive purposes. Accordingly, a range of illustrations showing the differences between a wooden and iron plough beam/*patela* supporting the coulter and the ploughshare, mechanical efficiency of the mould-boards and geometric expressions of the soil furrows were drawn up in the popular agricultural journals or institutional farm notes (Annual Report of the Sibpur Experimental Farm 1901–02, 1895). A lighter beam model or changes in the shape of the mould-board were frequently drawn up to show how these had a substantial effect on soil productivity. But the representation of ploughs as objects of knowledge was inherently complicated, given the combinations of mechanical complexity and the uses of both animal and human energies. It was obvious that plough designs had to be adapted to tropical environmental factors, but the illustrations were also pointing to teamwork and the complex energies that determined the uptake of newer plough designs.

In addition to providing the mechanical information, these illustrations indicated the points of techno-human engagement displaying in additional detail and often in separate images certain mechanical parts that were deemed by officials as either 'inefficient', labour-intensive or needed modification. Illustrations of the 'modified *nagar*' revealed two important illustration processes at work, constituting a scientific dialogue. Farm officials modified the plough designs by making different forms of adjustments, such as those relating to the shape and depth of furrows, movement of the bullocks, measurement of field gaps and unploughed land strips among others. These modifications conformed to existing peasant practices but were also meant to optimise output in relation to peasant needs. Illustrations of these modified versions of the plough, therefore, embedded a process of trust-building to match the innovations with peasant needs.

Plough designs were modified 'truthfully and faithfully' to provide useful and practical solutions for the purposes of improving agricultural production. An example of such accommodation was to illustrate those plough models that could be easily *repaired* (emphasis mine) by the local artisans and peasant communities, with confidence based on an understanding of the new knowledge on offer. Repair models represented a dialogue between the knowledge of the laboratory experts and those who acquiesced to new technology through field experience.

Another aspect of trust-building through illustrations of embodied technology referred to a faithful depiction of the plough bullocks that were often viewed as valuable as the peasant's family or household labour. The plough illustrations showed the different positions of the bullocks on the field that had to be adjusted in relation to the modified designs of ploughs. Farms experimented with the improvement of the mechanical structure of the plough in relation to the prevalent size of bullocks and the strength of cattle. One of the main difficulties regarding the use of improved ploughs was the relative smallness of bullocks generally used by Indian peasants. But some observers explained the resistance of Indian cultivators towards English implements in terms of the way they used bullocks. D.N. Reid a well-known English planter noted that the cultivator was delighted with the newly introduced Macrae's sub-soiler because he could easily get to the tails of the cattle. The cultivator could get more work out of his bullocks when he could reach over to twist the tails. Plough designs had to accommodate these everyday practices of the peasant. In the farm journals, the new plough designs were often juxtaposed with illustrations showing the peasant's intimacy with his cattle, when a new plough was used. These illustrations were meant to emphasise the priorities of a plough team for the peasant economy, instead of a solely focusing on diffusion of technology.

The examples of trust-building through exhibitions of illustrations of technology transfers in traditional village societies embodied certain characteristic features of a scientific dialogue that is reminiscent of an interface between science and culture. There were earlier instances of technical drawings showing the different parts of the traditional plough that were reshuffled to constitute an *ideal* picture but without a corresponding *real* object, that was available for scientific experiments. On the other hand, the real objects imported from English farms were put through a critical lens (Annual report of agricultural stations in charge of the Deputy Director of Agriculture Bengal for the year 1909–10, 1910). Illustrations of plough trials produced newer images that had to faithfully represent the technical modifications and the visual truth embodied in these changes. These new images often exhibited in public trials and in international agricultural shows were considered important mechanisms of technology transfer/dissemination.

24.2 Bullock Cart Illustrations and Rural Futures

As the bullock figured in different capacity through the late nineteenth and first half of twentieth century in the adaptive process of technological improvement, it was somewhat hardwired in the narrative of future rural reordering of space and options for communication. Numerous photos of the cart—a low-capital-intensive technology—appeared with the bullocks pulling off loads of goods as these were transferred across commercial routes that needed surveillance and maintenance. Until the second decade of the nineteenth century, reconstruction of land routes was considered the priority, given that carriage of produce was mainly through navigable rivers and the beaten tracks. Miserably inadequate was a typical expression in many petitions concerning roads. Misery apart, the petitions pointed to material and technical shortcomings, drawing attention to a distinction between roads and village tracks—'unbridged and unmetalled'.

Later decades into the second half of the twentieth century saw the rising importance of metalled and bridged public roads for the development of commerce and trade and for army movements. The question of an all-India bullock cart survey to examine the incidence of damage done by steel-tyred carts on roads brought into focus the utility of bullock carts but pitched the ongoing debate on animal strength in relation to traditional and modern methods of conveyance on village roads. For the survey, a census for standardised information was not considered necessary in lieu of local knowledge of the damage done by carts. The only type of surfacing which stood up to the heavily loaded steel tyre of the bullock cart was the cement concrete slab or track way. The bullock cart, therefore, continued to be the centre piece of the discussion, and fundamental changes to its design were not possible without resolving a range of conflicting demands and alternative views on standard goods vehicles. But there was scope for the rubber tyred bullock cart, carts with modern axle bearings, wood rimmed carts for use on village roads and other modifications and improvements (Silver Jubilee Souvenir on Road Making).

There are innumerable patterns of the country cart in use in India, but their general construction followed some basic principles. Almost all of them could be converted for pneumatic tyre requirement with minor modifications. The commentary on the adaptation of the indigenous cart to pneumatic tyres by W.S. Read, the superintendent of the cattle farm in Hissar,'s testifies to the pace of developing road-friendly vehicles that would reduce the overall cost of their maintenance. The reduced draught of vehicles with pneumatic tyres connotes a faster pace and a greater load capacity, thus increasing the pay load per mile. The cushion of air between the vehicle and the road reduces shock and prolongs the life of the vehicle. The roller bearings running on a steel axle gave several years more service than the soft iron axles. Despite these technical forays into prolonging the life of roads, the emphasis was on the length of the effective life of draught cattle. Here, the immediate and expedient connection between the materiality of roads and the non-human remained a plausible choice. Besides, the scale of adoption of the tyres was still small and limited to wealthy haulage contractors.

Road maintenance and adoption of pneumatic tyres expanded the remit and responsibilities of subsidies from rural reconstruction funds, banks, village societies and the big landowners. These subsidies were needed to protect the ordinary cultivator who was expected to fork out the cash for the tyres that were designed for the suitable uptake of carts available. The ordinary peasant was gradually expected to raise Rs 150 for a set of pneumatic tyres that in turn created normative demands for a new type of cart, the construction of which failed to match the skills of an average *mistri* or a local carpenter. The tyre companies had been slow in adapting to the existing vehicles and consequently mobilising labour for both repair and adaptable designs. Despite these initial shortcomings, the peasants had the ability to invest. With an investment of Rs 150, the peasant had a saving of 82 lbs in the total weight of the cart unladen. Road maintenance generated at the rural level at best added to two day's work for the carpenter and his friend and approximately Rs 8 for new material and a total Rs 11 minus the value of the old material removed from the cart.

The illustrations circulated through many road engineering associations such as in Bombay (present-day Mumbai) and Puna (presently Pune) and used to exemplify war-time discussions in forums like the Congress established the importance of cement concrete as the *future* road material, anticipated about a half-million tonnes of cement per annum required for road building after the Second World War. The efficiency of bullock carts, the urgency to change the design for improving roads opened the technicians to not just issues of technical materials, weights and measures but also to socio-economic needs and issues of right to use—for instance, engaging with a new kind of labour force, industrial materials and a new class of engineers.

II

The bullock cart survey undertaken under the auspices of the Council of the Indian Road Congress and its Bullock Cart subcommittee aimed to evolve a basic wheel incorporating essential requirements which could be compared to the wheels in use on the one hand, and wheels made to various designs to replace the old ones on the other hand. The only alternative was to choose a wheel without exceeding the cost and requiring greater tractive effort for saving in the wear and tear of road surfaces. Hence, the maintenance of road surface was not entirely related to material and technology but choices that would affect the carters. In addition, The IRC paper (No.137, p.187 para 19) recommended the body of the cart to be raised to the level of bullocks' necks. These newer interventions met the interests of the carter by saving on his expenses and bullocks; the community by saving roads too. Saving roads was thus linked to an individual's practical interests in wheel diameters and the community's interest in roads and bullocks.

Maintenance of roads was gradually brought into the fold of rural community entitlements and local decision-making. Here, local contingency and pragmatism was considered but more so the intervention of road users who claim a maximum saving in damage to roads so long a wheel of the same cost and traction was kept in operation. In 1948, the archived survey report mentions the structure of the bullock cartwheel that had no space for expensive springs.

The decision over a wheel diameter and savings on road surfaces was therefore an outcome of cost calculations that were deeply embedded in community sentiments.

By factoring in flexibility, certain issues of animal welfare were evident in a paper (no 128, IRC, Vol 12, No. 4). An IRC member BV Vagh from Mumbai commented on the reduction of injuries to bullocks' necks and damage to road surfaces by such impacts. In the process of these adaptations, there were explorations over short periods and short distances, fashionable to some extent without furnishing data on cost, maintenance and sustained performance. In addition, it was important to see the cartmen's reaction and the extent to which they provide work to the village wheel-wright industry. The consulting engineer to the Government of India (Roads) agreed to experiment on a similar set of wheels manufactured for field tests at the Pusa Agricultural Institute (New Delhi) by employing the same test procedure and variations. The bullock cart sub-committee members were, therefore, involved in a variety of calculations, compilations, charts and drawings and a survey of bullock cartwheels present in India. Mr J.A. Taraporevala who worked with BV Vagh had additionally designed a self-recording dynamometer for these tests that developed a reliable method of recording the experimental variations. The first series of tests on wheels from Sept 23, 1947, to Dec 10, 1947, was carried out at Pune where Taraporevala was also available for free discussion on numerous points.

Taraporevala's machine was, however, unable to cope with several variables that he did not account for, based on his standard expectations and calculations. A preliminary series of tractive efforts was carried out by employing bullocks in place of manual labour, enhancing the possibility of variables such as those unexpected non-human gestures—animals turning their necks sideways and up and down, starting with varying jerks and not keeping the same speed in the short distances used in the tests. It proved difficult to keep the driver from twisting the bullocks' tails for no reason, and it was impossible to keep off the flies—alien habits, and alien creatures proving to be 'environmental hazards'. Both habitual factors influenced the bullocks' movements and added to the difficulty of minimising the variables. Manual labour rather than automation was therefore factored in, and technical progress could not be based on assumed standardisation.

The survey of wheels poignantly pointed out (Annexure VIII p. 144, based on the comments received from the Bullock Cart Sub-Committee) that wheel diameters bore no relation to the height of the bullocks, and it was not generally accepted that wheel diameters should be chosen solely on considerations of cost, since the tractive effort depended on the angle of pull on the axle as transmitted from the yoke on bullocks' necks. Environmental factors such as an increase in the wheel diameter will influence the cost of a wheel appreciably. But carts in rural areas where the soil is sticky clay, all have narrow tyres which will cut through the clay and reduce the tractive effort. Hence, the improvisation experiments juggled with the interests of cost, labour and bullock rather than singularly focusing on the technical aspects of road building.

Fig. 24.7 Segregation of Traffic-Cement Concrete Roads for Cart Traffic

A later post-colonial survey in 1979 reveals a different picture of a more intimate relation between the bullock and road development. This intimacy may be based on nostalgia for the rural than on a reflection of real technical change in the intervening period of three decades in the post-colonial rural development. The nostalgic element in rural thinking was ingrained in a confession that carts represented a civilisational stage to modernity influenced by Gandhian village economics at the time. Despite the yawning gap of years between the two kinds of survey—one by the Road Congress in the colonial archive and the other by the post-colonial collections of independent India's Engineering College—there seemed to be a tacit agreement in how roads could be fashioned. Both surveys showed the technical emphasis in road maintenance, with vehicular objects related to the human or animal bodies. For the cart operations, impressions of the human or animal body co-existed as an abstract nuanced technical reference, with the more direct evidence of technical modifications, suitable for practical successes and local conditions (Fig. 24.7).

24.3 Conclusion

As an ideological process, the scientific reform of agriculture proceeded from 'within' and from practical inquiries. Methodologically, the scheme of practical inquiries and experiments were represented systematically in official illustrations of the scientific farm experiments. Illustrations represented the urge to understand local terminology and practical knowledge, mapping indigenous influence and a variety of conceptual, functional and procedural categories of agricultural knowledge. Studies on cultivation methods entailed further local intervention and opened new indices for agricultural improvement that moved beyond the initial ideas of a botanical progression of knowledge, and its corresponding relation with market strategies. More direct intervention in the methods of production implied a deeper understanding of existing agricultural practices. These local inquiries required experiments in Indian conditions using illustrations in survey methods.

The plough illustrations transcended the parameters of exact representation as was the case with natural history collections. These had coalesced various types of knowledge categories, blurring the boundaries of different levels and forms of expertise. English officials, for example, sought to demonstrate through elaborate illustrations, the difference between 'improved' and 'native' ploughs, comparing the crops grown by one method with those of the other. Officials aimed at the modification of local differences by the transference of better indigenous methods from one part of the country to another, by demonstrating the advantage of those that were more profitable methods. This implied 'scientific' judgements after all, and an assumed opposition between practical knowledge or ignorance and inhibitions and the 'rationality' of improved yield, maximum advantage or standard results obtained from agricultural experiments.

Plough illustrations not only systematically represented mechanical art, but also depicted subtly the details of technical instruction that arose because of trials, matches, experiments and values associated with exhibited objects. The depictions contextualised a dialogue between different categories of knowledge and praxis. In each trial case, for example, the illustrator made a conscious attempt to compare how different parts of an indigenous tool were modified in a new design, without totally compromising peasant's choices. The indigenous elements were represented as part of a system of instruction or modified suitably to be integrated into new methods of operation. Illustrations of the plough also revealed how different types of knowledge—those based on facts and rules, those depending on manipulative skills, intuitions, cultural negotiations or traditions—could be represented with equal vigour to sustain commercial interests in improving agricultural production.

Communication of technical knowledge in India had to rely on various models of visual culture such as those incorporating oral tradition, exhibitions, travelling images in the form of magic lanterns, demonstrations, trials and other genres of visual culture. Illustrations of the plough belonged to the genre of scientific works that applied the 'laws of science' to everyday problems. But technical innovations, in this case, also meant monitoring the progress of farm yield and its adoption by indigenous agencies. Despite the technical emphasis, the human factor was never completely forgotten in these visuals. Consequently, objects were always related to the human or animal bodies. For the plough operations, impressions of the human or animal body often co existed as an abstract nuanced technical reference, with the more direct evidence of technical modifications, suitable for practical successes.

Imaginations apart, these reformulations were also based on empirical truths that stemmed from both farm experiments and personal endeavours of farm illustrators, technical designers and those commissioned to record farm experiments. These men were driven by a desire to 'improve' agricultural implements, by pursuing knowledge about particularities embedded in indigenous practices. They deployed a range of visual rhetoric, either to bolster their own doubts about indigenous implements or to build a relationship of trust to communicate knowledge among the indigenous agencies. This trust-building exercise was an important function of illustrations for the dissemination of technical knowledge in a society where peasant literacy was tied to what I call 'itinerant modes' of communication gathered over trials and experiments, and not simply oral tradition.

The examples of the plough, and later the cartwheel, have shown the extent to which illustrations as marginal archival repositories served to bridge the communication of technology between the different worlds of the peasant, scientist, government and entrepreneurial interests. Later records of survey drawings of the cartwheel were based on comparing calculations that were not always contingent but reflected on labour, maintenance costs, supplies and repairs. Reading into these illustrations of the past had generated a wealth of empirical legacy, and truths consistent with dissemination of scientific knowledge involving indigenous agencies. The cart surveys of independent India stem from Kipling's colonial rural impressions, but the outpouring of rural nostalgia by post-colonial Indian scientists factored in peasant modes of communication geared to reconstructing the village, and in view of progressive urbanisation. Reading into the past through the lens of colonial archival documentation of illustrations creates a long shadow of layered rural impressions. The past lingering in the archive representing continuity and change can be, therefore, repurposed to suit contemporary needs.

Acknowledgements I am grateful to Prof Peter Robb (SOAS) for his comments on an earlier draft used in part for this article. The piece developed subsequently drawing from conference presentations on scientific illustrations held at University of Oxford and ESSHC, and further research supported by the European Research Council. I am responsible for all the shortcomings to present the research.

References

Anon. (1820). Common Country Plough, with the manner of ploughing (Water Colour, London: IOR, British Library, Add Or 5032).
Annual Report of the Sibpur Experimental Farm 1901–02. Calcutta: 1895–1908 (London: IOR, V/24/1541).
Annual report of agricultural stations in charge of the Deputy Director of Agriculture Bengal for the year 1909–10 (Calcutta: 1910).

Arnold D. (October 2005). 'Agriculture and 'Improvement' in early colonial India: a pre-history of development', *Journal of Agrarian Change*, 5, 4.
Bayly, C. A. (1996). *Empire and Information: Intelligence gathering and social communication in India, 1780–1870* (Cambridge: CUP).
Boserup, Ester. (1965). *The Conditions of Agricultural Growth: the Economics of Agrarian Change under Population Pressure*. http://www.biw.kuleuven.be/aee/clo/idessa files/Boserup1965.pdf. Accessed 17 April 2010.
Chatterjee, P. (2003). 'The Social Sciences in India', in Theodore H. Porter and Dorothy Ross (eds.), *The Cambridge History of Science: the Modern Social Sciences*, vol. 7, Cambridge: CUP.
Cohn, Bernard S. (1996). *Colonialism and its Forms of Knowledge: the British in India*, Princeton: Princeton University Press.
Edney, Matthew H. (1997). *Mapping an Empire: The Geographical Construction of British India 1765–1843* (Chicago & London: University of Chicago Press).
Godbole, S. S. (1914). 'Improvement of indigenous plough of Western India', *Bombay Agricultural Department Bulletin*, London British Library: India Office Records, V/25/500/252, No. 57.
Goddard, Nicholas. (1988). *Harvests of Change: The Royal Agricultural Society of England 1838–1988* (London: Quiller Press).
Grout, A. (1990). 'Geology and India, 1775–1805: an episode in colonial science', *South Asia Research* 10, pp. 1–18.
Hailey, H. R. C. (1918). 'Sale and Loan of Agricultural Implements', *Agricultural Journal of India*, 13, 2, pp. 319–332.
Henderson G. S. (1917). 'New agricultural implements for India', British Library London: India Office Records, V/25/500/123.
Henry, R. J. (1995). 'Technology Transfer and Its Constraints: Early warnings from agricultural development in colonial India' in Roy MacLeod and Deepak Kumar (eds.), *Technology and the Raj: Western Technology and Technical Transfers to India 1700–1947* (New Delhi: Thousand Oaks, Sage Publications).
Hodge, Joseph M. (2007). Triumph of the Expert: Agrarian Doctrines of Development and the Legacies of British Colonialism (Athens: Ohio University Press).
Illustrated London News. (6 February 1847). vol. 10, 249.
'Indigenous agricultural implements of India: an all-India survey'. (1960). *Indian Council of Agricultural Research* (New Delhi).
Krishi Sampad/Agricultural Resource. (1910). vol. 2, 11–12, p. 339.
Kumar, D. (1995). *Science and the Raj, 1857–1905* (Delhi: Oxford University Press).
Ludden, D. (ed.) (1994). *Agricultural Production and Indian History* (New Delhi: OUP), pp. 1–36.
Mollison, J. W. (1900). 'Manual of power tillage implements', *Bombay Agricultural Department Bulletin*, London British library: India Office Records, V/25/500/247/No.21.
Robb, P. G. (1998). 'Completing "our stock of geography", or an object "still more sublime": Colin Mackenzie's survey of Mysore, 1799–1810', *Journal of the Royal Asiatic Society*, 8, 2.
Yegna Narayan Aiyer, A. K. (1953). *Principles of crop husbandry in India*, Bangalore: India.
Sangawan, S. (1989). 'Trial of Strength', workshop on *Traditional Technologies in Indian Agriculture* (NISTADS: New Delhi).
Voelcker, J. A. (1893/1986). *Report on the Improvement of Indian Agriculture* (New Delhi: Agricole).

CHAPTER 25

Conclusion: Challenges of Social Research—A Way Forward

Alak Paul

From the beginning of human history, there have been differences in opinion on how research should be conducted. Philosophers such as Kuhn (1962, 1970), Foucault (1972, 1980) and Habermas (1987) have argued about the four concepts of research: ethics (axiology), epistemology, ontology and methodology (Guba 1990). Here ethics asks, how will I be a moral person in the world? Epistemology asks, how do I know the world? Ontology raises questions about the nature of reality and the nature of the human beings in the world; and methodology focuses on the best means for gaining knowledge about the world (Denzin and Lincoln 2000). Basic research aims to contribute to fundamental knowledge and theory (Patton 1990), but developing theory is a complex activity (Strauss and Corbin 1998). Theories are derived from the fieldwork process, are refined and tested during fieldwork and are gradually elaborated into higher levels of abstraction towards the end of the data collection phase (Bryman 1996). In social research, there are three major ingredients: the construction of theory, the collection of data and the design of methods for gathering data (Gilbert 2001). Social theory, along with social research, is of central importance in the social sciences (May 1997). Methodology in social research refers to the techniques and epistemological presuppositions that contribute to how information is identified and analysed about a research problem (Filstead 1979; Innes 2001). The quantitative

A. Paul (✉)
Department of Geography and Environmental Studies, University of Chittagong, Chittagong, Bangladesh
e-mail: paul.alak@cu.ac.bd

© The Author(s), under exclusive license to Springer Nature Switzerland AG 2023
N. Uddin, A. Paul (eds.), *The Palgrave Handbook of Social Fieldwork*, https://doi.org/10.1007/978-3-031-13615-3_25

researcher adopts the posture of an outsider looking in on the social world. Quantitative research is typically taken to be exemplified by social surveys and by experimental investigations (Bryman 1996). On the contrary, knowledge and theory are generated from empirical data in qualitative research (Bunne 1999) and oriented towards exploration and discovery (Patton 1990). Qualitative methods can be used to explore substantive areas about which little is known (Stern 1980), like people's lives, experiences, behaviours, emotions and feelings (Strauss and Corbin 1998). Like human geographers, social researchers have been involved in such debates, and there are several schools of thought on the best way to approach the relationship between society, space, place and environment (Kitchin and Tate 2000).

Inquiring about social issues or problems is the basics of social research where social researchers observe and analyse the 'world', using talk, text, photographs and so forth, depending on natural settings and people's experiences. Apart from general settings, social research is very much ideal for accessing vulnerable, stigmatized or hidden people through case studies, interviewing, participant observation, visual methods and interpretive analysis. Social researchers mostly depend on empirical information using moments and meanings of individual lives. However, research in natural settings like forests and wetlands is also considered a research area where observation is one of the prime methods. In both settings, fieldwork is a focused activity where researchers of anthropology, geography, psychology, political studies, natural science, history, women studies and so forth get the opportunity to talk or see or observe the participants or subjects. But, in social research, there are some concerns and challenging issues which should be addressed properly. For example, the validity crisis is one of the important controversies in contemporary social research. Ambiguity is very common in social research. Though researchers have some concepts about their existing literature and research questions, most of them have no idea what to know and what to uncover from their respondents or subjects. In many cases, the research questions and data collection procedures develop on the 'ground'. Due to flexibility in social research, researchers expect and produce many new data as unanticipated in the research. Some social researchers are not aware of ethical responsibilities. The sampling strategy is one of the challenging issues for social research. In social research, ambiguity is very common. Personal life and security might be affected while researching sensitive issues. Respondent's dishonesty about research issues may disrupt the progress of the research outcomes. Social and political factors can affect the outcome of social research. All these issues may involve some challenges to achieving their outcome.

In minimizing these challenges, researchers generally consider some issues to develop a good context. Self-wisdom, skill and support can play a big role to minimize 'field' challenges. Sampling has been an important topic in social research. A good sampling strategy would help for a better in-depth understanding of the research subject as well as a good representation of the whole population. Social researchers need to validate the data obtained from the respondents from other sources. Valid information from the respondents may come out through a good understanding between both. Sampling judgement should be employed by own wisdom and planning. Wisdom (judgement) and planning are the best solutions to select the research area, participants and sampling strategy. As most researchers use purposive sampling in social research, researchers need to be careful about the business with subjects. However, flexibility, sense of humour, consolation, dignity and respect, soft language, encouragement, facial expressions, emotional attachment and so forth are the common practical techniques that need to be involved between interviewer and interviewees in social research. Understanding is necessary between both parties through personal contact. Social research encourages researchers to be close with their research participants using soft language. Keeping flexibility in mind is a must for social researchers when they involve in fieldwork. They should maintain both a good sense of humour and consolation towards the interviewee and the issues to be discussed. Any aggressive or hostile attitudes may be considered disrespectful to interviewees. Even, (s)he should never try to exploit the respondents in any way. The dilemma of research ethics in social research needs to be considered. Researchers have the responsibility to keep the respondent's data confidential. Anonymity is an important component in social research where identity disclosure is being protected. In social research, researchers need to take proper consent/ permission before work or project. As a part of the responsibility, a researcher needs to keep privacy about the research issue and ensure the safety of the respondents from the 'outsiders'. Moreover, he or she needs to ensure that this research will not impinge/ impact his or her physical, mental or emotional health. This discussion presents the contemporary challenges of social research and its minimization procedures.

25.1 Challenges of Social Research

Social research involves an interpretive, naturalistic approach to the world. Social researchers always believe that good interpretations would come out from the individual. Various social, economic, political, demographic or environmental contexts or settings influence the challenges in social research. Various field and other challenges encountered by the authors are presented in the following.

Doing human geographical fieldwork in the water has many challenges and uncertainties which have been described by Ronan Foley in his recent field-based research with swimmers in Ireland using swim-along interviews. This will be exemplified in fieldwork-driven studies of surfing, kayaking, diving, sailing and swimming. He mentioned that research in the mobile settings of waters, both coastal and inland can be challenging, in terms of practice, ethics and the kinds of contemporary technologies used in such work. Moving beyond the body, blue spaces are sites of significant inhabitation and research in such spaces can have negative elements: invasion of spaces, privacy, access and place triggers. Doing research in the moving field of water, meant directly experiencing mobility and motility and getting caught up in the swirl and churn of the experience. Moreover, there are transgressive and risky blue space communities who seek danger either in their practice or in the spaces they go.

The fieldwork that Eric de Maaker conducted in the Garo Hills of Eastern Meghalaya, India, on death-related practices required close engagement with a limited number of people. He not only emphasized on 'trust' and 'rapport' required for the fieldwork but also made sure presence of multiple dimensions of the relationships among the concerned people in the field as traders, as kinsmen, or when acting by their religious responsibilities. In the beginning, he needed a research permit to do research in India. One of the things that he noted during his first weeks in the Garo Hills was the great disparity that existed between people's lifestyles in the towns, as compared to that in villages, especially since modern-day comforts were absent. There was no electricity, no telephone, and water had to be collected in a vessel or a bucket from a well. Most of the villagers had very little access to money, and would not be able to buy much from the shops or in the market. On the day they left, Eric suffered from a high fever, and it took about a month for him to recover from malaria.

Social researches sometimes become complex, scary and frustrating exercise where researchers feel highly dictated, especially when a researcher lacks a good understanding of the people and cultural constraints which Adebayo Adewusi faced in Nigeria. In the field, some social researchers face aggressive respondents, personal embarrassment, insulting words and physical injury. He conducted oral interviews and shared his practical experience on how cultural imperatives, wrong perceptions about research and researchers and other socio-economic and political factors can constitute major hurdles for researchers from gaining access to places and, most importantly, informants. Adebayo thinks that interviewees may change their minds to stop suddenly while talking to an interviewer. Sometimes, they consider the researcher as a stranger. Sometimes, interviewees feel curious about the payment for their responses to the interviewers. They might consider the study funded by either government or private organizations. He concluded that there might be some cultural distances between the interviewees and interviewer from the perspective of religion, caste, gender, ethnicity, residence and economic status, which hamper the progress of the study.

Social researchers sometimes find themselves in a vulnerable position such as violent encounters while undertaking fieldwork in an unknown dangerous field, like Nagaland, India. Debojyoti Das conducted fourteen months of ethnographic fieldwork in Nagaland under ceasefire with the hope to be normal where violence was part of everyday life propitiated by state and non-state actors in the disturbed borderland region, at the margins of the Indian state. But, unfortunately, he was caught up in a hostage situation while travelling with his interlocutor. The hostage was triggered by the local factional clash about development money that was spent on public works in the village funded by India's largest employment programme. During his fieldwork, it became increasingly difficult for him to detach himself from the everyday village life and politics of the field. Besides this, he was perturbed by another challenge in the field to find the right collaborators for his research. The researcher's lack of access to the study community creates challenges in finding good interlocutors for the field.

Anuradha Sen Mokharjee completed her ethnography of the experiences of the newly documented Indian citizens of the former Bangladeshi border enclaves that were exchanged between Bangladesh and India on 1 August 2015. It was difficult for her to enter the field without taking help from the local party leaders who resided in the enclaves, so she took help from the community-based activist organization headquartered on the Indian side of the border in the Dinhata subdivision of Cooch Behar that had a history of community activism. Anuradha felt unsettled and disappointed at the beginning of her fieldwork. During the fieldwork, the researcher expected support from her social environment. She faced threats in the field which led to emotional trauma; this is how social researchers put themselves into vulnerable situations during the fieldwork.

Ian G. Baird provided some information about five people from Laos, Thailand, Cambodia, the United States and Canada with whom he has developed long-term interview-based relationships. All these relationships have varied, although they have become normal for him, and he suspects that there are many others—some still lurking in the shadows—who have adopted similar approaches to engaging with long-term interview-based research, especially those who work on the oral history of various type. While there are plenty of articles written about advantages of interview methods, there has been surprisingly little written about the complex, messy and often unorthodox long-term interview-based relationships.

Experiencing a physical or mental illness can have devastating effects on data collection and the ability to participate in fieldwork settings, which Olea Morris faced in her fieldwork for her dissertation research in Mexico. She observed that the experience of the illness itself not only weakened her physically but also cultivated stress around her ability to successfully conduct research with her interlocutors. Despite her best intentions, her illness also strained relationships that had just begun to be formed. Some residents became frustrated with her demeanour, mistaking her lack of engagement (and appetite) for impoliteness. Travelling from one to the other location to meet the respondents for interviews becomes challenging and risky for a female researcher, especially who is an outsider in the study area. Moreover, female researchers' presence created curiosity in small towns and villages, and lonely roads, remotely located houses and offices became very risky for them.

Conducting fieldwork with a hidden population (in a black market) of human organs can be risky and challenging. Monir Moniruzzaman faced tremendous difficulties in his ethnographic research in Bangladesh on the illicit organ market, particularly in gaining access to organ sellers. Many sellers did not disclose their actions to or even share their stories with their family members, as selling body parts is considered an outlawed and repulsive act. In addition, sellers reside in every part of that country, so they are unknown to each other; as a result, he was unable to employ snowball sampling in locating them. While a key informant technique can be effective in gaining access to a hidden population, it can also be ethically and methodologically problematic. For example, searching kidney sellers through an organ broker posed several challenges. To what extent should the broker or middleman participate as a key informant? How should he be approached, persuaded and compensated? Why would he support research that might reveal, restrict or ruin his illicit business?

Sensitive research highly requires research integrity along with personal ethics and responsibility in handling confidential information mentioned by Pragna Paramita Mondal. Here are questions of access, research subjectivity, bias, the harm principle, informed consent and ethical negotiations in conducting social research on biomedical subjects, especially fieldwork on surrogacy in Kolkata and other cities of India. Although the research relied on the ethnographic format, there were certain deviations from traditional ethnographic methods based on endogenous conditions within the research site. It was not possible to stay with the surrogates that she interviewed and to conduct participant observation at a more proximal level. It was thus not only her research integrity but also her ethics and responsibility in handling confidential information that was being mapped out by the 'gatekeepers'. The other concern that she had to sort out through the different stages of the fieldwork was the aspect of interdisciplinarity that her work on surrogacy was meant to encompass. This interdisciplinarity was not only the basis of her research training and her approach to engaging in a field-oriented study of women in surrogacy, but it also related to the gap that she tried to address within the literature on Indian surrogacy.

Being a health geographer, Alak Paul spent more than six months in Bangladesh for extensive fieldwork using qualitative methods. He faced several problems during his 'sensitive' fieldwork when he worked with some socially marginalized and vulnerable people like sex workers, drug users, and so on. Before starting fieldwork, he had regular communication with local civil administration's high officials and high police officials of the study areas since he worked with some groups who are usually termed 'dangerous' by local people. Many locals advised him to keep in regular contact with the police to avoid potential dangers or harassment from drug users, sex workers or others. During the fieldwork, Alak regularly met with abusive language from the participants, bad experiences with these 'inaccessible' communities, anxiety for interview recording, wrong assumptions, misbehaviour, refusal to talk and so forth.

Minjune Song mentioned that social research has several limitations like using cross-sectional data that are not longitudinal or derived from a controlled setting, the limited sample size, accurate and honest measures from self-reported surveys and so forth.

Doing research with vulnerable communities in coastal Bangladesh always involves different kinds of challenges including emotional attachments versus professional detachment, objective analysis versus subjective interpretation and mere collective data versus doing something for them. In qualitative fieldwork, Kamal, Hassan and Uddin addressed that interactions with participants often take a long time and intense interaction. Researchers need to listen to participants' life histories which often make them upset, sad and anxious. Long engagement with participants and life histories, therefore, put them in ethical and moral dilemmas. The ethical challenges arise from relationships with participants, miscommunication between researchers and respondents and relational dynamics between researchers and collaborators. Researchers feel moral responsibilities of 'giving back' or helping 'vulnerable' people, but they have tittle option as the research plan focuses on completing fieldwork and data collection in a specific time rather than on helping people in vulnerable conditions. As a result, researchers would feel discomfort and guilty for not giving back to the research participants and not doing something that directly benefits them.

Research on gender-based violence involves risks and concerns for the researcher, especially while staying in the study area in a threatening environment. From the Bangladesh context, Nahid Rezwana mentioned that different types of physical risks are common for women researchers working on gender issues in developing countries. Sometimes researchers may feel threatened by harassment and even sexual abuse. She described the female aid workers who were discriminated against by the residents in continuing their daily basic routine, for example,. taking baths, going to the toilet, and so on. They had to leave the area without completing their plans of relief distribution and help to avoid further humiliation. Geographical location, culture, social attitude and especially gender perception among the studied social workers are factors that increase challenges and risks for the researcher.

For the purpose of feminist research, Ekata Bakshi focused mainly on refugee families in India who come from the then East Pakistan (now, Bangladesh) in the 70s. Although there are some difficulties to understand responses immediately, over time she realized the reasons for refusal and the inner sense of their conversations as well. She also understood that many of the second- and third-generation refugees, despite being aware of the fact that the event of displacement has affected and still affects their socio-economic and political conditions, do not want to use the term refugee for themselves because of the stigmatized connotations of the term. Moreover, some others simply did not want to tell the stories because they did not want to remember the past. A deeply perplexing moment in the research was reading silences, and it was difficult for her to read these responses immediately when she was engaged in using the oral history method.

Zuriatunfadzliah Sahdan examined the complexities of space and the everyday lives of women in domestic violence and how interventions might be made. As a Malay-Muslim woman, she was an outsider to the Indian participants, especially in terms of culture and religion. During the fieldwork, the staff in the shelter introduced her to the survivors as an intern. This position created a barrier between her and them. This is because interns in the shelter are often stereotyped as 'feminist', middle class, from overseas universities and who prefer to use English as the first language. In social research, respondents sometimes have some stereotyped mindset about the interviewer that she faced during her study in Malaysia, where most women were awkward about starting a conversation with her. There are also some ethical considerations in the use of photovoice, such as the risk of privacy invasion.

Researchers encounter a variety of challenges, vulnerabilities and experiences in the field, particularly while conducting research with another gender. Main Uddin found that when a male researcher talks to a woman, sometimes enthusiastic neighbours come and sit next to the woman and start sharing their opinions. He observed that the researchers and the informants are observed differently by people in the community based on age, gender, marital status, family status, dress code and body language. Participants don't like to see a male researcher and a young female informant talking in a particular place for a long time. Exploring female agency by the male researcher is a challenging endeavour, especially in a patriarchal Muslim society like rural Bangladesh. He was always wary not only of the reaction of community people but also of the women of the village when talking to them individually in separate places.

In every aspect of researching the Rohingya refugees, a conscious sense of contestation between academic and activist positioning always puts the researcher in a dilemma of ethical concerns. Nasir Uddin presented the experience of recording the traumatized narratives which put him in serious methodological changes as far as the code of ethics in ethnographic research are concerned. A refugee researcher upholds a strong sense of feeling for their demands, deep attachment to their pains, profound affection for their everyday struggle and a passionate mind for their everyday needs. As a human being, it was very difficult not to be emotionally biased, but he had to maintain academic professionalism. So, there is always an academic and activist conflict in his understanding, his interpretation, his writing and his analysis as far as the Rohingya research is concerned.

As a policy impact evaluation researcher in African contexts, Deo-Gracias Houndolo noted how high the risk of failure may be in moving research methods into the field. He observed that institutional preparation and stakeholders' engagement for application submission and getting the approval for data collection can delay research start and implementation. Conflict of interests may lead to the worst situation. Another serious challenge occurs when the methodology proposed by the research team is not known to members of the committee in charge of approving the fieldwork. The main challenge with questionnaires is their length, clarity of questions asked and the risk of endless changes that happens during the preparation phase concerning their structure, composition and format. However, he mentioned that sample selection, adaptation to cultural and religious norms, use of computer-based technology in areas with no Internet and electricity coverage, language challenges and so forth are the basic barriers in the field. Social researchers need to manage the shortage of time allocated for fieldwork, facing budget constraints, health issues in the field, tracking respondents, adapting to the high refusal rate of respondents and so forth.

Matteo Fumagalli tried to reflect on how his various and evolving identities and positionalities shaped his research, including his relationship with the participants and 'the field' broadly conceived. He used examples from three case studies of relevant ethnic minority groups in Central Asia, offering some degree of variation in terms of access and entry and the degree of openness and closure of the local research environment to discuss his positionality. Some of the reported challenges are peculiar/distinctive to the post-Soviet context, such as many authoritarian countries tending to regulate the possibility of conducting research by restricting entry (through visas); the harassment of friends and collaborators, defying exit; and the personal safety of local and international partners when conducting research. He said that the question of entry into this region is still an ethical, logistical and ultimately also a legal challenge.

Generally talking about sex is interesting to young men in Bangladesh as long as you do not ask about very personal, sensitive sexual practices. Sayed Md Saikh Imtiaz posited a very important methodological concern regarding his subjectivity as a researcher. No doubt dealing with subjectivity and positionality also needs to be substantiated by corresponding data collection methods specifically when researching sexual practices. Being a researcher, his subjectivity and the subjectivities of his informants required an initial agreement on certain points about breaking the socially desired rules (i.e. not to speak about sexuality openly, not to reveal the 'dirty little secrets'). Nevertheless, giving a 'thick description' of the subjective experiences to conduct the ethnographic fieldwork can ensure an alternative to the 'objectivity' of positivist research methodology while ensuring the reliability of the study.

Kapil Dahal carried out a multi-sited ethnographic study to generate information about health-seeking practices and to know about the health and wellbeing of Tarai Brahmin women in Nepal. He found that the nature of the relationship between the researcher and the participants over the period passes through the dialectical upheavals, and he would argue that, eventually, such a pattern contributes ultimately to the production of knowledge. He agreed that the relation between the researcher's positionalities and the research participants is fluid. The form of relatedness between the research partners and various spectrums between them, ultimately, at least for a reflective researcher, contributes to knowledge production.

Melati Nungsari observed that data collection in the field is often complicated by geographical challenges, ethical considerations, funding capacity and the recruitment of participants, especially people of hidden or vulnerable groups. She considered that incentives or payments for participants can play a positive role in having a successful project. Though there might be some issues of business with giving payments, respondents' enthusiasm and mental energy for joining the study may increase. Other than cash incentives, consumable foods or drinks or other gifts like educational aids for participant's kid(s), toiletries, and so on can be provided for an impactful project. Recruitment of interviewees for the study has some methodological challenges like sampling biases, underrepresentation of women as participants, and so on.

In India, official observation and recording through extensive field notes revealed the exotic perception of the tropical flora and the fauna. Sanjukta Ghosh demonstrated the drawings and paintings of the tropical environment, indigenous ways of life and artefacts of India were diligently depicted by a select group of artists, travellers, and some scientific professionals such as naturalists, who tried to combine their amateur interests with their careers in civil service. Scientific visualization in these early pursuits of object illustration had a looser interpretation and focused mainly on the direct comparison (flora, fauna, topographical details), showing the urge to maintain accuracy in scientific observation and research.

25.2 'Coping' with Fieldwork Challenges

To address many challenges in the fieldwork, social researchers need to cope physically and mentally to generate quality data. All field challenges can be minimized through the researcher's self-determination to achieve the final essence of the research. The following discussion presents the coping practices for managing fieldwork challenges that might be considered new reinterpretations of methodologies in social research using the narratives of the authors of this book.

There is a growing interest in research on and in the water, based on a recent turn in human geographical research towards blue space, especially in relation to a range of leisure practices that promote health and well-being detailed by Ronan Foley. Fieldwork in blue space needs more attention on how to research in the water because water is complex, mobile and an always unpredictable more-than-human element in such research. This can shape how and when the fieldwork can be done, as well as bring in other considerations such as risk and access. As swimming often produces an inversion of both person and place, it provides what might be termed a bathymetric understanding of space, providing depth, flow, but also a volumetric insight into the water in ways not possible on land. In addition, a deeper place engagement often leads to deeper place care and enhanced environmental awareness. Ronan thinks that this method possesses significant learning for the researcher from the exploration and discovery within field practice as well as the joy of sharing as a research tool; an emplaced noticing of how health and especially well-being emerged in those coastal and inland blue spaces.

Eric de Maaker achieved his best in the field by interacting with people over a prolonged period. Accompanied by a local folklorist he visited many places, notably in the east and west of the Garo Hills using public transport or on foot. Carrying backpacks with a sleeping mat and some food, he stayed over wherever they were invited, and he met a large number of people for making relationships for the years to come. He depended upon university-educated Garos for the fieldwork. He believed that the writing and films that have come out of the fieldwork and will most probably continue to emerge over the next couple of years will hopefully contribute to an appreciation for a rich culture among a broad audience. Eric tried to get organized, get established and sustain relationships in his fieldwork.

From the Nigerian context, Adebayo Adewusi mentioned how a determined researcher in the face of the tyrannies was able to navigate the convoluted system through understanding and adaptations dictated by the peculiarities of different communities without compromising the ethics of research. Researchers should conduct the study without compromising the ethics of research. As a historian, he preferred to gather as much information as may be available from different sources to avoid the risk of being misled in concluding. During the field, the interaction between the observer and the observed plays a significant role in data collection. He observed that interviewing becomes a suitable and standard data collection method across disciplines in social sciences, humanities and medical science over the years.

Fieldwork allows bridging connections with interlocuters, participants and informants. Debojyoti Das adopted a method of collaboration in which he shared his field notes with his interlocutors and solicited their opinion on what he wrote or thought about them. Such participation cleared many preconceptions about the community he lived in and over time he came to be recognized by village members as one of them. On one occasion, villagers announced that he is no longer an outsider. Such intimacy grew out of his participation in mundane activities, the sharing of food with residents and staying overnight with them in their paddy fields. This collaborative proactive instilled trust and fostered friendship with the villagers with whom he lived.

The emotions and experiences that follow field encounters are integral to the research process, with data emerging from the interplay of the researcher with the object of study. Anuradha Sen Mokharjee spent time with her interlocutors and her landlord's family to build a relationship of trust. She was aware that her interlocutors from the enclaves were used to talking to journalists as the former enclaves had received a wide reportage. She concluded that a fieldworker needs careful preparation, especially gaining an idea about people and their socio-cultural context in the field before starting the study.

Ian G. Baird demonstrated that interviewing can often occur over many years, and in a range of different contexts and formats. We need to acknowledge and embrace the inherent messiness of these sorts of research encounters. Everything from the topic of interest to the researcher, to the nature of past interactions, to the context of when and where the interviewer and interviewee meet, and many more factors, far more than it is possible to outline in detail here, are potentially important for determining how different interview experiences play out. These sorts of relationships are especially useful when investigating politically sensitive topics, or other topics that require a detailed understanding of the people involved. We need to make more space for interviewing based on long-term relationship-building to be better recognized as a legitimate, indeed a necessary method, for investigating a range of different topics in an array of variable contexts, ones that can only really be properly studied through multiple interactions over potentially many years.

Olea Morris suggested that illness—like other states of being that researchers might encounter—presents its range of possibilities for further ethnographic inquiry. She observed that it must be acknowledged that illness is just as much a part of the fieldwork landscape as any other condition common to the human experience. The experiences were not extraneous to her fieldwork experiences but represented formative points in her research process as a whole, as well as the communities with which she worked. Both experiences of illness in the field revealed broader patterns of relating that she might not have otherwise noticed, for example, gaps in communication between residents, latent biases, assumptions or diverse knowledge systems implicated in framing and treating illness. Experiencing illness as a collective phenomenon, rather than as an individual experience, had important ramifications for her rapport with her interlocutors as well as her capacity to collect information.

After guaranteeing the confidentiality, Monir Moniruzzaman explained his research project to the informants and sought their support in search of organ sellers. He upheld ethical integrity, promoted methodological innovation and minimized his respondents' risks, amidst facing serious challenges in locating kidney sellers in Bangladesh. Throughout his field notes, transcripts and publications, he used pseudonyms and released photographs of his respondents without revealing their faces to protect their identities and minimize any harm to them. He mentioned that ethnographers should be truthful to their interview subjects, minimize their risks and commit to the change by relentlessly exposing exploitation without revealing their identities.

In her sensitive research on Indian surrogacy, Pragna Paramita Mondal rephrased some of the critical questions asked to the participants to release their defensive attitudes and elicit more confident and open responses. She emphasized the first-hand experience of the 'learning by doing the process'. The nature of the data sought through interviews and the range of the enquiry thus continued to change and grow in newer directions and that added largely to the richness and potential of the research. The interdisciplinary tool was also useful in explaining her positionality as a researcher because some of her respondents were curious enough to ask her how her research would contribute to a field that specifically concerned doctors, medicine and medical technology.

Alak Paul observed that the interviewer needs to have trust in the interviewees in qualitative 'fieldwork'. On the contrary, the respondent has to be emotionally attached to the issue that helps grow convenience. Researchers need to be flexible for 'unexpected information' which might change the research direction. Even, both parties need to be sensible to research content and be respectful of each other's dignity and state of mind. He adopted no authoritarian or patronizing attitudes in his approach to them. During interviews he was sympathetic; good behaviour and simplicity, and sometimes some emotional expressions, also influenced them to share their untold stories. He never showed any aggressive or hostile attitudes in his questions and did not ask about any issues that they might consider disrespectful. He never tried to exploit these people in any way.

Minjune Song found that separation of data, inherently requiring a larger data pool, may account for such preconditioned trends that may skew results. A more systematic approach would be taken to rate school policy and its punishments on some standard metric, through questioning administrators or by self-conducting policy analysis. This effort, again, would require a large-scale study with a broader state-wide or national scope.

Research with vulnerable people and communities is complex as their vulnerabilities are intertwined with various social, economic, political and cultural factors. Kamal, Hassan and Uddin suggested broadening ethical measures to minimize researchers' dilemmas and challenges. In addition to that, informal support networks with colleagues, trusted friends and family members can minimize ethical dilemmas that arise from fieldwork with climate-vulnerable communities. If researchers become aware of local perceptions and perspectives about research, researchers and common research terminologies, they may avoid discomfort and confusion. However, the researchers minimize some of these dilemmas based on their experiences.

Nahid Rezwana discussed ensuring the interviewer's safety to avoid any unwanted circumstances and risks when conducting fieldwork that can affect the quality of data collection. Paying proper attention and taking measures in assessing researchers' risk, and making plans to ensure their safety while designing research projects, are the most common recommendations. She mentioned that researchers should spend more time in the study area and get familiar with the local people. He/she should attend invitations, talk with the locals doing daily shopping and visit local gatherings (water collection points, shared ponds, etc.) for a deeper understanding of local cultures. She recommended that the researcher should prepare with a second topic, which allows her/him to meet the curiosity of the residents who are not related to/involved in the study.

Feminist researchers, like Ekata Bakshi, focused to locate the lived experiences of women through a historical, contextual understanding of social, economic and political conditions. She emphasized trying to listen as closely as possible to deconstruct the dominant feminist subjectivity. During the course of her fieldwork, she became close to her respondents. She argues that it's possible to deconstruct the dominant feminist subjectivity by trying to listen as closely as possible and engage seriously with the 'Other's' narrative.

Zuriatunfadzliah Sahdan described the specific methodological techniques that would be used to minimize participants' risks and maximize benefits to them. She obtained signed permission from the participants to release the photos so that their photos could be posted or used in the exhibition, digital stories or on the website. The shelter management gave her a task assignment to facilitate engagement with the volunteers, and she was asked to teach them computing. The process of building rapport was easier once participants recognized her as a volunteer, as it made it easier for them to get to know each other. However, avoiding pride had helped her to connect with and understand her interviewees. In addition, many of the survivors shared stories once they trusted her, because she showed them empathy.

Main Uddin focused that researchers need to adopt various strategies for collecting expected data, especially when conducting ethnographic research. To conduct ethnographic research in an adverse environment, he hired one of his female anthropology students to work as his assistant in the field. The assistant conducted most of the individual discussions with women while he talked to men to understand their views about women's issues. He also talked to many women of different ages individually in separate places considering the situation and the sociability of the women. For that reason, he took a long time to understand the situation and to find out the liberal families where he can talk to women. He always waited for a trustworthy relationship and congenial environment for individual discussion with the women.

Nasir Uddin emphasized that refugee researchers should be careful between emotional attachment and professional detachment. He mentioned that an academic cannot be an activist or an activist cannot be an academic, but maintaining an intelligent balance between the two is essential to conduct good-quality research and produce relatively objective findings. It is more applicable in refugee research because refugees are structurally a vulnerable group of people which put the researcher into different forms of moral challenges and ethical dilemmas. However, to enhance the rights of the Rohingya people, he published many books and scientific and popular articles in different national and international media outlets. Nasir advocated for their repatriation, but it should be voluntary and dignified with legal recognition and social safety.

Deo-Gracias Houndolo realized that high-quality and dedicated field staff recruitment is essential for good fieldwork. He preferred to run proper pre-tests during the preparation phase and learn the lessons. Moreover, it is important to take action after the pre-test and pilot phase and do necessary questionnaire pruning, reduce the length of instruments and use 'focused instruments' for data collection. In some cases, it is required to translate survey instruments into other languages, namely local languages. Data collection in modern days uses either partially or entirely computer-assisted personalized interviews. It requires programming the instruments in ways that allow using a smartphone for data collection. This phase of fieldwork preparation requires designing the organigram of the field staff, conducting a pre-test of data collection instruments, a field visit to build contacts on the ground and organizing the recruitment of field staff (namely the enumerators and supervisors) and their training including a pilot survey.

Matteo Fumagalli raised the question of how academics should introduce themselves and their research to the participants. Although he was not able to reflect on how his ethnicity/race was viewed in the field or how it affected his research, he was aware that if he was at times distinguishable or indistinguishable it was because he also could come across as Russian/Slavic. He spent a few weeks reading local media and got language training. He has tried to shed light on selected experiences of entry, access, bans and returns to the field to reflect on his positionality as an international researcher. Taken together, all these speak to questions of power, hierarchies and inequalities, and the structures and systems that create, underpin and perpetuate them. He realized that researchers need to consider carefully the power they may represent to others in terms of access to money, publications, jobs or even just access point to the outside world.

Sayed Md Saikh Imtiaz collected as many examples as possible that helped him to analyse the phenomena and found commonalities, differences, patterns and structures. His field notes and diary entries regarding hot spot and cold spot helped him to minimize the biases. He employed the safeguards to protect the informants' rights: the research objectives were always articulated verbally and in writing so that they were clearly understood by the informants; written permission to proceed with the study as articulated was received from the informants where necessary; informants were informed of all data collection devices and activities; verbatim transcriptions and written interpretations and reports were made available to the informants; the informants' rights, interests and wishes were considered first when choices were made regarding reporting the data; and the final decision regarding informant anonymity rested with the informants themselves.

Kapil Dahal suggested that the researcher has to be sensitive to his specific participants along with their emotions, surprises and sometimes even discomforts, which can open up the ethnographer's horizon of thinking and data handing, approaching the situation and meaningfully engaging in the field. Kapil constantly made reflexive analyses of his relationship with his research participants and how that shapes his positionality in the field and reshapes the knowledge arising from the research. His reflection portrays the hesitation and shyness of the research participants whenever he had acted as 'the reluctant researcher'.

Melati Nungsari focused that social researchers should be aware of all ethical considerations, and they must give attention to the time, venue and method when collecting data in the field. Taking consent (informed or direct) from the respondents is very crucial in social research. For managing the issue of the legitimacy of informed consent, she proposed participatory methods in participant recruitment. Researchers should employ a variety of different methods of data collection for addressing the challenge of the under-representation of women.

Sanjukta Ghosh explained the challenges of historical methods of reading the colonial archives to locate indigenous voices and opinions. A literary reading of the visual in the form of alternate narratives of agency and empowerment can lead to entangled histories of science, colonial history and post-colonial society. In the case of technology transfers, such as the plough and the cartwheel, illustrations needed to be accurate and represent the object exact to its internal structure and exterior shape. Indigenous implements that were subject to survey, collection and used for purposes of engineering models belonged to this genre of scientific illustrations.

25.3 Concluding Remarks

Fieldwork in social research seems a lonely journey along with a set of uncertainties and different challenges for a researcher, and it involves numerous personal, emotional, moral, ethical and political issues and dilemmas to face. Social researchers often encountered identity difficulties or had to face physical risks along with the mental impacts. They have to adjust to the field environment including physical and realities without compromising data quality and efficient guidance to data enumerators while keeping a good research focus and data operation flexibility. An unfriendly environment in the field may appear before, during or after the fieldwork. Many researchers think that the power imbalance between the researcher and the participant is very much common in social research where interviewees think that the interviewer comes from an elite position which causes them to decline to participate in the study or provide a whimsical response. Social researchers should be aware of the sampling selection within a geographical location. The researcher should take informed consent for managing the privacy or confidentiality of the respondents. The relationship between researchers and participants should be close by building friendship and rapport for ensuring good-quality research and for having trust and empathy. Because of the complexities in a relationship with the respondents, a researcher must be aware of his positionality and subjectivity. It is important to mention that the researcher must respect the rights, needs, values and desires of the study informant or respondents. However, researchers should note down their challenges and strategies so that future researchers get an idea.

References

Bryman, A. (1996) *Quantity and quality in social research*, Routledge, London.

Bunne, M. (1999) Qualitative research methods in otorhinolaryngology, *International Journal of Pediatric Otorhinolaryngology*, 51, 1–10.

Denzin, N. K. and Lincoln, Y. S. (2000) *The handbook of qualitative research*, Second edition, Sage, London.

Filstead, W. J. (1979) Qualitative methods: a needed perspective in evaluation research, In T. D. Cook and C. S. Reichardt (eds) *Qualitative and quantitative methods in evaluation research*, Sage, Beverly Hills.

Foucault, M. (1972) *The archaeology of knowledge*, Tavistock, London.

Foucault, M. (1980) *Power/Knowledge: selected interviews and their writings 1972–1977*, Harvester, Brighton.

Gilbert, N. (2001) Research theory and method, In N. Gilbert (ed) *Researching social life*, Second edition, Sage, London.

Guba, E. G. (1990) The alternative paradigm dialogue, In E. G. Guba (ed) *The paradigm dialogue*, Sage, CA.

Habermas, J. (1987) The theory of communicative action, Vol. 2, *Lifeworld and System: a critique of functionalist reason*, Beacon Press, Boston.

Innes, M. (2001) Exemplar: Investigating the investigators- studying detective work, In N. Gilbert (ed) *Researching social life*, Second edition, Sage, London.

Kitchin, R. and Tate, N. J. (2000) *Conducting research in human geography: theory, methodology and practice*, Pearson, London.
Kuhn, T. S. (1962) *The structure of scientific revolutions*, University of Chicago Press, Chicago.
Kuhn, T. S. (1970) *The structure of scientific revolutions*, Second edition, University of Chicago Press, Chicago.
May, T. (1997) *Social research: issues, methods and process*, Second edition, Open University Press, Buckingham.
Patton, M. Q. (1990) *Qualitative evaluation and research methods*, Second edition, Sage, London.
Stern, P. N. (1980) Grounded theory methodology: its uses and processes, *Journal of Nursing Scholarship*, 12 (1), 20–23.
Strauss, A. and Corbin, J. (1998) *Basics of qualitative research: techniques and procedures for developing grounded theory*, Sage, London.

Index[1]

A

Abu-Lughod, 254, 254n2, 255, 255n4, 257
Abuse, 271, 272, 275, 277–281, 285, 291
Academics, 315–328
Activism, 316, 317, 320
Adjustments, 332, 335, 336, 338, 340–346
African, 331–346
Agency, 295–309
Agroecological, 121, 419, 420
Amateur, 417–419
Amsterdam, 378, 378n9, 380–382
Anthropology, 254
Archival, 417–438
Autobiography, 182

B

Bahujan, 257, 260
Baseline, 332, 345
Bhadralok, 259, 259n12, 262
Bingo, 305
Bioethics, 2, 3, 8–11, 162, 168, 177
Body language, 10
Brothel, 184–188, 191, 192

C

Case study, 54
Caste, 255–261, 256n7, 256n8, 259n12, 263, 264n16, 265n17, 266, 267
Central Asia, 347–362
Challenges, 331–346, 441–456
Chaperon, 245–246, 249
Chotolok, 259
Clandestine, 140, 141
Class, 255, 256n7, 258, 263, 267
Coastal Community, 221–223, 225–228, 230
Collective data, 219
Colonial knowledge, 417, 418
Communities, 349, 350n3, 351–352, 357, 358, 360, 361
Congregation
Consent, 407, 408, 411
Contestation, 315–317, 320, 322, 325, 328
COVID-19, 410, 412
Cox's Bazar, 318, 319n5, 326n12
Cross-cultural, 106
Cross-sectional data, 215
Customs and culture, 47

[1] Note: Page numbers followed by 'n' refer to notes.

D

Dalal, 140, 148–154, 156
Dalit, 255–258, 260
Data, 331–346
Decolonization, 70
Deterrence theory, 197, 201, 202, 204, 210, 211, 216
Dhaka, 299, 302
Diaspora, 319, 319n8, 319n9, 319n10
Dilemmas, 219–232, 322, 324, 325, 327, 328
Disaster-prone, 240
Domestic, 271–291
Domestic violence, 12, 13, 238, 242, 243

E

Eclogue, 305
Empowerment, 71, 271–291
En-casted, 253–268
Enclave, 86–98, 100
Endanger
Enthusiastic, 129
Entrapment, 285–288
Enumerator, 332, 333, 337, 339–346
Epidemiology, 182
Epistemological, 181
Epistemology, 219, 220
Equality, 271
Ethical, 405–409, 412
Ethical challenges, 9, 11
Ethnocentric, 391
Ethnographer, 315–328
Ethnographic, 122, 124, 133, 296, 298, 299, 301–303, 308, 367–370, 372, 374, 382, 383
Ethnography, 7, 8, 17, 18, 141–143, 155, 156, 253–255, 254n2
Etiology, 182, 394
Evidence, 331, 332
Exceptional, 79

F

Female researchers, 296–299, 303
Feminist, 162, 170, 253–258, 254n1, 254n3, 256n7, 256n8, 261, 262, 264, 265, 267, 268
Fieldwork/field work, 332–335, 337–339, 341–346
Flexibility, 442, 443, 456

Flood-prone, 241, 242
Folklorist, 39
Framework, 267, 268
Fundamental, 271, 315, 321

G

Garo Hills, 444, 450
Gatekeeper, 110, 112, 113
Gender-based, 271, 272, 447
Gender identity, 296, 298, 299, 305
Genocide, 320–322
Geocoded reflections, 105
Geographical location, 413
Grounded theory, 377

H

Health geography, 181–183, 194
Health measures, 347, 359
Hidden population, 8, 9
Homophily, 410
Hypothesis, 202, 204–206, 208–213

I

Idiosyncrasy, 54
Illness, 445, 452
Immune group, 11
Incentive, 408, 409, 414
Incongruous, 61
India, 444–447, 450
Indigenous, 302
Indigenous communities, 418
Influx, 318–320, 318n2, 325
Instruments, 332, 334–338
Interactive interviewing, 105
Interbeing, 121–133
Inter-disciplinary, 19
Interlocutors, 5, 6, 8, 123, 124, 131, 133
Interpretation, 219

J

Jhum, 79

K

Kashta, 261, 262
Key Enlightenment, 418

L
Labour, 253–268
Lingua franca, 392
Linguistic, 163
Local, 318, 319, 319n4, 319n5, 324–327, 327n13

M
Malaysia, 272, 273, 276, 277, 281, 290
Male researchers, 296–299, 301, 303
Management, 338, 340, 343–346
Manhandle, 55
Marginalization, 88, 89, 95
Marginalized, 221–223, 225, 229, 231
Marijuana, 199, 202, 203, 214
Medical geography, 181
Methodological, 161–164, 168, 177, 182, 183
Methodology, 441, 448–450
Migrants, 259, 261, 264
Migration, 55, 64, 300, 302, 304, 308
Migrant village, 299, 302
Milieu, 301, 308, 309
Minority, 347–362
Misrepresentation, 272
Moral dilemmas, 3, 6, 11
Musafir, 77
Muslim society, 296, 301, 306, 308

N
Nagar, 420, 422, 426–429, 431
Nang heritage, 73
Narratives, 318–322, 320n11
National cake, 66
Neurobiological, 202, 214, 216

O
Object, 315, 316, 323, 327, 328
Objective analysis, 219
Observer, 380, 382
Ontological, 183
Ontology
Opposite gender, 296, 298, 299, 301
Oral history, 253, 254, 258, 260

P
Pandemic, 348, 359, 360, 362, 407, 410, 412
Pathogens, 122
Patriarchal politics
Peer educators, 184, 187
Peer influence, 197–216
Perpetrator, 273, 274, 277, 281, 284, 285, 288–290
Phase, 373–375, 377, 383
Photovoice, 271–291
Plough illustration, 419, 422, 429, 430, 432, 437
Positionality, 389–401
Prejudices and taboos, 10
Preparations, 332–339, 345
Prestige, 370, 379
Procedural ethics, 220, 227
Progressive, 257, 258
Prostitution, 239
Provocation, 277, 281, 291

Q
Qualitative approach, 220
Questionnaire, 336–344

R
Rakhine, 319n7, 321–324
Rapport, 38
Rashidpur, 295, 300, 303, 305–309
Rashunia, 295, 299
Recruitment, 337
Reflexive, 348, 352, 354
Reflexivity, 367–384
Refuge, 273
Refugees, 315–328, 447, 448, 454
Remote sensing, 335, 336
Repatriation, 327, 327n13
Replacement, 342, 343, 346
Research gatekeeper, 243
Respectability, 262, 265–267
Risk, 447, 448, 451–453, 456
Rohingya, 316–327, 318n2, 319n3, 319n4, 319n6, 319n7, 319n8, 319n9, 319n10, 327n13

S

Samarkand, 356–358
Sampling frame, 335, 345
Sangster, Joan, 253, 254, 267, 268n19
Savarna, 256–258, 256n7, 256n8, 261–268
Scholarship, 348, 350, 353–356
Secondary data, 331, 335, 337, 345
Self-reflexivity, 12
Sensationalistic, 146
Sensorial ethnographic approaches, 8
Setting, 79
Settlement, 64, 65
Sexual abuse, 12
Sexuality, 367–384
Singling out, 347
Snowballing, 10, 183, 186, 187
Snowball sampling, 8
Social research, 441–456
Social taboo, 240–242, 247, 250
Socio-ecological, 181
Socio-economic, 370, 372, 373, 375–379, 377n8, 382
Songsareks, 39, 40, 43, 47, 48
Soviet, 349–351, 354, 356, 358n4, 360
Stakeholders, 161, 163–165, 170, 172, 175, 333–335
Stigmatization, 141
Strategies, 296, 299, 303–306
Subjective, 220
Surrogacy, 161–177, 446, 452
Surveys, 332–337, 339–345
Survivor, 273, 274, 276, 281–285, 288–291
Syndicate, 192

T

Tajik minority, 349
Taka, 139, 140, 140n1, 147, 149, 151, 153, 154, 158
Teknaf, 318–320, 318n2, 319n3, 319n4, 322, 324–327, 327n13
Topographical, 417, 419
Trafficking zone, 192
Traumatized, 74
Tribe, 41
Trustworthy, 298, 301, 305–307, 309

U

Ukhia, 318–320, 318n2, 319n3, 319n4, 322, 324–327, 326n12, 327n13
Undialectical, 391

V

Vice-versa, 223
Victim, 316, 320–322, 326
Violence, 271–291, 444, 447
Virtual interviews, 106
Vulnerability, 222–224
Vulnerable, 442, 444–447, 449, 453, 454

W

West Bengal, 259
Workstation, 245, 246, 249

Z

Zero tolerance policy, 197, 198, 201, 214, 215

Printed in the United States
by Baker & Taylor Publisher Services